# FINANCIAL ECONOMICS

# FINANCIAL ECONOMICS

## WITH APPLICATIONS TO INVESTMENTS, INSURANCE AND PENSIONS

EDITOR | HARRY H. PANJER

PHELIM P. BOYLE
SAMUEL H. COX
DANIEL DUFRESNE
HANS U. GERBER
HEINZ H. MUELLER
HAL W. PEDERSEN
STANLEY R. PLISKA
MICHAEL SHERRIS
ELIAS S. SHIU
KEN SENG TAN

THE ACTUARIAL FOUNDATION
*Preparing for tomorrow's possibilities*

**Library of Congress Cataloging-in-Publication Data**

Financial economics : with applications to investments, insurance and
   pensions / Harry H. Panjer, editor : Phelim P. Boyle . . . [et al.].
      p.  cm.
    Includes bibliographical references and index.
    ISBN 0-938959-48-4 (alk. paper)
    1. Finance.  2. Investments.  3. Insurance.  I. Panjer, Harry H.
  II. Boyle, Phelim P.
  HG174.F496   1998
  332—dc21                  97-27424
                                     CIP

ISBN 0-938959-48-4
Printed in the United States of America
03 02 01 00 99 98    5 4 3 2 1

Editor: David Anderson
SOA Liaison: Barbara Simmons, ELS, Publications Manager
Assistant Technical Editor: John Carey

# FOREWORD

From its organization in 1994, The Actuarial Foundation has characterized its activities by four words: research, education, communication, and partnership. The early meetings of the Board of Trustees were devoted to identifying projects that could be described by these words.

The idea of publishing a major textbook on financial economics, with applications in insurance, investments and pensions, seemed to meet the specifications. The explosive growth of the theory of financial economics in the past half-century guaranteed the research relevance of the project. It was equally clear that actuaries need to enhance their education about these new ideas if the profession is to keep its eminent position in planning and managing financial security systems. A high-quality book with emphasis on applications would send a powerful communication that actuaries have the intellectual tools to solve modern financial security problems.

The partnership characteristic that the Foundation sought was realized in two ways. First, Lincoln National Corporation endorsed the plan and became a full partner in funding the project. Second, a partnership team of outstanding authors was recruited. The recruiting was done by Harry H. Panjer, editor of this book and at that time Research Director of the Foundation. The author team was a far-flung partnership with members from three continents, four nations, and eight universities. These two key partnerships were forged in 1995.

The Actuarial Foundation is grateful to its many generous supporters, as well as Lincoln National Corporation and the author team, and is confident that this book will help support the work of actuaries in the next millennium.

Cecil D. Bykerk, F.S.A.
Chair, Board of Trustees
The Actuarial Foundation

June 1998

Ian M. Rolland, F.S.A.
Trustee, The Actuarial Foundation
Chairman of the Board, CEO and
President, Lincoln National Corporation

v

# CONTENTS

# LIST OF FIGURES

# LIST OF TABLES

# PREFACE

The field of financial economic theory has mushroomed both in scope and in applications in recent years. This book attempts to capture some key elements of this theory, with a strong emphasis on applications in investments, insurance and pensions—the three key areas of activity for the actuarial profession, which is the principal audience of this book.

Since the landmark work of Harry Markowitz in the 1950s, financial risk management has become more and more mathematically formalized. Professor Markowitz, along with Professors Merton Miller and William Sharpe, won the Nobel Prize in economics in 1990 for his pioneering work. Professor Sharpe contributed to the development of the capital-asset-pricing model. The breakthrough developments in option-pricing theory of Fischer Black and Myron Scholes in 1973 triggered the explosion of the entire field of financial derivatives, in theory and in practice. The 1997 Nobel Prize in economics was awarded to Scholes (Black having passed away in 1995) and Robert Merton. Merton contributed to the development of general equilibrium theory and the pricing of financial assets, including derivative securities. Other key Nobel Prize winners whose work is examined in this book are Kenneth Arrow (1971) and Gerard Debreu (1983). The term "Arrow-Debreu security" is used widely in financial economic theory.

Derivative securities, such as options, are special types of a larger class of financial contracts that depend on the outcome of some underlying variable or variables. Thus, certain nonforfeiture options in insurance contracts are options that can be valued using a framework similar to that of options on stocks or bonds. Pension plans that guarantee a defined benefit can be viewed as providing an annuity contract with a guarantee for each plan member.

Hence, actuaries should have a good working knowledge of financial economics to manage risk, not only on the asset side of the balance sheet but also on the liability side. This book provides that knowledge. Although the principal audience is actuaries, no doubt the book will be useful to anyone interested in the theory with an additional emphasis on insurance and pension applications.

This book focuses on discrete time rather than continuous time. Continuous-time models are appealing because they can lead to more tractable results; however, the level of mathematical rigor required is beyond the scope of this book. Furthermore, it can be argued that, in practice, we actually deal in discrete time even though the time interval may be small—one day, one hour, or even one minute. So why not treat the real world as being in discrete time and build models directly in discrete time? Finally, when continuous-time models do not lead to tractable results such as closed-form formulas, the approximations required to solve them generally depend on discretizing time so that computers can be used to generate numerical values.

"Financial Markets" (Chapter 1) and "Derivative Securities" (Chapter 2) provide the background for markets and securities, including insurance and pensions. These two chapters also introduce many concepts that are more formally developed in later chapters. The reader with little knowledge in the field should read these two chapters thoroughly before proceeding to the later, more technical treatments of the same and related topics.

"Interest Rate Risk and Immunizations" (Chapter 3) covers an area near the heart of actuarial practice, namely, asset-liability management using classical immunization theory, often called duration analysis. This chapter covers the main ideas and refers the reader to other sources in the actuarial, economics, and finance literature for additional reading.

"Equilibrium" (Chapter 4) deals with how individual buyers and sellers arrive at prices in a market. Equilibrium is reached when these agents cannot improve their positions by additional trading. The theory depends upon using utility to describe the welfare of the agents. Equilibrium pricing (or valuation) is shown to be directly related to risk-neutral or no-arbitrage valuation in Chapter 5.

"No-Arbitrage Pricing Theory" (Chapter 5) shows how prices of some securities are obtained when the price dynamics of related primitive securities are already known. The prices can be obtained as expected present values by using a special set of "probabilities" known as the risk-neutral or equivalent martingale probability measure. The probability measure is labeled as the $Q$ measure, whereas the true physical probability measure (often known as nature's probability measure) is consistently labeled the $P$ measure. In the one-period framework, only linear algebra is used. Probability concepts are introduced in the multiperiod case in which the evolution of information needs to be carefully treated. The fundamental theorem of asset pricing is introduced here and later in several forms. It appears again in Chapter 11, which is, in part, a more advanced treatment of the topics in Chapter 5.

"Options and Other Derivatives" (Chapter 6) introduces the numerous types of options and the practical applications of the no-arbitrage pricing theory developed in

Chapter 5 (and Chapter 11). Binomial lattice models are used extensively to describe price movements. American options (which allow for early exercise) are considered; more rigorous treatment is deferred to Chapter 11. Various risk statistics are introduced, and hedging methods are discussed.

"Term Structure Models" (Chapter 7) discusses models of the term structure of interest rates and the application to the valuation of cash-flow streams. Lattice models are used extensively. Details of implementation of some popular models such as the Black-Derman-Toy model are given. Included in applications are callable bonds, mortgage-backed securities, and single-premium deferred annuities.

"Portfolio Selection" (Chapter 8) deals with portfolio analysis in discrete time. It is based on the pioneering work of Markowitz, from which we have the capital-asset-pricing model and mutual fund separation theorems. Applications focus on pension fund investment with or without institutional constraints on allowable investments. Included in the chapter is a treatment of the multiperiod situation with a risk-neutral computational approach. In general, the solution requires linear or quadratic programming.

"Investment Return Models" (Chapter 9) considers, in rather general terms, stochastic investment return models in long-term models of the $P$ measure, which actuaries use for simulating the future. Well-known models, such as the Wilkie model, depend on many interrelationships among various economic variables. Many considerations in model building are discussed. These models are particularly useful in developing projections of pension or insurance over long periods.

"Option Pricing in Continuous Time" (Chapter 10) introduces this concept. While most books use the convergence of a binomial model process to a Brownian motion, this chapter uses a rather uniquely actuarial approach. Stock price movements are assumed to follow a geometric shifted Poisson process; hence, the price jumps at any point in (continuous) time. Option pricing is developed in this framework. Results for the special case of Brownian motion are obtained as limits. As in Chapter 6, many different types of options are considered.

"No-Arbitrage Pricing Theory—Advanced" (Chapter 11) deals with several topics whose treatment has been deferred from earlier chapters, so that the reader does not get bogged down (and possibly stop reading). The advanced treatment of option-pricing theory requires a detailed use of many concepts, such as partitions, filtrations, and adapted processes. This chapter employs these concepts in re-deriving many results from Chapter 5 in the more general framework. A background of the necessary probability theory is given in Appendix A. Chapter 11 also includes more advanced treatment of forward and futures contracts as well as American options, because more advanced probability concepts such as stopping times are involved.

Exercises ranging from elementary to rather difficult are included at the end of each chapter. Numerical answers for many exercises are given in Appendix B. Most numerical exercises allow the reader to check his or her understanding of the formulas developed in the text. Exercises requiring proofs complement the text material, either by filling in parts of proofs not done in the text or by adding to the text to provide additional insight.

The technical level gradually increases though the book. The book is written at a level appropriate for persons with actuarial training. It is more mathematical than most MBA-level texts but at a level lower than that of some well-known books in the field. It is intended that the reader will develop a good insight into the material (and be able at some future stage to contribute to the field!). The book is suitable for a two-semester course at the early graduate school level.

Although the group of authors is large, we have tried to homogenize the notation, the terminology, and the technical level by having more than one author work on each chapter. Thus authors are not identified with specific chapters. Several rewrites of the material were done to accomplish the objective of uniformity.

A large number of persons have been helpful in reading various drafts of the individual chapters. They have provided valuable feedback to the authors by pointing out errors and making specific suggestions for improvements. Their contributions are gratefully acknowledged. Unfortunately, not all their suggestions for specific content materials could be incorporated into the book because of size and scope limitations. In addition, students at several universities around the world have been subjected to early drafts of some of the chapters. We beg their forgiveness!

This project would not have gotten off the ground without the financial (and moral) support of The Actuarial Foundation and Lincoln National Corporation.

Undoubtedly there are still (as yet undetected) errors in the book. These remain the responsibility of the editor. If you detect errors, please let us know so that corrections can be made in future printings.

*Harry Panjer*
*Waterloo, Ontario*
*May 1998*

# About the Authors

**Phelim P. Boyle**, Ph.D., F.I.A., F.C.I.A., holds the J. Page Wadsworth Chair of Finance at the University of Waterloo and is the Director of the Centre for Advanced Studies in Finance. He has also taught at the University of British Columbia and the University of Illinois at Urbana-Champaign. He received his Ph.D. from Trinity College, Dublin. Dr. Boyle is the author of *Options and the Management of Financial Risk* and numerous papers in finance and actuarial science. He is editor of *Advances in Futures and Options Research*, finance editor of *Management Science*, as well as an associate editor of nine journals including *Journal of Risk and Insurance, Insurance: Mathematics and Economics, Mathematical Finance*, and *The Journal of Derivatives*. Among numerous awards for research, he received the first Halmstad Prize for the best paper in actuarial literature in 1978 and the Centennial Award of the International Actuarial Association in 1995.

**Samuel H. Cox**, Ph.D., F.S.A., is Professor of Actuarial Science and Risk Management and Insurance at Georgia State University. He earned his B.A. and M.S. degrees at Texas Christian University and Ph.D. at Louisiana State University, all in mathematics. Dr. Cox is a Chartered Property and Casualty Underwriter. He is editor of the *North American Actuarial Journal* and Vice-Chairperson of the Education and Research Section Council of the Society of Actuaries. He is coauthor of several textbooks and has published scholarly papers in mathematics, actuarial science, insurance, and finance.

**Daniel Dufresne**, Ph.D., A.S.A., is Senior Lecturer at the Centre for Actuarial Studies in the Department of Economics at the University of Melbourne, Victoria, Australia. He previously taught actuarial science and probability theory at Université Laval and

Université de Montréal in Canada. He received his Ph.D. from City University, U.K. Dr. Dufresne's interests are mathematical finance, stochastic calculus, and distribution theory. He has published research papers in the *Journal of the Institute of Actuaries*, the *Scandinavian Actuarial Journal*, *Bernoulli*, and *Advances in Applied Mathematics*, among others, as well as a book on pension mathematics.

**Hans U. Gerber**, Ph.D., A.S.A., is President of the Institute of Actuarial Science of the University of Lausanne. He is a coauthor of the Society of Actuaries text, *Actuarial Mathematics*, and author of the monographs, "An Introduction to Mathematical Risk Theory" and "Life Insurance Mathematics," which has been published in five languages. Dr. Gerber is editor of *Insurance: Mathematics and Economics* and the *Journal of the Swiss Association of Actuaries* and an associate editor of the *North American Actuarial Journal*. He has published almost 100 papers, primarily in risk theory and applied probability and more recently in mathematical finance. In 1995, he won the Centennial Award of the International Actuarial Association and the annual prize of the Society of Actuaries for a paper that he coauthored with Elias S. Shiu.

**Heinz H. Mueller**, Ph.D., is Professor of Mathematics at the University of St. Gallen, Switzerland. He has also taught at the universities of Zurich, Geneva, and Lausanne. He specializes in mathematical economics, economic theory, and financial economics. Some of his publications have appeared in *Journal of Economic Theory*, *Insurance: Mathematics and Economics*, and the *ASTIN Bulletin*.

**Harry H. Panjer**, Ph.D., F.S.A., F.C.I.A., is Professor of Actuarial Science at the University of Waterloo. He received his Ph.D. from the University of Western Ontario and previously taught at the University of Texas and at Western Ontario. He is coauthor of three other books in actuarial science, including most recently *Loss Models: From Data to Decisions*. He has published more than 40 papers, mostly in actuarial science. He is an associate editor of the *North American Actuarial Journal*, the *Journal of Risk and Insurance*, and *Insurance: Mathematics and Economics*. He has served in several leadership positions in actuarial professional organizations including President of the Canadian Institute of Actuaries and Vice-President of the Society of Actuaries. He has received prizes for papers from the Society of Actuaries, the Canadian Institute of Actuaries, and the *Journal of Risk and Insurance*.

**Hal W. Pedersen**, Ph.D., A.S.A., is Assistant Professor of Actuarial Science at Georgia State University and holds a Ph.D. in finance from Washington University in St. Louis. He has previously been on the faculty at the University of Manitoba. He was a joint recipient of the Halmstad Prize and has published scholarly papers in *Transactions* *of the Society of Actuaries, Insurance: Mathematics and Economics*, and *Journal of Financial Markets*. Dr. Pedersen's research activities are in financial economics and the application of financial economics to insurance problems.

**Stanley R. Pliska**, Ph.D., is Professor of Finance at the University of Illinois at Chicago. Formerly, he taught at Northwestern University and worked in the aerospace industry. He received a B.S. degree in aeronautical engineering from the Massachusetts Institute of Technology and both an M.S. degree in statistics and a Ph.D. in operations research from Stanford University. Dr. Pliska has published more than 40 research papers in applied probability, stochastic control theory, and finance, notably, "Martingales and Stochastic Integrals in the Theory of Continuous Trading," coauthored with J. Michael Harrison. He is also author of the textbook *Introduction to Mathematical Finance: Discrete Time Models* and coeditor of the book *Mathematics of Derivative Securities*. Dr. Pliska is founder and editor of *Mathematical Finance*.

**Michael Sherris**, M.B.A., F.I.A., F.I.A.A., A.S.A., is Professor of Actuarial Studies at the University of New South Wales in Sydney, Australia. He has published in actuarial and insurance journals including *Scandinavian Actuarial Journal, Journal of the Institute of Actuaries, North American Actuarial Journal*, and *Journal of Risk and Insurance* and is an associate editor of the *North American Actuarial Journal*. He is author of the book *Money and Capital Markets: Pricing, Yields and Analysis*. Before becoming an academic, he worked in the finance industry.

**Elias S. Shiu**, Ph.D., A.S.A., is Principal Financial Group Foundation Professor of Actuarial Science at the University of Iowa. He received his doctorate from the California Institute of Technology. Dr. Shiu is an editor of *Insurance: Mathematics and Economics* and an associate editor of the *Journal of Actuarial Practice* and the *North American Actuarial Journal*. From 1991 to 1994 he served as a member of the Investment Section Council of the Society of Actuaries. He won the Halmstad Prize in 1991 with Hal W. Pedersen and A.E. Thorlacius and in 1996 with Hans U. Gerber. With Hans U. Gerber, he received the 1995 Annual Prize of the Society of Actuaries.

**Ken Seng Tan**, Ph.D., A.S.A., is Assistant Professor of Actuarial Science at the University of Waterloo. He holds a Ph.D. degree from the University of Waterloo. He has coauthored several papers in finance and has published papers in *Management Science, The Journal of Derivatives*, and *Risk*. Together with Phelim P. Boyle and Corwin Joy, Dr. Tan published one of the first papers applying quasi-Monte Carlo methods to finance. In 1997 his paper "Applications of Scrambled Low Discrepancy Sequences to Exotic Options," coauthored with Phelim P. Boyle, was awarded a prize at the 7th AFIR International Colloquium.

# Chapter 1
## Financial Markets

### Section 1.1
### Introduction

The finance and insurance industries have much in common. The different tools these industries provide their customers for managing financial insurable risks rely on the same two fundamental concepts: risk pooling and risk transfer. Further, the valuation techniques in both financial and insurance markets are formally the same: the fair values of a security and an insurance policy are the discounted expected values of the cash flows they provide their owners. Scholars and practitioners recognize these commonalities. Not surprisingly the markets have converged recently; for example, some insurance companies offer mutual funds and life insurance tied to stock portfolios, and some banks sell annuities. These developments require that insurance company managers, owners, and customers understand financial markets and their relation to insurance markets.

Risk pooling and risk transfer in insurance and finance take place in markets. When an insurance company sells fire insurance, risk of loss is transferred from the property owner to the insurance company. To ensure its ability to pay insurance losses as promised, the insurance company must have initial capital, which may be provided through the sale of shares to investors. The investors bear the risk that the company collects adequate premiums to cover losses. Risk transfers from property owners to the shareholders occur through two transactions: one in the insurance market as the risks are pooled by the company, and a second in the stock market as the company sells its stock. This simple example shows that the complete picture of insurance operations involves financial markets in an important way.

Understanding finance and insurance, and how they are related, begins with financial markets. In Chapter 1 we emphasize financial markets, but we also discuss insurance markets. The fundamental markets for stocks, bonds, insurance, and annuities are covered in detail. In later chapters we assume that you have a good understanding of these fundamentals.

Financial markets provide traders and investors the opportunity to buy and sell financial assets such as stocks, bonds, and mutual fund shares. Securities derived from real or financial assets, or even from liabilities, may also trade in financial markets; these are called *derivative securities* or simply *derivatives*. Options on stocks, interest rate swaps, and grain futures are examples of derivatives based on assets. Insurance companies hedge their liability risks (for example, a portfolio of homeowners contracts covering residences in Florida) with reinsurance agreements that spread the risks to other insurers. Thus, reinsurance is a derivative in the sense that it is "derived" from the direct insurer's portfolio of policies.

Financial assets and derivatives have a variety of sources. There are products from different sources that are practically identical: for example, some banks issue annuities to individuals just as life insurers do. Some life insurance companies issue guaranteed interest contracts to pension plans, in competition with banks.

We need some properties to categorize these complex markets. One common property of financial markets is the intangible nature of the product. Financial products are merely contracts describing the buyer's and seller's rights and obligations. Example of such contracts include a U.S. Treasury bill (T-bill), a fire insurance policy, a stock certificate, or an option to buy 100 shares of stock at a guaranteed price. These contracts allow the owner to make a claim against the contract writer or issuer under future conditions specified in the contract. Contracts may also allow the issuer certain rights; for example, callable bonds allow the issuer to repay the debt early.

Market structure and arrangements that facilitate transactions also characterize markets. The most fundamental type of market is a *barter* market. Barter is an exchange of goods or services; but the lack of currency and lack of standardization of quality and quantity of goods make these transactions awkward. Commodity barter is an ancient practice that is still used; for example, in 1991 Pepsico bartered Pepsi Cola for vodka and obsolete Russian submarines.

The next level of sophistication is a *cash* market in which goods are purchased with cash and carried away, called a *cash-and-carry* market; the local grocery store is an example. A *spot* market is more refined than a cash-and-carry market in the sense that the goods are categorized and described as to quality and quantity, but they are not actually delivered at the point of sale. An agricultural commodity exchange is a good example of a spot market. Spot markets go back a long time; one of the oldest was the rice markets of eighteenth-century Japan, according to Schaede [169] and others.[1] Spot-market buyers and sellers do not deal with each other. Instead, they agree to pay a specified price through an exchange. The terms of sale provide for delivery of the specified goods within a few days at a specified place. Modern stock markets are examples of spot markets.

Securities markets have some special features of ownership and trading. In many stock and bond markets, ownership is recorded with the issuer. This allows the issuer to send stock dividends and bond coupons to the proper person. Securities handled this way are called *registered securities*. Alternatively, the security may allow the issuer to pay the person in possession (or bearer) of the bond. Securities handled this way are called *bearer securities*. In the U.S., most stocks and bonds are registered securities. The *primary market* for a security refers to the transaction between the issuer (creator of the security) and the first owner. The *secondary markets* are created when one owner sells the security, rather than holding it to maturity.

*Futures and forward markets* are similar to spot markets except that the time of delivery may be many months or more in the future. Thus, futures and forward contracts are agreements to purchase something in the future for a set price. The contract specifies at the time it is written all terms of the transaction, such as the quantity and quality of goods sold, the price of the goods, the time and place of delivery, and payment of the purchase price. Futures contracts are often settled in cash, as an alternative to physical delivery of the underlying asset. Futures contracts are traded through exchanges such as the Chicago Mercantile Exchange (CME), the Chicago Board of Trade (CBOT), and the London Futures and Options Exchange. Futures are standardized contracts; but forward contracts are usually customized to the needs of traders by a broker or dealer.

Brokers and dealers differ somewhat in their operations. Dealers act as principals in a securities transaction, whereas brokers act as an intermediary between buyers and sellers. Brokers arrange trades and match buyer and seller, usually without taking on market risk. Brokers may use an exchange to execute the transaction, or they may find both buyer and seller among their own clients. The broker never owns the traded security and thus never has exposure to risk of an adverse price movement. Typically the broker charges commissions to both buyers and sellers. In contrast, dealers own inventories of securities that they offer to customers on a bid-ask spread basis. For example, a dealer may offer to buy a security for 100 per unit, in effect bidding 100 per unit. At the same time, the dealer may offer to sell the identical security for 101 per unit, asking 101. Some customers buy for 101, and some sell for 100; the dealer profits on the spread of $1 = 101 - 100$. Because the dealer has an inventory of securities, it takes on the

---

[1]Schaede writes about the fascinating rice markets in eighteenth-century Japan; they had many of the characteristics of modern markets, such as futures, marking-to-market, and clearinghouses.

risk that the market value of its inventory declines. Of course, the value of the inventory could increase, providing a profit to the dealer. Dealers intend to profit from trading like brokers, but unlike brokers they participate in the market as buyers and sellers.

*Option markets* are similar to futures markets, but they provide an additional feature: option buyers exchange cash for price risk. This is a common way to protect against adverse price movements. The cash payment obligates a trader to perform under the contract even if the outcome is unfavorable.

Futures and options written on commodities, financial assets, and indices are examples of *derivative contracts*, or simply *derivatives*, so called because they are based on other assets, indices, or contracts. Options and futures are widely available, often traded 24 hours a day, facilitated by the major financial centers around the world. For example, futures written on the Japanese Nikkei stock index are traded in Chicago, as well as in Japan, and futures written on U.S. T-bills are traded in Singapore, Tokyo, London, New York, and Chicago. Table 1.1 shows some major financial markets.

### TABLE **1.1** │ *Examples of Financial Markets*

| Exchange-Traded | Over-the-Counter |
|---|---|
| *Assets* | |
| Stocks, bonds, commodities | Stocks, private placement, commodities, insurance, annuities, certificates of deposit, and mutual funds |
| *Asset-Backed Derivatives* | |
| Futures on bonds, stock indices, and currency, options on stocks and futures | Forwards on currency, options on stocks, bonds, futures, indices, currency swaps, and interest rate swaps |
| *Liability-Based Derivatives* | |
| Catastrophe insurance options | Insurance-linked bonds, reinsurance |

Table 1.1 is not intended to imply that derivatives are not assets, which they certainly are. The table is a convenient way of classifying assets. As with any financial asset, the obligation conferred on one party is a liability to that party, whereas the right conferred on the other party is an asset. Similarly, insurance futures and options are assets to one party but liabilities to another.

*Swaps*, in which two parties exchange cash flows, are traded *over-the-counter* (OTC) in markets organized by dealers. Options are also offered by OTC dealers, although there is more option trading through exchanges. These products may be customized to the traders' needs by the dealers. OTC markets exist for options, swaps, and forward contracts. Generally, the OTC markets are not as liquid as exchanges. *Liquidity* refers to the ease with which transactions occur. There may be default risk in an OTC derivative because the contract is with a specific party, not an exchange. Degree of interplay between markets varies; for example, the currency markets for OTC forwards and exchange-traded futures are highly integrated. Exchanges and OTC dealers are constantly innovating, creating new products that they hope their customers will use to hedge risky positions or to seek speculative profits. A good example of this innovation is the catastrophe insurance option contract that has been developed by the CBOT since 1992 (see the Chicago Board of Trade booklet [36] for a description of these products). Indeed, most exchanges offer free booklets and brochures describing their products and services.

# Section 1.2
# Stock Markets

Corporations issue stock (or share) certificates that convey rights to the registered owner, the stockholder (or shareholder). The owners have a claim on the earnings of the company, and the owners elect the board of directors, who appoint the company managers. The board of directors sets the policy for paying out earnings, called dividends, to stockholders. Instead of paying dividends, the available funds might be used to invest in company projects. If the company has projects available that are more attractive than those available in the marketplace, the board would be acting in the owners' interest by retaining earnings rather than paying cash dividends. Of course, the owners would expect their shares to increase in market value as a result of reinvesting earnings. The shareholders are not liable to the company's creditors if the company becomes bankrupt. The most the shareholders can lose is the price they paid for the shares.

## SECTION 1.2.1 | SUPPLY OF STOCKS

Shares are created in several ways. When a company is created, its owners typically supply capital to get it started and receive shares for their investment. At this point the company is privately held; its shares can be transferred, but it is not publicly traded. In most countries, public trading of shares is regulated by the government, mainly to prevent fraud and to facilitate orderly transfer of ownership. To become publicly traded, a privately held company requires the services of an investment banker. The investment banker engages attorneys, accountants, marketing specialists, and others who arrange for public sale of the firm's stock. This procedure is called an *initial public offering* (IPO).

The transfer of a firm from government ownership to ownership of publicly traded shares is also an IPO, although the term *privatization* is used to describe it. Privatizations of large and small state-owned businesses were used frequently in the transitions of the economies of Russia and other newly independent states of the former Soviet Union and its allies. For example, the government of Poland took state-owned companies, including its monopolistic insurance company, into nongovernment ownership. These privatizations create publicly traded shares where none existed previously, even though the firm was owned by the people through the government. A mutual insurance company is privately held since it is owned by its policyholders and the shares are not publicly traded. In recent years, several mutual life insurers have changed their ownership form to stock companies in order to raise capital. This is called *demutualization*. Demutualizations involve creating tradable shares that may be publicly traded or held privately.

Stock also is created when an existing company issues new shares, which will result in additional capital being paid into the firm and increasing the number of claimants on earnings. A company can also split its stock. For example, a firm may offer to exchange three shares of new stock for each share of old stock. The market price of the new shares would adjust to one-third of the price of an old share. Typically, there is no new capital paid in, and ownership is not diluted by a stock split.

These transactions can be reversed. For example, a publicly traded company can become privately held, which is something like a reverse IPO. Often the purchase is financed by borrowing money, which is secured by future earnings of the acquired firm, by selling some operations of the firm, or both. This is called a *leveraged buyout* or LBO. The buyers plan to run the company for a number of years, improve its efficiency, and take it public at a higher value than when it was purchased; for example, RJR Nabisco was purchased outright for $25 billion in October 1988 by Kohlberg Kravis Roberts and Company, a leveraged buyout specialist. LBOs are complex, expensive transactions and require the services of investment bankers, accountants, lawyers, and other consultants. The RJR transaction resulted in investment banker fees of almost $400 million. The total cost of the transaction was almost $1 billion, including interim borrowing costs (see Post [147]).

A stock insurance company can change to a mutual form of ownership, which is called *mutualization*; this is the reverse of demutualization. These transactions, like IPOs and LBOs, are expensive and involve actuaries, accountants, and lawyers, as well as investment bankers. Moreover, transactions involving insurance companies require approval of both insurance regulators and securities regulators. Many U.S. savings and loan institutions (sometimes called thrifts), which were originally organized as mutual corporations, have demutualized. Some are now traded on exchanges, and others are owned by holding companies.

## SECTION 1.2.2 | STOCK TRANSACTIONS

Stock or share certificates, regardless of how they are created, are *negotiable*, meaning the certificate owner can transfer ownership to another person without permission of the certificate issuer. As a result, an active secondary market for them developed. Secondary markets consist of exchange trading and OTC trading. The first negotiable stock certificate was created in Amsterdam in 1608 by the Dutch East India Company. In the U.S., there are two major stock exchanges, the New York Stock Exchange (NYSE) and the American Stock Exchange, as well as regional exchanges. Generally the exchange owners are brokers, and their employees trade on behalf of clients, who may be individuals or institutions such as pension funds and insurance companies. Stocks are also traded over-the-counter. The National Association of Securities Dealers Automated Quotation system (Nasdaq)[2] handles most OTC stock transactions in the U.S. electronically. There are also direct transactions between individuals or institutions; these are neither dealer nor exchange transactions. For example, a pension plan may exchange a stock portfolio with a life insurance company for an annuity. No brokers or dealers are involved in the transaction.

Communication stretches across networks, and some exchanges offer computerized trading. Exchanges are organizations whose owners have the right to trade on the exchange. Nasdaq, in contrast, is a network of dealers who trade on behalf of their customers or on their own. Trades made through exchanges incur commissions, charged to both the buyer and seller. OTC trades incur costs implied by the bid-ask spread set by the dealer, as we described in general terms earlier. See Elton and Gruber [54] for a more elaborate discussion.

The cash-flow diagram for stocks is shown in Figure 1.1. The initial offering of stock brings a price of $S_0$, and the stockholder is entitled to future dividends, denoted $D_n$. In the U.S., stocks that pay dividends pay them quarterly. The stock is traded in a secondary market, either exchange or OTC, and the new owner gets the future dividends.

***Market Orders.*** Most transactions in exchange or OTC markets are the result of market orders. The owner of 100 shares of Aetna common stock can sell them by placing a market order. The owner's broker will try to get the best immediately available price but makes no guarantee to the seller. If recent trades were observed at 70 per share, the seller can expect to get approximately 70. The situation is analogous for a buyer, who places an order for a specific number of units of the asset and must pay the price that prevails in the market. This is the most common trade in other markets too, including bond, option, and futures markets. In the U.S., a market order

---

[2]Although NASDAQ is the acronym, it is usually referred to as Nasdaq.

FIGURE **1.1** | *Stock Cash Flow*

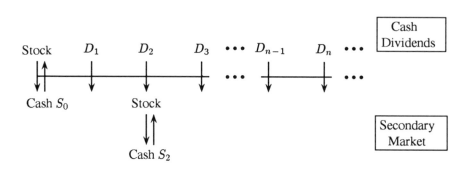

expires at the end of the trading day, unless the trader specifies another expiration date.

*Limit Orders.* A limit order is designed to reduce the price uncertainty of a transaction. The owner of 100 shares of Aetna places a limit order, for example, by telling the broker to sell at 71. The broker will execute the sale only if a bid of 71 or higher is available for 100 shares of Aetna. Less uncertainty as to price exists, but the transaction may not be executed at all. Limit buys are analogous.

*Stop Orders.* A stop-loss order is a delayed market order. The seller specifies a price $X$, below the current market price, and an expiration date $T$. If the stock trades at a price below $X$ before $T$, the order becomes a market sell order. A stop order to buy shares is also a delayed market order. The order becomes a market buy order if $S_t \geq X$ at a time $t \leq T$.

*Short Sales.* Typically traders who deal through a broker do not take delivery of their shares. For their convenience, the shares are held by the broker "in street name." This means that the broker is listed as owner in the issuing company's records, and the broker has a contractual obligation to its customer to pass on dividends, protect the certificate, etc. The broker receives dividends, stock splits, and so on and passes them on to the trader. Thus, the brokers have an inventory of shares on hand held for customers. A trader who wants to sell a stock, but does not own it, can borrow the stock out of a broker's inventory and sell it in the marketplace. This is called a short sale. A trader may want to sell short as part of an arbitrage, or the trader may want to speculate that the price of the stock will decline. Another possibility is that a short sale is needed to hedge the performance of the trader's portfolio of stocks.

The short seller must eventually buy the stock in the market and return it. In the meantime, any stock dividends that are paid must be credited to the account from which the stock was borrowed; these funds come from the short seller's account. Electronic registration of securities has made short selling easier.

***Buying on Margin.*** Brokers accommodate traders by paying short-term interest, that is, money market rates, on cash held in traders' accounts. They also facilitate borrowing to finance purchases of securities, which are held as collateral for the loan. In the U.S., the Federal Reserve Board regulates margin buying, and, of course, brokers may impose limits as well.

To be more specific, suppose the investor borrows an amount $B$ from the broker to buy $n$ shares of stock with a price per share $S$. The investor owns the shares, but they are held as collateral until the loan is repaid. The investor's *equity* is $nS - B$, which changes as the market price of the stock changes. If the investor's equity drops below zero, there is not enough collateral to cover the loan. To provide a cushion, the broker requires that the collateral total, called the maintenance margin account, always be at least a given fraction $p$ of the market value of the stock. Thus, $nS - B \geq pnS$ is required.

The amount of borrowing initially is limited to $nS - B \geq qnS$, where $q > p$ is a fraction used to define the initial amount of borrowing; with the terms rearranged, this can be stated as $B \leq (1 - q)nS$. In the U.S., typically $q = 50\%$, so the limit of margin buying is $B \leq nS/2$.

Because the relation $nS - B \geq pnS$ must be maintained throughout the term of the loan, it can lead to margin calls. If the stock price drops below the critical value determined by $nS = B(1 - p)^{-1}$, the investor must act to restore adequate collateral. This might mean reestablishment of the original level by paying down the loan, selling the shares, or adding assets (usually cash but it could be additional stock or even bonds) to the collateral. Refer to an investment textbook such as that by Bodie et al. [18] for detailed information on margin buying and short selling.

***Short Seller's Margin.*** When a trader sells a stock short, the broker borrows stock, sells it for the investor, and puts the cash from the sale in the investor's account. The cash proceeds, plus a cushion to protect the broker against an increase in the stock price, have to be held as collateral to ensure that the investor can buy the stock back to complete the transaction. If the stock price goes up, the short seller loses cash because more cash must be put under the broker's control. Because the broker must stand behind the trade, short traders must have adequate cash (or securities) on deposit as collateral to cover losses due to price increases in the borrowed security.

Note that this use of the term "margin" in a short-selling context is quite different from buying on margin. Short sellers do not borrow cash, as margin buyers do. Instead, they borrow stock and put up cash deposits to guarantee return of the borrowed stock.

Suppose the investor sells an asset short. The asset may be a stock or bond with a current market price of $S_0 = \$70$ per share. Suppose also that the investor wants to sell short $n = 100$ shares. The broker borrows the assets from other accounts and sells them, and the cash (equal to $nS_0 = \$7,000$) is put into the investor's account with the broker. The investor must eventually buy the assets in the open market and return them to the accounts from which they are borrowed. The broker needs assurance that there will be cash on hand to buy the assets back, so the cash from the sales remains as collateral. An additional amount of cash (or liquid securities such as T-bills) $A$ is also required as a cushion against the possibility of an increase in the market price of the asset (which would mean that it would cost more than $nS_0$ to buy it back). This is called the initial margin requirement, and it is specified at a fraction $u$, say, $u = 0.5$, of the initial market value of the sale $nS_0$. Thus, initially, $A = unS_0 = \$3,500$.

The investor's equity $E$ in the position is the total collateral $nS_0 + A$ less the market value of the liability to buy back the assets $nS_1$, where $S_1$, say, $S_1 = \$75$, is the new price per share of the asset. Thus, $E = nS_0 + A - nS_1 = \$3,000$. The broker requires that the equity always be at least a given fraction $v < u$, say, $v = 0.3$, of the market value of the assets: $E \geq vnS_1 = \$2,250$ or $nS_0 + A - nS_1 \geq vnS_1$.

The fraction $v$ is the maintenance margin requirement. If the equity $E$ falls below the required maintenance margin $vnS_1$, then an additional deposit of collateral is required. How much depends on the broker's rules. It would not be unreasonable to re-quire reestablishment of the original margin ratio. If the investor does not deposit addi-tional collateral, the broker may take some cash from the account and buy back enough of the securities to reduce the liability to a level that meets the margin requirement.

If the share price at time 1 remains unchanged ($S_0 = S_1$), the margin require-ment is still $A = unS_0$. Because $v < u$, the maintenance requirement is met at time 1.

Usually the collateral bears interest for the investor. The broker may offer a money market account in which the collateral is deposited, or the broker may allow the investor to purchase T-bills and hold them as collateral. The additional interest can count toward the margin requirement if it is needed and should be taken into account when the investor recognizes the rate of return of the trade. See Bodie et al. [18] and Kellison [111] for detailed descriptions of short selling.

# Section 1.3
## Money Market Securities

Corporations and governments borrow short term by issuing securities with a year or less to maturity. These securities make up the money market. We will discuss briefly Treasury bills, certificates of deposit, repurchase agreements, and the London

Interbank Offered Rate (LIBOR). The LIBOR is the rate at which large banks in London are willing to lend money to each other. There are many sources for more detailed descriptions of money market products; for example, see Fabozzi and Fabozzi [57], Jones and Fabozzi [101], and Elton and Gruber [54].

***Treasury Bills.*** In the U.S., the New York Federal Reserve Bank issues Treasury bills in weekly auctions. T-bills are issued in face amounts starting at $10,000. They are *discount* (zero-coupon) securities, meaning they do not pay coupons; the only payment is the face amount at maturity. Two maturities are issued weekly: 13 weeks and 26 weeks. Every 4 weeks, 52-week bills are also auctioned, which sell at a discount from face value. The cash-flow diagram for a T-bill is shown in Figure 1.2. The bank issues the bill and takes the investor's cash, the price of the bill $S_t$, at the time of issue $t$. At the maturity date $T$, the bank must take back its bill and pay the bearer of the bill its face amount $F$ in cash.

**FIGURE 1.2** | *T-Bill Cash Flow*

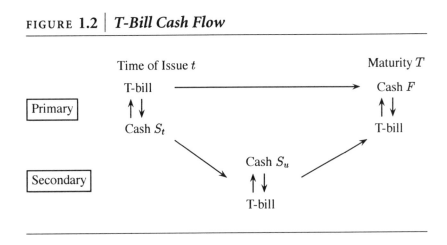

These are the primary transactions that define the bill. Secondary transactions take place at times $u$ at prices $S_u$ where $t < u < T$. T-bill ownership is easily transferable, thus allowing a secondary market, which is run by dealers who trade T-bills on a bid-ask spread basis. U.S. government securities dealers include Bank of America, Goldman Sachs, Merill Lynch, Morgan Stanley, and Prudential Securities.

T-bills are very close to being cash because there is no doubt that the Federal Reserve will take back its bill at maturity and pay the face amount. If the owner needs cash before maturity, the bill can be easily sold in the secondary market.

Newspapers such as *The Wall Street Journal* report daily the bid-ask for typical OTC quotations as of the previous business day. Table 1.2 is a typical report.

Cash-market T-bill price quotes are in terms of discount from face value per $100 of face value. For example, a T-bill maturing on November 16 has an ask T-bill

TABLE **1.2** │ *Treasury Bills*

| Maturity | Days to Maturity | Bid | Ask | Change | Ask Yield |
|---|---|---|---|---|---|
| Sep 14 1995 | 2 | 5.46 | 5.36 | +0.04 | 5.45 |
| Sep 21 | 9 | 5.68 | 5.58 | +0.02 | 5.67 |
| Sep 28 | 16 | 5.40 | 5.30 | ... | 5.40 |
| Oct 05 | 23 | 5.40 | 5.30 | +0.02 | 5.41 |
| Oct 12 | 30 | 5.39 | 5.35 | +0.03 | 5.46 |
| Oct 19 | 37 | 5.40 | 5.36 | +0.03 | 5.46 |
| Oct 26 | 44 | 5.38 | 5.34 | +0.03 | 5.46 |
| Nov 02 | 51 | 5.36 | 5.32 | +0.04 | 5.45 |
| Nov 09 | 58 | 5.35 | 5.33 | +0.02 | 5.47 |
| Nov 16 | 65 | 5.37 | 5.35 | +0.03 | 5.48 |
| Nov 24 | 73 | 5.36 | 5.34 | +0.02 | 5.49 |
| Nov 30 | 79 | 5.31 | 5.29 | +0.01 | 5.44 |
| Dec 07 | 86 | 5.36 | 5.34 | +0.02 | 5.50 |
| Dec 14 | 93 | 5.35 | 5.33 | ... | 5.48 |
| Dec 21 | 100 | 5.34 | 5.32 | +0.03 | 5.49 |
| Dec 28 | 107 | 5.24 | 5.22 | +0.02 | 5.39 |
| Jan 04 1996 | 114 | 5.32 | 5.30 | +0.01 | 5.48 |
| Jan 11 | 121 | 5.35 | 5.33 | +0.01 | 5.50 |
| Jan 18 | 128 | 5.37 | 5.35 | +0.02 | 5.54 |
| Jan 15 | 135 | 5.35 | 5.33 | ... | 5.53 |
| Feb 01 | 142 | 5.35 | 5.33 | ... | 5.54 |
| Feb 08 | 149 | 5.35 | 5.33 | ... | 5.53 |
| Feb 15 | 156 | 5.35 | 5.33 | ... | 5.55 |
| Feb 22 | 163 | 5.35 | 5.33 | ... | 5.55 |
| Feb 29 | 170 | 5.30 | 5.28 | ... | 5.51 |
| Mar 07 | 177 | 5.34 | 5.30 | +0.01 | 5.55 |
| Apr 04 | 205 | 5.35 | 5.33 | +0.01 | 5.57 |
| May 02 | 233 | 5.36 | 5.34 | ... | 5.59 |
| May 30 | 261 | 5.37 | 5.35 | +0.02 | 5.61 |
| Jun 27 | 289 | 5.31 | 5.29 | +0.01 | 5.56 |
| Jul 25 | 317 | 5.36 | 5.34 | +0.01 | 5.63 |
| Aug 22 | 345 | 5.35 | 5.33 | +0.02 | 5.64 |

Source: *The Wall Street Journal*, September 11, 1995.

yield of 5.35%.[3] If the face value is $1,000,000, the cash price is determined by the formula

$$\text{Price} = \text{Face}\left(1 - \text{Yield}\,\frac{\text{Days to Maturity}}{360}\right).$$

Thus, the cash price for $1,000,000 of November 16 T-bills is

$$\text{Price} = 1,000,000\left(1 - 0.0535\,\frac{65}{360}\right) = \$990,340.$$

The formula is merely an accepted convention for mapping prices uniquely to yields. The use of a 360-day year as a convention in the U.S. probably has its roots in the era before inexpensive calculators and personal computers, but there is no incentive to change it now. In principle, we could simply use prices and ignore yields. The prices would determine equivalent yields, found by solving the equation for the yield:

$$\text{Yield} = \frac{1,000,000 - 990,340}{1,000,000} \times \frac{360}{\text{Days to Maturity}} = 5.35\%.$$

This is the discount yield, which is appropriate for zero-coupon bonds sold at a discount from face value. To facilitate comparing yields with other securities, the newspaper also reports the annualized yield, as an annualized effective interest rate over the remaining life of the bond. The calculation is based on the ask price and is called the Ask Yield. For the November 16 maturity, the annualized rate for the 65-day period is determined as follows:

$$\text{Ask Yield} = \frac{1,000,000 - 990,340}{990,340} \times \frac{365}{65} = 5.48\%.$$

The equivalent continuously compounded interest rate $r$ over the 65-day period is determined by the equation $990,340\,e^{r(65/365)} = 1,000,000$, so $r = 5.45\%$. In the U.S., the term *bond equivalent yield* means two times the effective yield per half-year, that is, the annual yield compounded semiannually. Because U.S. bonds pay semiannual coupons, the bond equivalent yield gives a rate comparable to the annualized effective yield per coupon period. For this example, the bond equivalent yield is $2y = 5.53\%$, where $y = e^{0.5r} - 1$.

T-bills are very good collateral. They are very liquid, in the sense that bid-ask spreads in the secondary market are small, and they are ideal as a short-term, safe

---

[3]Note a 2-day variation in the Days to Maturity column. This allows 2 days for delivery.

place to invest cash. The large face amounts make it difficult for individuals to buy them directly, but money market mutual funds that invest heavily in T-bills and other good quality short-term securities are easily accessible.

The U.S. T-bill market is the largest and most liquid in the world, but the governments of many other countries also issue T-bills. The Bank of Canada offers 3-, 6-, and 12-month T-bills. Canadian T-bills are discount instruments; that is, they trade at a discount from face value, like U.S. T-bills. However, the convention for quoting prices is different: Canadian T-bill quotes are in terms of yield, using a 365-day year, whereas the U.S. T-bill uses a 360-day year. For example, a 65-day $1,000,000 Canadian T-bill selling for $990,340 would be quoted at 5.48%, whereas the equivalent U.S. T-bill is quoted at 5.35%. A 360-day year is used in some European markets. The Japanese government issues T-bills that are modeled on the U.S. T-bill; their maturities are 3 and 6 months, and the minimum size is 10 million yen.

The interest rates implied by government bonds are usually called risk-free rates. "Default-free" would be a better term than risk-free because the investors' rate of return does have elements of risk. Bond investors face *reinvestment risk* since they do not know what rates will prevail when cash flows are received. The degree of reinvestment risk increases with the term of the contract. Another measure of risk is simply variance of return. From this view, even very short-term default-free zero-coupon bonds are "risky." One way to think of this is to imagine a planned investment of 1 per week for each of the the next 10 weeks. Each unit is to be invested at the prevailing 90-day T-bill rate. The actual rates $r_1, \ldots, r_{10}$ obtained are uncertain at the time we plan the investment. Based on studies of interest rates, we can develop beliefs about the probability distribution of $r_1, \ldots, r_{10}$. Nevertheless, the financial outcome of our plan is uncertain, a definitely risky situation.

Frequently we use a constant, default-free interest rate for a model or plan, although we know in practice rates vary from day to day. This is often called the "risk-free" interest rate—a useful simplification. A less hypothetical constant rate is obtained by matching the model or plan's time horizon to a zero-coupon government bond. The yield to maturity of the bond is used as the "risk-free" rate for the model.

***Certificates of Deposit.*** Banks borrow short term by issuing negotiable certificates of deposit, called CDs. The face amounts are usually $10,000,000 or more. Like T-bills, CDs are short term with a maturity of 1 year or less, they are bearer securities, and they pay no coupons. The issuing bank agrees to pay the face amount plus specified interest at maturity. CDs are easy to trade, like T-bills, and there is a secondary market for them. The prices of CDs determine equivalent interest rates, in the same way that T-bill prices determine interest rates.

However, CDs are more risky and not as liquid as T-bills; therefore the price of a CD will be lower than the price of a T-bill with the same maturity and same cash payment at maturity. The corresponding CD-determined interest rate will be higher than the default-free rate. U.S. banks issue CDs in smaller denominations for the individual investor market, and the Federal Deposit Insurance Corporation insures them against the bank's default up to $100,000. Merrill Lynch makes a secondary market for these smaller denomination CDs.

*Repurchase Agreements.* Securities dealers make a market for repurchase agreements, called *repos*. Repos are formed with T-bills or other securities as collateral. A dealer uses repos to earn interest on surplus securities. For example, a dealer offers to sell a $10,000,000 5-month T-bill to an investor for $9,705,000 with a repurchase clause in the contract requiring return of the T-bill 14 days later at a price of $9,727,000. In effect the dealer is borrowing $9,705,000 for 14 days and paying interest of $22,000. This amounts to a loan, for which the lender holds the T-bill as collateral. Dealers also take the other side, creating a reverse repo, under which the dealer buys a security agreeing to sell it later at a fixed price. A dealer whose supply of T-bills is low could use a repo to get securities to meet a short-term commitment. Repos are important because they expand the possibilities for trading the underlying security.

*London Interbank Offered Rate.* The LIBOR is used by London banks for mutual lending and is used as a short-term interest rate quoted in the European money markets for Eurodollar transactions. The average of rates offered by five major banks for 1-, 3-, and 6-month and 1-year deposits are quoted in the financial press. For example, *The Wall Street Journal*'s "Money Rates" column of September 11, 1995, quotes the 6-month LIBOR rate as 5-7/8%. The LIBOR is quoted on an interest-added (simple interest) basis using a 360-day year and the actual number of days on deposit. This means, for example, that a London bank will accept 1 million U.S. dollars now and promise to pay principal and interest 6 months hence in the amount of

$$\text{Principal} + \text{Interest} = 1,000,000 \left( 1 + 0.05875 \, \frac{182}{360} \right) = 1,029,701$$

because there are 182 days to maturity and a year is assumed to have 360 days.

*Other Money Market Securities.* The securities we described above, as well as commercial paper and bankers' acceptances, are covered in greater detail by Fabozzi and Fabozzi [57], Marshall [130], Siegal and Siegal [183], and Marshall and Bansal [131]. These securities are not exchange traded; rather, they are traded in dealer markets or offered by banks. However, the exchanges offer derivative products based on these securities, and as a service to their clients they offer information on money market securities (see Besant [6], for example).

# Section 1.4
# Bond Markets

The long-term borrowing needs of corporations and governments are met by issuing bonds. A corporation typically uses an investment banker to issue bonds as do some local and state governments. The federal governments of the U.S., Canada, and other countries issue bonds through central banking systems. The bond contracts provide periodic coupon payments and redemption value at maturity to the bondholder. Bondholder rights are easily transferable, facilitating secondary markets. Most bonds in the U.S. are traded over-the-counter, but there are some exchange-traded bonds.

In the case of corporate bonds, the stockholders, who have the original claim on corporate earnings, promise in the bond contract to pay bondholder interest before taking dividends. This dual claim on corporate earnings is a source of conflict between stockholders and bond owners. The bond contract has to be strong enough to convince investors that the debt will be repaid. A weaker promise makes the contract less valuable and hence lowers the bond's market price.

Federal government bonds are backed by the credit of the government. Some governments have defaulted on debt or suspended interest payments, but the bonds of the U.S., Canada, Japan, and European federal governments are usually considered default free. Cities, states, counties, and their agencies also issue bonds. Investors must ascertain government creditworthiness as they consider prices. Liquidity is another important factor; for example, a bond issued by a city in Texas may not be as liquid as an equivalent bond issued by a large corporation because the city's creditworthiness is not as widely known. Thus, the lack of liquidity affects the price. We would expect the city's bonds to sell at a lower price than the corporation's, other things being equal.

We use the following terminology for bond parameters, which may be familiar. The contract provides a redemption value $C$, to be paid at a maturity date $T$, a coupon rate $c$, and a face amount $F$. These parameters define the cash flow promised to the bondholder (see Figure 1.3). Most bonds have a redemption value equal to the face value, $C = F$, on the maturity date.

FIGURE **1.3** │ *Cash Flow Promised to Bondholder*

A bond is *callable* if the issuer (the borrower) has the right under the terms of the contract to repay the debt before the normal redemption date. Callable bonds give the borrower an option to refinance the debt; the option is likely to be exercised when interest rates decline after the bond is issued. Upon early redemption, the contract may require a penalty payment to the bondholder, in addition to the redemption value and coupon payment then due. In this case we would have $C > F$.

The bond contract trades in a secondary market after it is issued. Let $P$ denote the market price at time $t$. The rights to the future cash flows ($N = T - t$ coupons and the redemption value) can be obtained by paying $P$ to the current owner. The *yield to maturity* is the interest rate $y$ for which the price is equal to the discounted future bond cash flows,

$$P = \frac{1 - (1 + y)^{-N}}{y} \, cF + (1 + y)^{-N}C.$$

This bond formula assumes pricing on coupon-paying dates, not between coupon dates. Otherwise, adjustment for accrued interest is necessary.

In the U.S., Canada, the U.K., and Japan, bonds typically pay semiannual coupons, so the timing of cash flows is $cF$ each half-year, $y$ is the rate of interest effective per half-year, and $N$ is the number of half-years to maturity. In other countries, coupons may be annual or even quarterly; for example, German bonds pay annual coupons, and some U.K. bonds pay quarterly coupons.

The market value of a callable bond with no penalty payment is less than or equal to the market value of an otherwise identical noncallable bond. The difference is the market value of the call option provided to the borrower; it cannot be negative. However, if all traders believe that the borrower will not exercise the call option, then the two bonds should trade at the same price, other things being equal.

U.S. Treasury bonds issued after November 1984 are noncallable. Callable bonds were issued earlier and remain in the market. The government of the U.K. issues callable bonds, but the Australian government issues only noncallable bonds.

The U.S. and Canadian governments now assign registration numbers to each coupon and principal payment of some bonds, with maturities as long as 30 years. This allows the individual payments to be traded, creating long-term, zero-coupon, default-free bonds. The U.S. program is called the STRIP (Separate Trading of Registered Interest and Principal Securities) program, and the securities are called *strips* (see also Section 2.8.1).

The Australian, Canadian, British, and American governments issue indexed bonds with coupons that are adjusted to reflect inflation in the economy. A person who depends on bonds for future consumption might find these attractive since they are designed to keep pace with consumer price changes.

# Section 1.5
# General Return Model

Let $S_t$ denote the price of an asset at time $t$. Since real-world prices are positive, we require $S_t > 0$. The change in price $S_t - S_a$ is the capital gain to the owner who buys at time $a$ and sells at a later time $t$, ignoring transaction costs such as commissions to brokers. Additional benefits may accrue to the owner. For example, if the asset is a stock, there may be dividends paid during $(a, t]$. If the asset is a bond, there may be coupons paid. However, some assets are costly to hold. For example, if the asset is a piece of real estate, there may be expenses such as insurance and property taxes to pay.

Let $D(a, t)$ denote the accumulated cash distributed to the owner during the period, with the understanding that if the owner pays out cash, $D(a, t)$ is negative. The effective return over the period is the total gain $S_t - S_a + D(a, t)$ divided by the price at the beginning of the period $S_a$. Thus, the continuously compounded, annualized return $R(a, t)$ solves the equation

$$e^{(t-a)R(a,t)} = \frac{S_t + D(a, t)}{S_a}.$$

This equation assumes dividends that are paid at the end of period, or that they are reinvested during the period and accumulated to the end of the period.

At time $a$, the price $S_t$ is a random variable. Investors have information on which to form opinions about the distribution of prices and its moments. Thus, the model allows for uncertainty of future prices while specifying certain statistical distributions for returns.

The period $(a, t]$ is usually a month, week, or day. If all the measurement periods are of the same length, such as days, we can use the shorter notation $R_t = R(t-1, t)$.

The simplest probabilistic example of asset price movements is the single-period model. Consider an asset traded at two times $t < T$, which we think of as now $t$ and later $T$. The two times, or dates, define a single period, and so this is often described as a single-period model. The asset pays no dividends and requires no carrying costs in this model. Let $S = S_t$ denote the current asset price, and let $\tau = T - t$. The probability distribution describing the return $R = R(t, T)$ is as simple as possible while still being random, a Bernoulli random variable. This means the return takes one of only two possible values:

$$R = \begin{cases} u, & \text{with probability } p \\ d, & \text{with probability } 1 - p \end{cases}$$

where $u$, $d$, and $p$ are model parameters. The two corresponding values of the price are given as follows:

$$S_T = \begin{cases} Se^{u\tau}, & \text{with probability } p \\ Se^{d\tau}, & \text{with probability } 1 - p. \end{cases}$$

The parameters $u$, $d$, and $p$ can be estimated by observing spot price movements. The symbol $u$ suggests an upward price movement, and $d$ suggests downward. Actually, both movements can be "up" in the sense that $Se^{d\tau}$ can be greater than $S$; one movement is just greater than the other: $Se^{u\tau} > Se^{d\tau}$. Models using this framework are discussed in several later chapters.

In a multiple-period setting, the model asset has one price change per trading period, the periods are equally spaced, and the prices are observed (i.e., trading is allowed) at the end of each period. Let $t_k = t + k\Delta$, for $k = 1, \ldots, N$, denote the times when prices are observed. The future prices are modeled by specifying the joint distribution of returns for the $N$ periods.

For the *binomial model* in which there is only one up or one down movement in each period, the return $R$ can be obtained by counting the random number of up and down movements: $R(t, T) = uK + d(N - K)$ where $K$ is the number of up price movements and $K$ is a binomial random variable with parameters $N$ and $p$. The model is specified once the parameters $p$, $N$, $u$, and $d$ are given. The binomial model is used extensively in later chapters.

# Section 1.6
# Interest Rates

The market prices for bonds, certificates of deposit, and other money market securities determine equivalent interest rates, called *spot market* interest rates or simply spot rates. The spot rates that correspond to differing maturities imply values for interest effective between future maturities; these are called *forward rates*. The one-period interest rate that may turn out to be available in the market during a future period is called the *short rate* applicable to the period. Applying these ideas to a coupon-bearing bond gives rise to yet another interest rate, the *yield to maturity*, which we introduced in Section 1.4. In this section we make these ideas precise in two settings. The first assumes that all rates are compounded once per period, and the second version uses continuous compounding. Of course, the same ideas can be developed for other compounding frequencies.

## SECTION 1.6.1 | COMPOUNDING ONCE PER PERIOD

Consider securities that are traded at times $t = 0, 1, 2, \ldots$, equally spaced and beginning now with $t = 0$. The price now of a security with a single future payment of 1 at time $t = k$ is denoted $P(0, k) = P(k)$. The corresponding spot rate $s_k$ is defined implicitly by

$$(1 + s_k)^{-k} = P(k)$$

or explicitly by

$$s_k = \frac{1}{P(k)^{1/k}} - 1.$$

For example, *The Wall Street Journal* of September 11, 1995, gave rates for guaranteed investment contracts (GICs) as shown in Table 1.3.

TABLE **1.3** | *Guaranteed Investment Contracts*

|         | 1 Year | 2 Years | 3 Years | 4 Years | 5 Years |
|---------|--------|---------|---------|---------|---------|
| Index   | 5.67%  | 5.85%   | 6.00%   | 6.15%   | 6.25%   |

Source: *The Wall Street Journal*, September 11, 1995.

GICs can take many different forms, but the most common type is a *bullet contract*, according to Walker [201]. Bullet contracts require a single deposit (the price) and provide a single lump-sum payment at maturity, which is described by a preset guaranteed interest rate. The interest rate is quoted on a basis of one compounding per year.

Consider five bullet GIC contracts, with maturities 1, 2, 3, 4, and 5 years, which provide guaranteed interest as indicated by the index in Table 1.3. The prices are not given; rather, the table gives the spot rates directly: for example, $s_1 = 0.0567$, $s_2 = 0.0585$, and so on. Prices, if needed, can be calculated by the fundamental relation given above. Forward rates, implied by the spot rates, apply to each of the five single-year periods; these are denoted $f_0, f_1, \ldots, f_4$. The spot rate $s_1 = 5.67\%$ covers the same period as $f_0$. For the initial period, the spot and forward rate concepts coincide, and $s_1 = f_0$. The first period of the 2 years covered by the 2-year spot rate $s_2$ is covered by $s_1$. The second forward rate applies to the second period, and the defining relation between spot and forward rates determines the forward rate:

$$(1 + s_2)^2 = (1 + s_1)(1 + f_1) = (1 + f_0)(1 + f_1).$$

As Babbel and Merrill [2] point out, the spot rate $s_2$ is in a sense an "average" of the implied forward rates $f_0$ and $f_1$ because $1 + s_2$ is the geometric average of $1 + f_0$ and $1 + f_1$. Taking logarithms of the above relation shows that $\log(1 + s_2)$ is the arithmetic average of $\log(1 + f_0)$ and $\log(1 + f_1)$. For the GIC data we compute the forward rate $f_1$ directly: $f_1 = (1 + s_2)^2/(1 + s_1) - 1 = (1.0585)^2/1.0567 - 1 = 6.03\%$. Using the general relation between forward and spot rates

$$(1 + s_k)^k = (1 + s_{k-1})^{k-1}(1 + f_{k-1}) = \prod_{j=0}^{k-1}(1 + f_j),$$

we successively compute the implied forward rates for the GIC data example as follows:

$$f_2 = \frac{(1 + s_3)^3}{(1 + s_2)^2} - 1 = \frac{(1.0600)^3}{(1.0585)^2} - 1 = 6.30\%,$$

$$f_3 = \frac{(1 + s_4)^4}{(1 + s_3)^3} - 1 = \frac{(1.0615)^4}{(1.0600)^3} - 1 = 6.60\%,$$

$$f_4 = \frac{(1 + s_5)^5}{(1 + s_4)^4} - 1 = \frac{(1.0625)^5}{(1.0615)^4} - 1 = 6.65\%.$$

This illustrates how spot rates determine forward rates. Spot rates are observed in the market in the case of GICs. For other securities, prices are observed, and we must compute the equivalent spot rate. Forward rates might not be observed in the market. However, if there is a forward contract written on a bond to be delivered in the future, the delivery price would be the same as the price implied by the spot rates, that is, the forward rate; otherwise we say there is an "arbitrage" opportunity (see Section 2.2).

Short rates are the one-period market rates that arise in future periods. They should be distinguished from forward rates. At $t = 0$, we can calculate the forward rates implied by spot market prices (or spot rates), but we can only estimate or conjecture as to what market rates will prevail in the future. Thus, at $t = 0$, we know the current short rate $r_0$; it is the same as $s_1$ and $f_0$. However, we do not observe $r_1$, the rate available at $t = 1$ for investment from $t = 1$ to 2, until $t = 1$. Thus, the short rates $r_1, r_2, \ldots$ are not revealed by the market until times $t = 1, 2 \ldots$. In contrast, the forward rates $f_1, f_2, \ldots$ are known at $t = 0$; they are the market's consensus at $t = 0$ of short rates that might prevail in the future.

We can use an interest rate model that gives a probabilistic connection to successive short rates to project or forecast future short rates. For example, Hull [98] and Duffie [50] describe a collection of such models, some of which we discuss in later chapters. To whet the reader's appetite, we present here a discrete-time analog to the *Vasicek model* [200] (see Hull [98] for a description of similar models). In this model short rates are generated recursively: $r_0$ is the current short rate. The recursion relation is

$$r_{k+1} = r_k + a(b - r_k) + \sigma Z_k$$

where $b$ denotes the "long-run" short rate and $a$ is a parameter measuring the intensity of the pull of $b$ on $r_k$. $Z_0, Z_1, \ldots$ are independent standard normal random variables and $\sigma$ is a positive constant. This is an autoregressive model of order 1, AR(1), in time-series terminology. The model parameters $a$, $b$, and $\sigma$ might be estimated from spot market data. The development of interest rate models is complex, and there are a variety of approaches. We develop these ideas in later chapters.

Simulating or modeling future short rates, and even future term structure curves, is important in practical actuarial work in which simulation is used for valuation of interest-sensitive life insurance products, for asset-liability management, and for solvency/regulatory purposes.

For zero-coupon bonds, the yield to maturity and spot rate for a given market price are equivalent concepts. However, when the bond pays coupons, its yield to maturity is a weighted average of spot rates corresponding to its coupon payment data. For example, consider a bond paying $cF$ at $t = 1, 2, \ldots, N - 1$ and $cF + C$ at time $t = N$. The yield to maturity, $y$, satisfies

$$P = cF \sum_{k=1}^{N}(1 + y)^{-k} + (1 + y)^{-N}C = cF\,\frac{1 - (1 + y)^{-N}}{y} + (1 + y)^{-N}C.$$

On the other hand, each coupon satisfies

$$cF\,P(k) = cF(1 + s_k)^{-k}$$

so that

$$P = cF \sum_{k=1}^{N}(1 + s_k)^{-k} + (1 + s_N)^{-N}C.$$

This illustrates the relation between yield to maturity of a coupon bond and the term structure defined by spot rates.

## SECTION 1.6.2 | CONTINUOUS COMPOUNDING

Let $P(t, T)$ denote the market price at time $t$ for a risk-free zero-coupon bond that pays 1 at its maturity, time $T > t$. The price determines the spot rate $s(t, T)$ implicitly by the equation $e^{-(T-t)s(t,T)} = P(t, T)$, or explicitly by

$$s(t, T) = \frac{-1}{T - t} \log P(t, T).$$

Yields, spot, and short rates corresponding to other compounding frequencies are defined analogously. For example, the semiannual spot rate $s^{(2)} = s^{(2)}(t, T)$ is defined by

$$\left(1 + \frac{s^{(2)}}{2}\right)^{-N} = P(t, T)$$

where $N$ is the number of half-years in the period $(t, T]$. Usually time is measured in years, so $N = 2(T - t)$ is the number of compounding periods in $T - t$ years.

Yields, like all interest rates, are quoted on an annual basis, but the compounding frequency depends on the customs of the market. For example, in the U.S. coupon-bearing bonds pay coupons twice per year, and yields to maturity are quoted in the financial press as annual rates compounded twice per year. Comparable spot rates would be based on compounding twice per year.

The *yield to maturity* of a bond can change depending on the maturity, the risk of default by the borrower, transaction costs, the security's coupon rate, and the frequency of interest compounding. The *term structure of interest rates* shows how interest rates vary with yield to maturity. A realization of this relationship is published in the financial press each business day; for example, *The Wall Street Journal* publishes a column called "STRIPS" that gives the yield to various maturities of zero-coupon bonds. These are considered to be risk free because they are collateralized by coupon-bearing U.S. government bonds.

The following model formalizes the relation between prices, yields, and forward rates. The curve $\{s(t, T); T \geq t\}$ is the term structure of interest rates at time $t$. The *instantaneous forward rates* $\{f(t, T); T \geq t\}$ implied by the term structure are defined implicitly by the equation

$$s(t, T) = \frac{1}{T - t} \int_t^T f(t, u)\, du$$

or equivalently

$$P(t, T) = \exp\left[-\int_t^T f(t, u)\, du\right].$$

Clearly, $s(t, t) = f(t, t)$ and $P(t, t) = 1$. The first equation can be interpreted by saying that the yield to maturity over $(t, T]$ is the average of the forward rates over the same period. In classical actuarial notation, when interest rates are deterministic, the forward rate is the force of interest $\delta_u$.

The notations are related by $\delta_u = f(t, u)$ so that the forward rate $f(t, u)$ does not depend on $t$. In this case, $\delta_u = f(t, u) = f(u, u) = s(u, u)$. So $\delta_u$ can also be thought of as the *continuously compounding short rate* or the *instantaneous spot rate*.

In this book we recognize that interest rates evolve stochastically through time and must be functions of two time variables. The classical actuarial notation is not rich enough for our purposes.

Multiplying both sides of the first equation by $T - t$ and differentiating with respect to $T$ gives the explicit representation

$$f(t, T) = \frac{\partial}{\partial T}[(T - t)s(t, T)].$$

The instantaneous forward rate $f(t, s)$ has discretely compounded equivalents. For example, the one compounding per period forward rate $f_k$, as described in the previous section, is related to the continuously compounded forward rate with $t = 0$:

$$1 + f_k = \frac{(1 + s_{k+1})^{k+1}}{(1 + s_k)^k}$$

$$= \frac{\exp\left[-\int_0^k f(0, s)\, ds\right]}{\exp\left[-\int_0^{k+1} f(0, s)\, ds\right]}$$

$$= \exp\left[\int_k^{k+1} f(0, s)\, ds\right].$$

This section has introduced methods to describe returns over a number of years on bonds, certificates of deposit, and other money market securities by spot rates, yield rates, and forward rates. In the next section we consider returns in a context that is more general in that it includes stocks in addition to money market securities. It is less general, however, in that it applies only to returns over a single period.

## Section 1.7
## Risk and Return:
## The Markowitz Model

According to the Markowitz [129] model, the total risk of an asset is measured by its variance over a planning period $[t, T]$. Thus, this Markowitz model is a one-period market model, which focuses on the relation between the two moments of a return variable $R$:

$$\mu = E[R],$$
$$\sigma^2 = Var(R).$$

Sharpe [175] allows portfolio selection on the basis of risk measured relative to the market portfolio $M$, which is defined by the statistic beta

$$\beta = \frac{\text{Cov}(R, R_M)}{\sigma_M^2}$$

and which is a widely diversified portfolio representative of the market as a whole. The mean, variance, and beta of the return distribution can be estimated by observing return outcomes over a period of time. Markowitz and Sharpe consider the risk-versus-return relation for portfolios of assets for which we can take these statistics as given.

Stock price and return data are widely available for publicly traded companies. For example, the Center for Research in Security Prices (CRSP) at the University of Chicago manages and distributes the CRSP databases, which include monthly stock price and return data for all stocks traded on the New York Stock Exchange dating back to 1926. In addition, CRSP has daily price and return data available for NYSE, American Stock Exchange, and Nasdaq securities dating back to 1962. In addition, return data are available for many corporate and government bonds, so there are adequate data on a rich array of basic securities that we can consider for inclusion in a portfolio.

Let $R_1, R_2, \ldots, R_N$ denote the return for a given universe of $N$ assets, $\sigma_{i,j}$ denote the covariance of $R_i$ and $R_j$, and $\Sigma$ be the $N \times N$ matrix with $(i, j)$-th element $\sigma_{i,j}$. This covariance matrix is symmetric, and its diagonal elements are the variances.

A portfolio is constructed from the $N$ given assets by specifying the percentage of the value of the portfolio that is invested in each asset. For example, if we have a universe of three assets from which to form a portfolio, and 500 monetary units to invest, then we might put 200 in asset 1, 250 in asset 2, and 50 in asset 3. The corresponding percentages (40%, 50%, and 10%) determine the portfolio. Under the assumptions commonly used, the scale of investment does not affect the percentages in the sense that investors with the same risk-return preferences will select the same portfolios regardless of the size of their investments. Thus, in specifying a portfolio, we need only specify the percentage invested in each security. We let $x_i$ denote the percentage invested in the $i$-th asset; it is called the weight of asset $i$ in the portfolio.

The return on the portfolio is denoted by $R_p$. The portfolio return is the weighted average of the individual security returns:

$$R_p = \sum_{i=1}^{N} x_i R_i .$$

Thus, the expected portfolio return and variance can be calculated in terms of the weights and the statistics of the securities as follows:

$$\mu_p = \sum_{i=1}^{N} x_i E[R_i] = \sum_{i=1}^{N} x_i \mu_i,$$

$$\sigma_p^2 = \text{Var}(R_p) = \text{Cov}(R_p, R_p) = \sum_{i=1}^{N} x_i \text{Cov}(R_i, R_p)$$

$$= \sum_{i=1}^{N} x_i \sum_{j=1}^{N} x_j \text{Cov}(R_i, R_j) = X^T \Sigma X.$$

The portfolio variance is a function of the vector of weights $X^T = [x_1, x_2, \ldots, x_N]$ and the covariance matrix $\Sigma = [\sigma_{i,j}]$.

An efficient portfolio is one that is not dominated by another portfolio; that is, it is a portfolio for which there is no other portfolio with lower variance and an equal or higher expected return. Figure 1.4 illustrates the concept of efficiency and the associated notion of portfolio dominance. Note that portfolio $B$ dominates portfolio $A$ since it offers the same variance but has a higher expected return. Similarly, portfolio $B$ dominates portfolio $C$ since it offers the same expected return but a lower variance. The basic portfolio problem is to find the maximum portfolio return for a given variance or the minimum portfolio variance for a given portfolio return. These optimal portfolios are said to be mean-variance-efficient portfolios.

### FIGURE 1.4 │ *Risk and Return Relations*

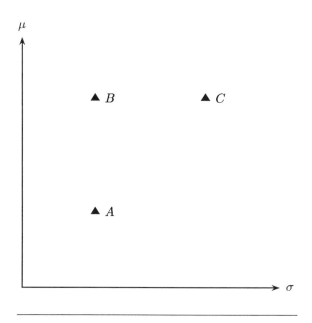

A number of variants of the general portfolio problem exist. One particular variant can be formulated as follows: Given a required portfolio target return $\mu_p$, and a set of $N$ securities with expected returns and covariance matrix $\Sigma$, determine the portfolio weights $X$ in order to minimize the risk measure $\sigma_p^2 = X^T \Sigma X$ subject to two constraints:

$$\sum_{i=1}^{N} x_i = 1$$

and

$$\sum_{i=1}^{N} x_i \mu_i = \mu_p.$$

This last constraint holds for short time periods or for a time period in which no rebalancing of the asset mix is allowed. Technical aspects of rebalancing a portfolio over time are discussed in later chapters.

Note that we did not constrain the value of a weight to be nonnegative. What would be the significance of a solution for which one of the weights is negative, say, $x_1 < 0$? Instead of buying enough of asset 1 so that it made up $100x\%$ of our portfolio, we should *sell short* enough of asset 1 so that we have $100 - 100x_1 > 100\%$ of our planned investment available to invest in other assets. Specifically, suppose we have 500 to invest, and $x_1 = -0.1$, $x_2 = 0.5$, $x_3 = 0.6$. Then we would sell enough units of asset 1 to obtain $500(-x_1) = 50$ in cash at the beginning of the period. This gives us 550 to invest in assets 2 and 3. We do not have to own asset 1 to sell it short. As we discussed earlier, we can borrow asset 1, sell it, buy it back at the end of the period, and return it to its owner. Now we can invest $500x_2 = 250$ in asset 2 and $500x_3 = 300$ in asset 3, a total of 550 in assets 2 and 3 and $-50$ in asset 1.

The first constraint simply requires that the portfolio be 100% invested in the $N$ risky securities being considered for inclusion in the optimal portfolio. The second constraint selects the target return for the portfolio whose variance is to be minimized. Often a portfolio is subject to restrictions on the percentage of funds to be invested in given assets. One such restriction is to forbid short selling a specific asset, say, asset 1. Then we must solve the optimization problem, subject to the additional constraint $x_1 \geq 0$. Another common constraint is to limit the percentage invested in a given class of assets; for example, a given industrial class such as computer technology stocks might be limited.

These constraints can be incorporated into the model easily. As an illustration, suppose $J$ is the subset of indices $j$ for which asset $j$ cannot be sold short and $C$ is the subset corresponding to computer technology stocks. We can set up the problem of finding an optimal portfolio, subject to no short selling of asset $j$ in class $J$, and subject to investing no more than 10% in class $C$ as follows. Determine the portfolio weights $X$ to minimize $\sigma_p^2 = X^T \Sigma X$ subject to the following constraints:

$$1. \quad \sum_{i=1}^{N} x_i = 1$$

$$2. \quad \sum_{i=1}^{N} x_i \mu_i = \mu_p$$

$$3. \quad \sum_{i \in C} x_i \leq 0.10$$

$$4. \quad x_i \geq 0, \quad \text{for all } j \in J.$$

Of course, potentially different minimum variance portfolios can be determined for each target return we might select. In fact, we can graph an entire set of efficient portfolios, plotting the points $(\sigma_p, \mu_p)$ by solving the portfolio problem for different values of $\sigma$ corresponding to a range of values of required return $\mu_p$. This graph is called the *efficient frontier* for the given portfolio of $N$ assets.

If the underlying assets are all positively correlated, there is a lower limit to the portfolio variance. Some risk persists even though the portfolio is diversified to the extent that is possible or desired. Suppose that we select a portfolio with return $R_p$ and now look outside the original universe from which the portfolio was selected. If there is a security $H$ for which $\text{Cov}(R_p, H) < 0$, then we can reduce portfolio variance by bringing $H$ into the portfolio. This is described by Boyle [22], who uses it to illustrate the value futures, options, reinsurance, and other derivatives offered to investors as methods of managing their risks. This is illustrated by the risk-and-return exercises at the end of this chapter.

# Section 1.8
## Insurance and Annuities

Insurance companies collect cash payments from customers in exchange for promises to pay for benefits under future contingent circumstances. Two examples are worth keeping in mind. First, property owners buy insurance that will compensate them for future damage to their property due to fire or windstorm. Second, investors purchase annuities that will provide future retirement income. In each case, the insurer invests the collected premiums, pays expenses, and prepares to pay customer claims as they occur. The insurer's portfolio of risks, the collection of policies it has issued, will have more stable financial values to the extent that the risks are uncorrelated. The asset portfolio model that we describe in Section 1.7 has an analog for insurance liabilities, which we discuss in later chapters.

## SECTION **1.8.1** | INSURANCE PORTFOLIOS

Bowers et al. [19] describe a model of an insurance transaction in their introduction to risk theory. In this model an individual purchases a contract that obligates the insurance company to pay future covered claims over the period $(0, T]$. Let $N(t)$ denote the number of claims paid since the policy is issued ($t = 0$); the size of the $i$-th claim is $X_i$. Thus, the customer pays $P$ at the time the policy issued, in exchange for $N(T)$ future payments as shown in Figure 1.5. The insurance cash-flow model suggests that insurance has much in common with other financial contracts, such as stock certificates. The future cash flow is uncertain as to size $X_i$ and time $t_i$, but to some degree this is true of stock dividends and bond redemptions. The important differences lie in the nature of the contracts, not their cash flows.

FIGURE **1.5** | *Insurance Portfolios*

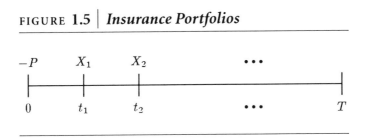

The major difference is the lack of a secondary market for insurance contracts. The property owner cannot transfer its policy to a third party because the insurance company reserves the right to approve, or *underwrite*, the person holding the contract. The insurer would not issue a fire insurance policy to a known arsonist, and it reserves the right, via contract language, to make sure the policy is not transferred to such an unsuitable person. This illustrates the personal nature of insurance contracts, which prevents the making of a secondary market for most insurance products, especially those contracts that are similar to traditional property insurance.

Life insurance products emphasizing savings compete directly with investment products such as bank certificates of deposit. Nevertheless, until very recently there was no secondary market for life insurance of any kind. In the early 1990s, the *viatical* market emerged in the U.S. Viatical companies buy policies from policyholders who are terminally ill for a fraction of the death benefit. In addition to the new viatical companies, the insurance industry has also entered this market (see Connolly [39]). Thus, there is at this time only a small, specialty, secondary market for individual life insurance contracts.

Although there is no secondary market for most direct insurance buyers, the insurers themselves transfer their liabilities to other insurers with reinsurance and occasionally even trade portfolios of insurance policies among themselves.

## SECTION 1.8.2 | ANNUITIES

In the spectrum of insurance products, at the other extreme from personal property insurance, we find investment-oriented contracts such as single-premium deferred annuities (SPDAs) and guaranteed investment contracts (GICs). These products were developed by U.S. and Canadian life insurers in the late 1970s. Although they provide mortality guarantees, SPDAs, and to a greater extent GICs, are designed and marketed as investment vehicles. The SPDA is intended primarily for the individual market. The insurance company receives an initial deposit $P$ and promises to return a fund value $F_n$ on the $n$-th anniversary. The primary guarantee is that the credited interest rate $i_k$ in each year will equal or exceed the contractual value; for example, a typical guarantee is 8.5% for 2 years and 4% for the following 6 years. Secondary guarantees provide for early surrender values and annuity purchase rates.

Typically, the GIC owner is a pension plan, or a trust company that invests funds of its pension plan clients. The pension plan makes a large deposit with the insurer, typically much larger than SPDA deposits. The insurer promises to pay a prespecified rate of return for a specific number of years, and the contract is customized to the needs of the plan and can contain a variety of options (see Walker [201] for details). However, the essential feature is the interest rate guarantee. For example, consider a GIC purchased at time 0 for 100 and promising to pay 10% for 2 years (see Figure 1.6). The maturity value is $100(1.10)^2 = 121$. What happens if market interest rates rise? If, after 1 year, the market rate for 1 year is 12%, the GIC customer may want its cash back. Although there is a surrender value $F_1$ available, most likely it will be less than the market value of the GIC holder's claim at time 1, which is $121(1.12)^{-1} = 108$. The insurer would have to liquidate assets at a time when rates are high and their market values low—hence the surrender penalty.

### FIGURE 1.6 | *Interest Rate Guarantee*

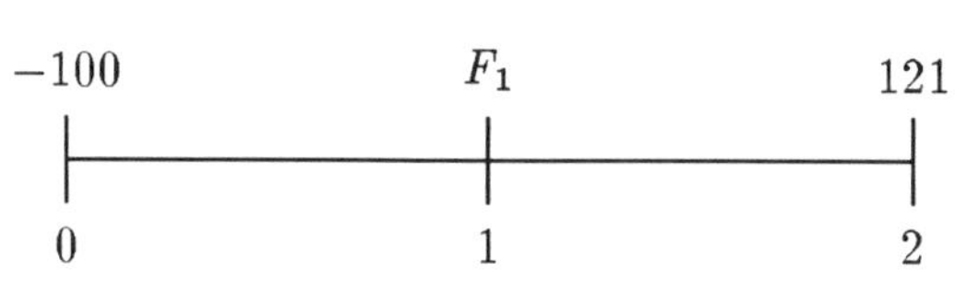

A pension plan investment manager has skills and opportunities not available to most individuals. For example, a pension plan could effectively sell its GIC in a secondary market by using its established reputation (or other collateral it may have) with a broker to enter an agreement allowing the plan to borrow 108 at time 1 and repay 108, plus interest, equaling 121 at time 2. The plan gets the market value 108 in cash and repays the loan with the GIC proceeds at time 2. Thus, to a pension plan with good financial market contacts, surrender penalties might not mean very much. In addition, SPDA (except variable SPDA) and GIC transactions are not subject to securities regulation in the U.S.

Annuity payments and life insurance policy values can be linked to a stock index. Equity investments historically have performed well over long holding periods. This linkage is attractive because annuity and life insurance owners are usually investing long term. In the U.S. these products combine the tax advantage of normal life insurance products (no tax paid until cash benefits are received) with an inflation hedge provided by equity returns. In 1995 and 1996, over 30 U.S. companies brought out equity-linked annuities. U.K. and European insurance companies introduced equity-linked life insurance in the 1980s.

The linkage comes from options on the stock index. To illustrate, we consider a single-premium deferred annuity with an initial deposit of $P$. Let $I(n)$ denote the value of the index at the beginning of policy year $n + 1$. The company guarantees the value $P \times I(1)/I(0)$ at the end of the first contract year if the index goes up. More important, it guarantees $P$ at the end of the year, even if the index declines. In other words, if the index drops, $I(1) < I(0)$, the customer has a minimum guaranteed policy value of $P$. In this case the insurance company has to pay the customer the difference $P \times [I(0) - I(1)]/I(0)$. We see later that this is the same payment as a put option on the index. In effect, the insurance company has provided the customer with a 1-year put option on the index. The contract value at the end of the first year can be written as $\max\{P, P \times I(1)/I(0)\}$, and it is said to be "reset" at this value. Some annuities are reset more frequently than annually. A minimum guaranteed return is commonly provided.

The reason why the insurance company can provide the put option is because a stock index such as the S&P 500 index is an index of stock prices (see Chapter 2). The index does not take into account the dividends paid by the stocks; these dividends can be used to buy the option. If the dividends are not sufficient to pay for the put option and expenses, then the company should write a contract providing less than 100% of the index return or make other policy modifications.

In the second policy year, a new guarantee applies to the beginning-year contract value, which amounts to a second option. Thus, for each contract year (or each reset period), the company is providing another option. Such an equity index annuity is equivalent to an annuity providing a portion of the stock index return and a bundle of 1-year options, which the insurance company builds into the contract. The insurer can hedge the risk of the options granted through the contract in the market for futures or options on the index. U.S. products use the S&P 500 index, for which there is a very active options market. The managers of these products must have a very good understanding of financial economics in order to evaluate the options included in the annuity or life insurance contract and to hedge the risk.

# Section 1.9
# Conclusion

Pooling of risks and contractual risk transfers are fundamental to finance and insurance, and both techniques normally involve financial markets. Stocks and bonds are the fundamental financial instruments. Stocks are traded on exchanges or over-the-counter. Stock transactions take various forms including market orders, limit orders, stop orders, short selling, and margin buying. Short-term government and corporate debt is traded in the money markets. The most important money market securities are T-bills, CDs, and repos. Long-term debt is traded in the bond markets, both on exchanges and to a greater extent over-the-counter.

We have defined the concepts of risk and return of an asset. For bond markets we discussed interest rates, the term structure of interest rates, and forward rates, and we discussed the relation between risk and return in an intuitive way. Finally, we have discussed insurance and annuities sufficiently to illustrate some connections with the financial markets. The main goal of the book is to elaborate on these various concepts and ideas. In Chapter 2 we continue with a discussion of securities and insurance that are derived from other securities and insurance.

# Section 1.10
# Exercises

### Exercise 1.1 (Money Markets)
a. Use the T-bill ask yields in Table 1.2 to determine the (continuously compounded) risk-free interest rate $r$:
   (i) For the period September 12 to January 4, 1996, and
   (ii) For the period September 12 to August 22, 1996.
b. Write a spreadsheet program to calculate the value of $r$ corresponding to each of the maturity dates $T$ in Table 1.2. Draw the graph of $r$ as a function of the time to maturity $T - t$, where $t$ is September 12. Use the ask prices.

### Exercise 1.2 (Risk, Return, and Portfolios)
a. For each stock described in Table 1.4, calculate the effective return for each month using a spreadsheet. Calculate the sample mean and covariance matrix of the

TABLE 1.4 | *Stock Price and Dividend Data*

| Year | Month | Apple Computer | | Homestake Mining | | FPL Group | |
|------|-------|-------|----------|-------|----------|-------|----------|
| | | Price | Dividend | Price | Dividend | Price | Dividend |
| 1987 | Dec | 42 | 0 | 17.625 | 0 | 28.625 | 0 |
| 1988 | Jan | 41.5 | 0 | 14 | 0.05 | 31.875 | 0 |
| 1988 | Feb | 43 | 0.08 | 18 | 0 | 30.875 | 0.53 |
| 1988 | Mar | 40 | 0 | 14.625 | 0 | 29 | 0 |
| 1988 | Apr | 41 | 0 | 14.625 | 0 | 28.75 | 0 |
| 1988 | May | 41.5 | 0.08 | 15.25 | 0.05 | 30.625 | 0.55 |
| 1988 | Jun | 46.25 | 0 | 15.125 | 0 | 30.5 | 0 |
| 1988 | Jul | 44.375 | 0 | 15 | 0.05 | 30.375 | 0 |
| 1988 | Aug | 39.875 | 0.08 | 14.25 | 0 | 29.875 | 0.55 |
| 1988 | Sep | 43.25 | 0 | 14.5 | 0 | 31.25 | 0 |
| 1988 | Oct | 38.625 | 0 | 13.5 | 0.05 | 31.5 | 0 |
| 1988 | Nov | 37.625 | 0.1 | 13 | 0 | 30.5 | 0.55 |
| 1988 | Dec | 40.25 | 0 | 12.625 | 0 | 31.125 | 0 |
| 1989 | Jan | 37.75 | 0 | 13 | 0 | 31.5 | 0 |
| 1989 | Feb | 36.25 | 0.1 | 14.5 | 0.05 | 29.875 | 0.55 |
| 1989 | Mar | 35.625 | 0 | 13.875 | 0 | 29.75 | 0 |
| 1989 | Apr | 39 | 0 | 13 | 0 | 30.625 | 0 |
| 1989 | May | 47.75 | 0.1 | 12.75 | 0.05 | 31.25 | 0.57 |
| 1989 | Jun | 41.25 | 0 | 13.25 | 0 | 30.875 | 0 |
| 1989 | Jul | 39.75 | 0 | 12.625 | 0 | 32.875 | 0 |
| 1989 | Aug | 44.5 | 0.1 | 14.625 | 0.05 | 31.5 | 0.57 |
| 1989 | Sep | 44.5 | 0 | 15.5 | 0 | 31.625 | 0 |
| 1989 | Oct | 46.5 | 0 | 16.625 | 0.05 | 33.375 | 0 |
| 1989 | Nov | 44.25 | 0.11 | 18.75 | 0 | 33.75 | 0.57 |
| 1989 | Dec | 35.25 | 0 | 19.125 | 0 | 36.375 | 0 |
| 1990 | Jan | 34 | 0 | 21.5 | 0.05 | 34 | 0 |
| 1990 | Feb | 34 | 0.11 | 19.625 | 0 | 32.875 | 0.57 |
| 1990 | Mar | 40.25 | 0 | 18 | 0 | 32.125 | 0 |
| 1990 | Apr | 39.375 | 0 | 16.375 | 0 | 29.75 | 0 |
| 1990 | May | 41.25 | 0.11 | 19.375 | 0.05 | 31.625 | 0.59 |
| 1990 | Jun | 44.75 | 0 | 18.25 | 0 | 30.625 | 0 |
| 1990 | Jul | 42 | 0 | 19.375 | 0.05 | 30.625 | 0 |
| 1990 | Aug | 37 | 0.11 | 20.25 | 0 | 27.25 | 0.59 |
| 1990 | Sep | 29 | 0 | 21.625 | 0 | 27.625 | 0 |
| 1990 | Oct | 30.75 | 0 | 18 | 0.05 | 28 | 0 |

*(Continued)*

TABLE **1.4** | *(Continued)*

| Year | Month | Apple Computer Price | Apple Computer Dividend | Homestake Mining Price | Homestake Mining Dividend | FPL Group Price | FPL Group Dividend |
|---|---|---|---|---|---|---|---|
| 1990 | Nov | 36.75 | 0.12 | 17.25 | 0 | 27.75 | 0 |
| 1990 | Dec | 43 | 0 | 19.25 | 0 | 29 | 0.59 |
| 1991 | Jan | 55.5 | 0 | 15.5 | 0.05 | 28.75 | 0 |
| 1991 | Feb | 57.25 | 0.12 | 16.25 | 0 | 29.75 | 0.59 |
| 1991 | Mar | 68 | 0 | 15.875 | 0 | 30.25 | 0 |
| 1991 | Apr | 55 | 0 | 14.25 | 0 | 30.25 | 0 |
| 1991 | May | 47 | 0.12 | 14.875 | 0.05 | 30.5 | 0.6 |
| 1991 | Jun | 41.5 | 0 | 16.75 | 0 | 30.375 | 0 |
| 1991 | Jul | 46.25 | 0 | 16.875 | 0.05 | 31.875 | 0 |
| 1991 | Aug | 53 | 0.12 | 14.625 | 0 | 32.75 | 0.6 |
| 1991 | Sep | 49.5 | 0 | 15.5 | 0 | 33.625 | 0 |
| 1991 | Oct | 51.5 | 0 | 15.875 | 0.05 | 34.625 | 0 |
| 1991 | Nov | 50.75 | 0.12 | 16.25 | 0 | 34.625 | 0.6 |
| 1991 | Dec | 56.375 | 0 | 16 | 0 | 37 | 0 |
| 1992 | Jan | 64.75 | 0 | 16 | 0.05 | 34.375 | 0 |
| 1992 | Feb | 67.5 | 0.12 | 15.5 | 0 | 33.75 | 0.6 |
| 1992 | Mar | 58.25 | 0 | 12.75 | 0 | 33.375 | 0 |
| 1992 | Apr | 60.125 | 0 | 11.625 | 0 | 34.75 | 0 |
| 1992 | May | 59.75 | 0 | 12.625 | 0.05 | 34.875 | 0.61 |
| 1992 | Jun | 48 | 0.12 | 13.125 | 0 | 34.875 | 0 |
| 1992 | Jul | 46.75 | 0 | 14.625 | 0.05 | 38 | 0 |
| 1992 | Aug | 46 | 0.12 | 13.25 | 0 | 36 | 0.61 |
| 1992 | Sep | 45.125 | 0 | 13.875 | 0 | 36.375 | 0 |

returns on these stocks. (The data for this exercise came from *RealData* by Kolb and Wilson [115].)

b. Use results of (a) and the optimization feature of spreadsheet software (for example, Solver in Excel™) to solve for a minimum variance portfolio of Apple Computer and Homestake Mining providing an expected return of 1.5% per month. Recalculate for a range of monthly returns running from 1% to 3% in increments of 0.5%, and save the values of the standard deviation of return corresponding to each level of expected return. Draw a graph using the chart feature of the spreadsheet, showing standard deviation on the horizontal axis and return on the vertical axis. This is the efficient frontier defined by Apple Computer and Homestake Mining.

c. Rework (b), but this time allow investing in FPL Group also. Plot both frontiers on the same set of axes.

## Exercise 1.3 (Cash-Flow Matching)

Table 1.5 gives the market prices of U.S. Treasury bonds for various maturities. Determine how much of each bond to buy on September 11, 1995, in order to create, from the combined coupon and maturity cash flows, a portfolio that pays $1,000,000 in each year 1996 through 2005. To keep it simple, assume that coupons are annual (rather than semiannual), that all of the bonds mature on September 11, and that the $1,000,000 payments are due September 11. Calculate the market value of the portfolio.

### TABLE 1.5 | *Treasury Bonds*

| Rate | Month | Year | Bid | Asked | Yield Asked |
|------|-------|------|--------|--------|-------------|
| 7.000 | Sep | 1996 | 101:10 | 101:12 | 5.63 |
| 5.500 | Sep | 1997 | 99:12 | 99:14 | 5.79 |
| 4.750 | Sep | 1998 | 96:22 | 96:24 | 5.93 |
| 7.125 | Sep | 1999 | 103:28 | 103:30 | 6.02 |
| 8.750 | Aug | 2000 | 111:12 | 111:14 | 6.03 |
| 7.875 | Aug | 2001 | 108:21 | 108:23 | 6.10 |
| 6.375 | Aug | 2002 | 101:05 | 101:07 | 6.16 |
| 5.750 | Aug | 2003 | 97:00 | 97:02 | 6.23 |
| 7.250 | Aug | 2004 | 106:19 | 106:21 | 6.27 |
| 10.750 | Aug | 2005 | 132:04 | 132:06 | 6.33 |

Source: *The Wall Street Journal*, September 11, 1995.

## Exercise 1.4 (Term Structure of Interest Rates)

For the bonds in Table 1.5, estimate the spot interest rates based on asked prices over the period September 1995 to September 2005. Plot the graph of the spot rate as a function of maturity. This is the term structure of interest rates. For simplicity, assume that the coupons are paid annually rather than semiannually.

## Exercise 1.5 (Efficient Set Mathematics)

Suppose that two risky investments are available: Fund $A$ with expected return $\mu_A$ and standard deviation $\sigma_A$, and Fund $B$ with expected return $\mu_B$ and standard deviation

$\sigma_B$. The correlation coefficient of the returns is $\rho_{A,B}$. Let $x$ represent of the percentage of the investor's portfolio invested in $A$, and $1 - x$ the percentage invested in $B$.

a. Show that the portfolio's expected return is $x\mu_A + (1 - x)\mu_B$ and that its standard deviation is

$$\sqrt{x^2\sigma_A^2 + 2x(1 - x)\rho_{A,B}\sigma_A\sigma_B + (1 - x)^2\sigma_B^2}.$$

b. Consider two securities with $\mu_A = 0.14$, $\sigma_A = 0.06$, $\mu_B = 0.08$, $\sigma_B = 0.03$, and $\rho_{A,B} = 0.7$. Use (a) to make a table of values of the portfolio return and its standard deviation for values of $x$ ranging from $-1$ to $1$ in increments of $0.1$. Plot the graph of these pairs of points with the standard deviation on the horizontal axis and the return on the vertical axis. Rework this exercise for values of $\rho_{A,B}$ running from $-1$ to $1$ in increments of $0.25$. Plot all the graphs on the same set of axes, and label them according to the value of $\rho_{A,B}$.

---

### Exercise 1.6 (Short Sales)

An investor sells 100 shares of Aetna short at 70 dollars per share. The broker requires an initial margin of 50% on the short position, and the investor earns 3% per year on margin funds.

a. One month later the investor buys 100 shares of Aetna at 68 and returns them to the broker. The margin is released. Calculate the investor's rate of return on the 1-month transaction.

b. Rework (a), but this time assume the price is 72 at the end of the month, and no additional margin is required.

Note: In the U.S., the proceeds from the sale cannot earn interest for the short seller by government regulation. The additional margin normally does earn interest. For this exercise, assume the transaction is not subject to U.S. regulations and that the short seller earns interest on the sale proceeds plus the additional margin.

---

### Exercise 1.7 (Margin Call)

An investor purchases 500 shares of common stock at $20 per share on a margin of 50%, subject to a maintenance margin of 35%. Calculate the price at which the investor would first get a margin call.

---

### Exercise 1.8 (Bond Equivalent Yield)

A company purchases a Treasury bill with 60 days to maturity and a face amount of $100,000 for a price of $98,375. Calculate the bond equivalent yield.

## Exercise 1.9 (Simulating Short Rates)

In a discrete-time analog to the Vasicek model, short rates are generated recursively; $r_0$ is the current short rate. The recursion relation is

$$r_{k+1} = r_k + a(b - r_k) + \sigma Z_k$$

where $b$ denotes the "long-run" short rate and $a$ is a parameter measuring the intensity of the pull of $b$ on $r_k$, $Z_0, Z_1, \ldots$ are independent standard normal random variables, and $\sigma$ is a positive constant. The model parameters $a$, $b$, and $\sigma$ might be estimated from spot market data. Calculate the expected value and variance of $r_{k+1}$, conditionally, given $r_k$.

# CHAPTER 2
## DERIVATIVE SECURITIES

## Section 2.1
## Introduction

A derivative is a security that pays its owner an amount that is a function of the values of other securities, called the underlying securities. The derivative is "derived" from the underlying security. In this chapter, we discuss the most important derivatives: forwards, futures, options, and swaps. If insurance is a security, then reinsurance is a derivative security. We include a discussion of reinsurance because the analogy to options is so strong.

The most important technique for valuation of derivatives is based on trading the derivative, the underlying securities, and a default-free bond. If the prices of the bond and underlying securities are known and a certain combination of them replicates the payoffs provided by the derivative, then, assuming the trading is "efficient," the market price of the derivative should be the same as the price of the combination of bonds and underlying securities. This is the so-called "no-arbitrage" pricing concept. In this chapter we give an intuitive, simple introduction to these ideas, beginning with arbitrage. In some markets there are not enough underlying securities to replicate the derivative; in this case, valuation methods based on market equilibrium can be applied. We develop in later chapters both arbitrage pricing and market equilibrium methods in more generality and with proper rigor.

The term *arbitrage* refers to the possibility of making a trading gain with no chance of loss. Markets, such as the U.S. stock market, that are easy to access and attract many sophisticated traders should not offer many arbitrage opportunities. We explain the basis for this view of such markets. In developing market models, it is almost always assumed that there are no arbitrage opportunities.

To understand arbitrage in concrete terms, consider two investment vehicles $A$ and $B$ with current prices, at time $t$, denoted by $A_t$ and $B_t$. Suppose that there are no cash payments to owners during $(t, T)$ and let $A_T$ and $B_T$ denote their market values at time $T$. These values at time $T$ are random as viewed from time $t$, but suppose that we can be sure now that, whatever happens in the future, $B_T$ will exceed $A_T$. If the price $B_t$ is less than $A_t$, an arbitrage could be constructed as follows: a trader could sell asset $A$ now, getting $A_t$ as cash while incurring an obligation to pay $A_T$ at time $T$. Since $B_t$ is less than $A_t$, the trader can buy asset $B$ with the cash from selling asset $A$ and have a positive amount $A_t - B_t$ left over. The benefit from buying asset $B$ is $B_T$ at time $T$, which is adequate to cover the trader's liability to pay $A_T$. This is an arbitrage because the trader has a sure profit $A_t - B_t > 0$ now and no liability to pay in the future since $B_T - A_T \geq 0$. Thus, in a market with no arbitrage, we can conclude that if $B_T \geq A_T$ with probability one, then $B_t \geq A_t$.

A double application of this yields a useful formulation: two assets (or securities, portfolios, liabilities, and so on) with identical cash flows in the future have the same current price in an arbitrage-free market. This is sometimes called the *law of one price*. We use it in our discussions of the pricing of futures and options and other derivative securities.

Are stock markets such as the NYSE and derivative markets such as those operated by the CBOT so efficient that there are no arbitrage opportunities? There is no easy answer. Evidence can be found that methods based on models based on a no-arbitrage assumption, such as stock-option pricing models, work well in practice. With easy access to markets and well-informed traders, we would think that there is little opportunity for arbitrage profits. Common sense tells us that prices should adjust quickly to eliminate arbitrage profits.

Some persistent anomalies, however, seem to indicate a presence of arbitrage profits. Many researchers in finance have reported finding that stock returns are persistently substantially higher in January than in other months, and the effect is greater for small firms. This contradicts market efficiency because an investor can "beat the market" by buying a portfolio of small-firm stocks in December and finance it by selling short a portfolio of large-firm stocks. Researchers have found anomalies in how investors react to announcements concerning firms, including investor reaction to earnings announcements, initial public offerings, and acquisitions. Elton and Gruber [54] discuss the evidence on efficiency in detail.

Most of this book, like the rest of the financial theory literature, is based on the assumption that markets are arbitrage free, for two main reasons. First, there is no simple way to allow for individual or firm-specific behavioral differences; for example, we do not know how to include investor psychological differences. Second, the assumption gives results that often work well, even though there can be some market anomalies.

# Section 2.2
## Forward Contracts

The next level of market sophistication beyond spot markets are markets that involve contracting for a trade to be executed in the future. These are forward, futures, and option markets. A *forward* contract specifies contract terms at time $t$ at which the contract is written for a transaction that is to take place at some time $T$ in the future. The contract specifies the quantity and quality of the goods as well as other details such as place of delivery, and it is usually a personal contract, customized to the needs of one of the parties and not easily transferable to a third party.

Forward contracts can be written on commodities, financial assets such as stocks and bonds, indices, or currency exchange rates. In practical terms, they are not as significant as futures contracts, a similar exchange-traded contract, which we describe in the next section. However, forward contracts are important, especially in the currency markets, and they are easier to describe than futures. A good understanding of forward contracts will pave the way for our discussion of futures and options. (For a brief history of the development of commodities forward trading in the U.S., see the *Commodity Trading Manual* [6].)

The forward traders view the current market and see the price $S_t$ of the traded asset as well as related information. They agree now to trade the asset at a price of $F(t, T)$ at time $T$. As time approaches $T$, the asset price turns out to be $S_T$. The forward buyer must pay $F(t, T)$ for the asset even if the market price is lower; that is, $S_T < F(t, T)$, and the seller must deliver the asset for a price of $F(t, T)$ even if it would be more advantageous to sell in the cash market where the price might be higher. Both parties must honor the contract, regardless of how the market actually turns out. This gives rise to a problem: each trader must be assured that the other party can and will perform on the contract, rather than default.

Forward contracts are often arranged by brokers or dealers. For example, in the currency exchange market, some banks serve as dealers. When an individual or firm enters into a currency forward contract with a bank, the bank's default is not much of a problem. The bank stands behind the forward contract just as it does its other obligations. However, the bank may be concerned about the other party's ability to perform. The bank may ask for a credit history or require a deposit of assets to back up the forward contract. The following example shows the use of a currency forward to hedge exchange rate risk.

### SECTION 2.2.1 | EXAMPLE: CURRENCY FORWARDS

Suppose that a Canadian insurance company issues an investment contract for which it accepts 90 million U.S. dollars from a U.S. pension trust and promises to return

100 million U.S. dollars, the deposit with interest, 1 year later. Ignoring details of the insurer's investment plan for the deposit, we simply assume that the insurer comes up with Canadian dollars, from the investment or elsewhere, sufficient to meet its investment contract obligation.[1] The insurer knows when it issues the investment contract that 1 year later it will have to buy 100 million U.S. dollars to meet its investment contract obligation. To lock in the rate of exchange, it opens a forward contract with a bank. The insurer and the bank then agree that 1 year later, the insurance company will buy 100 million U.S. dollars at a rate of 1.25 Canadian dollars per 1 U.S. dollar.

This is the forward price: $F(t, T) = 1.25$. The insurer will have to honor the terms of the forward contract, buying at 1.25, even if the market price of U.S. dollars turns out to be less, say, $S_T = 1.20$, 1 year later. If the market price is 1.20, the insurer pays 125 million Canadian dollars for 100 million U.S. dollars with a market value of only 120 million Canadian dollars. It loses 5 million Canadian dollars. But if the price moves up, the bank will nevertheless have to deliver U.S. dollars at the 1.25 price. For example, if the price goes to 1.30, the bank must deliver 100 million dollars U.S., with a market value of 130 million Canadian, in exchange for 125 million Canadian. It loses 5 million dollars Canadian. Table 2.1 illustrates some of the possible outcomes for the insurer and the bank, and the graph of the buyer's gain under a forward contract, as a function of the market price of the underlying asset at the time the forward expires, is shown in Figure 2.1.

### TABLE 2.1 | *Currency Forward Example*

| $S_T$ | Market Value of U.S.$100 million | Insurer's Gain | Bank's Gain |
|-------|----------------------------------|----------------|-------------|
| 1.00 | 100,000,000 | −25,000,000 | 25,000,000 |
| 1.05 | 105,000,000 | −20,000,000 | 20,000,000 |
| 1.10 | 110,000,000 | −15,000,000 | 15,000,000 |
| 1.15 | 115,000,000 | −10,000,000 | 10,000,000 |
| 1.20 | 120,000,000 | − 5,000,000 | 5,000,000 |
| 1.25 | 125,000,000 | 0 | 0 |
| 1.30 | 130,000,000 | 5,000,000 | −5,000,000 |
| 1.35 | 135,000,000 | 10,000,000 | −10,000,000 |
| 1.40 | 140,000,000 | 15,000,000 | −15,000,000 |
| 1.45 | 145,000,000 | 20,000,000 | −20,000,000 |
| 1.50 | 150,000,000 | 25,000,000 | −25,000,000 |

The market value and gains are in Canadian dollars.

---

[1] We ignore default risk and transaction costs.

FIGURE **2.1** | *Forward Buyer's Gain*

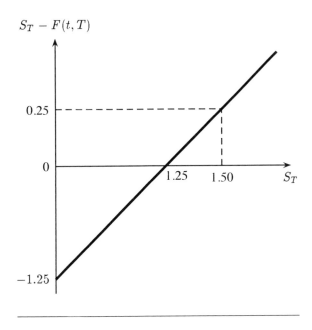

SECTION **2.2.2** | CHANGING FORWARD RATES

A forward-contract dealer, such as the bank in the example, makes a profit on its bid-ask spread. This is a cost traders pay to compensate the dealer for providing the transaction, a form of transaction cost. The dealer offers to buy, or bids, one price and offers to sell, or asks, at a higher price. The dealer stands behind its contracts, and it bears the risk that other parties default. The dealers manage default risk by checking creditworthiness or requiring collateral deposits. We frequently ignore bid-ask spreads and default risk in introductory mathematical models because they make it difficult to focus on the essential features of the markets.

Thus, we now assume that buyers and sellers get the same price, that there are no defaults on forward contracts, and that there are no arbitrage trades involving the underlying asset and forward contracts. From one day to another, the forward market changes, just like spot market prices change. For example, in January, $t = 0$, the price for U.S. dollars delivered in December may be 1.25 Canadian dollars, $F(0, 1) = 1.25$. By July that price may have changed so that the dealer then asks 1.20 or $F(0.5, 1) = 1.20$. As December nears, the forward prices converge to the spot price because of the law of one price.

The law of one price implies that the asset price is the same regardless of how it is purchased: in the cash market or under the terms of a forward contract.

To illustrate, we take an extreme case. Imagine a forward contract with the price set at time $t$, the afternoon before it matures at $T = t + \varepsilon$. The price $F(t, T)$ must be equal to the market price $S_T$. If $F(T - \varepsilon, T) > S_T$, then we would buy cheap in the cash market for $S_T$ the next morning and simultaneously sell in the forward market for $F(T - \varepsilon, T)$, making a sure profit. If the prices were reversed, we would just reverse the trades. Thus, we find that to avoid arbitrage across the markets, the prices must be the same when the forward contract matures; $F(T, T) = S_T$ because there is no uncertainty.

In Section 1.6 we introduced the concept of a forward interest rate. To see the relation forward interest rates bear to a forward contract written on a bond in a no-arbitrage setting, consider a forward contract written at time $t = 0$ that calls for delivery at time $t = k$ of a zero-coupon bond with $n$ years to maturity and a maturity value of 1. Let $F = F(0, k)$ denote the forward-contract price at time $t = 0$. Consider two strategies for investing over the period $(0, k + n]$:

1. Open the forward contract, agreeing to buy the $n$-year bond at time $k$. It costs nothing to open the forward contract except some small transactions costs, which we ignore. Simultaneously buy a zero-coupon bond maturing at time $k$ for a face amount equal to $F$, the forward price of the $n$-year bond. The forward contract costs $FP(k) = F(1 + s_k)^{-k}$, where $s_k$ is the spot rate at time 0 for a $k$-period discount bond. It provides cash at time $k$, which exactly meets the commitment to buy the bond to be delivered at time $k$. Buy the $n$-year bond under the terms of the forward contract at time $k$. The compound result of the two bond purchases is a payment of 1 at time $n + k$, at a cost of $FP(k)$ at time 0.

2. At time 0, buy the bond that matures at time $n + k$ with maturity value of 1. It costs $P(n + k)$.

The two strategies have the same future cash flows. By the no-arbitrage principle, the initial prices are equal. Thus, $FP(k) = P(n + k)$, or

$$F(0, k) = \frac{P(n + k)}{P(k)} = \frac{(1 + s_{n+k})^{-(n+k)}}{(1 + s_k)^{-k}} = \frac{1}{(1 + f_k) \cdots (1 + f_{n+k-1})},$$

where $f_k, f_{k+1}, \ldots$, are the implied one-period forward rates. In the case of a forward contract written on bonds, the forward price is the discounted maturity value, discounted at the appropriate forward interest rates. The forward prices come from the forward market, where the forwards are written on bonds and offered by dealers. The forward interest rates are implied by spot market prices for bonds, and the two markets are linked by the no-arbitrage property. The following discussion elaborates a relation between spot and forward markets in a general context.

## SECTION 2.2.3 | RELATION BETWEEN SPOT AND FORWARD MARKETS

Here we develop the fundamental relation between cash prices $S$ and forward prices $F$, following the approach of Stoll and Whaley [186]. Consider two buying strategies: the first is a purchase of an asset in the spot market. At time $t$ there is a cash payment of $S_t$. The asset may provide dividends, coupons, or other cash flows to the asset owner, but it may require more of the owner's cash flows, such as storage costs. Assume that the timing and amount of these cash flows are known to traders at time $t$, and that the the net cash flows to the owner accumulate at time $T > t$ to a known aggregate value denoted by $D(t, T)$. Thus, at time $T$, the buyer can liquidate the position by selling the asset for $S_T$ and end up with a total value of $S_T + D(t, T)$.

The second buying strategy is to enter into a forward contract, agreeing to pay $F = F(t, T)$ at time $T$, and at the same time depositing the present value of the future payment price plus the present value of $D(t, T)$ in a savings account that pays interest on savings at an annualized rate of $r = R(t, T)$. The cash flow at time $t$ is a payment of

$$\frac{F + D(t, T)}{e^{(T-t)r}}.$$

This is the value, ignoring the relatively small transaction cost to enter a forward contract. At time $T$, the savings account has accumulated to $F + D(t, T)$, an amount sufficient to fulfill the obligation under the forward contract and match the accumulated net benefits of ownership of the asset during $(t, T)$. At time $T$, the buyer pays $F$ and receives the asset, which has a market value of $S_T$.

Under the second strategy the buyer also has a total market value of $S_T + D(t, T)$. Thus, the two strategies have the same payoffs at time $T$, so by the law of one price, they must have the same price at time $t$. We find that

$$\frac{F + D(t, T)}{e^{(T-t)r}} = S_t,$$

which is usually written as

$$F(t, T) = S_t e^{(T-t)r} - D(t, T).$$

When the asset is a physical asset such as wheat, $D(t, T)$ is the accumulated value of storage costs, a negative value. This relationship was developed for commodities before futures on financial assets were so popular. Among commodity traders, $-D(t, T)$ is called the "carrying cost" of the spot asset. For financial assets, the carrying cost is often zero or negative; that is, $D(t, T) \geq 0$. We rewrite

$$F(t, T) = S_t e^{(T-t)r} + D(t, T) = S_t e^{(T-t)b} \qquad (2.2.1)$$

where $b$ is the aggregate carrying cost, including interest opportunity costs, compounded continuously over the life of the futures contract. This is known as the *cost of carry relation* between futures and spot prices.

Some assets provide additional value to the owner, beyond the present value of $D(t, T)$. For example, industrial consumers of copper may hold it for convenience; an unplanned shortage may require shutting down a process that is costly, so it pays to have an excess of copper on hand. An asset that provides this value to some traders is called a *convenience asset*. The additional value must be recognized in the relation between future and spot prices of convenience assets. In this book, we deal exclusively with financial securities, so we do not deal further with convenience yield. (See Siegal and Siegal [183] for a discussion of future and spot prices of convenience assets.)

# *Section 2.3*
# *Futures Market Model*

The customized or personal nature of forward contracts makes it difficult to change a position.[2] The customer must go to the dealer to make special arrangements to resolve a forward obligation early, that is, before the scheduled maturity. This form of illiquidity was the principal reason for the development of futures (see Besant [6]). A *futures* contract is similar to a forward in that it sets the price of a trade to take place in the future, but it is different in other respects. Futures contracts are offered through exchanges and are standardized with regard to maturity, size, and underlying asset or index. Despite these strengths, futures contracts may not exactly fit the needs of a particular trader.

Forwards are usually customized to the needs of each party. The forward contract may be arranged by a broker or dealer, who may or may not stand behind the contract. Also, no marking-to-market occurs, a requirement for futures that we explain below. Thus, default risk can be present but is not found in futures contracts.

---

[2]The forward trader need not be a real person; a corporation such as a bank or insurance company can enter into these contracts. The contracts are personal in the sense that they are tailored to meet specific needs.

A market for forwards may not be readily available, so a forward position may not be as liquid as a futures position. Because forward contracts are not marked-to-market as futures contracts are, gains and losses are not realized until settlement of the forward position (see Table 2.2).

TABLE **2.2** | *Forward Versus Futures Contracts*

|  | Forward | Futures |
| --- | --- | --- |
| Type of market | Dealer or broker | Exchange |
| Liquidity | Low | High |
| Contract form | Custom | Standard |
| Performance guarantee | Creditworthiness | Mark-to-market |
| Transactions costs | Bid-ask spread | Fees or commissions |

Currency markets are the most highly developed of all forward markets. Although there are currency futures available, because of the standardization, they cannot always provide an optimal hedge; for example, the International Monetary Market offers Japanese yen futures with delivery in March, June, September, and December. A transaction requiring dollars for yen in August cannot be completely hedged with these futures contracts, but a forward contract calling for delivery on the transaction date could be arranged through a bank or broker, hedging the risk completely. The forward and futures traders face the possibility that the price will move against their contract position. Options contracts allow traders to avoid this risk by paying an up-front fee.

Some futures contracts are settled in cash. For example, the stock index futures discussed below are settled in cash at the closing market value of the underlying index on the last trading day of the futures contract. There is no actual "delivery" of the index stocks, and market participants are required to deposit an initial performance margin. Futures performance margins are similar to the margins a short seller must establish and maintain, as we described earlier. However, both parties to a futures contract, the long and the short, must establish margins. Futures performance margins (usually no more than 10% of the contract face amount) are good-faith deposits to ensure performance of the contractual obligations. The margin can be put up in securities such as stocks or bonds. While the futures position is open, traders collect gains and pay losses daily.

As a simplified example, suppose future prices on an asset are quoted in dollars and cents, with the "tick," or minimum price movement, being 5 cents. Suppose a trader opens a long futures position on day 1. The contract calls for delivery of 100 units of the asset at a price of 50 dollars per unit on day 60, thus, $F(1, 60) = 50$.

Assume that the trader has an account balance of 1,000 on day 1. Table 2.3 illustrates how daily settlement prices change the account.[3]

TABLE **2.3** | *Mark-to-Market*

| Day | Account Value | Settlement Price | Contract Value |
|-----|---------------|------------------|----------------|
| 1 | 1,000 | 50.00 | 5,000 |
| 2 | 1,050 | 50.50 | 5,050 |
| 3 | 1,150 | 51.50 | 5,150 |
| 4 | 1,150 | 51.50 | 5,150 |
| 5 | 1,000 | 50.00 | 5,000 |
| 6 | 900 | 49.00 | 4,900 |

Now, suppose that at the end of day 2, the futures price is $F(2, 60) = 50.50$. The trader's long position improved since the contract allows buying at $5,000 something that the market says will be worth $5,050. Because profit is recognized daily in futures markets, the buyer's account is increased by $50 and the seller's decreased by $50 at the end of day 2. Each of the traders' future prices (their contractual values) are adjusted to reflect the account adjustments. This means that at the end of day 2, the trader has an obligation to buy at 50.50 per unit at maturity—which is equivalent to the original position if we ignore the time value of money. The trader has $50 in cash to adjust the original obligation ($5,000) for the goods up to $5,050. The $50 of favorable price movement is recognized the day it occurs, whereas in the forward market, it is recognized only at maturity. If the price moves against the trader, the trader's account is decreased.

During trading day 6, the trader holding the long position calls the broker and closes the position, essentially opening a second futures position, this one short. The two exactly offset each future price change, and so the trader is simply taken out of the market as soon as the (long) counterparty for the new short position enters the market, allowing the original long to be released. The account is cash, usually credited a daily interest rate, and it is available in cash to the trader, subject to an account minimum to be held in reserve for future adverse price movements. The gain on a short position is just the negative of the gain on the long position; they sum to zero.

Futures contracts are opened and closed through brokers who have access to the exchange. The brokers charge commissions or fees for their services. The contract initial position need not be maintained until the contract matures. A trader closes a futures position by notifying the broker. To end an obligation early, a trader who

---

[3]We ignore other transactions, interest, and other actions that could change the account.

is initially a buyer becomes both a buyer and seller, having a net future obligation of zero, and similarly, a seller closes out a position by becoming both a seller and a buyer. Figure 2.2 illustrates the buyer's gain on a long futures position opened at $F(t, T) = 50$ as a function of the settlement price. The settlement price at 80 in Figure 2.2 is only an illustration; a 60% price movement would be rare.

FIGURE **2.2** | *Long Futures Payoff*

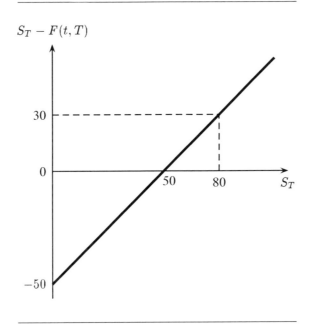

Futures prices are reported in newspapers. For example, *The Wall Street Journal* devotes several pages to futures prices. The format for reporting is standardized to some extent: newspapers do not report contract details such as place of delivery or quality of delivered goods. Such details are available from the exchange that offers the contract. As a second example of the reporting of futures prices Table 2.4 shows the prices of U.S. Treasury bond futures as they appeared on August 6, 1992.

Prices are quoted in dollars and thirty-seconds, per hundred dollars of face value; the tick is a thirty-second. The contract calls for delivery of a noncallable $100,000 U.S. Treasury bond with at least 15 years remaining to maturity. An otherwise similar callable bond may be delivered if it has at least 15 years to its first call date. The prices and yields reported in the table are quoted on a hypothetical 20-year noncallable bond with an 8% coupon. If a contract is settled by delivery, the seller has a choice of bonds of various coupons and maturities to deliver. The Chicago Board of Trade requires cash adjustments to reflect the value of differences in coupon and maturity of the actual bond delivered and the hypothetical 8% coupon, 20-year bond.

TABLE **2.4** | *Treasury Bonds (CBOT): $100,000*

| | Open | High | Low | Settle | Change | Yield Settle | Change | Open Interest |
|---|---|---|---|---|---|---|---|---|
| Sep 1992 | 105-08 | 105-28 | 105-03 | 105-10 | +2 | 7.484 | −0.006 | 316,752 |
| Dec | 104-04 | 104-22 | 103-31 | 104-05 | +2 | 7.593 | −0.006 | 42,303 |
| Mar 1993 | 103-00 | 103-18 | 102-28 | 103-01 | +2 | 7.700 | −0.007 | 15,596 |
| June | 102-08 | 102-13 | 101-30 | 101-30 | +2 | 7.807 | −0.006 | 11,599 |
| Sep | 100-29 | 101-13 | 100-29 | 100-29 | +2 | 7.909 | −0.006 | 1,433 |
| Dec | 99-25 | 100-13 | 99-25 | 99-30 | +2 | 8.006 | −0.007 | 389 |
| Sep 1994 | . . . | . . . | . . . | 97-19 | +2 | 8.248 | −0.006 | 100 |

Source: *The Wall Street Journal*, August 6, 1992.

The first column indicates the month in which the futures contract requires delivery. The contract gives the short trader the choice of any business day during the specified month. The next three columns give the future's opening price and its high and low for the day. The next two columns give the settlement price at which contracts were marked-to-market and its change from the prior trading day's settlement price. The next two columns give the same information in terms of yield to maturity instead of price. The last column indicates how many contracts have been opened (and not closed by taking an offsetting position).

## SECTION **2.3.1** | HEDGING SPOT PRICES
### IN THE FUTURES MARKET

To illustrate the use of futures contracts to manage spot price risk, take a fictitious example, in which ABC Corporation plans to raise capital in the bond market by issuing bonds for 10 million U.S. dollars. Assume that it is now August and the issue is planned for December. Currently investors require a yield of 7% on ABC's bonds. To get $10 million, ABC plans to issue 20-year 7% coupon bonds in December. Thus, the company plans to sell in the corporate bond spot market just enough to raise $10 million, provided the spot price for its bonds still corresponds to a 7% yield. If the bonds sold now, they would sell at par, yielding $10,000,000 in capital (less the issue costs, which we will ignore). ABC wants to lock in this amount of capital. They could do it with certainty if a futures market existed for its commodity like the one for wheat farmers. No futures market has been created for corporate bonds, but a reasonable substitute can be found: the futures market for $100,000 U.S. government 20-year, 8% coupon, noncallable bonds, which we described earlier.

ABC sells in the futures market, not its own bonds, but U.S. government bonds. The August financial press reports that December U.S. bonds are trading at 114-07. The tick is one thirty-second, and the decimal equivalent is 114.21875. This corresponds to a contract price of $114,218.75 and a yield to maturity of 6.7%. This is what traders think in August about the December bond market. ABC sells short 100 futures contracts, promising to deliver 100 U.S. T-bonds (of face amount $100,000) at a price of $114,218.75 each. The company pays a broker a modest fee and puts up a margin of $300,000 (the initial requirement is $3,000 per contract).

Suppose corporate bond yields increase to 7.5% in December. The corresponding price of ABC 7% coupon bonds drops to 94.86 per 100 of face value. This is a loss of 5.14 per 100, or a total shortfall of $514,000 on the entire issue. The ABC issue of 7% coupon bonds raises only $9,486,000. The U.S. bond market also drops. The required yield is 7.2%, corresponding to a price of 108-13. The cash price of the U.S. bonds ABC delivers under the terms of the futures contract is only $108,406.25 versus $114,218.75 required by the futures contract. This is a gain of $5,812.50 per contract, for a total of $581,250. Thus, ABC has a cash total of $581,250 + $9,486,000 = $10,067,250, a little more than the required $10,000,000. Table 2.5 displays these results.

TABLE 2.5 | *Spot and Bond Futures Prices*

### U.S. Bond Futures

| Date | Quoted Price | Yield | Contract Price |
|------|--------------|-------|----------------|
| August | 114-07 | 6.7% | $114,218.75 |
| December | 108-13 | 7.2% | $108,406.25 |
| Gain on 1 short futures contract: | | | $5,812.50 |
| Gain on 100 short futures contracts: | | | $581,250 |

### ABC Bond Prices

| Date Calculated | Yield | December Price |
|-----------------|-------|----------------|
| August | 7.0% | $10,000,000 |
| December | 7.5% | $9,486,000 |
| Loss relative to expectations: | | $514,000 |

What if bond prices rise? If so, ABC's bond issue raises more than 10 million dollars, but the company will have a loss in the futures market. The net result is still about 10 million dollars. ABC used a *cross hedge*: it went short in the U.S. bond futures market to hedge its own natural long position in the corporate bond spot market. ABC does not actually have to deliver bonds to settle the futures; it can simply close out the futures contract in the futures market before delivery. The exchange will sort out the details. Only a small percentage of traded futures are settled by delivery.

SECTION **2.3.2** │ FUTURES ON T-BILLS

The futures contract calls for delivery of a 3-month (also called 90-day or 13-week) bill. Consider a May futures contract that calls for delivery of a 3-month $1,000,000 U.S. T-bill 2 months later in July. In the U.S. and Canada, futures prices are in terms of discounted face values. Suppose that the current quoted spot price is 95 or 5% in terms of annualized discount yield; that is, the May price of a T-bill that can be delivered in July is 95. In May the bond must have 5 months to maturity; let us say it has 150 days to maturity. What is the corresponding no-arbitrage futures price $F(t, T)$? The price 95 corresponds to a contract price of $S_t = 1,000,000[1 - (0.05)150/360] = 979,167$ in May. No benefits or costs are associated with owning in May a T-bill that matures in October. Thus, the carrying cost is zero.

The risk-free interest rate $r$ over the period of the futures contract can be determined by looking at the price in May of a T-bill maturing in July. Suppose the yield for this bill is 4%; this implies a contract price of $993,333. Thus, $e^{r(T-t)} = 1,000,000/993,333 = 1.00671$ for the 2-month period May to July. The fundamental price relationship expressed by (2.2.1) with $b = r$ applies as follows:

$$F = S_t e^{r(T-t)}$$

$$= 979,167(1.00671) = 985,739.$$

Because prices are always quoted on an annualized basis, the corresponding future price is found by applying the formula relating contract prices and yields:

$$\text{Contract Price} = \text{Face Amount} \times \left(1 - \text{Yield}\, \frac{\text{Days to Maturity}}{360}\right)$$

$$985,739 = 1,000,000 \times \left(1 - y\, \frac{90}{360}\right).$$

This implies $y = 5.70\%$, and the quoted price is $100 - 5.70 = 94.30$ per 100 of face value. If the futures price were different, there would be a trade that would make a sure profit (ignoring transaction costs).

For example, suppose that in May the futures price for July T-bills is too low, say, at 93, relative to the spot T-bill price of 96 for July and 95 for September maturities. We would immediately buy at 93 in the futures market and sell at 95 in the spot market. The cash from the sale of the September T-bill, $979,167 is invested in a $1,000,000 July T-bill. When it matures we will have $979,167(1,000,000/993,333) = 985,739$ in cash, and it will be time to take delivery under the terms of the futures contract. We will pay $1,000,000[1 - 0.07(0.25)] = 982,500$ for a 90-day T-bill, which leaves us $3,239 in cash, and we have a T-bill maturing in September, which exactly replaces the T-bill we sold in May. This is an arbitrage. Anyone with a T-bill maturing in September can make a sure profit of $3,239, realized in July, merely by trading in May. This makes September T-bills more valuable. These arbitrage opportunities are noticed by traders, prices will adjust, and the opportunities will disappear, according to efficient market advocates.

## SECTION 2.3.3 | STOCK INDEX FUTURES

One of the most widely known stock price indices is the Dow Jones Industrial Average (DJIA). The DJIA is the average of 30 stock prices of U.S. companies including American Express, IBM, and Sears Roebuck. A second popular stock price index is the Standard & Poors 500, which is an average of 500 stock prices. Others are the New York Stock Exchange Composite Index, the Major Market Index (MMI), the Toronto Stock Exchange 300 (a composite of 300 hundred Canadian corporate stocks), the Nikkei Stock Average (an index of Japanese stocks), and the Financial Times Actuaries Index (FTSE). No futures contracts are written on the DJIA, but there are popular futures contracts written on the S&P 500, the NYSE Composite Index, the MMI, and the Nikkei.

The Chicago Mercantile Exchange offers futures and options on the Nikkei stock average and the MMI, which is an average of 20 blue-chip stock prices. We will describe the MMI futures contract; the other stock index future contracts are similar.

A single MMI futures transaction amount is the MMI multiplied by $250. Prices are quoted in decimals, and a tick is 0.05, which reflects a price change of $12.50 per contract. Hedging a blue-chip stock portfolio, protecting it from a decline in stock prices, is a natural use of MMI futures. As an illustration, suppose a fund manager decides to protect a $22.5 million blue-chip stock portfolio. To completely protect a market value of $22.5 million, the manager should "sell" the portfolio at its current price by opening $n$ short MMI futures contracts, where $n$ is determined so that the current face amount of the futures is $22.5 million. This means that $n(250)S_t = \$22.5$ million, where $S_t$ is the current MMI value; for example, if the current futures price for the index is 450.00, the manager should go short 200 contracts. Table 2.6 illustrates the position, assuming the blue-chip market declines.

### TABLE 2.6 | *Stock Spot and Futures Prices*

|  | **Cash Market** | **Futures Market** |
|---|---|---|
| Now | $22.5 million | Short 200 contracts at 450<br>= $22.5 million |
| Later | $20.95 million | Close out at 420 = $21 million |
| Result | $1.55 million loss | 200(250)(450 − 420)<br>= $1.5 million gain |
| Net change: | Loss of $50,000 | |

The portfolio loss in the cash market was offset by a gain in the futures market. The hedge was not perfect because the MMI does not have the same stocks in the same proportions as the portfolio. The fundamental cost of carry relation (2.2.1) has a specific form applied to stock index futures. For these contracts it is usually assumed that the stock dividends are paid continuously throughout the year, at a known constant annual rate, denoted by $d$. The net cost of carry is $b = r - d$, and the cost of carry relation is

$$F(t, T) = S_t e^{(r-d)(T-t)}.$$

The dividend rate $d$ is normally greater than the risk-free interest rate $r$.

In this section we have described several futures contracts and illustrated how they can be used to hedge financial outcomes. We have discussed anticipatory hedges and portfolio protection as examples. In each of these, the change of spot prices is matched by an opposite change in the futures market. The investor or hedger may need the offset from the futures position only if prices move in one direction. Option contracts can provide this sort of protection; the option-contract trade is executed only if it favors the contract owner. The owner gets someone to take the risk of having to buy or sell under unfavorable conditions by paying an up-front fee. We discuss the details next.

# Section 2.4
# Options

Forward and futures markets are more complex than spot markets, because they offer traders a way to manage risk that is not available in spot market trading. For example, a company planning to issue bonds can hedge against a market price drop by selling bond futures. The futures contract locks in a price for the bonds, avoiding adverse consequences of a price decline, but it also prevents the company from taking advantage of a price increase. An option contract provides a hedger with the same protection against the unfavorable price movement, without interfering with the benefit of a price increase. This "win-only" outcome is obtained by paying a premium to the other trader when the contract is opened.

As a specific example, consider a contract to buy bonds at a price of 70 that is obtained at time $t$ and matures at time $T$. The contractual price 70 is analogous to the futures price $F(t, T)$. This contractual price is called the *exercise price*, or sometimes the *strike price*. Let the price of the underlying asset at time $t$ be denoted by $S_t$ and the exercise price by $K$. The long position gain on the futures is $S_T - K = S_T - 70$, but an option contract owner will exercise the right to buy at 70 only if $S_T > 70$.

The option owner gains on the option position as the bond price increases. For example, a change in the bond price from 70 to 80 increases the exercise value to the owner from 0 to 10. Thus, the owner's rights increase in market value as the bond price increases. The value available to the owner by exercising the option is called the *exercise value*, or the *intrinsic value*. The exercise value as a function of the closing price is shown in Figure 2.3. The gain on a similar futures contract is exactly the same over the range of prices that are favorable to the buyer (prices in excess of 70). However, for those prices at which the futures buyer has a loss (prices less than 70), the option buyer does not exercise the option to buy bonds, and so avoids the loss. To entice the seller into such an agreement, the long option trader makes a cash payment, called the *premium*, to the other trader. This is the option's price, paid at the time the owner obtains the rights.[4] It is not contemporaneous with the exercise value. The right to buy or sell under the terms of the option expire when the owner exercises the option.

FIGURE **2.3** | *Call Option Exercise Value*

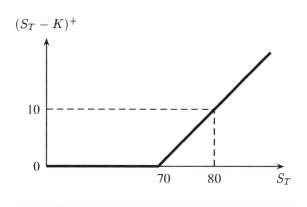

Denote $S$ as the price of the asset on which the option is written and $K$ as the exercise price. The market determines $S$; subscripts denote its values at various times. The option contract specifies the exercise price $K$; its value does not usually change with time. If the right to buy is considered at time $T$, the owner can obtain $S_T - K$ provided $S_T > K$ by buying under the terms of the option and immediately selling in the cash market. If the price $S_T$ is below $K$, the option will not be exercised. We say that its exercise value is zero. Its intrinsic value may be zero, but the market value of the option is positive, because there is a possibility that at a later time, the market

---

[4] All exchange-traded options work this way, with the exception of the Sydney Future Exchange options. SFE options are marked-to-market like futures contracts.

price will rise above the exercise price. A compact way of writing the exercise value uses the function

$$(z)^+ = \max(z, 0) = \begin{cases} z, & \text{if } z > 0 \\ 0, & \text{if } z \leq 0. \end{cases}$$

Thus, the exercise value can be written as $(S - K)^+$. The contract may allow the option owner to exercise the right to buy (or sell) *on or before* the contract expires at $T$. This added flexibility allows the long option owner to claim a value $(S_u - K)^+$ at $u \leq T$.

An option is analogous to a fire insurance contract written on a building. The insurance company accepts a premium at time $t$ in exchange for the promise to pay fire damage $S_u$ at time $u \leq T$ in excess of a deductible $K$ for fires occurring no later than $T$. The cash available to the fire insurance owner is $(S_T - K)^+$ when the fire occurs at $u \leq T$. The analogy is useful, but not perfect. It is useful because it illustrates the mathematical similarity of options to insurance; it is not perfect for at least two reasons. First, fire insurance is customized and personal; the fire insurance policy owner cannot transfer rights granted under the policy to a third party. In contrast, option rights are easily traded in exchanges. Second, the fire insurance policy may not expire when the fire damage is paid, but exchange-traded options expire when exercised.

## SECTION 2.4.1 | TERMINOLOGY OF OPTION CONTRACTS

Option contracts appear in many areas of modern finance. Organized markets offer standardized contracts. For example, the Chicago Board Options Exchange offers options on stocks. Options on tangible assets such as wheat, corn, and oil are traded in commodity exchanges. Options on bonds and currency exchange rates are traded in OTC markets and exchanges. Customized option contracts occur in other important financial settings, such as performance options, which are often part of a corporate manager's or a professional baseball player's compensation. Customized options are also written on real estate, jet airliners, and other expensive real assets to facilitate transfer of ownership. Other business contracts such as insurance policies, lease agreements, and employment contracts often have embedded options.

The option contracts traded in organized markets are easier to evaluate than customized options because they are standardized, and because the markets are more efficient. Efficient markets do not allow arbitrage. This allows traders to price option contracts on stocks, for example, by constructing a portfolio of stocks and bonds that replicates the option's future payoffs, and then pricing the portfolio. The option must have the same price as the portfolio, otherwise an arbitrage trade would be available. We focus on exchange-traded options, but the ideas and terminology often apply to options that arise in other situations. The terminology distinguishes contract features such as put versus call and American versus European, which we discuss next.

A *call option* on a stock is a contract that provides to the owner of the option the right to buy 100 shares of stock at a fixed price. The option expires after a specified date; the time remaining is called the term of the option. We use $\tau$ to denote the time to expiration: $\tau = T - t$; here $t$ is the current time.

A *put option* provides the owner the right to sell 100 shares of stock at a specified price during the term of the option. If the market value $S$ of the asset on which the option is written is less than the exercise price $K$, then the owner will exercise the right to sell at $K$ an asset obtainable in the cash market at a lower price $S$. The option owner buys in the cash market and simultaneously sells under the terms of the option contract. Of course, if the cash price is too high, the owner does not exercise the option. Thus, the exercise value of a put option is the excess, if any, of the specified price over the market price of the stock; that is, $(K - S)^+$.

Another option feature is the exercise style: we discuss two, *European* and *American*. European-style options can be exercised only on the expiration date specified in the contract. American-style options can be exercised at any time before or at expiration. Stock options are usually American style, as are most options traded in the U.S. European options are important in the U.S., because they are also traded there and because they are easier to evaluate.[5]

The value of a European-style option may be a good approximation to an otherwise identical American option. A common technique is to evaluate an American option as if it were European, because we have relatively simple methods for evaluating them. The approximation may be poor, in which case additional work is required to determine the added value of the early exercise privilege. Note that for two otherwise identical contracts, the American option is worth at least as much as the European option because it includes all the rights of the European option.

If $S$ is 80 per share, and $K$ is 70 per share, then using the rights provided under the call option contract would result in a gain of 10 per share. The option owner would pay 70 for a share, which could be sold immediately in the stock market for 80. The rights under the call option must be worth at least 10 per share if the option rights can be exercised immediately. Because we are considering options that are traded in markets, the owner has an alternative to exercising: the option may be sold in the options market.

---

[5]The Chicago Mercantile Exchange options on the S&P 500 are European style, as are some of the currency options traded on the Philadelphia Exchange. The CBOT catastrophe insurance options are European. In addition, OTC options can be European style.

Let $c$ and $p$ denote the prices of a European call and put option, respectively, and let $C$ and $P$ denote the call and put prices of an otherwise identical American option. Then $C > c$ and $P > p$. We can write that in general $C \geq S - K$ because the American option can be exercised immediately to obtain $S$ for a price of $K$ (or it could be held to a later time). The option owner has no obligation to buy if the price is lower than $K$, so $C$ is always nonnegative. Thus, we have $C \geq (S - K)^+$. Similarly, $P \geq (K - S)^+$ for the put option.

## SECTION 2.4.2 | PUT-CALL PARITY

In option markets that satisfy the assumptions described below, European put and call options are related by an equation called *put-call parity*. The equation relates prices ($p$, $c$, $S$, and $e^{-rt}$) so that, if three are known, the put-call parity relation provides a means of determining the fourth. Usually, $S$ and $r$ are given, so knowing the value $p$ determines $c$ and vice versa. Five assumptions are required for put-call parity:

A.1　There are no dividends payable on the underlying asset.

A.2　Borrowing and investing at a known risk-free rate $r$ is available to traders.

A.3　There are no transaction fees or taxes.

A.4　Short selling and borrowing are allowed. Securities are traded in any quantity, including fractional amounts. (That is, a trader need not hold a whole number of stocks. The number of stocks can be any real number, positive or negative.)

A.5　There are no arbitrage opportunities in or across the asset and option markets.

This "no-arbitrage" environment forces a relation between European put and call options written on the same asset and having the same maturity and exercise price. This means that the portfolio consisting of a long call and a short put, which costs $c - p$ at time $t$, has a payoff of

$$(S_T - K)^+ - (K - S_T)^+$$

$$= \begin{cases} S_T - K, & \text{if } S_T > K \\ 0, & \text{if } S_T \leq K \end{cases} - \begin{cases} 0, & \text{if } S_T > K \\ K - S_T, & \text{if } S_T \leq K \end{cases}$$

$$= S_T - K$$

at time $T$. The payoff $S_T - K$ at time $T$ can be obtained without using options: buy the asset, which costs $S$ at $t$, and borrow $Ke^{-r(T-t)}$. The net cost is $S - Ke^{-r(T-t)}$, and the resulting payoffs at time $T$ are identical to the portfolio of a long call and a short put. Because there are no arbitrage trades, we have

$$c - p = S - Ke^{-r(T-t)}. \tag{2.4.1}$$

This is called the put-call parity relation for European options, often written as[6]

$$c + Ke^{-r(T-t)} = S + p. \tag{2.4.2}$$

The most important result in option-pricing theory is the formula developed by Black and Scholes [16] and the hedging technique that underlies it. Merton [133] contributed substantially to the development of this theory. Black and Scholes assume that the spot price follows a geometric Brownian motion. This means that the rate of return (measured continuously)[7] on the spot asset over the period $(t, T]$ has a normal distribution with mean $\mu(T - t)$ and variance $\sigma^2(T - t)$, where $\mu$ and $\sigma$ are constant, and that the returns over disjoint time intervals are statistically independent. This is the so-called *random walk model* often associated with stock price movements.

Many formulas have been developed that are analogous to the Black-Scholes formula but based on different distributional assumptions. Gerber and Shiu [74] have developed an elegant method of deriving such formulas. The simplest of these analogs is the Bernoulli distribution, which is used to illustrate the fundamental hedging argument underlying all these formulas. It can also be used as an alternative means of deriving the Black-Scholes formula by taking limits appropriately.

### SECTION 2.4.3 | OPTION VALUATION

Option-valuation methods, especially the Black-Scholes model, form one of the most important areas of modern finance. The rigorous mathematical development provided in later chapters is required for a proper treatment of these methods. However, the fundamental ideas can be described using simple models. The market value of a European-style derivative contract based on the spot (underlying) asset is equal to a combination of market values of the spot asset and the default-free bond.

Let $S = S_t$ denote the current asset spot price, let $\tau = T - t$ be the term of the option in years, and let $r$ be the instantaneous (continuously compounded) rate of interest of the default-free bond. The distributional assumption on the return $R = R(t, T)$ is that it is Bernoulli, so it takes one of two values. It is convenient to describe the two corresponding values of the spot price as follows:

$$S_T = \begin{cases} Se^{u\tau}, & \text{with probability } \pi \\ Se^{d\tau}, & \text{with probability } 1 - \pi \end{cases}$$

---

[6]This shows that a portfolio consisting of one European call option plus cash equal to the discounted value of the strike price has the same value at time $T$ as another portfolio consisting of one share and one European put option.

[7]Or equivalently, the logarithm of 1 plus the rate of return for the period.

where $u$, $d$, and $\pi$ are given parameters, which could be estimated by observing spot price movements, and $d < u$. Because of the no-arbitrage principle, $d \leq r \leq u$ (see Exercise 2.1).

The derivative is defined by a contract so that its cash flow, or payoff to its owner at time $T$, is a known function of the spot price. Let $f(s)$ denote the function, so the derivative pays $f(S_T)$ at maturity. For example, the function defining a call option is $f(s) = (s - K)^+$, and a put option is defined by $f(s) = (K - s)^+$, where $K$ is the exercise price and $s$ is the asset spot price at the time of exercise. The valuation scheme is to reproduce the option's payoff with a portfolio of the spot asset and the risk-free (i.e., default-free) investment.

With this in mind, let $n$ be the number of units of the spot asset in the portfolio and let $B$ denote the number of dollars borrowed at the risk-free rate. If $n > 0$, we have a long position in the spot asset. If $n < 0$, we have a short position. Similarly, a positive value of $B$ represents the amount of borrowing, and a negative value represents the amount of saving (i.e., lending) at the default-free rate. The current price per unit is $S$, and therefore the value of $n$ units is $nS$.

The market price of the portfolio at time $t$ is $nS - B$, and its value to the owner at maturity $T$ is $nS_T - Be^{r\tau}$. The values of $n$ and $B$ are to be determined so that the maturity values are the same as the derivative's values. Let $f_u = f(Se^{u\tau})$ and $f_d = f(Se^{d\tau})$. Matching the payoffs at maturity gives two equations:

$$nSe^{u\tau} - Be^{r\tau} = f_u,$$
$$nSe^{d\tau} - Be^{r\tau} = f_d.$$

The solution is

$$nS = \frac{f_u - f_d}{e^{u\tau} - e^{d\tau}}$$

and

$$B = e^{-r\tau}\left(\frac{f_u e^{d\tau} - f_d e^{u\tau}}{e^{u\tau} - e^{d\tau}}\right).$$

The corresponding portfolio of the spot asset and default-free borrowing exactly duplicates the derivative's payoffs. This portfolio is called the *hedge portfolio* because it perfectly hedges the derivative. Since there are no arbitrage opportunities, the price of the derivative is the same as the price of the hedge portfolio, $nS - B$, which simplifies to

$$nS - B = e^{-r\tau}[q f_u + (1 - q) f_d] \tag{2.4.3}$$

where

$$q = \frac{e^{r\tau} - e^{d\tau}}{e^{u\tau} - e^{d\tau}}.$$

Equation (2.4.3) can be interpreted as the expected present value at time $t$ of the derivative's payoff at time $T$, provided the probability distribution of $S_T$ is adjusted:

$$S_T = \begin{cases} Se^{u\tau}, & \text{with probability } q \\ Se^{d\tau}, & \text{with probability } 1 - q \end{cases}$$

where $q$ is determined by the market-anticipated stock prices. Thus, the derivative's price is $c = e^{-r\tau}E[f(S_T)]$, where the expectation is calculated using a special distribution. For this distribution,

$$E[S_T] = q\,Se^{u\tau} + (1 - q)\,Se^{d\tau} = Se^{r\tau}.$$

This first-moment condition suggests that, relative to this distribution, the stock price is expected to accumulate at the risk-free rate. Sometimes the distribution is called the risk-neutral distribution (see Exercises 2.1–2.4 for details).

For a particular contract, the valuation formula can be simplified further. For a call option, $f(s) = (s - K)^+$, and the price formula simplifies:

$$c = e^{-r\tau}[f_u q + f_d(1 - q)]$$

so that

$$c = \begin{cases} 0, & \text{if } K \geq Se^{u\tau} \\ e^{-r\tau}q(Se^{u\tau} - K), & \text{if } Se^{d\tau} < K < Se^{u\tau} \\ e^{-r\tau}[q\,Se^{u\tau} + (1 - q)\,Se^{d\tau} - K], & \text{if } K \leq Se^{d\tau}. \end{cases}$$

The generalization to multiple periods leads to the binomial option model. Rather than one price movement in the interval $[t, T]$, suppose there are two independent identically distributed annualized return variables. This means that $R(t, t_2)$ and $R(t_2, T)$ both have the following values:

$$R(t, t_2) = R(t_2, T) = \begin{cases} \dfrac{u\tau}{2} & \text{with probability } \pi \\ \dfrac{d\tau}{2} & \text{with probability } 1 - \pi \end{cases}$$

where $t_2 = (t + T)/2$ is the midpoint of the interval.

The annualized return variable is $R(t, T) = Nu/2 + (2 - N)d/2$, where $N$ is binomial with parameters 2 and $\pi$. The asset price at $t_2$ is $Se^{u\tau/2}$ or $Se^{d\tau/2}$. The price $S_T$ at maturity $T$ is $Se^{u\tau}$, $Se^{d\tau}$, or $Se^{(u+d)\tau/2}$. At time $t_2$, the value of a derivative defined by a function $f(s)$ of the stock price $s$ is given by the one-period model, so we know its price conditionally on the asset price at $t_2$.

Consider the function $g(s)$ of the asset price defined as follows:

$$g(s) = e^{-r\tau/2}E[f(S_T) \mid S_{t_2} = s].$$

The value of the derivative $f$ at $t$ is the same as the value of the one-period derivative $g$ because they have the same values at time $t_2$. Thus, the value of $f$ by the one-period model applied to $g$ is obtained by iteration:

$$e^{-r\tau/2}E[g(S_{t_2})] = e^{-r\tau}E[E[f(S_T) \mid S_{t_2}]]$$
$$= e^{-r\tau}E[f(S_T)].$$

Formally the valuation equation is the same as the one-period model. The mathematical difference is that the return random variable $R = R(t, T)$ is not based on a Bernoulli variable, but on a binomial random variable $N$ with parameters 2 and $(e^{r\tau/2} - e^{d\tau/2})/(e^{u\tau/2} - e^{d\tau/2})$. The extension to a return random variable

$$R(t, T) = N\frac{u}{n} + (n - N)\frac{d}{n}$$

based on a binomial random variable $N$ with parameters $n$ and

$$p = \frac{e^{r\tau/n} - e^{d\tau/n}}{e^{u\tau/n} - e^{d\tau/n}}$$

yields the binomial option-pricing model. For a call option ($f(s) = (s - K)^+$), Cox and Rubinstein [45] derive the following formula, a simplification of $c = e^{-r\tau}E[f(S_T)]$:

$$c = S\Pr(S_T > K; n, p) - Ke^{-r\tau}\Pr(S_T > K; n, p_1)$$

where

$$p_1 = \frac{e^{u\tau/n} - e^{(u+d-r)\tau/n}}{e^{u\tau/n} - e^{d\tau/n}}.$$

An appropriate limit of the binomial model yields the Black-Scholes model in which the distribution of the return is normal, although this is not the method used by Black and Scholes [16].[8] We will develop these option-valuation formulas in later chapters. At this point, we merely state the Black-Scholes valuation formula for call and put options and discuss some of its properties.

## SECTION 2.4.4 | BLACK-SCHOLES OPTION MODEL

Consider a European call option on a non-dividend-paying stock. The exercise price is $K$, and the option is exercised $\tau$ years from now. The current stock price is $S$, and the stock price on the exercise date is $S_T = Se^{\tau R}$, where $R$ is the instantaneous rate of return. All assumptions for put-call parity (A.1 through A.5 of Section 2.4.2) remain in force here. In addition, for the Black-Scholes model, the return random variable $R$ is normally distributed with variance $\sigma^2\tau$. The current market prices of the call and put options are given by the formulas

$$c = S\,N(d_1) - Ke^{-r\tau}\,N(d_2),$$

$$p = Ke^{-r\tau}\,N(-d_2) - S\,N(-d_1) \qquad (2.4.4)$$

where

$$d_1 = \frac{\log(S/K) + (r + \sigma^2/2)\tau}{\sigma\sqrt{\tau}},$$

$$d_2 = d_1 - \sigma\sqrt{\tau}$$

and $N(x)$ denotes the cumulative standard normal distribution function. The exercises at the end of the chapter provide several illustrative examples.

If the underlying stock pays a dividend during the life of the option, then formulas (2.4.4) are not valid without modification. In case the stock pays dividends continuously at a known constant continuously compounded rate $\phi \geq 0$, the formulas can be generalized. The stockholder obtains dividends (payable continuously) at the rate $\phi S_s$ at time $s$, $t \leq s \leq T$, and invests it in more shares of stock. An initial holding of 1 share of stock at time $t$ grows to $e^{\tau\phi}$ shares at $T$. Therefore, a fraction $e^{-\tau\phi}$ of shares at $t$ grows to 1 share at $T$. The cost at $t$ is $e^{-\tau\phi}S$, and the value at $T$ is $S_T$. Instead of investing $S$ at $t$ in a non-dividend-paying share, we invest less in a dividend-paying stock and continuously buy more shares with the dividends. In either case we end up with the same value $S_T$. This suggests that the Black-Scholes formulas (2.4.4) can be applied here by simply replacing $S$ everywhere by $e^{-\tau\phi}S$. Gerber and Shiu [74] show that this is indeed the case (see Exercise 2.9 for the details of the substitution).

---

[8]See Boyle [22] for a concise history of the Black-Scholes model and a more elaborate discussion of its properties. In 1997 Scholes received the Nobel Prize in economics for this work.

# Section 2.5
# Swaps

The financial markets have grown both in terms of trading volume and in terms of the variety of instruments available. The brokers, dealers, commercial banks, and investment banks have responded to the demands of their customers with customized instruments, which have sometimes developed into standard products. For example, the first interest rate swap and the first currency rate swap were initiated in London in 1981. By 1983 swaps were firmly established with a combined principal outstanding of about $5 billion, which grew to over $2.5 trillion in 1990 and to $30–$40 trillion in 1995. However, due to netting (offsetting of the cash flows), the actual money that trades hands is only 1%–2% of these amounts.

Improvements in computers and communication systems have played an important role in the development of derivative contracts. Very complex contracts can now be evaluated using powerful computers, which were not available for commercial use only a few years ago. Communications satellites and computers allow rapid transfer of information and ideas.

The demand for derivatives continues as customers seek to use capital more efficiently and to manage risk at lower cost, and derivatives can be used to enter new markets or create an arbitrage. OTC derivative contracts are distinct from exchange-traded options in that they can be customized to the needs of the buyer. Because of their importance in risk management, we discuss a few specific derivatives: swaps, caps, and floors. (Marshall and Bansal [131] and Fabozzi and Fabozzi [57] provide additional detailed reading.)

## SECTION 2.5.1 | INTEREST RATE SWAPS

First we describe a "plain vanilla" interest rate swap, which is a contract between two parties, called counterparties, requiring them to make interest payments to each other over the term of the contract. The first pays interest to the second at a fixed rate, whereas the second pays interest at a floating rate to the first. The contracts are usually arranged through a broker or dealer, without the counterparties dealing directly with each other. The dealer makes a profit on a spread between the rates. The cash payments are determined by multiplying the interest rate times a face amount of principal specified in the contract, called the *notional principal*. Consider as a concrete example that a dealer offers to clients the following 10-year swap:

Floating-rate payer:    Pay 6-month LIBOR and receive fixed 8.60%

Fixed-rate payer:        Pay fixed-rate 8.80% and receive 6-month LIBOR.

The contract calls for semiannual payments and has a notional principal of $10 million. The floating-rate payer agrees to pay floating interest every 6 months in the amount of $10 million × LIBOR/2; for example, if the LIBOR rate on the payment date is 8%, the interest payment would be $400,000. The floating-rate payer receives fixed interest every 6 months of $430,000. The fixed-rate payer pays $440,000 every 6 months and receives $10 million × LIBOR/2. Once the contract is arranged, the dealer has no interest rate risk. The dealer's profit comes from the spread on the quoted fixed rates. In the example, it amounts to $10,000 every 6 months for 10 years.

Dealer-organized markets exist for swaps. The market can change so that swaps become more or less valuable. The position can be closed out like a futures position, although the swap market is not as liquid as exchange-traded futures. A party to a swap can end the obligation before the term of the swap by taking an offsetting position or by a cash transaction with the dealer. For example, consider the fixed payer's position as interest rates move up. Suppose that after 2 years the market for an 8-year swap is described as follows:

Floating-rate payer:    Pay 6-month LIBOR and receive fixed 10.60%

Fixed-rate payer:        Pay fixed-rate 10.80% and receive 6-month LIBOR.

The fixed payer can open a new swap agreeing to pay floating 6-month LIBOR and receive fixed 10.6%. The floating payments cancel, and the net fixed cash flow is $530,000 − $440,000 = $90,000 per 6 months, or $180,000 per year, in favor of the original fixed payer. Instead of opening a new swap at current rates, the fixed payer might negotiate a single sum to terminate the contract early. If rates have moved against the fixed payer, it would have to pay the dealer to terminate the obligation early.

## SECTION 2.5.2 | APPLICATIONS

Consider a life insurance company that has an obligation to pay floating-rate interest to annuity policyholders but holds fixed-rate assets. As long as the floating-rate liability remains stable, and below its return on its assets, the insurance company will earn a profit. The company can use a swap to convert its interest rate liability from floating to fixed. This protects it from an increase in the floating rate without a costly change to its asset portfolio.

Suppose that the insurance company has agreed to pay a floating 10-year T-bond rate plus 1% on $100 million of annuity deposits for a term of 5 years. It can arrange a swap agreeing to pay a fixed rate for 5 years and receive floating 10-year T-bond rates for 5 years. The fixed rate would depend on the market conditions at the time the swap is arranged. Thus, the insurance company has used a swap to convert its floating-rate liability to a fixed-rate liability.

Reverse swaps can be used to convert fixed-rate debt to floating-rate debt. A bank can have assets consisting of floating-rate mortgages and liabilities consisting of fixed-rate bonds. A swap can be arranged so that the bank pays floating rate and receives a fixed rate, creating a better asset/liability match.

## SECTION 2.5.3 | CURRENCY SWAPS

In a currency swap the notional amounts are specified in different currencies. This is handled by exchanging the notional amounts at the beginning of the swap and returning them at the end. For example, a dealer may offer the following 5-year swaps:

Floating-rate payer:   Pay 6-month LIBOR and receive fixed 8.5% on German marks

Fixed-rate payer:   Pay fixed 8.6% on German marks and receive 6-month LIBOR.

Consider a floating-rate payer, counterparty $A$. Initially $A$ pays the notional principal in German marks to the dealer and receives the equivalent notional amount of dollars. Suppose that the notional amounts are DM (Deutsche Marks) 15 million and U.S. $10 million, and the swap calls for semiannual payments. On each settlement date $A$ pays $10 million $\times$ LIBOR/2 and receives DM 15 million $\times$ 4.25%. At the end of 5 years, the notional principals are returned: $A$ receives the notional DM 15 million and pays $10 million. This swap would be attractive if $A$ can borrow marks for 5 years at a fixed rate below 8.5% and $A$ needs floating-rate financing. The swap allows $A$ to convert fixed to a floating rate and take advantage of its ability to borrow marks at a favorable rate. The fixed-rate payer, $B$, would accept this because it can borrow marks only at a fixed rate exceeding 8.6%, and it needs fixed-rate mark financing.

A fixed-rate dollar obligation can be converted to a fixed-rate obligation in marks with two swaps. The first swap is an interest rate dollar-based swap of fixed-dollar coupons for floating-dollar coupons. The second is a currency swap of floating dollars for fixed marks. The result is fixed-dollar payments swapped for fixed-mark payments. There are other types of swaps based on commodity prices, stock indices, and so on.

The basic idea is the same as that described above for interest rate swaps and currency swaps. Swaps have many uses; their main advantage is that they allow more efficient transfer of risk than would be possible if the underlying assets and liabilities had to be traded to achieve the same positions. We expect to see more innovation in this field; for example, swaps might be used to allow traders to exchange cash-flow liabilities arising from insurance contracts, which could make for more efficient allocation of capital and transfer of risk in insurance markets. The CBOT began to offer insurance futures and options in 1992 for just these reasons. We briefly discuss these and other insurance derivatives in Section 2.9.

## SECTION 2.5.4 | COVERED INTEREST RATE ARBITRAGE

The introductory example above illustrates a general relationship if there is to be no arbitrage in currency markets. Let $E_t$ denote the cash market rate in dollars for 1 unit of currency $A$ at time $t$, and let $F(t, T)$ denote the forward price in dollars at time $t$ for delivery of 1 unit of currency $A$ at time $T$. Let $r_A$ and $r$ denote the risk-free interest rates denominated in currency $A$ and dollars, respectively.

One way to convert 1 unit of currency $A$ at time $t$ to dollars at time $T$ is through the cash market. This will produce $E_t e^{(T-t)r}$ dollars at time $T$. Another way is to open a forward position, invest in currency $A$, and then deliver under the forward contract. This results in $e^{(T-t)r_A} F(t, T)$ ignoring all transaction costs. These two strategies must give the same result, or there would be an arbitrage, namely:

$$E_t e^{(T-t)r} = e^{(T-t)r_A} F(t, T). \qquad (2.5.1)$$

An alternative way to express the same result is called the *covered interest rate arbitrage relation*. Borrow 1 unit of currency $A$ at rate $r_A$, convert to dollars obtaining $E_t$, and invest at rate $r$ to obtain $E_t e^{(T-t)r}$ in dollars at time $T$. At time $t$, also open a forward contract to receive $e^{(T-t)} r_A$ units of currency $A$ at time $T$ to be used to repay the loan amount. The cost in dollars per unit of currency $A$ at time $T$ is $F(t, T)$ for a total cost of $e^{(T-t)r_A} F(t, T)$. If there is cash left over after repaying the loan, we have arbitrage. If there is not enough cash, we could make an arbitrage by interchanging the roles of currency $A$ and dollars. Thus, using the no-arbitrage principle, we have (2.5.1).

In addition to futures and forwards, there are currency swaps, options on currency rates, and options on currency futures. The fundamental properties that we discussed earlier apply to the currency derivatives as well. Currency and interest rate hedging instruments are widely available in organized exchanges (standardized futures and options) as well as through brokers and dealers (customized forwards and swaps).

# Section 2.6
# Caps and Floors

Interest rate caps and floors are contracts designed to limit the amount of interest payable on a floating-rate loan. Section 2.5.1 describes how a floating-rate loan can be exchanged for a fixed-rate loan using an interest rate swap, thus eliminating any uncertainty in interest payable in each period. Interest rate caps and floors provide a mechanism to limit the variability of the floating rate without eliminating it completely.

It is convenient to begin with a simplified contract known as an *interest rate caplet*. A caplet is a contract that provides an upper limit on the interest payable on the loan in a single period. Suppose you borrow money on a floating-rate basis for 2 years. The interest rate during the first year is specified on the loan date, but the interest rate for the second year depends on the prevailing 1-year rate in 1 year. Obviously, if interest rates rise sharply during the first year, this will result in a higher loan rate during the second year. One way to protect against an interest rate movement is to purchase an interest rate caplet that specifies the maximum rate (the cap rate) for the second year. If the prevailing rate for the second year exceeds the cap rate, the interest payment during the second year will be based on the cap rate.

Thus, the interest rate caplet can be viewed as a single European call option on the level of interest rate. The underlying "asset" is the 1-year interest rate that will be charged 1 year in the future. Of course, the caplet contract also specifies other relevant details such as the amount of the loan.

A series of caplets of different maturities tied together in a single security is called an *interest rate cap*, the effect of which is to limit the maximum the borrower will be paying as interest in each future payment. Thus, the cap is composed of a series of European call options. Suppose an investor borrows $1 million over a 4-year term with annual interest payments that depend on the prevailing reference rates.[9] The principal is to be repaid at the end of 4 years. Suppose the relevant floating annual interest rates over the term of the loan turn out to be 5%, 6%, 7%, and 6.5%. Under the floating-rate loan, the annual interest payments over the 4 years are $50,000, $60,000, $70,000, and $65,000. If the borrower had purchased an interest rate cap with a cap rate of 6% resetting yearly for the 4 years, the revised interest payments would have been $50,000, $60,000, $60,000, and $60,000.

An *interest rate floor* (a series of *floorlets*) is similar to an interest rate cap except that it provides a lower limit on the interest rate charged in each period on the floating-rate loan. If the lender issues a floating-rate loan with a floor, then the lender is

---

[9]Often the LIBOR rate is used as the reference rate.

guaranteed an investment return at least equal to the rates set by the floor. Thus, an interest rate floor resembles a portfolio of European put options on the level of interest rates.

Caps and floors provide protection for a series of future payments. A cap might be attractive to a borrower with a floating-rate loan. For example, suppose a corporation issues bonds with face amount $10 million having coupons determined by the 6-month LIBOR rate on the coupon payment date. The company faces the risk of high future coupon payments. Buying a cap protects against this risk. Suppose the cap rate is 8.6%. Then the corporation's net payment, coupon minus cap payment, is $1/2 \times \min(0.086, \text{LIBOR}) \times \$10$ million on any payment date. Thus, the cap provides a maximum on the corporation's net payment, just as if the bond were written with a floating coupon subject to a maximum of 8.6%.

Floors are analogous to put options. For the above example, a floor written on 6-month LIBOR with a floor rate of 8.6% provides the owner with $1/2 \times \max(0, 0.086 - \text{LIBOR}) \times \$10$ million on each payment date. A floor might be attractive to a lender who does not want to bear the risk of low future coupon payments. Such a lender might simultaneously buy a floating-rate bond and a floor. Of course, this would be equivalent to buying a bond with floating payments subject to a contractual minimum of 8.6%.

Interest rate caps and floors can be combined to provide an *interest rate collar*, which guarantees the net interest rate paid will lie between the upper limit (cap rate) and the lower limit (floor rate). Thus, an interest rate collar can be thought of as a long position in a cap and a short position in a floor. In the limit, as the cap rate approaches the floor rate, the floating-rate loan becomes transformed into a fixed-rate loan.

It is important to note that caps and floors provide protection against adverse movements in the floating rate. Thus, there is a cost associated with them. This cost may be embedded in the cost of the loan through an adjustment in the interest rate, or it may be a separate up-front charge.

Caps and floors are often embedded in other contracts. Bonds with minimum or maximum constraints on floating-rate coupon payments have embedded caps and floors. Caps and floors, like swaps, can also be arranged on a stand-alone basis by brokers or dealers. The pricing of the interest rate caps and floors is discussed in Chapter 7.

# *Section 2.7*
# *Reinsurance*

Insurance companies collect cash premiums from customers in exchange for contracts that oblige the insurer to make future payments conditionally on future contingent events. For various reasons, insurers buy insurance, which is called reinsurance, to transfer some of the risks they have assumed under the contracts issued to their customers. There are several terms used to help describe these complex transfers. The customer, who bears the risk, buys insurance from a *direct insurer* or *primary insurer*. The primary insurer *cedes* risk when it buys reinsurance to cover its directly written policies. The primary insurer is also called the *ceding company*; the insurer selling the coverage to the ceding company is the *reinsurer*. The amount of coverage retained by the ceding company is called its *net retention* or *retention limit*; the amount of coverage provided by the reinsurer is the *cession*. These terms are defined relative to a specific transaction. An insurance company can be a reinsurer in one transaction and a primary insurer in another.

The relations are even more entangled than this initial description suggests for two reasons. First, reinsurers may buy reinsurance on the coverage they provide to primary insurers. This is called a *retrocession*. Second, a primary insurer may buy reinsurance from several companies to cover the same primary risk. Figure 2.4 illustrates graphically how complex the reinsurance market can be; it is based on an example Straub [187] gives in describing non-life-reinsurance transactions. The risks are insured by two primary insurers, A and B. Company B passes some of the risk to reinsurers C, D, and E. Reinsurer C passes a retrocession of its share to another reinsurer F, a *retrocessionaire* in this transaction. Reinsurer D shares its share with G and H, while E shares with H and I. F and I further complicate matters with retrocessions to H.

The transactions between insurers, reinsurers, and retrocessionaires are often facilitated by reinsurance brokers. This secondary market is essentially a market for insurance derivative contracts, that is, contracts whose future payments are functions of the payments under a primary insurance contract. This is analogous to the OTC markets for forwards and swaps on interest rates and currency exchange rates. The primary insurer swaps its contingent future payments (or a portion of them) with the reinsurer in exchange for fixed cash payments. The analogy is strengthened when we recognize that reinsurance and swaps are both custom contracts, often arranged by brokers, rather than standardized exchange-traded derivatives.

The practical details of the reinsurance of life insurance, health insurance, and annuities in the U.S. are described by Tiller and Fagerberg [193], and property and casualty reinsurance is described by Patrik [142]. The following mathematical model applies to many reinsurance transactions, both life and non-life.

The primary insurer accepts a premium of $P$ at time $t = 0$ and agrees to pay future covered losses $X_1, X_2, \ldots, X_N$, which the insured customer incurs before $t = T$. The assumption is that the random variables $N$ (claim count or frequency) and $X_1, X_2, \ldots, X_N$ (claim amounts or severity) are independent and that the claim amounts are identically distributed for fixed $N$. The aggregate claim amount is the random sum $Y = X_1 + X_2 + \cdots + X_N$.

FIGURE **2.4** | *Reinsurance Transactions*

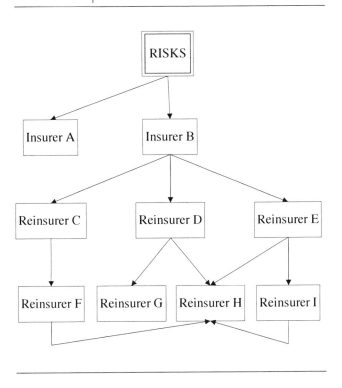

The purpose here is to use the model to describe reinsurance transactions. See one of the numerous actuarial texts that treat this model in detail, including those written by Bühlmann [32], Bowers et al. [19], Gerber [70, 71], Panjer and Willmot [140], and Klugman, Panjer, and Willmot [112].

The reinsurer can offer insurance on a per-claim basis or an aggregate basis. For a per-claim contract the reinsurer can simply agree to pay a proportion $\alpha$ of each covered claim ($0 < \alpha \leq 1$). The premium would be the same proportion $\alpha$ of the direct insurer's premium $P$; the reinsurer can offer a commission $c$ to the ceding company to recognize the ceding company's cost in obtaining the direct business. Thus, the reinsurer would receive cash equal to $\alpha P - c$ and promise to pay $\alpha X_1 + \alpha X_2 + \cdots + \alpha X_N = \alpha Y$ in the future.

Often the reinsurer's payment is a more complex function of the loss. For example, suppose that the direct policy is a group medical policy. The reinsurer may pay only in the case of a very large medical loss. Suppose this limit is $d$. Then the reinsurer pays nothing if the ceding company's incurred loss $X$ is less than $d$. It pays $\alpha(X - d)$ if $X > d$. In addition, the reinsurer's aggregate payment may be capped.

A form of reinsurance written on the aggregate loss $Y$ is called *stop-loss* reinsurance. In its simplest form, the reinsurer pays $Y - d$ when aggregate losses exceed the deductible $d$, called the *attachment point*; it pays nothing otherwise. The ceding company pays a premium at $t = 0$ to receive the payment $(Y - d)^+$ at $t = T$. The contract suggests the same mathematical structure as a call option on the ceding company's portfolio. However, the reinsurance market's economic characteristics are different from the markets for options on assets, such as stocks and bonds. For example, reinsurance is not easily traded, and the reinsurance contracts are personal and nonnegotiable. Exchange-traded options on stocks and bonds, on the other hand, are easily traded. Moreover, reinsurers often bundle expertise and services, such as underwriting, with the promise to pay.

Reinsurance is often written with a contractual maximum payment. Such a stop-loss reinsurance policy specifies contractual values $d$ and $m$ that define the reinsurer's payment to the insurance company. If the aggregate loss is less than $d$, there is no payment to the insurer. For aggregate losses between $d$ and $m$, the reinsurer pays $Y - d$. If the aggregate losses exceed $m$, then the reinsurer pays $m - d$. The reinsurer's payment is denoted compactly as $f(Y)$, where $f$ is the function defined by the equation

$$f(y) = \begin{cases} 0, & \text{if } y < d \\ y - d, & \text{if } d \le y < m \\ m - d, & \text{if } y > m. \end{cases}$$

The parameters $d$ and $m - d$ are usually specified in the reinsurance treaty. For example, if $d = 20$ million and $m = 25$ million, in insurance terms, we say that the reinsurer covers 5 million in excess of 20 million. Insurance-based securities such as the CBOT insurance options have payments that are similar to reinsurance (see Section 2.9).

# Section 2.8
# Securitization of Assets

In securitizing a portfolio of assets, the aggregate portfolio cash flow is divided into segments, creates contracts that promise to pay the cash flow contractually defined for each segment, and sells the contracts. The owner of the assets sells its rights to future cash flow from the underlying assets. As an example, consider a bank with a portfolio of consumer debt (e.g., credit-card debt). It may wish to sell the cash flow, or a portion of it, to improve its risk-based capital position, without getting out of the consumer credit business. It can dedicate a block of loans to a set of securities and sell the securities. The loans on the asset side of the bank's balance sheet are offset by a liability to pay loan cash flow to the security owners, and the bank has increased cash from the sale of the securities.

There are many variations of securitization, and a variety of motivations. We discuss three of them in detail: T-bond-backed securities, mortgage-backed securities, and securitization of life insurance policy loans.

## SECTION 2.8.1 | T-BOND-BACKED SECURITIES

We begin with a simple illustrative example. Consider five U.S. T-bonds selected from the September 11, 1995 edition of *The Wall Street Journal*, as shown in Table 2.7.

TABLE 2.7 | *Treasury Bonds*

| Rate | Month | Year | Bid | Asked | Asked Yield |
|------|-------|------|-----|-------|-------|
| 7.000 | Sep | 1996 | 101:10 | 101:12 | 5.63 |
| 5.500 | Sep | 1997 | 99:12 | 99:14 | 5.79 |
| 4.750 | Sep | 1998 | 96:22 | 96:24 | 5.93 |
| 7.125 | Sep | 1999 | 103:28 | 103:30 | 6.02 |
| 8.750 | Aug | 2000 | 111:12 | 111:14 | 6.03 |

Source: *The Wall Street Journal*, September 11, 1995.

Suppose we own a $100 face amount of each bond, and we want to create zero-coupon bonds. In 1996 we get $33.125 = 7 + 5.5 + 4.75 + 7.125 + 8.75$ in coupons and 100 in principal, so we can be certain of having 133.125 in September 1996. These bonds pay semiannual coupons, but they are all paid by September. The aggregate annual cash flow is shown in Figure 2.5. The owner of the coupon bonds sells five zero-coupon bonds with face amounts $133.125, 126.125, \ldots, 108.75$ and maturities in $1996, 1997, \ldots, 2000$. This is effectively selling the total portfolio cash flows in the zero-coupon market.

Merrill Lynch and other investment banks created such zero-coupon derivatives ("zeros") in the 1980s because there was a demand for default-free zero-coupon debt. In 1984 the U.S. Treasury started the STRIP (Separate Trading of Registered Interest and Principal of Securities) program, which allows separate trading of coupon and principal T-bond cash flows. The Canadian government has a program similar to the U.S. STRIP program (see Jones and Fabozzi [101] for more information on U.S. and Canadian STRIPs).

A new 30-year T-bond with a coupon rate of 10% and a face value of 100 becomes 61 separately registered securities when it enters the STRIP program, 60 coupon payments of 5, and 1 principal payment of 100. The separated coupons and principal securities are called "strips." Only bonds with 10 or more years to maturity enter the program, but as they mature they provide zeros of shorter maturities. Currently,

FIGURE **2.5** | *T-Bond-Backed Zero-Coupon Bonds*

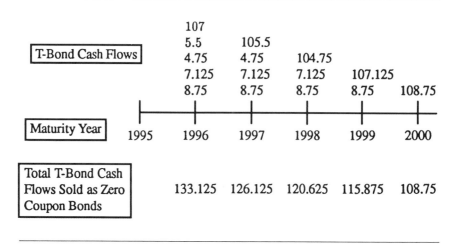

strips can have maturities as short as a few days. Investment banks continue to offer their own T-bond-backed zeros. On September 11, 1995, there were strips with nearly the same maturities as our T-bond-backed zeros. It is interesting to compare the market value of the T-bonds with the price we might get if we sold the cash flow as zeros.

The market value on September 8 of the five coupon T-bonds in the example was 512.625 bid and 512.9375 ask. From the September 11, 1995 *Wall Street Journal* report of STRIP trading, we have the values shown in Table 2.8.

TABLE **2.8** | *U.S. Treasury Strips*

| Maturity | Bid | Asked | Asked Yield |
| --- | --- | --- | --- |
| Aug 1996 | 95:9 | 95:10 | 5.26 |
| Aug 1997 | 89:16 | 89:18 | 5.82 |
| Aug 1998 | 84:06 | 84:09 | 5.94 |
| Aug 1999 | 79:07 | 79:10 | 5.99 |
| Aug 2000 | 74:13 | 74:16 | 6.07 |

The strip with maturity August 1996 sells for $95:9 = 95 - 9/32 = 95.28125$, so the example's 1996 zero could be sold for about $133.125 \times 0.9528125 = 126.84$. The 1997 zero could be sold for about $126.125 \times 0.895 = 112.88$. If we sold all the example's T-bond-backed zeros at STRIP prices, we would get a total of 513.94, slightly more than the market value of the T-bonds.

## SECTION 2.8.2 | MORTGAGE-BACKED SECURITIES

A mortgage is a loan requiring periodic payments of principal and interest with real estate as collateral. A residential mortgage, for the U.S. market, means a single-family home or multiple-family home with no more than four families occupying the property. Commercial mortgages have commercial property such as an apartment building or store as collateral. We limit our discussion to residential mortgages, because this is the most important segment of the market and the securitization of other mortgages is similar.

Most mortgages are issued with a fixed interest rate for a period of 15 to 30 years in the U.S. and for periods of 6 months to 5 years in Canada. They require level monthly payments of interest and principal based on amortization periods of 25 or more years. In the U.S., until *adjustable-rate* mortgages were introduced in the 1980s, all home mortgages were conventional. The adjustable-rate mortgage was introduced as a means of shifting most of the interest rate risk to the borrower as interest rate variability increased.

The adjustable-rate mortgage requires the monthly payment to be reset each year, after an initial period of several years during which it is fixed by the initial interest rate. For example, the initial monthly payment for a 30-year 6% mortgage loan of $100,000 is[10]

$$\frac{100,000}{a_{\overline{360}|\,0.005}} = 599.55$$

where the initial rate is reset at the beginning of the fourth year.

The mortgage contract specifies that the reset rate is the prevailing U.S. Treasury 1-year bill yield plus 2%. If the new rate is 7%, the new monthly payment is determined using the new rate. With the outstanding balance of 96,084 after 3 years, the new monthly payment is

$$\frac{96,084}{a_{\overline{360}|\,0.00583}} = 660.88.$$

The lender retains some interest rate risk because the mortgage contract limits the increase in the interest rate, or it provides a lifetime cap on the mortgage interest rate. Each year, after the initial fixed period, the monthly payment is recalculated to adjust the yield to the lender to reflect the market conditions. The monthly payment can go up or down, subject to a contractual maximum and minimum.

---

[10]The symbol $a_{\overline{n}|\,i}$ denotes the present value one period before the first payment of an annuity paying 1 per period for $n$ periods. Thus, $a_{\overline{n}|\,i} = v + v^2 + v^3 + \cdots + v^n$ where $v = (1+i)^{-1}$.

The U.S. Federal Housing Administration and other federal agencies insure qualifying mortgages against the borrower's default, eliminating the investor's credit risk. To qualify for insurance, a mortgage must satisfy several conditions: It must be long term, it must have a level payment with no early repayment penalty to the borrower, and it cannot provide a right to demand early repayment of the debt to the lender. Thus, the conventional qualified mortgage, although it conveys no credit risk to the lender, has substantial interest rate risk. As interest rates fall, borrowers can refinance, returning the principal to the lender at a time when interest rates are lower than the rate at which the mortgage was issued. There are costs to refinancing, but when rates fall enough, borrowers have a financial incentive to refinance.

Mortgage securitization shifts the refinancing risk to investors through the securities market. In other countries, the mortgage regulations and practices are often different; for example, in Canada mortgages do not normally allow borrowers to repay early without penalty. We will discuss three U.S. mortgage-backed securities:
1.    Pass-through securities
2.    Stripped mortgage-backed securities
3.    Collateralized mortgage-backed obligations.

***Pass-Through Securities.*** Government agencies are authorized by law to purchase mortgage loans and issue securities that provide the security owner with a claim on the pooled monthly mortgage cash flow. One purpose of this repackaging is to allow for a more efficient allocation of interest rate risk. Primary mortgage lenders usually have short-term liabilities (demand deposits); so, for most of them, mortgage assets are not well matched to their liabilities. However, a life insurance company with long-term liabilities may want to have mortgage-backed securities in its asset portfolio.

The mortgage borrowers make their monthly payments to the pool administrator. The pool collects the cash, deducts administrative fees, and passes the cash to the security owners on a pro-rata basis. For example, if there are 10 securities issued on the pool, each security owner gets one-tenth of the aggregate monthly cash flow, less fees. If a mortgage is repaid during the month, the repaid principal is paid to the security owners along with the monthly cash flow. Thus, the security owners bear the interest rate risk.

Valuation of a pass-through security requires knowing the rates and maturities of the pooled mortgages. This and other information is provided to potential purchasers. An actuarial approach would involve modeling the lifetime of a mortgage and considering the cash flow to be a cash-refund annuity. The difficulty (and the distinction from mortality-dependent cash flow) is that the mortgage lifetime depends on the interest rate environment. The other mortgage-backed securities present the same valuation problems; that is, the cash flows are *interest sensitive*. Other mortgage-backed securities, *non-pass-throughs*, come with a wide variety of payment features—so wide that it is said that no two securities are exactly alike. They can be very complex. We describe only two in an idealized form. The concepts involved are apparent without too much complexity. The first is a stripped MBS, and the second is a CMO.

***Stripped Mortgage-Backed Securities.*** A stripped MBS divides the payments from pooled mortgages into classes rather than distributing it on a pro-rata basis. For example, the *interest-only* class receives the interest paid by the pooled mortgages each month. The *principal-only* class receives the principal paid each month. Consider a representative mortgage in the pool. The principal outstanding at the beginning of the month is $100,000, the interest rate is 6%, and the level monthly payment is $600. Then, ignoring fees, the interest-only class is allocated $100,000 \times 0.06/12 = \$500$ this month from this mortgage. The principal-only class receives the principal paid with respect to the pool mortgage, $600 - 500 = 100$ if the mortgage is not repaid during the month. If the mortgage loan is repaid during the month, the principal-only class gets 100,000. The two classes receive similar payments from each mortgage with an outstanding balance at the beginning of the month.

The stripped pass-through security owners bear the interest rate risk of the pool, but it is allocated differently than it is for straight pass-throughs. The interest-only class receives interest until all the mortgages are repaid. Refinancing activity increases with falling interest rates, so the downside for interest-only security owners arises with declining interest rates. The principal-only class benefits from a decline in interest rates because refinancing means principal-only security owners receive their principal sooner. Thus, the stripped pass-through divides pool cash flow into segments that give a pure reflection of the result of an increase or decrease in interest rates. This is more flexible than a straight pass-through and appeals to at least as many investors. After all, an investor who wants a straight pass-through could simply buy shares of both interest-only and principal-only classes.

***Collateralized Mortgage Obligations.*** A CMO redistributes the interest rate risk two ways. First, like a stripped pass-through, the pool supports interest-only and principal-only securities. In addition, the collateralized mortgage obligation, consisting of several *tranches*, specifies the order in which the principal prepayments to the pool are to be allocated to the tranches. Interest payments normally go to all tranches. This system of tranches results in the tranches maturing in a specified order. As a hypothetical illustration, consider a pool of mortgages with an outstanding principal of $200 million supporting two tranches. Each tranche has a par amount of $100 million, meaning that the tranche owners each receive $100 million in principal. However, the first tranche, *A*, is paid all principal payments to the pool before the second tranche, *B*, gets any principal. Only after tranche *A* owners receive $100 million in principal payments do tranche *B* owners begin to get principal payments. Thus, *A* is a pro-rata pass-through, not for the entire pool, but the first $100 million of principal repaid. *B* is like an interest-only security until *A* is paid up, at which time it becomes a pro-rata pass-through on the remaining mortgages. The tranches *A* and *B* could be further divided into interest-only and principal-only securities.[11]

Securitization of the mortgage industry has allowed investors to enter the mortgage market without having to be (or own) a mortgage originator. Insurance companies and pension funds have become substantial investors in mortgage-backed securities. Thus, securitization has allowed for a better allocation of interest rate risk and provided a more efficient way for capital to enter the home-financing industry. The securitization technique is important for actuaries because the resulting products are used by insurance companies and because the technique can be applied to other asset classes. Perhaps the most important reason is that the expertise required to design and value these securities is fundamentally actuarial in nature.

## SECTION 2.8.3 | POLICY-LOAN-BACKED SECURITIES

Consider a long-term life insurance contract with a level annual premium and a death benefit paid upon death. The annual premium is essentially an average of expected future benefits and expense, while the expected cost of death benefits usually increases with age. The company starts out collecting a premium in excess of the benefit costs, but eventually the expected cost of benefits exceeds the level premium. U.S. regulators require that, in addition to the death benefit, this type of life insurance must pay a benefit, called the cash surrender value, upon early surrender of the contract, and they specify a regulatory minimum value. In effect, cash surrender values provide embedded options to the policyholder.

To provide policyholders access to the cash value without canceling the insurance policy, the policy also provides a loan option. The policyholder can borrow from the insurance company up to the policy cash surrender value without surrendering the policy; the loan is collateralized by the cash surrender values. The policyholder continues to pay premiums and, in addition, pays interest on the loan as specified in the policy.

Traditionally companies offered fixed-rate policy loans, but as interest rate volatility increased in the 1970s and 1980s, most companies started issuing policies that specified an indexed loan interest rate. When the loan interest rate is fixed, the policy loan provision is an interest rate call option. The value of the option increases with the volatility of interest rates; it was not until many policyholders began to exercise their options that companies recognized the value of these options. The industry response was to eliminate the option by making the loan rate variable.

---

[11] Students of life contingencies will notice the similarities the tranches have to multiple life annuities that provide benefits as a function of the order of death of the lives.

## SECTION 2.8.4 | MECHANICS OF THE LOAN PROVISION

The loan provision works as follows: Suppose that the cash surrender value at the beginning of policy year $[k-1, k)$, just before paying the premium due at $k-1$, is $_{k-1}CV$. Let $i$ be the policy loan interest rate. The policyholder has the following three options:

1. Surrender the policy, make no premium payments, and take the cash value $_{k-1}CV$. The company has no further obligation beyond paying the cash value.
2. Pay the premium keeping the policy in force and borrow $L$ from the company, subject to $L(1+i) \leq {}_kCV$.
3. Pay the premium, and do not exercise the loan option.

If the loan is not repaid at the end of the policy year, interest is added to the amount of the loan automatically. As long as the outstanding balance of the loan is less than the corresponding cash surrender values, the loan is fully collateralized.

Policyholders take out policy loans for several reasons. There is a financial incentive to exercise the loan provision when the policyholder can invest at a rate in excess of $i$. For example, suppose 1-year T-bills are available at yields greater than $i$. The policyholder can exercise the loan option for the maximum amount available and buys 1-year T-bills. At the end of the year, if the T-bills are redeemed and the loan is repaid, the policyholder makes a gain. The insurance policy is just where it would have been if there had been no loan.

If the policyholder dies while the loan is outstanding, the company reduces the death benefit by the amount of the loan, but the T-bill can be sold to offset the reduction. There may be some difference in tax treatment, but the financial incentive remains. Borrowing from the policy to purchase a bond still provides cash for emergencies, since the T-bills can be sold to offset the reduction in the death benefits.

Thus, when interest rates are above loan interest rates, policyholders should exercise the loan option. As life insurers found during periods of high interest in the 1970s and 1980s, many policyholders will respond if interest rates move well above policy loan rates. In addition, policy loan options are exercised when there is no financial advantage. For example, most policies allow the policyholder to elect to have the loan provision triggered automatically when a premium is overdue. This is convenient for both the policyholder and the company. Thus, there is always some loan activity, but it should increase to a maximum when the rates of interest paid on consumer savings are greater than policy loan rates.

## SECTION 2.8.5 | POOLING LOANS

Outstanding policy loans appear on the insurance company's financial statement as assets, at the face amount of the loan. Securitization of a portfolio of policy loans allows the company to sell them. One reason for doing this is to get cash to reduce the cash strain induced by policy loan activity. There may be a tax advantage when the loans are sold at a loss relative to their statement value. These reasons led to a very large securitization of policy loans by the Prudential Insurance Company of America in 1987. The Prudential transaction was based on a selected pool of policies with outstanding policy loans totaling about $600 million. The policy loan interest and principal payments formed the cash flow to support securities that were sold to investors as private placements.

A special purpose corporation (SPC) was formed to issue the securities and simultaneously purchase the loan cash flow from the Prudential. The Prudential administers the cash flow, collecting payments in a manner that is transparent to the policyholder and passing it to the SPC. Cash from the sale of the securities compensates the company for assigning future loan cash flow to the SPC. The SPC issued six bonds with a face amount of about $445 million and an equity security in December 1987. The six bonds are sequential tranches, similar to collateralized mortgage obligation tranches discussed in the last section. The equity investors purchased the right to residual cash flows after all the tranches have been paid. The Prudential securitization borrowed concepts from the securitization of mortgage loans, but it employed new features too. Since policy loan securitization was new, security buyers had no experience with loan repayment rates. To reduce the repayment risk to security owners, the securities provided for minimum and maximum repayment schedules. If actual repayments fell behind the minimum schedule, the Prudential promised to advance the needed cash to meet the required payments to security owners. Cash-flow simulations indicated that the Prudential was very unlikely to be called on to advance payments. If repayments were more rapid than the maximum, the SPC would invest the excess cash flow in a GIC. The SPC bought a 54-year GIC from an AAA-rated Swiss bank to provide security owners with evidence that the SPC would be able to perform on these promises.

The history of this transaction appears in the *Record of the Society of Actuaries* (see Shante et al. [171]). We know of no other policy loan securitization, although the transaction seems to have been successful, and Prudential officials have said they would do it again in appropriate circumstances. Perhaps high interest rates might make them attractive again someday. However, since the value of the loan option in newer policies is zero, the magnitude of the problem created by increased exercise activity is steadily decreasing, and the costs of a policy loan securitization are substantial (it involves investment bankers, lawyers, accountants, and actuaries, in and outside the company, in addition to other company staff and management). Therefore, it may be a long time before we see another policy loan securitization. However, the securitization process is, in principle, applicable to liabilities as well as assets. Activity in liability securitization increased in the 1990s, although the concept is much older. Goshay and Sandor [77] proposed reinsurance futures 20 years before the Chicago Board of Trade introduced insurance futures.

# Section 2.9
# Securitization of Insurance Liabilities

There are two approaches to securitization of insurance liabilities:

1. Exchange-traded options on the aggregate losses of a portfolio of risks
2. Bonds with coupon and principal based on aggregate losses of a portfolio of risks.

For the first approach, we briefly describe the catastrophe insurance options traded at the CBOT based on the pamphlet *PCS Catastrophe Insurance Options* [36], and we use the bonds described by Tilley [197] to illustrate the second. The trade press reports other approaches, such as borrowing agreements triggered by aggregate losses in a portfolio. However, these two examples are adequate to illustrate the actuarial and financial principles needed for liability securitization.

## SECTION 2.9.1 | INSURANCE OPTIONS

In May 1990 the Chicago Board of Trade announced a novel insurance futures and option complex. It provided insurance companies with a hedge against their insurance risk, and it provided investors an opportunity to profit from insurance risk. One of these, a contract based on catastrophe insurance, was moderately successful. In September 1995, the CBOT replaced the insurance contract by a better design, called PCS catastrophe insurance options. PCS stands for Property Claim Services, an independent company to which the industry reports claims. The contracts behave like property catastrophe stop-loss reinsurance on a portion of the industry's property risk in a region of the U.S.

To illustrate this, consider a hypothetical insurance company that has sold property insurance in Florida. Let $X$ denote the aggregate loss that the company incurs during the period $(t, T)$. Consider a stop-loss reinsurance policy covering $m - d$ in excess $d$. The reinsurer's payment $f(X)$, which we discussed in Section 2.7, can be written as

$$f(x) = (x - d)^+ - (x - m)^+.$$

(We leave the verification of this relation as an exercise.) Thus, the reinsurance contract has the same mathematical structure as a portfolio of two call options (one long with exercise price $d$ and one short with exercise price $m$). If call options were written on the insurance company's losses, the reinsurance payment could be duplicated with two calls. A portfolio of two call options created in this way is a call option spread. A CBOT option spread has exercise values, which are analogous to reinsurance payments. In 1996 the CBOT offered spread contracts, whereas in early 1997 it offered only call options. Of course, a trader can construct a spread as we just described, so it may be less complicated and just as useful to offer only call options.

However, the CBOT insurance options are not the same as options on assets, such as stocks and bonds, because the underlying insurance is not traded. Moreover, the insurance options differ from traditional reinsurance in that they are written on the industry's portfolio, not the portfolio of a single company. We must keep these issues in mind when using CBOT options as reinsurance. In addition, reinsurance is not easily traded, and reinsurance contracts are customized and nontransferable. The CBOT options are easily traded, and they are not customized. Moreover, as mentioned earlier, reinsurers provide expertise and services, such as underwriting, as well as the promise to pay.

The CBOT options are written on nine loss ratios calculated by Property Claim Services. Thus, the underlying "asset" on which the options are written is not an asset at all: it is the loss ratio on a specific set of insurance policies. An insurance company would have to know the correlation of its own policies with those underlying the index loss ratio to use the CBOT options as a hedge. Although it may require some effort and the hedge is not perfect (as reinsurance is), an insurance company might buy call spreads if they were cheaper than reinsurance.

The CBOT has been careful to point out to insurance regulators and customers that it is not an insurance company. It merely aligns buyers and sellers.

If insurance companies are the natural buyers of call spreads, who are the sellers? The CBOT points to statistical studies that show that the underlying loss ratio is not correlated with the stock market (see Froot et al. [67] and Lane [117]). It suggests that investing in catastrophe options diversifies the investor's portfolio in a way that is difficult to do with stocks; that is, selling catastrophe call options should provide returns that, on average, are not correlated with returns on stocks.

This may be better than simply buying shares in a reinsurance company. Selling catastrophe options has lower transaction costs than buying reinsurance shares. It is more of a "pure" play in that it concentrates on catastrophe risk, whereas a share of a reinsurer provides a claim on all earnings of which catastrophe business may be a small portion. All of these are reasons investors such as life insurance companies and pension funds might invest in insurance options or other insurance derivatives.

We now turn to the details of the PCS option contract, following the CBOT pamphlet [36]. The underlying index is one of the following PCS loss indices: National, Eastern, Northeastern, Southeastern, Midwestern, Western, Florida, Texas, and California. Each PCS loss index reports PCS estimates for insured industry losses resulting from catastrophic events in the area and loss period covered. PCS provides each index daily. Each PCS loss index represents the sum of then-current PCS estimates for insured catastrophic losses in the area and loss period covered divided by $100 million.

The loss period is the time during which a catastrophic event must occur in order for resulting losses to be included in the index. The California and Western indices have annual loss periods; other indices have quarterly loss periods. The development period is the time after the loss period during which PCS estimates continue to affect the PCS indices. PCS option users can choose either a 6- or a 12-month development period. The PCS index value at the end of the chosen development period is the settlement value. The length of the development period is important because it can take many months to settle losses after an earthquake or hurricane.

Option premiums are quoted in points and tenths of a point. Each point equals $200, and so each tenth of a point equals $20; for example, a premium of 5.2 equals $1,040. All PCS options, which are European style, expire at 6:00 p.m. on the same day in which the settlement value of the underlying index is made publicly available, either 6 or 12 months after the loss period, depending on the development period of the option. For catastrophe insurance options, the buy/sell obligations settle in cash, like options written on stock-price indices. For the stock-price index options, the underlying index is widely disseminated and independently calculated. The PCS loss index plays the same role for catastrophe insurance options that the stock price index plays for stock index options.

Information about claims payments is very important to catastrophe insurance options traders. This may not be available to all traders, but daily catastrophe loss information is available from Property Claims Service. Of course, catastrophic events such as hurricanes also have an impact on option prices. We expect catastrophe insurance option prices to vary daily just as the more familiar futures prices of commodities and financial instruments do, even though the financial press does not publish actual loss data.

PCS options can help insurers and reinsurers protect their book of business against catastrophic losses. PCS options can act as a complement to traditional reinsurance, filling in the gaps when traditional coverage either is not available or costs too much. As an example, consider this report from the financial press during the week of March 29, 1996. Ten of the third-quarter Southeastern 200/250 call spreads sold for 1.8 points. This means there was a trader willing to buy and another trader was willing to sell at

$$1.8 \text{ points} \times \$200 \text{ per point} = \$360 \text{ per contract.}$$

The option provides protection for the index values between

$$200 \text{ points} \times \$100 \times \text{ million per point} = \$20 \text{ billion}$$

and $25 billion. The index reflects industry losses in the Southeastern region incurred during July, August, and September 1996 and settled during the 12 months following

September 1996. If the index settles below 200, the call option pays the owner nothing. If it settles at or above 250, it pays

$$(250 - 200) \times \$200 = \$10,000.$$

For an index value $I$ between 200 and 250, it pays $(I - 200) \times \$200$.

Thus, the call spread represents a fraction of a stop-loss reinsurance on the industry's Southeastern region exposure, covering $5 billion of losses in excess of $20 billion, incurred during the third quarter and settled within 12 months. In October 1996 the index was 16.4, corresponding to industry losses of $1.64 billion. The option was well out of the money at the end of the loss period. Loss development will probably not move the index into the money by September 1997, when the contract settles.

If an insurance company's loss exposure is 0.1% of the industry's exposure in the Southeastern region during the third quarter, then the 200/250 index spread corresponds to company losses in the range of $20 million to $25 million. The company might use the call spread as a substitute for stop-loss reinsurance of $5 million in excess of $20 million. One option pays zero to $10,000 over this range, so 500 contacts would cover zero to

$$500 \times \$200 \times (250 - 200) = \$5 \text{ million.}$$

The company would need to buy 500 contracts at a cost of

$$500 \times \$360 \text{ per contract} = \$180,000$$

to "cover" this exposure. Of course, it is not a perfect substitute for traditional reinsurance because the call spread is written on the industry's portfolio instead of the company's own loss exposures.

As appealing as the PCS options may seem, they clearly have a long way to go before they can be a competitive threat to traditional reinsurance. In March 1996, there were only about 2,800 outstanding insurance options; this is the open interest. By October 1996, this had increased to about 6,800. In comparison to other option markets, this is low volume. On the same date, the volume of options on U.S. interest rate futures exceeded 50,000, and there were more than 24,000 options on crude oil futures.

In summary, an insurance company might buy catastrophe call spreads as a substitute or supplement to traditional reinsurance. An investor or a reinsurer might sell call spreads if the prices were attractive. The risk of writing call spreads is very similar to the reinsurer's risk in writing traditional coverage on a proportion of the industry.

## SECTION 2.9.2 | CATASTROPHE REINSURANCE AS A HIGH-YIELD BOND

Most investment banks, some insurance brokers, and most large reinsurers developed OTC insurance derivatives by 1995. This is another form of liability securitization, but instead of exchange-traded contracts, these securities are handled like private placements or like forwards or custom options. Tilley [197] describes securitized catastrophe reinsurance in terms of a high-yield bond. Froot et al. [67] describes a very similar one-period product. These products illustrate how catastrophe risk can be distributed through capital markets. The description here is an abstraction and simplification; refer to the literature provided by the product developers for practical details.

Consider a reinsurance contract issued at $t$ for which the reinsurer agrees to pay a fixed amount $L$ at $T > t$ if a defined catastrophic event occurs. It pays nothing if there is no catastrophe. $L$ is known when the policy is issued. If $q_{cat}$ denotes the probability of a catastrophic event and $P$ the price of the reinsurance, then the "fair" value of the reinsurance is

$$P = \frac{1}{1 + i_f} L q_{cat}$$

where $i_f$ is the risk-free effective interest rate over the policy period. This defines a one-to-one correspondence between bond prices and the probability of a catastrophe. Because the reinsurance market will determine the price $P$, it is natural to call $q_{cat}$ the reinsurance market assessment of the probability of a catastrophe.

From where does the capital to support the reinsurer come? The reinsurer will have no customers unless it can convince them that it has capital at least equal to $L$. Suppose that just before it sells the reinsurance, the reinsurer borrows capital by issuing a defaultable bond. "Defaultable bond" is a fancy term for junk bond, a bond with a relatively high risk of default. Investors know when they buy a junk bond that it may default, but they buy it anyway because the bonds do not often default and they have higher returns than more reliable bonds.

The reinsurer issues enough bonds to raise an amount of cash $C$ determined so that

$$(P + C)(1 + i_f) = L.$$

This satisfies the reinsurer's customers: they see that the reinsurer has enough capital to pay for a catastrophe. The bondholders know that the bonds will be worthless if there is a catastrophe, in which case they get nothing. If there is no catastrophe, they get their cash back plus a coupon $R = L - C$.

The bond market will determine the price per unit of face value. In terms of discounted expected cash flow, the price per unit can be written in the form

$$\frac{1}{1+i_f}(1+c)(1-q_B)$$

where $c = R/C$ is the coupon rate and $q_B$ denotes the bondholders' assessment of the probability of default on the bonds. We can assume that the investment bank designing the bond contract sets $c$ so that the bonds sell at face value. Thus, $c$ is determined so that investors pay 1 to receive $1 + c$ a year later, if there is no catastrophe. This is expressed as

$$1 = \frac{1}{1+i_f}(1+c)(1-q_B).$$

Of course, default on the bonds and a catastrophe are equivalent events. The probabilities $q_B$ and $q_{cat}$ can differ because bond investors and reinsurance customers can have different information about catastrophes. The reinsurance company sells bonds once $c$ is determined to raise the required capital $C$. The corresponding bond market probability is found by solving for $q_B$:

$$q_B = \frac{c - i_f}{1 + c},$$

and the implied price for reinsurance is

$$P_B = \frac{1}{1+i_f}\frac{c-i_f}{1+c}L.$$

Provided the reinsurance market premium $P$ (the fair price determined by the reinsurance market) is at least as large as $P_B$, the reinsurance company will function smoothly. It will collect $C$ from the bond market and $P$ from the reinsurance market at the beginning of the policy period. The sum invested for one period at the risk-free rate, $(P + C)(1 + i_f)$, will be at least $L$, so the reinsurer has adequate capital. This is easy to see mathematically using the relation $R = L - C$.

So long as $P_B$ does not exceed $P$, or equivalently, so long as

$$q_{cat} \geq \frac{c - i_f}{1 + c},$$

an economically viable market will exist for reinsurance capitalized by borrowing in the bond market. In an efficient market with infinite capacity, the inequality would be expected to become an equality. However, these catastrophe products have been developed in response to limited reinsurer market capacity.

Borrowing (issuing bonds) to finance losses is not new. In the late 1980s when U.S. liability insurance prices were high and interest rates were moderate, some traditional insurance customers switched to self-insurance programs financed by bonds. Tilley [197], Froot et al. [67], and others imply that the same price relation between the catastrophe property reinsurance market and the bond market exists in the 1990s.

In summary, the reinsurer has adequate cash to pay the loss if a catastrophic event occurs. If no catastrophe occurs, the fund goes to the bond owners. From the bond owners' perspective, the bond contract is like lending money subject to credit risk, except the risk of "default" is really the risk of a catastrophic event. Note that the reinsurer has adequate cash at the beginning of the period to make the loss payment with probability one. Tilley describes this as a fully collateralized reinsurance contract.

This scheme is a simple version of how a traditional reinsurer works with these differences. The traditional reinsurance company investors buy shares of stock instead of bonds. Losses are based on a portfolio of risks rather than single exposure. Simplifying and specializing makes it possible to sell single exposures through the capital markets, in contrast to shares of stock of a reinsurer, which are claims on the aggregate of outcomes. Tilley [197] demonstrates this technique in a more general setting in which the reinsurance and bond are multiperiod contracts. This one-period model illustrates the key ideas.

# Section 2.10
# Conclusion

The financial markets for stock and bond derivatives are very successful in that they allow for efficient exchange of capital and risk. We have described in a simple, nonrigorous way how options on stocks can be replicated by a portfolio of bonds and stocks. Intuitively, the assumptions underlying the Black-Scholes method were applied to this situation, and we briefly discussed the resulting formula.

Reinsurance is analogous to an option, at least from a mathematical perspective. However, insurance (the underlying security) is not traded in an efficient market. This is one flaw in the analogy between insurance markets and financial markets. We know that care must be used in applying methods, such as the Black-Scholes option-pricing model, to insurance. Nevertheless, financial markets play an important role in valuing insurance products as diverse as equity-indexed annuities, discussed in Chapter 1, and "act of God bonds" discussed in this chapter.

Chapters 4 and 5 provide two different derivations of the Black-Scholes formula; there trading and arbitrage are presented in a more rigorous, multiple-period setting. The methods described in this and all later chapters are becoming more important for actuaries as life insurance companies continue to develop policies with embedded options. Securitization of insurance, such as the CBOT options, is more complex because the underlying insurance portfolio is not traded. Actuaries must appreciate market equilibrium pricing techniques to understand these developments; these are covered in Chapter 4.

# Section 2.11
## Exercises

### Exercise 2.1 (Arbitrage)

Let $S = S(t)$ denote the current asset spot price, and suppose that the price at time $T > t$ is Bernoulli:

$$S_T = \begin{cases} Se^{u\tau}, & \text{with probability } p \\ Se^{d\tau}, & \text{with probability } 1-p \end{cases}$$

where $\tau = T - t$. Let $r$ denote the continuously compounded risk-free annual rate of interest. Assume that the spot asset pays no dividends ($D = 0$). Show that the no-arbitrage principle implies that $d \leq r \leq u$.

### Exercise 2.2 (Bernoulli Stock Price Model)

For the Bernoulli model as described in Exercise 2.1 show that

$$E[S_T] = Se^{r\tau}$$

if and only if

$$p = \frac{e^{r\tau} - e^{d\tau}}{e^{u\tau} - e^{d\tau}}.$$

### Exercise 2.3 (Bernoulli Option Price Model)

Consider the Bernoulli model as described in Exercise 2.1. A European-style derivative security pays $f(S_T)$ at time $T$. Show that the derivative's price $c$ at time $t$ is

$$c = e^{-r\tau}E[f(S_T)]$$

where the "up" probability is set to the value described in Exercise 2.2.

## Exercise 2.4 *(Continuation of Exercise 2.3)*

The derivative is a European call option with exercise price $K$. Thus, $f(s) = (s - K)^+$. Show that

$$c = Sp' - e^{-r\tau} K p$$

where

$$p = \frac{e^{r\tau} - e^{d\tau}}{e^{u\tau} - e^{d\tau}}$$

and

$$p' = p e^{(u-r)\tau}$$

provided $Se^{d\tau} \leq K \leq Se^{u\tau}$. For $K < Se^{d\tau}$, $c = S - Ke^{-r\tau}$. For $K > Se^{u\tau}$, $c = 0$. Explain the meaning of the last two statements in your own words.

## Exercise 2.5 *(Binomial Return Model)*

Consider the binomial monthly return model: $R = uK + d(N - K)$, where $0 \leq d < u$ and $K$ is binomial with parameters $p$ and $N$.

a. Calculate $E[R]$ and $\text{Var}(R)$ in terms of the parameters $u$, $d$, $p$, and $N$.

b. Assume that $N = 25$ and $p = 0.5$. Use the method of moments based on the sample monthly returns for Apple Computer in Table 1.4 to estimate $u$ and $d$.

## Exercise 2.6 *(Investment Strategy)*

Consider the following dilemma of a U.S. pension fund manager. The current stock market seems to be underpriced, and the manager would like to invest the annual contribution in a diverse portfolio of U.S. stocks. It is now July, and the annual contribution of approximately $2,000,000 will be made in December. Describe a use of financial markets that resolves the dilemma. Reconsider your answer for a manager who wants to invest in Canadian or Japanese stocks.

## Exercise 2.7 *(Convertible Bonds)*

A *convertible* bond provides the bond owner with an option to convert the face amount of the bond to a fixed number of shares of stock of the company that issues the bond. A bond that pays only coupons and redemption value, with no convertibility option or call option, is called a *straight* bond. Consider the following information on a convertible bond:

---

| **Contract Information** | |
|---|---|
| Face amount | 1,000 |
| Annual coupon rate | 8% |
| Maturity | 20 years |
| Conversion value | 50 shares of stock |
| **Market Information** | |
| Current 20-year default-free interest rate | 9% |
| Bond rating | A |
| Current market yield on straight A bonds | 10% |
| Current market price of common stock | 18 per share |
| Current annual dividend rate | 1 per share |
| Current price of convertible bond | 950 |

---

a. Calculate the market value of the bond, ignoring the conversion option.

b. Calculate the conversion price per share if the bond is converted now. Compare it to the market price.

c. Suppose that exchange-traded call options are available on the company's stock. The current price for a 90-day call option on 100 shares of the stock with an exercise price of 20 dollars per share sells for $35. Calculate the implied stock volatility.

d. Use the stock price volatility from (c) to evaluate the conversion option.

e. Discuss the arbitrage possibilities assuming that straight bonds and stock options, as well as the convertible bond, are available to investors.

---

## Exercise 2.8 (Exchange Rates)

On January 1, 1993, $10,000 is invested in a German stock selling for 50 marks per share. The exchange rate is 2 marks/dollar. At the same time, a contract is entered into to deliver 20,000 marks for dollars on December 31, 1993, at the forward exchange rate of 1.9 marks/dollar. On December 31, 1993, the stock is selling at 60 marks, and the exchange rate is 1.8 marks/dollar. Ignoring transaction costs, calculate the dollar-denominated rate of return.

---

## Exercise 2.9 (Black-Scholes for Dividend-Paying Stocks)

A European call option on a dividend-paying stock has an exercise price of $K$. The option is exercised $\tau$ years from now. The current stock price is $S$, and the stock price on the exercise date is $S_T = Se^R$, where $R$ is the return. The stock pays dividends continuously at a known constant rate, $\phi \geq 0$. All assumptions for put-call parity

(A.1 through A.5) are in force. In addition, the return random variable $R$ is normally distributed with mean $(r - 1/2\,\sigma^2)\tau$ and variance $\sigma^2\tau$. The current market prices of the options are given by the formulas

$$c = Se^{-\phi\tau}\,N(d_1) - Ke^{-r\tau}N(d_2),$$

$$p = Ke^{-r\tau}N(-d_2) - Se^{-\phi\tau}\,N(-d_1) \qquad (2.11.1)$$

where

$$d_1 = \frac{\log\left(\frac{S}{K}\right) + \left(r - \phi + \frac{\sigma^2}{2}\right)\tau}{\sigma\sqrt{\tau}},$$

$$d_2 = d_1 - \sigma\sqrt{\tau},$$

and $N(x)$ denotes the standard normal distribution function.

Show that substituting $Se^{-\phi\tau}$ for $S$ in the Black-Scholes equations (2.4.4) yields the same formulas.

---

### Exercise 2.10 (Black-Scholes Option Formula)

Consider European call and put options on the S&P 500 index. The options have the same exercise price of 300, and they mature in 2 months. The average dividend yield is projected to be 3% per annum over the next 2 months. The risk-free rate is 8%, and the current index value is 310. (Note: In terms of the formulas in Exercise 2.9, $K = 300$, maturity $\tau = 0.1667$, $\phi = 0.03$, $r = 0.08$, $S = 310$.)

a. Calculate the call and put option prices when $\sigma = 0.20$.

b. Recalculate the call and put prices for values of the current index varying from 200 to 400 in increments of 10. Draw a graph of the results.

---

### Exercise 2.11 (Call Option Spread)

During the week of March 25, 1996, the third-quarter CBOT Southeastern call option 200/250 spread sold for 1.8 points. On October 21, 1996, the Southeastern index value was 16.4.

a. Calculate the intrinsic value (exercise value) of the call spread.

b. Calculate the value of industry losses corresponding to the index value 16.4.

c. How much would industry losses have to move to get the option into the money by the time it settles in 1997?

# Chapter 3
## Interest Rate Risk
## and Immunization

## Section 3.1
## Introduction

A financial intermediary such as an insurance company faces a problem in interest rate fluctuations. The term "C-3" risk was coined by C. L. Trowbridge, when he was chairperson of the Society of Actuaries Committee on Valuation and Related Matters, to denote the risk of losses due to changes in interest rates—changes in either the *level* of interest rates or the *shape* of the yield curve. (See Section 1.6 for a review of the basic terminology of interest rates and yield curves.) The letter "C" stands for "contingency." Trowbridge used the term "C-1" risk to denote the risk of asset defaults and decreases in market values of equity investments and the term "C-2" risk to denote mortality and morbidity risks—the risk of losses from increases in claims and from pricing deficiencies, other than those from C-1 and C-3 risks. Subsequently, the term "C-4" risk was added to denote accounting, managerial, social, and regulatory risks.

This chapter presents Redington's theory of immunization, which is a classical actuarial tool for managing interest rate risk, and discusses interest-sensitivity measures such as *duration, convexity,* and *M-squared.* By means of modern option-pricing theory, Redington's model is extended to the case of interest-sensitive cash flows.

A problem with Redington's model and many of its generalizations is that these models are not arbitrage free and hence not internally consistent. The hypothesis of such models implies the existence of riskless arbitrage opportunities with an infinite rate of return—the so-called "second derivative profit." The final part of this chapter presents a refinement of Redington's model without such riskless arbitrage opportunities.

# Section 3.2
## Interest Rate Risk

To understand what C-3 risk or interest rate risk means, consider a block of long-term life insurance or annuity policies and its associated assets. The *asset cash flow* (or *investment cash flow*) in any future time period is defined as the investment income and capital maturities (principal repayments) expected to occur in that time period. The *liability cash flow* (or *insurance cash flow*) in any future time period is defined as the sum of the policy claims, policy surrenders, and expenses minus the premium income projected to occur in that time period.

The *net cash flow* is defined as the difference between the asset cash flow and liability cash flow. A positive net cash flow means that the asset cash flow exceeds the liability cash flow, generating excess cash for (re)investment. If interest rates fall when the net cash flows are positive, the cash flows will have to be (re)invested at rates that are lower than the initial rates. This is called the *reinvestment risk*. On the other hand, negative net cash flows mean shortages of cash needed to meet liability obligations. A cash shortage requires the liquidation of assets or borrowing (within or without the company). If interest rates rise when the net cash flows are negative, capital losses can occur as a result of liquidation of bonds and other fixed-income securities whose values have fallen because of the increase in interest rates. This is called the *disinvestment risk*, or *price risk*.

The C-3 risk problem is further aggravated by the various interest rate options embedded in the assets and liabilities; that is, the asset and liability cash flows are functions of interest rates. When interest rates go up, policyholders are more likely to surrender their policies (in order to to reinvest the cash values elsewhere for higher return) or exercise their policy loan options. On the other hand, when interest rates fall, bonds are more likely to be called, and mortgages can be prepaid earlier than expected. In most of this chapter, we assume that there are no interest rate options embedded in the assets and liabilities and that the cash flows are fixed and certain. The treatment of interest-sensitive cash flows will be discussed briefly in Section 3.7 and then more extensively in Chapter 7.

# Section 3.3
## Cash-Flow Matching and Immunization

In a classical actuarial paper, Haynes and Kirton [86, p. 142] wrote:

> It is generally accepted that a life office should bear in mind the outstanding term of its existing liabilities when deciding upon the distribution of its assets with regard to date

of redemption—that if its assets are of longer date than its liabilities, a rise in interest rates will be harmful and a fall in interest rates beneficial, and vice versa. While accepting this principle, however, it is difficult in practice to determine where the optimum date-distribution of assets lies—the distribution which, so far as possible, will insulate the fund from the effect of fluctuations in the market rate of interest.

It is now understood that, in general, there are two approaches to the problem: *cash-flow matching* and *immunization*.

Cash-flow matching, or *dedication*, was formally suggested by the Dutch mathematical economist Tjalling C. Koopmans [116], when he was a refugee during the Second World War working for the Penn Mutual Life Insurance Company, for managing assets and liabilities in life insurance companies (Fisher [61, p. 22]). Algorithms for cash-flow matching can be found in papers by Hiller and Schaack [90] and by Kocherlakota, Rosenbloom, and Shiu [113, 114]. The basic problem is to determine the cheapest portfolio of fixed-income securities such that, for all periods in the planning horizon, the accumulated net cash flows are nonnegative. The model can be extended to allow borrowing and reinvestment, hence lowering the cost. The key technique in cash-flow matching is the method of *linear programming*.[1] Note that cash-flow matching techniques normally require the cash flows to be fixed and certain. We do not discuss cash-flow matching algorithms, although the linear programming formulation in Section 3.9, which arises from an immunization model, can be considered as a method for matching asset cash flows with liability cash flows.

The term "immunization" was coined in a 1952 paper entitled "Review of the Principles of Life-Office Valuations" by the British actuary Frank M. Redington [149], who was chief actuary of Prudential Assurance. Note from the title that the paper was supposed to be about valuation rather than strategies for matching assets and liabilities. In this historic paper, Redington suggested that actuaries should adopt a similar basis for the valuation of both assets and liabilities. He proposed that, to "immunize" the surplus value of a block of business against interest rate fluctuations, one should equate the *mean term* of the assets to that of the liabilities while requiring the cash flows from the assets to be more spread out than those from liabilities. Partly for this work, Redington was awarded a gold medal by the British Institute of Actuaries in 1968.

It turned out that Redington's concept of mean term had already appeared in the work of Frederick R. Macaulay [126], whose term "duration" is the standard

---

[1] Together with Leonid V. Kantorovich, Koopmans was awarded the 1975 Nobel Prize in economics for his independent discovery of linear programming and applications of linear programming to resource allocation problems.

terminology today. Incidentally, F. R. Macaulay's father was T. B. Macaulay, president of the Actuarial Society of America from 1899 to 1900. Two Nobel laureates in economics, Sir John Hicks [89] and Paul A. Samuelson [166], had also independently come up with the concept of duration. For historical reviews on immunization theory and duration analysis, see the papers by Weil [202], Fisher [61], Hawawini [85, pp. 1–30], and Bierwag, Kaufman, and Toevs [10]. Several books that deal solely with immunization theory and duration analysis are those by Hawawini [85], Kaufman, Bierwag, and Toevs [109], Granito [78], and Bierwag [9]. Two early papers that introduced the concept of immunization to North American actuaries were by Hickman [88] and Vanderhoof [199].

Note that some scholars (for example, Hawawini [85, pp. 4–5]) would argue that the concept of mean term or duration was anticipated by the British actuary George J. Lidstone [121], who discussed actuarial formulas such as

$$a_x^j - a_x^i \approx -\frac{j-i}{1+i}(Ia)_x^i \tag{3.3.1}$$

and

$$A_x^j - A_x^i \approx -\frac{j-i}{1+i}(IA)_x^i \tag{3.3.2}$$

(see also Jordan [102, p. 56, (2.49)]).

# Section 3.4
# *Redington's Theory of Immunization*

Consider a block of long-term insurance or annuity policies and its associated assets at time $t = 0$. For $t > 0$, let $A_t$ denote the asset cash flow expected to occur at time $t$; that is, the interest income, dividends, rent, capital maturities, repayments, and prepayments expected to occur at that time. Let $L_t$ denote the liability cash flow (or insurance cash flow) expected to occur at time $t$: the policy claims, policy surrenders, policy loan payments, policyholder dividends, expenses, and taxes, less premium income, policy loan repayments, and policy loan interest expected at that time. For a given interest rate $i$, the asset and liability present values are given by the sums

$$\sum_{t>0} \frac{A_t}{(1+i)^t} \tag{3.4.1}$$

and

$$\sum_{t>0} \frac{L_t}{(1+i)^t} \qquad (3.4.2)$$

respectively. Let $S(i)$ denote the surplus of this block of business, evaluated at the interest rate $i$. Because surplus or net worth is the difference between asset and liability values, we have

$$S(i) = \sum_{t>0} \frac{A_t}{(1+i)^t} - \sum_{t>0} \frac{L_t}{(1+i)^t}. \qquad (3.4.3)$$

We now consider the historical significance of (3.4.3). It was about 1800 when William Morgan of the Equitable Life Assurance Society (London) began to discuss valuation methods (Mitchell [136, pp. 6–7]):

> Morgan was the first actuary who could be called a professional actuary in the sense that the term is understood today. . . . Outstanding among Morgan's string of actuarial "firsts" were his setting up of a balance sheet to take account of a life insurance company's future liabilities and his appreciation of the significance of the results; his realization of the need to carry forward a margin of surplus to prevent the policyholder dividend system from breaking down; the classifying and measuring of the available sources of profit. . . . Morgan was also the first in a long succession of actuaries to have trouble from policyholders and directors who refused to appreciate the need of holding adequate reserves for paying future claims instead of paying higher dividends.

As Redington [150, p. 86] pointed out, Morgan "would have been astonished to learn how little progress was to be made" on valuation theory for the next 150 years. Before the appearance of Redington's 1952 paper, it did not seem obvious to most actuaries that "there should be consistency of treatment in the valuation of assets and liabilities," which Redington [150, p. 83] called the cardinal principle of valuation. (A notable exception in the early actuarial literature was D. P. Moll's [137] letter to the editor of the *Journal of the Institute of Actuaries*.) In making a valuation, actuaries assumed that the reported asset value was correct; their duty as actuaries was to find the right value of the liabilities. Redington's insight was that, because every insurance or pension liability is merely a stream of cash flows that can be regarded as the negative of asset cash flows, the same interest rate $i$ should be used to discount the asset and liability cash flows to determine their respective values. The surplus or net worth is, of course, the difference of these two values. His immunization theory follows immediately from this idea that there should be equal and parallel treatment in the valuation of assets and liabilities.

If (3.4.3) is the proper way to value the surplus of a block of business, the strategy for insulating the surplus against interest rate fluctuations merely becomes a consequence of "an elementary piece of differential calculus" (Redington [150, p. 85]). It follows from the definition of a derivative that

$$S(i + \Delta i) \approx S(i) + S'(i)\Delta i \qquad (3.4.4)$$

is an approximation formula for small $\Delta i$. Thus, by structuring assets and liabilities in such a way that

$$S'(i) = 0, \qquad (3.4.5)$$

we would have

$$S(i + \Delta i) \approx S(i);$$

that is, the surplus remains nearly the same or is "immunized" with respect to a small interest rate change of size $\Delta i$. If the cash flows are *not* functions of interest rates, then condition (3.4.5) is equivalent to

$$\sum_{t>0} \frac{t A_t}{(1 + i)^t} = \sum_{t>0} \frac{t L_t}{(1 + i)^t}, \qquad (3.4.6)$$

which says that the discounted asset and liability cash-flow streams have the same first moment. Formula (3.4.6) is the essence of Redington's immunization strategy.

Redington's model is a good first step toward solving the problem of interest rate risk. However, it is not an internally consistent model because it allows arbitrage opportunities (often called "free lunches" because there should be none). To see this, consider the three-term Taylor approximation formula

$$S(i + \Delta i) \approx S(i) + S'(i)\Delta i + \frac{1}{2}S''(i)(\Delta i)^2. \qquad (3.4.7)$$

It follows from (3.4.7) that structuring assets and liabilities such that condition (3.4.5) and

$$S''(i) > 0 \qquad (3.4.8)$$

hold would imply that, for small $|\Delta i|$,

$$S(i + \Delta i) > S(i). \qquad (3.4.9)$$

Hence, as the interest rate changes, the surplus automatically increases, resulting in a "second derivative profit." This automatic "free lunch" in the model arises from using the same interest rate $i$ to discount cash flows of all terms. That is, the model always assumes that the yield curves are flat, or that short- and long-term interest rates are always the same. A remedy for this model inconsistency is to replace the discount factor $(1 + i)^{-t}$ in (3.4.1) and (3.4.2) with $P(0, t)$, the price at time 0 of a $t$-period zero-coupon bond, as we do later in this chapter.

An implication of Redington's theory is the *barbell strategy*. A financial intermediary would issue medium-term liabilities or sell short (that is, hold a negative amount of) medium-term bonds, the resulting cash flows being $\{L_t\}$. Using the funds received, the intermediary invests in long- and short-term bonds, their combined cash flows being $\{A_t\}$, such that (3.4.6) is satisfied. Note that the cost to the financial intermediary is zero; that is,

$$S(i) = 0,$$

or equivalently,

$$\sum_{t>0} \frac{A_t}{(1 + i)^t} = \sum_{t>0} \frac{L_t}{(1 + i)^t}. \tag{3.4.10}$$

As soon as there is an interest rate movement, it sells the long- and short-term bonds and, with the proceeds of the sales, closes out its position in the medium-term bonds. It expects to have a positive profit because, with conditions (3.4.10) and (3.4.6) and the asset cash flows being more dispersed than the liability cash flows, we have

$$\sum_{t>0} \frac{t^2 A_t}{(1 + i)^t} > \sum_{t>0} \frac{t^2 L_t}{(1 + i)^t}, \tag{3.4.11}$$

which is equivalent to (3.4.8). Indeed, (3.4.7) implies that, the larger is the inequality (3.4.11), the larger is the change in the surplus, and hence the larger is the profit. Hence, the financial intermediary would invest in bonds of both very short and very long terms. In other words, it would try to mismatch its assets with its liabilities as much as possible. In Redington's model, this "barbell" strategy has an infinite rate of return because no fund is required from the financial intermediary for executing the strategy. The asset portfolio is funded entirely by the liability.

In discussing Redington's paper, C. D. Rich remarked [149, p. 319]:

> Immunization . . . was an outstanding example of the difference between actuarial theory and practice. How delightful it would be if the funds of a life office could be so invested that, on any change in the rate of interest—whether up or down—a profit would always emerge! But how difficult it would be to carry out to the full the investment policy implied by the theory of immunization.

## Section 3.5
## Duration, Convexity, and M-Squared

Various measures have been proposed in the literature for quantifying interest-rate sensitivity of a fixed-income security. In this section, we discuss some of these measures.

Let $\{A_t; t > 0\}$ be the cash-flow stream of a fixed-income security with current $(t = 0)$ price or market value $A$. As defined in Section 1.6.1, the *yield to maturity*, $y$, is the solution of the equation

$$A = \sum_{t>0} \frac{A_t}{(1+y)^t}.$$  (3.5.1)

We assume that the cash flows $\{A_t\}$ are fixed, and we consider the price $A$ as a function of $y$.

### Modified Dollar Duration
The derivative of the price with respect to the yield $y$ is

$$\frac{d}{dy}A = -\sum_{t>0} \frac{t A_t}{(1+y)^{t+1}},$$

which some authors call the *modified dollar duration* of the security.

### Modified Duration
The *modified duration* is defined as

$$-\frac{1}{A}\frac{d}{dy}A = -\frac{d}{dy}\log A.$$  (3.5.2)

### Macaulay Duration
The *Macaulay duration* is

$$D = \frac{1}{A}\sum_{t>0} \frac{t A_t}{(1+y)^t}$$

$$= -(1+y)\frac{d}{dy}\log A,$$  (3.5.3)

which differs from the modified duration by the factor $(1 + y)$. Let $r = \log(1 + y)$ denote the continuously compounded yield to maturity. In the actuarial literature, $r$ is called the *force of interest* and is usually denoted as $\delta$. Then

$$A = \sum_{t>0} e^{-rt} A_t,$$  (3.5.4)

and

$$D = \frac{1}{A} \sum_{t>0} te^{-rt} A_t$$

$$= -\frac{1}{A} \frac{d}{dr} A$$

$$= -\frac{d}{dr} \log A. \tag{3.5.5}$$

It can be shown (Exercise 3.3) that the Macaulay duration of an $n$-year mortgage with $m$ payments per year (and without default risk and prepayment option) is

$$\frac{1}{d^{(m)}} - \frac{n}{(1+i)^n - 1} \tag{3.5.6}$$

where $i$ is the effective annual interest rate for the mortgage and $(1 - d^{(m)}/m)^{-m} = 1 + i$. Similarly, the Macaulay duration of an $n$-year noncallable and default-free bond (Exercise 3.2), priced at par and with interest payable $m$ times each year, is

$$\ddot{a}_{\overline{n}|}^{(m)} = \sum_{j=0}^{mn-1} \frac{1}{m} (1+i)^{-j/m} = \frac{1 - (1+i)^{-n}}{d^{(m)}}. \tag{3.5.7}$$

In economics, the term *elasticity* means the percentage change in one variable with respect to a percentage change in another variable, or the ratio of the logarithmic derivatives of the two variables. Writing the right-hand side of (3.5.5) as

$$\frac{d \log A}{d \log(1+y)^{-1}}, \tag{3.5.8}$$

we see that the Macaulay duration (3.5.3) is the elasticity of the price $A$ with respect to the discount factor $(1+y)^{-1}$. This observation was made by Hicks [89, p. 186], who wrote:

> Now when we look at the form of this elasticity we see that it may be very properly described as the *Average Period* of the [payment] stream; for it is the *average length of time for which the various payments are deferred from the present, when the times of deferment are weighted by the discounted values of the payments.*

### Convexity

Recall that, in (3.4.7), there is a second derivative term. The quantity

$$C = \frac{1}{A} \frac{d^2}{dr^2} A$$

$$= \frac{1}{A} \sum_{t>0} t^2 e^{-rt} A_t \tag{3.5.9}$$

is called the *Macaulay convexity.*

**M-squared**

Following Fong and Vasicek ([64], [65]), we define the quantity *M-squared* as

$$M^2 = \frac{1}{A} \sum_{t>0} (t-D)^2 e^{-rt} A_t$$

$$= C - D^2, \tag{3.5.10}$$

and we claim that

$$\frac{d}{dr} D = -M^2. \tag{3.5.11}$$

To see this, we apply the quotient rule of calculus. The negative of the left-hand side of (3.5.11) is

$$\frac{d}{dr} \frac{A'}{A} = \frac{A'' A - (A')^2}{A^2}$$

$$= \frac{A''}{A} - \left( \frac{A'}{A} \right)^2,$$

which is the right-hand side of (3.5.10). It follows from (3.5.11) that, for a stream of fixed cash flows, its duration decreases as the interest rate increases, and its duration increases as the interest rate decreases. This is not necessarily the case for interest-sensitive cash flows. (This is a premature assertion since we have not yet extended the definition of duration to interest-sensitive cash flows; see (3.7.7) below.) In Exercise 3.10, you are asked to show that

$$\frac{d}{dr} M^2 = -\frac{1}{A} \sum_{t>0} (t-D)^3 e^{-rt} A_t. \tag{3.5.12}$$

**The Babcock Equation**

For a continuously compounded rate (or force) of interest $r$, the value of the cash-flow stream $\{A_t\}_{t>0}$ evaluated at time $T$ is

$$A(r, T) = \sum_{t>0} e^{r(T-t)} A_t$$

$$= e^{rT} \sum_{t>0} e^{-rt} A_t. \tag{3.5.13}$$

Hence, the quantity $A$ in (3.5.4) is $A(r, 0)$. Suppose that the interest rate changes from

$r$ to $r + \varepsilon$. Let the number $\rho$ be defined by the equation

$$\frac{A(r + \varepsilon, T)}{A(r, T)} = e^{\rho T}. \tag{3.5.14}$$

Then $\rho$ is the continuously compounded rate of return of the security due to the interest rate shock of size $\varepsilon$ over a period of length $T$. In other words, the quantity $\rho$ measures the gains or loss of the security due to a change in the interest rate of size $\varepsilon$ for a period of length $T$. We now show that $\rho$ can be approximately determined by means of $D$ and $M^2$. Because

$$A(r + \varepsilon, T) = \sum_{t>0} e^{r(T-t)} A_t e^{\varepsilon(T-t)} \tag{3.5.15}$$

and

$$e^{\varepsilon(T-t)} = e^{\varepsilon(T-D)} e^{\varepsilon(D-t)}$$
$$= e^{\varepsilon(T-D)} \left[ 1 + \varepsilon(D - t) + \frac{1}{2}\varepsilon^2(D - t)^2 + \cdots \right],$$

we have

$$A(r + \varepsilon, T) = e^{\varepsilon(T-D)} \sum_{t>0} e^{r(T-t)} A_t \left[ 1 + \varepsilon(D - t) + \frac{1}{2}\varepsilon^2(D - t)^2 + \cdots \right]$$
$$= e^{\varepsilon(T-D)} A(r, T) \left( 1 + 0 + \frac{1}{2}\varepsilon^2 M^2 + \cdots \right).$$

Hence, we have the approximate formula

$$\frac{A(r + \varepsilon, T)}{A(r, T)} \approx e^{\varepsilon(T-D)} \left( 1 + \frac{1}{2}\varepsilon^2 M^2 \right). \tag{3.5.16}$$

It follows from (3.5.14) and (3.5.16) that

$$\rho \approx \varepsilon \left( 1 - \frac{D}{T} \right) + \frac{1}{T} \log \left( 1 + \frac{1}{2}\varepsilon^2 M^2 \right)$$
$$\approx \varepsilon \left( 1 - \frac{D}{T} \right) + \frac{\varepsilon^2 M^2}{2T}. \tag{3.5.17}$$

Dropping the $\varepsilon^2$ term, we have

$$\rho \approx \varepsilon \left( 1 - \frac{D}{T} \right), \tag{3.5.18}$$

which is known as the Babcock equation [9, (5.8), (5B.9)] in the literature. With $T = D$, (3.5.17) simplifies as

$$\rho \approx \frac{\varepsilon^2 M^2}{2D},$$

$$(3.5.19)$$

which is positive.

### An Alternative Derivation

We conclude this section with another derivation of (3.5.17). Let $X$ be a random variable for which the moment generating function exists, and let $\mu$ denote its mean. For $j = 2, 3, \ldots$, let

$$\mu_j = E[(X - \mu)^j]$$

be the $j$-th central moment of $X$ (hence $\mu_2$ is the variance). We can expand the function $\log(E[e^{tX}])$, called the cumulant generating function of $X$, as a power series in $t$ as follows:

$$\log(E[e^{tX}]) = \log(E[e^{t\mu + t(X-\mu)}])$$

$$= \mu t + \log(E[e^{t(X-\mu)}])$$

$$= \mu t + \log\left(E\left[\sum_{n=0}^{\infty} \frac{t^n (X-\mu)^n}{n!}\right]\right)$$

$$= \mu t + \log\left(1 + \sum_{n=2}^{\infty} \frac{t^n \mu_n}{n!}\right)$$

$$= \mu t + \sum_{n=2}^{\infty} \frac{t^n \mu_n}{n!} - \frac{1}{2}\left(\sum_{n=2}^{\infty} \frac{t^n \mu_n}{n!}\right)^2 + \cdots$$

$$= \mu t + \frac{\mu_2 t^2}{2!} + \frac{\mu_3 t^3}{3!} + \frac{(\mu_4 - 3\mu_2^2)t^4}{4!} + \frac{(\mu_5 - 10\mu_2\mu_3)t^5}{5!} + \cdots.$$

$$(3.5.20)$$

Now, consider the random variable $X$ defined by

$$\Pr(X = t) = \frac{e^{-rt} A_t}{A(r, 0)}.$$

$$(3.5.21)$$

The probability distribution is well defined by virtue of (3.5.4) and gives the proportion of the security according to the discounted value of the cash flow at each time $t$.

Obviously,

$$E[X] = D, \tag{3.5.22}$$

$$E[X^2] = C, \tag{3.5.23}$$

and

$$\text{Var}(X) = M^2. \tag{3.5.24}$$

It follows from (3.5.15) that

$$\frac{A(r + \varepsilon, T)}{A(r, T)} = e^{\varepsilon T} \frac{A(r + \varepsilon, 0)}{A(r, 0)}$$

$$= e^{\varepsilon T} E[e^{\varepsilon X}].$$

Applying (3.5.14) and then (3.5.20), we get

$$\rho T = \varepsilon T + \log(E[e^{\varepsilon X}])$$

$$= \varepsilon T - \varepsilon D + \frac{1}{2}\varepsilon^2 M^2 - \cdots, \tag{3.5.25}$$

from which (3.5.17) follows.

# Section 3.6
# Multivariate Immunization Models

Some authors have proposed to extend Redington's model by assuming that the yield curve is a function of several variables or that the surplus is a function of several variables. Models with more variables or parameters should give a better representation of the real world. However, such models can contain arbitrage opportunities and hence are not internally consistent. To see this, we consider the surplus (or net worth) of a block of insurance or annuity business as a differentiable function of $n$ deterministic variables,

$$S(x_1, x_2, \ldots, x_n). \tag{3.6.1}$$

We now follow Redington's development in Section 3.4, but using multivariate calculus. Structuring the assets and liabilities such that

$$\frac{\partial}{\partial x_j} S(x_1, x_2, \ldots, x_n) = 0, \quad j = 1, 2, \ldots, n \tag{3.6.2}$$

(which generalizes (3.4.5)) would mean that the surplus remains nearly the same or is "immunized" for small changes in the independent variables $x_1, x_2, \ldots, x_n$; that is,

$$S(x_1 + \Delta x_1, x_2 + \Delta x_2, \ldots, x_n + \Delta x_n) \approx S(x_1, x_2, \ldots, x_n) \qquad (3.6.3)$$

for small values of $\Delta x_1, \Delta x_2, \ldots, \Delta x_n$. Furthermore, if the assets and liabilities are such that the $n$-by-$n$ (Hessian) matrix

$$H = \left( \frac{\partial^2 S}{\partial x_i \partial x_j} \right) \qquad (3.6.4)$$

is positive definite,[2] then it follows from the multivariate Taylor expansion theorem (the multivariate version of (3.4.7)) that

$$S(x_1 + \Delta x_1, x_2 + \Delta x_2, \ldots, x_n + \Delta x_n) > S(x_1, x_2, \ldots, x_n), \qquad (3.6.5)$$

meaning that there are automatic "free lunches" in the model.

Let us repeat a point made by Paul Milgrom in his discussion of Vanderhoof's [199, pp. 194–95] paper. For $t > 0$, let $s_t$ denote the $t$-period spot rate (see Section 1.6.1). Then the surplus is

$$S = \sum_{t>0} (A_t - L_t)(1 + s_t)^{-t}. \qquad (3.6.6)$$

If the spot rates can fluctuate independently (that is, if $\{s_t\}$ are independent variables), then the immunization condition

$$0 = \frac{\partial}{\partial s_\tau} S$$
$$= -\tau (A_\tau - L_\tau)(1 + s_\tau)^{-\tau-1} \qquad (3.6.7)$$

means that

$$A_\tau = L_\tau. \qquad (3.6.8)$$

Milgrom (see Vanderhoof [199, p. 195]) concluded: "The result is as we would expect—that we can only immunize against independent fluctuation in interest rates by having exact matching in our cash flows from investment and insurance operations."

---

[2]A square matrix $H$ is positive definite if $v^T H v > 0$ for all nonzero column vectors $v$.

For further discussions on multivariate duration analysis and immunization, see the papers by Chambers, Carleton, and McEnally [35], Ho [91], Falkenstein and Hanweck ([58], [59]), Litterman and Scheinkman [123], Prizman and Tian [148], Reitano [152, 153, 154, 155] and Willner [208].

# Section 3.7
## Interest-Sensitive Cash Flows

In this section, we introduce the case of interest-sensitive cash flows. This is a preview of and motivation for much of the material in the next several chapters, where details and proofs will be provided.

In the earlier sections, we made the assumption that the asset and liability cash flows, $\{A_t\}$ and $\{L_t\}$, are independent of interest rate fluctuations. This condition certainly does not hold for assets such as callable bonds, mortgage-backed securities (MBSs), and liabilities such as single-premium deferred annuities (SPDAs) and universal life insurance (UL). However, Redington's principle of equal and parallel treatment in the valuation of assets and liabilities should still apply. What we need is a more sophisticated method for valuing interest-sensitive cash flows.

The option-pricing theory of Fischer Black and Myron Scholes [16], which we discussed in Chapter 2, has been described as the most important single advance in the theory of financial economics in the 1970s. These authors derived a formula for valuing a European option on a non-dividend-paying stock by showing that the option and stock could be combined linearly to form a riskless hedge, which, by the *principle of no arbitrage*, must earn interest exactly at the risk-free rate. The theory for pricing stock options has been generalized and extended to include the pricing of debt options. In general, a debt security can be viewed as a risk-free asset plus or minus various contingent claims, which usually can be modeled as options. The option-pricing methodology can be applied to value interest-sensitive cash flows.

To help establish these ideas, we now describe a general setup of a finite discrete-time security market model. We assume that the market is frictionless and that trades occur only at the times $t = 0, 1, 2, \ldots$. Let $i_t$ denote the one-period risk-free interest rate, or *short rate*, at time $t$: if an investor invests \$1 at time $t$, the investor will receive $\$(1 + i_t)$ at time $t + 1$, $t = 0, 1, 2, \ldots$. We also assume that there is a finite number of primitive securities. Let $V_{j,t}$ denote the value of the $j$-th primitive security at time $t$ and let $C_{j,t}$ denote the dividend or interest payment for the $j$-th security at time $t$. (We assume that $V_{j,t}$ is the value of the security after the payment $C_{j,t}$ has been made.) Note that, as seen from time $s$, $s < t$, the quantities $i_t$, $V_{j,t}$, and $C_{j,t}$ are random variables.

We will show in subsequent chapters that the assumption of no arbitrage is *equivalent* to the existence of a probability measure under which the conditional expectation

$$E_t[V_{j.t+1} + C_{j.t+1}]$$

equals $(1 + i_t) V_{j.t}$, for $t = 0, 1, 2, \ldots$, and $j = 1, 2, 3, \ldots$. The subscript $t$ following the expectation operator E signifies that the expectation is taken with the knowledge of all information available up to time $t$. Because, at time $t$, the interest rate $i_t$ is known and not a random variable, this relationship can also be written as

$$V_{j.t} = E_t \left[ \frac{1}{1 + i_t} (V_{j.t+1} + C_{j.t+1}) \right]. \qquad (3.7.1)$$

The probability measure over which the expectation is taken, normally not the same as the actual or physical probability measure, is called a *risk-neutral* probability measure, or *equivalent martingale measure*. This result is called the *Fundamental Theorem of Asset Pricing* by Dybvig and Ross [53]. It follows from (3.7.1) that, for each $j$ and $n$,

$$V_j(0) = E \left[ \left( \sum_{t=0}^{n} \frac{C_{j.t+1}}{(1 + i_0)(1 + i_1) \cdots (1 + i_t)} \right) + \frac{V_{j.n+1}}{(1 + i_0)(1 + i_1) \cdots (1 + i_n)} \right]. \qquad (3.7.2)$$

In general, the value at time 0 of a (stochastic) cash-flow stream, $\{C_t; t = 1, 2, 3, \ldots\}$, which can be generated or replicated by the primitive securities, is given by

$$E \left[ \sum_{t \geq 0} \frac{C_{t+1}}{(1 + i_0)(1 + i_1) \cdots (1 + i_t)} \right]. \qquad (3.7.3)$$

A detailed proof is given in Chapter 11.

Note that for $n = 1, 2, \ldots$, the expectation

$$E \left[ \frac{1}{(1 + i_0)(1 + i_1) \cdots (1 + i_{n-1})} \right]$$

is $P(0, n)$, the time-0 price of an $n$-period noncallable default-free zero-coupon bond (with maturity value 1). The prices $\{P(0, n)\}$ are known at time 0 from the market, for example, by looking them up in the newspaper. It is natural to require that the prices $\{P(0, n)\}$ are replicated in any interest rate evolution model. This condition is a source of difficulty in model construction because the set of initial bond prices

$\{P(0, n)\}$ are exogenous parameters. In Chapter 7, we present binomial lattice interest rate models that satisfy this initial yield curve reproduction condition.

To emphasize that the cash flows and interest rates in (3.7.3) can be random, we rewrite (3.7.3) as

$$\sum_{\omega} \Pr(\omega) \left[ \sum_{t \geq 0} \frac{C_{t+1}(\omega)}{[1 + i_0][1 + i_1(\omega)] \cdots [1 + i_t(\omega)]} \right]. \tag{3.7.4}$$

Here each outcome $\omega$ can be identified as an *interest rate path* or *scenario path*; $\{i_0, i_1(\omega), i_2(\omega), \ldots\}$ and $\{C_1(\omega), C_2(\omega), C_3(\omega), \ldots\}$ are the one-period interest rates (short rates) and cash flows along the path $\omega$. To apply (3.7.4), we need to specify the risk-neutral probability measure and the short rates $\{i_t(\omega)\}$. Furthermore, as we just pointed out, the probability measure and the short rates should be such that the model can reproduce an exogenously prescribed set of initial bond prices $\{P(0, n)\}$; that is, the condition

$$P(0, n) = \sum_{\omega} \Pr(\omega) \left[ \frac{1}{[1 + i_0][1 + i_1(\omega)] \cdots [1 + i_{n-1}(\omega)]} \right] \tag{3.7.5}$$

is to hold for all $n$. It is relatively straightforward to construct arbitrage-free binomial lattices, as we will see in Chapter 7. However, some might complain that it could be very difficult to project the cash flows of certain assets or liabilities. To answer this objection, we quote Redington [151, p. 548]: "Absolute bedrock is to me the net difference between the income and the outgo $A_t - L_t$. The actuary who does not know the shape of this cash flow does not know his own company."

There are practical limitations in applying (3.7.4) to value a stream of path-dependent cash flows. For example, to value an MBS pool with 30-year mortgages, we need a model with 360 time periods, each time period corresponding to 1 month. In a corresponding binomial model, there are $2^{360}$ paths. This means that the summation $\sum_{\omega}$ in (3.7.4) has $2^{360}$ terms, which is computationally infeasible. Thus, we must estimate (3.7.4) by techniques such as the Monte Carlo simulation method using a representative sample of the $2^{360}$ paths; that is, we pick a subset $\Omega'$ of all interest rate paths and calculate

$$\frac{1}{\sum_{\omega \in \Omega'} \Pr(\omega)} \sum_{\omega \in \Omega'} \Pr(\omega) \left[ \sum_{t \geq 0} \frac{C_{t+1}(\omega)}{[1 + i_0][1 + i_1(\omega)] \cdots [1 + i_t(\omega)]} \right], \tag{3.7.6}$$

which is an approximation of the value of the cash flows $\{C_t\}$. A systematic procedure for selecting a subset of interest rate paths has been proposed by Ho [92].

**Option-Adjusted Duration and Convexity**

Duration and convexity can also be defined for interest-sensitive cash flows $\{C_t\}$. Usually, such interest-sensitivity measures are defined with respect to parallel shifts of the initial yield curve. Let $V$ be the value of the stochastic cash flows as determined by (3.7.3) or (3.7.4). We can numerically approximate the duration of interest-sensitive cash flows as follows:

1. Reinitialize the stochastic interest rate model with the initial yield curve shifted down by 50 basis points (0.5%).
2. Project the cash flows in this new interest rate model, calculate (or approximate) their expected discounted value, and denote it as $V_{-50}$.
3. Reinitialize the stochastic interest rate model with the initial yield curve shifted up by 50 basis points.
4. Project the cash flows in this new interest rate model, calculate their expected discounted value, and denote it as $V_{+50}$.

Then the *option-adjusted duration* (*effective duration* or *stochastic duration*) is approximated as

$$-\frac{V_{+50} - V_{-50}}{0.01\,V}, \tag{3.7.7}$$

and the *option-adjusted convexity* (*effective convexity* or *stochastic convexity*) is approximated as

$$\frac{V_{+50} - 2V + V_{-50}}{0.02\,V}. \tag{3.7.8}$$

To conclude this section, we quote James A. Tilley [194], who in his address to the 23rd International Congress of Actuaries pointed out that "understanding the asset allocation question should begin with an analysis of the market value of the relevant liabilities, and that the market value of the liabilities may best be represented by the theoretical value of the underlying cash flow obligations." Redington would most certainly have agreed with this statement. Except for reinsurance and certain catastrophe futures contracts, there is no active market for the exchange of insurance liabilities. It is difficult to actually come up with the market value of each insurance liability. However, by constructing an arbitrage-free valuation model, we can compute *relative* market values and price-sensitivity indexes (option-adjusted duration, convexity, etc.) for both assets and liabilities. Based on such information, we can design appropriate strategies for managing assets and liabilities. Indeed, without such a model, it would be hard even to estimate the values of the various options in the assets and liabilities.

## Section 3.8
## A Generalization of Redington's Theory

We now return to the less complicated situation in which the asset and liability cash flows are not interest sensitive in order to obtain a more tractable model for analyzing the change in surplus value after an instantaneous interest rate shock. Here we consider a refinement of Redington's model with the yield curves not assumed to be flat, and the interest rate shocks not necessarily small (see Fong and Vasicek [64], [65]; Shiu [181], [182]). Again, let $\{A_t\}$ and $\{L_t\}$ be the asset and liability cash flows of a block of business. These cash flows are (assumed to be) not interest sensitive. Let $N_t$ denote the net cash flow at time $t$,

$$N_t = A_t - L_t, \tag{3.8.1}$$

and let $S$ denote the current surplus,

$$S = \sum_{t>0} N_t P(0, t), \tag{3.8.2}$$

where $P(0, t)$ is the price at time 0 of a noncallable and default-free zero-coupon bond maturing for 1 at time $t$, $t \geq 0$. Consider an instantaneous shock to the term structure of interest rates, which changes the zero-coupon bond prices from $P(0, t)$ to $P^*(0, t)$, $t > 0$. Then the surplus value changes to

$$S^* = \sum_{t>0} N_t P^*(0, t). \tag{3.8.3}$$

The crucial assumption underlying (3.8.3) is that the cash flows are independent of interest rate fluctuations.

Redington's question was: *What are the conditions on the cash flows such that the surplus value will not decrease?* In other words, are there ways to ensure that

$$S^* \geq S? \tag{3.8.4}$$

Unfortunately, as pointed out by Rich, Milgrom, and others, it should not be possible that (3.8.4) holds for all interest rate shocks, unless

$$S^* = S$$

for all shocks; otherwise, there would be an arbitrage opportunity. As we saw in (3.6.7) and (3.6.8), the fact that the surplus remains unchanged for all possible interest rate shocks means that the net cash flows are zero; that is,

$$N_t = 0, \quad \text{for all } t > 0. \tag{3.8.5}$$

Next we will analyze the change in the surplus, $S^*-S$. Let $n_t$ denote the discounted value of the net cash flow $N_t$ with respect to the original term structure of interest rates,

$$n_t = N_t P(0, t). \tag{3.8.6}$$

Define the function

$$g(t) = \frac{P^*(0, t)}{P(0, t)} - 1. \tag{3.8.7}$$

Note that $g(0) = (1/1) - 1 = 0$. The change in surplus is

$$
\begin{aligned}
S^* - S &= \sum_{t>0} N_t P(0, t) g(t) \\
&= \sum_{t>0} n_t g(t).
\end{aligned}
\tag{3.8.8}
$$

For notational simplicity, we assume that the function $g$ is twice differentiable. By Taylor's formula with integral remainder,

$$g(t) = g(0) + g'(0)t + \int_0^t (t - w)g''(w)\, dw$$

(which can easily be verified by means of integration by parts). Hence, the change in surplus is

$$S^* - S = g'(0) \sum_{t>0} t n_t + \sum_{t>0} n_t \int_0^t (t - w)g''(w)\, dw. \tag{3.8.9}$$

To facilitate the interchange of the order of summation and integration in the last term of (3.8.9), we use the notation

$$x^+ = \max(x, 0). \tag{3.8.10}$$

Then

$$
\begin{aligned}
\sum_{t>0} n_t \int_0^t (t - w)^+ g''(w)\, dw &= \sum_{t>0} n_t \int_0^\infty (t - w)^+ g''(w)\, dw \\
&= \int_0^\infty \left[ \sum_{t>0} n_t (t - w)^+ g''(w) \right] dw.
\end{aligned}
$$

Now, suppose that the net cash flows $\{N_t\}$ satisfy either

$$\sum_{t>0} n_t(t-w)^+ \geq 0, \quad \text{for all positive } w, \tag{3.8.11}$$

or

$$\sum_{t>0} n_t(t-w)^+ \leq 0, \quad \text{for all positive } w. \tag{3.8.12}$$

Then, by the weighted mean value theorem for integrals, a positive number $\xi$ exists such that

$$\int_0^\infty \left[ \sum_{t>0} n_t(t-w)^+ g''(w) \right] dw = g''(\xi) \int_0^\infty \left[ \sum_{t>0} n_t(t-w)^+ \right] dw.$$

Reversing the order of integration and summation yields

$$\int_0^\infty \left[ \sum_{t>0} n_t(t-w)^+ \right] dw = \sum_{t>0} n_t \int_0^\infty (t-w)^+ dw$$

$$= \sum_{t>0} n_t \int_0^t (t-w) dw$$

$$= \sum_{t>0} n_t \frac{t^2}{2}. \tag{3.8.13}$$

Thus, subject to (3.8.11) or (3.8.12), we have a rather simple formula for the change in surplus due to an instantaneous interest rate shock:

$$S^* - S = g'(0) \sum_{t>0} t n_t + \frac{1}{2} g''(\xi) \sum_{t>0} t^2 n_t. \tag{3.8.14}$$

Furthermore, if (the asset and liability cash flows can be structured so that) the first moment of the present values of the net cash flows is zero,

$$\sum_{t>0} t n_t = 0, \tag{3.8.15}$$

or equivalently,

$$\sum_{t>0} t A_t P(0, t) = \sum_{t>0} t L_t P(0, t), \tag{3.8.16}$$

then (3.8.14) simplifies as

$$S^* - S = \frac{1}{2}g''(\xi)\sum_{t>0} t^2 n_t. \tag{3.8.17}$$

Redington's model can be viewed as the special case of parallel shifts in the yield curve. Here

$$P^*(0, t) = e^{ct}P(0, t) \tag{3.8.18}$$

or

$$g(t) = e^{ct} - 1$$

where the constant $c$, which can be positive or negative, denotes the amount of yield curve shift. Then (3.8.17) becomes

$$S^* - S = \frac{1}{2}\xi^2 e^{c\xi}\sum_{t>0} t^2 n_t. \tag{3.8.19}$$

Hence, if conditions (3.8.15) and (3.8.11) hold, we have

$$S^* \geq S \tag{3.8.20}$$

for any instantaneous parallel shift in the yield curve (for any value of $c$, large or small). Inequality (3.8.20) is analogous to (3.4.9). Note that (3.8.20) is not true for all interest rate shocks (or for all shifts in the yield curve). The present model, unlike Redington's, is internally consistent in this regard.

We now introduce several additional interest-sensitive measures and give some remarks about the model.

## Fisher-Weil Duration and Convexity

Condition (3.8.16) is a generalization of (3.4.6). The left-hand side of (3.8.16) is sometimes called the *Fisher-Weil dollar duration of the assets*, and the right-hand side, the *Fisher-Weil dollar duration of the liabilities*. The ratios

$$\frac{\sum_{t>0} t A_t P(0, t)}{\sum_{t>0} A_t P(0, t)}$$

and

$$\frac{\displaystyle\sum_{t>0} t^2 A_t P(0, t)}{\displaystyle\sum_{t>0} A_t P(0, t)}$$

are called the *Fisher-Weil duration* and *convexity of the assets.* Because of (3.8.13), the sum

$$\sum_{t>0} t^2 n_t, \qquad (3.8.21)$$

which is called the *Fisher-Weil dollar convexity of the surplus*, is nonnegative if (3.8.11) holds and nonpositive if (3.8.12) holds.

**Mean Absolute Deviation**
Because of the identity

$$x = x^+ - (-x)^+, \qquad (3.8.22)$$

we have

$$\sum_{t>0} n_t(t - w)^+ = \sum_{t>0} n_t(w - t)^+ \qquad (3.8.23)$$

if

$$S = \sum_{t>0} n_t = 0 \qquad (3.8.24)$$

holds in addition to (3.8.15). Furthermore, because

$$|x| = x^+ + (-x)^+, \qquad (3.8.25)$$

we have

$$\sum_{t>0} n_t(t - w)^+ = \sum_{t>0} n_t(w - t)^+ = \frac{1}{2} \sum_{t>0} n_t|t - w|. \qquad (3.8.26)$$

Therefore, under (3.8.24) and (3.8.15), the condition

$$\sum_{t>0} n_t|t - w| \geq 0, \quad \text{for all positive } w, \qquad (3.8.27)$$

is equivalent to (3.8.11). Fong and Vasicek [64] call (3.8.27) the *mean absolute deviation* (MAD) constraint. In the appendix to this chapter, we discuss the theory presented in this section further.

# Section 3.9
# Linear Programming Implementation

Because the sum

$$\sum_{t>0} n_t(t - w)^+$$

is a piecewise linear function of $w$, to verify conditions (3.8.11) or (3.8.12) we only need to check for those values of $w$ for which $n_w \neq 0$. Because there are only finitely many nonzero cash flows in practice, (3.8.11) or (3.8.12) merely represents finitely many linear inequalities. The model presented in the last section can be implemented by means of linear programming.

In view of (3.8.17),

$$S^* - S = \frac{1}{2}g''(\xi) \sum_{t>0} t^2 n_t,$$

we would want to structure the asset and liability cash flows such that the quantity

$$g''(\xi) \sum_{t>0} t^2 n_t \tag{3.9.1}$$

is as large as possible to maximize the new surplus value $S^*$. However, the factor $g''(\xi)$ depends on the interest rate shock, which one cannot predict. Because the quantity $g''(\xi)$ can be positive or negative, a more prudent strategy is to structure the cash flows such that the absolute value of the Fisher-Weil dollar convexity of the surplus,

$$\left| \sum_{t>0} t^2 n_t \right|, \tag{3.9.2}$$

is as small as possible, while subject to the conditions that give rise to (3.8.17) (i.e., while subject to (3.8.15) and (3.8.11), or (3.8.12)).

For simplicity assume that the cash flows occur only at the end of each time period. Let $A_{j,t}$ denote the cash flow at the end of the $t$-th period for an initial investment of $1 in the $j$-th fixed-income security. We assume that the securities are noncallable and default free. For each $j$,

$$1 = \sum_{t \geq 1} A_{j,t} P(0, t). \qquad (3.9.3)$$

Let $x_j$ denote the amount of money to be invested in the $j$-th security; then the aggregate asset cash flow at time $t$ is

$$A_t = \sum_j x_j A_{j,t}. \qquad (3.9.4)$$

The asset allocation problem, for a given stream of liability cash flows $\{L_t\}$ and a surplus value $S$, is to determine the "optimal" amounts $\{x_j\}$.

To formulate the linear program, we first need to guess which of (3.8.11) and (3.8.12) may hold. (If neither condition holds, then the linear programming model cannot be implemented.) Suppose that we think (3.8.11) would hold. Recall that the sum $\sum t^2 n_t$ is nonnegative if (3.8.11) holds. Hence, minimizing (3.9.2) is equivalent to minimizing $\sum t^2 n_t$, which, in turn, is equivalent to minimizing the asset Fisher-Weil dollar convexity $\sum t^2 A_t P(0, t)$ because the liability cash flows $\{L_t\}$ are assumed to be fixed. The linear programming problem is

$$\min_{x_j \geq 0} \sum_j x_j C_j$$

subject to

$$C_j = \sum_{t \geq 1} t^2 A_{j,t} P(0, t),$$

$$n_t = \left( \sum_j x_j A_{j,t} - L_t \right) P(0, t),$$

$$S = \sum_{t \geq 1} n_t,$$

$$\sum_{t \geq 1} t n_t = 0,$$

$$\sum_{t > k} (t - k) n_t \geq 0, \quad k = 1, 2, \ldots,$$

$$(3.9.5)$$

and other constraints that might be imposed. A typical constraint is that there is a maximum amount that can be invested in a particular bond. In view of (3.9.3), $C_j$ is the Fisher-Weil convexity of the $j$-th security. The last set of constraints in (3.9.5) is a reformulation of (3.8.11).

On the other hand, if we think that (3.8.12) would hold, then the linear programming problem is

$$\max_{x_j \geq 0} \sum_j x_j C_j$$

subject to

$$C_j = \sum_{t \geq 1} t^2 A_{j,t} P(0, t),$$

$$n_t = \left( \sum_j x_j A_{j,t} - L_t \right) P(0, t),$$

$$S = \sum_{t \geq 1} n_t,$$

$$\sum_{t \geq 1} t n_t = 0,$$

$$\sum_{t > k} (t - k) n_t \leq 0, \quad k = 1, 2, \ldots,$$

(3.9.6)

and any other necessary constraints.

# Section 3.10
# Appendix

The discussion in Section 3.8 can be phrased more succinctly in terms of inequalities satisfied by convex functions.

*Definition 3.10.1. A real-valued function g defined on an interval $(a, b)$, $-\infty \leq a < b \leq \infty$, is convex if for each pair of numbers $x, y \in (a, b)$, and for every $\alpha \in (0, 1)$, the inequality*

$$g(\alpha x + (1 - \alpha) y) \leq \alpha g(x) + (1 - \alpha) g(y)$$

(3.10.1)

*holds. The function g is strictly convex if $\leq$ in (3.10.1) is replaced by $<$.*

Graphically, condition (3.10.1) is that, if $x < t < y$, then the point $(t, g(t))$ lies below or on the line (chord) joining the points $(x, g(x))$ and $(y, g(y))$ in the plane. A differentiable function $g$ is convex if and only if the derivative $g'$ is a monotonically increasing function (Exercise 3.15), and that a twice-differentiable function $g$ is convex if and only if $g''$ is a nonnegative function (Exercise 3.16). For each fixed real number $w$, the *angle* function

$$g(t) = (t - w)^+$$

is convex.

**Definition 3.10.2.** *A signed measure defined on the Borel subsets of the interval $(a, b)$ is called a **Karamata measure** if*

$$\int_a^b d\mu(t) = \mu(a, b) = 0, \tag{3.10.2}$$

$$\int_a^b t\, d\mu(t) = 0, \tag{3.10.3}$$

*and*

$$\int_a^b (t - w)^+ \, d\mu(t) = \int_w^b (t - w)\, d\mu(t)$$

$$\geq 0, \quad \text{for each } w \in (a, b). \tag{3.10.4}$$

**Theorem 3.10.3 (Karamata [105]).** *Let $\mu$ be a signed measure defined on the Borel subsets of $(a, b)$. Then*

$$\int_a^b g(t)\, d\mu(t) \geq 0 \tag{3.10.5}$$

*for every convex function $g$, for which the integral exists, if and only if $\mu$ is a Karamata measure.*

To apply Karamata's theorem to immunization theory, we consider $g(t)$ defined by (3.8.7). In the case of a parallel shift of the yield curve by the amount $c$ (see (3.8.18)), we have

$$g(t) = e^{ct} - 1, \tag{3.10.6}$$

which is a convex function. Let $a$ be 0 and $b$ be a time after the occurrence of the last cash flow; define a measure $\mu$ on $(0, b)$ by

$$\mu(0, t] = \sum_{0 < \tau \leq t} n_\tau, \quad t \in (0, b), \tag{3.10.7}$$

which is the sum of the present values of all net cash flows up to time $t$. Then the change in surplus formula (3.8.8) becomes

$$S^* - S = \int_a^b g(t) \, d\mu(t). \tag{3.10.8}$$

We are interested in conditions on the cash flows such that inequality (3.8.4),

$$S^* - S \geq 0,$$

holds for some class of interest rate shocks that include (3.10.6). Karamata's theorem provides an answer for the class of interest rate shocks in which the function $g(t)$ is convex. Conditions (3.10.2) and (3.10.3) say that the asset and liability cash flows have identical present value and (dollar) duration. Condition (3.10.4) (or its equivalences to be discussed below) prescribes a dispersion relationship between the asset and liability cash flows.

The "only if" direction of Karamata's theorem is obvious. Conditions (3.10.2) and (3.10.3) necessarily follow from (3.10.5) because each linear function,

$$g(t) = k_1 + k_2 t,$$

is a convex function and the negative of a linear function is again a linear function. Condition (3.10.4) follows from (3.10.5) because the angle function, $(t - w)^+$, is convex.

The "if" direction of Karamata's theorem is a consequence of the following observation by Hardy, Littlewood, and Pólya [82, p. 150]: "It is intuitive, and easy to prove, that any convex and [uniformly] continuous function may be approximated by the sum of a linear function and a finite number of positive multiples of angles." The following result corresponds to (3.8.17).

**Proposition 3.10.4.** *Let $\mu$ be a Karamata measure on $(a, b)$. Then, for each twice-differentiable function $g$ on $[a, b]$, there is a number $\xi$ between $a$ and $b$ such that*

$$\int_a^b g(t) \, d\mu(t) = \frac{1}{2} g''(\xi) \int_a^b (t - c)^2 \, d\mu(t) \tag{3.10.9}$$

*where $c$ is any real number.*

**Proof.** *For* $t \in (a, b)$, *we have the Taylor formula with integral remainder*

$$g(t) = g(a) + (t - a)g'(a) + \int_a^b g''(w)(t - w)^+ \, dw. \qquad (3.10.10)$$

*Integration with respect to the measure* $\mu$ *and applying* (3.10.2) *and* (3.10.3) *yields*

$$\int_a^b g(t) \, d\mu(t) = 0 + 0 + \int_a^b \left[ \int_a^b g''(w)(t - w)^+ dw \right] d\mu(t)$$

$$= \int_a^b g''(w) \left[ \int_a^b (t - w)^+ \, d\mu(t) \right] dw. \qquad (3.10.11)$$

*Because of condition* (3.10.4), *we can apply the weighted mean value theorem for integrals to the right-hand side of* (3.10.11): *there exists a number* $\xi$ *between a and b such that*

$$\int_a^b g(t) \, d\mu(t) = g''(\xi) \int_a^b \left[ \int_a^b (t - w)^+ \, d\mu(t) \right] dw$$

$$= g''(\xi) \int_a^b \left[ \int_a^b (t - w)^+ dw \right] d\mu(t)$$

$$= g''(\xi) \frac{1}{2} \int_a^b (t - a)^2 \, d\mu(t). \qquad (3.10.12)$$

*Because of* (3.10.2) *and* (3.10.3), *the number a in the last integrand can be replaced by any constant c, yielding* (3.10.9).

Condition (3.10.4) in the definition of a Karamata measure can be replaced by other conditions. The integrand $(t - w)^+$ on the left-hand side of (3.10.4) can be replaced by convex functions such as $(w - t)^+$, $|t - w|$, and $\max(t, w)$. Because

$$t - w = (t - w)^+ - (w - t)^+$$

(which is (3.8.22)), it follows from (3.10.2) and (3.10.3) that

$$\int_a^b (t - w)^+ \, d\mu(t) = \int_a^b (w - t)^+ \, d\mu(t). \qquad (3.10.13)$$

Hence, (3.10.4) can be replaced by the condition that

$$\int_a^b (w - t)^+ \, d\mu(t) = \int_a^w (w - t) \, d\mu(t)$$

$$\geq 0, \quad \text{for each } w \in (a, b). \qquad (3.10.14)$$

Also, because of (3.8.25), condition (3.10.4) can be replaced by

$$\int_a^b |t - w| \, d\mu(t) \geq 0, \quad \text{for each } w \in (a, b), \tag{3.10.15}$$

which corresponds to the MAD constraint of Fong and Vasicek [64]. Note that Karamata [105] stated his theorem with condition (3.10.15).

Integration by parts yields

$$\int_w^b (t - w) \, d\mu(t) = \int_w^b \mu(t, b) \, dt \tag{3.10.16}$$

and

$$\int_a^w (w - t) \, d\mu(t) = \int_a^w \mu(a, t] \, dt. \tag{3.10.17}$$

Hence, condition (3.10.4) in the definition of Karamata measure can also be replaced by

$$\int_w^b \mu(t, b) \, dt \geq 0, \quad \text{for each } w \in (a, b), \tag{3.10.18}$$

or by

$$\int_a^w \mu(a, t] \, dt \geq 0, \quad \text{for each } w \in (a, b). \tag{3.10.19}$$

It follows from (3.10.13), (3.10.16), and (3.10.17) that

$$\int_a^w \mu(a, t] \, dt = \int_w^b \mu(t, b) \, dt, \quad \text{for each } w \in (a, b), \tag{3.10.20}$$

from which we obtain the following proposition.

**Proposition 3.10.5.** *Let $\mu$ be a signed measure on $(a, b)$, and (3.10.2) and (3.10.3) hold. If there exists $T \in (a, b)$ such that*

$$\mu(a, t] \geq 0, \quad \text{for each } t \in (a, T] \tag{3.10.21}$$

*and*

$$\mu(t, b) \geq 0, \quad \text{for each } t \in (T, b), \tag{3.10.22}$$

*then $\mu$ is a Karamata measure.*

To apply Proposition 3.10.5 to immunization theory, recall definition (3.10.7). Thus, if the asset and liability cash flows have identical present value ($S = 0$) and identical Fisher-Weil duration, and if there exists a positive number $T$ such that

$$\sum_{0<\tau\leq t} n_\tau \geq 0, \quad 0 < t \leq T, \tag{3.10.23}$$

and

$$\sum_{t<\tau} n_\tau \geq 0, \quad t > T, \tag{3.10.24}$$

then the measure $\mu$ defined by (3.10.7) is a Karamata measure. Hence, it follows from Karamata's theorem and (3.10.8) that, for any instantaneous interest rate shock with convex $g(t)$ (as defined by (3.8.7)), the changed surplus, $S^*$, is nonnegative, that is,

$$S^* \geq 0 = S.$$

This class of interest rate shocks includes all parallel shifts of the yield curve.

The conditions

$$\sum_{t>0} n_t = 0 \tag{3.10.25}$$

and

$$\sum_{t>0} t\, n_t = 0 \tag{3.10.26}$$

imply that the sequence of discounted net cash flows $\{n_t\}$, if not identically zero, has at least two sign changes. Consider the special case in which the sequence $\{n_t\}$ (or equivalently, the sequence of net cash flows $\{N_t\}$) has exactly two sign changes, and the pattern of the signs is of the form $+, -, +$. Then there is a positive number $T$ for which (3.10.23) and (3.10.24) hold. Hence,

$$S^* \geq 0 = S.$$

For a practical application, consider an insurance company that issues single-premium immediate annuity (SPIA) policies (see Shiu [182, p. 174]). It invests all premiums that it receives for the annuities in a noncallable and default-free bond or in a default-free mortgage with no repayment provision. The company has the policy of matching asset and liability durations. These two statements mean that (3.10.25) and (3.10.26) hold. Therefore, unless the asset and liability cash flows are matched exactly, the sequence $\{n_t\}$ has at least two sign changes. The (expected) annuity cash flows are decreasing with respect to time, but the cash flows from the bond or the mortgage are nondecreasing. Consequently, the liability has cash flows of longer date than those of the asset, and $\{N_t\}$ has exactly two sign changes with the pattern $-, +, -$. Since the sign pattern is the reverse of the above, we have

$$S^* \leq 0 = S$$

instead. In other words, the company will *lose* money under any instantaneous interest rate shock with a strictly convex function $g(t)$; such shocks include all parallel shifts.

The observation with respect to exactly two sign changes also gives us the Fisher-Weil [62] immunization theorem. Consider a liability of amount $L$, to be paid at time $T$, $T > 0$, and funded by a stream of asset cash flows, $\{A_t\}$, with the same present value,

$$L P(0, T) = \sum_{t>0} A_t P(0, t). \tag{3.10.27}$$

If the Fisher-Weil duration of the asset cash flows is $T$, that is, if

$$T = \frac{\sum_{t>0} t A_t P(0, t)}{\sum_{t>0} A_t P(0, t)} \tag{3.10.28}$$

$$= \frac{\sum_{t>0} t A_t P(0, t)}{L P(0, T)}, \tag{3.10.29}$$

then, under any instantaneous parallel shift of the yield curve, the asset value is sufficient to meet the liability value: for each real number $c$,

$$L P(0, T) e^{-cT} \leq \sum_{t>0} A_t P(0, t) e^{-ct}. \tag{3.10.30}$$

To prove (3.10.30), we note that here the net cash flows are

$$N_t = A_t, \quad \text{if } t \neq T$$

and

$$N_T = A_T - L.$$

Hence, unless the asset is a $T$-period zero-coupon bond matching the liability exactly, the sequence of net cash flows $\{N_t\}$ has exactly two sign changes, and the pattern is of the form $+, -, +$. It follows that, for each convex function $g$,

$$LP(0, T)g(T) \leq \sum_{t>0} A_t P(0, t)g(t), \qquad (3.10.31)$$

which is a more comprehensive result than (3.10.30), the conclusion of the Fisher-Weil [62] immunization theorem. We note that if $g$ is a concave function (that is, $-g$ is a convex function), then the inequality sign in (3.10.31) is reversed.

We now show that the famous Jensen's inequality is a consequence of Proposition 3.10.5 and Karamata's theorem. This inequality is used in subsequent chapters.

**Theorem 3.10.6 (Jensen's Inequality).** *Let F be a probability distribution function with $F(a) = 0$, $F(b) = 1$, and mean*

$$T = \int_a^b t \, dF(t). \qquad (3.10.32)$$

*Then, for each convex function $g$,*

$$\int_a^b g(t) \, dF(t) \geq g(T). \qquad (3.10.33)$$

**Proof.** *Let $\mu$ be the signed measure defined on $(a, b)$ with*

$$\mu(a, t] = F(t) - I_{(T,b)}(t), \quad t \in (a, b) \qquad (3.10.34)$$

*where $I(\cdot)$ denotes the indicator function. Then, for $t \in (a, T]$,*

$$\mu(a, t] = F(t) \geq 0.$$

*Furthermore, for $t \in (T, b)$,*

$$\mu(t, b] = -\mu(a, t]$$
$$= 1 - F(t)$$
$$\geq 0.$$

*Hence, it follows from Proposition 3.10.5 that $\mu$ is a Karamata measure. Inequality (3.10.33) now follows from Karamata's theorem.*

A corollary to Jensen's inequality is the Fisher-Weil [62] immunization theorem. Similar to (3.5.21), let $X$ be the random variable defined by

$$\Pr(X = t) = \frac{A_t P(0, t)}{L P(0, T)}. \tag{3.10.35}$$

By (3.10.29),

$$E(X) = T. \tag{3.10.36}$$

With $F(t)$ as the probability distribution function of $X$, inequality (3.10.33) is

$$\frac{\sum_{t>0} A_t P(0, t) g(t)}{L P(0, T)} \geq g(T),$$

which is equivalent to (3.10.31).

# *Section 3.11*
# *Exercises*

## *Exercise 3.1 (Duration)*

The ratio of the modified duration to the Macaulay duration is $(1 + y)^{-1}$, which is the same as the derivative $dy/dr$. Use this and the chain rule of calculus to reconcile the right-hand side of (3.5.2) with that of (3.5.5).

The next three exercises on Macaulay duration utilize actuarial compound-interest notation.

## *Exercise 3.2 (Bond Duration)*

a. Show that the Macaulay duration of an $n$-year noncallable and default-free bond, priced at par and with interest payable $m$ times per year, is (see (3.5.7))

$$i^{(m)}(I^{(m)}a)_{\overline{n}|}^{(m)} + \frac{n}{(1 + i)^n} = \ddot{a}_{\overline{n}|}^{(m)}$$

where $i$ is the effective annual rate of interest on the mortgage and $(I^{(m)}a)_{\overline{n}|}^{(m)} = \sum_{j=1}^{mn}(j/m^2)(1 + i)^{-j/m}$.

b. Write a computer program to compute $1,000\, \ddot{a}_{\overline{n}|}^{(2)}$ for $n = 5, 10, 15, 20$ and $i^{(2)} = 4\%, 6\%, 8\%, 10\%, 12\%$.

---

## Exercise 3.3 (Duration of a Fixed-Rate Mortgage)

a. Verify that the Macaulay duration of an $n$-year mortgage with $m$ payments per year (and without default risk and prepayment option) is

$$\frac{(I^{(m)}a)_{\overline{n}|}^{(m)}}{a_{\overline{n}|}^{(m)}} = \frac{1}{d^{(m)}} - \frac{n}{(1+i)^n - 1}.$$

b. Write a computer program to compute $1,000\,(I^{(12)}a)_{\overline{n}|}^{(12)}/a_{\overline{n}|}^{(12)}$ for $n = 10, 20, 30$ and $i^{(12)} = 5\%, 7\%, 9\%, 11\%$.

---

## Exercise 3.4 (Duration of an Adjustable-Rate Mortgage)

Consider a mortgage with an amortization period of $n$ years and payments made $m$ times per year. The interest rate is fixed for only $k$ years, $k \le n$, and will be reset at the then market rate. In the United States $k$ is usually 1, and in Canada $k$ is usually 5. Show that the Macaulay duration of such a mortgage is

$$\frac{\left(I_{\overline{k}|}^{(m)}a\right)_{\overline{n}|}^{(m)}}{a_{\overline{n}|}^{(m)}}$$

where $(I_{\overline{k}|}^{(m)}a)_{\overline{n}|}^{(m)} = \sum_{j=1}^{mn} \frac{\min(j, mk)}{m^2}(1+i)^{-j/m}$.

Assume that the valuation interest rate is the same as the fixed mortgage contract rate of interest

## Exercise 3.5 (Duration and Convexity)

Consider a portfolio of $n$ fixed-income securities, all having the same yield rate. For $j = 1, 2, \ldots, n$, let the Macaulay duration and convexity of the $j$-th security be denoted by $D_j$ and $C_j$, respectively. Let $p_j$ be the proportion of the value of $j$-th security in the portfolio; hence, $\sum_{j=1}^{n} p_j = 1$. Show that the duration and convexity of the portfolio are $\sum_{j=1}^{n} p_j D_j$ and $\sum_{j=1}^{n} p_j C_j$, respectively.

---

## Exercise 3.6 (M-squared)

Consider a portfolio of two fixed-income securities with the same yield rate. For $j = 1, 2$, let the Macaulay duration and $M$-squared of the $j$-th security be denoted by $D_j$ and $M_j^2$, respectively. Let $p_j$ be the proportion of the value of $j$-th security in the port-folio; hence, $p_1 + p_2 = 1$. It follows from Exercise 3.5 that the duration of the portfolio is $p_1 D_1 + p_2 D_2$. On the other hand, by (3.5.11) the $M$-squared of the portfolio is

$$-\frac{d}{dr}(p_1 D_1 + p_2 D_2) = -p_1 \frac{d}{dr} D_1 - p_2 \frac{d}{dr} D_2$$
$$= p_1 M_1^2 + p_2 M_2^2.$$

However, this result is obviously false because the $M$-squared of every zero-coupon bond is zero, and we can consider a portfolio consisting of two zero-coupon bonds with different maturity dates. Explain where the error occurs.

---

### Exercise 3.7 (Leveraging Surplus Duration by Mismatching)

Let $A$ and $L$ denote the present values of asset and liability cash flows, with $S = A - L > 0$ being the present value of the surplus. Let $D_A$,

$$D_L = \frac{1}{L} \sum_{t>0} te^{-rt} L_t,$$

and

$$D_S = \frac{1}{S} \sum_{t>0} te^{-rt}(A_t - L_t)$$

be the Macaulay durations of the assets, liabilities, and surplus, respectively. Show that
  (i) $S D_S = A D_A - L D_L$,
  (ii) $D_S = \frac{A}{S}(D_A - D_L) + D_L$,
  (iii) $D_S = D_A + \frac{L}{S}(D_A - D_L)$.

---

### Exercise 3.8 (Leveraging Surplus Convexity by Mismatching)

Repeat Exercise 3.6 with durations replaced by convexities.

---

### Exercise 3.9 (Immunizing Ratios)

With the notation in Exercise 3.7, show that the following conditions are equivalent to each other:
  (i) $D_A = D_L$,
  (ii) $D_A = D_S$,
  (iii) $D_L = D_S$,
  (iv) $\dfrac{d}{dr}\dfrac{A}{L} = 0$,
  (v) $\dfrac{d}{dr}\dfrac{S}{A} = 0$,
  (vi) $\dfrac{d}{dr}\dfrac{S}{L} = 0$.

(Hence, matching the asset duration with the liability duration is to "immunize" the asset-to-liability ratio, the surplus-to-asset ratio, and the surplus to liability ratio.)

## Exercise 3.10
Verify (3.5.12).

## Exercise 3.11
Verify the last step in the derivation of (3.5.20).

## Exercise 3.12
Use (3.5.20) to give an alternative derivation for (3.5.11) and (3.5.12).

## Exercise 3.13
Show that

$$\frac{A(r + \varepsilon, 0)}{A(r, 0)} = \exp\left(-\varepsilon D + \frac{1}{2}\varepsilon^2 M^2 - \cdots\right).$$

## Exercise 3.14 (Multivariate Immunization)
Assume that the asset and liability cash flows are such that condition (3.6.2) holds and the matrix $H$ defined by (3.6.4) is positive definite. Use the multivariate Taylor expansion theorem to derive the free-lunch condition (3.6.5).

## Exercise 3.15
Show that, if $g$ is a differentiable function, then $g$ is convex if and only if the derivative $g'$ is a monotonically increasing function.

## Exercise 3.16
Show that, if $g$ is a twice-differentiable function, then $g$ is convex if and only if $g''$ is a nonnegative function.

## Exercise 3.17
Let $\mu$ be a nontrivial measure on $(a, b)$ satisfying (3.10.4). Show that

$$\int_a^b (t - a)^2 \, d\mu(t) > 0.$$

Hint: $\int_a^b (t - a)^2 \, d\mu(t) = 2 \int_a^b \left[ \int_a^b (t - w)^+ \, d\mu(t) \right] dw.$

## Exercise 3.18

Let $\mu$ be a nontrivial Karamata measure on $(a, b)$. If the second derivative $g''$ is a strictly positive function ($g$ is strictly convex), show that

$$\int_a^b g(t)\, d\mu(t) > 0.$$

## Exercise 3.19

Show that condition (3.10.4) in the definition of Karamata measure can be replaced by

$$\int_a^b \max(t, w)\, d\mu(t) = w\mu(a, w] + \int_w^b t\, d\mu(t)$$

$$\geq 0, \quad \text{for all } w \in (a, b).$$

Hint: $2\max(t, w) = |t - w| + t - w$.

# CHAPTER 4
## EQUILIBRIUM PRICING

## Section 4.1
## Introduction

In modern finance, the two basic approaches to the pricing of securities are the no-arbitrage approach and the equilibrium approach. This chapter deals with the equilibrium approach. The no-arbitrage approach was introduced in Chapter 2 and is examined in detail in Chapter 5. This chapter begins with a brief description of both approaches and a discussion of their differences.

The no-arbitrage approach is widely used in pricing derivative securities. This approach is based on the no-arbitrage principle, which states that, in well-functioning financial markets, two securities that have the same payoffs must trade at the same price. This means that if we can replicate the payoff of a security using existing traded securities, we can price this security in terms of the existing traded securities. For example, in Section 2.5 we saw that in a one-period model the payoff from a call option could be replicated by a portfolio consisting of the underlying asset and the riskless bond. An investor should be indifferent between holding the call option and the replicating portfolio because both provide identical payoffs at the end of the period. Hence, the price of the call must be equal to the value of the replicating portfolio to prevent arbitrage. This example highlights a key requirement of no-arbitrage pricing: to apply this approach, it is necessary to be able to replicate the payoff using the existing marketed securities.

There are situations in which the no-arbitrage approach cannot be applied. One example is when a new security is introduced and this security cannot be replicated by the existing traded securities. In these situations, we cannot use no-arbitrage pricing, but we can use the equilibrium approach.

The equilibrium approach provides a more general framework for analyzing markets and pricing securities. It relates the prices of securities to more fundamental economic concepts and, in this sense, tells us where the prices come from. Hence, to apply this approach, we need to impose more structure than in the no-arbitrage approach, which simply takes the prices as given.

For the equilibrium model, we assume a one-period model in which a set of individuals (*economic agents*) trade securities. The characteristics of these securities are fixed at the outset. Each agent has an initial amount of resources or *endowment*. We assume that there is a financial market where agents buy and sell securities. Agents maximize their respective welfare by trading in the available securities. The equilibrium prices result from the optimizing actions of all the agents in the market. Equilibrium is reached when the prices are such that each agent's expected utility is maximized. When equilibrium is attained, the prices are such that no agent has an incentive to trade at these prices.

The equilibrium prices are related to the attributes of the agents in the economy, such as the endowments, beliefs, and preferences, as well as to the type and structure of the traded securities. If any of these change, the resulting equilibrium prices will, in general, change as well. If a market is in equilibrium, then, intuitively we can see it should not permit arbitrage opportunities. If a set of prices admits arbitrage, agents are able to improve their welfare at zero cost. This contradicts the property of an equilibrium that the agents' utilities are already maximized. Hence, the two approaches lead to consistent pricing.

The equilibrium approach plays an important role in modern finance. A number of the major pricing models can be derived using this approach. As we see later in this chapter, both the capital-asset-pricing model and the Black-Scholes option-pricing formula can be derived in this way. The equilibrium approach (in continuous time) also provides the basis for the derivation of the Cox-Ingersoll-Ross model, one of the best-known stochastic interest rate models.

We begin by discussing the expected utility hypothesis. This is a convenient way to model how individuals make decisions under uncertainty. We use it in our development of the equilibrium approach. Section 4.3 deals with a one-period model of financial markets. We show how the equilibrium prices of the traded securities depend on the characteristics of the underlying economy and that the price of a security can be expressed as the discounted expectation of its payoff, where the expectation is taken over a special probability measure. There is a similar type of formula for the price of a security in the no-arbitrage framework, in which the special measure is called a risk-neutral measure. In this case, the price can also be written as an expectation. Two important differences exist between the two valuation formulas.

In the equilibrium case, the actual payoff is adjusted by a risk factor, and the expectation is taken with respect to a different probability measure than for the no-arbitrage approach. This probability measure corresponds to realistic probabilities. It is important to appreciate the distinction between the two probability measures, as it is often critical for modeling future asset returns and the valuation of securities. Consequently, we discuss this distinction at the end of Section 4.3.

In Section 4.4, we show how the computation of equilibrium prices can be simplified. Under certain conditions, we can amalgamate the characteristics of each individual agent into one representative agent. We then derive the equilibrium prices in terms of the attributes of this representative agent and use the representative agent technique to derive two important finance models: the capital-asset-pricing model (Section 4.5) and the Black-Scholes formula in an equilibrium setting (Section 4.6). In Section 5.3 we discuss the multiperiod case.

# Section 4.2
# Decision Making under Uncertainty: The Expected Utility Hypothesis

Individuals often have to make choices under conditions of uncertainty. For our purposes, we assume that an agent's preferences for each outcome can be measured using a utility function. In this model, we assume economic agents act to maximize the expected value of this function. Agents compute the expected value using their own subjective probability beliefs about the future outcomes. The expected utility approach is a common way of modeling how individuals make decisions under uncertainty, but it is by no means the only approach. This approach enables us to model how agents make investment and insurance choices and to explore what governs such decisions.

This section introduces utility functions and discusses some applications. We assume that agents prefer more wealth to less wealth and that they do not like risk (that is, they are *risk averse*). These attributes can be reflected in the mathematical properties of the utility function of the individual agents. The property of risk aversion also has implications for an individual's investment choices. The basic intuition is that the more risk averse an investor is, the more the investor will invest in safer (less risky) assets. The expected utility approach can also shed light on the key determinants of insurance purchases. An individual who is risk averse will be willing to pay more than the expected value of the loss for insurance protection. We illustrate these applications with examples.

We first consider a single-period, discrete-time model where the outcome at the end of the period is uncertain. The period begins at time 0 and ends at time 1.

The decision maker is concerned with wealth at time 1 and maximizes the expected utility at time 1.[1] Thus, the quantity of interest is the agent's wealth at time 1.

We assume that the utility function, $u(x)$, where $x$ represents the amount of the agent's wealth, is strictly increasing and concave so that $u'(x) > 0$ and $u''(x) \leq 0$. An individual whose utility function is concave is said to be risk averse. Two commonly used measures of risk aversion are obtained from the utility function: the absolute risk aversion function, $R_A(x)$, and the relative risk aversion function, $R_R(x)$,

$$R_A(x) = -\frac{u''(x)}{u'(x)}, \qquad R_R(x) = x R_A(x) = -\frac{x u''(x)}{u'(x)} \qquad (4.2.1)$$

where $x$ represents the amount of the agent's wealth. These measures contain useful information about the decision maker's attitude to risk.

A simple example illustrates how the expected utility approach is used to model decision making.

**Example 4.2.1.** Suppose a decision maker has initial wealth at time 0 of $w$ units. Assume that there are two securities: a riskless security costing 1 unit and earning a rate of return of $i$ and a risky security also costing 1 unit. Suppose the risky security has two possible outcomes at time 1. Either it earns a rate of return of $i_u$ or it earns a rate of return of $i_d$. Suppose that the decision maker's subjective probability that the upstate, $u$, will occur is $p$ and the corresponding probability that the downstate, $d$, will occur is $(1 - p)$. We assume that the decision maker's utility function is $u(x)$. We can now compare the attractiveness of alternative investment strategies. If the agent invests exclusively in the riskless asset, the utility is $u(w(1 + i))$. If the decision maker invests exclusively in the risky asset, the expected utility associated with this decision is

$$pu(w(1 + i_u)) + (1 - p)u(w(1 + i_d)).$$

Comparing expected utilities, the investment in the risky asset will be more attractive if

$$pu(w(1 + i_u)) + (1 - p)u(w(1 + i_d)) > u(w(1 + i)). \qquad \blacksquare$$

The expected utility hypothesis can be used to rank these two investment alternatives. We remark that neither of these may be the best alternative; that is, it may be better to invest part of wealth at time 0 in the riskless asset and part in the risky asset. As we show later, the expected utility approach can be used to compute the optimal investment strategy for problems involving a portfolio of the available assets.

---

[1] In later sections, the utility function is defined over the agents' consumption at different points in time.

The expected utility approach can also be used to model insurance purchase decisions. We can obtain an equation for the maximum price an individual would be willing to pay for insurance coverage. Suppose the individual's total initial wealth is $w$, and suppose that this wealth is subject to a random loss $Y$ during the period, where $0 \leq Y < w$. An insurance contract is available that fully reimburses the individual for the incurred loss. The price (the insurance premium) for this contract is $\pi$ and is payable at time 0. We neglect the time value of money in this example to concentrate on the insurance aspects of the problem. If the individual decides not to buy insurance, the expected utility is $E[u(w - Y)]$. Note that this expectation is based on the investor's own subjective probability assessment of the loss. If the individual decides to purchase insurance, the time-1 wealth is no longer random but is $w - \pi$ since the insurer will reimburse the investor fully for any loss. In this case the utility at time 1 is $u(w - \pi)$. The individual will make the decision to buy insurance as long as

$$u(w - \pi) > E[u(w - Y)]. \tag{4.2.2}$$

The investor will always be willing to pay a premium that is higher than the expected value of the loss, $E[Y]$. This follows from Jensen's inequality.

**Theorem 4.2.1 (Jensen's Inequality).** *Suppose $u''(w) \leq 0$ and $X$ is a random variable; then*

$$u(E[X]) \geq E[u(X)]. \tag{4.2.3}$$

**Proof.** *Suppose $E[X] = \mu$ exists; the tangent line at point $(\mu, u(\mu))$ in Figure 4.1 can be expressed as*

$$y = u(\mu) + u'(\mu)(w - \mu).$$

*Since $u(w)$ is concave, the graph of $u(w)$ will lie below the tangent line. In other words,*

$$u(w) \leq u(\mu) + u'(\mu)(w - \mu) \tag{4.2.4}$$

*for all values of $w$. If $w$ is replaced by the random variable $X$, and the expectation is taken on each side of the inequality (4.2.4), we have $E[u(X)] \leq u(\mu)$, which is Jensen's inequality.*

Jensen's inequality implies that

$$u(w - E[Y]) \geq E[u(w - Y)].$$

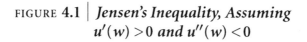

FIGURE **4.1** | *Jensen's Inequality, Assuming*
*u'(w) > 0 and u''(w) < 0*

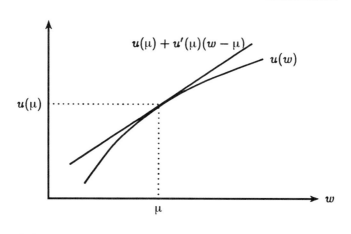

This means that a risk-averse individual will be willing to pay more than the expected value of the loss. In general, the more risk averse the individual, the higher the price the individual is willing to pay.

We can obtain an intuitive relationship between the size of this difference (of price and expected value) and the individual's risk aversion if we assume that the risk is "small" in the sense that third and higher central moments are negligible in comparison to the variance.

**Theorem 4.2.2.** *Consider a random variable Y with mean μ and variance $\sigma^2$ and for which higher central moments $\mu_3, \mu_4, \ldots$ are negligible relative to the variance. The maximum price that a risk-averse individual with wealth w is willing to pay to avoid a possible loss of Y is approximately*

$$\pi \approx \mu + \frac{\sigma^2}{2} R_A(w - \mu). \tag{4.2.5}$$

**Proof.** *The price satisfies*

$$u(w - \pi) = \mathrm{E}[u(w - Y)].$$

*Rewrite Y as $Y = \mu + zV$, where V is a random variable with mean 0. Then the price satisfies*

$$u(w - \pi) = \mathrm{E}[u(w - \mu - zV)] \tag{4.2.6}$$

*and is a function of z. Consider the Taylor series around $z = 0$:*

$$\pi = a + bz + cz^2 + \cdots.$$

*By setting $z = 0$ in (4.2.6), we see that $a = \mu$. Differentiating (4.2.6) once and setting $z = 0$ yields $b = 0$. Differentiating again and setting $z = 0$ yields*

$$c = \frac{1}{2} R_A(w - \mu) z^2 \operatorname{Var}(V).$$

*Ignoring all but the first three terms in the Taylor expansion yields the approximation*

$$\pi \approx \mu + \frac{1}{2} R_A(w - \mu) \, z^2 \operatorname{Var}(V)$$

$$= \mu + \frac{1}{2} R_A(w - \mu) \operatorname{Var}(Y)$$

$$= \mu + \frac{\sigma^2}{2} R_A(w - \mu).$$

Formula (4.2.5) is intuitive. It states that for small risks, the maximum risk premium for insurance is proportional to the product of the variance of the risk and the absolute risk aversion. In the economic literature, the quantity $\pi - \mu$ is sometimes called the *risk premium*. The intuition behind (4.2.5) is simple. For small risks, the risk premium is proportional to the product of the variance of the loss distribution and the individual's absolute risk aversion. Individuals with high levels of risk aversion are willing to pay higher insurance premiums than those with low levels of risk aversion. Formula (4.2.5) states that increases in the riskiness of the loss distribution (in the sense of increased variance) also increase the risk premium. This makes intuitive sense.

We now examine some commonly used utility functions. It is convenient to characterize these functions in terms of their risk aversion.

***Example 4.2.2 (Quadratic Utility).*** A particularly simple one is quadratic utility, given by

$$u(x) = x - \frac{x^2}{2b}, \quad \text{for } x < b,$$

$$u'(x) = 1 - \frac{x}{b},$$

$$u''(x) = -\frac{1}{b}. \tag{4.2.7}$$

■

We require the marginal utility to be positive. This is why we limit the range of $x$ to values such that $x < b$. For quadratic utility, the absolute risk aversion is

$$R_A(x) = \frac{1}{b - x}, \quad \text{for } x < b,$$

which is an increasing function of $x$ for $x < b$. This implies that quadratic utility functions exhibit increasing absolute risk aversion. Quadratic utility functions are extremely tractable. The reason is that the decision maker cares about only the first two moments (mean and variance) of a security's return. We will see in Chapter 8 that this assumption is related to the Markowitz mean-variance model of portfolio selection. On the other hand, quadratic utility functions do have a couple of disadvantages. First, we have seen that the range of the argument has to be restricted to ensure that the utility function is increasing. Second, the increasing risk aversion property is considered undesirable. This is because an agent who can allocate money between a risky asset and a risk-free asset will put a lower dollar amount of funds in the risky asset as wealth increases if the utility function exhibits increasing absolute risk aversion. This is generally considered unreasonable behavior.

**Example 4.2.3 (Exponential Utility).** The exponential utility function is used extensively in both finance and insurance applications. The function and its first two derivatives are, for $x > 0$,

$$u(x) = 1 - e^{-ax}, \quad a > 0$$
$$u'(x) = ae^{-ax},$$
$$u''(x) = -a^2 e^{-ax}. \tag{4.2.8}$$

The absolute risk aversion is equal to the constant $a$ for all wealth levels. ∎

**Example 4.2.4 (Power Utility).** Another common type of utility function is the power utility function. This function and its first two derivatives are, for $x > 0$,

$$u(x) = \frac{x^\alpha - 1}{\alpha}, \quad \alpha \in (0, 1),$$
$$u'(x) = x^{\alpha-1},$$
$$u''(x) = (\alpha - 1)x^{\alpha-2}. \tag{4.2.9}$$

The absolute risk aversion is

$$R_A(x) = \frac{1 - \alpha}{x},$$

which decreases with $x$. The relative risk aversion for the power utility function is

$$R_R(x) = 1 - \alpha,$$

which is a constant. The power utility function has decreasing absolute risk aversion, and this is deemed to be a more desirable property than increasing absolute risk aversion. This is because an agent who can allocate money between a risky asset and a risk-free asset will put a higher dollar amount of funds in the risky asset as the agent's wealth increases if the utility function exhibits decreasing absolute risk aversion. ∎

**Example 4.2.5 (Logarithmic Utility).** When $\alpha = 0$ in Example 4.2.4, the utility function becomes $u(x) = \log(x)$. Logarithmic utility and its derivatives are usually written as for $x > 0$,

$$u(x) = a \log x + b, \quad a > 0,$$
$$u'(x) = \frac{a}{x},$$
$$u''(x) = -\frac{a}{x^2}.$$

∎

We now discuss a simple asset allocation problem and show how to solve for the optimal investment proportions using the expected utility approach. We first assume the investor has power utility given by [2]

$$u(x) = \frac{x^\alpha}{\alpha}, \quad 0 < \alpha < 1.$$

The investor has initial wealth of $w$ and can allocate funds between two assets: a risky asset and a riskless asset. The current price of each asset is 1 unit. There are two possible states at time 1. If the upstate occurs, the risky asset pays an amount $1 + i_u$, and if the downstate occurs, the risky asset pays an amount $1 + i_d$. The riskless asset pays the same amount $(1 + i_f)$ in each state. The investor believes that the probability of the upstate is $p$ and the probability of the downstate is $(1 - p)$. Note that these are subjective probabilities. Thus, the estimate of the expected rate of return on the risky security is

$$m = pi_u + (1 - p)i_d.$$

From this equation the probabilities of the states can be expressed as

$$p = \frac{m - i_d}{i_u - i_d}, \quad 1 - p = \frac{i_u - m}{i_u - i_d}.$$

---

[2]The $-1$ in the numerator of $u(x)$ in Example 4.2.4 can be dropped without loss of generality.

It is natural to impose the condition that $m > i_f$, because otherwise a rational individual will never invest a positive amount in the risky asset. We also have the no-arbitrage conditions $(i_u > i_f > i_d)$ and $(i_u > m > i_d)$. Suppose that the investor puts a fraction $x$ of initial wealth in the risky asset. The investor's wealth in the upstate will be $w((1 + i_f) + x(i_u - i_f))$, and in the downstate will be $w((1 + i_f) + x(i_d - i_f))$. The investor's expected utility at time 1 will be

$$p\frac{\{w[(1 + i_f) + x(i_u - i_f)]\}^\alpha}{\alpha} + (1 - p)\frac{\{w[(1 + i_f) + x(i_d - i_f)]\}^\alpha}{\alpha}. \quad (4.2.10)$$

We find the optimal investment in the risky asset by determining the value of $x$ that maximizes the investor's expected utility. Since the function $u(x)$ is concave, the expected utility is also a concave function of $x$. Hence, the maximum is obtained by setting the first derivative of the expected utility equal to zero and solving for $x$. Because of the concavity, the second-order condition for a maximum is automatically satisfied. A little algebra shows that the optimal proportion $x^*$ is given by

$$x^* = \frac{(1 + i_f)(\theta - 1)}{i_u - i_f + \theta(i_f - i_d)} \quad (4.2.11)$$

where

$$\theta = \frac{[p(i_u - i_f)]^{1/(1-\alpha)}}{[(1 - p)(i_f - i_d)]^{1/(1-\alpha)}}.$$

Using the no-arbitrage conditions, it can be shown that $\theta \geq 1$ (see Exercise 4.1).

We note that the investment in the risky asset is always positive as long as $\theta > 1$. As $m$ tends to $i_f$, $\theta$ tends to 1, and the optimal proportion in the risky asset tends to zero. This makes sense. A risk-averse investor will prefer the riskless asset if it has the same return as the expected return on the risky asset. The optimal proportion in the risky asset will be less than 1 as long as $\theta < (1 + i_u)/(1 + i_d)$.

We can derive a more intuitive expression for the optimal proportion $x^*$ if we consider the continuous-time limit of this discrete-time model. To do this properly, we should first work out the optimal solution for the multiperiod case in which the securities have the same distribution of returns in each period. Because of the stationarity of the return distribution and because there are no transaction costs, it can be shown that the multiperiod case collapses to a series of identical single-period problems.[3] Hence, the optimal value of $x$ is the same at each time interval and is equal

---

[3]For details see the paper by Gennotte and Jung [69] in which this result is a special case of their more complicated problem.

to the value $x^*$ we obtained in (4.2.11) for the one-period problem. We now select the parameters of the discrete-time distribution of the risky asset so that we can obtain the desired limiting distribution. This approach is essentially the same one that permits us to obtain a normal distribution from a discrete-time random walk. We will use a similar approach in Chapter 6 to select the parameters of the discrete-time model so that, in the limit, the payoff on the risky asset has a lognormal distribution. Let there be $n$ time intervals each of length $h = 1/n$. Let $i_u$, $i_d$, $m$, $\sigma$, and $\mu$ satisfy

$$1 + i_u = e^{\sigma\sqrt{h}}, \qquad 1 + i_d = e^{-\sigma\sqrt{h}}, \qquad m = e^{\mu h} - 1.$$

The continuously compounded return $r$ is related to $i_f$ as follows:

$$e^{rh} = 1 + i_f.$$

These expressions for $i_u$, $i_d$, $i_f$, and $p$ are now functions of $h$. We can make these substitutions into (4.2.11) for $x^*$. If we take the limit as $h$ tends to zero, we obtain (see Exercise 4.5) the following expression for the optimal fraction in the risky asset:

$$x^* = \frac{\mu - r}{\sigma^2(1 - \alpha)}. \tag{4.2.12}$$

This expression for the proportion of risky assets in the portfolio was first obtained by Merton [132] using a continuous-time framework. The term on the right-hand side of (4.2.12) is called the *Merton ratio*. Merton[4] assumed that the return on the risky asset follows geometric Brownian motion with constant (over time) mean and volatility and that the investor has a power utility function. In addition, the market was assumed to be frictionless, eliminating all transaction costs.

This solution indicates that it is optimal for the investor to maintain a constant proportion of wealth in the risky asset. As time passes, the value of the risky asset changes, requiring the investor to rebalance the portfolio continuously to maintain the same constant proportion of wealth in the risky asset. Since there are no frictions such as transaction costs,[5] it is costless to rebalance the portfolio.

The Merton ratio has several intuitive properties:

- First, note that it can be written in words as

$$\text{Optimal proportion} = \frac{\text{Risk premium on risky asset}}{(\text{Variance})(\text{Relative risk aversion})}.$$

---

[4]In 1997, Robert Merton received the Nobel Prize in economics for his contribution to valuing financial instruments.

[5]For a discussion of how the inclusion of transaction costs affects the problem, see Gennotte and Jung [69] or Boyle and Lin [24].

- Second, note that the optimal fraction is proportional to $(\mu - r)$, the risk premium on the risky asset. Other things being equal, the higher the risk premium, the higher the fraction invested in the risky asset. As $\mu$ tends to $r$, the optimal fraction tends to zero. This makes sense because if the risky asset does not offer any additional expected return, the investors prefer the risk-free asset.

- Third, the optimal fraction invested in the risky asset is inversely proportional to the variance of the risky asset. As the variance increases, the fraction invested in the risky asset declines.

- Fourth, the optimal fraction is inversely proportional to $(1 - \alpha)$, the investor's relative risk aversion. As the investor becomes more risk averse, a lower fraction will be invested in the risky asset.

- Fifth, for $\alpha = 0$, the *growth optimum portfolio* results.[6] For given initial wealth $W_0 = w$, the growth optimum portfolio is obtained if we maximize

$$\mathrm{E}\left[\log\left(\frac{W_T}{w}\right)\right], \qquad (4.2.13)$$

where $W_T$ denotes wealth at time $T$. Using the notation

$$W_T = w(1 + i_1) \cdots (1 + i_T),$$

we obtain

$$\log\left(\frac{W_t}{w}\right) = \sum_{t=1}^{T} \log(1 + i_t).$$

Hence, under the i.i.d. assumption of the Merton model, (4.2.13) is equivalent to

$$\max \mathrm{E}\left[\log(1 + i_t)\right], \quad t = 1, 2, \ldots, T.$$

If the optimal value is denoted by $V_{\mathrm{max}}$, then for large $T$, the law of large

---

[6]The growth optimal portfolio was introduced by Hakansson [81], and it corresponds to the portfolio selected by an investor with log utility. It plays an important role in the Cox and Huang [42] application of martingale theory to the solution of the investor's consumption investment problem. For an analysis of the significance of the growth optimal portfolio, see Samuelson [167].

numbers implies that

$$\frac{1}{T} \sum_{t=1}^{T} \log(1 + i_t)$$

converges to $V_{max}$ with probability 1. This suggests that long-run portfolio strategies exceeding the equity exposure of the growth optimum portfolio are somewhat questionable.

One advantage of the Merton ratio is that it can be used to provide numerical estimates of the optimal fraction in the risky asset. Asset allocation problems are very important strategic decisions for both pension plans and individual investors. In the case of pension plans, a frequently quoted rule of thumb is 60% in stocks and 40% in bonds. It is instructive to insert some "ballpark" figures in the Merton ratio. Assuming the risky asset corresponds to a well-diversified common stock portfolio, historical estimates for the parameters might be $\mu = 10\%$, $\sigma = 20\%$. A long-run estimate of the riskless rate is 5%. There is a range of different estimates of $\alpha$ in the empirical finance literature, but based on the paper by Constantinides [40], take $\alpha = -1$. With these inputs, the value of the Merton ratio is 62.5%. By a remarkable coincidence, this is close to the 60% ratio quoted earlier.

For the given parameter values $\mu = 10\%$, $r = 5\%$, and $\sigma = 20\%$, the growth optimum portfolio has an equity exposure of 125%, implying borrowing at the rate $r$ to finance purchasing the equities in excess of 100%.

# Section 4.3
# One-Period Model of Securities Markets

In this section, we use a one-period model of a securities market with the following characteristics:

- There is no production in this model. Such models are known as exchange economies.
- There is a single perishable good that cannot be stored. We use this good as the unit of measurement.
- A security is a contract that specifies the amount of the consumption good in each future state.
- Securities have no risk of default.
- Agents maximize their expected utility of consumption by trading in the available marketed securities.

- The equilibrium prices in turn are set by the actions of the agents in the model.

We start by considering the case in which there is no uncertainty at time 1. In this case, the only security is the riskless asset. This setting allows us to interpret the interest rate in terms of the ratio of marginal utilities of the individual agents. We then consider the case in which there is uncertainty about the outcome at time 1, and we investigate the valuation of assets whose payoffs differ across different states of nature. In this case, the prices of such risky assets can be related to the marginal utilities of the individual agents.

## SECTION 4.3.1 | CERTAINTY MODEL

We start with a deterministic model. Even this simple model can generate some useful insights. In particular, we are able to derive a connection between the price of the pure discount bond and the parameters of the economy such as the agents' preferences and resources. A feature of the equilibrium approach is that we are able to derive expressions for asset prices in terms of other parameters of the economy. In this sense, the equilibrium approach is more basic than the no-arbitrage approach of Chapter 5, which assumes that the prices are given. Here we see where the prices come from. We develop an expression for the one-period interest rate in terms of the characteristics of a single agent.

Recall that there is no uncertainty at time 1. We assume that the agent has initial wealth $w$ and consumes $c_0$ at time 0 and $c_1$ at time 1. We assume that agents can borrow and lend at a market interest rate of $i_f$. We further assume that there is no risk of default, so that the interest rate is riskless. For now, we assume that this rate is given.

The agent is assumed to have an additively separable utility function for the consumption pattern $\{c_0, c_1\}$; that is,

$$u(c_0, c_1) = u_0(c_0) + u_1(c_1)$$

where $u_0(x)$ and $u_1(x)$ are increasing, concave, and twice differentiable. The utility function $u(c_0, c_1)$ is a function of consumption over two periods. The additive separability is a technical convenience.

The agent's objective is to maximize expected utility subject to the wealth constraint:

$$w \geq c_0 + \frac{c_1}{1 + i_f}.$$

This means that the total current consumption and discounted future consumption is financed by the agent's current wealth. To obtain the agent's optimal consumption pattern, we can apply the method of Lagrange multipliers. At optimality, this inequality becomes an equality since the concavity of the agent's utility function guarantees that the solution of the first-order conditions leads to a maximum. The solution to the agent's optimization problem is $\{c_0^*, c_1^*\}$, where

$$\frac{1}{1 + i_f} = \frac{u_1'(c_1^*)}{u_0'(c_0^*)}. \tag{4.3.1}$$

In equilibrium, the agent selects a consumption pattern to maximize expected utility, given the agent's resources and the market rate of interest. The left-hand side of (4.3.1) is the price of the one-period pure discount bond. The right-hand side is the marginal rate of substitution between time-1 consumption and time-0 consumption. The intuition here is that at the optimal allocation, the agent trades off consumption across time at a rate equal to the market rate of interest. Note that this example relates the price of the risk-free asset to the attributes of a particular agent.

Instead of assuming that the agent's endowment consists only of wealth at time 0, we could assume that the agent is entitled to $e_0$ at time 0 and $e_1$ at time 1. Then we solve the original optimization problem with the resource constraint

$$w = e_0 + \frac{e_1}{1 + i_f},$$

and there is no essential difference in the solution.

In this economy, the same pricing relation holds for each agent $i$ so that the utility functions on the right-hand side of (4.3.1) could more generally be subscripted by the index $i$. The left-hand side, on the other hand, does not depend on the index $i$ at all. This independence is a property of the market equilibrium interest rate. The market rate is determined by finding the equilibrium interest rate such that agents choose consumption patterns that maximize their individual expected utility and such that at this interest rate the market for the risk-free asset clears.

## SECTION 4.3.2 | MODEL OF SECURITIES MARKET
### WITH UNCERTAINTY

In this section, we analyze the one-period model under uncertainty. We assume that there is a given set of traded securities and show how the prices of these securities can be related to more fundamental economic variables. However, we start by assuming that the prices of the existing securities are given. We develop expressions for the price of a given security in terms of the attributes of an individual agent. Although the approach may seem a little abstract, these ideas form the basis for important pricing formulas that are of practical interest.

At time 1, the state of the economy is represented by a set of outcomes $\omega \in \Omega$. Suppose that there are $N$ securities that are specified by their payouts at time 1. A single perishable good exists, and we measure all prices and payoffs in units of this good. The time-1 payout on security $j$, in state $\omega$, is $X_j(\omega)$. We further assume there is no risk of default.

We assume that the securities in this economy are traded in a perfect frictionless market by a set of risk-averse economic agents. These agents buy and sell securities to maximize their individual expected utility functions. We describe how this happens in more detail below.

Each agent is assumed to receive an initial allocation or endowment of the consumption good, which consists of an amount $e_0$ at time 0 and an amount $e_1(\omega)$ at time 1 in state $\omega$.[7] The elements of the endowment process $\{e_0, \ e_1(\omega)\}$ are assumed to be nonnegative. Each agent is assumed to consume at time 0 and at time 1 only. The amounts available for consumption depend on the initial endowment and the trades made.

We consider a generic agent who consumes an amount $c_0$ of the consumption good at time 0 and an amount $C_1(\omega)$ at time 1 in state $\omega$. Suppose that this agent has an initial endowment of $e_0$ at time 0 and an endowment of 0 in each state at time 1; that is, $e_1(\omega) = 0$ for all $\omega$. If the agent makes no trades, the consumption pattern is $\{e_0, 0\}$. However, if the agent buys 1 unit of security $j$ for a price of $x_j$, the consumption pattern at time 0 and 1 becomes

$$\{e_0 - x_j, \ X_j(\omega)\}.$$

The current consumption is reduced by the price paid for the security $j$. Under this strategy, the agent is able to consume the amount $X_j(\omega)$ in state $\omega$ at time 1.

It is sometimes convenient to use the notion of a trading strategy to represent an agent's decisions. A trading strategy consists of an $N$-dimensional vector showing the net trades that the agent makes in each security. Different trading strategies lead to different consumption patterns. In solving for the agent's optimal consumption, it is sometimes preferable to conduct the optimization over the feasible set of trading strategies rather than directly over the consumption allocations. This is because the structure of the existing securities may permit the agent to attain only certain consumption allocations. For example, if the market is incomplete,[8] not all consumption patterns are attainable. However, if the market is complete, then all consumption allocations are attainable.

---

[7]We have used $e_1(\omega)$ rather than $E_1(\omega)$, even though consumption at time 1 is a random variable, because we want to reserve the symbol E for the expectation operator.

[8]See Chapter 5 for a detailed discussion of completeness. If the market is complete, then in the one-period case, all possible payoffs can be replicated using the existing securities. These will happen if the number of linearly independent traded securities is equal to the number of states.

We assume that agents make decisions to maximize their individual expected utilities. Each agent computes this expectation using the agent's own subjective probabilities. Two cases can be conveniently distinguished. In the first case, agents have different (heterogeneous) beliefs. Agent $i$ assigns his or her subjective probability $p_i(\omega)$ to state $\omega$. In the second case, agents have the same (homogeneous) beliefs. Each agent assigns the same probability $p(\omega)$ to a given state. We often label this set of probabilities the $P$ measure; it is also called *nature's measure* or the *physical measure*.

For the rest of this subsection, we assume that agents have heterogeneous beliefs. Agent $i$ is assumed to have the utility function

$$u_{i0}(c_{i0}) + u_{i1}(C_{i1}(\omega))$$

where $u_{i0}$ and $u_{i1}$ are increasing concave and twice differentiable. With these assumptions, the expected utility for agent $i$ is therefore

$$u_{i0}(c_{i0}) + \sum_{\omega} p_i(\omega) u_{i1}(C_{i1}(\omega)).$$

Each agent strives to maximize the agent's own expected utility. Given that the initial endowments are fixed and that there is no production in the economy, the only way to do this is by trading in the marketed securities.[9]

For now, consider the actions of agent $i$ and assume that this agent faces a fixed set of prices $x_j$, where $1 \leq j \leq N$. This means that agent $i$'s trades have no impact on the current market prices of the existing securities. This agent can alter his or her consumption pattern by buying and selling the marketed securities. Of course, the initial endowment acts as a constraint in this process. The possibilities available will also depend on the number and type of the traded securities. For example, if there is just one traded security, the possible consumption patterns are more limited than if there is a complete set of traded securities.

We now show how the prices of the traded securities can be derived from equilibrium considerations. We assume that each agent has already made his or her optimal trading decisions so that the consumption allocations are optimal for each agent. The prices that support this allocation are the equilibrium prices. When the system is in equilibrium, the prices and the consumption allocations are such that each agent's expected utility is maximized at these consumption allocations and prices. This means that there is no incentive for any agent to trade at these prices. We can exploit this fact in the case of our agent $i$ to derive a valuation formula. First, denote

---

[9]Indeed, as we see later, the trading actions of the agents help determine the prices of these securities in equilibrium.

the optimal consumption process in equilibrium by $\{c_{i0}^*, C_{i1}^*(\omega)\}$. Next, consider security $j$ with current price $x_j$.

We exploit the fact that the agent has already made the optimal investment decisions. By definition, any deviation from this position is no longer optimal. If the agent is offered a choice of buying any amount $\alpha$ of this security at time 0, the optimal choice will be $\alpha = 0$.

Assume that the agent purchases $\alpha$ units of security $x$ at time 0. Then the agent's consumption is $c_{i0}^* - \alpha x_j$ at time 0 and $C_{i1}^*(\omega) + \alpha X_j(\omega)$ at time 1 in state $\omega$. With this revised investment and consumption plan, the agent's expected utility becomes

$$u_{i0}(c_{i0}^* - \alpha x_j) + \sum_\omega p_i(\omega) u_{i1}(C_{i1}^*(\omega) + \alpha X_j(\omega)).$$

We now take the derivative of this expression with respect to $\alpha$ and obtain

$$-x_j u_{i0}'(c_{i0}^* - \alpha x_j) + \sum_\omega p_i(\omega) u_{i1}'(C_{i1}^*(\omega) + \alpha X_j(\omega)) X_j(\omega).$$

This expression must vanish for $\alpha = 0$, from which we obtain

$$x_j = \sum_\omega p_i(\omega) \frac{u_{i1}'(C_{i1}^*(\omega))}{u_{i0}'(c_{i0}^*)} X_j(\omega)$$

$$= \mathrm{E}^{P_i}[Z_i X_j]. \tag{4.3.2}$$

This last equation states that the current price of the security is equal to the expected value of the product of its future payoff and a random variable denoted here by $Z_i = u_{i1}'(C_{i1}^*(\omega))/u_{i0}'(c_{i0}^*)$. This random variable is equal to the agent's marginal rate of substitution (MRS).[10] The expectation in (4.3.2) is taken with respect to the subjective probabilities of the individual agent.

Equation (4.3.2) represents an important valuation result, and it forms the basis for many modern asset-pricing models. Note that we did not make any assumptions about the completeness of the securities market in deriving this result, so that it remains valid when the market is incomplete.

When agents have homogeneous beliefs, we can rewrite (4.3.2) as

$$x_j = \sum_\omega p(\omega) \frac{u_{i1}'(C_{i1}^*(\omega))}{u_{i0}'(c_{i0}^*)} X_j(\omega)$$

$$= \mathrm{E}^P[Z_i X_j]. \tag{4.3.3}$$

---

[10] The random variable $Z_i$ is also called a pricing kernel and is related to the state price density that we discuss in Chapter 5.

Equation (4.3.3) can be used to value any security in terms of its payoffs. We need considerably more information here than we require under the no-arbitrage approach to be developed in Chapter 5. In the no-arbitrage approach, all that is needed is the set of current prices of the traded securities. The equilibrium approach requires more in the way of assumptions than the no-arbitrage approach, but in return it provides a more powerful valuation tool.

We now use (4.3.2) to derive an explicit expression for a particular security, the Arrow-Debreu security, which pays exactly 1 unit of the consumption good in state $\omega$ at time 1, and zero in all other states. Let $\psi_\omega$ be the price of the Arrow-Debreu security associated with state $\omega$.[11] From (4.3.2), we have

$$\psi_\omega = p_i(\omega) \frac{u'_{i1}(C^*_{i1}(\omega))}{u'_{i0}(c^*_{i0})}. \tag{4.3.4}$$

This valuation equation is from the perspective of agent $i$. We can write an analogous expression for $\psi_\omega$ in terms of the attributes of any other agent, say, agent $k$. Since the left-hand side of (4.3.4), $\psi_\omega$, does not depend explicitly on the attributes of any individual agent, the right-hand side of (4.3.4) must be equalized across all agents in the economy. The interpretation of this observation is similar to the certainty case. The market price of 1 unit in state $\omega$ is equal to the marginal rate of substitution between present consumption and future consumption for every agent in the economy.

Let us consider a portfolio that consists of all the Arrow-Debreu securities. This portfolio pays precisely 1 unit at time 1 in each state. The unit discount bond also pays precisely 1 unit at time 1 in each state. Hence, these two securities have the same payouts, and so they must sell for the same price to avoid arbitrage. Thus, we have the following relationship:

$$\frac{1}{1+i_f} = \sum_\omega \psi_\omega = \sum_\omega p_i(\omega) \frac{u'_{i1}(C^*_{i1}(\omega))}{u'_{i0}(c^*_{i0})}. \tag{4.3.5}$$

We see in the next section that this relationship plays a fundamental role in the construction of the risk-neutral probability measure that is used extensively in Chapter 5.

We can also derive the basic valuation equation directly by solving the individual agent's optimization problem. We assume that there is a complete market of Arrow-Debreu securities.[12] Assuming that the prices are taken as given, we solve agent $i$'s

---

[11] If the market is complete, the price of this security is unique, as we see in Chapter 5.

[12] This means that there exists a traded Arrow-Debreu security for each possible outcome.

problem. We assume agent $i$'s initial endowment is $\{e_{i0}, e_{i1}\}$. The agent's problem is

$$\max_{c_{i0}, C_{i1}} \left\{ u_{i0}(c_{i0}) + \sum_{w \in \Omega} p_i(w) u_{i1}(C_{i1}(w)) \right\} \tag{4.3.6}$$

subject to the constraint that

$$c_{i0} + \sum_{w \in \Omega} \psi_w C_{i1}(w) = e_{i0} + \sum_{w \in \Omega} \psi_w e_{i1}(w)$$

where the initial endowment $w = e_{i0} + \sum_{w \in \Omega} \psi_w e_{i1}(w)$. We form the Lagrangian as follows:

$$u_{i0}(c_{i0}) + \sum p(w) u_{i1}(C_{i1}(w)) + \gamma_i \left[ e_{i0} + \sum \psi_w e_{i1}(w) - c_{i0} - \sum \psi_w C_{i1}(w) \right].$$

$$\tag{4.3.7}$$

To solve the agent's problem, we differentiate this Lagrangian with respect to the consumption variables because we can use these variables as choice variables when the market is complete. We obtain the following first-order conditions, which are both necessary and sufficient for the maximum, since the utility functions are assumed to be concave:

$$u'_{i0}(c_{i0}) = \gamma_i, \quad \text{for all } i,$$

$$p_i(w) u'_{i1}(C_{i1}(w)) = \gamma_i \psi_w, \quad \text{for all } i, w. \tag{4.3.8}$$

Taking the ratio of these last two equations, we recover (4.3.4). The $\gamma$'s are positive since the utility functions are increasing. Note that the $\gamma$'s are the Lagrangian multipliers for the initial endowment; hence, they depend on the initial endowment.

We now discuss the concept of equilibrium in more detail. We will see that in equilibrium the prices result from the individual optimizing actions of the agents in the economy. We do not assume that the securities market is complete. In this case it is more convenient to assume that the agents in the market optimize directly over trading strategies. The trading strategies can be used to alter the agents' consumption patterns. The following assumptions and conventions are used:

- There are $I$ agents in the economy. Each agent has a utility function that is of the form

$$u_{i0}(c_{i0}) + u_{i1}(C_{i1})$$

where the $u$'s are increasing concave and twice differentiable.

- Agent $i$ has an endowment process of $\{e_{i0}, e_{i1}\}$.
- There are $N$ securities in the market. Security $j$ has a payoff of $X_j(\omega)$ at time 1 in state $\omega$. The time-0 price of security $j$ is $x_j$. We denote the vector of time-0 prices by $\{x\}$.
- Agent $i$'s trading strategy is an $N$-dimensional vector of real numbers $\{\theta_i^1, \theta_i^2, \ldots, \theta_i^N\}$. The entire set of trading strategies for the group of $I$ agents is denoted by $\{\Theta\}$.

An equilibrium is a set of prices and trading strategies $\{x, \Theta\}$ such that the following conditions are satisfied:

- Given these prices and trading strategies, each agent's expected utility is maximized subject to the constraint imposed by the agent's initial endowment. This furnishes a total of $N \times I$ first-order conditions. For example, the first-order condition for agent $i$ in respect of $\theta_i^j$ is

$$
u_{i0}\left(e_{i0} - \sum_{n=1}^{N} \theta_i^n x_n\right) x_j = \sum_{\omega} p_i(\omega) u_{i1}\left(e_{1i} + \sum_{n=1}^{N} \theta_i^n X_n(\omega)\right) X_j(\omega).
$$

$$(4.3.9)$$

- The market for each security clears. This means that

$$
\sum_{i=1}^{I} \theta_i^n = 0, \quad \text{for } n = 1, 2, \ldots, N. \tag{4.3.10}
$$

The solution of the $N \times I$ first-order equations and the $N$ market-clearing conditions delivers the optimal trading strategies and the equilibrium prices. There are $N(I + 1)$ equations for the $N(I + 1)$ unknowns. The optimal trading strategies and the equilibrium prices enable us to compute the optimal consumption for each agent. Notice that we do not assume a complete market.

- The market-clearing conditions are consistent with the requirement that total consumption equals total endowment in each state. The total consumption at time 0 is

$$
\sum_{i=1}^{I}\left(e_{i0} - \sum_{n=1}^{N} \theta_i^n x_n\right).
$$

From the market-clearing condition, this is equal to the total endowment

$$
\sum_{i=1}^{I}(e_{i0}).
$$

The total consumption at time 1 in state $\omega$ is

$$\sum_{i=1}^{I} \left( e_{i1}(\omega) - \sum_{n=1}^{N} \theta_i^n X_i^n(\omega) \right).$$

From the market-clearing condition, this is equal to the total endowment at time 1 in state $\omega$ as

$$\sum_{i=1}^{I} e_{i1}(\omega).$$

The concept of equilibrium is an important one, and it is useful to discuss it a little further. Consider the following thought experiment. For each set of prices,[13] the agents determine those trading strategies that optimize their preferences. The equilibrium prices are those for which the optimal trading strategies equalize the supply of and the demand for each security. In other words, the global aggregate demand for each security is zero. We say that the given equilibrium is supported by these prices. In equilibrium, two important things happen. Each agent uses trading strategies that optimize the agent's preferences for the given market structure and prices. In addition, the market clears so that the purchases and sales of each security are in balance. The equilibrium is characterized by the prices and the optimizing trading strategies. Of course, these trading strategies generate specific consumption allocations for each agent. Sometimes it is convenient to focus on the trading strategies, and sometimes it is useful to focus on the consumption allocations.

The inputs that generate the equilibrium prices and trading strategies (or consumption allocations) are the initial endowments, the preferences and beliefs of the agents, and the security market structure. The equilibrium prices emerge from a constrained optimization problem that uses these inputs. Hence, the prices depend on these inputs, and so if the inputs are changed, the resulting prices and equilibrium allocations also change. For example, if we change the initial endowments, this also changes the resulting prices and equilibrium allocations. If we add a new security that cannot be replicated from the existing securities, the resulting prices and equilibrium allocations also change. Indeed, any change (however small) in the inputs can lead to a corresponding change in the prices and the equilibrium allocations.

The following example illustrates the concept of equilibrium. It shows how the equilibrium prices depend on the inputs to the model and how the nature of marketed securities available can affect the equilibrium allocations and prices.

---

[13]The process by which the prices get to equilibrium is beyond the scope of this book.

*Example 4.3.1.* We assume that there are three states at time 1. There are three agents in the model, and each agent has an initial endowment of 16 units at time 0 and 50 units at time 1 in each state. Each agent has the same utility function of the form

$$\sqrt{c} + \sqrt{C}.$$

The agents have different subjective probabilities of the states and are given as follows:

| Agent | State 1 | State 2 | State 3 |
|-------|---------|---------|---------|
| One   | 0.50    | 0.25    | 0.25    |
| Two   | 0.25    | 0.50    | 0.25    |
| Three | 0.25    | 0.25    | 0.50    |

To derive the equilibrium allocations, we need to specify the securities that are available for trading. We use two different assumptions here, which correspond to two different market structures. The first structure assumes that three Arrow-Debreu securities are traded. In this case, the securities market is complete. Even though this is a fairly simple problem, we have 15 unknowns. These consist of 12 consumption amounts (four for each agent) and the prices of the three securities. We also have 15 equations: nine first-order conditions corresponding to (4.3.4), three equations (one for each agent) that ensure that the market value of each agent's optimal consumption allocation is equal to the market value of the agent's original endowment, and three equations that ensure that the total aggregate consumption equals total aggregate endowment in each state. It suits our purpose better to present the optimal solution without wading through the details. We can confirm that in this case the equilibrium allocations for the three agents are as follows:

| Agent | Time 0 | State 1 | State 2 | State 3 |
|-------|--------|---------|---------|---------|
| One   | 16     | 100     | 25      | 25      |
| Two   | 16     | 25      | 100     | 25      |
| Three | 16     | 25      | 25      | 100     |

The price of the three Arrow-Debreu securities are each 0.2. We can confirm that these prices and the above allocations satisfy (4.3.4) for each agent and for each state. This means that each agent's expected utility is maximized. We can also confirm the other conditions for an equilibrium. Hence, the market for each security clears. In addition, the total amount of consumption in each state is 150 units, which equals the total endowment. Take agent one, for example. This agent has an endowment at time 1 of 50 units in all three states. To attain his or her desired consumption allocation, this agent sells Arrow-Debreu securities associated with states 2 and 3. The agent sells 25 units of each security, which produces an inflow of 10 units: 5 from the sale of each security. This amount is used to purchase 50 units of the state-1 Arrow-Debreu security. After the trades have taken place, the allocation at time 1 is 100 in state 1 and 25 in states 2 and 3, as shown above.

Furthermore, the sum of the prices of the Arrow-Debreu securities is equal to $(1+i_f)^{-1}$. Hence, the one-period riskless interest rate in this model is $2/3 = 0.66667$. The expected utility of agent one if the initial endowment were retained is

$$\sqrt{16} + \frac{1}{2}\sqrt{50} + \frac{1}{4}\sqrt{50} + \frac{1}{4}\sqrt{50} = 11.0711.$$

In contrast, the expected utility of this agent's assuming optimal consumption is 11.50. A similar improvement in welfare occurs for the other two agents. The existence of the market permits the agents to engage in more efficient risk sharing. The ability to trade in the market improves overall welfare.

By way of comparison, we now consider a second type of market structure that has a more restricted set of securities. We assume that the only security available in the market is the riskless security that pays 1 unit of the consumption good in each state. In this case the market is no longer complete. We can use the equilibrium approach to determine the optimal consumption allocation as well as the price of this bond. In this case there is just one security—the riskless bond. The trading strategy of each agent $i$ consists of the agent's investment in this security. The number of units of the security bought (or sold) by agent $i$ is $\theta_i^1$. From the market-clearing condition (4.3.10), we have

$$\theta_1^1 + \theta_2^1 + \theta_3^1 = 0.$$

From the first-order conditions (4.3.9), we have an expression for the time-0 price of the riskless security in terms of the valuation of each agent $i$:

$$\frac{1}{\sqrt{16 - \theta_i^1/(1+i_f)}} \frac{1}{1+i_f} = \frac{1}{\sqrt{50 + \theta_i^1}}.$$

We can write this in the form

$$\frac{1}{1+i_f} = \frac{\sqrt{16 - \theta_i^1/(1+i_f)}}{\sqrt{50 + \theta_i^1}}.$$

This equation is true for $i = 1, 2, 3$. Note that the right-hand side is a monotonically decreasing function of $\theta_i^1$. Since the left-hand side is independent of $\theta_i^1$, it follows that all the $\theta_i^1$'s are equal. However, since they sum to one, each $\theta_i^1$ must be zero. In this market the optimal solution is that there is no trading. Hence, the optimal allocation in this case is the initial endowment. We can use (4.3.5) to obtain the time-0 value of the riskless bond as

$$\frac{1}{2}\frac{\sqrt{16}}{\sqrt{50}} + \frac{1}{4}\frac{\sqrt{16}}{\sqrt{50}} + \frac{1}{4}\frac{\sqrt{16}}{\sqrt{50}} = \frac{\sqrt{16}}{\sqrt{50}} = 0.5657.$$

Note that this price corresponds to a riskless interest rate of 0.7678, which is higher than the corresponding rate when the market was complete. The example shows that the prices of the traded securities in general will depend on the market structure. We do not have enough information to determine the prices of the individual Arrow-Debreu securities in this case. All that we can say is the sum of the prices of the three Arrow-Debreu is equal to 0.5637. ∎

This example illustrates an important point. Suppose we had started with the second market structure in which the only traded security is the risk-free bond. Consider what happens if we propose to add the three Arrow-Debreu securities to this market. We cannot price these securities using the no-arbitrage approach because all we have is the riskless bond. To price these new securities, we can use the equilibrium approach. The introduction of the new securities changes the equilibrium allocations of the three agents. In addition, their introduction changes the price of the preexisting security. This discussion highlights an important difference between the equilibrium approach and the no-arbitrage approach. If the market is incomplete and we introduce a new security that cannot be written as a combination of the existing securities, we cannot price this security using the no-arbitrage approach. The price of this new security can be obtained from an equilibrium model, and the introduction of the security in general changes the prices of the preexisting securities.

## SECTION 4.3.3 | THE EQUILIBRIUM APPROACH AND RISK-NEUTRAL VALUATION

In the last section, we saw how the equilibrium approach can be used to value securities. We see in Chapter 5 that we can price a security using the no-arbitrage approach if we can replicate a security's payoff using existing traded securities. Many introductory treatments of option-pricing theory focus exclusively on the no-arbitrage approach in which the price is computed as an expectation based on the risk-neutral probabilities. These risk-neutral probabilities are synthetic constructs and should not be used for realistic projections of future cash flows. This distinction is sometimes not fully appreciated. One of the best ways of understanding the distinction is to examine the two valuation approaches. First, we discuss the two approaches and then mention some of the implications of the differences between them for investment modeling and actuarial applications.

As we have seen, the equilibrium approach can be used to determine the price of a security. We need to impose explicit assumptions on the model and solve for the optimal allocations to derive the prices of the securities. The valuation equations (4.3.2) or (4.3.3) express the current price of the security as the expectation of its payoff times a random variable. The valuation formula can be written from the perspective of any individual agent: this of course does not change the price. In this subsection, we consider a generic agent; for convenience we drop the subscripts. With this convention, we denote the agent's subjective probability measure as the $P$ measure.

In the no-arbitrage approach, the valuation is carried out using the risk-neutral measure, which was introduced in Chapter 2. We provide a more detailed treatment of the no-arbitrage valuation approach in Chapter 5. The essential result is that if there is no arbitrage, any security that can be replicated using existing traded securities can be priced by taking its discounted expected value under the risk-neutral measure. The risk-neutral measure represents a probability measure that is generated using the prices of the existing traded assets. This probability measure is often known as the $Q$ measure. In general, the $Q$ measure does not assign the same probabilities to the different outcomes as the $P$ measure does. Indeed, the probabilities under the $Q$ measure are usually somewhat unrealistic. It would be inappropriate to use the $Q$ measure probabilities for realistic projections of the future, for example, for asset return projections in conjunction with cash-flow (or dynamic solvency) testing.

We now trace the direct linkage between the equilibrium valuation formula and the risk-neutral formula. This will show the connection between the $P$ measure and the $Q$ measure. The equilibrium price of security $j$ as given by (4.3.3) can be written as

$$x_j = \sum_\omega p(\omega) X_j(\omega) Z(\omega). \tag{4.3.11}$$

We have dropped the subscript $i$ in the $Z$-function. Recall that $Z$ is the ratio of marginal utilities between time 1 and time 0. The riskless bond pays 1 unit in each state at time 1. We can find its current price from (4.3.11) as

$$\frac{1}{1 + i_f} = e^{-r} = \sum_\omega p(\omega) Z(\omega) \tag{4.3.12}$$

where $r$ is the continuously compounded risk-free interest rate. We recall that $Z(\omega)$

is always positive since it is the ratio of marginal utilities. We now define positive numbers $q(\omega)$, one for each state as follows:

$$q(\omega) = (1 + i_f)\, p(\omega)\, Z(\omega), \quad \text{for all } \omega \in \Omega. \tag{4.3.13}$$

We see that each $q(\omega)$ is positive. By virtue of (4.3.12), these $q(\omega)$'s sum to 1. We can use them to define a probability measure, and under this measure the valuation of security $j$ is

$$x_j = \frac{1}{1 + i_f} \sum_{\omega} q(\omega) X_j(\omega) = \frac{E^Q[X]}{1 + i_f}. \tag{4.3.14}$$

This last equation corresponds to the no-arbitrage valuation approach. Note that the $Q$ measure is the risk-neutral measure over which the expectation is taken. Note that these $q$ probabilities are derived from prices, and that they are in general different from the $p$'s. Indeed, the risk-neutral probabilities in general will not correspond to the individual beliefs of any agent in the economy. For instance, in the case of Example 4.3.1 it is easy to verify that the the risk-neutral probabilities are each equal to 1/3. None of the three agents had this set of probability beliefs.

Compare (4.3.3) and (4.3.14). In (4.3.3), the payoff from the security is multiplied by the pricing kernel, and the expectation is with respect to nature's measure, $P$. On the other hand, in (4.3.14), the expectation is of the unadjusted payoff, and it is taken with respect to the risk-neutral measure $Q$ and discounted at the risk-free rate. There is one situation when both coincide. Suppose that the agent who is featured in the valuation formula has a linear utility function. In this case, the agent is risk neutral, and both the $P$ and $Q$ measures coincide.

Suppose that a particular agent has a risk-neutral utility function given by

$$c + e^{-\rho} C$$

where $\rho$ is the rate of time preference. The term $e^{-\rho}$ measures the weight that the agent assigns to time-1 consumption. If we set $e^{-\rho} = e^{-r}$, then the $Q$ and $P$ measures coincide for this agent. Under these assumptions, (4.3.13) becomes

$$Z(\omega) = e^{\rho},$$

and so

$$q(\omega) = e^{-r} e^{\rho}\, p(\omega) = p(\omega).$$

This explains the origin of the term "risk-neutral measure."

In most traditional presentations of option pricing, the risk-neutral approach is emphasized because the no-arbitrage principle is generally used. However, the risk-neutral probabilities associated with this approach are artificial constructs that facilitate the valuation. In many actuarial and investment applications, realistic estimates of the distribution of future asset prices are required. These sorts of projections are discussed in Chapter 9. One application is in a stochastic simulation to test solvency levels for insurance companies. In such situations, using the risk-neutral probabilities is not appropriate. Realistic probabilities should be used instead.

Some other examples can help in highlighting the distinction between these two probability measures. In Chapter 7, we discuss the Black-Derman-Toy (BDT) stochastic interest rate model. This model takes as inputs the current term structure of bond prices and the current term structure of volatilities. From these inputs, we can construct the BDT valuation lattice, which can then be used to price interest rate derivatives. The probabilities used in the construction of this lattice are risk-neutral probabilities. They are synthetic constructs that give the correct current prices, but they will not give realistic probabilities. From the BDT lattice, we can compute the entire term structure at any node. If this lattice is used to simulate future interest rate paths, the scenarios so generated will not be realistic. The paths generated in this way may appear strange. This should not be surprising since the basic input probabilities were unrealistic. The no-arbitrage approach can furnish the current prices, but without some additional input it is incapable of providing realistic projections. This point is of relevance in many types of calculations in which the future distributions of particular assets or liabilities portfolios of assets (or liabilities) are required. Such situations would include solvency projections, asset-liability management, and value-at-risk calculations.

The importance of this distinction can also be illustrated using the Black-Scholes formula for a European call option. This formula appears throughout this book (see, for example, Sections 2.4.3 and 4.6). The call option price is given by (2.4.3). Remember that the integrals are based on the risk-neutral distribution for the underlying stock. The term $N(d_2)$ is the probability *under the risk-neutral density* that the call option will finish up in the money. This is not a realistic estimate of the true probability of this event. The actual probability that the call option will have a positive payoff when the option expires should be computed under realistic assumptions of the stock price's future distribution. We can make a related point about an American put option. This option can be exercised before maturity. To compute the "expected time until exercise," it would not be meaningful to use the risk-neutral distribution. Real-world probabilities should be used instead. In other words, the $P$ measure should be used, not the $Q$ measure.

# Section 4.4
# Models Based on a Representative Agent

The equilibrium approach can be used to derive the prices of the traded securities by solving for the prices and the optimal allocations that support this equilibrium. This will involve a very large set of equations because we need to satisfy simultaneously the first-order conditions for all the agents across all states. By making simplifying assumptions, we can take a shortcut to solving for the equilibrium prices and obtain the correct state prices by using the concept of a representative agent. We construct a much simpler parallel economy than the original economy and solve for the equilibrium prices in the new economy. The new economy is constructed so that it has the same equilibrium prices as the original economy. The key idea in the simplification is that there is only one agent in the parallel economy. The single agent is known as the representative agent. Under certain conditions, we can construct the representative agent's utility function from the utility functions of all the agents in the original economy. This agent is endowed with the aggregate endowment in each state. We then solve the simpler problem for the representative agent in the parallel economy and obtain the same prices that we would have obtained by solving a much more complicated problem involving all the agents. In this section, we describe the reasoning behind this approach and outline the main features of the solution procedure. We do not provide the details.[14]

We begin by discussing the construction of the representative agent's utility function. The following set of conditions are sufficient for this construction:

- Agents are assumed to have homogeneous probability beliefs.
- Agents have time-additive, state-independent, utility functions that are increasing concave and differentiable.
- The securities market is complete.

Under these assumptions, we can construct the utility function of the representative agent in terms of the utility functions of the individual agents. For the specific details of the construction, see Huang and Litzenberger [96, Chapter 5]. The weights assigned to the individual agents are related to their initial endowments. For now, we assume these weights correspond to the elements of a vector $\lambda = (\lambda_1, \ldots, \lambda_I)$. In fact, they are defined as follows:

$$\lambda_i = \frac{1}{\gamma_i}$$

---

[14]To do so would take us too far afield. The book by Huang and Litzenberger [96] describes the details of the representative agent model.

where the $\gamma_i$'s are as defined by (4.3.8). The representative agent's utility function is defined in terms of the individual agents' utility functions at time 0 and time 1 and the $\lambda$'s as follows:

$$v_0(x) = \max_{x_i > 0} \sum_{i=1}^{I} \lambda_i u_{i0}(x_i) \tag{4.4.1}$$

and

$$v_1(x) = \max_{x_i > 0} \sum_{i=1}^{I} \lambda_i u_{i1}(x_i) \tag{4.4.2}$$

where

$$x = \sum_{i=1}^{I} x_i.$$

With these definitions it can be shown that both $v_0(x)$ and $v_1(x)$ are strictly increasing, concave, and differentiable.

The representative agent is assumed to hold the aggregate endowment (which equals the aggregate consumption) in each state. The construction of the parallel economy is such that the state prices in the original economy are precisely equal to the corresponding state prices in the parallel economy. The state prices can be obtained more easily in the parallel economy from the first-order conditions of the representative agent. The representative agent's first-order conditions are satisfied when the agent holds the aggregate consumption in each state. This means that at the equilibrium state prices there is no incentive for the representative agent to trade.[15] The state prices are given by

$$\psi_\omega = p(\omega) \frac{v_1'\left(C_1^a(\omega)\right)}{v_0'\left(c_0^a\right)}. \tag{4.4.3}$$

In this equation, $c_0^a$ is the aggregate consumption at time 0, and $C_1^a(\omega)$ is the aggregate consumption at time 1 in state $\omega$. Note the similarity in structure with (4.3.4), which holds for all agents and all states in the original economy. We emphasize once more that, if we were to solve the full-scale equilibrium model in the original economy, the resulting equilibrium state prices also satisfy (4.4.3). In the original

---

[15] Of course, we should not take this too literally. There is no one for the agent to trade with, but the meaning is that at these prices the economy is in equilibrium.

economy, the equilibrium prices depend, in general, on the distribution of the initial endowments. If we change the initial endowments in the original economy, in general, we change the equilibrium allocations and the equilibrium prices.

The prices obtained in the parallel economy exhibit the same sensitivity to the distribution of initial endowments. In the parallel economy the equilibrium prices depend on the choice of $\lambda$, because the representative agent's utility function depends on the relative importance of the endowments of the individual agents through $\lambda$. Strictly speaking, we should signify that the representative agent's utility function depends on $\lambda$.

Under some conditions, the state prices obtained in a (complete) competitive securities market do not depend on the initial endowments. In these cases, we could rearrange the initial endowments and still observe the same prices. If this happens, we say that the economy has the *aggregation property*. The appropriate conditions can be expressed in terms of the properties of the individual agents' utility functions.

To state these conditions, we need to define a new concept: risk tolerance. Risk tolerance is the reciprocal of the absolute risk aversion. We denote it by $\tau(\cdot)$. Hence,

$$\tau(x) = -\frac{u'(x)}{u''(x)}.$$

If the risk tolerance is linear, it has the form

$$\tau(x) = a + bx. \tag{4.4.4}$$

We can readily verify that power utility functions and exponential utility functions have the property of linear risk tolerance. The coefficient $b$ in (4.4.4) is known as risk cautiousness. The sufficient conditions for aggregation can now be stated. The market exhibits the aggregation property if each agent in the economy has a utility function with linear risk tolerance, identical risk cautiousness, and the same rate of time preference. More complete details and proofs are available in Huang and Litzenberger [96]. If the aggregation property holds, the prices are independent of the initial endowments, and the calculation of the equilibrium prices is much simpler.

In summary, the introduction of a representative agent simplifies the computation of the prices of securities by solving a much simpler problem in a parallel economy. The derivations of many important pricing models in finance are based on the representative agent approach, for example, the Cox-Ingersoll-Ross [43] stochastic interest rate model. In the following two sections, we show how to derive two of the most important pricing models in modern finance using this framework: the capital-asset-pricing model and the Black-Scholes [16] option formula.

## Section 4.5
# Derivation of the Capital-Asset-Pricing Model

The representative agent approach provides a convenient method of deriving the capital-asset-pricing model (CAPM), a simple equilibrium pricing model. A powerful tool in both corporate and investment finance, CAPM gives us an intuitive way of representing the risk of a stock in terms of its "beta." The beta measures the risk of a stock in terms of its correlation with the market portfolio of all the assets in the economy.

Assume we have the required conditions for the existence of a representative agent. As we have seen, the Arrow-Debreu state prices can be expressed in terms of the marginal utility of this representative agent and the (assumed homogeneous) state probabilities. Consider security $j$, which pays an amount $X_j(\omega)$ at time 1 in state $\omega$. The current price of this security, $x_j$, is given by

$$x_j = \sum_\omega \psi_\omega X_j(\omega) = \sum_\omega p(\omega) \frac{v_1'[C_1^a(\omega)]}{v_0'(c_0^a)} X_j(\omega).$$

The first equation follows from the assumption of no arbitrage. The second follows from an application of (4.4.3). Hence, we can write the price in terms of an expectation over the $P$ measure:

$$x_j = E^P[ZX_j] \tag{4.5.1}$$

where $Z$ is the ratio of marginal utilities for the representative agent. We now express this in terms of returns. We denote the rate of return of security $j$ in state $\omega$ by $R_j(\omega)$, where

$$\frac{X_j(\omega)}{x_j} = 1 + R_j(\omega).$$

Dividing (4.5.1) by $x_j$, we obtain

$$1 = E[(1 + R_j)Z].$$

We can use the same procedure for the one-period bond. The corresponding result in this case is

$$1 = E[(1 + i_f)Z] = (1 + i_f)E[Z].$$

Using the properties of the expectation and the covariance operators, we find with some elementary algebra that

$$E[R_j] - i_f = -(1 + i_f)\text{Cov}(R_j, Z). \qquad (4.5.2)$$

The term on the left-hand side is the difference between the expected return on the security and the risk-free rate and is known as the risk premium. In principle, the risk premium can be either positive or negative.

Equation (4.5.2) relates the risk premium to a term involving the variable $Z$. Since $Z$ is not observable, this makes the formula difficult to apply. To remedy this, we introduce the market portfolio. In a one-period model, the aggregate consumption at time 1 is equal to the total wealth in the economy. For simplicity, we drop the superscripts on aggregate consumption and use $c_0$ and $C_1$ instead of $c_0^a$ and $C_1^a$. We define $R_m$, the rate of return on the market, by

$$1 + R_m(\omega) = \frac{C_1(\omega)}{c_0}. \qquad (4.5.3)$$

The rate of return on the market also satisfies an equation like (4.5.2), and hence

$$E[R_m] - i_f = -(1 + i_f)\text{Cov}(R_m, Z). \qquad (4.5.4)$$

Combining (4.5.2) and (4.5.4), we obtain

$$E[R_j] - i_f = \frac{\text{Cov}(R_j, Z)}{\text{Cov}(R_m, Z)} \left( E[R_m] - i_f \right). \qquad (4.5.5)$$

The ratio of the covariance terms can be simplified further if we make some additional assumptions. This can be done either by specifying the utility function or by making specific assumptions about the nature of the return distribution of the securities.

First, assume that the representative agent has a quadratic utility function. With this assumption, the random variable $Z$ can be written explicitly as

$$Z(\omega) = \frac{v_1'[C_1(\omega)]}{v_0'(c_0)} = \frac{b - C_1(\omega)}{b - c_0}.$$

With this substitution, we can simplify the covariance term as follows:

$$\begin{aligned}
\text{Cov}(R_j, Z) &= \text{Cov}\left( R_j, \frac{b - C_1}{b - c_0} \right) \\
&= \frac{-1}{b - c_0}\text{Cov}(R_j, C_1) \\
&= \frac{-c_0}{b - c_0}\text{Cov}(R_j, 1 + R_m) \\
&= \frac{-c_0}{b - c_0}\text{Cov}(R_j, R_m).
\end{aligned}$$

Using the same approach for the rate of return on the market portfolio, we find

$$\text{Cov}(R_m, Z) = \frac{-c_0}{b - c_0}\text{Var}(R_m).$$

Substituting the two expressions for the covariance into (4.5.5), we obtain

$$\text{E}[R_j] - i_f = \beta_j \left(\text{E}[R_m] - i_f\right) \tag{4.5.6}$$

where

$$\beta_j = \frac{\text{Cov}(R_j, R_m)}{\text{Var}(R_m)}.$$

This is the celebrated capital-asset-pricing model.

The CAPM relates the expected return on a security to the expected return on the market. The risk of the security is measured by beta, $\beta_j$. This risk is measured relative to the market portfolio. Note that the CAPM is an *ex ante* relationship in that it deals with expected returns. This model has found many useful applications in portfolio selection, investment modeling, and corporate finance. The CAPM is discussed further in Section 8.2.4. The book by Dumas and Alliaz [52] provides a critique of the model as well as a summary of empirical tests.

We can also derive the CAPM by assuming that the returns on all securities have a multivariate normal distribution. The return on the market portfolio, a linear combination of the returns on the individual securities, will also have a normal distribution for the market return $R_m$. A technical property of the normal distribution known as Stein's lemma is required.

**Lemma 4.5.1 (Stein's Lemma).** *If $X$ and $Y$ have a bivariate normal distribution and $g$ is differentiable, then*

$$\text{Cov}[g(X), Y] = \text{Cov}(X, Y)\,\text{E}[g'(X)].$$

**Proof.** *Recall that* $\text{Cov}[g(X), Y] = \text{E}_X\left[\text{E}_Y[(g(X) - \text{E}[g(X)])(Y - \text{E}[Y])|X]\right]$. *Apply integration by parts to confirm the lemma.*

We start as before from (4.5.5), and we use Stein's lemma to evaluate the covariance terms as follows:

$$\frac{\text{Cov}(R_j, Z)}{\text{Cov}(R_m, Z)} = \frac{\text{Cov}[R_j, v_1'(C_1)/v_0'(c_0)]}{\text{Cov}[R_m, v_1'(C_1)/v_0'(c_0)]}.$$

The right-hand side can be written as

$$\frac{\text{Cov}[R_j, v_1'(C_1)]}{\text{Cov}[R_m, v_1'(C_1)]}.$$

We can express $C_1$ in terms of $R_m$ from (4.5.3) to rewrite the last term as

$$\frac{\text{Cov}[R_j, v_1'(c_0(1 + R_m))]}{\text{Cov}[R_m, v_1'(c_0(1 + R_m))]}.$$

Now apply Stein's lemma to both covariance terms in the last ratio to obtain

$$\frac{\text{E}[v_1''(c_0(1 + R_m))]}{\text{E}[v_1''(c_0(1 + R_m))]} \frac{\text{Cov}(R_j, R_m)}{\text{Cov}(R_m, R_m)} = \frac{\text{Cov}(R_j, R_m)}{\text{Var}(R_m)}.$$

If we substitute this expression into (4.5.5), we obtain the same CAPM equation as before.

A great attraction of the CAPM is its simplicity. It relates the risk premium on a security to the product of the security's beta and the risk premium on the market portfolio. Note that the inputs to the CAPM are the expected returns on the security and in the market as well as the simple covariance and variance terms.

# Section 4.6
# The Black-Scholes Option Formula

In this section, we illustrate an application of the equilibrium approach to the valuation of derivative securities. We assume the existence of a representative agent. Given assumptions about the joint distribution of security payoffs and aggregate consumption, we can derive valuation formulas for the prices. To obtain solutions, we make explicit assumptions about the utility functions and the underlying distributions.

Under one set of assumptions, we can derive the important Black-Scholes pricing formula. To do this, we assume that the representative agent has a power utility function and that the stock price and aggregate consumption have a bivariate lognormal distribution. This derivation of the Black-Scholes formula in an equilibrium setting was first obtained by Rubinstein [165]. In this section, we use a more streamlined derivation.

We use the notation of the previous section. The representative agent's utility function is

$$v(c_0, C_1) = v_0(c_0) + v_1(C_1).$$

Under this representation the time-0 equilibrium price of a security that pays $S(\omega)$ in state $\omega$ is

$$s_0 = \frac{E^P[v_1'(C_1)S]}{v_0'(c_0)}. \tag{4.6.1}$$

The superscript $P$ indicates we are computing expectations using the $P$ measure, the physical measure. The price of a certain payment of 1 unit at time 1 is

$$e^{-r} = \frac{1}{1+i_f} = \frac{E^P[v_1'(C_1)]}{v_0'(c_0)} \tag{4.6.2}$$

where $r$ is the continuously compounded rate of interest. We can combine the last two equations to obtain the following valuation equation for $s_0$:

$$s_0 = \frac{1}{1+i_f} \frac{E^P[v_1'(C_1)S]}{E^P[v_1'(C_1)]}. \tag{4.6.3}$$

Now let us consider a derivative security whose time-1 payoff is given by $f(S(\omega))$. Then, by the same logic, we see that the current price $V(s_0, 0)$ of the derivative is

$$V(s_0, 0) = \frac{1}{1+i_f} \frac{E^P[v_1'(C_1)f(S)]}{E^P[v_1'(C_1)]}. \tag{4.6.4}$$

If we define $q(\omega)$ by

$$q(\omega) = \frac{p(\omega)v_1'(C_1)}{E^P[v_1'(C_1)]}$$

we see that the $q$'s are each strictly positive and that they sum to 1. Hence, they can be used to construct the probability measure that we call the $Q$ measure. The valuation equation for the price of the derivative security has the following compact expression in terms of the $Q$ measure:

$$V(s_0, 0) = e^{-r}E^Q[f(S)].$$

We now specify the explicit functional form of the utility function. We assume the representative agent's time-1 utility function is a power utility function with positive parameter $\alpha$ so that

$$v_1(C_1) = \frac{C_1^\alpha}{\alpha},$$

and we define a new random variable $Y$ by

$$e^Y = C_1^{\alpha-1}. \tag{4.6.5}$$

Making this substitution, we obtain

$$E^Q[f(S)] = \frac{E^P[e^Y f(S)]}{E^P[e^Y]}. \tag{4.6.6}$$

This equation shows that the expectation of the payoff under the $Q$ measure is proportional to the expectation of an adjusted payoff under the $P$ measure. It is now convenient to define $X$ by

$$S = s_0 e^X. \tag{4.6.7}$$

We see that $X$ corresponds to the continuously compounded rate of return on the security $s$. Now we assume that the joint distribution of $X$ and $Y$ is bivariate normal with moment generating function

$$M^P(t_1, t_2) = E^P[e^{t_1 X + t_2 Y}]$$

$$= \exp\left[\mu_1 t_1 + \mu_2 t_2 + \frac{1}{2}(\sigma_1^2 t_1^2 + \sigma_2^2 t_2^2 + 2\rho\sigma_1\sigma_2 t_1 t_2)\right]$$

where $\mu_1$ is the expected value of $X$, $\mu_2$ is the expected value of $Y$, $\sigma_1^2$ is the variance of $X$, $\sigma_2^2$ is the variance of $Y$, and $\rho$ is the correlation coefficient between $X$ and $Y$.

For subsequent analysis, it is convenient to have the explicit form of the moment generating function (mgf) of $X$ under the $Q$ measure, which we denote by $M^Q(t)$. We now show that this mgf can be expressed in terms of the mgf of the bivariate distribution under the $P$ measure:

$$M^Q(t) = E^Q[e^{tX}]$$

$$= \frac{E^P[e^{tX+Y}]}{E^P[e^Y]}$$

$$= \frac{M^P(t, 1)}{M^P(0, 1)}.$$

Thus, for the bivariate normal distributions $(X, Y)$ and the power utility, there is a simple expression for the mgf of $X$ under the $Q$ measure in terms of the mgf of the bivariate distribution under the $P$ measure. We substitute the explicit expressions for the bivariate mgf in the last expression to obtain

$$E^Q[e^{tX}] = \exp\left[(\mu_1 + \rho\sigma_1\sigma_2)t + \frac{1}{2}\sigma_1^2 t\right].$$  (4.6.8)

This shows that under the $Q$ measure the random variable $X$ is still normal with modified mean $\mu_Q$ where

$$\mu_Q = \mu_1 + \rho\sigma_1\sigma_2$$  (4.6.9)

and the variance $\sigma_1^2$ is unchanged. There is a consistency requirement that we can use to eliminate $\mu_Q$. This stems from the valuation equation for $S$ under the $Q$ measure. Recall that

$$s_0 = \frac{1}{1+i_f} E^Q[S]$$

$$= e^{-r} E^Q[S]$$

$$= s_0 e^{-r} E^Q[e^X]$$

$$= s_0 e^{-r} \exp\left(\mu_Q + \frac{1}{2}\sigma_1^2\right).$$

It follows that

$$\mu_Q = r - \frac{1}{2}\sigma_1^2.$$  (4.6.10)

Armed with this result, we can now price a derivative security such as a European call option. In this case, the payoff at time 1 is the maximum of $S - K$ and 0 so that

$$f(S) = [S - K]^+.$$

Hence, the current price of the call option is

$$V(s_0, 0) = \frac{1}{1+i_f} E^Q[(S - K)^+]$$

$$= e^{-r} E^Q[(s_0 e^X - K)^+]$$  (4.6.11)

where $X$ is a normal random variable. At this stage, it is convenient to drop the subscript on the variance of $X$ so that its distribution has the following parameters:

$$\text{Expected value} = r - \frac{1}{2}\sigma^2, \qquad \text{Variance} = \sigma^2.$$

The expectation in (4.6.11) can be written as an integral, which is evaluated in Example 10.6.1 with an appropriate change of the timescale. The result is

$$V(s_0, 0) = s_0 N(d_1) - K e^{-r} N(d_1 - \sigma) \tag{4.6.12}$$

where

$$d_1 = \frac{\log(s_0/K) + \left(r + \frac{1}{2}\sigma^2\right)}{\sigma}.$$

This is the well-known Black-Scholes formula for the price of a European call option. The derivation presented here is based on an equilibrium approach. The key assumptions are that the representative agent has a power utility function and that the security payoff $S$ and aggregate consumption $C_1$ have a bivariate lognormal distribution.[16]

Notice how the use of the basic valuation (4.6.6) for both the underlying asset and for the risk-free bond permitted us to eliminate the mean and variance of aggregate consumption as well as the expected return on the asset and the correlation coefficient. These transformations ultimately led us to the Black-Scholes formula, which depends on the risk-free interest rate. So, although the initial valuation equation started in terms of the $P$ measure, the ultimate formula ends up in terms of the $Q$ measure.

# Section 4.7
# Multiperiod Models of Security Markets

In this section, we consider equilibrium pricing when there are several periods. The key intuitions that were developed for the single-period case carry through to this case as well. Agents jointly determine equilibrium prices through their individual optimizing decisions. Equilibrium prices can be related to the other parameters of the economy such as individual beliefs and preferences. We can construct a representative

---

[16] Recall that we assumed that $X$ and $Y$ have bivariate normal distribution. By taking logarithms of (4.6.5) and (4.6.7), we have

$$\log(S) = X + \log(s_0) = X_1,$$

$$\log(C_1) = \frac{Y}{\alpha - 1} = Y_1.$$

Because $X$ and $Y$ have a bivariate normal distribution, $X_1$ and $Y_1$ also have a bivariate normal distribution. Hence $\log(S)$ and $\log(C_1)$ have a bivariate normal distribution. This means that $S$ and $C_1$ have a "bivariate lognormal distribution."

agent under the same assumptions as before. A security's price can be written as an expectation using nature's measure; it can also be written as an expectation using the risk-neutral measure.

The resolution of uncertainty in a multiperiod world can be posited in terms of an event tree or information structure. The framework here is similar to that introduced in Section 3.7. There is a finite discrete-time security market. The market is frictionless, and trading takes place only at times $0, 1, 2, \ldots, T$. We provide a more detailed description of how uncertainty is resolved over time in this model in Chapter 5. To give an idea of how this works, we consider a two-period example of an information tree in Figure 4.2.

FIGURE **4.2** │ *Event Tree for Two-Period Model*

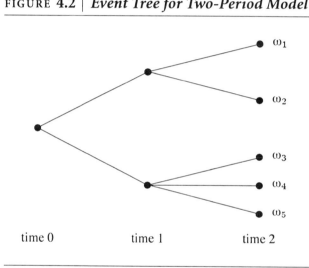

time 0             time 1             time 2

Note that at time 0, we know that the possible states of the economy are $\{\omega_1, \omega_2, \omega_3, \omega_4, \omega_5\}$. At time 1 in the top node the economy has two possible states $\{\omega_1, \omega_2\}$ and in the bottom node $\{\omega_3, \omega_4, \omega_5\}$. As time passes, uncertainty is resolved.

However, some new features of the multiperiod models are not present in the single-period model. In the one-period case, we had a single market at time 0. In the multiperiod case, we have the possibility of trading at future times at different nodes in the event tree. In order to make appropriate investment decisions at time 0, agents need to make conjectures about the prices that will be obtained at future times. It is easier to deal with situations in which these conjectures are consistent across all agents in the economy. This notion of consistency can be given a more precise meaning, as we see below.

Another novel feature of a multiperiod market is market completeness,[17] which can be thought of as follows. A market is said to be complete if every consumption pattern is attainable by an agent with arbitrary initial endowment. One way to obtain market completeness in a multiperiod model is to have enough independent securities. Another way is to have fewer securities but use the flexibility given by trading to adjust the positions. An agent can use the extra degrees of freedom to give a richer set of consumption opportunities. Thus, it is possible to have a smaller number of securities than the number of states and still have a complete market.

We assume a $T$-period model, and each agent has a time-additive utility function of the form

$$u(c_0, c_1, \ldots, c_T) = u_0(c_0) + u_1(c_1) + \cdots + u_T(c_T). \qquad (4.7.1)$$

The utility functions and the consumption amounts should be subscripted to denote the individual agents. To simplify the notation, we have not put in the subscripts here, and we assume all agents have homogeneous beliefs. Consider a generic security $j$ that pays dividends at the end of each time period.[18] Its *ex dividend* price at time $t$ and in state $\omega$ is $X_j(t, \omega)$, and it pays a dividend of $D_j(t, \omega)$ at time $t$ and state $\omega$. At time $T$, the security pays a liquidating dividend of $D_j(T, \omega)$, and it is then worth zero. We assume that all agents agree on the dividend process $D_j(t, \omega)$. In the equilibrium framework we consider, all agents also conjecture the same future prices for $x_j(t, \omega)$ at each future time and state. If the economy happens to reach this state, these conjectured prices will be realized. This type of equilibrium is known as a rational expectations equilibrium.

As in the one-period model, it is convenient to use the representative agent approach. Under the same conditions as for the single-period case, we can construct a utility function for the representative agent:

$$v(c_0, c_1, \ldots, c_T) = v_0(c_0) + v_1(c_1) + \cdots + v(c_T). \qquad (4.7.2)$$

The representative agent consumes the aggregate endowment in each period, and the equilibrium prices are such that the representative agent is content with this endowment. As such, the agent has no incentive to trade, and this is a determining feature of the equilibrium prices. We can obtain an explicit representation of the price of security $j$ in terms of its future dividends and the intertemporal marginal rate

---

[17]This is discussed more fully in Chapter 5.
[18]We adopt a minimalist approach to notation here because notation in the multiperiod case can be overwhelming.

of substitution (IMRS)[19] of the representative agent using the same approach as in Section 4.3. We exploit the fact that the representative agent has no incentive to trade at time $t$. The argument is similar to that leading to (4.3.2). If the agent purchases a fraction $\alpha$ of security $j$, then the agent's expected utility becomes

$$E^P \left[ v_t(c_t - \alpha x_j(t)) + \sum_{s=t+1}^{T} v_s(C_s + \alpha D_j(s)) \right].$$

Differentiating this expression with respect to $\alpha$, we obtain

$$-x_j(t)v_t'(c_t - \alpha x_j(t)) + E^P \left[ \sum_{s=t+1}^{T} v_s'(C_s + \alpha D_j(s)) D_j(s) \right].$$

This expression must vanish when $\alpha = 0$, which gives us

$$x_j(t) = E^P \left[ \sum_{s=t+1}^{T} \frac{v_s'(C_s)}{v_t'(c_t)} D_j(s) \right]. \tag{4.7.3}$$

This is the fundamental valuation equation. It expresses the current price as the expected value of future dividends, where the dividends are adjusted by the pricing kernel. The probability measure $P$ is nature's measure. The expectation on the right-hand side is conditional on the information available at time $t$.

This equation can be used to derive a recursive valuation formula that relates the current price to the expected value of the security at the end of the next period. We split the summation in (4.7.3) into two parts: the first corresponds to time $t+1$, and the second is the rest of the terms. Using the law of iterated expectations, we can express the second term in terms of $X_j(t+1)$. After some manipulations we obtain

$$x_j(t) = E^P \left[ \frac{v_{t+1}'(C_{t+1})}{v_t'(c_t)} (X_j(t+1) + D_j(t+1)) \right]. \tag{4.7.4}$$

This formula expresses the current asset price in terms of the expected value of the next period's price plus the next period's dividends adjusted by the $Z$ factor:

$$x_j(t) = E^P[Z(t+1)(X_j(t+1) + D_j(t+1))]. \tag{4.7.5}$$

---

[19]The ratio of the marginal utility at time $s$ to the marginal utility at some earlier time $t$ is known as the intertemporal marginal rate of substitution over the time period $(t, s)$.

These equilibrium pricing formulas should be contrasted with the corresponding valuation formulas in Chapter 5. In both cases, the current price of the security is equal to an expectation involving the future cash flows on the security. The formulas in this chapter are derived from an equilibrium model with a representative agent, and the expected values are taken with respect to the real-world probabilities (the $P$ measure). The formulas in Chapter 5 are derived from the no-arbitrage principle, and the expectations are taken with respect the risk-neutral measure (the $Q$ measure).

## Section 4.8
## Exercises

### Exercise 4.1
Show, using the no-arbitrage conditions, that $\theta \geq 1$ in (4.2.11) and that $\theta$ tends to 1 as $m$ tends to $i_f$.

### Exercise 4.2
Derive (4.3.1). Hint: Maximize the agent's expected utility over the decision variables $c_0$ and $c_1$ subject to the wealth constraint.

### Exercise 4.3
Derive (4.5.2).

### Exercise 4.4
Prove Stein's lemma, Lemma 4.5.1.

### Exercise 4.5
Show that if we substitute $i_u$, $i_d$, $i_f$, and $p$ as functions of $h$ into the expression for $x^*$ in (4.2.11) and take the limit as $h$ tends to zero, then we obtain (4.2.12).

### Exercise 4.6 (Exponential Utility, Normal Consumption)
Suppose that the representative agent has an exponential utility function and that the joint distribution of security, $S$, and aggregate consumption is bivariate normal. Show

using the approach of this section that the time-0 price of the European call option on this security is

$$V(s_0, 0) = (s_0 - Ke^{-r})N\left(\frac{s_0 e^r - K}{\sigma}\right) + e^{-r}\sigma N\left(\frac{K - s_0 e^r}{\sigma}\right).$$

## Exercise 4.7 (DARA Utility)

An individual's utility function displays *decreasing absolute risk aversion* when $R_A(\cdot)$ is a strictly decreasing function. Show that if an individual's utility function displays decreasing absolute risk aversion, then the third derivative of the individual's utility function must be positive. (Assume $u' > 0$ and $u'' < 0$.)

## Exercise 4.8 (IARA Utility)

An individual's utility function displays *increasing absolute risk aversion* when $R_A(\cdot)$ is a strictly increasing function. Construct a concave utility function with positive first and third derivatives that displays increasing absolute risk aversion.

## Exercise 4.9 (Insurance under DARA)

An individual has a utility function that is strictly increasing, strictly concave, and differentiable. At time 0, the individual owns two assets. One is subject to a fire hazard and is worth $H$. The other asset is indestructible and is worth $W_0$. The individual's subjective probability that there will be a fire is $p$. If there is a fire, the perishable asset is destroyed. Thus, at time 1, the individual's wealth will be $W_0$ with probability $p$ and $W_0 + H$ with probability $(1 - p)$. The individual can obtain full insurance by paying a premium $\pi$. Show that if the individual's utility function displays decreasing absolute risk aversion, the maximum acceptable insurance premium the individual is willing to pay decreases as $W_0$ increases. (Note that we do not include interest rates here to keep things simple.)

## Exercise 4.10 (DARA Utility)

An individual has a utility function that is strictly increasing, strictly concave, and differentiable. Assume there are just two available assets: a risky asset and a riskless asset. The individual has total initial wealth of $W_0$, which can be allocated between the two assets. Let $x$ be the optimal investment in the risky asset. Show that if the individual's utility function displays decreasing absolute risk aversion, $x$ increases as $W_0$ increases. In this case the risky asset is said to be a *normal good*. You purchase more of a normal good as your wealth increases.

## Exercise 4.11 (Exponential Utility)

An investor has exponential utility and initial wealth of $W_0$. There are two assets in the economy, and we are in a one-period model. The riskless asset has a rate of return of $r$. The risky asset has a normal distribution with an expected rate of return of $\mu$ and a variance of $\sigma^2$. Determine the optimal investments in the two assets.

## Exercise 4.12 (Representative Agent's Utility)

Show that the representative agent's utility function as defined by (4.4.1) and (4.4.2) is strictly increasing, concave, and differentiable. Given the construction of the representative agent's utility function, show that the state prices obtained from (4.4.3) correspond to the equilibrium state prices in the original economy.

## Exercise 4.13

Assume a one-period model. The aggregate consumption at time 0 is 8 units. There are three states at time 1, $\{\omega_1, \omega_2, \omega_3\}$. All agents have homogeneous beliefs, and the probability of each state is $1/3$. (This is the $P$ measure.) The aggregate consumption in these states is

$$C(\omega_1) = 64, \qquad C(\omega_2) = 27, \qquad C(\omega_3) = 125. \qquad (4.8.1)$$

The representative agent's utility function is of the form

$$v(c_0, C_1) = c_0^{1/3} + C_1^{1/3}. \qquad (4.8.2)$$

Suppose the three Arrow-Debreu securities are traded in this model. Compute the prices of these three securities. A traded asset exists that pays 1% of aggregate consumption at time 1 in each state. Find the price of this asset at time 0. Traded call and put options on this asset have the same strike price $K$. You are told that the call price is equal to the put price. Find $K$.

Compute the one-period riskless interest rate in this model. Can you give any suggestions as to why the riskless rate is so high in this example? Show that it is possible to construct a model in which the riskless rate is negative. What is the main feature of the model that would result in a negative riskless rate?

## Exercise 4.14

Assume a one-period model with a representative agent. Let $r$ be the continuous compounded interest rate. Use whatever approximations and assumptions necessary to obtain the following two different expressions for $r$:

> $r = -$ (expected rate of return in the marginal utility of aggregate wealth)
>
> $r = -$ (expected rate of return on aggregate wealth)
>
> $\quad + $ (covariance of the rate of return on aggregate wealth with
>
> $\qquad$ the rate of change in the marginal utility of wealth).

### Exercise 4.15

Suppose we have a multiperiod discrete-time model. A representative agent maximizes the expected utility of consumption. The utility function is of the form

$$v_0(c_0) + v_1(c_1) + \cdots + v_T(c_T). \tag{4.8.3}$$

Security $j$ has price $x_j(t)$ at time $t$ and pays a dividend of $D_j(s)$ at time $s$. Show that $x_j(t)$ can be written as

$$x_j(t) = \mathrm{E}\left[\sum_{s=t+1}^{T} \frac{v_s'(C_s)}{v_t'(C_t)} D_j(s)\right]. \tag{4.8.4}$$

We let $G_t$ denote the marginal rate of substitution of the representative agent from time $t-1$ to time $t$. Let $P(t, t+n)$ denote the value at time $t$ of the pure discount bond that pays 1 unit at time $t+n$. Show that

$$P(t, t+n) = \mathrm{E}\left[\Pi_{j=t+1}^{t+n} G_j\right]. \tag{4.8.5}$$

### Exercise 4.16

(Continuation of Exercise 4.15) We make three additional assumptions. First, we assume there is only one source of risk in the model. Second, we let $Y_t = \log G_t$ where the $\{Y_t\}$ have a multivariate normal distribution. Third, we assume that $Y_t$ obeys the following first-order autoregressive process

$$Y_t - \mu = \theta(Y_{t-1} - \mu) + \varepsilon_t \tag{4.8.6}$$

where $\mu = \mathrm{E}[Y_t]$, $\theta$ is a constant and the $\{\varepsilon_t\}$ are multivariate normal with

$$\mathrm{E}[\varepsilon_t] = 0, \quad \mathrm{Var}(\varepsilon_t) = \sigma_\varepsilon^2, \quad \text{and} \quad \mathrm{Cov}(\varepsilon_t, \varepsilon_s) = 0, \quad t \neq s. \tag{4.8.7}$$

With these assumptions show that the price of the pure discount bond may be written as

$$P(t, t+n) = \frac{P(0, t+n)}{P(0, t)} e^{\alpha_t + \beta_t} \tag{4.8.8}$$

where

$$\alpha_t = \sum_{j=1}^{t} \left[ \frac{g(t-j)^2 - g(t+m-j)^2}{2} \right] \sigma_j^2,$$

$$\beta_t = \theta g(n-1) \sum_{j=1}^{t} \theta^{t-j} \varepsilon_j,$$

$$g(k) = \sum_{j=0}^{k} \theta^j.$$

(The last two examples are based on a paper by Turnbull and Milne [198].)

# CHAPTER 5
## NO-ARBITRAGE PRICING THEORY

## Section 5.1
## Introduction

In this chapter, we study the fundamental concept of arbitrage and examine its implications for the pricing of cash-flow streams. Only the finite discrete-time and discrete-state theory is considered. A more advanced treatment of the topics in this chapter is given in Chapter 11.

The main result of this chapter, given in various versions, is the *Fundamental Theorem of Asset Pricing*, which says that "absence of arbitrage is equivalent to the existence of a strictly positive linear pricing rule." Separating hyperplane arguments underlie this result.

With some effort, all the results of this chapter can be expressed (and proved) without using probability concepts. However, employing probability has the advantages of (1) significantly shortening the proofs, (2) introducing concepts that are intuitively appealing, and (3) preparing you for the continuous-time case, where probability cannot be avoided. Relevant probabilistic concepts are introduced as needed.

## Section 5.2
## Single-Period Model

### SECTION 5.2.1 | DESCRIPTION OF THE MODEL

We begin with a finite number $N$ of securities or assets $S_1, S_2, \ldots, S_N$. In this section we consider only their values at times 0 and 1. At time 0, the investors know the time-0 values, but the time-1 values are random variables. These random variables are defined with respect to a sample space $\Omega = \{\omega_1, \omega_2, \ldots, \omega_M\}$ consisting of a finite number $M$ of "states of nature" or possible outcomes. At time 0, the investors know the list of these possible outcomes, but they do not know until time 1 which one will occur. There is also a probability measure $P$ satisfying $P(\omega) > 0, \omega \in \Omega$, although this will play a minor role throughout this section.

The price or value of security $j$, in state of nature $\omega$, at time $k$, is denoted as $S_j(k, \omega)$. We assume that these values are always nonnegative; in other words, they are *limited liability securities*, because their owner's financial liability is limited to the price paid for the security. Although we use the symbol $S$, these assets need not be stocks. They could be bonds, call options, or any of the other traded securities discussed in Chapter 2.

The time-0 prices of the securities are assumed to be strictly positive. Since $S_j(0, \omega)$ is the same for all $\omega \in \Omega$, we simply denote this common value as $S_j(0)$ and consider the row vector

$$S(0) = [S_1(0) \quad S_2(0) \quad \cdots \quad S_N(0)].$$

Meanwhile, it is convenient to organize the time-1 prices as the matrix

$$S(1, \Omega) = \begin{bmatrix} S_1(1, \omega_1) & S_2(1, \omega_1) & \cdots & S_N(1, \omega_1) \\ S_1(1, \omega_2) & S_2(1, \omega_2) & \cdots & S_N(1, \omega_2) \\ \vdots & \vdots & \vdots & \vdots \\ S_1(1, \omega_M) & S_2(1, \omega_M) & \cdots & S_N(1, \omega_M) \end{bmatrix}. \quad (5.2.1)$$

The evolution of the market in the model is illustrated in Figure 5.1.

Investors select a portfolio of the assets at time 0. The number of units of asset $j$ held from time 0 to time 1 is denoted by the numbers $\theta_j, \ j = 1, 2, \ldots, N$. If $\theta_j$ is positive, $\theta_j$ units of security $j$ are purchased. If $\theta_j$ is negative, $|\theta_j|$ units of security $j$ are sold short. We sometimes refer to the column vector

$$\theta = \begin{bmatrix} \theta_1 \\ \theta_2 \\ \vdots \\ \theta_N \end{bmatrix} \quad (5.2.2)$$

as a *trading strategy*. Then the value of the corresponding portfolio at time 0 is

$$S(0)\theta = \theta_1 S_1(0) + \theta_2 S_2(0) + \cdots + \theta_N S_N(0). \quad (5.2.3)$$

FIGURE **5.1** | *Evolution of the Market*

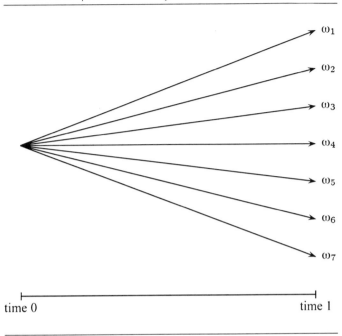

The time-1 value of this same portfolio will depend upon the state of nature. If state $\omega_j$ occurs, then the time-1 value is

$$\theta_1 S_1(1, \omega_j) + \theta_2 S_2(1, \omega_j) + \cdots + \theta_N S_N(1, \omega_j),$$

which is the $j$-th component of the column vector

$$S(1, \Omega)\theta = \begin{bmatrix} \theta_1 S_1(1, \omega_1) + \theta_2 S_2(1, \omega_1) + \cdots + \theta_N S_N(1, \omega_1) \\ \theta_1 S_1(1, \omega_2) + \theta_2 S_2(1, \omega_2) + \cdots + \theta_N S_N(1, \omega_2) \\ \vdots \\ \theta_1 S_1(1, \omega_M) + \theta_2 S_2(1, \omega_M) + \cdots + \theta_N S_N(1, \omega_M) \end{bmatrix}. \qquad (5.2.4)$$

Thus, from the time-0 perspective of the investors, the time-1 value of the portfolio corresponding to the trading strategy $\theta$ is the random variable whose outcomes are the components of the vector $S(1, \Omega)\theta$. Examples of single-period security models are found in Subsections 5.2.2 and 5.2.6.

Sometimes it is useful to designate security 1 as the *bank account* and stipulate that it is of the form

$$S_1(0) = 1 \quad \text{and} \quad S_1(1, \omega) = 1 + i, \quad \text{for all } \omega \in \Omega,$$

where the nonnegative number $i$ is interpreted as the *one-period interest rate* or the *short rate*. Here $S_1(1, \omega)$ is constant with respect to $\omega$, because in this case the short rate $i$ is fully known to the investors at time 0.

Subject to the assumptions that there are only one period and a finite number of states of nature, is this model reasonable from the economic point of view? Not necessarily, for in the next subsection we will see that arbitrage opportunities can exist.

## SECTION 5.2.2 │ ARBITRAGE AND THE FUNDAMENTAL THEOREM OF ASSET PRICING

Arbitrage is generally defined as "the simultaneous purchase and sale of the same securities, commodities, or foreign exchange in different markets to profit from unequal prices." Our definition of arbitrage expresses this idea mathematically.

*Definition 5.2.1. An **arbitrage opportunity** is a trading strategy $\theta$ such that* [1]

$$S(0)\theta \leq 0 \qquad and \qquad S(1, \Omega)\theta > \mathbf{0}. \tag{5.2.5}$$

*We say that a securities market model is **arbitrage free** if there are no arbitrage opportunities.*

Intuitively, a model admits an arbitrage opportunity if an investor can select a portfolio that costs nothing now, pays something to the investor at the end of the period in at least one state of nature, but never ends up with the investor having an obligation to pay.

Clearly arbitrage opportunities are unreasonable from an economic standpoint, for investors seeing them in the real world would probably want to establish such large positions that the prices would be affected in such a way that the arbitrage opportunities would be quickly eliminated. In other words, if investors were to find a trading strategy that started with no money and, without any risk of losing money, had the potential of a positive return, then their buy and sell orders, together with the principle of supply and demand, would cause the market prices to change quickly and the arbitrage opportunity to disappear. Thus, for our single-period model to

---

[1]Notation and inequalities for vectors: Let $x, y \in \Re^n$ denote $n$-dimensional vectors with $x_i$ and $y_i$ being the $i$-th component of $x$ and $y$. If $x_i \geq 0$, $i = 1, 2, \ldots, n$ we write $x \geq \mathbf{0}$ and say that $x$ is nonnegative. If $x$ is *nonnegative* and $x_i > 0$ for some $i$, we write $x > \mathbf{0}$ and say that $x$ is *positive*. If $x$ is positive and $x_i > 0$ for all $i$, we write $x \gg \mathbf{0}$ and say that $x$ is *strictly positive*. We write $x \geq y$ if $x - y \geq \mathbf{0}$, $x > y$ if $x - y > \mathbf{0}$, and $x \gg y$ if $x - y \gg \mathbf{0}$. Corresponding definitions are made for inequalities $\leq$, $<$, and $\ll$. We also define $\Re_+^n = \{x \in \Re^n \mid x \geq \mathbf{0}\}$ and $\Re_{++}^n = \{x \in \Re^n \mid x \gg \mathbf{0}\}$.

have a measure of economic realism, it is necessary to assume that it is arbitrage free.

**Example 5.2.1.** Suppose $M = N = 2$, $S(0) = [1 \ 1]$, and

$$S(1, \Omega) = \begin{bmatrix} 1+i & u \\ 1+i & d \end{bmatrix},$$

where $u$ and $d$ are numbers such that $d < 1 < u$. Thus, $S_1$ represents a bank account with short interest rate $i \geq 0$, whereas $S_2$ represents a stock whose final value is either $u$ ("up") or $d$ ("down"). Consider whether the trading strategy $\theta = [\theta_1 \ \theta_2]^T$ is an arbitrage opportunity. First, we must have $S(0)\theta \leq 0$, that is,

$$\theta_1 + \theta_2 \leq 0. \qquad \qquad (1)$$

Second, we must have $S(1, \Omega)\theta \geq 0$, that is,

$$(1+i)\theta_1 + u\theta_2 \geq 0 \qquad \text{and} \qquad (1+i)\theta_1 + d\theta_2 \geq 0.$$

Finally, to have $S(1, \Omega)\theta > 0$, at least one of these last two inequalities must be strictly positive.

If $\theta_2 \geq 0$ and these three inequalities all hold, then since $1 + i > d$, it follows that $\theta_1 \leq 0$ and

$$d\theta_2 \geq -(1+i)\theta_1 \geq -d\theta_1 \geq d\theta_2.$$

This means that $\theta_1 = \theta_2 = 0$. Hence, $\theta$ cannot be an arbitrage opportunity.

On the other hand, if $\theta_2 < 0$ and all three inequalities hold, then $\theta_1 > 0$ and

$$(1+i)\theta_1 \geq -u\theta_2 \geq u\theta_1.$$

This implies $1 + i \geq u$. Moreover, since $-u\theta_2 > -d\theta_2$, it follows that the third inequality is strict, which means $\theta$ is actually an arbitrage opportunity.

Conversely, suppose $1+i \geq u$. Then choose $\theta_1 = 1$ and $\theta_2 = -(1+i)/u \leq -1$ so that the first two inequalities will hold. Since $u > d$, the third inequality will hold in a strict fashion, and thus $\theta$ will be an arbitrage opportunity.

In summary, an arbitrage opportunity exists for this model if and only if $1 + i \geq u$, that is, if and only if the bank account's return is certain to be at least as great as the stock's return. ∎

**Example 5.2.2.** Suppose in Example 5.2.1, a stock with price 1.00 increases to 1.20 or decrease to 0.80 after one period. If the one-period rate of interest is 10%, then an investment of 1.00 in the bank account and 1.00 in the stock has current price $S(0) = [1.00 \ 1.00]$ and

$$S(1, \Omega) = \begin{bmatrix} 1.10 & 1.20 \\ 1.10 & 0.80 \end{bmatrix}.$$ ∎

As seen in the preceding examples, the existence of arbitrage opportunities for the single-period model depends on some algebraic calculations. Not surprisingly, these calculations can be organized into a concise, algebraic statement. What is surprising, however, is that, as explained in Subsection 5.2.4, the resulting statement has enormous implications for financial theory and practice. The following theorem is often called the *fundamental theorem of asset pricing* because it says that the absence of arbitrage is equivalent to the existence of a state price vector that prices all traded assets.

**Definition 5.2.2.** *A **state price vector** $\psi$ is a strictly positive row vector $[\psi(\omega_1), \psi(\omega_2), \ldots, \psi(\omega_M)]$ for which*

$$S(0) = \psi S(1, \Omega). \tag{5.2.6}$$

*Equivalently, $\psi$ is a random variable for which*

$$S_j(0) = \sum_{\omega \in \Omega} \psi(\omega) S_j(1, \omega), \quad j = 1, \ldots, N.$$

A state price vector expresses the current prices of traded assets as a positive linear combination of their uncertain cash flows at time 1. If there are fewer than $M$ assets with linearly independent payoff vectors at time 1, then $S(1, \Omega)$ is not of full rank. Hence, more than one solution of (5.2.6) may exist.

Before presenting the theorem, we should mention that the proof involves securities that pay one unit in one state of nature and nothing in all others. These are called *Arrow-Debreu securities* and were discussed in Chapter 4. For $m = 1, 2, \ldots, M$, the Arrow-Debreu security for outcome $\omega_m$ is a security that at time 1 pays 1 if outcome $\omega_m$ occurs, and 0 otherwise. In other words, the Arrow-Debreu security for outcome $\omega_m$ has payoff vector $e_m = [0, \ldots, 0, 1, 0, \ldots, 0]^T$ with the "1" in the $m$-th position.

Given an arbitrary Arrow-Debreu security with payoff vector $e_m$ at time 1, consider whether a trading strategy $\theta$ exists such that $S(1, \Omega)\theta = e_m$. If so, then we say $\theta$ and the corresponding portfolio *replicate* the payoff $e_m$. In a particular market model, none, some, or all of the Arrow-Debreu securities can be obtained from linear combinations of the assets $S_1, S_2, \ldots S_N$. If all Arrow-Debreu securities can be replicated in this way, then *any* time-1 payoff vector may also be replicated by some trading strategy. This is because the set of vectors $\{e_1, \ldots, e_M\}$ forms a basis of $\Re^M$. These ideas are utilized in the proof of the theorem.

**Theorem 5.2.3 (Fundamental Theorem of Asset Pricing).** *The single-period securities market model is arbitrage free if and only if there exists a state price vector.*

**Proof.** *Suppose that a state price vector* $\psi$ *exists. If* $S(1, \Omega)\theta > 0$, *then by* (5.2.6), $S(0)\theta = \psi S(1, \Omega)\theta > 0$. *Hence, all portfolios with positive payoff vectors at time* 1 *have positive prices at time* 0, *and the model is arbitrage free.*

*Conversely, suppose that the model is arbitrage free and that there are M assets with linearly independent payoff vectors at time* 1 (*a proof for the case where fewer than M of the assets have linearly independent payoff vectors will be deferred until Subsection* 5.2.7). *Thus,* $S(1, \Omega)$ *has full rank and* $N \geq M$. *There is no loss of generality in assuming that the first M assets are the linearly independent ones. We partition the vector* $S(0)$ *as follows:*

$$S(0) = [L(0) \vdots R(0)],$$

*where*

$$L(0) = [S_1(0) \quad S_2(0) \quad \cdots \quad S_M(0)]$$

*and*

$$R(0) = [S_{M+1}(0) \quad S_{M+2}(0) \quad \cdots \quad S_N(0)].$$

*Correspondingly, we partition the matrix* $S(1, \Omega)$ *as*

$$S(1, \Omega) = [L(1) \vdots R(1)],$$

*where*

$$L(1) = \begin{bmatrix} S_1(1, \omega_1) & S_2(1, \omega_1) & \cdots & S_M(1, \omega_1) \\ S_1(1, \omega_2) & S_2(1, \omega_2) & \cdots & S_M(1, \omega_2) \\ \vdots & \vdots & \ddots & \vdots \\ S_1(1, \omega_M) & S_2(1, \omega_M) & \cdots & S_M(1, \omega_M) \end{bmatrix}$$

*and*

$$R(1) = \begin{bmatrix} S_{M+1}(1, \omega_1) & S_{M+2}(1, \omega_1) & \cdots & S_N(1, \omega_1) \\ S_{M+1}(1, \omega_2) & S_{M+2}(1, \omega_2) & \cdots & S_N(1, \omega_2) \\ \vdots & \vdots & \ddots & \vdots \\ S_{M+1}(1, \omega_M) & S_{M+2}(1, \omega_M) & \cdots & S_N(1, \omega_M) \end{bmatrix}.$$

*Because* $L(1)$ *is invertible, we can define the M-dimensional row vector* $\psi = L(0)L(1)^{-1}$.

*For an arbitrary Arrow-Debreu security having time-1 payoff $e_m$, consider the trading strategy* $\theta = [(L(1)^{-1}e_m)^T, 0, \ldots, 0]^T$, *which calls for a nontrivial position in the first M securities but no position in any of the last N − M securities. Note that*

$$S(1, \Omega)\theta = L(1)L(1)^{-1}e_m = e_m,$$

*so* $\theta$ *replicates the payoff* $e_m$. *Since* $e_m > 0$ *and there are no arbitrage opportunities, it follows that this replicating portfolio's time-0 price*

$$S(0)\theta = L(0)L(1)^{-1}e_m = \psi e_m$$

*is strictly positive. Hence, the m-th component of the vector* $\psi$ *is strictly positive. Since m is arbitrary, we conclude that every component of* $\psi$ *is strictly positive.*

*Next consider*

$$\psi S(1, \Omega) = L(0)L(1)^{-1}[L(1) \vdots R(1)] = [L(0) \vdots L(0)L(1)^{-1}R(1)].$$

*If $N = M$, $S(0) = L(0)$ (and there is no $R(1)$); we have found a state price vector. For $N > M$, since the columns of $L(1)$ form a basis of $\Re^M$, an $M \times (N − M)$ matrix $K$ exists such that $R(1) = L(1)K$. Because the model is arbitrage free, the prices of the $N − M$ redundant securities must equal the cost of the unique portfolio of the linearly independent assets that produce the same payoffs at time 1. Algebraically, this means*

$$R(0) = L(0)K = \psi L(1)K = \psi R(1).$$

*We finally obtain*

$$\psi S(1, \Omega) = \psi[L(1) \vdots R(1)] = [\psi L(1) \vdots \psi R(1)]$$
$$= [L(0) \vdots R(0)] = S(0). \qquad \blacksquare$$

For a general single-period model, it is difficult to provide intuition for why the absence of arbitrage opportunities should imply the existence of a state price vector. Easier to understand is the important special case of the following subsection. Before turning to that, however, it is worthwhile to reconsider Example 5.2.1.

***Example 5.2.1 (continued).*** Consider whether a state price vector exists, that is, a strictly positive solution $(\psi_1, \psi_2)$ for the system (writing $\psi_j$ for $\psi(\omega_j)$)

$$1 = (1 + i)\psi_1 + (1 + i)\psi_2,$$
$$1 = u\psi_1 + d\psi_2.$$

The solution is easily found to be

$$\psi_1 = \frac{1 + i - d}{(1 + i)(u - d)}, \qquad \psi_2 = \frac{u - (1 + i)}{(1 + i)(u - d)}.$$

Because we have already assumed that $i \geq 0$ and $u > 1 > d > 0$, we conclude that a state price vector exists if and only if $u > 1 + i$. Note that this is precisely the condition that we earlier found to be equivalent to the absence of arbitrage. ∎

**Example 5.2.2 (continued).** In Example 5.2.1, the state price vector has elements

$$\psi_1 = \frac{1.10 - 0.80}{1.1(1.20 - 0.80)} = \frac{30}{44},$$

$$\psi_2 = \frac{1.20 - 1.10}{1.1(1.20 - 0.80)} = \frac{10}{44}.$$

∎

## SECTION 5.2.3 | RISK-NEUTRAL PROBABILITY MEASURES

Throughout this subsection, assume security $S_1$ is a bank account, as introduced in Subsection 5.2.1. In other words, assume $S_1(0) = 1$ and $S_1(1, \omega) = 1 + i$ for all $\omega \in \Omega$, where the number $i \geq 0$ is the one-period interest rate.

Given a state price vector $\psi$ (see Definition 5.2.2), we can always define the quantities

$$Q(\omega) = (1 + i)\psi(\omega), \qquad \omega \in \Omega, \tag{5.2.7}$$

and note all these quantities are strictly positive for all $\omega$. Thus, (5.2.6) becomes

$$S_j(0) = \sum_{\omega \in \Omega} \frac{Q(\omega) S_j(1, \omega)}{1 + i}, \qquad \text{for } j = 1, \ldots, N. \tag{5.2.8}$$

In particular, for $j = 1$ we have

$$S_1(0) = 1 = \sum_{\omega \in \Omega} Q(\omega). \tag{5.2.9}$$

Hence, it is convenient to interpret $Q(\omega)$ as a probability associated with the state of nature $\omega$, in which case $Q$ should be interpreted as a probability measure on the sample space $\Omega$.

Also note that the quantity $S_j(1, \omega)/(1 + i)$ can be interpreted as the *discounted* (to time 0) time-1 price of security $j$ if the state of the world is $\omega$. Hence the right-hand side of (5.2.8) can be interpreted as the *expected discounted price* of security $k$, where the expectation is computed with respect to the probability measure $Q$, not the original probability measure $P$.

In summary, starting with a state price vector, we have constructed what is called a *risk-neutral probability measure*.

**Definition 5.2.4.** *A risk-neutral probability measure is a probability measure $Q$ on $\Omega$ such that*

a. $Q(\omega) > 0$, *for all $\omega \in \Omega$*

b. *Equation (5.2.8) holds for $j = 2, \ldots, N$.*

Thus, a risk-neutral probability measure is a strictly positive probability measure under which the expected discounted price of any security equals the initial price of the same security.

What about the converse? Starting with a risk-neutral probability measure $Q$, can we construct a state price vector $\psi$? The answer is yes. By defining $\psi$ using (5.2.7), the requirement that the probabilities sum to one becomes

$$1 = \sum_{\omega \in \Omega} Q(\omega) = \sum_{\omega \in \Omega} \psi(\omega)(1 + i) = \sum_{\omega \in \Omega} \psi(\omega) S_1(1, \omega),$$

which is the first row of (5.2.6). Furthermore, (5.2.7) for $j \geq 2$ becomes the $j$-th row of (5.2.6). Hence, when there is a bank account, the existence of a state price vector is equivalent to the existence of a risk-neutral probability measure.

Our conclusions can be summarized as follows:

**Theorem 5.2.5.** *Suppose security 1 is a bank account. Then the following are equivalent:*

a. *The single-period model is arbitrage free.*

b. *There exists a state price vector.*

c. *There exists a risk-neutral probability measure.*

**Example 5.2.1 (continued).** We can readily see that security 1 is a bank account. By (5.2.7) and the earlier results, we thus have (denoting $Q(\omega_m) = q_m$)

$$q_1 = \frac{1 + i - d}{u - d} \quad \text{and} \quad q_2 = \frac{u - (1 + i)}{u - d}.$$

Note that $q_1 + q_2 = 1$. Moreover, both quantities are strictly positive if and only if $u > 1 + i$, the condition we already obtained for the absence of arbitrage. Finally, note that for the expected discounted price of security 2 we have

$$\frac{q_1 S_2(1, \omega_1)}{1 + i} + \frac{q_2 S_2(1, \omega_2)}{1 + i} = \frac{1 + i - d}{u - d} \frac{u}{1 + i} + \frac{u - (1 + i)}{u - d} \frac{d}{1 + i}$$
$$= \frac{u - d}{u - d} = 1 = S_2(0),$$

which is (5.2.8) for $j = 2$. ∎

***Example 5.2.2 (continued).*** In Example 5.2.1, the risk-neutral probabilities are

$$q_1 = \frac{1.10 - 0.80}{1.20 - 0.80} = \frac{3}{4},$$
$$q_2 = \frac{1.20 - 1.10}{1.20 - 0.80} = \frac{1}{4}.$$

From this it can be seen that the discounted expected value of the stock cash flows is

$$\frac{1}{1.10}\left[\frac{3}{4}1.20 + \frac{1}{4}0.80\right] = 1.00,$$

which is the current price of the stock. ∎

## SECTION 5.2.4 | VALUATION OF CASH FLOWS

A principal purpose of securities market models is to derive the time-0 value of future uncertain cash flows. In the case of single-period models, such a cash flow can be simply described by a random variable $X$ representing the time-1 payment. In other words, $X(\omega)$ is the time-1 payment that occurs if $\omega \in \Omega$ turns out to be the state of the world. Sometimes $X$ is called a *contingent claim*, and it can readily be used to model European options, as will be seen in Chapter 6. This subsection considers the time-0 value of the cash flow $X$ in the context of arbitrage-free single-period models.

The first important principle is the idea of cash-flow replication. We say that the trading strategy $\theta$ *replicates* the cash-flow vector $X = [X(\omega_1), \ldots, X(\omega_M)]^T$ if

$$S(1, \Omega)\theta = X.$$

By considering the components of this vector equation, we can say equivalently that the trading strategy $\theta$ replicates the cash-flow random variable $X$ if

$$\sum_j S_j(1, \omega)\theta_j = X(\omega), \quad \text{all } \omega \in \Omega.$$

We also say that the cash flow $X$ is *attainable* if it can be replicated by some trading strategy. Thus, if a cash flow is attainable, then a trading strategy exists such that the time-1 value of the corresponding portfolio coincides with the cash flow $X$ in every state of nature $\omega \in \Omega$. Note that this concept was introduced in Subsection 5.2.2, where the cash flows were Arrow-Debreu payoffs $e_m$.

The second important principle is the idea of arbitrage pricing: if the cash flow $X$ is attainable, then its time-0 value must equal the time-0 value of its replicating portfolio. This is because the introduction of a cash flow is like adding to the model a new security having time-1 price $X$ and some time-0 price, say $\pi$. If $\pi$ is not equal to the time-0 value of the replicating portfolio, then this augmented single-period model (obtained by adding in the new security) will not be arbitrage free.

To see this, suppose $\pi > S(0)\theta$, that is, you can buy or sell at time 0 a position in the cash flow at a price that is greater than the initial value of the replicating portfolio. In this case the arbitrageur would sell the cash flow at time 0, thereby collecting $\pi$ dollars and promising to deliver $X(\omega)$ dollars at time 1 if state $\omega \in \Omega$ occurs. The arbitrageur would also take a long position in the replicating portfolio, costing $S(0)\theta$ dollars but leaving a net profit of $\pi - S(0)\theta > 0$ dollars. At time 1, the arbitrageur will have the obligation to pay $X$, but this will be precisely equal to $S(1, \Omega)\theta$, the time-1 value of his portfolio, so the net obligation will be precisely zero. The arbitrageur will thus have made a profit of $\pi - S(0)\theta > 0$ without needing initial funds and without any risk of losing money. Thus, the condition $\pi > S(0)\theta$ is unreasonable from the economic point of view. Similarly (this is left to the reader to verify), the condition $\pi < S(0)\theta$ is unreasonable from the economic point of view. Only when $\pi = S(0)\theta$ will the augmented single-period model be free of arbitrage opportunities.

These results are summarized as follows:

**Theorem 5.2.6.** *In an arbitrage-free, single-period model, the time-0 value of an attainable cash flow $X$ is equal to the time-0 value of the portfolio that replicates $X$.*

But there is a more remarkable consequence of the fundamental theorem of asset pricing. Consider the state price vector $\psi$. If $S(1, \Omega)\theta = X$, then $\psi S(1, \Omega)\theta = \psi X$. However, we also have $S(0)\theta = \psi S(1, \Omega)\theta$ from (5.2.6), hence

$$S(0)\theta = \psi X.$$

This says that the time-0 price of the replicating portfolio, and thus the time-0 value of the cash flow $X$, is equal to $\psi X$, a quantity that can be computed by knowing the state price vector $\psi$ without any knowledge of the replicating trading strategy $\theta$ itself.

If security 1 is a bank account with short interest rate $i \geq 0$, then by (5.2.7) the time-0 value of the cash flow $X$ is

$$\psi X = \sum_{\omega \in \Omega} \psi(\omega) X(\omega) = \sum_{\omega \in \Omega} \frac{Q(\omega) X(\omega)}{1 + i}.$$

This says that the time-0 value of $X$ is equal to the expected discounted value of $X$, where the expectation is computed using the risk-neutral probability measure. This principle, first encountered in Section 3.7, is called *risk-neutral valuation* and has enormous implications for the valuation of options, as we see in Chapter 6.

We conclude this subsection with a summarizing theorem, another look at our familiar examples, and some final remarks.

**Theorem 5.2.7.** *In an arbitrage-free, single-period model, the time-0 value of an attainable cash flow $X$ is equal to $\psi X$, where $\psi$ is the state price vector. If, in addition, security 1 is a bank account with short interest rate $i \geq 0$, then*

$$\psi X = \sum_{\omega \in \Omega} \frac{Q(\omega) X(\omega)}{1 + i},$$

*where $Q$ is the risk-neutral probability measure.*

**Example 5.2.1 (continued).** Suppose the model is arbitrage free (that is, $u > 1 + i$) and consider an arbitrary cash flow $X$. Easy algebraic equations will verify that

$$S(1, \Omega)\theta = X = [X(\omega_1), X(\omega_2)]^T$$

will always have the solution $\theta = S(1, \Omega)^{-1}X$, so every possible cash flow will be attainable in this example. Since $S(0) = [1 \quad 1]$, the time-0 value of $X$ will be $[1 \quad 1]S(1, \Omega)^{-1}X$. In view of Theorem 5.2.7, this will also equal

$$\psi X = \frac{1 + i - d}{(1 + i)(u - d)} X(\omega_1) + \frac{u - (1 + i)}{(1 + i)(u - d)} X(\omega_2)$$

$$= \frac{1 + i - d}{u - d} \frac{X(\omega_1)}{1 + i} + \frac{u - (1 + i)}{u - d} \frac{X(\omega_2)}{1 + i}$$

$$= q_1 \frac{X(\omega_1)}{1 + i} + q_2 \frac{X(\omega_2)}{1 + i}. \qquad \blacksquare$$

**Example 5.2.2 (continued).** In Example 5.2.1, if we wish to price a call option with a strike price of 1.10, then the cash flows are $X(1) = 0.10$, $X(2) = 0.00$ and the option's price is

$$\frac{3}{4} \frac{0.10}{1.10} + \frac{1}{4} \frac{0.00}{1.10} = \frac{3}{44}.$$

Note that $S(1, \Omega)\theta = X$ is

$$\begin{bmatrix} 1.10 & 1.20 \\ 1.10 & 0.80 \end{bmatrix} \begin{bmatrix} \theta_1 \\ \theta_2 \end{bmatrix} = \begin{bmatrix} 0.10 \\ 0.00 \end{bmatrix},$$

yielding $\theta_1 = -2/11$ and $\theta_2 = 1/4$. This means that the option is replicated by borrowing 2/11 and investing 1/4 in the stock. This results in a net investment of

3/44, the price of the option. At the end of the period $(2/11)1.10 = 0.20$ is owed. If the stock increases in value to $(1/4)1.20 = 0.30$. After repayment of the borrowing the net cash flow is 0.10. Similarly, if the stock goes down, the 1/4 in stock is worth only 0.20, with a net cash flow of 0. This demonstrates that the combination of borrowing and investment in the stock replicates the call option on the stock. ∎

Bear in mind that the preceding theory for valuing cash flows applies only for cash flows that are attainable. If a cash flow cannot be replicated by some trading strategy, then arbitrage arguments cannot be used to determine the cash flow's value. Instead, the equilibrium pricing methods of Chapter 4 must be employed.

How do we check whether a cash flow $X$ is attainable? There is rarely a shortcut; usually, we must investigate whether $S(1, \Omega)\theta = X$ has a solution $\theta$. However, as illustrated with the preceding example, sometimes a single-period model is such that every cash flow is attainable. This is the subject of the following subsection.

## SECTION 5.2.5 | COMPLETENESS IN THE SINGLE-PERIOD MODEL

*Definition 5.2.8.* *An arbitrage-free market model is said to be* **complete** *if for every cash-flow vector* $X \in \Re^M$ *there exists some trading strategy* $\theta \in \Re^N$ *such that*

$$S(1, \Omega)\theta = X.$$

Thus, in complete markets we can construct a portfolio that replicates any prescribed contingent cash flow, in which case every cash flow can be priced by arbitrage. The following theorem provides a useful necessary and sufficient condition for the model to be complete.

*Theorem 5.2.9.* *Suppose a single-period model is arbitrage free. Then the model is complete if and only if there is a unique state price vector.*

*Proof.* *Suppose the model is complete but there are two distinct state price vectors, say,* $\psi$ *and* $\bar{\psi}$. *Since every cash flow is attainable, there must exist some attainable cash flow X such that* $\psi X \neq \bar{\psi} X$. *But this contradicts Theorem 5.2.6, for X cannot have two distinct time-0 values in an arbitrage-free model.*

*Conversely, suppose that the model is not complete. Then there is some* $X \in \Re^M$ *for which there is no* $\theta \in \Re^N$ *such that* $S(1, \Omega)\theta = X$. *Thus, the rank of* $S(1, \Omega)$ *is strictly smaller than M. This in turn means that the M rows of that matrix are linearly dependent, so there is a nonzero* $\phi \in \Re^M$ *such that* $\phi S(1, \Omega) = 0$. *Since the model is arbitrage free, there is at least one state price vector, say* $\psi$. *For any real number* $\varepsilon \neq 0$

*so small that* $\psi + \varepsilon\phi \gg 0$, *we get*

$$(\psi + \varepsilon\phi)S(1, \Omega) = \psi S(1, \Omega) + \varepsilon\phi S(1, \Omega) = \psi S(1, \Omega) = S(0),$$

*showing that the number of state price vectors is infinite.* ∎

The proof of this theorem also shows that, when the securities market model is complete, the price of the Arrow-Debreu security for outcome $\omega$ is equal to $\psi(\omega)$. Combining the fundamental theorem of asset pricing with this theorem gives the following result: *a single-period model is arbitrage free and complete if and only if there exists a unique state price vector.*

If, in addition, security 1 is a bank account, then we have the following result, the proof of which is left to you.

**Corollary 5.2.10.** *Suppose security 1 in a single-period model is a bank account. Then this model is arbitrage free and complete if and only if the risk-neutral probability measure is unique.*

We see that in a complete arbitrage-free market each contingent cash flow has a unique price. The next subsection gives some examples with incomplete markets.

## SECTION 5.2.6 | APPLICATIONS OF THE FUNDAMENTAL THEOREM OF ASSET PRICING

For a given securities market model we may compute all state price vectors by determining all strictly positive solutions of

$$S(0) = \psi S(1, \Omega).$$

As long as the securities market model is arbitrage free, the fundamental theorem of asset pricing assures us that at least one strictly positive solution of this equation exists. We can try to find all possible state price vectors.

**Example 5.2.3.** Let us compute all state price vectors for the securities market model

$$S(0) = [1 \quad 1], \qquad S(1, \Omega) = \begin{bmatrix} 2 & 0 \\ 2 & 0 \\ 2 & 4 \\ 2 & 4 \end{bmatrix}.$$

This market model consists of two assets, each with initial price 1. There are four possible states of nature, one corresponding to each row of $S(1, \Omega)$. A solution

$\psi = [\psi_1, \psi_2, \psi_3, \psi_4]$ of the linear equation $S(0) = \psi S(1, \Omega)$ is equivalent to solving

$$2\psi_1 + 2\psi_2 + 2\psi_3 + 2\psi_4 = 1,$$
$$4\psi_3 + 4\psi_4 = 1.$$

As this is an underdetermined system, its solution will involve two parameters. One parameterization of the solutions is as follows:

$$\psi_4 = t,$$
$$\psi_3 = \frac{1}{4} - t,$$
$$\psi_2 = s,$$
$$\psi_1 = \frac{1}{4} - s.$$

The requirement that a state price vector be strictly positive imposes the refinements that $0 < t < 1/4$ and $0 < s < 1/4$. Thus, the collection of all state price vectors for this model is the set $H$ of all vectors of the form $[1/4 - s, s, 1/4 - t, t]$ for $s$ and $t$ satisfying $0 < s < 1/4$ and $0 < t < 1/4$, that is,

$$H = \left\{ \left[ \frac{1 - 4s}{4}, s, \frac{1 - 4t}{4}, t \right] \middle| (s, t) \in W \right\}$$

where

$$W = \left\{ (s, t) \middle| 0 < s < \frac{1}{4}, 0 < t < \frac{1}{4} \right\}$$

is the parameter region for the model. ∎

**Example 5.2.4.** Consider the following securities market model, which differs only slightly from the preceding example:

$$S(0) = \begin{bmatrix} 1 & 1 \end{bmatrix}, \qquad S(1, \Omega) = \begin{bmatrix} 2 & 0 \\ 2 & 0 \\ 2 & 4 \\ 2 & 3 \end{bmatrix}.$$

We can compute all strictly positive solutions of the equation $S(0) = \psi S(1, \Omega)$ to characterize the state price vectors in this model. Proceeding as in the preceding example, we find that the set of all state price vectors for this model is

$$H = \left\{ \left[ \frac{1 - 4s - t}{4}, s, \frac{1 - 3t}{4}, t \right] \middle| (s, t) \in W \right\}$$

where

$$W = \left\{ (s, t) \middle| 0 < s, \quad 0 < t < \frac{1}{3}, \quad \frac{4s + t}{4} < \frac{1}{4} \right\}.$$ ∎

Suppose that a new security is to be introduced into an existing incomplete securities market model. If the resulting securities market model is to remain arbitrage free, we know from the Fundamental Theorem of Asset Pricing that a state price vector must still exist. Such a state price vector must be consistent with the original securities market model, so a state price vector for the augmented securities market model must be chosen from the collection, denoted $H$, of state price vectors for the original model. Consequently, a new security having time-1 price vector $c$ may be introduced in an arbitrage-free fashion if and only if its time-0 price equals $\psi c$ for some $\psi \in H$.

For instance, over what range of time-0 prices would the security with time-1 price vector

$$c = [1 \quad 0 \quad 0 \quad 1]^T$$

be introduced into the securities market model of Example 5.2.4 such that the resulting model is arbitrage free? The answer is the set of current prices $\psi c$ that is compatible with the set $H$; that is, $\psi \in H$. Since

$$\psi c = 1 \left( \frac{1}{4} - s - \frac{1}{4} t \right) + 0s + 0 \left( \frac{1}{4} - \frac{3}{4} t \right) + 1t$$

$$= \frac{1}{4} - s + \frac{3}{4} t,$$

the range of possible time-0 prices for this new security is then

$$\left\{ \frac{1}{4} - s + \frac{3}{4} t \middle| (s, t) \in W \right\}.$$

Some simple calculations then show that

$$\left\{ \frac{1}{4} - s + \frac{3}{4} t \middle| (s, t) \in W \right\} = \left( 0, \frac{1}{2} \right).$$

Therefore, the new security with time-1 price vector $c$ may be introduced at any initial price in $(0, 1/2)$, and the resulting securities market model will be arbitrage free.

## SECTION 5.2.7 │ PROOF OF THEOREM 5.2.3 (COMPLETED)

The proof of the "only if" part of Theorem 5.2.3 given in Subsection 5.2.2 assumed that there are $M$ assets with linearly independent payoff vectors at time 1. Here we provide a proof for the other case, namely, where fewer than $M$ of the assets have linearly independent payoffs, that is, for the case $N < M$.

One difficulty in proving this result lies in constructing a state price vector when the securities market model is arbitrage free. This construction is based on adding assets to the model to obtain an extended arbitrage-free securities market model which will ultimately have full rank, thereby placing us back in the domain of the earlier proof.

Recall that arbitrage means there exists a trading strategy or portfolio $\theta$ such that

$$\begin{bmatrix} S(1) \\ -S(0) \end{bmatrix} \theta > 0.$$

(For simplicity, the matrix $S(1, \Omega)$ is now written as $S(1)$.)

Therefore, an arbitrage can occur if and only if a portfolio $\theta$ exists such that either

$$\boxed{\begin{aligned} S(1)\theta &> 0 \\ -S(0)\theta &\geq 0 \end{aligned}} \tag{5.2.10}$$

or

$$\boxed{\begin{aligned} -S(0)\theta &> 0 \\ S(1)\theta &\geq 0 \end{aligned}}. \tag{5.2.11}$$

Thus, there is no arbitrage if and only if

$$\text{whenever } S(1)\theta > 0, \quad \text{we cannot have } -S(0)\theta \geq 0$$

or

$$\text{whenever } -S(0)\theta > 0, \quad \text{we cannot have } S(1)\theta \geq 0,$$

that is,

$$S(1)\theta > 0 \quad \Rightarrow \quad S(0)\theta > 0 \tag{5.2.12}$$

or

$$-S(0)\theta > 0 \quad \Rightarrow \quad \text{at least one coordinate of } S(1)\theta \text{ is negative.}$$

For simplicity we assume that we have an asset with strictly positive payments; then arbitrage of type (5.2.11) implies (5.2.10). Hence, we must check only that condition (5.2.12) holds, to ensure that the model is arbitrage free.

Consider an arbitrage-free model $S$ with a strictly positive asset to which we seek to add an unspanned standard basis vector $e_i$ as an additional asset. By "unspanned" we mean that the vector $e_i$ must not be in span$\{S(1)\}$, which is the linear subspace spanned or generated by the column vectors in $S(1)$. It is assumed that the rank of $S(1) = S(1, \Omega)$ is less than $M$, so we may assume $N < M$.

The as yet unknown time-0 price of the unspanned asset will be denoted by $\alpha$. It follows from condition (5.2.12) that there is no arbitrage in the extended model if and only if

$$\left.\begin{aligned} S(1)\theta + e_i > 0 &\quad\Rightarrow\quad S(0)\theta + \alpha > 0 \\ S(1)\theta - e_i > 0 &\quad\Rightarrow\quad S(0)\theta - \alpha > 0. \end{aligned}\right\} \tag{5.2.13}$$

Since $\{S(1)\theta | \theta \in \Re^N\} = \{-S(1)\theta | \theta \in \Re^N\}$, we may reformulate (5.2.13) as

$$\left.\begin{aligned} S(1)\theta < e_i &\quad\Rightarrow\quad S(0)\theta < \alpha \\ S(1)\theta > e_i &\quad\Rightarrow\quad S(0)\theta > \alpha. \end{aligned}\right\} \tag{5.2.14}$$

Therefore, the price that is assigned to the new security must be larger than the price of all portfolios it dominates and smaller than the price of all portfolios it is dominated by if the extended model is to be arbitrage free. We thus consider the quantities $L$ and $U$, which are defined in terms of two linear programs :

$$\boxed{\begin{aligned} L &= \max S(0)\theta \\ &\text{subject to} \\ &S(1)\theta \leq e_i \end{aligned}} \tag{5.2.15}$$

and

$$\boxed{\begin{aligned} U &= \min S(0)\theta \\ &\text{subject to} \\ &S(1)\theta \geq e_i \end{aligned}}. \tag{5.2.16}$$

Note that we have replaced "$<$" by "$\leq$" because we assume that $e_i \notin$ span$\{S(1)\}$. Also, $L \geq 0$ because $\theta \equiv 0$ satisfies the constraint $S(1)\theta \leq e_i$.

It follows from (5.2.15) and (5.2.16) and the no-arbitrage condition that $L$ is less than or equal to $U$. Also, the quantity $U$ is always finite when we have a strictly positive asset. If $b$ is the $i$-th component of the strictly positive asset, then buying at least $1/b$ units of the asset will result in a payoff that dominates $e_i$. Then the (finite) cost of this asset will be an upper bound on $U$. Hence, $U$ is finite and $0 \leq L \leq U < \infty$.

Next let us analyze the relationship between the two linear programs and thus the gap between $U$ and $L$. We know that $\{S(1)\theta \geq e_i\}$ and $\{S(1)\theta \leq e_i\}$ are convex sets, each of which is the intersection of a finite number of half spaces. Therefore each set has a finite number of extreme points. Since $L$ is finite, we know from the theory of linear programming that the linear programs (5.2.15) and (5.2.16) have optimal solutions at one of the extreme points in the respective sets $\{S(1)\theta \geq e_i\}$ and $\{S(1)\theta \leq e_i\}$. In particular, (5.2.15) is solved by a portfolio at an extreme point, say $\theta_1^*$. Similarly, since $U$ is finite, (5.2.16) is solved by a portfolio $\theta_2^*$ at an extreme point. Because $e_i \notin \text{span}\{S(1)\}$, we have

$$S(1)\theta_1^* < e_i < S(1)\theta_2^*,$$

which means

$$S(1)(\theta_2^* - \theta_1^*) > 0.$$

Because there are no arbitrage opportunities, it follows that

$$S(0)(\theta_2^* - \theta_1^*) > 0.$$

Thus, we see that

$$L = S(0)\theta_1^* < S(0)\theta_2^* = U.$$

Hence, we have $L < U$, whenever $e_i \notin \text{span}\{S(1)\}$. Therefore, we have shown that there is always a choice for $\alpha$ such that

$$L < \alpha < U$$

and (5.2.14) is satisfied. Therefore we can add one nonredundant (that is, unspanned) asset to the model in an arbitrage-free manner.

By induction we can extend the model as many times as necessary, each time preserving the arbitrage-free property, until the extended model is such that the resulting $S(1, \Omega)$ has full rank. At this point we know that a state price exists by the proof of Theorem 5.2.3 in Subsection 5.2.2. This establishes the general version of the fundamental theorem of asset pricing for single-period models.

## SECTION 5.2.8 | SINGLE-PERIOD EXTENSION EXAMPLE

We now illustrate the preceding discussion with a concrete example. We have indicated how our arbitrage-free model with fewer than $M$ linearly independent assets can be extended to a model that is arbitrage free and has $M$ linearly independent assets. The following example illustrates this procedure. Suppose

$$S(1) = \begin{bmatrix} 1 & 0 \\ 1 & 1 \\ 1 & 0 \\ 1 & 3 \end{bmatrix} \qquad \text{and} \qquad S(0) = [1 \quad 1].$$

Note that $e_1 = [1 \ 0 \ 0 \ 0]^T \notin \text{span}\{S(1)\}$ since the span of the two assets is parameterized by

$$\begin{bmatrix} 1 & 0 \\ 1 & 1 \\ 1 & 0 \\ 1 & 3 \end{bmatrix} \sim \begin{bmatrix} s \\ s+t \\ s \\ s+3t \end{bmatrix}.$$

We thus begin the extension process by adding the asset with time-1 payoff vector equal to the standard basis vector $e_1$. To determine a price at which to add $e_1$ we must compute

$$U = \min S(0)\theta \quad \text{subject to} \quad S(1)\theta \geq e_1,$$
$$L = \max S(0)\theta \quad \text{subject to} \quad S(1)\theta \leq e_1.$$

To compute $U$, we solve linear program (5.2.16), which is

$$\boxed{\begin{aligned} &\min \theta_1 + \theta_2 \\ &\text{subject to} \\ &\theta_1 && \geq 1 \\ &\theta_1 + \theta_2 && \geq 0 \\ &\theta_1 && \geq 0 \\ &\theta_1 + 3\theta_2 && \geq 0 \end{aligned}}.$$

By inspection we see that the optimal solution is $\theta_1 = 1$ and $\theta_2 = -1/3$, in which case $U = 1 - 1/3 = 2/3$. Similarly, linear program (5.2.15) is

$$\boxed{\begin{aligned} &\max \theta_1 + \theta_2 \\ &\text{subject to} \\ &\theta_1 && \leq 1 \\ &\theta_1 + \theta_2 && \leq 0 \\ &\theta_1 && \leq 0 \\ &\theta_1 + 3\theta_2 && \leq 0 \end{aligned}}.$$

The optimal solution here is $\theta_1 = 0$ and $\theta_2 = 0$, in which case $L = 0$.

Therefore, we can add to the model the asset with time-1 payoff vector $e_1$ at any initial price $\alpha \in (0, 2/3)$, and the extended model will be arbitrage free. We set $\alpha = 1/4$. Consequently, the extended arbitrage-free model is

$$S(0) = \begin{bmatrix} 1 & 1 & \frac{1}{4} \end{bmatrix}, \qquad S(1) = \begin{bmatrix} 1 & 0 & 1 \\ 1 & 1 & 0 \\ 1 & 0 & 0 \\ 1 & 3 & 0 \end{bmatrix}.$$

To add a fourth asset, we note that $e_2 \notin \text{span}\{S(1)\}$ since the span of the three assets is parameterized by

$$\begin{bmatrix} 1 & 0 & 1 \\ 1 & 1 & 0 \\ 1 & 0 & 0 \\ 1 & 3 & 0 \end{bmatrix} \sim \begin{bmatrix} s + u \\ s + t \\ s \\ s + 3t \end{bmatrix}.$$

We therefore continue the extension process by adding an asset with time-1 payoff vector $e_2$. To determine an initial price of this additional asset, we must compute

$$U = \min S(0)\theta \quad \text{subject to} \quad S(1)\theta \geq e_2$$

and

$$L = \max S(0)\theta \quad \text{subject to} \quad S(1)\theta \leq e_2.$$

This requires the solution of the following linear programs, which can be solved by any standard linear programming software package:

$$\begin{aligned}
&\min \theta_1 + \theta_2 + \tfrac{1}{4}\theta_3 \\
&\text{subject to} \\
&\theta_1 \qquad\quad + \theta_3 \qquad \geq 0 \\
&\theta_1 + \theta_2 \qquad\qquad \geq 1 \\
&\theta_1 \qquad\qquad\qquad \geq 0 \\
&\theta_1 + 3\theta_2 \qquad\qquad \geq 0
\end{aligned}$$

$$\begin{aligned}
&\max \theta_1 + \theta_2 + \tfrac{1}{4}\theta_3 \\
&\text{subject to} \\
&\theta_1 \qquad\quad + \theta_3 \qquad \leq 0 \\
&\theta_1 + \theta_2 \qquad\qquad \leq 1 \\
&\theta_1 \qquad\qquad\qquad \leq 0 \\
&\theta_1 + 3\theta_2 \qquad\qquad \leq 0
\end{aligned}$$

A solution of the first is $\theta_1 = 3/2$, $\theta_2 = -1/2$, and $\theta_3 = -3/2$, giving $U = 5/8$. The solution of the second is $\theta_1 = 0$, $\theta_2 = 0$, and $\theta_3 = 0$, giving $L = 0$. Therefore, we can add an asset with time-1 payoff vector $e_2$ at any initial price $\alpha \in (0, 5/8)$, and the extended model will be arbitrage free. We will set $\alpha = 1/4$. Consequently, the extended arbitrage-free model is

$$S(1) = \begin{bmatrix} 1 & 0 & 1 & 0 \\ 1 & 1 & 0 & 1 \\ 1 & 0 & 0 & 0 \\ 1 & 3 & 0 & 0 \end{bmatrix}, \qquad S(0) = \begin{bmatrix} 1 & 1 & \dfrac{1}{4} & \dfrac{1}{4} \end{bmatrix}.$$

We now have an arbitrage-free model with $M = 4$ linearly independent assets. Therefore, as we have seen, the unique state price vector for this model is

$$\psi = S(0)S(1)^{-1}.$$

We can do the algebra or make an educated guess to find that

$$\psi = \begin{bmatrix} \dfrac{1}{4} & \dfrac{1}{4} & \dfrac{1}{4} & \dfrac{1}{4} \end{bmatrix}.$$

Thus, we have found a state price vector from the extended model that will also serve as a state price vector for the original model:

$$S(1) = \begin{bmatrix} 1 & 0 \\ 1 & 1 \\ 1 & 0 \\ 1 & 3 \end{bmatrix}, \qquad S(0) = \begin{bmatrix} 1 & 1 \end{bmatrix}.$$

This discussion has numerically illustrated our argument that every arbitrage-free model has a state price vector. Another approach to the Fundamental Theorem of Asset Pricing is given in Section 7.2.10.

# Section 5.3
# The Multiperiod Model

We now become more realistic and consider multiperiod models of securities markets. There is not much new to learn; the fundamental principles of arbitrage in the context of single-period models go a very long way in the study of multiperiod models.

On the other hand, there is still much to learn. This is largely due to the complex nature of actual securities markets, thereby causing a realistic multiperiod model to be very complicated in terms of its elements and the notation. The theory of stochastic processes helps, because it standardizes some terminology and thereby facilitates communication between model builders and analysts; but this means that you must study some prerequisite material.

Because there is so much to learn about the fundamentals of multiperiod models, this subject is presented in two stages. In this section we focus on an important basic case in which one security is a bank account and the other securities, which can be thought of as stocks, pay no dividends. Furthermore, in this section we focus on the financial economics, the underlying intuition, and the basic results while deemphasizing the mathematical details and rigor. In Chapter 11, we study the general situation using more sophisticated mathematics.

## SECTION 5.3.1 | DESCRIPTION OF THE MODEL

As with the single-period model, there is a sample space $\Omega = \{\omega_1, \omega_2, \ldots, \omega_M\}$ consisting of $M < \infty$ states of nature. Representing the investor's beliefs is a probability measure $P$ satisfying $P(\omega) > 0$ for all $\omega \in \Omega$. There are $T < \infty$ time periods, giving rise to $T + 1$ time points denoted by $k = 0, 1, \ldots, T$.

There are $N < \infty$ primitive securities or assets $S = \{S_1, S_2, \ldots, S_N\}$. Here $S_j(k, \omega)$ denotes the time-$k$ price of security $j$ if the underlying state of the world is $\omega \in \Omega$. Since $\omega \to S_j(k, \omega)$ is a function on the sample space, the time-$k$ price of security $j$ should be viewed as a *random variable*, simply denoted $S_j(k)$. Because $S_j(k)$ is a random variable for each time $k = 0, 1, \ldots, T$, the collection

$$S_j = \{S_j(k); \quad k = 0, 1, \ldots, T\}$$

should be viewed as a *stochastic process*. For each $\omega \in \Omega$, we call the function $k \to S_j(k, \omega)$ a *sample path* of the stochastic process $S_j$. Finally, the collection $S = \{S_1, S_2, \ldots, S_N\}$ of stochastic processes should be viewed as a *vector-valued stochastic process*.

We call security $S_1$ the *bank account*, and it plays a special role. Throughout this section it is assumed that $S_1(0, \omega) = 1$ and that $k \to S_1(k, \omega)$ is a nondecreasing function for all $\omega \in \Omega$. Hence, the random variable $S_1(k)$ represents the money in the bank account at time $k$ if one dollar is deposited at time 0. Moreover,

$$i_k = \frac{S_1(k + 1)}{S_1(k)} - 1$$

will always be nonnegative. The random variable is called the *one-period interest rate* or the *short rate*, since it is the interest rate that is applied to deposits from time $k$

to time $k + 1$. Thus, $\{i_k; k = 0, 1, \ldots, T - 1\}$ is another stochastic process. An important special case is when $i_k = i$ is constant with respect to both time and the state of the world, in which case the bank account is the deterministic quantity $S_1(k) = (1 + i)^k, k = 0, 1, \ldots, T$.

***Example 5.3.1 (Binomial Stock Price Model).*** Building on Example 5.2.1, suppose there are just two securities: a bank account $S_1$ with constant short rate $i \geq 0$ and a risky security $S_2$ which each period either goes up by the factor $u > 1$ or goes down by the factor $d, 0 < d < 1$. Hence, through $T$ periods there will be $2^T$ possible sample paths for $S_2$, and so for the sample space $\Omega$ it is appropriate to have $M = 2^T$ states of nature $\omega$, with each $\omega$ corresponding to a particular sequence of up- and down-jumps. Assuming $S_2(0)$ is a fixed scalar, the random variable $S_2(k)$ thus takes one of the $k + 1$ values

$$S_2(0)u^k, \; S_2(0)u^{k-1}d, \ldots, S_2(0)ud^{k-1}, \; \text{or} \; S_2(0)d^k.$$

Of course, the deterministic bank account satisfies $S_1(k) = (1 + i)^k$ for all $k$.

Suppose that each up-jump occurs with probability $p$ and each down-jump occurs with probability $1 - p$, for some positive number $p$ that is less than 1. Moreover, suppose all these jumps are independent of each other. Then

$$P(\omega) = p^n(1 - p)^{T-n}$$

if the state of nature $\omega$ corresponds to precisely $n$ up-jumps and $T - n$ down-jumps. Furthermore, $S_2(k)$ will have the *binomial probability distribution*; in particular, for $k = 1, 2, \ldots, T$,

$$P(S_2(k) = S_2(0)u^n d^{k-n}) = \binom{k}{n} p^n (1 - p)^{k-n}, \quad n = 0, 1, \ldots, k,$$

where

$$\binom{k}{n} = \frac{k!}{n!(k - n)!}$$

is the number of states of nature with $n$ up-jumps and $k - n$ down-jumps. ∎

In the single-period model, we assumed that at time 0 the investors did not have any idea about the true state of nature (beyond what corresponds to the probability measure $P$). Moreover, we assumed that the investors learn the true state of nature $\omega$ at the end of the period. We make these same assumptions for the multiperiod model; that is, the investors start out thinking every $\omega$ is possible, and they learn the true $\omega$ at time $T$, at the end of the last period.

However, there is a key difference with respect to single-period models: for multiperiod models we must specify how the investors learn about the true state of nature at intermediate points of time. To see this, consider Example 5.3.1. One possibility is that investors observe and remember all past and present security prices. In this case, at each intermediate time they realize that states of nature that do not correspond to the observed sample path are impossible. On the other hand, if two or more states of nature have sample paths that coincide up to an intermediate point in time, then knowledge of the true $\omega$ will be uncertain at that time. For instance, suppose the first jump is "up" and the second is "down." Then investors at time 2 can rule out all paths which start out up-up, down-down, or down-up. Alternatively, another possibility is that the investors observe all security prices but they are forgetful, paying attention to only the present prices. In this case investors rule out only states of nature that correspond to unobserved prices at that time. For instance, if the risky security starts out with an up- and then a down-jump, then at time 2 the investors only know that sample paths which start out up-up or down-down are impossible. For a precise model, it is necessary to specify how information becomes known to the investors. The following assumptions will be in force throughout this section:

- The investors observe all prices, and they remember all past and present observations.
- The investors start off at time 0 with full knowledge about $\Omega$, $P$, and the values of $S_j(k, \omega)$ for all $j$, $k$, and $\omega$. The price $S_j(0, \omega)$ is constant with respect to $\omega$; for the investors at time 0 any $\omega$ is possible.
- There is a unique sample path for each $\omega \in \Omega$, so at time $T$ the investors know the true state of nature.
- Finally, at intermediate points of time, $k < T$, no additional information is given to the investors that would help them learn the true state of nature.

***Example 5.3.1 (continued).*** Suppose $T = 2$ so $\Omega = \{\omega_1, \omega_2, \omega_3, \omega_4\}$. Suppose $\omega_1$, $\omega_2$, $\omega_3$ and $\omega_4$ correspond to up-up, up-down, down-up, and down-down, respectively. Then if the first jump by $S_2$ is an up-jump, the investors realize states $\omega_3$ and $\omega_4$ are impossible, although they remain uncertain about whether the true state is $\omega_1$ or $\omega_2$. ∎

As just seen in the example, the information known by the investors at each point in time can be nicely described by a subset $\mathcal{H}$ of the sample space $\Omega$ (using probabilistic terminology, $\mathcal{H}$ is an *event*), with the elements of $\mathcal{H}$ being all those outcomes or states of nature $\omega \in \Omega$ that are still "alive" at that point in time. For instance, in Example 5.3.1, $\mathcal{H} = \Omega$ at $k = 0$; $\mathcal{H}$ is either $\{\omega_1, \omega_2\}$ or $\{\omega_3, \omega_4\}$ at $k = 1$; and $\mathcal{H}$ is either $\{\omega_1\}$, $\{\omega_2\}$, $\{\omega_3\}$, or $\{\omega_4\}$ at $k = 2$. This pattern holds for more general multiperiod models; the information known by the investors at a point in time can be equated to a subset of $\Omega$. And since the information is based upon the history of past and present security prices, these subsets will be called *histories*.

Also notice from Example 5.3.1 that if $\mathcal{H}_k$ is a time-$k$ history, then the history $\mathcal{H}_{k+1}$ at time $k+1$ will be a subset of $\mathcal{H}_k$. After all, if $\omega \in \mathcal{H}_{k+1}$ is alive at time $k+1$, then it must have been alive at time $k$. Hence, the multiperiod submodel for how information becomes known to the investors has the form of a tree. Each node corresponds to a particular history or subset of $\Omega$. At the root of the tree is node $\Omega$, corresponding to time 0. From this one branch goes to each of the histories, that is, nodes, that is possibly at time 1. In general, from each time-$k$ node or history one branch goes to each of the possible successor time-$(k+1)$ nodes or histories. Finally, at the top of the tree are the time-$T$ nodes, one for each state of nature $\omega \in \Omega$. Note the unique path from the time-0 node to each of the time-$T$ nodes. Figure 5.2 illustrates an example of an information structure.

The collection of possible time-$k$ histories for a model clearly forms a *partition* of the sample space, for each $\omega \in \Omega$ corresponds to a unique time-$t$ history. We let $\mathcal{P}_k$ denote the collection of the time-$k$ histories that are possible, and we view $\mathcal{P}_k$ as a partition of $\Omega$.

We soon will find it necessary to compute various conditional expectations given the information known to the investors at a point in time. We let $E[X|\mathcal{H}]$ denote the conditional expectation of the random variable $X$ given the history $\mathcal{H}$; since $\mathcal{H}$ is simply an event, we thus have

$$E[X|\mathcal{H}] = \frac{\sum_{\omega \in \mathcal{H}} X(\omega) P(\omega)}{\sum_{\omega \in \mathcal{H}} P(\omega)}. \tag{5.3.1}$$

We also let $E[X|\mathcal{P}_k]$ or $E_k[X]$ denote the collection of all conditional expectations of the form $E[X|\mathcal{H}]$, where $\mathcal{H} \in \mathcal{P}_k$.

In conclusion, our multiperiod securities market model is now fully specified. All the data for a model are organized in terms of the basic elements $\Omega$, $P$, and $S$. With our assumption that the investors observe and remember all past and present security prices, we can deduce and construct the tree-like information submodel that will play an important role in the remainder of this chapter. More complicated multiperiod models are developed in Chapter 11, but we get considerable insight from our simple version. The next step is to consider trading strategies.

## SECTION 5.3.2 | SELF-FINANCING TRADING STRATEGIES

Having fully specified the multiperiod securities market model, we now need to describe trading strategies and the values of the corresponding portfolios. Let $\theta_j(k, \omega)$ denote the number of shares or units of security $j$ held from time $k$ to time $k+1$, and denote

$$\theta(k, \omega) = [\theta_1(k, \omega), \theta_2(k, \omega), \dots, \theta_N(k, \omega)]^T.$$

FIGURE 5.2 │ *Information Structure*

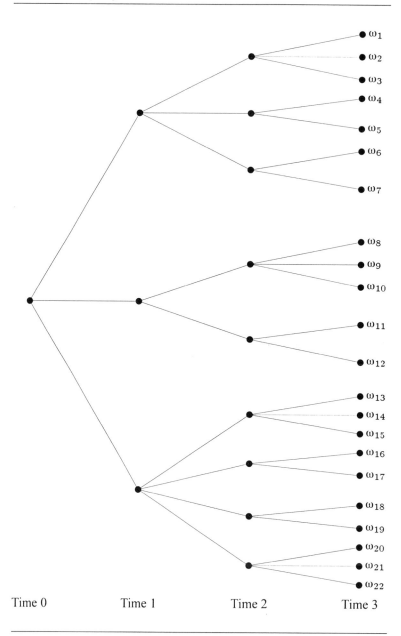

Time 0       Time 1       Time 2       Time 3

We want $\theta(k, \omega)$ to be a function of $k$ to allow the investor to adjust the portfolio positions from time to time. We also want $\theta(k, \omega)$ to be a function of $\omega$, so the investor can take different positions at time $k$ for different time-$t$ histories. In other words, we want to allow $\theta(k, \omega_1)$ to be different from $\theta(k, \omega_2)$ if the sample paths of the securities through time $k$ under $\omega_1$ are different from the sample paths through time $k$ under $\omega_2$. But we need to be careful here; although we want the investors to be able to use all available information, we do not want them to be fortune tellers. Consequently, we require $\theta(k, \omega)$ to be identical or constant for all $\omega$ having the same time-$t$ history. In other words, $\theta(k, \omega_1)$ and $\theta(k, \omega_2)$ must be the same if the sample paths of the securities through time $k$ under $\omega_1$ are the same as the sample paths through time $k$ under $\omega_2$. After all, if the investors are uncertain about whether $\omega_1$ or $\omega_2$ is the true state of nature, then they should not establish a different position for $\omega_1$ than for $\omega_2$.

Notice that $\theta(k) = \theta(k, \cdot)$, a vector of functions on the sample space $\Omega$, can be regarded as a vector of random variables. Consequently,

$$\theta = \{\theta(k); \quad k = 0, 1, \ldots, T - 1\}$$

can be regarded as a vector-valued stochastic process, where component $j$ specifies the position in security $j$ as a function of times and the observed history. Any $\theta$ of this form can be conveniently referred to as a *trading strategy*.

Because $S(k, \omega)$ is a row vector and $\theta(k, \omega)$ is a column vector, it follows from their definitions that the scalar

$$V^\theta(k, \omega) = S(k, \omega)\theta(k, \omega), \quad k = 0, 1, \ldots, T - 1 \tag{5.3.2}$$

represents the time-$k$ value of a portfolio for state $\omega$ just after any transactions that might have been made at time $k$. Moreover, the random variable $V^\theta(k) = V^\theta(k, \cdot)$ represents the time-$k$ value of this same portfolio, and

$$V^\theta = \{V^\theta(k); \quad k = 0, 1, \ldots, T - 1\}$$

is the corresponding stochastic process. The superscript $\theta$ is meant to be a reminder that the value of any portfolio depends upon the underlying trading strategy.

Similarly, we can consider the value of a portfolio just before any time-$k$ transactions. For state $\omega$ this is

$$V^\theta(k^-, \omega) = S(k, \omega)\theta(k - 1, \omega), \quad k = 1, 2, \ldots, T, \tag{5.3.3}$$

and the corresponding random variable is $V^\theta(k^-) = V^\theta(k^-, \cdot)$.

Note that there is no requirement that $V^\theta(k^-) = V^\theta(k)$. In other words, money might be flowing into or out of the portfolio at time $k$. We define

$$c^\theta(k, \omega) = \begin{cases} -V^\theta(k, \omega), & k = 0 \\ V^\theta(k^-, \omega) - V^\theta(k, \omega), & k = 1, \ldots, T - 1 \\ V^\theta(k^-, \omega), & k = T. \end{cases} \tag{5.3.4}$$

Then the random variable $c^\theta(k) = c^\theta(k, \cdot)$ represents the *cash flow* out of the portfolio at time $k$, $k = 0, 1, \ldots, T$. We call

$$c^\theta = \{c^\theta(k); \quad k = 0, 1, \ldots, T\}$$

the *cash-flow process* corresponding to trading strategy $\theta$.

A trading strategy $\theta$ is said to be *self-financing* if $c^\theta(1) = c^\theta(2) = \cdots = c^\theta(T-1) = 0$. This means no money is added to or withdrawn from the portfolio except at times 0 and $T$. Self-financing trading strategies play a special role, as will be seen in the next subsection. In anticipation of this, a convenient and common convention sets $V^\theta(T) = V^\theta(T^-)$ for all trading strategies $\theta$, enabling us to interpret the stochastic process

$$V^\theta = \{V^\theta(k); \quad k = 0, 1, \ldots, T\}$$

as giving all the time-$k$ values of the portfolio corresponding to trading strategy $\theta$.

**Example 5.3.1 (continued).** With $T = 2$ and $\omega_1$, $\omega_2$, $\omega_3$ and $\omega_4$ corresponding to up-up, up-down, down-up, and down-down, respectively, for a trading strategy to be admissible, we must have

$$\theta_j(0, \omega_1) = \theta_j(0, \omega_2) = \theta_j(0, \omega_3) = \theta_j(0, \omega_4) = \theta_{0j}, \quad j = 1, 2$$

for two scalars $\theta_{01}$ and $\theta_{02}$, since all states of nature have the same time-0 history. If the first move by $S_2$ is an up-jump, then at time 1, states $\omega_1$ and $\omega_2$ are still alive, which means that we must have

$$\theta_j(1, \omega_1) = \theta_j(1, \omega_2) = \theta_{uj}, \quad j = 1, 2$$

for two scalars $\theta_{u1}$ and $\theta_{u2}$. On the other hand, the first move might be a down-jump, which leads to the requirement

$$\theta_j(1, \omega_3) = \theta_j(1, \omega_4) = \theta_{dj}, \quad j = 1, 2$$

for two scalars $\theta_{d1}$ and $\theta_{d2}$.

Assuming all these requirements are met, note that $\theta$ will be self-financing if and only if

$$S(1)\theta(0) = S(1)\theta(1).$$

Both sides of this equation are random variables, so it must hold for all $\omega \in \Omega$. For $\omega_1$ and $\omega_2$ this equation says

$$(1 + i)\theta_{01} + S_2(0)u\theta_{02} = (1 + i)\theta_{u1} + S_2(0)u\theta_{u2}.$$

For $\omega_3$ and $\omega_4$ this equation says

$$(1 + i)\theta_{01} + S_2(0)d\theta_{02} = (1 + i)\theta_{d1} + S_2(0)d\theta_{d2}.$$ ∎

### SECTION 5.3.3 | THE FUNDAMENTAL THEOREM OF ASSET PRICING

The primary purpose of this subsection is to present and explain a multiperiod version of the fundamental theory of asset pricing, which has the same form as the single-period version, Theorem 5.2.3, but with multiperiod generalizations of three principal notions: arbitrage, state price vectors, and risk-neutral probability measures.

Just as with single-period models, an arbitrage opportunity is a trading strategy that starts with zero dollars and has a final portfolio value that might be strictly positive but cannot be negative. To be precise:

**Definition 5.3.1.** *A multiperiod securities market model admits* **arbitrage** *if there is a self-financing trading strategy* $\theta$, *called an* **arbitrage opportunity**, *such that*
1.     $V^\theta(0) = S(0)\theta(0) \leq 0$
2.     $V^\theta(T) = S(T)\theta(T - 1) \geq 0$
3.     $V^\theta(T) = S(T)\theta(T - 1) \neq 0.$

Note that (2) and (3) together is the same as saying, with the notation of Section 5.2, that $S(T)\theta(T - 1) > \mathbf{0}$. In other words, $V^\theta(T)$ is a nonnegative random variable that is strictly positive in at least one state of nature $\omega$. Also note that the trading strategy $\theta$ constituting the arbitrage opportunity must be self-financing, for if the cash flow at intermediate points in time is allowed to be nonzero, then we lose the idea that an arbitrage opportunity is a strategy for transforming zero wealth into a riskless profit. Clearly, multiperiod models that permit arbitrage opportunities are unreasonable from the economic point of view.

Turning to the notion of risk-neutral probability measures for multiperiod models, recall the single-period requirement (5.2.8), which can be interpreted by saying that the expected value of the time-1 discounted price of each security (other than the bank account) is equal to the initial price of the security, where this expectation is computed with the risk-neutral probability measure, not the original one. To extend the requirement to multiperiod models we need to worry about each individual period, not just the initial and final times 0 and $T$. To explain this properly, it is necessary to introduce two concepts about stochastic processes.

**Definition 5.3.2.** *A stochastic process* $X = \{X(k); k = 0, 1, \ldots, T\}$ *is said to be* **adapted** *to the information submodel* $\{\mathcal{P}_k; k = 0, 1, \ldots, T\}$ *if, for each k, there is a function such that* $X(k, \omega)$ *can be expressed as this function of the time-k history, for all* $\omega \in \Omega$.

In other words, investors, who know the past and present security prices at each time $k$ (and who also know the function $(k, \omega) \rightarrow X(k, \omega))$ must be able to deduce the time-$k$ value of $X$. Since the time-$k$ knowledge of the investors is captured by some history $\mathcal{H}$, a subset of the sample space $\Omega$, Definition 5.3.2, says for an adapted process $X$ the function $\omega \rightarrow X(k, \omega)$ must be constant on each possible time-$k$ history $\mathcal{H}$. That is, if $\omega_1 \in \mathcal{H}$ and $\omega_2 \in \mathcal{H}$ for some time-$k$ history $\mathcal{H}$, then $X(k, \omega_1) = X(k, \omega_2)$.

**Definition 5.3.3.** *A stochastic process* $X = \{X(k); k = 0, 1, \ldots, T\}$ *is said to be a* **martingale** *if it is adapted and*

$$\mathrm{E}[X(k+1)|\mathcal{P}_k] = X(k), \quad k = 0, 1, \ldots, T-1.$$

In other words, the conditional expectation of a martingale's value in the next period, given any current history, is equal to the current value of the martingale. The wealth of a gambler who plays a fair game is an example of a martingale. Note that the single-period requirement (5.2.8) is a special case of this: just take $k = 0$ and replace $X$ by the discounted security price.

We are now about ready to present the multiperiod definition of risk-neutral probability measures. These will be defined in terms of discounted security prices, which are obtained by taking the ordinary prices $S_j(k)$, $j = 2, 3, \ldots, N$, and dividing by the prices $S_1(k)$ of the bank account at the same point in time:

$$\frac{S_j}{S_1} = \left\{ \frac{S_j(k)}{S_1(k)}; k = 0, 1, \ldots T \right\}, \quad j = 2, 3, \ldots, N.$$

**Definition 5.3.4.** *A* **risk-neutral probability measure** *is a probability measure $Q$ on $\Omega$ satisfying*
a.      $Q(\omega) > 0$, *all* $\omega \in \Omega$
b.      $S_j/S_1$ *is a martingale under $Q$ for* $j = 2, 3, \ldots, N$.

Note that although the discounted prices may be martingales under $Q$, they may not be under the original probability measure $P$, because under $P$ the conditional expected discounted price next period, given a current history, may fail to equal the current discounted price.

We also remark that, for obvious reasons, risk-neutral probability measures are often called *martingale measures*.

We now come to the third and final principal notion in the fundamental theorem of asset pricing, the notion of state price vectors. Recall that for single-period models we had the simple expression (5.2.6) relating initial and final security prices. To extend this to multiperiod models we again must worry about each period and each possible history for each period, not just the initial and final times 0 and $T$.

Consequently, we need to speak of a state price process, not just a state price vector that is a simple random variable. In particular, we have the following definition:

**Definition 5.3.5.** *A stochastic process* $\psi = \{\psi(k); k = 0, 1, \ldots, T\}$ *is said to be a* **state price process** *if the following four conditions hold:*

a.   $\sum_{\omega \in \Omega} \psi(0, \omega) = 1$

b.   *It is adapted*

c.   *It is strictly positive*

d.   $\sum_{\omega \in \mathcal{H}} \psi(k, \omega) S_j(k, \omega) = \sum_{\omega \in \mathcal{H}} \psi(k+1, \omega) S_j(k+1, \omega)$          (5.3.5)

*for all time-k histories* $\mathcal{H}$, *all* $k = 0, 1, \ldots, T-1$, *and all* $j = 1, 2, \ldots, N$.

Note that the requirement (5.2.6) for single-period state price vectors is a special case of this since one can take $k = 0$ and $\mathcal{H} = \Omega$ (recall that $S_j(0, \omega)$ is constant for all $\omega \in \Omega$). Additional insight about state price processes and their links with risk-neutral probabilities will be provided shortly, but now we are ready to present the main result of this subsection.

**Theorem 5.3.6 (Fundamental Theorem of Asset Pricing).** *For a multiperiod model of a securities market that satisfies the assumptions of this section, the following are equivalent:*

a.   *The model is arbitrage free*

b.   *There exists a state price process*

c.   *There exists a risk-neutral probability measure.*

A rigorous proof of the theorem is deferred until Chapter 11, and there the proof will be for multiperiod models that are somewhat more general than the kind studied here. Instead, the balance of this subsection will be devoted to the presentation of some useful economic insights.

A good way to understand this theorem is to appeal to the single-period results and to realize that the multiperiod model consists of single-period models that are pasted together like a tree according to the underlying information structure. We find one component single-period model for each possible history at each possible time before $T$. If any component single-period model has an arbitrage opportunity, then so does the multiperiod model (do nothing until a selected event occurs; if it does, follow the single-period arbitrage strategy, putting any profits in the bank account until time $T$). Conversely, if the multiperiod model has an arbitrage opportunity, then some single-period component must have a single-period arbitrage opportunity (which can be identified by looking for the first period when the multiperiod portfolio value is nonzero).

Hence, if the multiperiod model is arbitrage free, a one-period, risk-neutral probability measure must exist for each component single-period model. These one-period probabilities correspond to conditional probabilities for the multiperiod model, one probability for each branch of the information tree structure. Each $\omega \in \Omega$ corresponds to a unique path in the information tree; multiplying the conditional probabilities along each path gives the $Q(\omega)$'s and thus the risk-neutral probability measure. Conversely, starting with a risk-neutral probability measure we can compute the conditional probabilities and thus the single-period probability measures for each of the component single-period models. From this, we conclude that each component single-period model is arbitrage free, in which case so is the whole multiperiod model.

The same kind of argument can be used to show that the multiperiod model is arbitrage free if and only if there exists a state price process. Instead of taking this direction, however, we establish the explicit connections between state price processes and risk-neutral probability measures, analogous to single-period relationships (5.2.7).

Starting with a risk-neutral probability measure $Q$, we can define a stochastic process $\psi = \{\psi(k); k = 0, 1, \ldots, T\}$ by taking

$$\psi(k, \omega) = \frac{Q(\mathcal{H}) 1_{\mathcal{H}}(\omega)}{\#\mathcal{H} S_1(k, \omega)}, \tag{5.3.6}$$

where $\mathcal{H}$ is any time-$k$ history, $\#\mathcal{H}$ denotes the cardinality of $\mathcal{H}$ (the number of states of nature it contains), and $1_{\mathcal{H}}$ is the indicator function

$$1_{\mathcal{H}}(\omega) = \begin{cases} 1, & \omega \in \mathcal{H} \\ 0, & \text{otherwise.} \end{cases}$$

Thus, $\psi(k, \omega)$ equals $Q(\mathcal{H})/[\#\mathcal{H} S_1(k, \omega)]$ if $\mathcal{H}$ is the time-$k$ history such that $\omega \in \mathcal{H}$. By considering all time-$k$ histories, (5.3.6) defines $\psi(k, \omega)$ for all $\omega \in \Omega$; varying $k$ from 0 to $T$ gives the full specification of the stochastic process $\psi$.

Clearly $\psi$ is strictly positive. It is also adapted, because $S_1(k, \omega)$ and thus the right-hand side of (5.3.6) are constant with respect to $\omega$ on the event $\mathcal{H}$. To conclude that $\psi$ is a state price process, it remains to demonstrate that (5.3.5) is satisfied.

To show this, consider arbitrary $j, k$, and time-$k$ history $\mathcal{H}$, and let $\mathcal{H}(\omega)$ denote the time-$(k + 1)$ history containing $\omega \in \mathcal{H}$. Then for the right-hand side of (5.3.5) we have

$$\sum_{\omega \in \mathcal{H}} \psi(k + 1, \omega) S_j(k + 1, \omega) = \sum_{\omega \in \mathcal{H}} \frac{Q(\mathcal{H}(\omega)) S_j(k + 1, \omega)}{\#\mathcal{H}(\omega) S_1(k + 1, \omega)}. \tag{5.3.7}$$

Next consider all the time-$(k + 1)$ histories that can possibly follow $\mathcal{H}$, and denote these by $\mathcal{H}_i$, $i = 1, 2, \ldots, I$, and recall that these form a partition of $\mathcal{H}$. Since

$$\sum_{\omega \in \mathcal{H}_i} \frac{Q(\mathcal{H}(\omega))}{\#\mathcal{H}(\omega)} = \sum_{\omega \in \mathcal{H}_i} \frac{Q(\mathcal{H}_i)}{\#\mathcal{H}_i} = Q(\mathcal{H}_i), \quad i = 1, 2, \ldots, I$$

and since $S_j(k + 1, \omega)$ and $S_1(k + 1, \omega)$ are constant on each $\mathcal{H}_i$, which will be denoted $S_j(k + 1, \mathcal{H}_i)$ and $S_1(k + 1, \mathcal{H}_i)$, respectively, it follows from (5.3.7) that

$$\sum_{\omega \in \mathcal{H}} \psi(k + 1, \omega) S_j(k + 1, \omega) = \sum_{i=1}^{I} Q(\mathcal{H}_i) \frac{S_j(k + 1, \mathcal{H}_i)}{S_1(k + 1, \mathcal{H}_i)}. \tag{5.3.8}$$

Meanwhile, in a similar fashion, the left-hand side of (5.3.5) is

$$\begin{aligned}
\sum_{\omega \in \mathcal{H}} \psi(k, \omega) S_j(k, \omega) &= \sum_{\omega \in \mathcal{H}} \frac{Q(\mathcal{H}) S_j(k, \omega)}{\#\mathcal{H} S_1(k, \omega)} \\
&= \frac{S_j(k, \mathcal{H})}{S_1(k, \mathcal{H})} \sum_{\omega \in \mathcal{H}} \frac{Q(\mathcal{H})}{\#\mathcal{H}} \\
&= \frac{S_j(k, \mathcal{H})}{S_1(k, \mathcal{H})} Q(\mathcal{H}), \tag{5.3.9}
\end{aligned}$$

where the middle equality is true because $S_j(k, \omega)$ and $S_1(k, \omega)$ are constant on $\mathcal{H}$. But $Q$ is a risk-neutral probability measure, so for $\omega \in \mathcal{H}$

$$\frac{S_j(k, \omega)}{S_1(k, \omega)} = \sum_{i=1}^{I} \frac{Q(\mathcal{H}_i)}{Q(\mathcal{H})} \frac{S_j(k + 1, \mathcal{H}_i)}{S_1(k + 1, \mathcal{H}_i)};$$

because $Q(\mathcal{H}_i)/Q(\mathcal{H})$ is just the conditional probability that the time-$(k+1)$ history is $\mathcal{H}_i$ given that the time-$k$ history is $\mathcal{H}$. Hence, the right-hand sides of (5.3.8) and (5.3.9) are equal, so we conclude that the left-hand sides are equal and that $\psi$ is a state price process.

Conversely, given a state price process $\psi$ we can use (5.3.6) to define the strictly positive quantities $Q(\mathcal{H})$. Taking $k = 0$ and $j = 1$ in (5.3.9) we see that $Q(\Omega) = 1$ (recall $S_1(0, \omega) = 1$). Taking $j = 1$, general $k$, (5.3.8), (5.3.9), and (5.3.5), we see that

$$Q(\mathcal{H}) = \sum_{i=1}^{I} Q(\mathcal{H}_i),$$

where $\mathcal{H}$ and $\mathcal{H}_i$ are histories as defined above. In particular, taking $k = T - 1$ we conclude that $Q(\omega) > 0$ for all $\omega \in \Omega$ and that $\sum_{\omega} Q(\omega) = 1$. Thus, $Q$ is a probability measure. Finally, taking these same equations for $j \geq 2$ gives the conditional expectation relationships that establish the discounted prices as martingales under $Q$, so $Q$ is indeed a risk-neutral probability measure.

We now present an alternative argument showing that the existence of a risk-neutral probability measure implies the model is arbitrage free. This argument is of interest not only because it provides additional understanding about the fundamental theorem of asset pricing, but also because two secondary results along the way are useful for future purposes. These intermediate results are stated as two propositions.

**Proposition 5.3.7.** *If Q is a risk-neutral probability measure and if $\theta$ is a self-financing trading strategy, then the discounted value of the corresponding portfolio satisfies*

$$\frac{V^\theta(k)}{S_1(k)} = E^Q\left[\frac{V^\theta(k+1)}{S_1(k+1)}\bigg|\mathcal{P}_k\right], \quad k = 0, 1, \ldots, T-1. \tag{5.3.10}$$

This says that the discounted value of the portfolio corresponding to a self-financing strategy is a martingale under a risk-neutral probability measure. To see why it is true, note that

$$E^Q\left[\frac{V^\theta(k+1)}{S_1(k+1)}\bigg|\mathcal{P}_k\right] = E^Q\left[\frac{V^\theta((k+1)^-)}{S_1(k+1)}\bigg|\mathcal{P}_k\right]$$

$$= E^Q\left[\frac{S(k+1)\theta(k)}{S_1(k+1)}\bigg|\mathcal{P}_k\right]$$

$$= E^Q\left[\frac{S(k+1)}{S_1(k+1)}\bigg|\mathcal{P}_k\right]\theta(k)$$

$$= \frac{S(k)}{S_1(k)}\theta(k)$$

$$= \frac{V^\theta(k)}{S_1(k)},$$

where the first equality is because $\theta$ is self-financing, the second follows from (5.3.3), the third is because the random vector $\theta(k)$, fully specified by any time-$k$ history, can come out of the expectation, the fourth is due to (b) in Definition 5.3.4, and the last follows from (5.3.2).

Proposition 5.3.7 can be generalized by using a basic principle of probability theory. By the law of iterated expectations we have that

$$E^Q\left[\frac{V^\theta(k+2)}{S_1(k+2)}\bigg|\mathcal{P}_k\right] = E^Q\left[E^Q\left[\frac{V^\theta(k+2)}{S_1(k+2)}\bigg|\mathcal{P}_{k+1}\right]\bigg|\mathcal{P}_k\right],$$

which says that the conditional expectation of discounted prices two periods in the future, given current information, is equal to the conditional expectation, given the same information, of the conditional information of the same prices given the information that will be available next period (a fair gamble over two periods is fair over each of the two successive periods). But the inside conditional expectation on the right-hand side equals $V^\theta(k+1)/S_1(k+1)$ by Proposition 5.3.7, so using this proposition a second time leads to

$$E^Q\left[\frac{V^\theta(k+2)}{S_1(k+2)}\Big|\mathcal{P}_k\right] = \frac{V^\theta(k)}{S_1(k)}.$$

This argument can be extended to an arbitrary number of future periods, thereby obtaining the following useful result:

**Proposition 5.3.8.** *If Q is a risk-neutral probability measure and if $\theta$ is a self-financing trading strategy, then the discounted value of the corresponding portfolio, which is a martingale under Q, satisfies*

$$\frac{V^\theta(k)}{S_1(k)} = E^Q\left[\frac{V^\theta(t)}{S_1(t)}\Big|\mathcal{P}_k\right] \tag{5.3.11}$$

*for all $0 \le k \le t \le T$.*

Incidentally, as was pointed out earlier, $V^\theta(k)/S_1(k)$ is a martingale under the risk-neutral probability measure, and so the preceding argument shows that the requirement $X(k) = E[X(t)|\mathcal{P}_k], 0 \le k \le t \le T$, is equivalent to the one in Definition 5.3.3 for $X$ to be a martingale.

Armed with Proposition 5.3.8, it is easy to see why the existence of a risk-neutral probability measure $Q$ precludes the presence of any arbitrage opportunities. Suppose $\theta$ is a self-financing trading strategy satisfying $V^\theta(T) \ge 0$ and $V^\theta(T) \ne 0$. Then applying Proposition 5.3.8 with $k = 0$ and $t = T$, and recalling that the bank account process is strictly positive, we realize that $V^\theta(0)$ must be strictly positive. Hence, $\theta$ cannot be an arbitrage opportunity.

We conclude this subsection with a calculation of the risk-neutral probability measure and the state price process for our familiar example.

**Example 5.3.1 (continued).** Just as with the single-period model Example 5.2.1, the multiperiod binomial stock price model is arbitrage free if and only if $u > 1 + i > d > 0$. If this condition holds, then

$$q = \frac{1+i-d}{u-d}$$

and $1 - q$ define the risk-neutral conditional probabilities of up- and down-jumps, respectively, for each component single-period model. It follows (see the discussion of this example in Subsection 5.3.1) that the risk-neutral probability is

$$Q(\omega) = q^n(1 - q)^{T-n}$$

if the state of nature $\omega$ corresponds to exactly $n$ up-jumps and $T - n$ down-jumps. To specify the state price process, note that if $\mathcal{H}$ is a time-$k$ history corresponding to a particular sequence $n$ up-jumps and $k - n$ down-jumps, then

$$Q(\mathcal{H}) = q^n(1 - q)^{k-n}$$

and $\#\mathcal{H} = 2^{T-k}$, in which case for $\omega \in \mathcal{H}$

$$\psi(k, \omega) = \frac{q^n(1 - q)^{k-n}}{2^{T-k}(1 + i)^k}. \qquad \blacksquare$$

## SECTION 5.3.4 | VALUATION OF EUROPEAN OPTIONS AND OTHER CASH FLOWS

As we stated in the context of single-period models (see Subsection 5.2.4), a primary purpose of securities market models is to derive the time-0 values of future uncertain cash flows. For single-period models, the principal result (see Theorem 5.2.7) states that if a cash flow is attainable, then its time-0 value equals the expected discounted value of the cash flow, with this expectation computed with a risk-neutral probability measure. It is important to note, with one exception, that the same kind of result holds for multiperiod models, even though a cash flow may involve payments at two or more points in time.

Three kinds of cash flows are discussed in this subsection. The simplest kind, called a *contingent claim* or *European option*, is one where the cash flow occurs at a single point in time. As with single-period models, such a cash flow is fully described by a random variable $X$, with the interpretation that the owner of this cash flow receives $X(\omega)$ dollars at the designated point of time if state of nature $\omega$ pertains.

The valuation of European options will be studied shortly, but first we mention the other two kinds of cash flows. Slightly more complicated than European options are cash-flow streams described by an adapted stochastic process

$$c = \{c(k); \quad k = 1, 2, \ldots, T\}.$$

Here the owner of the cash-flow stream receives $c(k, \omega)$ dollars at time $k$ if $\omega$ is the state of nature, for $k = 1, 2, \ldots, T$. Since the cash-flow stream is simply the sum of $T$ European options, its value is simply the sum of the values of these corresponding European options. Cash-flow streams are studied at the end of this subsection.

The third kind of cash flow is also described by an adapted stochastic process such as $c$ above, but the interpretation is much different. These are called American options. Here the owner must choose, in real time, a single *exercise date* $\tau$, thereby receiving $c(\tau)$ dollars. In other words, if the owner has not exercised already, then at time $k$, and based upon the time-$k$ history, the owner can either exercise right away, thereby receiving $c(k)$ dollars, or continue for at least one more period. Since the owner can exercise at most once, American options can be viewed as generalizations of European options. And since the rational owner of an American option will want to choose the exercise date so as to maximize, in some sense, the cash received, the valuation of American options is rather complicated. Consequently, we postpone the study of American options until Chapters 6 and 11.

We now return to the study of European options. As stated earlier, a European option is a random variable $X$ representing the cash payment to the owner at a designated point in time $T$. For example, if $S_j$ is a designated security, then

$$X(\omega) = [S_j(T, \omega) - K]^+$$

is a European option called a *call option*. It represents the right for the owner of this option to purchase one share of security $j$ for $K$ dollars at time $T$. Call options and many other kinds of European options are studied extensively in Chapter 6. The aim here is to simply present the basic theory for their valuation.

As with single-period cash flows, we say that the self-financing trading strategy $\theta$ and the corresponding portfolio *replicate* the European option $X$ if

$$V^\theta(T) = X,$$

that is, $V^\theta(T, \omega) = X(\omega)$, all $\omega \in \Omega$. This means there is some trading strategy such that, without adding or removing money at intermediate points in time, the final value of the portfolio coincides with the case flow, regardless of the state of nature.

We say that a European option is *attainable* if it can be replicated by some self-financing portfolio. So just as we saw for single-period models, the idea of arbitrage quickly leads us to the following conclusion:

**Theorem 5.3.9.** *In an arbitrage-free multiperiod model, the time-0 value of an attainable European option $X$ is equal to the time-0 value of the portfolio that replicates $X$.*

For anyone who has already studied Subsection 5.2.4, the next conclusion should come as no surprise. First, notice that $V^\theta(T) = X$ if and only if

$$\frac{V^\theta(T)}{S_1(T)} = \frac{X}{S_1(T)}. \tag{5.3.12}$$

Second, recall (see Proposition 5.3.7) that the discounted value of a self-financed portfolio is a martingale under a risk-neutral probability measure $Q$, so the expectation under $Q$ of the left-hand side of (5.3.12) must equal (see Proposition 5.3.8) $V^\theta(0)/S_1(0) = V^\theta(0)$. But $V^\theta(0)$ is the time-0 value of the European option $X$, so using (5.3.12) again we have established the first part of the following theorem.

**Theorem 5.3.10.** *In an arbitrage-free multiperiod model having risk-neutral probability measure $Q$, the time-0 value of an attainable European option $X$ is equal to $\mathrm{E}^Q[X/S_1(T)]$. This value can also be expressed in terms of the state price process $\psi$, because*

$$\mathrm{E}^Q\left[\frac{X}{S_1(T)}\right] = \sum_{\omega \in \Omega} \psi(T, \omega) X(\omega). \tag{5.3.13}$$

Equation (5.3.13) follows from (5.3.6) with $k = T$. In this case the time-$T$ histories are of the form $\mathcal{H} = \{w\}$, so

$$\psi(T, \omega) = \frac{Q(\omega)}{S_1(T, \omega)}.$$

Consequently,

$$\mathrm{E}^Q\left[\frac{X}{S_1(T)}\right] = \sum_{\omega \in \Omega} \frac{Q(\omega)}{S_1(T, \omega)} X(\omega) = \sum_{\omega \in \Omega} \psi(T, \omega) X(\omega).$$

We now turn to the valuation of cash-flow streams that are described by an adapted process $c = \{c(k); k = 1, 2, \ldots, T\}$. A (not necessarily self-financing) trading strategy $\theta$ and the corresponding portfolio $V^\theta$ are said to *replicate $c$* and to *finance $c$* if

$$c^\theta(k) = c(k), \quad k = 1, 2, \ldots, T \tag{5.3.14}$$

(note $c^\theta$ is defined by (5.3.4)). The cash-flow stream $c$ is said to be *attainable* if it can be replicated by some trading strategy $\theta$.

Just as with attainable European options, if a cash-flow stream $c$ can be financed by a trading strategy $\theta$, then arbitrage arguments can be used to conclude that the time-0 value of $c$ must equal the time-0 value $V^\theta(0)$ of the portfolio that corresponds to $\theta$. For instance, if this cash-flow stream were to sell at a higher price, then at time 0 an alert arbitrageur would sell at this higher price a contract to deliver this cash-flow stream, begin the strategy $\theta$ at a lower cost, and place the difference in the bank account. At each subsequent point in time the arbitrageur would fulfill the cash-flow obligation by withdrawing money from the portfolio according to $\theta$, ending up at time $T$ having fulfilled all the cash-flow obligations and with a positive amount of money in the bank.

This is an arbitrage opportunity, and one would also exist if the time-0 value of $c$ were less than the time-0 value of the replicating portfolio. We thus have the following theorem:

**Theorem 5.3.11.** *In an arbitrage-free multiperiod model, the time-0 value of an attainable cash-flow stream $c$ is equal to the time-0 value of the portfolio that finances $c$.*

There are simple formulas for the value of a cash-flow stream, analogous to those for European options in Theorem 5.3.10. To see this, first consider the simple case where $T = 2$, so (see (5.3.4))

$$V^\theta(1^-) - V^\theta(1) = c(1); \qquad (5.3.15)$$

that is, the time-1 reduction in portfolio value is equal to the out-going cash flow $c(1)$, and

$$V^\theta(2^-) = c(2); \qquad (5.3.16)$$

that is, the time-2 portfolio value is $c(2)$. Meanwhile, note that

$$V^\theta(0) = E^Q\left[\frac{V^\theta(1^-)}{S_1(1)}\right],$$

because we can apply the familiar argument that the expectation under the risk-neutral probability measure of the discounted value of the portfolio just before any time-1 transactions is equal to the initial value of the portfolio (see Proposition 5.3.7). Combining this with (5.3.15) gives

$$V^\theta(0) = E^Q\left[\frac{c(1)}{S_1(1)}\right] + E^Q\left[\frac{V^\theta(1)}{S_1(1)}\right]. \qquad (5.3.17)$$

Using a slight variation of Proposition 5.3.7 again together with (5.3.16) gives

$$\frac{V^\theta(1)}{S_1(1)} = E^Q\left[\frac{V^\theta(2^-)}{S_1(2)}\Big|\mathcal{P}_1\right] = E^Q\left[\frac{c(2)}{S_1(2)}\Big|\mathcal{P}_1\right].$$

Substituting this into (5.3.17) and using the principle of iterated conditional expectations, we obtain

$$V^\theta(0) = E^Q\left[\frac{c(1)}{S_1(1)}\right] + E^Q\left[E^Q\left[\frac{c(2)}{S_1(2)}\Big|\mathcal{P}_1\right]\right]$$

$$= E^Q\left[\frac{c(1)}{S_1(1)}\right] + E^Q\left[\frac{c(2)}{S_1(2)}\right]. \qquad (5.3.18)$$

In view of Theorem 5.3.11, we finally conclude that the time-0 value of an attainable cash-flow stream is equal to the expected discounted value of the cash flows, with this expectation computed with a risk-neutral probability measure.

This cash-flow stream valuation principle holds for any number of time periods (see Theorem 5.3.12 below). First, however, consider how to express the value of a two-period cash-flow stream in terms of the state price process $\psi$.

Suppose $T = 2$ and (5.3.18) applies. By taking $c(2)$ in place of $X$ in Theorem 5.3.10, it follows that

$$E^Q\left[\frac{c(2)}{S_1(2)}\right] = \sum_{\omega \in \Omega} \psi(2, \omega)c(2, \omega). \tag{5.3.19}$$

But for the other term on the right-hand side of (5.3.18), which has $S(1)$ instead of $S(2)$ in the denominator, we need to do some more work. This argument is a bit abstract, for it involves time-1 histories and the defining property (see Definition 5.3.5) of state price processes, so you may find it useful to visualize the information tree structure for a generic two-period model.

Recall that $\mathcal{P}_1$ denotes the collection of time-1 histories $\mathcal{H}$ and that (since the process $c$ is assumed to be adapted) the function $\omega \rightarrow c(1, \omega)$ is constant over each $\mathcal{H} \in \mathcal{P}_1$. Let $c(1, \mathcal{H})$ denote this constant value, and, similarly, let $S_1(1, \mathcal{H})$ denote the constant value of $S_1(1, \omega)$ on each $\mathcal{H} \in \mathcal{P}_1$. Starting out with the same argument used to derive (5.3.13), we then have

$$E^Q\left[\frac{c(1)}{S_1(1)}\right] = \sum_{\omega \in \Omega} \frac{c(1, \omega)}{S_1(1, \omega)} Q(\omega)$$

$$= \sum_{\omega \in \Omega} \frac{c(1, \omega)}{S_1(1, \omega)} \psi(2, \omega) S_1(2, \omega)$$

$$= \sum_{\mathcal{H} \in \mathcal{P}_1} \frac{c(1, \mathcal{H})}{S_1(1, \mathcal{H})} \sum_{\omega \in \mathcal{H}} \psi(2, \omega) S_1(2, \omega)$$

(visualization of an information tree will help with the understanding of this last equality). We now apply the defining property (5.3.5) of the state price process $\psi$ (taking $k = 1$) to obtain

$$E^Q\left[\frac{c(1)}{S_1(1)}\right] = \sum_{\mathcal{H} \in \mathcal{P}_1} \frac{c(1, \mathcal{H})}{S_1(1, \mathcal{H})} \sum_{\omega \in \mathcal{H}} \psi(1, \omega) S_1(1, \omega)$$

$$= \sum_{\omega \in \Omega} \psi(1, \omega)c(1, \omega).$$

Finally, we combine this with (5.3.18) and (5.3.19) to conclude

$$V^\theta(0) = \sum_{\omega \in \Omega} \sum_{k=1}^{2} \psi(k, \omega) c(k, \omega).$$

Again, this argument can be extended to any number of periods, and so we have the following:

**Theorem 5.3.12.** *In an arbitrage-free multiperiod model having risk-neutral probability measure Q and state price process $\psi$, the time-0 value of an attainable cash-flow stream c is equal to*

$$E^Q\left[ \sum_{k=1}^{T} \frac{c(k)}{S_1(k)} \right] = \sum_{\omega \in \Omega} \sum_{k=1}^{T} \psi(k, \omega) c(k, \omega).$$

**Example 5.3.1 (continued).** Suppose for some functions $f_k : \mathfrak{R} \to \mathfrak{R}$ that

$$c(k) = f_k(S_2(k)), \quad k = 1, 2, \ldots, T.$$

Since

$$Q(S_2(k) = S_2(0) u^n d^{k-n}) = \binom{k}{n} q^n (1-q)^{k-n}, \quad n = 0, 1, \ldots, k,$$

it follows that the time-0 value of the cash-flow stream is

$$E^Q\left[ \sum_{k=1}^{T} \frac{c(k)}{S_1(k)} \right] = E^Q\left[ \sum_{k=1}^{T} f_k(S_2(k))(1+i)^{-k} \right]$$

$$= (1+i)^{-k} \sum_{k=1}^{T} \sum_{n=0}^{k} \binom{k}{n} q^n (1-q)^{k-n} f_k\left(S_2(0) u^n d^{k-n}\right). \quad (5.3.20)$$

Alternatively, to derive this expression by using the state price process $\psi$, let $E_{nk}$ denote the event that exactly $n$ of the first $k$ moves are up-jumps, for $n = 0, 1, \ldots, k$; $k = 1, 2, \ldots, T$. Then

$$c(k, \omega) = f_k(S_2(0) u^n d^{k-n}), \quad \text{all } \omega \in E_{nk},$$

$$\psi(k, \omega) = \frac{q^n (1-q)^{k-n}}{2^{T-k}(1+i)^k}, \quad \text{all } \omega \in E_{nk}$$

(see the preceding discussion of this example), and thus the time-0 value of the cash-flow stream is

$$\sum_{\omega \in \Omega} \sum_{k=1}^{T} \psi(k, \omega) c(k, \omega) = \sum_{k=1}^{T} \sum_{n=0}^{k} \sum_{\omega \in E_{nk}} \frac{q^n (1-q)^{k-n}}{2^{T-k}(1+i)^k} f_k(S_2(0) u^n d^{k-n}).$$

This is the same as (5.3.20), because $\binom{k}{n}$ is the number of distinguishable time-$k$ histories featuring $n$ up-jumps and $k - n$ down-jumps, and each of these histories has $2^{T-k}$ states of nature $\omega$, so $E_{nk}$ has $\binom{k}{n} 2^{T-k}$ states of nature $\omega$.

Note that if $f_k = 0$ for $k = 1, 2, \ldots, T - 1$, then $c$ is the same as a European option. ∎

## SECTION 5.3.5 | COMPLETENESS IN THE MULTIPERIOD MODEL

The notion of completeness for multiperiod models is very similar to the notion for single-period models (see Definition 5.2.8):

**Definition 5.3.13.** *An arbitrage-free multiperiod model is said to be* **complete** *if every adapted cash-flow stream c is financed by some trading strategy* $\theta$.

If you know that the model is complete, then you automatically know that every cash-flow stream and European option can be valued as in Theorems 5.3.10 and 5.3.12. On the other hand, if you know the model is not complete, then it is necessary to verify that the cash-flow stream or European option to be priced is attainable before you can apply these theorems. If a cash-flow stream is not attainable, then for its valuation we must resort to equilibrium pricing, as described in Chapter 4. Thus, it may be important to know whether a multiperiod model is complete.

The single-period results presented in Theorem 5.2.9 and Corollary 5.2.10 generalize in a natural way to our multiperiod situation.

**Theorem 5.3.14.** *For an arbitrage-free multiperiod model, the following are equivalent:*
a.    *The model is complete.*
b.    *The state price process* $\psi$ *is unique.*
c.    *The risk-neutral probability measure Q is unique.*

We can see without much difficulty why this theorem is true. The equivalence of (b) and (c) follows from (5.3.6) and the accompanying discussion.

If the model is complete, then for arbitrary $\bar{\omega} \in \Omega$ the European option $X = 1_{\bar{\omega}}$ that pays 1 at time $T$ if state $\bar{\omega}$ occurs but pays nothing otherwise is attainable. By Theorem 5.3.10, the time-0 price of this Arrow-Debreu security, that is, European option, is

$$E^Q\left[\frac{X}{S_1(T)}\right] = \frac{Q(\bar{\omega})}{S_1(T, \bar{\omega})}.$$

This shows that $Q$ must be unique.

Conversely, if the risk-neutral probability measure $Q$ is unique, then so too must be the risk-neutral conditional probabilities associated with each of the single-period submodel components corresponding to the information tree structure. By Corollary 5.2.10, this means every component single-period submodel is complete. This in turn means that given any time-$k$ history $\mathcal{H}$ and any adapted cash flow $c$ a vector $\theta \in \Re^N$ exists such that

$$\sum_{j=1}^{N} S_j(k, \omega)\theta_j = c(k+1, \omega), \quad \text{all } \omega \in \mathcal{H}.$$

Finally, by pasting together the various pieces of the trading strategy in an appropriate way (the details are omitted, since they are not difficult to understand, only messy), it can be shown that the cash flow $c$ can be financed. Because $c$ was arbitrary, this shows the model is complete.

**Example 5.3.1 (continued).** Because all the single-period component submodels are identical and complete, then the whole multiperiod model is complete, and the risk-neutral probability measure and the state price process are unique. ∎

# Section 5.4
# Conclusion

The pricing of financial instruments based on the principle of no arbitrage is a key paradigm in modern financial economics. Another key paradigm is the equilibrium pricing theory discussed in Chapter 4. The principle of no arbitrage originates from the following economic consideration: As opportunities for "free lunches" arise, they quickly disappear as they are recognized. Arbitrageurs move very rapidly to take advantage of supply-and-demand differences in various markets.

In this chapter, we introduce no-arbitrage securities market models in the simplest possible framework: the single-period and multiperiod models with a finite set of possible outcomes (finite state space). In the single-period model, we restricted the mathematics to elementary linear algebra and linear programming. In the multiperiod case, we found it more efficient to introduce probability concepts, even though it is possible to express and prove all results without using probability. In particular, because trading is allowed at all future points in time (a finite number of discrete points), the history of the process (a finite number of possible histories) plays a critical role. Thus, the probability concepts introduced include partitions, adapted processes, and martingale measures.

The treatment of the principle of no arbitrage can be done in a more general mathematical framework. In Chapter 11 much of the multiperiod model is reexamined, and many more results are derived. However, in this book we avoid the continuous-time and continuous state-space framework except for what is introduced through the Poisson process in Chapter 10.

The treatment of continuous-time models normally requires yet another level of mathematical sophistication, requiring tools such as continuous-time stochastic processes, Ito's calculus, Girsanov's theorem, and so on. We avoid this because several additional chapters would be required and many concepts are better understood in the discrete-time framework. In addition, in any model-building exercise, discrete time points are usually assumed to better represent the real world of trading. In any case, a discretization of time is required for computer implementation. However, we hasten to add that there are many advantages in using continuous-time models, such as the availability of elegant closed-form formulas. Indeed, most of the important no-arbitrage term structure of interest rates models are based on the continuous-time approach.

# *Section 5.5*
# *Exercises*

## *Exercise 5.1*

Consider a one-period security market model. There are two assets, a bond and a stock. The interest rate is assumed to be 0 so that the bond sells for $1 and pays $1 at the end of the period. The stock price is assumed to have the following binomial evolution:

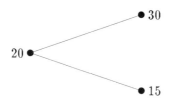

Consider a put option written on the stock with strike price $23. Calculate the price of the put option. Give a brief description why the price you have computed is the price of the put option.

## Exercise 5.2

Consider a one-period security market model. There are two assets, a bond and a stock. The interest rate is assumed to be 0 so that the bond sells for $1 and pays $1 at the end of the period. The stock price is assumed to have the following trinomial structure:

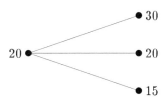

Consider a call option written on the stock with strike price $23. Is it possible to calculate the price of the call option from arbitrage considerations alone? Support your answer with a brief description why. Is it possible to derive bounds, based on the absence of arbitrage, for the price of the call option? The call option obviously will have a positive price not exceeding $7. Devise an argument to determine the tightest bounds on the option price that can be obtained from arbitrage considerations alone. Do this problem graphically without using the fundamental theorem of asset pricing. [Hint: Form portfolios containing either long or short positions in the call option and use the fact that if the payoffs from a portfolio are nonnegative, then its price must be nonnegative. Be sure to determine if strict inequality is obtained in the bounds you derive.]

## Exercise 5.3

Rework Exercise 5.2 using the fundamental theorem of asset pricing.

## Exercise 5.4

Consider an asset market in which two assets, corporate bonds and risk-free government bonds, are defined. The continuously compounded rate of interest on risk-free bonds is 8%, and the corporate bond is currently priced at $65. If the government is able to balance its budget, the corporate bond will go to 110, but if it fails, the corporate bond will go to $38. Another possibility is that because of the government's inability to balance the budget, the company will be unable to service its debt (due to high corporate borrowing costs) and go bankrupt. Consequently, there is a third state in which the company goes bankrupt and defaults on its bonds. What is the most an investor would pay for a call option on the corporate bond with a strike price of $85?

## Exercise 5.5

A one-period arbitrage-free model has two assets with the following price evolution:

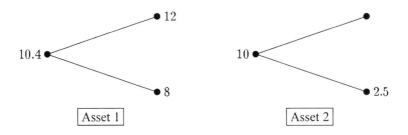

A call option on asset 1 with a strike price of 9 has a price of 1.8.

a. Compute the state prices implicit in this model.

b. Compute the risk neutral probabilities for this model.

c. Compute the implied rate of interest for this model.

d. The price of a call option on asset 2 is 2.4. What is the strike price of this call option?

## Exercise 5.6

Consider a one-period securities market model given by

$$S(0) = \begin{bmatrix} \dfrac{1}{2} & \dfrac{5}{6} & \dfrac{1}{6} \end{bmatrix}, \qquad S(1) = \begin{bmatrix} 1 & 2 & 0 \\ 1 & 3 & 0 \\ 1 & 0 & 1 \\ 0 & 0 & 0 \end{bmatrix}.$$

Is this model arbitrage free? Does a state price vector exist for this model? If so, calculate one explicitly.

## Exercise 5.7

Consider a one-period securities market model. At the end of the period the economy will either be "good" or "bad." There are two assets in this model. The first asset pays $4 if the economy is good and $1 if the economy is bad. The second asset pays $1 if the economy is good and $4 if the economy is bad. At the beginning of the period (time 0) the first asset sells for $2.25 and the second asset sells for $1.50. An investor would like to receive $1 if the economy is good and nothing if the economy is bad. Is there a portfolio of assets 1 and 2 that has the payoffs the investor would like? What are the portfolio holdings of asset 1 and asset 2 that give a portfolio with the payoffs the investor would like? What is the price of this portfolio?

## Exercise 5.8

Consider a one-period securities market model. There are two assets, a bond and a stock. The interest rate is assumed to be 0 so that the bond sells for $1 and pays $1 at the end of the period. The stock price is assumed to have the following trinomial evolution:

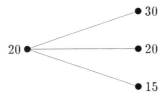

Your company has decided to market an investment product that protects investors from adverse investment performance in the stock. This asset has the payoffs

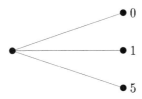

What is the range of prices at which this new asset could be introduced into the market such that there would be no arbitrage opportunities?

## Exercise 5.9

Determine all state price vectors for the one-period securities market model

$$S(0) = [0.7 \quad 0.3], \qquad S(1) = \begin{bmatrix} 1 & 2 \\ 1 & 10 \end{bmatrix}.$$

## Exercise 5.10

a. Determine if the following one-period securities market model is arbitrage free:

$$S(0) = [1 \quad 2 \quad 10], \qquad S(1) = \begin{bmatrix} 1 & 12 & 0 \\ 1 & 3 & 0 \\ 1 & 0 & 0 \\ 1 & 0 & 10 \end{bmatrix}.$$

b. If we change the payoffs of the assets to

$$S(1) = \begin{bmatrix} 1 & 12 & 0 \\ 1 & 3 & 0 \\ 1 & 0 & 0 \\ 1 & 0 & 20 \end{bmatrix},$$

keeping $S(0)$ as before, is the resulting single-period securities market model arbitrage free? If so, exhibit a state price vector for the model.

## Exercise 5.11

Consider a one-period model with three traded assets. The payoffs and current prices of each asset are as shown on the following trees:

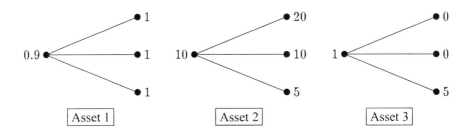

The chief actuary of the company you are currently employed by believes that asset 2 is "overdue for a big price swing" and has "suggested" that you find a way for the company to benefit from this "insight." You have decided that an appropriate portfolio for taking advantage of big price changes in asset 2 is a straddle position consisting of one call option on asset 2 with strike price 10 and one put option on asset 2 with strike price 10.

a. What is the price of a call option on asset 2 with strike price 10? What is the price of a put option on asset 2 with strike price 10? What is the cost of the straddle portfolio you decide to adopt?

b. Draw a tree labeling the payoffs of the straddle portfolio in each state and the cost of the straddle portfolio at time 0. Compute the return on investment for the straddle portfolio in each state.

c. Portfolios with very high rates of return in a few states and little value in most states are said to be "leveraged." You have no sooner set up the portfolio than the chief actuary calls you in. "Leveraged option portfolios are the bread and butter of this company," he informs you, "but the regulators are being a nuisance, so I want you to adjust our straddle portfolio by adding put options [on asset 2 with strike price 10] so that the return on investment in the lowest state is equal to the return on investment in the highest state." After you carry this out, what will be the return on investment in each state for the modified portfolio?

---

### Exercise 5.12

A securities market model follows the binomial stock price model. You are given that $u = 1.2$, $d = 0.91$, $i = 0.07$, and the initial stock price is 20. Compute the price of a European put option on the stock that expires in four periods and has a strike price of 17.

# CHAPTER 6
## OPTIONS AND OTHER DERIVATIVES

## Section 6.1
## Introduction

This chapter covers the discrete-time valuation of options and other derivatives excluding term structure derivatives. The no-arbitrage valuation results of Chapter 5 are first used to value standard European derivatives with a payoff at a fixed expiration date. These include standard European call and put equity options. The binomial model is used to value these options.

The main features of some of the more popular exotic options are described along with a discussion of aspects of their valuation. These options include digital options, Asian options, lookback options, barrier options, and exchange options. The valuation of American-style options that allow early exercise is outlined after a discussion of the effect of early exercise on option valuation.

In practice, derivatives are valued using different numerical procedures depending on whether they are European or American and whether or not the option payoff is path dependent. The binomial model is a commonly used method. A variety of other numerical techniques exist that can be used for option valuation including lattice models and Monte Carlo simulation. For many exotic options, the existence of path dependence and the resulting numerical complexity requires the use of numerical techniques, some of which are outlined and discussed.

The risk management of a portfolio of derivatives requires a knowledge of the sensitivity of the portfolio to the various factors that influence its value. A number of risk statistics such as the delta, gamma, theta, and vega are useful for this purpose and are also used for the hedging of derivatives. These various risk statistics are defined along with a discussion of their use.

The valuation of derivatives is generally based on an arbitrage-free model and the assumption that the derivative security can be replicated using a self-financing portfolio of traded securities. Derivative valuation models generally assume that there are no market frictions such as transaction costs and that there are no taxes. If the derivative cannot be replicated using existing traded securities, then other valuation approaches such as those covered in Chapters 4 and 10 are required.

Finally, we provide examples in which option valuation techniques have been applied to value insurance and pension liabilities.

The literature and textbooks on derivative valuation are extensive. This chapter only covers the main concepts. Readers are referred to any of the recent texts on derivatives such as Boyle [22], Chriss [38], Hull [98], Ritchken [157], and Jarrow and Turnbull [100] for more details. Cox and Rubinstein [45] provides a practical coverage of option pricing. Dothan [48], Duffie [50], Huang and Litzenberger [96], and Ingersoll [99] provide more advanced treatments.

# *Section 6.2*
# *Valuation of Derivative Securities*

In this section we discuss the basic valuation result for European derivative instruments within the no-arbitrage framework. The theoretical framework for this approach was developed in Chapter 5. The key idea is that if we can replicate a cash flow (payoff) using existing traded securities, then we can obtain the price of this cash flow using no-arbitrage arguments. We first consider the simple one-period model with two distinct outcomes and two assets. In this case, the result becomes very intuitive because any payoff at time 1 can be replicated using a portfolio of the two assets. We concentrate first on the replication approach and demonstrate its natural connection with hedging. Indeed, if we use the replication approach, we obtain both the value of the derivative and the hedging strategy at the same time. Then we show how the valuation relation can be expressed in terms of the equivalent martingale measure.

## SECTION 6.2.1 | DERIVATIVE PRICING:
## THE ONE-PERIOD MODEL

We first analyze the one-period model where there are two assets and two outcomes. We denote the asset prices by $S_1$ and $S_2$, which refer to as the *primitive securities*. Their time-0 prices are $S_1(0)$ and $S_2(0)$. At time 1, their prices are $\{S_1(1, \omega_j), S_2(1, \omega_j)\}$ where $\omega_j$, $j = 1, 2$, denotes the states at time 1. We assume that all the prices are strictly positive. To ensure a complete market, the returns on these securities must be linearly independent. This implies that the payoff matrix is nonsingular so that its determinant is nonzero.

Suppose we have a derivative security whose payoff at time 1 is a function of the two primitive securities so that

$$V(1, \omega_j) = g(S_1(1, \omega_j), S_2(1, \omega_j)), \quad j = 1, 2. \tag{6.2.1}$$

We now construct a portfolio of the two primitive securities that has the same value as the derivative security in each state at time 1. Assume the portfolio consists of $\theta_1$ units of $S_1$ and $\theta_2$ units of $S_2$. To ensure that the portfolio has the same payoff as the derivative in each state at time 1, we must have

$$V(1, \omega_1) = \theta_1 S_1(1, \omega_1) + \theta_2 S_2(1, \omega_1), \tag{6.2.2}$$

$$V(1, \omega_2) = \theta_1 S_1(1, \omega_2) + \theta_2 S_2(1, \omega_2). \tag{6.2.3}$$

This is a system of two linear equations in two unknowns. A unique solution must exist because of the complete market assumption. The solution is

$$\theta_1 = \frac{V(1, \omega_2) S_2(1, \omega_1) - V(1, \omega_1) S_2(1, \omega_2)}{S_1(1, \omega_2) S_2(1, \omega_1) - S_1(1, \omega_1) S_2(1, \omega_2)}, \tag{6.2.4}$$

$$\theta_2 = \frac{V(1, \omega_1) S_1(1, \omega_2) - V(1, \omega_2) S_1(1, \omega_1)}{S_1(1, \omega_2) S_2(1, \omega_1) - S_1(1, \omega_1) S_2(1, \omega_2)}. \tag{6.2.5}$$

We note that the denominator is the same in both expressions and that this quantity is nonzero because of the complete market assumption.

The next step in the argument draws on the no-arbitrage assumption. If there is no arbitrage, then the time-0 value of the portfolio must be equal to the time-0 price of the derivative. If this were not the case, we could make arbitrage profits with a zero initial investment contradicting the no-arbitrage assumption. Hence, the time-0 value $V(0)$ of this derivative security is

$$V(0) = \theta_1 S_1(0) + \theta_2 S_2(0) \tag{6.2.6}$$

where the $\theta$'s are given by (6.2.4) and (6.2.5).

This valuation formula and its derivation illustrate some important ideas. Note that the derivative is expressed as a *portfolio* of the primitive securities with the positions in the securities given by $\theta_1$ and $\theta_2$. This derivation also shows the natural connection between the replication strategy and the valuation equation.

We can confirm that (6.2.6) gives the correct result for some simple special cases. Suppose the derivative's value at time 1 is equal to the price of $S_1$ at time 1 in each state. Then

$$V(1, \omega_j) = S_1(1, \omega_j), \quad j = 1, 2. \tag{6.2.7}$$

In this case (6.2.4) and (6.2.5) yield

$$\theta_1 = 1, \qquad \theta_2 = 0. \tag{6.2.8}$$

Hence, $V(0) = S_1(0)$, which is what we would have predicted.

Suppose instead that

$$V(1, \omega_j) = -S_2(1, \omega_j), \quad j = 1, 2. \tag{6.2.9}$$

In this case (6.2.4) and (6.2.5) yield

$$\theta_1 = 0, \qquad \theta_2 = -1 \tag{6.2.10}$$

and hence $V(0) = -S_2(0)$. Again this confirms what we would have predicted.

We have seen that a critical step in the derivation of the valuation equation (6.2.6) relies on the no-arbitrage assumption. We saw in Chapter 5 that the absence of arbitrage is equivalent to the existence of an equivalent probability measure known as the equivalent martingale measure. We affirm this connection in this one-period model below. When there are just two assets, we can use simple economic arguments to find the conditions that must be satisfied by the prices so that the market is arbitrage free. It is convenient to simplify the notation. Because the prices are assumed strictly positive, positive numbers $\{u_1, d_1, u_2, d_2\}$ exist such that

$$S_1(1, \omega_1) = S_1(0)u_1, \qquad S_2(1, \omega_1) = S_2(0)u_2, \tag{6.2.11}$$
$$S_1(1, \omega_2) = S_1(0)d_1, \qquad S_2(1, \omega_2) = S_2(0)d_2. \tag{6.2.12}$$

Thus, an initial investment of 1 unit in $S_1$ will amount to $u_1$ if state $\omega_1$ occurs and $d_1$ if state $\omega_2$ occurs. An initial investment of 1 unit in $S_2$ will amount to $u_2$ if state $\omega_1$ occurs and $d_2$ if state $\omega_2$ occurs. Because the market is complete, it is impossible to have

$$u_1 = d_1 \quad \text{and} \quad u_2 = d_2.$$

Hence, without any loss of generality (for instance, by switching asset 1 and 2 or by switching state 1 and 2), we may assume $u_1 > d_1$. Notice that, in general, we cannot simultaneously impose both conditions $u_1 > d_1$ and $u_2 > d_2$. For example, if security 1 is a risky stock and security 2 is a risk-free bond maturing at time 1, then at time 1, we have $S_2(1, \omega_1) = S_2(1, \omega_2) = 1$, so that $u_2 = d_2$.

We can rewrite the basic valuation equation (6.2.6) using this new notation as

$$V(0) = \frac{d_1 - d_2}{u_2 d_1 - u_1 d_2} V_u + \frac{u_2 - u_1}{u_2 d_1 - u_1 d_2} V_d \qquad (6.2.13)$$

where we let $V_u = V(1, \omega_1)$ and $V_d = V(1, \omega_2)$.

We now impose the no-arbitrage condition and use a direct approach to find the restrictions it imposes on prices and hence on the $u$'s and the $d$'s. We know from Chapter 5 that the no-arbitrage conditions correspond to the existence of a risk-neutral or equivalent martingale measure. Here we use a different approach that leads to the same result.

There are different cases to consider. If there is no arbitrage and the market is complete, then we cannot have $u_1 = u_2$.[1] Hence, we must have either

$$\text{Condition A:} \quad u_2 > u_1 \qquad (6.2.14)$$

or

$$\text{Condition B:} \quad u_1 > u_2. \qquad (6.2.15)$$

If condition A holds, the no-arbitrage condition implies that $d_1 > d_2$. Assume that $d_1 \leq d_2$. At time 0 we take a long position in $S_2$ and sell short $S_1$ such that the initial value of the portfolio is zero. The payoff from this strategy is guaranteed to be always positive no matter which state occurs. Because the cost of setting up the portfolio is zero, this violates the no-arbitrage assumption. Hence, our original assumption is violated. Therefore, we must have

$$d_1 > d_2.$$

We use a similar argument to show that if Condition B holds, the no-arbitrage condition implies that

$$d_2 > d_1.$$

Assume that $d_2 \leq d_1$. We take a long position in $S_1$ and sell short $S_2$ so that the initial value of the portfolio is zero. The payoff from this strategy is guaranteed to be always positive no matter which state occurs. Since the cost of setting up the portfolio is zero this violates the no-arbitrage assumption. Hence, our original assumption is violated.

---

[1] You are asked to show why this must be the case.

Therefore, we must have

$$d_2 > d_1.$$

In summary, the no-arbitrage condition implies that if $u_2 > u_1$, then

$$d_2 < d_1, \tag{6.2.16}$$

and if $u_1 > u_2$, then

$$d_2 > d_1. \tag{6.2.17}$$

We now show how the no-arbitrage conditions enable us to rewrite the valuation equation in terms of expectations with respect to an equivalent martingale measure. Rewrite (6.2.13) as

$$V(0) = \frac{u_1(d_1 - d_2)}{u_2 d_1 - u_1 d_2} \frac{V_u}{u_1} + \frac{d_1(u_2 - u_1)}{u_2 d_1 - u_1 d_2} \frac{V_d}{d_1}. \tag{6.2.18}$$

Under either Condition A or Condition B, the no-arbitrage condition delivers a formula for the price of the derivative as an expectation. In fact, there are two formulas corresponding to the use of either security as the numeraire. Let us define the coefficients of the normalized $V$'s on the right-hand side of (6.2.18) as

$$q_1 = \frac{u_1(d_1 - d_2)}{u_2 d_1 - u_1 d_2}, \qquad 1 - q_1 = \frac{d_1(u_2 - u_1)}{u_2 d_1 - u_1 d_2}.$$

Because the market is complete, $q_1$ is well defined. Then (6.2.18) can be written as

$$V(0) = q_1 \frac{V_u}{u_1} + (1 - q_1) \frac{V_d}{d_1}. \tag{6.2.19}$$

If there is no arbitrage, then we can show that $0 < q_1 < 1$. The proof is as follows. If there is no arbitrage, then either (6.2.16) or (6.2.17) holds. If (6.2.16) holds, it follows that $q_1$ is strictly positive because both the numerator and denominator of the corresponding fractions in terms of the $u$'s and $d$'s are strictly positive. If (6.2.17) holds, it follows that $q_1$ is strictly positive because both the numerator and denominator of each quantity are strictly negative.

We can also give a geometric proof that the no-arbitrage conditions imply that $0 < q_1 < 1$. Consider two vectors $\boldsymbol{u} = (u_2, u_1)^T$ and $\boldsymbol{d} = (d_1, -d_2)^T$. In fact, $u_2 d_1 - u_1 d_2 = \boldsymbol{u}^T \boldsymbol{d}$ and the sign of $\boldsymbol{u}^T \boldsymbol{d}$ is determined by the cosine of the angle between $\boldsymbol{u}$ and $\boldsymbol{d}$. If there is no arbitrage then, either condition (6.2.16) or condition (6.2.17) holds. In the first case , $d_1 - d_2 > 0$, $u_2 - u_1 > 0$, and the angle between $\boldsymbol{u}$

and $d$ is strictly greater than zero and is strictly less than $\pi/2$. Therefore, we have that $0 < q_1 < 1$. Similarly, under condition (6.2.17), we have $d_1 - d_2 < 0$, $u_2 - u_1 < 0$, and the angle between $u$ and $d$ is strictly greater than $\pi/2$ and is strictly less than $\pi$. In this case, the cosine is negative, and once more $0 < q_1 < 1$.

If we divide across by $S_1(0)$, we can express (6.2.19) in terms of an expectation as follows:

$$\frac{V(0)}{S_1(0)} = E^{Q_1}\left[\frac{V(1)}{S_1(1)}\right] \qquad (6.2.20)$$

where $V(1)$ denotes the value of the derivative security at time 1, $S_1'(1)$ denotes price of asset 1 at time 1, and $Q_1$ denotes the probability measure. We see that this corresponds to the result we obtained in Chapter 5. If we normalize the prices using security 1 as the numeraire, the current price of the derivative is equal to its expected future price. Thus, the normalized price processes form a martingale.

We can obtain a corresponding formula when $S_2$ is used as the numeraire. The derivation is basically the same; we just give the results. Starting from (6.2.13), we can write

$$V(0) = \frac{u_2(d_1 - d_2)}{(u_2 d_1 - u_1 d_2)}\frac{V_u}{u_2} + \frac{d_2(u_2 - u_1)}{(u_2 d_1 - u_1 d_2)}\frac{V_d}{d_2}. \qquad (6.2.21)$$

Let the coefficient of $V_u/u_2$ be $q_2$ and the coefficient of $V_d/d_2$ be $1 - q_2$. As before, these coefficients sum to 1. The no-arbitrage condition delivers the result that these coefficients are both positive. Hence, they can be used to represent probabilities. The valuation equation then becomes

$$V(0) = q_2\frac{V_u}{u_2} + (1 - q_2)\frac{V_d}{d_2}, \qquad (6.2.22)$$

and this corresponds to the use of security two as numeraire. Note that we still get the same value for $V(0)$ as (6.2.20) because both correspond to different rearrangements of the original valuation equation (6.2.6).

The above argument relies on a replication argument. The replication of the derivative's payoff is feasible because the market is complete. To equate the current price of the derivative to the current value of the replicating portfolio, we need the no-arbitrage assumption. This approach to valuation shows clearly the connection between the pricing formula and the replication strategy. If you can replicate a security and there is no arbitrage, then you can price the security. The positions in the traded assets that give the replicating portfolio are given by the coefficients in (6.2.6). If an institution wishes to replicate the derivative $V$, the weights of the primitive securities in the replicating portfolio are given by $\theta_1$ and $\theta_2$. We also showed how starting from the replication strategy we could obtain a valuation formula for the current price of the derivative in terms of expectations. We showed how either asset can be used as the numeraire and although the probability measures differ, the price of the security is the same.

**Example 6.2.1.** Suppose we have two securities $S_1$ and $S_2$. Their initial prices are each 100, and their price evolution is given in Figure 6.1.

**FIGURE 6.1** | *Security Price Lattices $S_1$ and $S_2$ in Example 6.2.1*

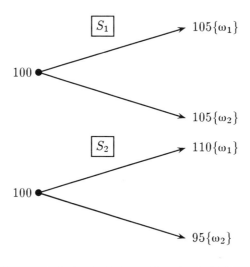

We note that security 1 is riskless.

a.     This system does not admit arbitrage. We know from Chapter 5 that the absence of arbitrage is equivalent to the existence of the $Q$ measure under which the normalized process forms a martingale. We normalize with the riskless security. Under this normalization, we obtain Figure 6.2.

If the process $\{S_2/S_1\}$ is to be a martingale, then the probabilities under the $Q$ measure are given by

$$1 = q\frac{110}{105} + (1-q)\frac{95}{105}$$

where $q$ is the probability of reaching state 1 under the $Q$ measure. Solving this equation, we find that $q = 2/3$. This means that the $Q$ measure exists. If we had found a value of $q$ outside the interval $(0, 1)$, then a valid $Q$ measure would not exist, and there would have been an arbitrage opportunity.

FIGURE **6.2** | *Normalized Security Price Lattices $S_1$ and $S_2$ in Example 6.2.1*

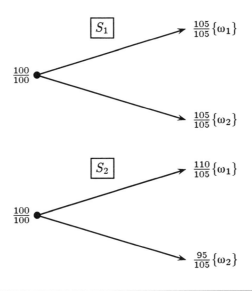

Notice that under this measure, the normalized price processes for both securities are martingales. For security 1 we have

$$E^Q \left[ \frac{S_1(1)}{S_1(1)} \,\middle|\, \mathcal{P}_0 \right] = \frac{2}{3}\frac{105}{105} + \frac{1}{3}\frac{105}{105} = 1 = \frac{S_1(0)}{S_1(0)},$$

and for security 2 we have

$$E^Q \left[ \frac{S_2(1)}{S_1(1)} \,\middle|\, \mathcal{P}_0 \right] = \frac{2}{3}\frac{110}{105} + \frac{1}{3}\frac{95}{105} = 1 = \frac{S_2(0)}{S_1(0)}.$$

Indeed, the price of any derivative security whose payoff depends on securities 1 and 2 will also be a martingale under this $Q$ measure if we normalize its price by the riskless asset.

b.      We can use this approach to value a European call option on asset two. Suppose that the strike price of the call is 104. The payoff from the call option at time 1 is

| State | Payoff from European Call |
|---|---|
| $\omega_1$ | $\max[110 - 104, 0] = 6$ |
| $\omega_2$ | $\max[95 - 104, 0] = 0$ |

If the call price at time 0 is denoted by $c(0)$, then its normalized price process is a martingale. Hence,

$$\frac{c(0)}{100} = \frac{2}{3}\frac{6}{105} + \frac{1}{3} \times 0 = 0.038095 \,.$$

The call price $c(0)$ is therefore 3.8095. ∎

## SECTION 6.2.2 | THE MULTIPERIOD MODEL

We now extend the single-period model discussed in the last section to the multiperiod case. Now there are several trading dates labeled $\{t = 0, 1, \ldots, T\}$. We assume the existence of a multiperiod securities markets with $M$ distinct *primitive* securities $\{S_1, S_2, \ldots, S_M\}$. We assume a frictionless market and that the information structure corresponds to that in Chapter 5. To price a cash flow, we need two basic conditions to be satisfied:

1. The securities market must not admit arbitrage.
2. We must be able to replicate the payoff using the traded securities.

We saw that the necessary and sufficient conditions for no-arbitrage are provided by the first fundamental theorem of asset pricing. The theorem states that the absence of arbitrage is equivalent to the existence of an equivalent martingale measure. For the second condition to be satisfied, there must exist a trading strategy that can replicate the payoff. We assume in this section that both conditions are satisfied.

We also assume, for now, that the primitive securities do not pay dividends. We consider the pricing of European derivatives; these derivative securities do not have early exercise provisions. Examples of such derivatives include European options and forward contracts. Consider a European derivative that has a payoff at time $T$ of $g(T) = g(S_1(T), S_2(T), \ldots, S_M(T))$. Suppose its value at time $t$ is $V(t)$ and let us use security 1 as numeraire. We have

$$V(t) = S_1(t)\mathrm{E}^Q\left[\frac{g(T)}{S_1(T)}\,\middle|\,\mathcal{P}_t\right] \tag{6.2.23}$$

where $Q$ is a probability measure, equivalent to the real-world probability measure $P$, under which $\{S_j(t)/S_1(t); t = 0, 1, \ldots, T, j = 1, 2, \ldots, M\}$ is a martingale.

For this formula to be valid, we must be able to replicate the payoff from the derivative using the existing securities. Hence, the price of the derivative can also be represented as a portfolio of the traded securities

$$V(t) = \theta_1 S_1(t) + \theta_2 S_2(t) + \cdots + \theta_M S_M(t). \tag{6.2.24}$$

As time passes, the weights on the replicating portfolio are adjusted according to the trading strategy. At maturity, the value of the portfolio will be exactly equal to $g(T)$.

To derive the trading strategy, we need to work backwards in a dynamic fashion and determine the appropriate portfolio weight at each time and state. In many cases, it is more convenient to determine the price of the derivative from (6.2.23).

We now use (6.2.23) to price a standard European call option. In general, options can be based on several assets. For simplicity, let us consider a standard call based on security 2. In this case

$$g(T) = [S_2(T) - K]^+$$

where $K$ is the exercise price of the option.

If we denote the value of this call option at time $t$ by $c(t)$, then from (6.2.23) the price of the option at time $t < T$ will be

$$
\begin{aligned}
c(t) = V(t) &= S_1(t) \mathrm{E}^Q \left[ \frac{[S_2(T) - K]^+}{S_1(T)} \, \bigg| \, \mathcal{P}_t \right] \\
&= S_1(t) \mathrm{E}^Q \left[ \frac{[S_2(T) 1_{S_2(T)>K}]}{S_1(T)} \, \bigg| \, \mathcal{P}_t \right] - S_1(t) K \mathrm{E}^Q \left[ \frac{1_{S_2(T)>K}}{S_1(T)} \, \bigg| \, \mathcal{P}_t \right].
\end{aligned}
$$

$$(6.2.25)$$

This valuation formula applies even if interest rates are stochastic. Exercise 6.2 requires derivation of the equivalent expression for the value of a European put option, $p(t)$.

If we assume that the numeraire is a bank account or money market fund earning the one-period interest rate during each period with an initial value at time 0 of one unit, then

$$S_1(t) = B_t = (1 + i_0)(1 + i_1) \cdots (1 + i_{t-1}) \qquad (6.2.26)$$

$$= \exp(r_0 + r_1 + \cdots + r_{t-1}). \qquad (6.2.27)$$

The value of a European derivative, with payoff $g(T)$ at time $T$, can then be written as

$$
\begin{aligned}
V(t) &= B_t \mathrm{E}^Q \left[ \frac{g(T)}{B_T} \, \bigg| \, \mathcal{P}_t \right] \\
&= \mathrm{E}^Q \left[ \frac{g(T)}{(1 + i_t)(1 + i_{t+1}) \cdots (1 + i_{T-1})} \, \bigg| \, \mathcal{P}_t \right] \\
&= \mathrm{E}^Q \left[ e^{-(r_t + r_{t+1} + \cdots + r_{T-1})} g(T) \, \bigg| \, \mathcal{P}_t \right].
\end{aligned}
$$

$$(6.2.28)$$

If we further assume that the interest rate on the bank account, expressed as a continuously compounded rate, is constant and equal to $r$ per period, then the value of the derivative simplifies to

$$V(t) = e^{-r(T-t)} \mathrm{E}^Q[g(T) \,|\, \mathcal{P}_t], \qquad (6.2.29)$$

and the value of a standard European call option on security 2 is

$$c(t) = e^{-r(T-t)}\{E^Q[S_2(T)1_{S_2(T)>K}] - K E^Q[1_{S_2(T)>K}]\}.$$

Of course, to get explicit expressions for these prices we need to know the future distribution of asset returns in order to take expectations.

From Chapter 5, we also know that since the market is arbitrage free, then the price of a standard European option can also be expressed in terms of a strictly positive state price process $\{\psi(k, \omega)\}$ as

$$V(0) = \sum_{\omega \in \Omega} \psi(T, \omega)g(T, \omega) \qquad (6.2.30)$$

so that the value of a European call option on security 2 with expiration at time $T$ and strike price $K$ can be written as

$$c(0) = \sum_{\omega \in \Omega} \psi(T, \omega)[S_2(T, \omega) - K]^+$$

with an equivalent expression for a put option.

***Example 6.2.2.*** Consider the following model with $T = 2$, and $\Omega = \{\omega_1, \omega_2, \omega_3, \omega_4\}$, two securities denoted by $S_1$ and $S_2$ with prices as given in the following table and with $S_1(0) = S_2(0) = 100$:

| $\omega$ | $S_1(1, \omega)$ | $S_2(1, \omega)$ | $S_1(2, \omega)$ | $S_2(2, \omega)$ |
|---|---|---|---|---|
| $\omega_1$ | 105 | 110 | 110 | 120 |
| $\omega_2$ | 105 | 110 | 100 | 100 |
| $\omega_3$ | 100 | 95 | 95 | 95 |
| $\omega_4$ | 100 | 95 | 100 | 90 |

Figure 6.3 sets out these prices on a lattice for each security.

a.   Our first step is to show that this price system does not admit arbitrage. This will be the case if an equivalent martingale measure exists. Use security 1 as the numeraire. In this case, the lattice for the normalized price process is given in Figure 6.4. The one-period risk-neutral probabilities $q(i, j)$ at time period $i$ are also shown in the same figure. For there to be no arbitrage, each

FIGURE **6.3** | *Security Price Lattices $S_1$ and $S_2$ in Example 6.2.2*

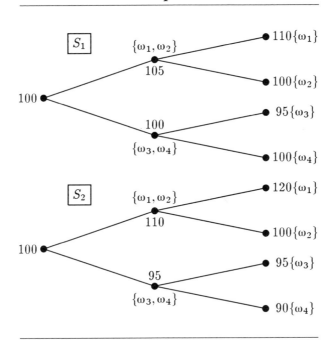

FIGURE **6.4** | *Normalized Price Process in Example 6.2.2*

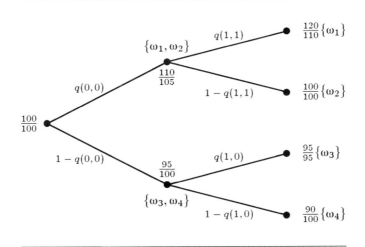

of these probabilities must be in the interval $(0, 1)$. The equations for these probabilities are

$$\frac{110}{105} = q(1, 1)\frac{120}{100} + [1 - q(1, 1)]\frac{100}{100},$$

$$\frac{95}{100} = q(1, 0)\frac{95}{95} + [1 - q(1, 0)]\frac{90}{100},$$

$$\frac{100}{100} = q(0, 0)\frac{110}{105} + [1 - q(0, 0)]\frac{95}{100},$$

and the corresponding solutions are

$$q(1, 1) = \frac{11}{21},$$

$$q(1, 0) = \frac{1}{2},$$

$$q(0, 0) = \frac{21}{41}.$$

Note that all these probabilities are in the interval $(0, 1)$ so that there is no arbitrage in the price system. We can construct the $Q$ measure as follows:

$$Q(\omega_1) = q(0, 0)q(1, 1) = \frac{11}{41},$$

$$Q(\omega_2) = q(0, 0)[1 - q(1, 1)] = \frac{10}{41},$$

$$Q(\omega_3) = [1 - q(0, 0)]q(1, 0) = \frac{10}{41},$$

$$Q(\omega_4) = [1 - q(0, 0)][1 - q(1, 0)] = \frac{10}{41}.$$

b.  We now show how to construct the Arrow-Debreu state prices for this example. The price at time 0 of a security that pays 1 unit at time 2 in state $\omega_1$ and 0 elsewhere is given by

$$\frac{\psi(2, \omega_1)}{S_1(0)} = Q(\omega_1)\frac{1}{S_1(2, \omega_1)}.$$

Hence,

$$\psi(2, \omega_1) = \frac{11}{41} \times \frac{100}{110} = \frac{10}{41}.$$

The other three state prices vectors can be obtained in the same way to give the following table.

| $\omega$ | $\psi(2, \omega)$ |
|---|---|
| $\omega_1$ | 10/41 |
| $\omega_2$ | 10/41 |
| $\omega_3$ | 200/779 |
| $\omega_4$ | 10/41 |

To confirm that this is a state price vector, we calculate the price at time 0 of security 2 using its time-2 payoffs as

$$120 \times \frac{10}{41} + 100 \times \frac{10}{41} + 95 \times \frac{200}{779} + 90 \times \frac{10}{41} = 100$$

as it should. Similarly for the security 1, time-2 payoffs, we can verify that their price at time 0 is also 100 under this state price vector.

c.  We now illustrate using the result in part (b) to value European derivatives. Consider a European call option on asset 2 with an exercise price of 100 and an expiration of $T = 2$. The payoff on this option is given in the following table.

| $\omega$ | $g(2, \omega) = [S_2(2) - 100]^+$ | $g(2, \omega)/S_1(2)$ |
|---|---|---|
| $\omega_1$ | 20 | 18/99 |
| $\omega_2$ | 0 | 0 |
| $\omega_3$ | 0 | 0 |
| $\omega_4$ | 0 | 0 |

Using (6.2.23), the value will be

$$S_1(0)E^Q\left[\frac{[S_2(2) - 100]^+}{S_1(2)} \,\middle|\, \mathcal{P}_0\right] = 100 \times \frac{18}{99} \times \frac{11}{41} = 4\frac{36}{41}.$$

This value can be verified using (6.2.30) and the state price vector given in (b) to get $20 \times 10/41 = 4.878049$.

d.  In general, we can use these results to price other derivative payoffs at time $T = 2$. Consider a derivative with payoffs at time 2 equal to $S_2(2)^2$. The payoffs are given in the following table.

| $\omega$ | $g(2, \omega)$ |
|---|---|
| $\omega_1$ | 14,400 |
| $\omega_2$ | 10,000 |
| $\omega_3$ | 9,025 |
| $\omega_4$ | 8,100 |

We can easily verify that the value of this security in the model is 10,243.90.

It is also possible to determine the trading strategies that finances the cash flows of derivatives in the model. These trading strategies give the replicating or hedge portfolio for the derivative. For the derivative with payoffs at time 2 equal to $S_2(2)^2$ you are asked to verify (see Exercise 6.1) that the following is a self-financing trading strategy:

$$\theta_1(1, \{\omega_1\omega_2\}) = -240, \qquad \theta_2(1, \{\omega_1\omega_2\}) = 340,$$

$$\theta_1(1, \{\omega_3\omega_4\}) = -45, \qquad \theta_2(1, \{\omega_3\omega_4\}) = 140,$$

$$\theta_1(0) = -186.34146, \qquad \theta_2(0) = 288.78049. \qquad \blacksquare$$

# Section 6.3
# The Binomial Option-Pricing Model

The binomial option-pricing model provides a powerful and flexible tool for option valuation. It represents the simplest and best known example of a multiperiod valuation model. In the binomial model, there are two primitive securities. Here we assume they are a risky asset (the stock) and a riskless security (the bond). The stock price movements are very simple. Given a stock price at time $t$, there are just two possible stock prices at time $t + 1$. The distribution of these one-period returns on the stock is constant both across time periods and across different states. Because of the simple structure of the model, we can derive compact closed-form expressions for the value of European options. In addition, we can use a recursive approach to valuation that is extremely convenient for numerical work. We now provide more details and discuss the formula for the valuation of European derivatives in this model.

We assume there are $N$ time periods with each time period of size $h$ so that the the time to maturity of the derivative is $T = Nh$. We let $S(n)$ denote the risky asset price at time period $n$. Let $t = nh$. With slight abuse of notation, we sometimes write $S(t) \equiv S(n)$, where $S(t)$ and $S(n)$ denote respectively the asset price at time $t$ and time period $n$. Consequently, we also have $S(T) \equiv S(N)$ depending on the timescale. This notation will be used interchangeably throughout the rest of this chapter.

We further denote the ratio of two successive stock price changes by $R(n)$:

$$R(n) = \frac{S(n)}{S(n-1)}, \quad n = 1, 2, \ldots, N.$$

Under the binomial model, $R(n)$ is equal to either $u$ or $d$ where $u$ and $d$ are constants. After two time periods, there are three possible stock prices $\{S(0)u^2, S(0)ud, S(0)d^2\}$. After $n$ time periods, there are $n+1$ possible stock prices

$$S(j) = S(0)u^j d^{n-j}, \quad j = 0, 1, \ldots, n.$$

The risk-free asset is denoted by $B$ with prices, $\{B_i; i = 0, 1, \ldots, T\}$, with $B_i = \exp(ihr)$ where $r$ is the continuously compounded interest rate per year, which is assumed to be constant.

By construction, the model is arbitrage free and complete. The arbitrage-free condition is guaranteed by imposing the condition

$$u > e^{rh} > d.$$

The market is complete because at any time step there are two linearly independent securities and two states. Thus, there exists a *unique* probability measure $Q$, equivalent to the actual probability measure $P$, for which $\{S(n)/B_n\} = \{e^{-rnh}S(n)\}$ is a martingale with $Q[R(n) = u \mid \mathcal{P}_{n-1}] = q$ and $Q[R(n) = d \mid \mathcal{P}_{n-1}] = 1 - q$ where $q = (e^{rh} - d)/(u - d)$.[2]

For the binomial model, we know that the value at time 0 of a European derivative with expiration at time $T$ and payoff equal to some function $g(S(N))$ of the asset is

$$V(0) = \mathrm{E}^Q[e^{-rNh}g(S(N))]$$

$$= e^{-rNh} \sum_{j=0}^{N} \binom{N}{j} q^j (1-q)^{N-j} g(S(0)u^j d^{N-j}). \tag{6.3.1}$$

This is an explicit formula that could be used for numerical work. However, we will see that a better method for numerical computations exists.

---

[2]Note that $Q[\cdot] = \mathrm{Pr}^Q[\cdot]$.

## SECTION 6.3.1 | EUROPEAN CALL AND PUT OPTIONS

We now use the binomial model to value standard call and put options. For a European call option with exercise price $K$, the payoff at time $T = Nh$ is

$$g(N) = [S(N) - K]^+ = [S(0)u^j d^{(N-j)} - K]^+, \quad j = 0, 1, \ldots, N.$$

Let $m$ be the smallest integer value of $j$ that makes $S(N) = S(0)u^j d^{(N-j)}$ greater than $K$. This is the asset price for which the call option is "in-the-money" for the first time and is the smallest value of $j$ for which $[S(N) - K]$ is positive. The payoff on the call option will be zero for values of $j$ less than $m$ because the call option is "out-of-the-money" for these values. Thus, $m$ is the smallest integer such that

$$S(0)\, u^m d^{N-m} > K.$$

Taking logarithms and rearranging gives $m$ as the smallest integer such that

$$m > \frac{\log[K/(d^N S(0))]}{\log(u/d)}.$$

The binomial model value of a European call option can then be written as

$$c(0) = e^{-rNh} \left[ \sum_{j=m}^{N} \binom{N}{j} q^j (1-q)^{N-j} [u^j d^{N-j} S(0) - K] \right]$$

$$= S(0)\Phi(m;\, N, q^*) - K e^{-rNh} \Phi(m;\, N, q) \tag{6.3.2}$$

where

$$\Phi(m;\, N, p) = \sum_{j=m}^{N} \frac{N!}{j!(N-j)!} p^j (1-p)^{N-j}$$

is the complementary binomial distribution function and $q^* = qu \exp(-rh)$. You are asked to verify this result in Exercise 6.3.

  Notice the similarity between (6.3.2) and the Black-Scholes option-pricing formula given in Chapter 2 and derived in Chapter 4 in a discrete-time equilibrium framework. Also note that the expression for the call price can be regarded as a portfolio consisting of a long position in the stock and a short position in the riskless asset. This also implies that a call option payoff can be replicated (matched) with weights given by the coefficients of $S(0)$ and $K \exp(-rNh)$ in (6.3.2).

*Example 6.3.1.* We now consider the valuation of a derivative that pays the value of a security if the security price is above a specified amount (say, $K$) at expiration and zero otherwise. We denote the security by $S$ and assume we are in a binomial world. The value of such a derivative is $\exp(-rT)E^Q[S(N, \omega)1_{S(N,\omega)\geq K}]$. This value is equal to the first term in (6.3.2) for the binomial model; that is, $S(0)\Phi(m; N, q^*)$. This is equal to $S(0)E^{Q*}[1_{S(N,\omega)\geq K}]$, where $Q^*\{R(n) = u|\mathcal{P}_{n-1}\} = q^* = uq\exp(-rh)$. We can easily verify that $q^*$ also lies in the interval $(0, 1)$. We have

$$e^{-rNh}E^Q[S(N, \omega)1_{S(N,\omega)\geq K}] = e^{-rNh}\left[\sum_{j=m}^{N}\binom{N}{j}S(0)u^j d^{N-j}q^j(1-q)^{N-j}\right]$$

$$= S(0)\left[\sum_{j=m}^{N}\binom{N}{j}\left(\frac{u}{e^{rh}}q\right)^j\left(\frac{d}{e^{rh}}(1-q)\right)^{N-j}\right].$$

Because $\{\exp(-rnh)S(n)\}$ is a martingale under $Q$ and $que^{-rh} + (1-q)de^{-rh} = 1$, the derivative's value can be written in terms of $q^*$ as

$$S(0)\left[\sum_{j=m}^{N}\binom{N}{j}(q^*)^j(1-q^*)^{N-j}\right] = S(0)E^{Q*}[1_{S(N,\omega)\geq K}]$$

$$= S(0)Q^*\{S(N, \omega) \geq K\}.$$

Note that $Q^*$ is the equivalent martingale measure when we use security $S$ as the numeraire. The normalized price process, $\{\exp(rnh)/S(n)\}$, is a $Q^*$ martingale and the normalized price process, $\{\exp(-rnh)S(n)\}$, is a $Q$ martingale. ∎

A European put option has payoff at maturity $[K - S(N)]^+$. An expression for the value of this put option is

$$p(0) = e^{-rNh}E^Q[[K - S(N)]^+]$$

$$= e^{-rNh}\left[\sum_{j=0}^{m-1}\binom{N}{j}q^j(1-q)^{N-j}[K - u^j d^{N-j}S(0)]\right]$$

$$= e^{-rNh}K[1 - \Phi(m; N, q)] - S(0)[1 - \Phi(m; N, q^*)]. \qquad (6.3.3)$$

It is easy to confirm the put-call parity result for European non-dividend-paying options. A long call option plus a short put option, each with the same expiration date and exercise price, will have value $c(0) - p(0)$. If we substitute the expressions for $c(0)$ and $p(0)$ from (6.3.2) and (6.3.3), we find that

$$c(0) - p(0) = S(0) - Ke^{-rNh}.$$

This result is known as *put-call parity*. Note also that this is the same as the value of a forward contract on the asset with forward price $K$ and delivery at time $T$.

*Example 6.3.2.* This example concerns the valuation of a three-period European call option using the binomial model. One time unit corresponds to 1 month. The initial asset price is 100, and the option has an exercise price of 100. Under the binomial model, the price is assumed to either increase by the factor $u = 1.05943424$ or fall by the factor $d = 0.94390002$ over the unit time interval of length 1 month so that $h = 1/12 = 0.0833333$. In Section 6.3.3 we see the origin of these $u$ and $d$ values. The continuously compounded riskfree interest rate is assumed to be 5% per year. We illustrate how to calculate the price of this option.

Because $N = 3$, $h = 1/12$, and $r = 0.05$, the discounting factor becomes $\exp(-rT) = \exp(-rNh) = \exp(-3r/12) = 0.9875778$. Obviously the no-arbitrage condition $u > e^{rh} > d$ is satisfied. We also have that

$$q = \frac{e^{rh} - d}{u - d} = \frac{1.00417536 - 0.94390002}{1.05943424 - 0.94390002} = 0.52170984$$

and

$$q^* = \frac{u}{e^{rh}}q = 0.55041907.$$

The value for $m$ is the smallest integer for which

$$m > \frac{\log[K/(d^N S(0))]}{\log(u/d)} = \frac{\log[100/(0.94390002^3 \times 100)]}{\log(1.05943424/0.94390002)} = 1.50$$

so that $m = 2$. Applying (6.3.2) we have

$$100 \times 0.5753723 - 100 \times 0.9875778 \times 0.5325443 = 4.94433.$$

Hence, this is the current price of the European call option. ∎

The value of an option can also be calculated using the recursive valuation procedure developed in Chapter 5. In practice, the recursive valuation procedure is more efficient for numerical work.

## SECTION 6.3.2 | CONTINUOUS-TIME LIMIT OF THE BINOMIAL OPTION-PRICING MODEL

The binomial model is a useful valuation model in its own right. The continuous-time limit of the binomial model is the Black-Scholes model. The argument that derives the continuous-time limit of the binomial model uses a result that is well known in probability. If a particle starts at the origin and follows a random walk its distribution at the end of $N$ time steps is a binomial distribution. In the limit as the size of the time step gets smaller and $N$ becomes larger, the distribution tends to normality. If we take the limit of a random walk, we obtain Brownian motion.

For now both $N$ and $h$ are fixed. When we start considering the limit, we will let both $N$ and $h$ vary but in such a way that their product remains constant. We let $\{X_0, X_1, \ldots, X_{N-1}\}$ be a Markov process with two states and values $\log(u)$ and $\log(d)$. The transition matrix is

$$\begin{bmatrix} q & q \\ 1 - q & 1 - q \end{bmatrix}$$

where

$$q = \frac{e^{rh} - d}{u - d}.$$

Thus, if the stock price at time $t = ih$, $i = 0, 1, \ldots, N-1$ is $S(t)$, the possible stock prices at the next trading date $t + h = (i + 1)h$ are $S(t)e^{X_i}$. Indeed, the stock price at time $T$ is

$$S(0)e^{\sum_{i=0}^{N-1} X_i} = S(0)e^{Y}$$

where $Y = \sum_{i=0}^{N-1} X_i$. The distribution of the terminal stock prices (under the $Q$ measure) is governed by the distribution of $Y$. The time-0 value of a European derivative that pays $g(S(T))$ at time $T$ is

$$V(0) = e^{-rNh} E^Q[g(S(0)e^{Y})]. \tag{6.3.4}$$

This equation corresponds to (6.3.1). Because $Y$ is the sum of $N$ independent and identically distributed random variables it is easy to obtain the first two moments of $Y$. The expectation of $Y$ is

$$E^Q[Y] = N\left[\log(d) + q \log\left(\frac{u}{d}\right)\right], \tag{6.3.5}$$

and the variance of $Y$ is

$$\text{Var}^Q(Y) = Nq(1 - q)\left[\log\left(\frac{u}{d}\right)\right]^2. \tag{6.3.6}$$

To show that in the limit the binomial distribution converges to the Black-Scholes model, we should demonstrate that the discrete-time distribution converges to an appropriate continuous-time distribution. In the Black-Scholes model, the logarithm of the ratio of the terminal stock price to the initial stock price has a normal distribution under the $Q$ measure. Therefore,

$$\log \frac{S(T)}{S(0)}$$

is normally distributed with expected value $(r - \sigma^2/2)T$ and variance $\sigma^2 T$.

We show first how the parameters of the discrete-time binomial distribution can be selected so that the first two moments of $Y$ converge to the first two moments of the continuous-time distribution, the normal distribution. For this to happen, we must have

$$N\left[\log(d) + q \log\left(\frac{u}{d}\right)\right] \rightarrow \left(r - \frac{1}{2}\sigma^2\right)T \tag{6.3.7}$$

and

$$Nq(1-q)\left[\log\left(\frac{u}{d}\right)\right]^2 \rightarrow \sigma^2 T \tag{6.3.8}$$

as $N \rightarrow \infty$, $h \rightarrow 0$ with $Nh = T$. The choice of the parameters $u$, $d$, and $q$ as functions of $h$ will dictate the behavior of the left-hand sides of (6.3.7) and (6.3.8). For the one-period model to preclude arbitrage, we require that

$$u > e^{rh} > d, \tag{6.3.9}$$

and in this case the probability $q$ is given by

$$q = \frac{e^{rh} - d}{u - d}. \tag{6.3.10}$$

When we select

$$u = e^{\sigma\sqrt{h}} \quad \text{and} \quad d = e^{-\sigma\sqrt{h}}, \tag{6.3.11}$$

the no-arbitrage condition becomes

$$\sigma > r\sqrt{h} = r\sqrt{\frac{T}{N}} > -\sigma. \tag{6.3.12}$$

For plausible parameter values, this condition is satisfied.[3] We insert these values for $u$, $d$, and $q$ in the left-hand sides of (6.3.7) and (6.3.8) and take expansions in term of $h$. We ignore third and higher-order terms in $h$ and take the limit as $h \to 0$ and $N \to \infty$ so that their product $Nh = T$. If we do this, it is straightforward to show that the mean of $Y$ on the left-hand side of (6.3.7) converges to the continuous-time limit on the right-hand side and that the variance of $Y$ on the left-hand side of (6.3.8) converges to the continuous-time limit on the right-hand side.

To complete the derivation, we need to show for this limiting procedure that the discrete-time approximation converges to the normal distribution. Note that we are not just adding another random variable to the sum, $Y$, and keeping all the other parameters constant. When we increase $N$ by an additional step, the parameter $h$ changes, and each of $u$, $d$, and $q$ changes. This changes all the $X$'s in the sum. In this case one needs a special form of the central limit theorem that requires some technical conditions. In the present case, these technical conditions are satisfied, and the proof goes through. In other words, we can show that the distribution of $Y$ tends to normality as $N$ becomes large. As a consequence, the discrete-time binomial valuation model converges to the continuous-time Black-Scholes model. It would take us too far afield to give the details of the proof. Duffie [49] gives a more rigorous proof of this result.

The value of $N$ used in the binomial model must be large enough to ensure accurate answers. As $N$ increases, the binomial model value eventually converges to the continuous-time option values with an appropriate selection of parameters. A number of techniques can be used to speed up convergence of the binomial model. Broadie and Detemple [27] examine the speed and accuracy of a large number of numerical techniques. We provide a numerical example to illustrate the convergence of the binomial model.

**Example 6.3.3.** This example uses the same parameters that were used to construct Example 6.3.2. We start by showing the origin of the $u$ and $d$ values in Example 6.3.2. Recall that this is a 3-month European call option with an initial asset price of 100, strike price of 100, riskless rate 5% per year. Suppose that the value of $\sigma$ is 20% per year. If we assume that $u$ and $d$ are given by (6.3.11), then for monthly periods, $h = 1/12$, we obtain the numerical values for $u$ and $d$ employed in Example 6.3.2.

The value of the European call option in Example 6.3.2 can also be calculated using the binomial model for differing values of $N$. Note that as $N$ changes, the values of $d$, $u$, and $q$ are also changed. Table 6.1 shows the call option values for $N = 10$, 11, 20, 21, 50, 51, 100, 101, 200, 201, 500, and 501. It is interesting to note that even

---

[3]We can see that if $N$ is large enough, the condition will be satisfied. We discuss this issue in Section 6.3.3.

after 500 time intervals the values have not converged to two-decimal-place accuracy. The binomial model values converge to the Black-Scholes option value of 4.615 for sufficiently large $N$. Table 6.2 gives the values of the call option using an average of the binomial model option values for $N$ and $N + 1$. Notice how much faster the answer converges. ∎

TABLE **6.1** │ *Rate of Convergence of the Binomial Model in Example 6.3.3*

| $N$ | Call Option Value |
|-----|-------------------|
| 10 | 4.51656 |
| 11 | 4.70366 |
| 20 | 4.56541 |
| 21 | 4.66125 |
| 50 | 4.59508 |
| 51 | 4.63398 |
| 100 | 4.60503 |
| 101 | 4.62457 |
| 200 | 4.61001 |
| 201 | 4.61981 |
| 500 | 4.61300 |
| 501 | 4.61693 |
| Black-Scholes | 4.615 |

TABLE **6.2** │ *Rate of Convergence of the Binomial Model in Example 6.3.3*

| $N$ | Average of Call Option Values for $N$ and $N+1$ |
|-----|-------------------------------------------------|
| 10 | 4.61011 |
| 20 | 4.61333 |
| 50 | 4.61453 |
| 100 | 4.61480 |
| 200 | 4.61491 |
| 500 | 4.61496 |
| Black-Scholes | 4.615 |

## SECTION **6.3.3** │ BINOMIAL MODEL PARAMETERS

In this subsection, we discuss some aspects of selecting the binomial model parameters. We continue to use $N$ time intervals and specify the maturity as $T$ years. The length of each time interval is therefore $h = T/N$ years. In practice, $N$ needs to be chosen large enough to ensure accurate answers for values and risk statistics. Even for short-term, standard options, a choice of $N = 100$ might not be large enough (see Example 6.3.3). Longer-term options and exotic options could require a much higher value for $N$ to ensure sufficient accuracy. Interest rates are usually quoted as per-year rates, so we assume that $r$ is a per-year rate.

The values of $u$ and $d$ are often chosen according to (6.3.10) and (6.3.11) as

$$u = e^{\sigma\sqrt{h}}, \qquad d = \frac{1}{u}, \quad \text{and} \quad q = \frac{e^{rh} - d}{u - d} \qquad (6.3.13)$$

where $\sigma$ is the annual "volatility." The volatility is the standard deviation of the continuously compounded return on the underlying asset and $r$ is the continuously compounded interest rate (per year) in the model. We saw that this selection of parameters ensures that, in the limit, as the number of time intervals increases the option values will converge to the Black-Scholes formula price.

Selecting $d = 1/u$ is a sufficient condition for a recombining resulting model. The number of distinct values for the underlying asset price after $i$ time intervals is then $(i + 1)$. If the binomial model is not recombining then the number of distinct values for the underlying asset price after $n$ time intervals is $2^n$ and grows exponentially. There are obvious computational advantages to using a recombining model. In general, $u$ and $d$ could vary over time intervals. The situation is illustrated in Figure 6.5 where $u(i)$ and $d(i)$ are the up- and down-jumps at time period $i$. In this situation, the binomial model will not recombine unless $d(i+1)u(i) = u(i+1)d(i)$ for all periods $i$.

FIGURE 6.5 | *Binomial Model with u and d Varying over Time Periods*

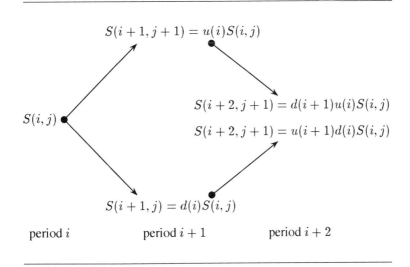

$$S(i + 1, j + 1) = u(i)S(i, j)$$

$$S(i, j)$$

$$S(i + 2, j + 1) = d(i + 1)u(i)S(i, j)$$

$$S(i + 2, j + 1) = u(i + 1)d(i)S(i, j)$$

$$S(i + 1, j) = d(i)S(i, j)$$

period $i$ period $i + 1$ period $i + 2$

When valuing a derivative security using the binomial model the values of $r$ and $\sigma$ are assumed known from market data or estimated from historical data in the case of the volatility. The length of the time interval $h$ is selected to ensure accurate numerical answers. When (6.3.13) is used to calculate the binomial model parameter values, the value used for $h$ can result in a computed martingale "probability" greater than 1. This will occur if $h > (\sigma/r)^2$, and the binomial model will not be arbitrage free. The answers produced by the model are not correct in this case. Exercise 6.4 requires you to show this.

A number of alternative methods of selecting the binomial parameters ensure that the model is arbitrage free. As we mentioned earlier, the choice in (6.3.11) always works when $N$ is large enough. In continuous time, the model most often used for asset prices is the lognormal distribution. It is possible to select the parameters $u$, $d$, and $q$ to equate the expected value and variance of the price change under the martingale measure with the corresponding expected value and variance of the continuous (lognormal) distribution. Assume that $Z$ has a normal distribution with mean $(r - \sigma^2/2)h$ and variance $\sigma^2 h$ so that $X = e^Z$ has a lognormal distribution. Then

$$E[X] = E[e^Z] = e^{rh} \quad \text{and} \quad E[X^2] = E[(e^Z)^2] = (e^{rh})^2 e^{\sigma^2 h}.$$

If the mean and variance[4] of $X$ are to equal those of the continuous lognormal distribution, then $u$, $d$, and $q$ must be selected so that

$$qu + (1-q)d = e^{rh} \quad \text{and} \quad qu^2 + (1-q)d^2 = (e^{rh})^2 e^{\sigma^2 h}. \qquad (6.3.14)$$

As discussed in Chapter 5, it is important to check that $q$ is between 0 and 1 and that $u$ and $d$ are positive for any selection of parameters to ensure that the binomial model is arbitrage free. A parameter choice consistent with (6.3.14) that ensures the martingale probabilities are between 0 and 1 is

$$q = \frac{1}{2}, \quad u = e^{rh}\left(1 + \sqrt{e^{\sigma^2 h} - 1}\right), \quad \text{and} \quad d = e^{rh}\left(1 - \sqrt{e^{\sigma^2 h} - 1}\right). \qquad (6.3.15)$$

Notice that for this choice, we always have $u > \exp(rh) > d$. In addition, this choice ensures that both (6.3.7) and (6.3.8) are satisfied. We now present an example to illustrate some of these points with a low volatility and a high riskless rate.

***Example 6.3.4.*** Assume that the continuously compounded risk-free rate is 15% per year, the volatility of the rate of return on the underlying asset is 5% per year, the term

---

[4]Notice that matching the first two moments of the distribution is equivalent to matching both the mean and variance of the distribution.

to expiration is 3 years, and the number of time intervals is $N = 20$. If we determine the binomial model parameters using (6.3.13) we obtain $h = 3/20 = 0.15$, $u = \exp(0.05\sqrt{0.15}) = 1.019554$, $d = 0.980821$, $\exp(rh) = 1.022755$, and $q = 1.082655$ so that the model will not be arbitrage free. Note that we require $d < \exp(rh) < u$ for an arbitrage-free model. In this case, $\exp(rh) > u$ so that it violates the no-arbitrage condition. Thus, the risk-free asset dominates the underlying asset. If we instead use (6.3.15) we obtain $q = 0.5$, $u = 1.042562$, and $d = 1.002948$, and now we have $d < \exp(rh) < u$ and the model will be arbitrage free. Note that it is not necessary for $d < 1$ and $u > 1$ for an arbitrage-free model. ∎

We remark that (6.3.15) would give rise to a negative value for $d$ for some parameter values. In practice, selecting $u$, $d$, and $q$ according to (6.3.13) will always work for large $N$.

## SECTION 6.3.4 | RECURSIVE VALUATION

Recall from Chapter 5 that the value of a European derivative in the binomial model can be written in terms of a recursive valuation relation that applies for each time interval as

$$V(i, j) = e^{-rh}[q V(i + 1, j + 1) + (1 - q) V(i + 1, j)] \qquad (6.3.16)$$

where $j$ is the number of times that the ratio of two successive price changes $R(k)$ has taken the value $u$ for $0 < k \leq i$. This is often referred to as the number of up-jumps in the asset price. In the binomial model, the recursion commences on the expiration date of the derivative with $V(N, j) = g(S(N)) = g(S(0)u^j d^{N-j})$ for each value of $j$. For European derivatives, a binomial model formula can be derived without the need to use this recursive formula as given in (6.3.1). However, the recursive approach is more suitable for programming on a computer and is a better numerical approach than evaluating (6.3.1) directly.

This recursive valuation approach is simple to program and can easily handle more general derivatives such as American-style derivatives and derivatives on assets paying income at discrete dates.

**Example 6.3.5.** Consider the 3-month European call option in Example 6.3.2 with an exercise price of $100. Figure 6.6 shows the binomial model asset prices and the values of the option in brackets using (6.3.16). Recall that we have $u = 1.059434$, $d = 0.943900$, $\exp(rh) = 1.004175$, and $q = 0.521710$. Note also that $d < \exp(rh) < u$ so that the model is arbitrage free. We also have $\exp(-rh) = 0.995842$ and $1 - q = 0.478290$.

On the option expiry date, the value is given by $V(N, j) = [S(N, j) - K]^+$, $j = 0, 1, \ldots, N$ where $K = 100$. The nodes in the binomial model lattice in

Figure 6.6 are labeled $A$ to $F$. The recursive calculations for each node are as follows (values for $V$ are shown to four decimal places but calculated with higher accuracy):

$F$: $V(2, 2) = 0.995842(0.521710 \times 18.911 + 0.478290 \times 5.9434) = 12.6559$

$E$: $V(2, 1) = 0.995842(0.521710 \times 5.9434 + 0.478290 \times 0.0000) = 3.0878$

$D$: $V(2, 0) = 0.995842(0.521710 \times 0.0000 + 0.478290 \times 0.0000) = 0.0000$

$C$: $V(1, 1) = 0.995842(0.521710 \times 12.6559 + 0.478290 \times 3.0878) = 8.0460$

$B$: $V(1, 0) = 0.995842(0.521710 \times 3.0878 + 0.478290 \times 0.0000) = 1.6043$

$A$: $V(0, 0) = 0.995842(0.521710 \times 8.0460 + 0.478290 \times 1.6043) = 4.9443.$

FIGURE **6.6** │ *Binomial Model Values for Example 6.3.5*

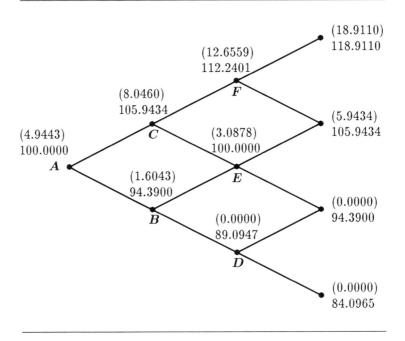

Note that $V(0, 0)$ agrees with the earlier calculation for the option in Example 6.3.2. ∎

Finance books dealing with continuous-time models frequently derive the Black-Scholes partial differential equation, which corresponds to the discrete-time recursive valuation relation given in (6.3.16). To show this, we now consider, in a nonrigorous way, the limiting form of this recursive valuation procedure. Cox and Rubinstein [45] provide more details. Assume that $V$ is a continuous function of the underlying asset price $S$ and time $t$ and that the partial derivatives $V_S = \partial V / \partial S$, $V_{SS} = \partial^2 V / \partial S^2$, and $V_t = \partial V / \partial t$ exist. The approach is to expand the two $V$ terms on the right-hand side of (6.3.16) of the value of the derivatives (corresponding to two different states) in terms in the Taylor series. This ultimately results in the following partial differential equation:

$$rV(t) = rS(t)V_s + \frac{1}{2}\sigma^2 S(t)^2 V_{ss} + V_t. \tag{6.3.17}$$

This is the Black-Scholes partial differential equation, which can be derived formally in the continuous-time model. Continuous-time valuation is discussed in Chapter 10 where you are asked to derive this partial differential equation as the limit of a self-financing condition in Exercise 10.14.18.

## SECTION 6.3.5 | TRADING STRATEGIES

We saw in Section 6.2 how to determine the weights of the replicating portfolio in a one-period model. In this section we give the explicit form of the replicating portfolio for any node of the multiperiod binomial tree. It is convenient to use the notation of Chapter 5 for the corresponding trading strategy. We will see that in the multiperiod model the same equations give the portfolio weights at each node of the tree.

We use the notation of the previous sections and assume that we are at node $(i, j)$ in the tree where the price of the risky asset is $S(i, j)$. The time step is of length $h$ and $ih = t$. One time step later at $(i + 1)h$, the price of the risky asset will be $S(i + 1, j + 1) = S(i, j)u$ if an "up-jump" occurs, and price of the risky asset will be $S(i + 1, j) = S(i, j)d$ if a "down-jump" occurs. It is a feature of the binomial model that $u$ and $d$ do not vary throughout the tree. The second asset is the money market account, which earns a continuously compounded rate of $r$. At node $(i, j)$ its price is $B(i, j) = \exp(irh) = \exp(rt)$. The derivative security has a price $V(i + 1, j + 1)$ at node $(i + 1, j + 1)$, and it has a price $V(i + 1, j)$ at node $(i + 1, j)$. The replicating portfolio has a terminal payoff exactly equal to that of the derivative security. This portfolio has $\theta_1$ units in the money market account and $\theta_2$ units in the risky asset. These weights vary by node and are indexed using the same notation. At node $(i, j)$, the value of the replicating portfolio is

$$\theta_1(i, j)e^{rih} + \theta_2(i, j)S(i, j). \tag{6.3.18}$$

We know the values of the $\theta$'s at the maturity date, and so we can work backwards through the tree to get the values at an earlier node. At each node we solve two linear equations for the two $\theta$'s. The equations are similar to those we saw earlier in Section 6.2. If the "upstate" at time $(i + 1)h$, we have

$$V(i + 1, j + 1) = \theta_1(i, j)e^{-r(i+1)h} + \theta_2(i, j)S(i, j)u,$$

and if the "downstate" occurs, we have

$$V(i+1, j) = \theta_1(i, j)e^{-r(i+1)h} + \theta_2(i, j)S(i, j)d.$$

Indeed, we can use (6.2.4) and (6.2.5) with appropriate modifications to write the results:

$$\theta_1(i, j) = e^{-r(i+1)h}\frac{uV(i+1, j) - dV(i+1, j+1)}{u - d}, \qquad (6.3.19)$$

$$\theta_2(i, j) = \frac{V(i+1, j+1) - V(i+1, j)}{(u - d)S(i, j)}. \qquad (6.3.20)$$

We often refer to $\theta_2$ as the delta of the derivative. We now give a numerical example that illustrates how the $\theta$'s can be computed.

***Example 6.3.6.*** We can determine the trading strategy for the European call option in Example 6.3.2. The binomial model prices were calculated in Example 6.3.5, and Figure 6.6 sets out the resulting values. Working backwards recursively, we can determine the trading strategy that replicates the option using (6.3.20) and (6.3.19). The results for each of the nodes are as follows:

*Node F*

$$\theta_2(2, 2) = \frac{18.9110 - 5.9434}{118.9110 - 105.9434} = 1.000,$$

$$\theta_1(2, 2) = 0.9875778\,\frac{18.9110 \times 0.9439 - 5.9434 \times 1.0594}{0.9439 - 1.0594} = -98.7578.$$

Note that in this case the option expires in the money at the end of the period, and the replicating portfolio involves holding a unit of the underlying asset. This is financed by a short position in the money market account that is the same as borrowing. Since the value of the money market account at this node is $\exp(2r) = 1.008368$, the amount of the borrowing is $98.7578 \times 1.008368 = 99.5842$. This borrowing accumulates to 100 at expiry, which is the exercise price of the option. We then have at Node $E$:

*Node E*

$$\theta_2(2, 1) = \frac{5.9432 - 0.0000}{105.9433 - 94.3900} = 0.5144,$$

$$\theta_1(2, 1) = 0.9875778\,\frac{5.9432 \times 0.9439 - 0.0 \times 1.0594}{0.9439 - 1.0594} = -47.9539.$$

In this case, $\theta_2$ is equal to 0.5144 units of the underlying asset, and this portfolio is financed by a short position in the money market account (borrowing). For Node $D$, we have:

*Node D*

$$\theta_2(2, 0) = 0.0,$$
$$\theta_1(2, 0) = 0.0.$$

Because the option expires worthless regardless of what the underlying asset does from this node, the self-financing portfolio to replicate the option involves zero holding in both the underlying asset and the money market account. Finally, for Nodes $C$, $B$, and $A$:

*Node C*

$$\theta_2(1, 1) = \frac{12.6559 - 3.0878}{112.2401 - 100.0000} = 0.7817,$$

$$\theta_1(1, 1) = 0.991701 \frac{12.6559 \times 0.9439 - 3.0878 \times 1.0594}{0.9439 - 1.0594} = -74.4588.$$

*Node B*

$$\theta_2(1, 0) = \frac{3.0878 - 0.000}{100.0000 - 89.0947} = 0.2832,$$

$$\theta_1(1, 0) = 0.991701 \frac{3.0878 \times 0.9439 - 0.0 \times 1.0594}{0.9439 - 1.0594} = -25.0180.$$

*Node A*

$$\theta_2(0, 0) = \frac{8.0460 - 1.6043}{105.9434 - 94.3900} = 0.5576,$$

$$\theta_1(0, 0) = 0.995842 \frac{8.0460 \times 0.9439 - 1.6043 \times 1.0594}{0.9439 - 1.0594} = -50.8117.$$

Thus, the initial trading strategy to replicate the option requires a long position of 0.5576 units of the underlying asset for each call option, and this is financed by a short position (borrowing) in the money market account at $-50.8114$ units (each worth \$1 at time 0). The cost of establishing this trading strategy is $0.5576 \times 100 - 50.8114 = \$4.944$ per call option, which is the value of the option determined using the recursive valuation relationship (Example 6.3.5) and the binomial formula (Example 6.3.2). ∎

## SECTION 6.3.6 | DIVIDENDS AND OTHER INCOME

In this section, we analyze the impact of dividend payments from the underlying asset on the valuation of derivatives. We are concerned with the cases when the underlying asset is a share of common stock or a stock market index. We discuss some details of how dividends are paid, mention some common assumptions concerning dividend policy, and review how the basic valuation formulas are modified when the asset pays dividends. We start with a general discrete-time framework and then specialize to the well-known binomial model. It turns out that we need strong assumptions on the nature of the dividend payments in order to retain the simplicity of the binomial model. In particular, we need to assume that the dividend payments are proportional to the underlying asset price. As usual, we ignore market imperfections such as taxes.

Common stocks generally make dividend payments at regular intervals. If the stock price is 100 just prior to the dividend payment and the stock pays a dividend of 1 unit, then we say that the *cum-dividend* price is 100, the dividend is 1, and the *ex-dividend* price is 99. Over a short time horizon such as 1 year, we can make a good estimate of a stock's future dividend. However, forecasts for longer time periods become less certain.

A stock index is based on a portfolio of several or many stocks. In some countries such as the U.S., the dividend payment dates are spread throughout the year. In other countries such as Japan, companies tend to pay their dividends on the same dates. The incidence of the dividend cash flow on a stock market index will depend on the characteristics of the underlying stocks.

At this stage, it is useful to recall some facts about the pricing and hedging of derivative securities when the underlying asset pays dividends. We assume a discrete-time model with $N$ equal time intervals of length $h$. The notation for the $N+1$ time points is

$$\{t_0 = 0, t_1 = h, t_2, \ldots, t_N = Nh = T\}.$$

We also assume there is a risky security with ex-dividend price $S(i, \omega)$ at time $t_i = ih$ in state $\omega$ and that the dividend payment at time $t_i$ in state $\omega$ is $D(i, \omega)$. Note that all investors in the market at time 0 are assumed to agree on the size of the dividend for all $i$ and $\omega$. We assume the numeraire is the money market account $B$ and that the short rates are deterministic. We also assume the market does not admit arbitrage. The ex-dividend price of $S$ at time $ih$ can be written as follows:

$$\frac{S(i)}{B_i} = \mathrm{E}^Q\left[\left.\frac{S(i+1) + D(i+1)}{B_{i+1}}\right| \mathcal{P}_i\right]. \tag{6.3.21}$$

It follows from the law of iterated expectations and repeated application of this formula that

$$\frac{S(i)}{B_i} = \mathrm{E}^Q\left[\left.\sum_{k=i+1}^{N} \frac{D(k)}{B_k} + \frac{S(N)}{B_N}\right| \mathcal{P}_i\right]. \tag{6.3.22}$$

This equation has already appeared in Chapter 3 (3.7.2) and in Chapter 5. It expresses the price of a security at time $t_i$ as the expected discounted value of its dividends during the interval $(t_i, T]$ and the expected discounted value of its market price at time $T$.

If we have a derivative security that can be replicated using the existing traded securities then it can be priced using the martingale property. Suppose the payout on the derivative (assumed European) at maturity time $T = Nh$ is $g(S(N))$, then its price at time $t_i$ is

$$\frac{V(i)}{B_i} = E^Q\left[\frac{g(S(N))}{B_N}\,\middle|\,\mathcal{P}_i\right]. \tag{6.3.23}$$

The price of the European derivative depends on the distribution of the ex-dividend asset price at time $T$.

We now specialize this framework to the case of the binomial model. One of the most appealing features of the standard binomial model is that the parameters $u$, $d$, and $q$ are invariant across time and state and that the tree is recombining. We illustrate what assumptions are required to retain the recombining property when the underlying asset pays dividends. Assume we are now at time $t_{i-1} = (i-1)h$, in state $j$, where $1 < i < N$ and $j = 0, 1, \ldots, i-1$. One period later, at time $t$, the stock price will be in either state $j+1$ or state $j$. We denote the dividend at time period $i$ in state $j$ by $D(i, j)$. If we assume a binomial model with a constant probability $q$ of an up-jump, we have from (6.3.16)

$$S(i-1, j) = e^{-rh}\{q[S(i, j+1) + D(i, j+1)] + (1-q)[S(i, j) + D(i, j)]\}. \tag{6.3.24}$$

The ex-dividend asset price is equal to the discounted expected value of the cum-dividend asset price one period later.

If we construct the usual binomial lattice with the standard parameters $u$ and $d$, we have

$$S(i, j+1) + D(i, j+1) = S(i-1, j)u, \tag{6.3.25}$$
$$S(i, j) + D(i, j) = S(i-1, j)d. \tag{6.3.26}$$

There is a drop in the asset prices at nodes where there is a dividend payment. The next example illustrates this point.

**Example 6.3.7.** Consider a three-period model with $N = 3$ and $h = 1$. The initial stock price is 100. The risk-free rate is zero (for simplicity). The values of $u$ and $d$ are

$$u = 1.25 \quad \text{and} \quad d = 0.8.$$

There is just one dividend date at time 2. At time 2, the stock pays a constant dollar dividend of 10. We wish to value a European call option that has a strike price of 100. First, we construct the price lattice for S. Observe that there is a discontinuity in the asset price at time 2 and that at time 3 the lattice does not recombine. It is easy to verify that $q = 4/9$. We display the binomial tree for this example in Figure 6.7. We also indicate the ex-dividend and option prices at each node. The option prices are obtained by the recursive valuation formula. The time-0 call price is equal to 11.8793. ∎

FIGURE **6.7** | *Effect of Constant Dividend Values*
*on the Binomial Lattice for Example 6.3.7*

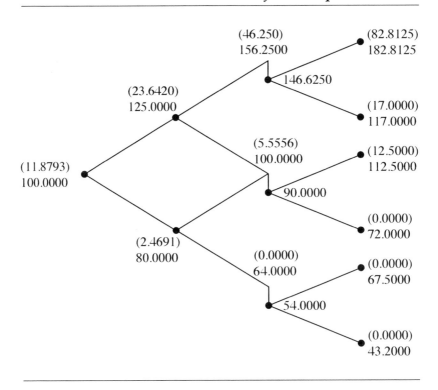

If there are several discrete dividends the calculations become very cumbersome using this type of lattice. We now investigate what sort of dividend policy will lead to a recombining lattice for the ex-dividend price process. Assume we are at time $t_{i-1}$ and there is a dividend payment at time $t_i$. The ex-dividend tree will recombine if starting at node $(i-1, j)$ an up movement followed by a down movement leads to the same node as a down movement followed by an up movement. For this to happen we must have

$$[S(i-1, j)u - D(i, j+1)]d = [S(i-1, j)d - D(i, j)]u. \quad (6.3.27)$$

This implies that

$$\frac{D(i, j+1)}{D(i, j)} = \frac{u}{d}. \quad (6.3.28)$$

This will be the case if the dividend is proportional to the cum-dividend stock price. Note that this also means that the dividend is proportional to the ex-dividend stock price. We can illustrate this with a modification of the previous example.

**Example 6.3.8.** Consider the same three-period model as in Example 6.3.7. The initial stock price is 100. The risk-free rate is zero. The values of $u$ and $d$ are as before; that is, $u = 1.25$ and $d = 0.8$.

At time 2, the stock pays a constant dollar dividend of 10% of its cum-dividend price. We display the binomial tree for this example in Figure 6.8. In this case the lattice recombines, and the time-0 call price is 10.7682. For larger lattices with more time steps, the recombining property simplifies the calculations. The option price at each node is obtained by the recursive valuation formula. ■

FIGURE **6.8** | *Effect of Proportional Dividend Values on the Binomial Lattice for Example 6.3.8*

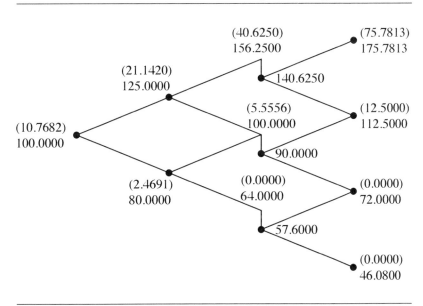

We now assume there is a dividend payable at each node and that the dividend is proportional to the stock price at that node. In this case we show that the ex-dividend stock prices also form a binomial lattice, which we call the revised lattice. The revised lattice (under our dividend assumption) does not have any vertical drop in the lattice and is easy to construct. It can be used for the valuation of derivatives. We will see that the up movements and the down movements in the revised lattice are a constant proportion of the corresponding movements in the original lattice. We will also see that under the risk-neutral measure the ex-dividend stock price has an expected growth equal to the risk-free rate minus the dividend yield.

The stock price movement from a generic node $(i-1, j)$ to its successor nodes $(i, j+1)$ and $(i, j)$ are

$$S(i-1, j)u = S(i, j+1) + D(i, j+1) = S(i, j+1)[1 + \lambda(h)]$$

and

$$S(i-1, j)d = S(i, j) + D(i, j) = S(i, j)[1 + \lambda(h)]$$

where $\lambda = \lambda(h) = D(i, j)/S(i, j)$ represents the dividend yield. Note that we have assumed that the dividend is proportional to the ex-dividend stock price.[5] The dynamics of the ex-dividend stock price are

$$S(i, j+1) = S(i-1, j)\frac{u}{1+\lambda} = S(i-1, j)u_1 \tag{6.3.29}$$

and

$$S(i, j) = S(i-1, j)\frac{d}{1+\lambda} = S(i-1, j)d_1. \tag{6.3.30}$$

Here $u_1$ and $d_1$ denote the binomial parameters for the dynamics of the ex-dividend stock price where

$$u_1 = \frac{u}{1+\lambda}$$

and

$$d_1 = \frac{d}{1+\lambda}.$$

---

[5] Alternatively, we could define $\lambda$ such that it is proportional to the cum-dividend price.

The binomial jump parameters in the revised lattice are a constant proportion of those in the original lattice. We can now rewrite the basic recursive valuation equation (6.3.24) as

$$S(i - 1, j) = e^{-rh}[qS(i - 1, j)u_1(1 + \lambda) + (1 - q)S(i - 1, j)d_1(1 + \lambda)].$$

This equation can be simplified and made more intuitive if we use a continuously compounded growth rate for the dividends and set

$$1 + \lambda(h) = e^{\delta h}.$$

With this substitution, we have

$$S(i - 1, j) = e^{-(r-\delta)h}[qS(i - 1, j)u_1 + (1 - q)S(i - 1, j)d_1]. \tag{6.3.31}$$

We see that the ex-dividend stock price stock prices has parameters $u_1$ and $d_1$ and that the ex-dividend stock prices grow at a rate of $r - \delta$. When we divide this equation across by the stock price we obtain an expression for $q$ in terms of $u_1$, $d_1$, and $\delta$:

$$q = \frac{e^{(r-\delta)h} - d_1}{u_1 - d_1} = \frac{e^{rh} - d}{u - d}.$$

Note that the risk-neutral probability $q$ has not changed. The next example illustrates the construction of the lattice for the ex-dividend price process.

***Example 6.3.9.*** Consider the same three-period model as in Examples 6.3.7 and 6.3.8 except that the dividend ($\lambda = 1/9$) is payable at the end of each period. In this case, $u_1 = 1.125$ and $d_1 = 0.72$. The revised lattice for the ex-dividend stock price is displayed in Figure 6.9. ∎

We next consider the valuation of a call option on an asset providing a continuously compounded income yield of $\delta$ using the binomial model. Its value at time 0 is

$$c(0) = e^{-rNh}E^{Q}[[S(N, j) - K]^{+}|\mathcal{P}_0]$$

where $S(N, j) = S(0)u_1^j d_1^{N-j}$ and $\{e^{-(r-\delta)ih}S(i)\}$ is a martingale under $Q$. We have

$$c(0) = e^{-rNh}\left[\sum_{j=m}^{N}\binom{N}{j}q^j(1-q)^{N-j}[S(0)u_1^j d_1^{N-j} - K]\right]$$

$$= e^{-rNh}S(0)\left[\sum_{j=m}^{N}\binom{N}{j}q^j(1-q)^{N-j}(u_1^j d_1^{N-j})\right] - e^{-rNh}K\Phi(m; N, q).$$

FIGURE **6.9** │ *The Revised Lattice for Example 6.3.9*

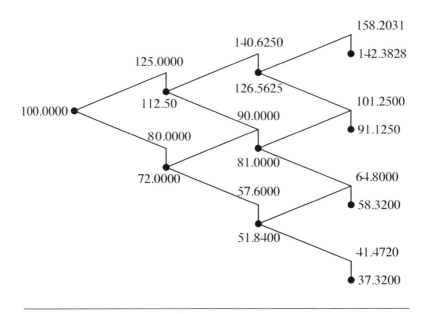

We know that under $Q$, we have (from (6.3.31))

$$q u_1 e^{-(r-\delta)h} + (1-q) d_1 e^{-(r-\delta)h} = 1$$

so that if we take $q^* = u_1 e^{-(r-\delta)h} q$, then

$$c(0) = e^{-\delta Nh} S(0) \Phi(m; N, q^*) - e^{-r Nh} K \Phi(m; N, q). \qquad (6.3.32)$$

The corresponding equation for the European put option on an asset with a constant dividend yield is

$$p(0) = e^{-r Nh} K[1 - \Phi(m; N, q)] - e^{-\delta Nh} S(0)[1 - \Phi(m; N, q^*)]. \qquad (6.3.33)$$

As the time interval $h$ tends to zero and $N$ tends to $\infty$ in such a way that $Nh = T$, these formulas for the prices of the call and put options become

$$c(0) = S(0) e^{-\delta T} N(d_3) - K e^{-r T} N(d_4) \qquad (6.3.34)$$

and

$$p(0) = K e^{-r T} N(-d_4) - S(0) e^{-\delta T} N(-d_3) \qquad (6.3.35)$$

where

$$d_3 = \frac{\log[\,S(0)e^{-\delta T}/K\,] + (r + \sigma^2/2)\,T}{\sigma\sqrt{T}}$$

and

$$d_4 = d_3 - \sigma\sqrt{T}.$$

Note that in this case the put-call parity relationship is

$$c(0) - p(0) = S(0)e^{-\delta T} - Ke^{-rT}. \qquad (6.3.36)$$

We now present an example that deals with options on a stock market index.

**Example 6.3.10.** Suppose the current level of the S&P 500 Index is 800. We want to find the prices of 5-year European call and 5-year European put values on this index. In both cases the strike price is also 800. We assume that the continuously compounded annual interest rate is 6% and that the dividend yield is 2.5% per year. The assumed annualized volatility is 17%. Note that this is the volatility of the price index (the ex-dividend prices).

We use the revised binomial lattice for the price index, which we assume to be an ex-dividend price index. If $h$ is the time interval, then the values of $u_1$ and $d_1$ are

$$u_1 = e^{\sigma\sqrt{h}} \quad \text{and} \quad d_1 = e^{-\sigma\sqrt{h}}.$$

The recursive equation for the value of a derivative, $V(i-1,\,j)$, based on this lattice is

$$V(i-1,\,j) = e^{-rh}\,[q\,V(i,\,j+1) + (1-q)\,V(i,\,j)]$$

where

$$q = \frac{e^{(r-\delta)h} - d_1}{u_1 - d_1}.$$

If the number of time intervals equals 100, we have

$$h = 0.05, \qquad u_1 = 1.038745, \qquad d_1 = 0.962700, \qquad q = 0.5135308.$$

For this example the European call and put prices are as in the following table.

| N | Call | Put |
|---|---|---|
| 100 | 164.33 | 50.98 |
| 500 | 164.55 | 51.20 |
| 1,000 | 164.56 | 51.22 |

These prices converge to their continuous time limit given by (6.3.34) and (6.3.35), which are 164.59 and 51.25. ∎

This approach can also be used to value options on foreign currencies. We can treat the foreign currency as a dividend-paying stock in which the dividend yield corresponds to the foreign interest rate. The analogy is that an investor who purchases the option on the foreign currency does not receive the "income" from the foreign currency during the life of the option just as an investor who purchases an option on a dividend-paying stock does not receive the dividends on the stock during the life of the option.

***Example 6.3.11.*** Consider a 1-year European put option on the U.S. dollar/U.K. pound exchange rate. We take the perspective of a U.S. investor. The put option has an exercise price of \$1.50 (per pound). The payoff on this option will be $(1.5 - X)^+$ U.S. dollars where $K$ is the dollar/pound exchange rate. The current exchange rate is U.S.\$1.50 (per pound). The U.S. interest rate is 5.5% per year, and the interest rate is 7.5% per year (both are continuously compounded rates). The volatility of the sterling exchange rate is 15% per annum. The value of this put option using the binomial model can be calculated from (6.3.3). Taking $N = 50$, we have

| | |
|---|---|
| $h$ | 0.02 |
| $u$ | 1.0214398 |
| $d$ | 0.9790102 |
| $e^{(r-\delta)h}$ | 0.9996001 |
| $q$ | 0.4852708 |
| Put value | 0.098416 |

The following table gives the values for the binomial model value for different values of $N$.

| $N$ | Currency Put Option Value |
|-----|---------------------------|
| 50 | 0.09842 |
| 51 | 0.09924 |
| 100 | 0.09863 |
| 101 | 0.09904 |
| 500 | 0.09880 |
| 501 | 0.09888 |

The Black-Scholes value is 0.099 to three decimal places.                    ■

# Section 6.4
## Exotic Derivatives

There is a range of derivative contracts other than the standard put and call options that have become very popular in recent years. Such contracts are often referred to as "exotic" derivatives. For example, many types of equity-indexed annuities in the United States have included embedded exotic options in their structures. The payoff of an equity-indexed annuity might be based on the average of the S&P 500 index over a prespecified investment horizon.

The valuation of exotic options using a discrete-time model such as the binomial model can involve significant computational problems in practice. This is because most exotic options are path dependent and they can depend on several assets. Derivatives with values that depend on the path of asset prices are called path dependent. In a binomial model, this implies that the number of prices to be stored and the computations required for valuation grow exponentially. Path-dependent European options can be valued using simulation or some other path-sampling procedure. For American-style options that allow early exercise, these path-sampling procedures require modification in order to determine if it is worth exercising the derivative early. In these cases, it is necessary to use numerical approximation techniques. These computational issues are discussed in Section 6.6. The valuation technique largely depends on whether or not the derivative value is path dependent and whether the derivative allows for early exercise. In this section, we outline the main types of exotic derivative contracts.

## SECTION 6.4.1 | DIGITAL (BINARY) AND GAP OPTIONS

Digital options have payoffs that depend on whether the underlying asset value is above or below a fixed amount on the expiration date. A cash-or-nothing call (put) pays a fixed amount, $X$, if the underlying asset value $S(T)$ is above (below) the exercise price $K$ and nothing otherwise. The payoff for a European cash or nothing call with expiration $T$ is $X\{1_{S(T)>K}\}$ and has value $V(0) = e^{-rT}X Q[S(T) > K|\mathcal{P}_0]$ where $\{e^{-rt}S(t)\}$ is a martingale under $Q$.

An all-or-nothing call (put) pays the asset value if the terminal asset price is above (below) the exercise price or zero otherwise. Example 6.3.1 derived the value of an asset-or-nothing call. These options are often included as part of a structured contract.

Other digital options include one-touch all-or-nothing options where the option pays if the underlying asset value goes above (below for a put) the exercise price during the life of the option.

Gap options have similar payoffs to standard options except that the payoff is only made if the asset price on the expiration date is above or below a strike price different from that used for the payoff. Thus, a gap call option has payoff $S(T) - K$ if $S(T) > H$ and zero otherwise. Because $H$ is not equal to $K$, there is a jump or "gap" in the payoff at the price $H$ and hence the name.

## SECTION 6.4.2 | ASIAN OPTIONS

These options have payoffs that depend on the average price of the underlying asset during the life of the option. They have become popular contract features in some types of equity-indexed products in the United States. They are also used extensively in foreign currency and interest rate options markets where options on the average exchange rate or the average interest rate during a time period, referred to as average rate options, provide valuable hedging features for investors, insurance companies, and corporate treasurers.

Average price call options pay the difference between the average price of the underlying asset during the life of the option and the exercise price provided this is positive and zero otherwise. The payoff can be written as $(S_{ave} - X)^+$ where $S_{ave}$ is the average underlying price as defined in the contract. An average price put option pays $[X - S_{ave}]^+$ at expiration.

Asian options can also use averages for the exercise price. These are floating strike options. An average strike call option pays $[S(T) - S_{ave}]^+$, and an average strike put pays $[S_{ave} - S(T)]^+$ at expiration where $S(T)$ is the price at maturity. The definition of the average price needs to specify the period over which averaging takes place, the number of points used in the average, and the type of averaging used. Most

Asian options use arithmetic averages and can be based on an average over the full term of the option or over a shorter period.

The binomial model can, in principle, be used to value Asian options. On the expiration date, it is necessary to calculate the average price for each state in the model where each state represents a path of asset prices. This means that the number of possible values to be calculated is $2^N$. Even if $N$ were chosen to be as small as 20, then the number of values would be $2^{20}$, which would require lengthy computation.

### SECTION 6.4.3 | LOOKBACK OPTIONS

The payoff on a lookback option depends not only on the underlying asset price (or rate) at expiry but also on the maximum or minimum asset price during the life of the option. A lookback call option pays $[S(T) - S_{min}]^+$ at expiration where $S_{min}$ is the minimum asset value during the life of the option, and a lookback put option pays $[S_{max} - S(T)]^+$ where $S_{max}$ is the maximum asset value during the life of the option. Thus, a lookback call essentially guarantees purchase of the asset at the lowest price during the life of the option, and a lookback put allows sale of the asset at the maximum price. Lookbacks with less frequent sampling intervals for determining $S_{min}$ and $S_{max}$ will be cheaper. This follows because the volatility of $S_{min}$ and $S_{max}$ will be higher for more frequent sampling. Intuitively, the higher frequency of sampling increases the chances of observing more extreme asset prices.

Lookback options present similar problems for valuation using the discrete binomial model as for Asian options because the maximum or minimum value depends on the sequence of up- and down-jumps. In a similar way, the sampling interval used for sampling the underlying asset price for the purposes of determining the maximum (minimum) value is also important. The binomial model can be used to value lookback options. An option value is determined for each distinct value of the maximum underlying asset value. A rule linking the maximum values over each time interval in the model is then used along with the recursive valuation procedure. Babbs [3] demonstrates how to use the binomial model to value lookback options. His method simplifies the computations and is quite accurate.

*High-water mark* options are also based on the maximum price of the underlying asset. For call options, the payoff at maturity is $[S_{max} - K]^+$ where $S_{max}$ is the maximum price of the asset. Options with these features are found in equity-indexed annuities.

### SECTION 6.4.4 | BARRIER OPTIONS

Barrier options have payoffs that depend on whether or not the value of the underlying asset reaches a barrier before expiry. Knockout options are options that become worthless or pay a fixed rebate if the asset value reaches a barrier but otherwise have payoffs identical to a standard option. A down-and-out call option is a knockout option that becomes worthless or pays a fixed rebate if the asset value falls below a barrier, $X$, but otherwise is the same as a call option with payoff $[S(T) - K]^+$ at expiry. A down-and-out put option has payoff $[K - S(T)]^+$ provided the underlying asset value does not fall below the barrier $X$, otherwise it becomes worthless or pays a fixed rebate. The rebate is paid when the barrier is reached.

A down-and-in option comes into existence if the underlying asset value reaches the barrier; otherwise, the option will expire worthless. An up-and-out option becomes worthless if the asset value reaches the barrier value during the life of the option, and an up-and-in option comes into existence if the underlying asset reaches the barrier and otherwise expires worthless. There are also double knockouts that cease to exist if the asset price reaches either barrier.

Barrier options can be valued using the binomial model. As an example, for knockout options the value of the option is set to zero whenever the underlying asset value exceeds the knockout barrier. In valuing a barrier option, it is necessary to allow for the frequency with which the underlying asset price is sampled in order to determine if the barrier has been crossed. Less frequent monitoring makes knockout options more expensive and knockin options less expensive. Boyle and Lau [23] develop a binomial model for valuing barrier options, and Kat and Verdonk [108] develop a more accurate adjusted binomial model that averages two binomial model prices.

Note that a standard call option is the sum of a down-and-out option and a down-and-in option with the same exercise price and barrier. Hence,

$$C(K) = DOC(X, K) + DIC(X, K)$$

where $C(K)$ is the value of a call with strike $K$, $DOC(X, K)$ is the value of a down-and-out call with strike $K$, and barrier $X$, and $DIC(X, K)$ is the value of a down-and-in call with the same strike and barrier.

Given that the standard call can be valued using the binomial model, it is only necessary to value the down-and-out option because the down-and-in option can be derived from these two values; that is,

$$DIC(X, K) = C(K) - DOC(X, K).$$

### SECTION 6.4.5 | OPTIONS ON THE MAXIMUM AND MINIMUM

Options on the maximum (or minimum) of a number of assets are sometimes called rainbow options. These contracts have values that depend on the joint distribution of the asset values. Options on the maximum (or minimum) of several assets often arise as part of a structured security. These contracts pay the maximum value of several underlying assets. Bond futures contracts allow the sold position to choose from a range of different bonds to deliver. In this case the short position will select the bond cheapest to deliver. These futures contracts contain an option on the minimum of the different bonds in the deliverable set of bonds specified in the contract. Outperformance options pay the maximum return on two or more assets or market indexes.

Valuation of these options requires an extension of the binomial model to incorporate the other assets. For a complete market, if the option is on $n$ assets, then a $(n + 1)$ jump multinomial model will be required. This adds to the computation time required for valuing these options.

A European option on the maximum of two assets is equivalent to holding one of the assets plus a European option to exchange this asset for the other asset since $\max[S_1(T), S_2(T)] = S_1(T) + [S_2(T) - S_1(T)]^+$.

## SECTION 6.4.6 | CLIQUETS

A cliquet option is a series of standard call options that pays the annual increase in the underlying asset. The strike resets at the beginning of each year. The return of a cliquet call option is given by $\prod_{i=1}^{N} \max[S(i)/S(i-1), 1] - 1$.

## SECTION 6.4.7 | QUANTOS

Quanto is a shortened expression for "quantity adjusted option." These are guaranteed exchange-rate contracts in which the payoff on a foreign currency derivative is converted to the domestic currency at a fixed exchange rate. Thus, the payoff on a quanto European call option on a foreign asset with guaranteed exchange rate $X$ would be $X[S_f(T) - K_f]^+$ where $S_f(T)$ is the value of the foreign asset in foreign currency at expiry and $K_f$ is the strike price in foreign currency.

## SECTION 6.4.8 | OTHER EXOTICS

There are many other types of exotic options. These are often found in structured securities, but they can also be individually structured in the OTC market for investors. These include compound options, which are options on other options. Chooser options are options to buy either a call or a put option so that the holder can select the option they require on exercise depending on the asset price. Spread options have payoffs based on the difference in two asset prices.

Options that permit exercise before their maturity date are known as American options. We discuss American options in the next section.

# Section 6.5
# American Options

### SECTION 6.5.1 | EARLY EXERCISE

In this section we derive some general restrictions on the prices of American options. We use these to make statements about when it is rational to exercise an American call option early. These general results, first derived by Merton [133], do not involve any distributional assumptions concerning the underlying asset. The basic principle used to derive these results is the no-arbitrage principle. The first result provides bounds for the price of an American call option. The second provides conditions when it is *not* optimal to exercise an American call option, which leads to a discussion of when it is rational to exercise a call option early.

We assume that the underlying asset, $S$, pays known cash disbursements (dividends). The price of the asset at time $t$ is $S(t)$. We consider a standard American call option on $S$ with exercise price $K$ and expiring at time $T$. Let the price of this option be $C(t)$. Our first result provides upper and lower bounds for this option. These are

$$S(t) \geq C(t) \geq [S(t) - K]^{+}. \tag{6.5.1}$$

We deal first with the lower bound. Note that the call value can never be negative. The payment from the call option contract at expiration or prior exercise will be either a positive amount or zero. To prevent riskless arbitrage, such a contract must sell for a nonnegative amount. The key point here is that options have value. The American call option cannot be worth less than $S(t) - K$. If it were, an investor could purchase the option, exercise it immediately, and receive a riskless profit. Hence, we have obtained the lower bound.

We now show why the American call price must not exceed the asset price. Suppose that it does. In this case an investor could purchase 1 unit of the underlying asset and sell (write) an American call option. This generates an immediate profit given our assumption. Because the option is American, its owner could exercise it before expiration at time $T_1$, say, where $T_1 \leq T$. In this case the investor receives $K$ upon exercise as a clear profit because the long asset position is precisely offset by the liability under the option contract. The same argument can be used if the option is in the money at expiration. If the option expires out of the money, then the investor has no liability under the option contract but still owns 1 unit of the asset. In all three cases, the investor makes a riskless profit with a negative net investment. Because this strategy gives rise to a riskless profit, our initial assumption must be false, and so the result follows. Hence, we have obtained the upper bound.

The lower bound is expressed in terms of the $\geq$ symbol. We are able to characterize the conditions when this holds as an equality and when it holds as an inequality. We can obtain a more precise statement of the lower bound for the American call that relates to dividend payment dates. The first result is the following:

*The value of an American call option must be strictly greater than* $[S(t) - K]^+$ *at any time other than the expiry date or just immediately before there is a dividend payment from the underlying asset.*

Because the option value is always strictly positive, this statement is true if the asset price lies below the strike price. Hence, we can assume that $S(t) > K$. Suppose that the American call value is exactly equal to

$$S(t_1) - K$$

at some time $t_1$ in between dividend dates. Assume that the next dividend will be made at time $T_1$. An investor can realize arbitrage profits in these circumstances by purchasing the call option, shorting the underlying asset, and investing the strike price $K$ in a pure discount bond that matures at time $T_1$. By assumption this strategy requires no initial investment because the net amount available after setting up the position is zero. The position is closed out immediately prior to the dividend date at time $T_1$. The proceeds from the riskless bond will be

$$\frac{K}{P(t_1, T_1)} > K$$

where we have assumed that the interest rate is positive. The investor can either sell the call option or exercise it at time $T_1$ depending on which is the more profitable. In any case the investor will have made a riskless profit, and so our initial assumption must be false. This proves the result that the call price at time $t_1$ is strictly greater than $S(t_i) - K$.

It follows from this last result that a rational investor will not exercise an American call between dividend payment dates. We have seen that the value of an American call is always strictly greater than its exercise value at times other than ex-dividend dates or the option expiration date. Therefore, between dividend payment dates, a rational investor would prefer to sell the call rather than exercise it. Hence, the only times that an American call should be rationally exercised is just before the asset goes ex-dividend.

This result enables us to derive some useful insights. Note that if the underlying asset makes no dividend payments then it is never optimal to exercise the option early. In these circumstances, the value of an American call will be equal to the value of its European counterpart. This equivalence holds only for simple American options on one asset. The discussion above on the optimal exercise strategy for an American call option on an asset indicates that the only time the call will be exercised prematurely is just before a payment is to be made on the underlying asset. Suppose that this happens at time $t$. It is clearly not optimal to exercise the call at this time for all possible asset prices. In particular, if the option is out of the money, its exercise value is zero and a rational investor would not exercise it in such circumstances. In other words, if it is rational to exercise an American call option, the option will certainly be in the money. However, the fact that the option is in the money is not a sufficient condition for early exercise. There will be a range of values of the underlying asset, for which it is optimal to exercise the option. The lower endpoint of this range corresponds to the asset price at which the call owner will be indifferent to exercising the option and retaining it. Denote this critical asset price by $S^*(t)$, and denote the instant before the payment date by $t^-$ and the instant after the payment is made by $t^+$. Let $D(t)$ denote the dividend payment at time $t$. We assume the asset price falls by the amount of the dividend, after the payment is made, so that

$$S(t^+) = S(t^-) - D(t).$$

$S(t^-)$ is called the cum-dividend price, and $S(t^+)$ is called the ex-dividend price. If the owner of the call exercises it just before the payment, at time $t^-$, the value of the call is

$$S(t^-) - K.$$

Note that this amount is positive because a rational investor will only exercise the option if it is in the money. If the option is not exercised it may still be in the money. If the option is left unexercised it will be worth $C(t^+)$ where the asset price used to compute the option value is $S(t^+)$. Because a rational investor will pursue an optimal strategy the call value just before the payment date will be the larger of these two values, that is,

$$\max[S(t^-) - K, C(t^+)]. \tag{6.5.2}$$

The critical asset price is the asset price that makes these two values equal. Hence, $S^*(t^-)$ is the solution of

$$S^*(t^-) - K = C(t^+). \tag{6.5.3}$$

To summarize, we have shown that it is optimal to exercise an American call just before a payment date if the asset price exceeds a critical value. If the asset price lies below the critical value, then it is not optimal to exercise the call even immediately before the payment date. Obviously there is a range of asset prices over which premature exercise is not optimal. In particular, if the call option is out of money, it will never be optimal to exercise it early. By continuity there is a range of asset prices (those below the critical asset price) over which early exercise will not be optimal. Note that there is a critical asset price associated with each payment date that depends on the parameters of the option contract, such as strike price and time until maturity.

Unlike American call options, American put options may be optimally exercised at any time. Consider two put options, one American and one European that are otherwise identical. Suppose the asset price drops to zero and the contracts have 1 year left. It makes sense to exercise the American put because the maximum amount obtainable at maturity is the strike price. (The holder of the European contract has to wait until expiration.) By continuity there is a range of asset prices for which early exercise is optimal. At each time there is a critical asset price below which it is optimal to exercise the American put. The locus of these points forms the *early exercise boundary*.

## SECTION 6.5.2 | NUMERICAL VALUATION OF AMERICAN OPTIONS USING THE BINOMIAL METHOD

In this section we discuss the numerical valuation of American options using the binomial method. To begin, we consider an American put option on a non-dividend-paying stock. Later we discuss the valuation of American call options. Recall that unless the underlying stock pays dividends it is never rational to exercise an American call option early. We have already seen that if an American call option is exercised early, this will only happen just prior to a dividend payment date.

We consider a two-period binomial model using the same notation and conventions as before. In particular, the up movement is denoted by $u$ and the down movement is denoted by $d$. We examine the valuation of an American put option in this model, and discuss conditions when it is rational to exercise the put option early. If the option is held to maturity, then the values of the American put option and its European counterpart are equal. We now suppose we are at time 1 in state 0.

Figure 6.10 shows the value of the put option at expiration for part of the lattice. We assume the option has not been exercised at node $(1, 0)$ so that with risk-neutral probability $q$ the option will expire at time period 2 with a payoff of $[K - S(2, 1)]^+$ or with risk-neutral probability $1 - q$ the option will expire with a payoff of $[K - S(2, 0)]^+$. From the risk-neutral valuation (or from (6.3.16)), the value of the European put option at node $(1, 0)$ is

$$p(1, 0) = e^{-rh}\{q[K - S(1, 0)u]^+ + (1 - q)[K - S(1, 0)d]^+\}. \qquad (6.5.4)$$

The American put option, on the other hand, has the added advantage that it can be exercised at node $(1, 0)$ and the owner of the option will receive an amount of

FIGURE **6.10** | *Stock Price Dynamics*

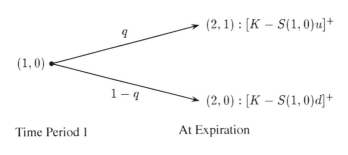

$(2, 1) : [K - S(1, 0)u]^+$

$q$

$(1, 0)$

$1 - q$

$(2, 0) : [K - S(1, 0)d]^+$

Time Period 1                         At Expiration

$[K - S(1, 0)]^+$. Therefore, the value of the American put option, at node $(1, 0)$, $P(1, 0)$, must be the greater of these two values; that is,

$$P(1, 0) = \max\{[K - S(1, 0)]^+, \, p(1, 0)\}$$
$$= \max\{K - S(1, 0), \, e^{-rh}(q[K - S(1, 0)u]^+$$
$$+ (1 - q)[K - S(1, 0)d]^+)\}.$$

The exercise price $K$ will lie either between the next two successive stock prices in the lattice or else above both or below both. Thus, the exercise price $K$ will either be greater than $S(1, 0)u$, lie between $S(1, 0)u$ and $S(1, 0)d$, or be less than $S(1, 0)d$:

$$K > S(1, 0)u,$$
$$S(1, 0)u > K > S(1, 0)d,$$
$$S(1, 0)d > K.$$

If the first case occurs, then the put option is in the money at both the nodes $(2, 0)$ and $(2, 1)$. In this case $p(1, 0)$ is equal to

$$Ke^{-rh} - S(1, 0).$$

However, we can see that this is less than the value of the American option. If it were exercised immediately at node $(1, 0)$, its value would be

$$K - S(1, 0).$$

Thus, in the first case we have

$$P(1, 0) = K - S(1, 0) > Ke^{-rh} - S(1, 0) = p(1, 0).$$

Next, go directly to the third case. If the third case occurs, then the put option is worth zero at both the nodes $(2, 0)$ and $(2, 1)$. In this case $p(1, 0)$ is also worth zero. However, we can also see that in this case the value of the American option is also zero at node $(1, 0)$. If it were exercised immediately, the payoff would be

$$K - S(1, 0).$$

But in view of our assumptions this amount is negative. Hence, it would not be rational to exercise the American put option at this node in these circumstances.

We have seen that if the stock price is low—lower than the exercise price at the up node, it always pays to exercise the American put at node $(1, 0)$. Furthermore, we have seen that if the stock price is high—higher than the exercise price at the down node, it never pays to exercise the American put at node $(1, 0)$.

In the second case, we will find a range of stock prices over which it is rational to exercise the American put early. Indeed, we will determine the break-even stock price at which the investor is indifferent between exercising the American put and holding on to it.

We now assume that the second condition holds so that the put is in the money at the lower node $(2, 0)$ and worth zero at the top node $(2, 1)$. The critical stock price at time 1, $S^*(1)$, is the price that satisfies

$$K - S^*(1) = e^{-rh}(1 - q)[K - S(1, 0)d].  \tag{6.5.5}$$

Therefore, we have

$$S^*(1) = K\frac{1 - e^{-rh}(1 - q)}{1 - e^{-rh}(1 - q)d}.  \tag{6.5.6}$$

Note that the critical stock price depends only on time and is independent of the state.

The critical stock price can be interpreted as the cutoff price between the decision to exercise or to hold the option alive. For an American put option, it is always optimal to exercise the option immediately when the stock price is lower than some critical stock price. For an American call option, it is always optimal to exercise the option immediately when the stock price is higher than some critical stock price.

The analysis can be extended to an $n$-period binomial model. The option payoff function at time period $i$ in state $j$ is $g(S(i, j))$. The following analysis applies to both call and put options. We first revisit one of the pricing techniques we used for standard European options in the binomial framework. The binomial valuation formula given by (6.3.1) can be understood as follows: the value of the European option depends only on the terminal stock prices at expiration; it is therefore natural to start considering the valuation at expiration $T = Nh$. In the binomial model, there are only $N + 1$

possible terminal stock prices. In each state $j$, stock price, $S(N, j) = S(0)u^j d^{N-j}$, as well as the option payoff, $V(N, j) = g(S(N, j))$, are computed. We require $j$ up-jumps and $N - j$ down-jumps to move from node $(0, 0)$ to node $(N, j)$. The probability of this event happening is $q^j(1 - q)^{N-j}$ with a total of $\binom{N}{j}$ such paths. The option payoff is adjusted by these factors as well as the discounting factor $e^{-rNh}$ to determine the time-0 value (present value) of the option pertaining to state $j$. This procedure is repeated for all other states, and the sum of these values is the required time-0 European option value.

We have already seen how the period by period recursive valuation formula also gives the current price of a European option. Not only is this recursive method better from a computational viewpoint, but it also provides the flexibility we need to handle America options.

In the recursive method, we first determine the option values at expiration $V(N, j) = g(S(N, j))$, $j = 0, 1, \ldots, N$. Rather than discounting $V(N, j)$ directly to time 0, we proceed backward in time, one step at a time. We use (6.3.16) to determine $V(N - 1, j)$, for $j = 0, 1, \ldots, N - 1$. This procedure is used repeatedly for $i = N - 1, N - 2, \ldots, 0$, $j = 0, 1, \ldots, i$ so that we eventually obtain $V(0, 0)$. The option value $V(0, 0)$ is the required time-0 option value and is equivalent to $c(0)$ for the European call option or $p(0)$ for the European put option.

Algebraically, the above procedure can be represented recursively as

$$V(i, j) = e^{-rh}[q V(i + 1, j + 1) + (1 - q) V(i + 1, j)] \qquad (6.5.7)$$

for $i = N - 1, N - 2, \ldots, 0$, $j = 0, 1, \ldots, i$ and $V(N, j) = g(S(N, j))$.

Observe that to determine $V(i, j)$, (6.5.7) requires $V(i + 1, j + 1)$ and $V(i + 1, j)$ to have been determined in the earlier computation at time $(i + 1)$. Furthermore, we need $1 + 2 + \cdots + (N + 1) = (N + 1)(N + 2)/2$ node calculations in (6.5.7) to determine $V(0, 0)$ as opposed to only $N + 1$ node calculations for (6.3.1).

We now discuss how to modify the above algorithm to handle the early exercise feature. What distinguishes the American options from the European options is that at each node $(i, j)$, the holder of the option must make a decision on whether to exercise the option immediately and receive a payoff of $g(S(i, j))$ or to keep the option alive. In this context, we assume that the investor is rational and optimally exercises the option to maximize gain.

Evaluating the American option becomes the classical optimal stopping time problem. This involves determining the *critical stock price boundary* of the option. This boundary consists of the critical stock prices at each future time over the life of the option. The dynamic programming approach provides a means of approximating the critical stock price at each time period. This method works as follows. Assuming the American option is still alive at expiration, the option payoffs $V(N, j)$ are computed.

At time period $N - 1$ in state $j$, we must make an optimal decision on whether to exercise the option based on the condition that the option is still alive. Such a decision is resolved by comparing the exercise value to the holding value of the option. The exercise value corresponds to the value obtained from immediately exercising the option whereas the holding value corresponds to the value of the option assuming it is kept alive, that is, not exercised. Let $E(i, j)$ denote the exercise value and $H(i, j)$ denote the holding value of the option at time period $i$ in state $j$. Therefore, we have

$$E(i, j) = g(S(0)u^j d^{i-j})$$

and

$$H(i, j) = e^{-rh}[qV(i+1, j+1) + (1-q)V(i+1, j)].$$

We now describe where the $V$ functions in the last equation come from. When the immediate-exercise value is greater than the holding value of the option, the option should be exercised, otherwise the option will be kept alive. The option value in node $(i, j)$ must correspond to the greater of these two values; that is,

$$V(i, j) = \max\{E(i, j),\ H(i, j)\}. \tag{6.5.8}$$

We can start the procedure at time $N$ because we know that

$$V(N, j) = g(S(N, j)),$$

assuming the option is still alive at node $(N, j)$. The above recursive procedure is repeated for $i = N-1, N-2, \ldots, 0, \ j = 0, 1, \ldots, i$. Then $V(0, 0)$ is the required American option value at time 0.

As long as we move backward in time and maximize the option value at each state, the dynamic programming approach optimizes the decision making. This method provides an estimate of the American option value that converges to the continuous-time American option as the number of time periods increase (see Chapter 5).

It should be emphasized that in the case of an American call option with discrete dividend dates, early exercise occurs only on ex-dividend dates. The procedure is similar to that which we described earlier.

***Example 6.5.1.*** Assume gold has a current price of $400 and a volatility of 5% per year. The risk-free interest rate is 6% per year and is assumed to be constant and deterministic. A put option on 1 ounce of gold with a 2-month expiration date has an exercise price of $401 and can be exercised at the end of each month. We use a two-time-interval binomial model to illustrate the recursive valuation of this option. The parameters of the binomial model are (using (6.3.13)) the following:

| $N$ | 2 |
|---|---|
| $h$ | 0.083333 |
| $u$ | 1.014538 |
| $d$ | 0.985670 |
| $e^{rh}$ | 1.005013 |
| $q$ | 0.670024 |

The results from the recursive valuation are shown in Figure 6.11. The value of the option is 2.429. Note that for the nodes (1,0), (2,0), and (2,1) the option would be exercised early. ∎

FIGURE **6.11** | *Recursive Valuation of American Put Option for Example 6.5.1*

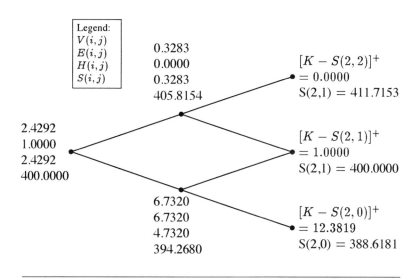

Most exotic options are path dependent since their values often depend on the path of the asset prices. Conceptually path-dependent derivatives that allow early exercise can be valued using the same procedure as for a standard non-path-dependent derivative. However, the computation of American option prices for many path-dependent options using these procedures can be slow. Thus, the practical valuation of path-dependent derivatives requires the use of approximate techniques that allow efficient and accurate calculation of values and the hedging statistics. Some of these techniques are discussed in the next section. Broadie and Detemple [27] provide a detailed coverage and comparison of most methods that have been proposed for American option valuation.

# Section 6.6
# Numerical Methods

Numerical methods have become very important in finance. There are several reasons why this has happened. First, the underlying models that describe the evolution of the prices of the basic securities and the relevant state variables have become more sophisticated. Second, the types of securities and their associated derivative offspring have become more complex. To compute the prices and risk sensitivities of these instruments high-dimensional integrals often have to be evaluated. Third, advances in risk management technology and practice now mandate more comprehensive and intricate analyses at the portfolio level. For example, due to regulatory requirements, many financial institutions are currently devoting considerable resources to setting up systems to compute Value at Risk (VAR).[6] These VAR calculations can involve thousands of different variables. The continuing improvement in computing power has made many calculations feasible that would have been impossible even a few years ago.

A wide range of numerical methods are available for these purposes, which we now discuss in turn. First, there are problems that have closed form or analytical solutions, but even in these cases we usually still require numerical work. Even when analytical expressions are available, some numerical algorithm must usually be invoked to complete the calculation. For example, the Black-Scholes formula furnishes a closed-form expression for the price of a European call option on a non-dividend-paying stock. However, to obtain numerical values we still need to evaluate two cumulative normal distribution functions. There are many derivative contracts for which analytical solutions do not appear to exist. However, for many cases of interest the price of the derivative is governed by a partial differential equation (PDE): Zvan, Forsyth, and Vetzal [214] have applied modern techniques from the PDE literature to derive efficient methods for the pricing of certain types of exotic options. The disadvantage of PDE methods is that they can only deal with a small number of state variables.

---

[6]For a comprehensive and accessible overview of Value at Risk models and implementation issues, see Duffie and Pan [51].

In 1979, the paper by Cox, Ross, and Rubinstein [44] introduced and popularized the use of lattice (or tree) methods in computational finance. This is essentially a finite difference method, but it resonates well with basic finance intuition. In the backward recursion, the value of the derivative at a given time interval is equal to its discounted expected value at the next time interval when the discounting is at the one-period risk-free rate. Lattice methods are widely used for different types of derivatives including interest-sensitive derivatives. This method works best if the tree is *recombining*. Thus, it is not an efficient method for models involving non-Markovian state variables, for example, the general versions of the Heath, Jarrow, and Morton [87] model. Like PDE methods, lattice methods are most suitable for situations in which the number of state variables is small.

Many problems of interest involve large numbers of state variables. Examples include mortgage-backed securities and other path-dependent securities. In these cases, the price of a derivative security whose payoff is a function of these state variables can be written as a multidimensional integral. For such problems, the Monte Carlo method provides a powerful and flexible tool. The Monte Carlo method is usually straightforward to implement, and because of the unprecedented improvements in computer efficiency it can now be applied to a wide range of complex problems. Even so, problems still remain for which the standard Monte Carlo approach is computationally burdensome. Various techniques have been proposed to speed up the convergence.

In the next section we discuss some simple lattice-type approximations. In the following section we briefly review the standard Monte Carlo approach and discuss methods that can be used to speed up the efficiency of this method.

## SECTION 6.6.1 | LATTICE MODELS

Lattice models approximate the distribution of the underlying asset with a discrete distribution. The binomial model considered earlier in this chapter is the lattice model most often used in practice. The models are called lattice models because the prices at future dates, when connected together, appear on a lattice. They are also referred to as "trees." The points on the lattice at the end of each time interval in the lattice are referred to as the nodes in the lattice, and the connection between the nodes on the tree are called branches of the tree (and also for the lattice). Each node corresponds to a state of the world in the model.

The lattice can be constructed as a complete market discrete-time model. However, for numerical computation it is not necessary to use the complete markets discrete-time model. It is usually assumed that underlying asset prices follow a continuous process and that the discrete models are approximations to the continuous-time results. In this case, the numerical accuracy of the discrete models as the time interval is made shorter is an important issue as is the speed of computation. For the binomial model, as the time interval is made smaller the model value for a call option does not converge smoothly to the continuous-time value (Kamrad and Ritchken [104]). This was shown in Example 6.3.2.

Boyle [21] has suggested a trinomial lattice. Note that after two time intervals in the binomial model there are three nodes and this is equivalent to a trinomial model with a time interval equal to two binomial time intervals. Kamrad and Ritchken [104] demonstrate that a trinomial lattice with $n$ time intervals often requires less computation and produces more accurate answers than a binomial lattice with $2n$ time intervals. Broadie and Detemple [27] demonstrate that, after allowing for the speed-accuracy tradeoff, the trinomial method is only slightly better than the binomial method except for long maturities. For longer maturities, the trinomial method can perform worse than the binomial. The convergence of the trinomial lattice to the continuous-time value can be more stable for lower values of $n$.

In the trinomial model, we have

$$R(t) = \begin{cases} u & \text{with probability } q_u \\ m & \text{with probability } 1 - q_u - q_d \\ d & \text{with probability } q_d \end{cases}$$

where $u = e^{\lambda\sigma\sqrt{h}}$, $m = 1$, and $d = e^{-\lambda\sigma\sqrt{h}}$ with $\lambda$ selected to ensure that the model is arbitrage free with positive martingale probabilities.

Cho and Lee [37] suggest a method of selecting the parameters for the trinomial model by matching the first, second, and third moments of a lognormal distribution for the asset price. They use $u = \exp[(r - \sigma^2/2)h + \lambda\sigma\sqrt{h}]$, $m = \exp[(r - \sigma^2/2)h]$, and $d = \exp[(r - \sigma^2/2)h - \lambda\sigma\sqrt{h}]$. The martingale probabilities $q_u$ and $q_d$ and the value for $\lambda$ are determined by equating the three noncentral moments using

$$q_u u + (1 - q_u - q_d)\, m + q_d d = e^{rh},$$
$$q_u u^2 + (1 - q_u - q_d)\, m^2 + q_d d^2 = e^{2rh+\sigma^2 h},$$
$$q_u u^3 + (1 - q_u - q_d)\, m^3 + q_d d^3 = e^{3rh+3\sigma^2 h}.$$

The lattice models are constructed so that the branches recombine, that is, $ud = du$, which allows efficient calculation of standard derivatives. A similar requirement applies for the trinomial lattice. In the parameter selection above, $ud = du = m^2$. This results in a path-independent lattice with values of the asset at the various nodes of the lattice depending only on the value of $i$ at that node.

A trinomial lattice is also used for the joint distribution required to value derivatives whose cash flows depend on two primitive asset values. Section 6.8.2 describes a pension application using such a model as well as simulation.

The speed and accuracy of binomial methods is significantly enhanced using Richardson extrapolation (Broadie and Detemple [27]).

## SECTION 6.6.2 | MONTE CARLO SIMULATION

In the previous section, we discussed the use of lattice model for derivative pricing. This method becomes computationally burdensome for certain types of exotic options. It is also difficult to apply when the payoff depends on several several state variables. In these circumstances, the Monte Carlo simulation is often convenient. In this section we provide a brief discussion of this method and discuss ways of making it more efficient.

We have seen that the value of a standard European call can be written as an expectation of its payoff. This expectation can be written as an integral, and more complex securities can be written as multiple integrals. That Monte Carlo method furnishes a useful tool for the valuation of these securities.

For simplicity, consider the valuation of a standard European call option. In this case, the price can be written as an one-dimensional integral. The payoff at maturity is integrated over the terminal distribution of the stock price. In the Black-Scholes case, this distribution is lognormal.

The first step is to generate $N$ values from the terminal distribution. In practice, we would use a suitable random number generator to generate these values. For each stock price in the sample, we compute the maturity value of the option. This value is zero if the terminal asset price lies below the strike price, and the difference between the terminal asset price and the strike price otherwise. In this way, we can compute the value of the option at maturity. We next take the average of the $N$ simulated terminal call option values. The Monte Carlo estimate is obtained by discounting this average at the risk-free rate over the remaining life of the contract. We can also use this method to compute the variance of the estimate. The estimate converges to the true value as $N$ becomes large. This follows from the strong law of large numbers. Furthermore, the distribution of the estimate tends to normality as $N$ becomes large from the central limit theorem. This means that we can obtain confidence limits on the accuracy of the estimate, a very useful feature in numerical work.

We now illustrate the application of the Monte Carlo methods to the valuation of general European options. Recall that the value of a European derivative is $V(0) = e^{-rT} \mathrm{E}^Q[g(S(T)) \,|\, \mathcal{P}_0]$. A sample of $N$ equally likely values of $\hat{g}_i(S(T))$ is simulated, and

$$\hat{V}(0) = \frac{1}{N} \sum_{i=1}^{N} e^{-rT} \hat{g}_i(S(T))$$

is the estimate of the derivative value. The variance of the estimate is

$$s^2 = \frac{1}{N-1} \sum_{i=1}^{N} [e^{-rT} \hat{g}_i(S(T)) - \hat{V}(0)]^2,$$

and the standard error is $s/\sqrt{N}$.

The same approach can be used to price more complicated structures such as mortgage-backed securities and Asian options. The Monte Carlo method provides a powerful and flexible tool for such problems and is normally easily implemented. It is also well suited for the valuation of European options, but the valuation of the American option poses some challenges. However, significant progress has been made in this area in recent years (see papers by Tilley [196], Barraquand and Martineau [5], and Broadie and Glasserman [29]).

We have seen that the standard error of the Monte Carlo estimate is proportional to $N^{-1/2}$.[7] This implies that to increase the accuracy by a factor of 10, we need to increase the number of simulations by 100-fold. Instead of increasing the number of simulation runs, there are several techniques that can be used to increase the accuracy of the estimate. These techniques are generally known as *variance reduction techniques*.

### Antithetic Variable Technique

Suppose an (unbiased) estimator, $\bar{f}$, is obtained by averaging a pair of unbiased estimators ($f_1$, $f_2$); that is,

$$\bar{f} = \frac{f_1 + f_2}{2}.$$

The variance of the resulting unbiased estimator becomes

$$\text{Var}(\bar{f}) = \frac{\text{Var}(f_1) + \text{Var}(f_2)}{4} + \frac{\text{Cov}(f_1, f_2)}{2}.$$

This shows that the variance of the estimator $\bar{f}$ is smaller than the corresponding estimators $f_1$ or $f_2$ when $\text{Cov}(f_1, f_2) < 0$. Hence, it is desirable to use two unbiased estimators that are highly negatively correlated. Suppose a sequence of independently and identically distributed uniform numbers, $u_i$, are used to drive the simulation for computing $f_1$. If $u_i$ is uniformly distributed on $[0, 1]$, then $1 - u_i$ is also

---

[7]This convergence rate is independent of the dimension of the problems.

uniformly distributed on $[0, 1]$. An antithetic estimator $f_2$ can be obtained by using the antithetic sequence $1 - u_i$. The method, however, does not always guarantee a variance reduction in general unless the function is monotone with respect to each underlying uniform number.

### Control Variate Technique

The basic idea underlying this method is to replace the problem under consideration by a similar but simpler problem that has an analytic solution. The solution of the simpler problem is used to increase the accuracy of the solution to the more complex problem. The key element in this method is that the control variate chosen must be highly correlated with the problem under consideration. For instance, suppose we are interested in simulating an arithmetic Asian option. A natural candidate of the control variate is a corresponding Asian option with geometric averaging because in this case a simple closed-form solution is available.

### Stratified Sampling

Stratified sampling involves breaking the sampling region for the random variates into $m$ disjoint subregions. Monte Carlo simulation is used to estimate each sub-region separately. The idea of this technique is to take more observations in the parts of the region that are more "important" rather than by sampling over the whole distribution.

### Low-Discrepancy Methods

The method of quasi-random or low-discrepancy sequences is based on using deter-ministic points that are as uniformly distributed as possible instead of the pseudo-random numbers used in Monte Carlo simulation. Joy, Boyle, and Tan [103] and Paskov and Traub [141] demonstrate that this method can produce faster convergence to derivative values than the conventional Monte Carlo simulation.

### Path Dependency

Simulation is used for the calculation of path-dependent derivative prices where the use of a nonrecombining lattice would not be computationally feasible. Valuation of American-style derivatives is not as straightforward using simulation. The main reason for this is that on each simulated path of prices it is not possible to read-ily determine if the option should be exercised early. To do this, it is necessary to determine $\max[E(i, j), H(i, j)]$, but the value of $H(i, j)$ can only be directly evaluated along a single path. Tilley [196] has developed a "path-bundling" proce-dure that can be used to approximate the value of American-style derivatives using simulation.

# Section 6.7
# Hedging

Derivatives are used by company treasurers and investment managers to manage or hedge a physical exposure to an underlying asset. Dealers who write derivatives are concerned with managing the risk in a portfolio of derivatives. The standard approach to hedging is based on the concepts underlying immunization against interest rate movements. This is referred to as dynamic hedging because the portfolio used to hedge the derivative is rebalanced in a dynamic manner.

The self-financing trading strategy in the binomial model determines the composition of the hedge portfolio. An examination of (6.3.14) shows that the delta is the discrete approximation of the partial derivative of the derivative value with respect to the asset price.

Any pricing model, including the binomial model, is only an approximation to the real world. The sensitivity of the model values to the assumptions of the model are important in practice. These sensitivities are called risk statistics and include the delta, gamma, theta, vega, and rho for a derivative.

## SECTION 6.7.1 | DELTA, $\Delta$

The delta ($\Delta$) of a derivative is a measure of the sensitivity of its price to changes in the underlying asset. It is equal to the number of units of the underlying asset in the replicating portfolio. For the binomial model we have

$$\Delta(i, j) = \frac{V(i + 1, j + 1) - V(i + 1, j)}{(u - d) S(i, t)}.$$

If a portfolio of underlying assets and derivatives is constructed so that the portfolio delta is zero, then the portfolio is delta neutral. Using the assumptions of the model, if the underlying asset value changes, then the value of a delta-neutral portfolio will not change since it is perfectly hedged.

In practice, the delta is sometimes approximated by extending the tree backwards:

$$\Delta(i, j) = \frac{V(i, j + 1) - V(i, j - 1)}{(u^2 - d^2) S(i, t)}.$$

This is a better approximation to the continuous-time delta (see Pelsser and Vorst [144]). Deltas are positive for call options, representing long positions on the asset, and for put options the deltas are negative, representing short positions. Recall that in the Black-Scholes model the price of a call option is

$$c(0) = S(0)N(d_1) - Ke^{-rT}N(d_2),$$

$$d_1 = \frac{\log[S(0)/K] + (r + \sigma^2/2)T}{\sigma\sqrt{T}},$$

$$d_2 = d_1 - \sigma\sqrt{T}$$

where the notation corresponds to the usual conventions. The delta of the call option in this case is equal to $N(d_1)$. It is also true that delta is equal to the sensitivity (partial derivative) of the call option price with respect to the stock price (see Exercise 10.14.19).

## SECTION 6.7.2 | GAMMA, $\Gamma$

Gamma ($\Gamma$) is an estimate of the sensitivity of the delta to changes in the underlying asset value. It is calculated in the binomial model as

$$\frac{\Delta(i+1, j+1) - \Delta(i+1, j)}{S(i+1, j+1) - S(i+1, j)} = \frac{\Delta(i+1, j+1) - \Delta(i+1, j)}{(u-d)S(i, j)}.$$

Pelsser and Vorst [144] provide alternative expressions for the gamma of a portfolio. If a portfolio is constructed so that the portfolio gamma is zero, then the portfolio is *gamma neutral*. A delta- and gamma-neutral portfolio can provide a better hedge than can a delta-neutral portfolio.

In the continuous-time Black-Scholes model the gamma of a European call option on a non-dividend-paying stock is

$$\Gamma = \frac{\Phi(d_1)}{S_0\sigma\sqrt{T}} \tag{6.7.1}$$

where $\Phi(\cdot)$ is the standard normal density function.

## SECTION 6.7.3 | THETA, $\Theta$

The theta ($\Theta$) measures the time decay in the value of a derivative. It is calculated in the binomial model as

$$\Theta = \frac{V(i+2, j+1) - V(i, j)}{2h}.$$

Other sensitivities are often calculated in practice when managing a portfolio of derivatives. Because the binomial model assumes that the interest rate and the volatility are constant when in practice they are not, it is important to determine the sensitivity of the portfolio value to changes in the model assumptions for these parameters. The sensitivity to changes in the interest rate is called "rho," and the sensitivity to the changes in the volatility is called "vega."

*Example 6.7.1.* We use the binomial model to calculate the delta, gamma, and theta for a 1-year European put option on the U.S. dollar/U.K. pound exchange rate with an exercise price of $1.50 (per pound), a 3-month U.S. interest rate of 5.5% per year, a 3-month U.K. interest rate of 7.5% p.a, a current exchange rate of $1.50, and a volatility of the sterling exchange rate of 15% per year (this is the put option from Example 6.3.11). Using 50 time intervals and the binomial model formula for a put option (6.3.3) gives a put price of 0.09842 and the values in the following table.

| Node $(i, j)$ | $(1, 0)$ | $(1, 1)$ | $(2, 0)$ | $(2, 1)$ | $(2, 2)$ |
|---|---|---|---|---|---|
| $T$ | 49 | 49 | 48 | 48 | 48 |
| $m$ | 26 | 25 | 26 | 25 | 24 |
| $S(i, j)$ | 1.46852 | 1.53216 | 1.43769 | 1.50000 | 1.56501 |
| $V(i, j)$ | 0.11354 | 0.08260 | 0.12998 | 0.09636 | 0.06820 |

From the table the estimates of delta, gamma, and theta are the following (answers have been calculated using more decimal places than shown in the table):

$$\Delta = \frac{0.08260 - 0.11354}{1.53216 - 1.46852} = -0.48608,$$

$$\Gamma = \frac{\dfrac{0.06820 - 0.09636}{1.56501 - 1.5} - \dfrac{0.09636 - 0.12998}{1.5 - 1.43769}}{1.53216 - 1.46852}$$

$$= 1.67232,$$

$$\Theta = \frac{0.09636 - 0.09842}{2 \times 0.02} = -0.05150.$$

More accurate estimates of these values can be obtained using larger values of $T$. The following table gives values for delta, gamma, and theta for larger values of $T$.

| $N$ | $\Delta$ | $\Gamma$ | $\Theta$ |
|---|---|---|---|
| 100 | −0.48576 | 1.65709 | −0.05109 |
| 101 | −0.48538 | 1.64877 | −0.05085 |
| 500 | −0.48551 | 1.64512 | −0.05077 |
| 501 | −0.48544 | 1.64349 | −0.05073 |

∎

## SECTION 6.7.4 | COMPUTING RISK SENSITIVITIES USING SIMULATION

If simulation is used for derivative valuation, then it is not a simple matter to compute the risk statistics. The risk statistics are sensitivities of the derivative value to the underlying variables in the model. Numerical estimates of these derivatives can be calculated using simulation. The same random numbers are used for the calculation of the risk statistics as are used to value the derivative. The delta is estimated by calculating the value of the derivative for a small change in the initial underlying asset value using simulation, and the change in the derivative value divided by the change in the underlying asset value is an estimate of the delta. A similar procedure can be used for the other risk statistics. In practice, it is essential to use variance-reduction techniques for risk statistic calculations to improve the accuracy and speed of calculation. Using a crude simulation technique produces unreliable estimates of the risk statistics, especially for the gamma. See Broadie and Glasserman [28] for a better approach of estimating risk statistics using simulation.

## SECTION 6.7.5 | DYNAMIC HEDGING

Hedging a derivative position involves taking an offsetting position in a replicating, self-financing portfolio of traded securities. If the underlying asset is used for the replicating portfolio, then for a bought call option this is hedged using a short position in the underlying asset equal to the delta time of the underlying asset value and an investment in the money market account equal to the difference between the call option value and the cost of delta of the underlying asset. To hedge a put option, which involves a replicating portfolio with a short position in the underlying asset, it is necessary to hold a long position in the underlying asset equal to the absolute value of the delta of the option times the underlying asset value and to finance this with funds from the money market account.

The hedge portfolio is rebalanced for the binomial model at the end of each time period, because the asset price is assumed to be traded only at the end of the time periods in the model. In practice, trading takes place continuously during a trading day, and so the hedging position needs to be rebalanced reasonably frequently. The more frequently the hedge position is rebalanced, the better the hedge of the derivative, but the transactions costs will also be higher in practice. Because of transaction costs and other factors, it is not possible to perfectly hedge a derivative using the underlying asset. If other derivative securities related to the derivative being hedged are traded, then it will often be better in practice to hedge using these securities because the transaction costs are normally much lower in the derivative markets and the liquidity higher than in the underlying asset.

*Example 6.7.2.* Consider the put option in Example 6.5.1 on gold. The time-2 interval binomial model for the gold price with the value of the option is given in Figure 6.11.

The delta for the option at time 0 is

$$\Delta = \frac{0.32833 - 6.732036}{405.815371 - 394.267964} = -0.554558 \, .$$

Assume that you have written a 2-month put option on gold with a strike of 401. To hedge this position you will need a long position in an equivalent put option generated using the replicating position for a put. The replicating position at time 0 for one put option will be a short position of $-0.554558$ ounces of gold generating $0.554558 \times 400 = 221.8232$ and an investment in a money market account for an amount of $221.8232 + 2.42922 = 224.2524$.

At the end of the first month, if the gold price increases, then the hedge position will be worth

$$-0.554558 \times 405.815371 + 224.2524 \times 1.005013 = 0.3283$$

which is sufficient to purchase the written put option at the model price.

If the gold price decreases to 394.267964, then the hedge position will be worth

$$-0.554558 \times 394.267964 + 224.2524 \times 1.005013 = 6.73212,$$

and once again the put option is hedged.

Now consider what happens when the hedge portfolio is rebalanced at the end of the first month. If the price increases to 405.815371, then the new delta (hedge ratio) is

$$\frac{0 - 1.0}{411.715287 - 400.00} = -0.08536,$$

so that $0.554558 - 0.08536 = 0.469198$ ounces of gold must be purchased costing $0.469198 \times 405.815371 = 190.4077$. The hedge portfolio must remain self-financing so that the money market account is reduced by this amount to $224.2524 \times 1.005013 - 190.4077 = 34.9689$. Thus, the hedge position for the written put becomes a short position of $-0.08536$ ounces of gold with value $0.08536 \times 405.815371 = 34.6404$ and an investment in the money market account of 34.9689.

At the end of the second month if the gold price rises to 411.715289, then the hedge portfolio will be worth

$$-0.08536 \times 411.715287 + 34.9689 \times 1.005013 = 0.0000,$$

which is the same as the written put option which expires out of the money.

If the price falls to 400.00, then the hedge portfolio will be worth

$$-0.08536 \times 400.0 + 34.9689 \times 1.005013 = 1.0000,$$

which is exactly sufficient to provide the net payoff to the holder of the option who will rationally exercise the option in this case.

Now consider what happens if the gold price falls to 394.267964 at the end of the first month. In this case the holder of the option will exercise the option, and it will be necessary to buy the asset for 401. If the hedge portfolio is rearranged to produce an offsetting position in the underlying asset, then an additional short position of 1.0000 − 0.554558 or 0.44544 ounces of gold will be required. This will produce a money market account balance of $224.2524 \times 1.005013 + 0.44544 \times 394.267964 = 401.00$, which is exactly sufficient to meet the contracted obligation under the written put.

In practice, the hedge portfolio must be rebalanced more frequently since price changes occur much more frequently than monthly as assumed in this example. ∎

### SECTION 6.7.6 | STATIC HEDGING AND PATH-DEPENDENT OPTIONS

For many path-dependent derivatives, the use of a dynamic hedge based on the delta of the derivative can require a large amount of trading in the underlying asset, especially as the underlying asset value comes close to a boundary such as the barrier for barrier options. This problem also occurs as standard options reach expiration and the option is close to the money. The gamma of the derivative is high in these, cases indicating that the hedge portfolio based on the delta is likely to change significantly as the underlying asset value changes.

A technique that can be used to handle these situations is the static hedge. A static hedge of standard traded options with differing exercise prices and expiration dates is established at the initial date. This static hedge is not intended to be rebalanced, hence the name "static" hedge. We can use standard options with differing exercise prices and expiration dates to replicate the payoffs of path-dependent options at the critical price levels such as at the barriers and at expiration.

### SECTION 6.7.7 | OTHER FACTORS

In the valuation models in this chapter the derivative security is priced using an arbitrage-free model and a self-financing replicating portfolio of traded assets. In such a model a derivative security can be considered to be a redundant security and need not exist because it appears to provide nothing more than is currently available in the market of traded securities. In practice we know that options and other derivatives are not redundant for a host of reasons and that they serve a valuable role for corporate treasurers, financial managers, and investment fund managers.

There are many reasons that options and other derivatives have a valuable economic role to play. Derivative securities often provide an efficient means of achieving payoffs that are not readily available in markets or a more efficient means of achieving these payoffs. Thus, options and other derivatives help complete markets. Path-dependent options can provide a hedge against stochastic volatility. Derivatives often have a different tax and regulatory treatment of underlying assets and can provide an efficient means of managing tax and regulations for businesses. The transaction costs of using derivatives are usually much less than those of a self-financing replicating portfolio, which involves the costs of rebalancing the amount held in the underlying asset. Thus, derivatives can achieve payoffs more efficiently than the replicating portfolio.

The model assumptions used to value derivatives do not hold exactly in practice. For many options these factors are not significant or the model can be made more realistic to take these factors into account. Many standard equity derivative valuation models assume constant volatility and deterministic interest rates. These assumptions can be relaxed and need to be allowed for when valuing long-dated options. It is well known that the volatility observed in market prices for options varies with the exercise price and maturity date of the option. This is referred to as the volatility smile or volatility skew. Stochastic volatility models have been developed that provide a better representation of market prices than the constant volatility models. Stochastic interest rate models, as covered in Chapter 7, can also be used in derivative valuation although the valuation becomes more complex. As mentioned earlier, these factors are important for longer-dated options such as those that life insurance and pension funds will be interested in to manage the risks in their liabilities.

In practice, the valuation of derivatives needs to make an allowance for transaction costs since there will be a tradeoff between how well the derivative is replicated with frequent rebalancing and the costs incurred in doing this. The replication of a derivative will also be based on a model for the underlying asset price, and situations exist where the real-world behavior of the asset price is not the same as the model. More general models have been developed to handle these situations. These issues, although very important, are beyond the scope of this chapter.

# *Section 6.8*
## *Insurance and Pension Examples*

### SECTION 6.8.1 | INSURANCE PRODUCTS

Life insurance products contain a variety of options. Insurance products can contain maturity guarantees in which the policyholder is guaranteed a minimum of a return of premiums, sometimes with a low rate of interest on maturity. These products also guarantee a return of premiums, perhaps with a low rate of interest, on death or withdrawal as required under nonforfeiture laws in some countries. These maturity guarantees, minimum death, and withdrawal benefits are embedded options. The premium income from such products is usually invested in a mix of assets including equities. The returns are allocated to the products as dividends (or bonuses), or a formula specifies the return as a function of an equity index. Thus, if the assets backing the policies fall in value below the guarantee, the life insurance company will incur a loss on death and withdrawal payments. Valuation of these insurance products requires account to be taken of the decrement and survival probabilities as well as the embedded options. If the product guarantees a minimum surrender benefit, then allowance must be made for withdrawal decrements in the valuation. These withdrawals are often interest sensitive so that the withdrawal rate can depend on the market values of financial assets or their returns.

Equity-linked insurance products contain a variety of options in their product design. Equity-indexed annuities and equity-indexed life insurance provide returns linked to an equity index such as the S&P 500 index. Typically these products provide the policyholder with a proportion of the return on the index and guarantee a percentage of the premium with a low rate of interest, for example, a product that provides 100% of the S&P 500 return based on the highest value of the index over the term of the policy with a guarantee of 90% of the premium with 3% annual interest.

We assume that the decrement rates and the cash flow of the benefit payment are independent. Denote the cash flow of the benefit for time interval $t$ as $B(t)$ and the probability of payment at the end of time interval by $p(t)$.[8] The value of the benefits is

$$\sum_{t=1}^{T} e^{-rt} p(t) E^Q[B(t) \mid \mathcal{P}_0]$$

where $Q$ is an equivalent martingale measure.

In practice if $p(t)$ is a mortality rate then we would expect this to be independent of $B(t)$. However, withdrawal rates are likely to depend on $B(t)$ and perhaps other factors. In practice these benefits are complex and require careful evaluation. Because of the dependence between decrements and benefit values it is usually necessary to use simulation to value these benefits.

---

[8] In actuarial notation,

$$p(t) = \begin{cases} {}_{t-1|}q_u, & \text{for } t < T \\ {}_{T-1|}q_u + {}_T p_u = {}_{T-1} p_u, & \text{for } t = T. \end{cases}$$

## SECTION **6.8.2** | PENSION PLANS

Many pension plans offer retirement, resignation, and death benefits that have option features, for example, the maximum of two alternative benefit amounts based on a multiple of service or salary or the accumulation of defined contributions. The "greater of" benefit for a member who joined a fund at age $x$ years, on retirement from the fund after a membership of $T$ years, when the life is aged $x + T$, will be the greater of

$D(T) =$ a fixed multiple of final salary for each year of service or part thereof
(*defined benefit*),

or

$A(T) =$ the accumulation of contributions as a fixed percentage of salary at the crediting rate during membership time of $T$ (*defined contribution*).

Death, disability, or withdrawal benefits need not be based on the maximum of these two benefits, but this is the assumption here.

The benefit as a multiple of final salary is $D(T) = TkS(T)$ where $T$ is membership in years, $k$ is the salary multiple for the value of the benefit at exit, and $S(T)$ is the salary at time $T$ for a member who entered aged $x$. In practice the defined benefit is based on a multiple of final average salary, often in the 3 years before exit. This would mean that value of the benefit depends on the salary over the 3 years before retirement. The salary at exit is a function of the salary growth rate from the age at entry to the age at exit. The accumulation benefit depends on the history of salary growth rates as well as the fund earning rates during membership of the fund and is path dependent.

Assuming benefit payments are made at the end of the time interval, the valuation model time interval is of length $h$ years, and there are $N = T/h$ time intervals, then the value of the benefit can be written as

$$\sum_{i=0}^{N-1} e^{-r(i+1)h} \, p(i+1) E^Q[\max\{A(i), D(i)\} \mid \mathcal{P}_0]$$

where $p(i)$ is the expected proportion of the lives age $x$ that will receive the benefit at the end of time interval $i$ of membership in the fund. In the last time interval, this includes the survivors who retire along with the deaths and withdrawals in this last time interval. In a complete market valuation model, we assume that there are three primitive securities: $S_2$, $S_3$, and a money market account. The accumulation benefit and the defined benefit are functions of the history of the asset values $S_2$ and $S_3$. Under the equivalent martingale measure $Q$, we know that $\{e^{-rih} S_2(i)\}$ and $\{e^{-rih} S_3(i)\}$ are martingales. The correlation between the assets and hence the benefit values must be allowed for in the valuation.

Sherris [179] applies a number of derivative pricing techniques to the valuation of these benefits. Two variables are modeled in order to value these benefits. One is the salary growth rate, and the other is the crediting rate for the accumulation of contributions. A trinomial lattice model is developed with two state variables. These are the salary growth rate and the crediting rate. The assets $S_2$ and $S_3$ have values that are functions of these state variables, and the martingale requirement under the $Q$ measure is used to determine their relative expected returns for the valuation model. A lattice is constructed for these state variables using the $Q$ measure for a complete markets model.

In a discrete model, the general form of the lattice for the salary growth rate, $s$, and the crediting rate, $f$, is as shown in Table 6.3, where $d_{ij}$ is the proportional change in the current value of state variable $j$ for the $i$-th branch. Each of the lattice branches can be written in terms of an increase at the risk-adjusted expected change plus a random jump.

TABLE **6.3** | *Complete Markets Trinomial Lattice for Two State Variables*

| Current Node Value | Next Time Period Node Values | Probability |
|---|---|---|
| $[s_t, f_t]$ | $[(1 + d_{1s})s_t, (1 + d_{1f})f_t]$ | $p$ |
| $[s_t, f_t]$ | $[(1 + d_{2s})s_t, (1 + d_{2f})f_t]$ | $q$ |
| $[s_t, f_t]$ | $[(1 + d_{3s})s_t, (1 + d_{3f})f_t]$ | $1 - p - q$ |

The jumps in the trinomial lattice can be constructed in a number of different ways. It is necessary to ensure that the jumps used for the state variables have the required means, variances, and correlation. To do this, jumps are generated with zero means, variances of one, and zero correlation. These jumps form an orthogonal martingale and are referred to as an orthogonal basis. For the two state variables case, the orthogonal basis denoted by $Z_{ij}$ is given in Table 6.4. This is used with (6.8.1) and (6.8.2) to construct a trinomial lattice for the proportional increases in the state variables in Table 6.3.

In Table 6.3, the proportional increase in $s$ and $f$ over any time period is given by $(1 + d_{ij})$ where the subscript $i$, $\{i = 1, 2, 3\}$ indicates the branch of the lattice and subscript $j$ indicates the state variable for which the jump applies. For each branch $i = 1, 2$, and 3 the corresponding value for $d_{ij}$, for $j = s$ and $f$, are given by (6.8.1) and (6.8.2) respectively:

$$d_{is} = \mu_s h + \sigma_s \sqrt{h} Z_{is}, \qquad (6.8.1)$$

$$d_{if} = \mu_f h + \sigma_f \sqrt{h}(\rho Z_{is} + \sqrt{1 - \rho^2} Z_{if}) \qquad (6.8.2)$$

TABLE **6.4** | *Orthogonal Basis, $Z_{ij}$, for the Trinomial Lattice*

| Branch $i$ | $Z_{ij}$ | | Probability of Branch |
|:---:|:---:|:---:|:---:|
| | $j = s$ | $j = f$ | |
| 1 | $\dfrac{}{\sqrt{3/2}}$ | $\dfrac{}{\sqrt{1/2}}$ | 1/3 |
| 2 | 0 | $-2\sqrt{2}$ | 1/3 |
| 3 | $-\sqrt{3/2}$ | $\sqrt{1/2}$ | 1/3 |

where $\mu$ is the annualized expected change under the $Q$ measure, $\sigma$ is the annualized standard deviation, $\rho$ is the correlation coefficient, and $Z$ is the standard normal distribution.

In the "greater of" benefits case, the lattice will not recombine because the benefit value is path dependent. This leads to a very large number of nodes and computational difficulties. Without using an approximation to the lattice this approach is impractical for such benefit valuations because of the computation time and memory requirements. Simulation is a better method in this case.

The valuation can be carried out using simulated sample paths by calculating benefit values along individual paths for the salary growth rate and the crediting rate, multiplying the benefit values by decrement rates along the path, and discounting these values at the relevant risk-free interest rates. The benefit values for each path are then averaged to obtain an estimate of the present value of the benefit payments. This valuation procedure is a pathwise valuation procedure that allows for decrements.

In carrying out the valuation, the assumption was made that interest rates are deterministic. Another factor to note is that securities do not trade that exactly hedge the salary inflation and crediting rate risk in the greater-of benefits so that it is hard to argue that complete markets exist for replicating these benefits. In this case, it is necessary to allow for a price of risk of the state variables in the simulation. In the equations for the salary growth rate and the crediting rate given below, the price of risk is denoted by $\lambda_s$ for the salary growth rate and $\lambda_f$ for the crediting rate. Note that the resulting difference equations are only appropriate for valuation purposes and not for projection purposes. This is because the adjustment for the price of risk introduced into the expected change of the state variables generates future values for discounting at the risk-free interest rate and not values from the actual distribution of future benefit payments, that is, based on the $P$ measure. Note that in the complete markets case the adjustment for the price of risk results in an equivalent martingale $Q$ measure for valuation.

Simulation was implemented using a monthly time interval. The salary was generated using the difference equation $\text{Salary}_{t+h} = \text{Salary}_t(1 + hs_{t+h})$. The defined benefit was then calculated as $D_t = k \times$ service $\times$ Salary$_t$, where $k$ is the benefit accrual rate for each year of service and service is calculated from age at entry to the age at death or retirement. The accumulated contribution was determined using the difference equation

$$A_{t+h} = A_t(1 + hf_t) + c \times h \times \text{Salary}_t$$

where $c$ is the defined contribution rate for the member.

The rate of salary growth at time $t + h$, $s_{t+h}$ was derived from the stochastic difference equation

$$s_{t+h} = s_t + (\alpha_s + b_s s_t - \lambda_s \sigma_s s_t^{\gamma_s})h + \sigma_s s_t^{\gamma_s}\sqrt{h}Z_s.$$

This formulation allows several alternate distributions to be generated for the salary growth rate depending on the choice of the parameter $\gamma_s$. In practice, the parameter values should be estimated from empirical data including data on traded financial assets that price similar risks to those of the "greater-of" benefit. In this example, the aim was to illustrate how different the valuation results were compared with the standard deterministic actuarial valuation assumptions. For this reason, the study used a range of parameter values to examine the sensitivity of the results to these assumptions.

The crediting rate at time $t + h$ was generated from the equation

$$f_{t+h} = f_t + (\alpha_f + b_f f_t - \lambda_f \sigma_f f_t^{\gamma_f})h + \sigma_f f_t^{\gamma_f}\sqrt{h}(\rho Z_s + \sqrt{1 - \rho^2}Z_f)$$

where $Z_s$ and $Z_f$ are independent standard normal random variates. The correlation between the rate of salary growth and the crediting rate is given by $\rho$.

The results of the valuations indicated that standard deterministic valuations as often used by actuaries can understate the value of these option features in retirement benefits by as much as 35%. These applications indicate the usefulness and the importance of the financial economics approach to actuarial problems.

# Section 6.9
# Exercises

(Assume interest rates are continuously compounded unless the question states otherwise.)

### Exercise 6.1
Verify that the trading strategy given in Example 6.2.2 part (d) finances the derivative cash flows.

## Exercise 6.2

Derive an equivalent expression to (6.2.25) for a put option.

## Exercise 6.3

Derive (6.3.2) and show all intermediate steps in the derivation.

## Exercise 6.4

Show that if $h > (r/\sigma)^2$ and the binomial model parameters are selected using (6.3.13), then $q > 1$.

## Exercise 6.5

A European derivative pays the square of the asset price in 3 months' time. The current price is $20, and the asset price has a volatility of 15% per year. The continuously compounded interest rate is 7% per year. Use the binomial model with three time intervals to calculate the value of this derivative. Determine the self-financing portfolio for the first time interval and an estimate of the delta for the derivative. How do your answers change if 20 time intervals are used?

## Exercise 6.6

Derive the binomial option pricing model formula for a European call option using the recursive valuation relation given in (6.5.7).

## Exercise 6.7

Value a 3-month European call option on a dividend-paying stock with current price $50 and exercise price of $51. The dividend is due at the end of 1 month and is equal to $2.50. The volatility of the stock is 12%, and the continuously compounded risk-free interest rate is 5% per year for bonds less than or equal to 1 month to maturity and 5.5% for bonds more than 1 month to maturity. Use the binomial model with 3 time intervals.

## Exercise 6.8

Calculate the value of the option in Exercise 6.7 using a three-period binomial model if it allows for early exercise. Calculate the delta, gamma, and theta for this option.

## Exercise 6.9

Determine the value of an European put option on the geometric average of the price of a stock with current price $20, strike price $20, continuously compounded risk-free rate 7.5% per year, volatility 25% per year, and time to maturity 6 months. The geometric average uses the current value plus the value at the end of each month to the date of calculation of the average (sampling frequency is monthly). No dividends are due on the stock over the next 6 months. Use a monthly time interval and a binomial model. Calculate the value if the put option were American style.

## Exercise 6.10

Use simulation to calculate the value of the European put option in Exercise 6.9. Under the $Q$ measure assume that the continuously compounded rate of growth over any month is independently and normally distributed with mean $(0.075 - 0.5 \times (0.25)2) \times (1/12)$ and variance $(0.25)2 \times 1/12$. Use both 100 and 1,000 sample paths to estimate $E^Q[C(T)]$ and calculate the standard error of your estimate.

## Exercise 6.11 (Insurance Policy Maturity Guarantee)

A life insurance company issues 10-year maturity single premium equity-linked policies under which the company guarantees a return of the premium with 2% per year interest on maturity. The company invests the single premiums less an initial charge for the guarantee into an equity fund. The return earned on the equity fund is paid as a bonus at the end of each year. Use a binomial model to calculate the cost of the maturity guarantee for a single premium of $10,000, assuming that the equity fund has a volatility of 20% per year, that the risk-free rate is 5% per year, and that all policyholders survive to maturity.

## Exercise 6.12

Describe how the life insurance company in Exercise 6.11 could guarantee that it will be able to meet its investment guarantee on maturity of the policy.

## Exercise 6.13 (Annuity Guarantees)

A life insurance company issues annuities under which the income payments are indexed to the Consumer Price Index with a guaranteed minimum rate of annuity increase of 3% per year. Payments are made annually in arrears.

a. Show that the payment at time $t$ is equivalent to the payment on a zero-coupon bond plus an option on the inflation index.

b. Ignoring mortality, calculate the cost of this guarantee for a 5-year annuity with initial annual payment of $10,000. Assume that the Consumer Price Index has a volatility of 2% per year and that the risk-free interest rate is 5% per year. Use a binomial model to calculate the value of the annuity guarantee. You should assume that there is an active market in CPI indexed zero-coupon government bonds with "real" yields of 4% per year and that $e^{-rt}$ times the value of this indexed zero-coupon bond is a martingale under the $Q$ measure used to value the guarantee.

c. Discuss how the insurance company should invest to match its annuity liability.

## Exercise 6.14 *(Minimum Death Benefits)*

A life insurance company issues an equity-linked single-premium life insurance policy. On death or withdrawal the company guarantees a return of the gross single premium. The company invests the single premium less initial expense charges (the cost of the death or withdrawal guarantee) into an equity fund with a volatility of 20% per year. On maturity the policy pays the value of the amount in the equity fund with the same guarantee of a minimum return of gross premium. Death and withdrawal payments are made at the end of each year, and the following table gives the expected death and withdrawal rates for these policies.

| Year | Death and Withdrawals (% of in Force at Start of Year) |
|------|--------------------------------------------------------|
| 1 | 15 |
| 2 | 10 |
| 3 | 5 |
| 4 | 5 |
| 5 | 5 |
| 6 | 5 |
| 7 | 5 |
| 8 | 2 |
| 9 | 2 |
| 10 | 2 |

The risk-free interest rate on zero-coupon securities is 5% per year for a 1-year maturity, 5.5% per year for a 2-year maturity, and 6% per year for a 3-or-more-year maturity. Calculate the cost of this guarantee using a binomial model for equity returns.

# CHAPTER 7
## TERM STRUCTURE MODELS

## Section 7.1
## Introduction

Stochastic term structure or interest rate models are widely used for two main purposes. The first is to study the future value of a portfolio of fixed-income assets and liabilities. With interest rates subject to all the shocks and random forces of the world's economy, the future values of a realistic fixed-income portfolio are highly uncertain. But a realistic stochastic model of interest rates, combined with simulation or other numerical methods, can be used to provide useful estimates of the probability distribution of the portfolio's future value.

The second main purpose of interest rate models is to serve as a tool for the pricing and hedging of interest rate derivatives. The buying and selling of interest rate derivatives, often for the purpose of hedging the risks of a business organization, has recently become a huge industry. Sophisticated mathematical models are playing a significant role in this development. Just as stochastic models of stock prices are used to provide theoretical formulas for puts and calls, stochastic models of interest rates are also used to provide theoretical values for the prices of swaptions, caps, and floors.

In practice, most stochastic interest rate models are formulated in continuous time. As with continuous-time models of stock prices, this tendency seems to be due to the convenience of describing a model with just a few parameters as well as the possibility of obtaining concise formulas for derivative prices. Nevertheless, discrete-time interest rate models, the subject of this chapter, are important to study for several reasons. First, several important discrete-time models are widely used. Second, most important ideas and concepts about interest rate models can be learned in the discrete-time context, where the mathematics are much easier. Third, many continuous-time models are usually solved with numerical procedures on a computer by discrete-time models that approximate continuous-time models.

Section 7.2 presents some basic preliminaries about interest rates, and Section 7.3 provides a theoretical description of some basic interest rate derivatives. This presentation builds on some concepts introduced in Chapter 2, especially Section 2.5 on swaps and Section 2.6 on caps and floors. Section 7.4, the core of this chapter, presents the fundamental theory of stochastic interest rate models; it relies heavily on the arbitrage-pricing theory of Chapter 5. The development of theory is carried forward into Section 7.5, which studies the valuation of interest rate derivatives. Section 7.5 thus is dependent on Section 3.7, which introduced the notion of interest-rate-sensitive cash flows, and on Chapter 6, which discusses puts and calls on common stocks.

Section 7.6 considers an important class of discrete-time interest rate models, namely, binomial lattice models, especially those by Ho and Lee [93] and Black, Derman, and Toy [13]. A "case study" implementation of the Black-Derman-Toy model is derived in Section 7.7.

The chapter concludes with four sections on miscellaneous topics. Although interest rate futures (see Section 2.3) are derivatives, they have some special features, and so they are treated separately in Section 7.8. The remaining sections deal with valuation of financial instruments with interest-sensitive cash flows such as callable bonds, mortgage-backed securities, and deferred annuity products.

## Section 7.2
## Yield Curves, Forward Rates, Zero-Coupon Bonds

A basic requirement of any interest rate model is that it must be capable of giving the current price or value of a deterministic cash flow. For example, consider a default-free bond that pays a coupon $C$ at times $t = 1, \ldots, T$ and the face value $F$ at time $t = T$. The time-0 price $B$ of this bond is equal, of course, to the present value of this cash flow; that is, $B$ is equal to the $T$-fold sum of the present value of the $T$ payments. To compute these present values, we must know the corresponding interest rates, one for each payment date. This sequence of interest rates is called the *yield curve* or *term structure*; it must be specified at each point in time as part of the interest rate model.

The time-$t$ value of the yield curve is denoted by $\{Y(t, t + s); s = 0, 1, \ldots\}$. Here $Y(t, t + s) \geq 0$ is the riskless interest rate for an investment from time $t$ to time $t + s$, so that \$1 invested at time $t$ accumulates to $[1 + Y(t, t + s)]^s$ dollars at time $t + s$. The yield in the special case when $s = 1$ is called the *short rate* and is denoted $i_t = Y(t, t + 1)$. Moreover, the time-$t$ present value of \$1 paid at time $t + s$ is $[1 + Y(t, t + s)]^{-s}$. Thus, in particular, the time-0 price of the above bond is

$$B = \sum_{s=1}^{T-1}[1 + Y(0, s)]^{-s}C + [1 + Y(0, T)]^{-T}(C + F). \qquad (7.2.1)$$

For instance, with $T = 3$, $C = 6$, $F = 100$, $Y(0, 1) = 5\%$, $Y(0, 2) = 5.8\%$, and $Y(0, 3) = 6.4\%$, we have $B = 5.7143 + 5.3602 + 87.9997 = 99.0742$.

Keep in mind that the various interest rates associated with a yield curve are distinct, in general, from the yield-to-maturity of a bond (see Section 1.4 where the latter is discussed). The yield-to-maturity is the number $y$ such that

$$B = \sum_{s=1}^{T-1}[1 + y]^{-s}C + [1 + y]^{-T}(C + F). \qquad (7.2.2)$$

For instance, for the numerical example in the preceding paragraph the yield-to-maturity of the bond is $y = 6.3486\%$, which is different from $Y(0, 3) = 6.4\%$.

The time-$t$ present value of \$1 paid at time $t + T$, as introduced above, should be viewed as the time-$t$ price of a zero-coupon bond (also called a *pure discount bond*) that has face value \$1 when it matures at time $t + T$. This price is denoted $P(t, t + T)$, so that

$$P(t, t + T) = [1 + Y(t, t + T)]^{-T}, \qquad (7.2.3)$$

which is consistent with (7.2.1) when $C = 0$ (i.e., the coupon payment is zero) and the face value $F = 1$. This is also consistent with (7.2.2), so, in fact, $Y(t, t + T)$ is also the yield-to-maturity of a zero-coupon bond that matures at time $t + T$. Note that $P(t, t + T) \geq 0$, $P(t, t) = F = 1$, and $P(t, t + T)$ is a nonincreasing function of $T$ (see Exercise 7.1). Zero-coupon bonds are actual securities that are commonly traded in the economy, although, in general, the face values are not necessarily equal to one (but it is conventional in the interest-rate-modeling business to focus on zero-coupon bonds having face values equal to one, since the price of any other pure discount bond is a simple multiple).

The time-$t$ yield curve and (7.2.3) give rise to the *time-t curve of zero-coupon prices*, namely, $\{P(t, t+s); s = 0, 1, \ldots\}$. For instance, if the yield curve has $Y(0, 1) = 5\%$, $Y(0, 2) = 5.8\%$, and $Y(0, 3) = 6.4\%$, then $P(0, 1) = 0.9524$, $P(0, 2) = 0.8934$, and $P(0, 3) = 0.8302$. Conversely, knowing the prices of all the zero-coupon bonds, it is simple to infer the yield curve, because solving (7.2.3) for $Y$ in terms of $P$ gives

$$Y(t, t + T) = \left[ \frac{1}{P(t, t + T)} \right]^{\frac{1}{T}} - 1. \qquad (7.2.4)$$

For instance, if $P(0, 1) = 0.94$, $P(0, 2) = 0.89$, and $P(0, 3) = 0.83$, then $Y(0, 1) = 6.38\%$, $Y(0, 2) = 6.00\%$, and $Y(0, 3) = 6.41\%$. Thus, knowing the yield curve is equivalent to knowing the curve of all zero-coupon prices. Because the yield curve must be part of any interest rate model, the same must be said for all the prices of all the zero-coupon bonds.

Equivalent to these two curves is a third: the curve of forward short rates. Consider $F(t, t + T, t + T + \tau)$, the *forward interest rate* that is arranged at time $t$ for a riskless loan beginning at time $t + T$ and ending at time $t + T + \tau$. For instance, if the arrangement made at time $t$ is to borrow $1 at time $t + T$, then $[1 + F(t, t + T, t + T + \tau)]^\tau$ dollars must be repaid at time $t + T + \tau$.

It turns out by an arbitrage argument that there is a simple relationship between $F(t, t + T, t + T + \tau)$ and the time-$t$ curve of zero-coupon bond prices. Consider the problem of investing $1 from time $t$ to time $t + T + \tau$ in a riskless fashion. There are two ways to do this. You could buy $P(t, t + T + \tau)^{-1}$ units of the zero-coupon bond that matures at time $t + T + \tau$, an investment that becomes worth $P(t, t + T + \tau)^{-1}$ dollars at time $t + T + \tau$. Or you could buy $P(t, t + T)^{-1}$ units of the zero that matures to $P(t, t + T)^{-1}$ dollars at time $t + T$ and then, at time $t + T$, invest the $P(t, t + T)^{-1}$ dollars at the forward interest rate $F(t, t + T, t + T + \tau)$ from time $t + T$ to time $t + T + \tau$. With this second strategy you will have $P(t, t + T)^{-1}[1 + F(t, t + T, t + T + \tau)]^\tau$ dollars at time $t + T + \tau$.

Because both strategies are riskless and start with $1, both strategies must yield the same amount at time $t + T + \tau$, or an arbitrage opportunity would exist. This means that

$$P(t, t + T + \tau)^{-1} = P(t, t + T)^{-1}[1 + F(t, t + T, t + T + \tau)]^\tau,$$

which is the promised relationship between forward interest rates and the curve of zero-coupon bond prices. Thanks to (7.2.3), this immediately gives a useful relationship between forward interest rates and the yield curve as

$$[1 + Y(t, t + T + \tau)]^{T+\tau} = [1 + Y(t, t + T)]^T [1 + F(t, t + T, t + T + \tau)]^\tau. \qquad (7.2.5)$$

Equation (7.2.5) shows clearly how the invested funds accumulate under the various interest rates under the two strategies considered in the arbitrage argument.

Equation (7.2.5) also shows clearly that by knowing the time-$t$ yield curve, all the time-$t$ forward interest rates can be computed, and vice versa. For example, if $Y(0, 1) = 5\%$, $Y(0, 2) = 5.8\%$, and $Y(0, 3) = 6.4\%$, then (7.2.5) with $t = 0$ and

$T = 0$ gives $F(0, 0, \tau) = Y(0, \tau)$ (because if the loan starts right away, then the forward rate is the same as the ordinary yield), whereas $T = 1$ gives $F(0, 1, 2) = 6.61\%$ and $F(0, 1, 3) = 7.11\%$ and $T = 2$ gives $F(0, 2, 3) = 7.61\%$.

Before illustrating the converse, we note that to deduce the time-$t$ yield curve, knowledge of the forward interest rates for just one-period loans suffices (i.e., when $\tau = 1$); these are called the *forward short rates* and are denoted

$$f(t, t + T) = F(t, t + T, t + T + 1), \quad T = 0, 1, \ldots.$$

To see how the curve of forward short rates can be used to deduce the yield curve, take (7.2.5) with $\tau = 1$:

$$[1 + Y(t, t + T + 1)]^{T+1} = [1 + Y(t, t + T)]^{T}[1 + f(t, t + T)]. \quad (7.2.6)$$

With $T = 0$ this gives

$$1 + Y(t, t + 1) = 1 + f(t, t),$$

which shows that the forward short rate coincides with the ordinary short rate $i_t$ when the forward loan starts immediately, as one should expect. Taking $T = 1$ in (7.2.6) gives

$$[1 + Y(t, t + 2)]^2 = [1 + Y(t, t + 1)][1 + f(t, t + 1)]$$
$$= [1 + f(t, t)][1 + f(t, t + 1)].$$

Therefore an induction argument can be used to show that, in general, for $s = 1, 2, \ldots$ we have

$$[1 + Y(t, t + s)]^s$$
$$= [1 + f(t, t)][1 + f(t, t + 1)] \cdots [1 + f(t, t + s - 1)]. \quad (7.2.7)$$

This proves that if you know the time-$t$ curve of forward short rates, then both the yield curve and (by (7.2.3)) the curve of zero-coupon bond prices are known as well. For instance, if $f(0, 0) = 5\%$, $f(0, 1) = 5.2\%$, and $f(0, 2) = 5.4\%$, then $Y(0, 1) = 5\%$, $Y(0, 2) = 5.1\%$, and $Y(0, 3) = 5.23\%$.

Using (7.2.3) to substitute $P(t, t + s)$ for $Y(t, t + s)$ in (7.2.7) gives

$$P(t, t + s)$$
$$= [1 + f(t, t)]^{-1}[1 + f(t, t + 1)]^{-1} \cdots [1 + f(t, t + s - 1)]^{-1}. \quad (7.2.8)$$

This is a useful expression for the price of a zero-coupon bond in terms of the current curve of forward short rates.

In summary, all three curves are equivalent, and so with knowledge of any one of them, the current value of a deterministic cash flow can be worked out by computing its present value.

What about random cash flows, such as cash flows where the payment amounts depend on future interest rates that, in turn, evolve in a stochastic manner? To value random cash flows we need a stochastic model describing how one, and thus all three, of the curves evolve. This subject was introduced in Section 3.7, and it is our focus in Section 7.4. But, first, we present some examples of stochastic cash flows that are important in the interest rate context.

# Section 7.3
# Swaps, Swaptions, Caps, and Floors

To gain an appreciation for the type of interest rate model that needs to be developed, this section describes some of the principal interest rate derivatives.[1]

Suppose a party is paying a floating-rate loan issued some time in the past. Perhaps, due to new circumstances, the party now prefers to have a fixed-rate loan. Although the party could refinance the loan, an alternative is to enter into a swap agreement.

A *swap* is an agreement between two parties to exchange cash flows. In a "plain vanilla" swap, one party pays the second party's floating-rate interest payments, while the second party pays the first party's fixed-rate interest payments, with both payments based on the same principal amount. The payments (actually the net payment) are exchanged each period for a set number of periods. The fixed interest rate is set in advance, and the floating rate is based on the short rate $i_t = Y(t, t + 1)$.

There are two variations to the structure of the floating-rate payments. Either the floating-rate payment at a point in time is based on the rate for the period that just ended (the swap is *settled in arrears*), or the floating-rate payment is based on the rate for the period that is about to begin (the swap is *settled in advance*). Usually, the interest rate exchanges begin with the period when the agreement is reached, but there are also *forward start* swaps in which the interest rate exchanges begin at a future period.

The value of a swap for each of the parties must be based on the net cash flow, and so the value to one party will equal the negative of the value to the other party. The value of a *payer* swap is from the perspective of the party paying the fixed rate and receiving the floating rate. The value of a *receiver* swap is from the perspective of the other party.

---

[1] Before proceeding, you may wish to review Sections 2.5 and 2.6 on swaps, caps, and floors.

To make some of these ideas more precise, we develop a mathematical expression for the cash flow associated with a payer forward start swap settled in arrears, using the notation developed in the preceding section. Assume that the principal is $1, the fixed interest rate is denoted $\kappa$, the swap agreement is made at time 0, the initial payment exchange occurs at time $s$, and the last exchange occurs at time $\tau$. Because this is a payer swap settled in arrears, at time $t$ the party involved pays $\kappa$ dollars and receives $i_{t-1} = Y(t-1, t)$ dollars. Thus, the net cash flow received by the party is

$$i_{t-1} - \kappa, \quad t = s, s+t, \ldots, \tau. \tag{7.3.1}$$

Of course, if the swap is based on a principal amount other than $1, the net cash flow is simply that amount times (7.3.1). For instance, if the principal is $1,000,000, the fixed interest rate $\kappa$ is 6%, and the short rates observed at times $t = 1, 2, \ldots$ are 6.0%, 6.2%, 6.5%, 6.3%, 5.9%, $\ldots$, then the cash flows of a forward start payer swap, settled in arrears with initial payment at time 3, are $2,000, $5,000, $3,000, $-$1,000, $\ldots$, respectively.

Note three features of this cash flow. First, since the short rate $i_t$ is random, so is the net cash flow. Thus, the value of this swap cannot be determined by taking the simple net present value. As will be shown in a later section, the value of this swap is equal to the *expected* present value of the future net cash flow, with the expectation computed with respect to the *risk-neutral probability measure*.

Second, note that the time-$t$ value, denoted $v_t$ for $t = 0, 1, \ldots, \tau$, of this swap will evolve in a stochastic manner in response to the stochastic evolution of the short rate $i_t$. For example, if the short rate goes up, then the swap agreement becomes more valuable for the party paying the fixed rate.

Third, the value of this swap depends upon the fixed interest rate $\kappa$. For small values of $\kappa$, the initial value $v_0$ will be positive, whereas for large values of $\kappa$ the initial value $v_0$ will be negative, and for just the right value of $\kappa$, $v_0$ will equal zero. This particular value of $\kappa$ is called the *(forward) swap rate*, and it is customary to make this the choice for the fixed interest rate in the swap agreement. In other words, it is customary for the choice of $\kappa$ in the swap agreement to be such that $v_0 = 0$.

Another kind of interest rate derivative called a *swaption* is an option on a swap. As indicated above, the value $v_t$ of a payer forward swap should be viewed as a stochastic process. With the initial payment date $s$ of the swap set for a future period, the party paying a fixed rate may be hesitant about committing to the swap agreement, because the short rate might drop, making the swap's value negative. This party therefore might be interested in paying for the option to enter into the swap agreement, with the exercise date equal to time $s - 1$, the beginning of the period when the first interest rate payments occur. Such an option is just like a European call on the time-$(s - 1)$ value of the payer swap, in which the exercise price of this call is zero. This is called a *payer swaption*, and the time-$(s-1)$ payoff of this European call is precisely $\max\{0, v_{s-1}\}$. We are interested in the time-$t$ value of this swaption for $t \le s - 1$.

A *receiver swaption* is just like a payer swaption, except that it is defined with respect to a receiver swap. It is like a European call on the value of the receiver swap, with exercise price zero and exercise date equal to the beginning of the period when the first payment occurs. Consider next the receiver swap that corresponds to the payer swap having value $v_t$. As explained earlier, the value of this receiver swap is $-v_t$. Thus, the value of this receiver swaption on the exercise date is precisely $\max\{0, -v_{s-1}\}$. But $\max\{0, v_{s-1}\} - \max\{0, -v_{s-1}\} = v_{s-1}$, and thus we have by the law of one price (i.e., by arbitrage considerations) the following *parity* relationship: *for each time $t < s$, the price of the payer swaption minus the price of the receiver swaption is equal to the price of the forward payer swap.* In particular, since swaption values are always nonnegative, the value of a payer swaption is always greater than the price of the corresponding payer swap. This makes economic sense: you get the swap's cash flows if "good" states of the world occur but not if "unfavorable" states occur.

To understand the interest rate derivatives called caps and floors, consider a party that has borrowed $1 and is paying each period at the floating rate of interest. This party is content with paying the floating rate but is interested in buying an "insurance policy" that will pay off the difference between the short rate and some "cap" amount $\kappa$ in any period the rate exceeds the cap; nothing will be paid if the short rate is less. This "policy," called a *cap*, is for a specified number of consecutive periods, say, from time $t = s$ to time $t = \tau$. A cap with $s > 1$ is called a *forward start* cap. Just like swaps, caps can be settled in arrears or in advance, depending on whether the time-$t$ payment is based upon the short rate for the period ending at $t$ or the period beginning at $t$, respectively.

The payment at any point of time is called a *caplet*, that is, a cap is a string of caplets. Moreover, a caplet is just like a European call option on the short rate $i_t = Y(t, t+1)$ with exercise price $\kappa$. For instance, in the case of a caplet settled in arrears at time $t$, $t = s, s+1, \ldots, \tau$, the time-$t$ payoff is

$$\max\{0, i_{t-1} - \kappa\}. \tag{7.3.2}$$

Notice the similarity between this and (7.3.1) for the cash flow of a payer swap. As with (7.3.1), if the principal amount is other than $1, then the payoff of a caplet is simply that amount times (7.3.2). Clearly, the payments associated with a cap are random. For instance, if the principal is $1,000,000, the cap $\kappa = 6\%$, and the short rates observed at times $t = 1, 2, 3, \ldots$ are 6.0%, 6.2%, 6.5%, 6.3%, 5.9%, $\ldots$, then the cash flows of a forward start cap, settled in arrears with initial payment at time 3, are $2,000, $5,000, $3,000, $0, $\ldots$, respectively. We are especially interested in the value of a cap at time $t = 0$, when the cap can be purchased.

Interest rate derivatives called *floors* are just like caps, except that they are comprised of *floorlets*, each of which is like a European put option on the short rate. Floors might be of interest to a party who loaned some money at a floating rate and is worried about declining interest rates. In the case of a floorlet settled in arrears at time $t$, the time-$t$ payoff, for $t = s, s + 1, \ldots, \tau$, is

$$\max\{0, \kappa - i_{t-1}\}.$$

Note that

$$\max\{0, i_{t-1} - \kappa\} - \max\{0, \kappa - i_{t-1}\} = i_{t-1} - \kappa.$$

By the law of one price, this means the price of a caplet minus the price of a floorlet equals the value of the payment $i_{t-1} - \kappa$. Moreover, in view of (7.3.1) and the fact that caps and floors are strings of caplets and floorlets, we have the following parity relationship: *the price of a cap minus the price of a floor equals the price of a payer swap.*

Interest rate derivatives such as those discussed in this section are based on random cash flows, so we would like to be able to derive their prices. However, to derive the price of a particular derivative, we do not necessarily need to rely on "first principles." Instead, a parity relationship can sometimes be used to give the price of the derivative of interest in terms of the known prices of other derivatives, just as the price of an ordinary put can be expressed in terms of the price of an ordinary call, their common exercise price, a discount factor, and the price of the underlying security.

# Section 7.4
## Arbitrage-Free Interest Rate Models

As discussed in Section 7.1, there are two main purposes for developing an interest rate model. First, an investor is considering a portfolio of fixed-income securities (in general, some are assets, others are liabilities), and the investor is interested in the stochastic evolution of the value of this portfolio. The price of each security is a function of the current yield curve, so a model for the stochastic evolution of the yield curve (or, as explained in Section 7.2, of either the curve of zero-coupon bond prices or the curve of forward short rates) is sufficient. In other words, we must have a stochastic process model for the whole vector of yields, with one component for each possible maturity. In particular, the model must include, at least implicitly, a stochastic characterization of the short rate (which is one end of the yield curve). Moreover, since the yield curve is equivalent to a curve of zero-coupon bond prices, the model must also include (again, at least implicitly) a stochastic characterization of the price of at least one zero-coupon bond, say, the one that matures at time $T < \infty$ with face value $1.

The second purpose for developing an interest rate model is to work out the price of an interest rate derivative. As seen in the preceding section, interest rate derivatives often have payoffs that depend on the evolution of the short rate, so again this must be included in our interest rate model. But is this enough? Can the price of common interest rate derivatives be worked out simply by knowing a stochastic model of the short rate? The answers are no, because, as with the pricing of ordinary puts and calls on stocks, the concept of arbitrage-pricing theory and the existence of one or more primitive securities are fundamental to derivative-pricing theory. A trading strategy must exist, one involving the primitive securities and the borrowing or lending of money at the short rate, which replicates the derivative, in which case the price of the derivative is equal to the value of the replicating portfolio.

Thus, our interest rate model must include the short rate as well as at least one primitive security. For this security, we fix the time horizon $T$ and take the zero-coupon bond maturing at time $T$ with face value \$1. We now apply what we discussed in Chapter 5 about arbitrage-free securities markets and see how far we can get.

Consider a finite sample space $\Omega = \{\omega_1, \ldots, \omega_M\}$, a specified probability measure $P$ on this sample space, and a sequence of trading dates $t = 0, 1, \ldots, T$. There is also a fixed sequence $\{\mathcal{P}_t\}$ of partitions (that is, there is a fixed filtration) that describes how information is revealed to the investors. Also in accordance with Chapter 5, the price process $S = \{S_t; t = 0, 1, \ldots, T\}$ of our primitive security is assumed to be adapted to the filtration, which means that at each time (here it is convenient to denote time with a subscript) $t$, the investors know the past and present values of this zero-coupon bond. To reconcile this notation with that of Chapter 5, we have $S_t = S_2(t) = P(t, T)$ for $t = 0, 1, \ldots, T$.

The short rate process $i = \{i_t; t = 0, 1, \ldots, T - 1\}$ is also assumed to be adapted. Of course, $i_t = Y(t, t + 1)$ is the interest rate pertaining to loans from time $t$ to time $t + 1$. The short rate should be thought of as the interest paid by a money market account or a bank account. Corresponding to this is the money market process $B = \{B_t; t = 0, 1, \ldots, T\}$, where $B_0 = 1$ and

$$B_t = (1 + i_0)(1 + i_1) \cdots (1 + i_{t-1}), \quad t = 1, \ldots, T.$$

Thus, $B_t$ can be interpreted as the amount of money in the bank account at time $t$ if \$1 is deposited at time 0. Because money can also be borrowed at the short rate, $B_t$ can also be interpreted as the amount that must be paid back to the bank at time $t$ if \$1 is borrowed from time 0 to time $t$. Note that the process $B$ is adapted. In Section 5.2, the notation for the bank account is $S_1(t)$. Hence $B_t = S_1(t)$.

Now that we have specified the principal ingredients of our interest rate model, the next step is to make sure that there are no arbitrage opportunities, that is, that there are no trading strategies that start with \$0 and, without any possibility of ending up negative, that have a positive chance of ending up with a positive amount of money.

Clearly, the existence of an arbitrage opportunity is inconsistent with having a good model of a securities market that is in economic equilibrium.

As explained in Chapter 5, for there to be no arbitrage opportunities, it is necessary and sufficient that some probability measure $Q$ exist that is equivalent to the original probability measure $P$ and such that the discounted security price is a martingale under $Q$. Now, the discounted security price is $S_t/B_t$, so by the definition of a martingale the condition that must be satisfied by our model is

$$\frac{S_t}{B_t} = E^Q\left[\frac{S_\tau}{B_\tau}\bigg|\mathcal{P}_t\right], \quad 0 \le t \le \tau \le T \tag{7.4.1}$$

where $E^Q$ denotes expectation with respect to the probability measure $Q$. If a probability measure $Q$ satisfies (7.4.1), it is called a *risk-neutral* probability measure or a *martingale* measure. To summarize these points, our term structure model must be such that (7.4.1) is satisfied when we take $S_t = P(t, T)$.

***Example 7.4.1.*** Consider a simple model with $T = 2$, $\Omega = \mathcal{P}_0 = \{\omega_1, \ldots, \omega_4\}$, $P(\omega) > 0$ for all $\omega \in \Omega$, $\mathcal{P}_1 = \{\{\omega_1, \omega_2\}, \{\omega_3, \omega_4\}\}$, $\mathcal{P}_2 = \{\{\omega_1\}, \{\omega_2\}, \{\omega_3\}, \{\omega_4\}\}$, $i_0 = 6\%$, and values for $i_1$ as indicated in the following table.

| $\omega$ | $i_1(\omega)$ | $B_2(\omega)$ | $S_1 = P(1,2)$ |
|---|---|---|---|
| $\omega_1$ | 5% | 1.1130 | 0.9524 |
| $\omega_2$ | 5 | 1.1130 | 0.9524 |
| $\omega_3$ | 7 | 1.1342 | 0.9346 |
| $\omega_4$ | 7 | 1.1342 | 0.9346 |

Of course, $S_2 = P(2,2) = 1$, $B_0 = 1$, and $B_1 = 1.06$. The values for $B_2$ are displayed in this table; they are computed from $i_0$ and $i_1$. The values for $S_1 = P(1, 2)$, which are also displayed in this table, are also implied by the values of $i_1$, because (7.2.3) must be satisfied when $t = T = 1$.

All that remains is the specification of $S_0 = P(0, 2)$. Suppose $S_0 = 0.92$. Equation (7.4.1) with $t = 0$ and $\tau = 1$ gives

$$0.92 = E^Q\left[\frac{S_1}{1.06}\bigg|\mathcal{P}_0\right] = E^Q\left[\frac{S_1}{1.06}\right]$$

for some probability measure $Q$. Denoting $q = Q(\omega_1) + Q(\omega_2)$, this equation can be rewritten as

$$0.92 = q\frac{0.9524}{1.06} + (1-q)\frac{0.9346}{1.06} = 0.8817 + 0.0168q.$$

The unique solution is $q = 2.2798$, which is clearly incompatible with the existence of a probability measure $Q$ satisfying (7.4.1).

Because no risk-neutral probability measure exists for this model, an arbitrage opportunity must exist. For example, at time 0, sell short the zero-coupon bond, receiving 0.92 dollars, and invest the 0.92 dollars in the bank account at 6%. At time 1, you will have $(1.06)(0.92) = 0.9752$ dollars in the bank account, more than enough to cover your short position in the zero-coupon bond, regardless of whether $S_1 = 0.9524$ or 0.9346.

Suppose, however, that $S_0 = P(0, 2) = 0.89$. Now, with $t = 0$ and $\tau = 1$, (7.4.1) becomes

$$0.89 = 0.8817 + 0.0168q,$$

the unique solution of which is $q = 0.4940$. Because $0 < q < 1$, this is compatible with the existence of a probability measure $Q$ satisfying (7.4.1) for all $t$ and $\tau$. In fact, any probability measure satisfying $Q(\omega_1) + Q(\omega_2) = 0.4940$ will work (as can be verified), provided $Q(\omega) > 0$ for all $\omega \in \Omega$. Moreover, other values for $S_0$ are also compatible with the existence of a risk-neutral probability measure, as will be left for you to investigate. ∎

Note that we cannot be indiscriminate in the specification of the short-rate and zero-coupon bond processes; they must be chosen in such a way that a risk-neutral probability measure $Q$ exists. We suppose hereafter that this is the case. (Section 7.6 will give some guidance about how to choose these processes in a suitable way.) Working on this assumption, we find that (7.4.1) has some remarkable consequences.

First, consider (7.4.1) for $\tau = T$ so that, with $S$ the price of the discount bond maturity at time $\tau$, $S_\tau = 1$. Multiplying through by $B_t$, (7.4.1) becomes

$$S_t = P(t, T) = \mathrm{E}^Q \left[ \frac{B_t}{B_T} \middle| \mathcal{P}_t \right] \tag{7.4.2}$$

$$= \mathrm{E}^Q[(1 + i_t)^{-1}(1 + i_{t+1})^{-1} \cdots (1 + i_{T-1})^{-1} | \mathcal{P}_t]$$

where the last equality follows from the definition of the bank account process $B$. Note the similarity between this and (7.2.8) for the price of a zero in terms of the forward short rates. Equation (7.4.2) shows that the price of our primitive security, the zero-coupon bond, can be expressed as a conditional expectation under the risk-neutral probability measure of an expression involving the short-rate process.

What about zero-coupon bonds with maturities $\tau < T$? If our model is complete (see Chapter 5), then given any time $\tau \le T$ and any time-$t$ payoff $X$ that is known to the investors at time $\tau$ (i.e., the contingent claim $X$ is $\mathcal{P}_\tau$-measurable), a trading strategy exists involving the bank account and $P(\cdot, T)$ such that the portfolio with time-$t$ value $V_t$ satisfies $V_\tau = X$ for all $\omega \in \Omega$. In particular, taking $X = 1$ for arbitrary $\tau < T$, we see that with a complete model we can replicate the payoff of the zero-coupon bond that matures at time $\tau$. By the law of one price, the value $V_t$ of the replicating portfolio must coincide with the price $P(t, \tau)$ for all $t \leq \tau$. Thus, if the model featuring the short-rate process $i$ and the primitive zero-coupon bond $P(\cdot, T)$ is complete, then the price processes of all the other zero-coupon bonds are automatically included.

What are the prices of these other zero-coupon bonds? Because the discounted value of any portfolio in an arbitrage-free model is a martingale under a risk-neutral probability measure $Q$, the discounted price of any zero-coupon bond is as well. This gives rise to a relationship just like (7.4.2):

$$P(t, \tau) = E^Q \left[ \frac{B_t}{B_\tau} \,\middle|\, \mathcal{P}_t \right] \tag{7.4.3}$$

$$= E^Q[(1 + i_t)^{-1}(1 + i_{t+1})^{-1} \cdots (1 + i_{\tau-1})^{-1} \mid \mathcal{P}_t], \quad 0 \leq t < \tau \leq T.$$

This equation for the price of an arbitrary zero-coupon bond is of fundamental importance for interest rate models.

Suppose, however, that the original interest rate model, consisting of just the short interest rate process and the primitive zero-coupon bond having maturity $T$, is not complete. Then it might be impossible to replicate time-$\tau$ payoffs of $1 for some $\tau < T$, which means the price process of the corresponding zero-coupon bond is not already included in the model. It must be added manually. In other words, it is necessary to specify the price processes of each zero-coupon bond that is missing from the model, making sure, of course, that arbitrage opportunities are not inadvertently introduced. How is this done, making sure not only that no arbitrage opportunities are introduced but also that the terminal value of the security equals one? The secret is to use relationship (7.4.3): this will give a price process whose discounted value is a martingale under the risk-neutral probability measure.

In summary, we now have our interest rate model. Its main ingredients are a short-rate process and a primitive zero-coupon bond whose maturity equals the planning horizon, chosen in an arbitrage-free way. If this preliminary model is complete, then the prices of all the other zero-coupon bonds are included. If the model is not complete, then the prices of the missing zeros must be introduced in accordance with (7.4.3). In either case, we have an arbitrage-free model for the stochastic behavior of the curve of zero-coupon bond prices and thus of the yield curve (via (7.2.4)) and of the curve of forward short rates (via (7.2.6)).

You may have realized that there is an alternative approach to building an interest rate model. As an alternative to the "conventional" approach just described, we could start with just a model of the short-rate process along with the selection of a probability measure that is adopted as the risk-neutral probability measure $Q$. Then (7.4.3) could be used to introduce all the prices of all the zero-coupon bonds. This "risk-neutral" approach has some advantages, such as being simpler to implement (with the conventional approach, specifying the primitive zero-coupon bond without adding an arbitrage opportunity can be tricky). It also lends itself well to the pricing and hedging of interest rate derivatives.

On the other hand, the risk-neutral approach is a bit circuitous if the purpose of the model is to understand the evolution of interest rates under the real-world probability measure $P$. This is because, with the risk-neutral approach, we have poor control over the sample paths of all the zero-coupon bond prices. Even if the real-world probability measure $P$ is not specified until the final step (having specified how prices and interest rates evolve in each state of the world $\omega$, the final step is to choose $P(\omega)$), it may be difficult to achieve the desired statistical properties of the interest rates. In principle, the risk-neutral approach may provide an excellent real-world model, but this procedure can be awkward or difficult for some purposes.

**Example 7.4.2.** Consider, as an illustration of the conventional approach, a three-period model with $\Omega$ having 12 states of the world. The short-rate process and the price process of the bond maturing at time $T = 3$ are as indicated in the following table:

| $\omega$ | $i_0$ | $i_1$ | $i_2$ | $P(0,3)$ | $P(1,3)$ | $P(2,3)$ |
|---|---|---|---|---|---|---|
| $\omega_1, \omega_2$ | 5% | 6% | 6.5% | 0.864 | 0.8900 | 0.9390 |
| $\omega_3, \omega_4$ | 5 | 6 | 5.5 | 0.864 | 0.8900 | 0.9479 |
| $\omega_5, \omega_6$ | 5 | 5 | 5.5 | 0.864 | 0.9070 | 0.9479 |
| $\omega_7, \omega_8$ | 5 | 5 | 4.5 | 0.864 | 0.9070 | 0.9569 |
| $\omega_9, \omega_{10}$ | 5 | 4 | 4.5 | 0.864 | 0.9246 | 0.9569 |
| $\omega_{11}, \omega_{12}$ | 5 | 4 | 3.5 | 0.864 | 0.9246 | 0.9662 |

The information submodel is the one generated by these processes, so

$$\mathcal{P}_1 = \{\omega_1, \omega_2, \omega_3, \omega_4\} \cup \{\omega_5, \omega_6, \omega_7, \omega_8\} \cup \{\omega_9, \omega_{10}, \omega_{11}, \omega_{12}\}$$

and

$$\mathcal{P}_2 = \{\omega_1, \omega_2\} \cup \{\omega_3, \omega_4\} \cup \{\omega_6, \omega_6\} \cup \{\omega_7, \omega_8\} \cup \{\omega_9, \omega_{10}\} \cup \{\omega_{11}, \omega_{12}\}.$$

This model is arbitrage free, because a risk-neutral probability measure exists. Actually, many risk-free probability measures exist; the one we take is $Q(\omega) = 1/12$, all $\omega \in \Omega$ (use (7.4.2) to verify that this is indeed a martingale measure as well as to identify alternative choices for the martingale measure $Q$).

This model is not complete. In particular, it is not possible to replicate the zero-coupon bond that matures at time $t = 2$. To see this, first note that the relationship $P(1, 2) = (1 + i_1)^{-1}$ gives $P(1, 2) = 0.9434$, when $i_1 = 6\%$, $P(1, 2) = 0.9524$ when $i_1 = 5\%$, and $P(1, 2) = 0.9615$ when $i_1 = 4\%$ (however, the value of $P(0, 2)$ is unclear). Next, consider the trading strategy that starts at time $t = 0$ by investing $a$ dollars at the spot rate at 5% and buying $b$ units of the zero-coupon bond maturing at $T = 3$. At time $t = 1$, the value of this portfolio is $(1.05)a + P(1, 3)b$, so to replicate the bond maturing at time $t = 2$, we must have

$$(1.05)a + P(1, 3)b = P(1, 2), \quad \text{all } \omega \in \Omega.$$

This amounts to a system of three equations (one corresponding to each value of $P(1, 2)$) in the two unknowns ($a$ and $b$). You can verify that this system has no solution.

We must finish our interest rate model by specifying the price process of the bond maturing at time $t = 2$, in this case, $P(0, 2)$. With $Q(\omega) = 1/12$, all $\omega \in \Omega$, (7.4.3) gives $P(0, 2) = 0.9071$. ∎

A crucial lesson to be learned from this example is that when the preliminary model is not complete, the specifications of the zero-coupon bonds maturing before $T$ are not unique (here the choice $P(0, 2) = 0.9071$ was not unique). This is because the choice of the risk-neutral probability measure in incomplete models is not unique, and thus the specification of the zero-coupon bond prices from (7.4.3) will not be unique.

The simplest kind of interest rate model is one in which the short rate evolves in a binomial fashion (see Section 7.6). Before turning to this specific class of models, however, we look at how general models can be used to value interest rate derivatives.

# Section 7.5
# Valuation of Interest Rate Derivatives

In this section, we explain valuation of interest rate derivatives. One of the themes introduced in Section 7.3 and developed further here is the idea that the price of one kind of derivative can often be expressed in terms of the price of another kind of derivative; this is illustrated for the derivatives introduced in Section 7.3.

Throughout this section we assume that the interest rate model has the risk-neutral probability measure $Q$. Moreover, we assume that the model is complete, which means, as explained in Chapter 5, the time-$t$ price $\pi_t$ of any time-$\tau$ contingent claim $X$ (that is, a random variable whose value is known to the investors at time $\tau$)

is given by (see Theorem 5.3.10)

$$\pi_t = B_t E_t^Q \left[ \frac{X}{B_\tau} \right]$$

where, as usual, $B_t$ denotes the time-$t$ value of the bank account process and $E_t^Q$ denotes conditional expectation with respect to the risk-neutral probability measure $Q$ given the information available at time $t$. Moreover, the time-$t$ value of a cash flow, that is, of a collection of contingent claims, is the simple sum of the prices of the corresponding contingent claims.

For example, consider the cash flow associated with a payer forward start swap settled in arrears in which, as shown in (7.3.1), the cash flow is $(i_{u-1} - \kappa)$ from $u = s$ to time $u = \tau$. Thus, the time-$t$ value $v_t$ of this cash flow is

$$v_t = E_t^Q \left[ \sum_{u=s}^{\tau} (i_{u-1} - \kappa) \frac{B_t}{B_u} \right], \quad 0 \le t < s < \tau \le T.$$

This abstract expression can be transformed into something much more useful by using the fact that $i_{u-1} = P(u-1, u)^{-1} - 1$:

$$v_t = E_t^Q \left[ \sum_{u=s}^{\tau} \{ P(u-1, u)^{-1} - (1 + \kappa) \} \frac{B_t}{B_u} \right]$$

$$= E_t^Q \left[ \sum_{u=s}^{\tau} \frac{B_t}{B_u P(u-1, u)} \right] - (1 + \kappa) E_t^Q \left[ \sum_{u=s}^{\tau} \frac{B_t}{B_u} \right]$$

$$= \sum_{u=s}^{\tau} E_t^Q \left[ \frac{B_t}{B_u P(u-1, u)} \right] - (1 + \kappa) \sum_{u=s}^{\tau} P(t, u)$$

where the last equality uses (7.4.3).

Finally, using $P(u-1, u)^{-1} = (1 + i_{u-1}) = B_u / B_{u-1}$ again, we obtain

$$v_t = \sum_{u=s}^{\tau} E_t^Q \left[ \frac{B_t}{B_{u-1}} \right] - (1 + \kappa) \sum_{u=s}^{\tau} P(t, u)$$

$$= \sum_{u=s}^{\tau} P(t, u-1) - (1 + \kappa) \sum_{u=s}^{\tau} P(t, u).$$

Thus, the time-$t$ value of our swap is a simple function of the time-$t$ curve of zero-coupon bond prices. This result could also have been obtained with a simple arbitrage argument, but we wanted to illustrate the risk-neutral valuation approach.

Introducing the notation

$$C_u = \begin{cases} \kappa, & u = s, \ldots, \tau - 1 \\ 1 + \kappa, & u = \tau, \end{cases}$$

we see that the value of the swap can be expressed as

$$v_t = P(t, s - 1) - \sum_{u=s}^{\tau} P(t, u) C_u. \tag{7.5.1}$$

Because $C_u$ can be interpreted as the time-$u$ payment of a coupon-paying bond with coupon rate $\kappa$, face value 1, and initial date $s$, (7.5.1) says that the time-$t$ value of the swap equals the discounted value of $1 minus the discounted value of the coupon-paying bond. In particular, if $t = s - 1$, then $v_t$ equals one minus the time-$t$ price of the coupon bond.

As explained in Section 7.3, the swap rate is the value of $\kappa$ such that $v_0 = 0$. Thus, the swap rate is given by

$$\kappa = \frac{P(0, s - 1) - P(0, \tau)}{P(0, s) + \cdots + P(0, \tau)}.$$

**Example 7.5.1.** Consider a payer forward start swap that is settled in arrears and based on the model in Example 7.4.2. The fixed rate is $\kappa = 4.5\%$, the initial cash flow is at time $s = 2$, and the second and final cash flow occurs at time $\tau = 3$. Moreover, suppose the swap is based upon $1,000,000 principal.

Now, $C_2 = 0.045$ and $C_3 = 1.045$, so, using (7.5.1), the time-0 value of the swap to the party paying a fixed rate is

$$v_0 = (1,000,000)[0.9524 - (0.9071)(0.045) - (0.864)(1.045)] = \$8,700.$$

Since this is positive, the swap rate must be larger than 4.5%. In fact, the swap rate is

$$\kappa = \frac{P(0, 1) - P(0, 3)}{P(0, 2) + P(0, 3)} = \frac{0.9524 - 0.864}{0.9071 + 0.864} = 4.99\%.$$

For future purposes we can also compute the value of the swap at time 1. In view of (7.5.1) this is

$$v_1 = (1,000,000)[1 - P(1, 2)(0.045) - P(1, 3)(1.045)].$$

We therefore have

$$v_1 = \begin{cases} 10^6[1 - (0.9434)(0.45) - (0.89)(1.045)] = \$27,500, & i_1 = 6\% \\ 10^6[1 - (0.9524)(0.045) - (0.907)(1.045)] = \$9,300, & i_1 = 5\% \\ 10^6[1 - (0.9615)(0.045) - (0.9246)(1.045)] = -\$9,500, & i_1 = 4\%. \end{cases}$$

The higher the floating rate, the more the swap is worth to the party paying a fixed rate. ∎

For $t \le s - 1$, the time-$t$ price $\pi_t$ of a payer swaption (see Section 7.3) is

$$\pi_t = E_t^Q \left[ \frac{B_t}{B_{s-1}} \max\{0, v_{s-1}\} \right]$$

$$= E_t^Q \left[ \frac{B_t}{B_{s-1}} \max\left\{ 0, 1 - \sum_{u=1}^{\tau} P(s-1, u)C_u \right\} \right]$$

where the last equality was obtained by using (7.5.1) with $t = s - 1$. This result has a convenient interpretation: a payer swaption is the same as a European put option on a coupon bond, where the exercise price is 1, the exercise date is $s - 1$, and the coupon bond has face value one and pays at the coupon rate $\kappa$ from time $s$ to time $\tau$. Thus, if the price of a put option on a coupon bond can be computed, then so can the price of a swaption.

**Example 7.5.2.** Consider a payer swaption that is based on the swap of Example 7.5.1 and the interest rate model of Example 7.4.2. The exercise date is $(s - 1) = 1$, at which time the payoff is

$$\pi_1 = \max\{0, v_1\} = \begin{cases} 27,500, & i_1 = 6\% \\ 9,300, & i_1 = 5\% \\ 0, & i_1 = 4\% \end{cases}$$

where $v_1$ is the time-1 value of the payer swap, as computed in Example 7.5.1. By the risk-neutral valuation formula displayed above, the time-0 value of this swaption (recall $Q(\omega) = 1/12$, all $\omega \in \Omega$) is

$$\pi_0 = E^Q \left[ \frac{B_0}{B_1} \pi_1 \right] = \frac{1}{1.05} E^Q[\pi_1]$$

$$= 0.9524 \left[ \left( \frac{1}{3} \right)(27,500) + \left( \frac{1}{3} \right)(9,300) + \left( \frac{1}{3} \right)(0) \right]$$

$$= \$11,683.$$

The corresponding receiver swaption is worth \$9,500 at time 1 if $i_1 = 4\%$, but it is worth nothing at time 1 otherwise. Using risk-neutral valuation again, the time-0 value of the receiver swaption must be $(0.9524)(1/3)(9,500) = \$3,016$. Note that this verifies the swaption parity relationship, because the payer option value minus the receiver option value equals \$8,667, which equals the swap price computed in Example 7.5.1, up to round-off error. ∎

What about the price of a caplet? In view of (7.3.2), the time-$t$ price of a caplet settled in arrears at time $\tau$ is, for $t < \tau$,

$$\pi_t = B_t E_t^Q \left[ \frac{\max\{0, i_{\tau-1} - \kappa\}}{B_\tau} \right].$$

This can be evaluated from the joint conditional probability distribution of $i_{\tau-1}$ and $B_\tau$. Note, however, that $B_\tau = B_{\tau-1}(1 + i_{\tau-1}) = B_{\tau-1}/P(\tau - 1, \tau)$, so this becomes

$$\pi_t = B_t E_t^Q \left[ \frac{\max\{0, i_{\tau-1} - \kappa\} P(\tau - 1, \tau)}{B_{\tau-1}} \right].$$

This says that the time-$\tau$ payoff $\max\{0, i_{\tau-1} - \kappa\}$, a quantity that is fully known to the investors at time $\tau - 1$, is exactly the same as this value discounted to time $\tau - 1$, that is, the same as the time-$(\tau - 1)$ payoff $\max\{0, i_{\tau-1} - \kappa\} P(\tau - 1, \tau)$.

Using $i_{\tau-1} = P(\tau - 1, \tau)^{-1} - 1$ again, we now obtain

$$\pi_t = B_t E_t^Q \left[ \frac{\max\{0, P(\tau - 1, \tau)^{-1} - 1 - \kappa\} P(\tau - 1, \tau)}{B_{\tau-1}} \right]$$

$$= B_t E_t^Q \left[ \frac{\max\{0, 1 - (1 + \kappa) P(\tau - 1, \tau)\}}{B_{\tau-1}} \right]$$

$$= B_t E_t^Q \left[ \frac{(1 + \kappa) \max\{0, (1 + \kappa)^{-1} - P(\tau - 1, \tau)\}}{B_{\tau-1}} \right].$$

Thus, a caplet with cap rate $\kappa$ settled in arrears at time $\tau$ is the same (up to the factor $(1 + \kappa)$) as a European put on the zero-coupon bond $P(\cdot, \tau)$ with exercise date $\tau - 1$ and exercise price $(1 + \kappa)^{-1}$. If one can be evaluated, then the other can as well.

The situation for floorlets is symmetric; they are equivalent to calls on zero-coupon bonds. The prices of caps and floors, of course, are equal to sums of prices of individual caplets and floorlets.

***Example 7.5.3.*** Consider a cap based on the interest rate model of Example 7.4.2. With a cap rate of $\kappa = 4.5\%$, a principal of \$1,000,000, the initial payment at time 2, and the final payment at time 3, this cap is closely related to the swap in Example 7.5.1.

This cap comprises two caplets. The first caplet has a time-2 payment

$$\pi_2 = \begin{cases} 15,000, & \omega \in \{\omega_1, \ldots, \omega_4\} \\ 5,000, & \omega \in \{\omega_5, \ldots, \omega_8\} \\ 0, & \omega \in \{\omega_9, \ldots, \omega_{12}\}. \end{cases}$$

Using the formula displayed above, its time-0 value is

$$\pi_0 = (1{,}000{,}000)(1)E^Q\left[\frac{1.045}{1.05}\max\{0, (1.045)^{-1} - P(1,2)\}\right]$$

$$= (995{,}238)\left[\frac{1}{3}\max\{0, 0.9569 - 0.9434\}\right.$$

$$\left. + \frac{1}{3}\max\{0, 0.9569 - 0.9524\} + \frac{1}{3}\max\{0, 0.9569 - 0.9615\}\right]$$

$$= \$5{,}971.$$

Alternatively, we can compute the time-0 value of this first caplet with risk-neutral valuation:

$$\pi_0 = E^Q\left[\frac{\pi_2}{B_2}\right]$$

$$= \frac{(1/3)(15{,}000)}{(1.05)(1.06)} + \frac{(1/3)(5{,}000)}{(1.05)(1.05)} = \$6{,}004,$$

which differs from the earlier result only by round-off error.

The second caplet has a time-3 payment

$$\pi_3 = \begin{cases} 20,000, & \omega \in \{\omega_1, \omega_2\} \\ 10,000, & \omega \in \{\omega_3, \ldots, \omega_6\} \\ 0, & \omega \in \{\omega_7, \ldots, \omega_{12}\}. \end{cases}$$

Using the displayed equation again, its time-0 value is

$$\pi_0 = (1{,}000{,}000)(1.045)E^Q\left[\frac{\max\{0, 0.9569 - P(2,3)\}}{B_2}\right]$$

$$= (1{,}045{,}000)\left(\frac{1}{6}\right)[0.0161 + 0.0081 + 0.0082 + 0 + 0 + 0]$$

$$= \$5{,}641.$$

Alternatively, using risk-neutral valuation,

$$\pi_0 = E^Q \left[ \frac{\pi_3}{B_3} \right] = \frac{1}{6} \left[ \frac{20{,}000}{1.1853} + \frac{10{,}000}{1.1742} + \frac{10{,}000}{1.1631} \right]$$

$$= \$5{,}666,$$

which differs from the preceding computation only by a round-off error.

Thus, the time-0 value of the whole cap, up to round-off error, is $5{,}971 +$ $5{,}641 = \$11{,}612$. Because the time-0 value of the corresponding swap is $8{,}700, from the parity relationship mentioned in Section 7.3, we see that the corresponding floor has a time-0 value equal to $11{,}612 - 8{,}700 = \$2{,}912$ (up to round-off error). ∎

# Section 7.6
# Binomial Interest Rate Models

As with discrete-time stock price models, the simplest discrete-time interest rate models that can be constructed are ones in which the short interest rate evolves according to a recombining binomial lattice. In this section we will study this approach, highlighting two special cases, the Ho and Lee [93] model and the Black, Derman, and Toy [13] model. A generalization of the Ho and Lee model was developed by Pedersen, Shiu, and Thorlacius [143].

In the recombining binomial lattice, with $T$ periods, there are exactly $T + 1$ possible values of the short rate at time $T$. The idea is that at time $t$, $t = 0, 1, \ldots, T-1$, the short rate $i_t$ takes one of exactly $t + 1$ prespecified (and distinct: no two of the $t+1$ values are the same) values, which we denote $i(t, 0), i(t, 1), \ldots, i(t, n), \ldots, i(t, t)$. Moreover, if $i_t = i(t, n)$, then in the next period the short rate takes one of only two values, either $i_{t+1} = i(t + 1, n)$ or $i_{t+1} = i(t + 1, n + 1)$.

This model should be viewed graphically as a binomial tree (or lattice). There are exactly $t + 1$ nodes corresponding to time $t$, for $t = 0, 1, \ldots, T$. For each $t$, the $t + 1$ time-$t$ nodes are labeled $(t, 0), (t, 1), \ldots, (t, n), \ldots, (t, t+1)$. For each $t < T$, node $(t, n)$ has exactly two directed branches or arcs proceeding out, with one going to node $(t + 1, n)$ and the other going to node $(t + 1, n + 1)$. Thus, for $t > 0$, node $(t, n)$ has one or two entering branches; if $0 < n < t$, then one comes from node $(t - 1, n - 1)$ and another comes from node $(t - 1, n)$, whereas if $n$ equals 0 or $t$, then node $(t, n)$ has exactly one entering branch.

The sample path for the short-rate process $i$ corresponds to a path through the binomial tree, starting at node $(0, 0)$ and proceeding to one of the time-$T$ nodes. There are exactly $2^T$ routes through this tree, each corresponding to one state of the world $\omega \in \Omega$. In an obvious manner, node $(t, n)$ is identified with short-rate value $i(t, n)$, so that if the path through the tree goes through node $(t, n)$, then the sample path satisfies $i_t = i(t, n)$. For instance, if the path is $(0, 0)$, $(1, 0)$, $(2, 1)$, $\ldots$, then the corresponding sample path is $i_0 = i(0, 0)$, $i_1 = i(1, 0)$, $i_2 = i(2, 1)$, $\ldots$. A generic lattice is displayed in Figure 7.1.

FIGURE **7.1** | *The Binomial Interest Rate Lattice*

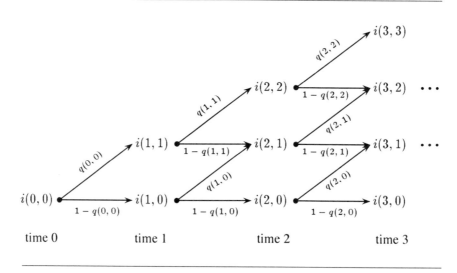

Thus far, we have specified the sample space $\Omega$ and the short-rate process $i$. For the next step in the construction of the interest rate model, we are going to take the risk-neutral approach and specify the martingale measure $Q$. We could assign probabilities in an arbitrary fashion to each of the $2^T$ states of the world in $\Omega$, that is, to each of the sample paths, but we are going to make an important, simplifying assumption: the short-rate process $i$ evolves like a Markov chain under the risk-neutral probability measure $Q$.

The Markov property means that if you know the past and present values of the short-rate process, then all that matters as far as future values are concerned is the current value of the short rate. In particular, if the current value of the short rate is $i_t = i(t, n)$, then the conditional probability of the event $i_{t+1} = i(t + 1, n + 1)$ can depend on $(t, n)$, but it is independent of the path leading up to node $(t, n)$. Thus, it suffices to define one conditional probability for each node of the binomial tree with $t < T$, the conditional probability of an "up-jump":

$$q(t, n) \equiv Q(i_{t+1} = i(t + 1, n + 1) \mid i_t = i(t, n)), \quad 0 \leq n \leq t < T.$$

Of course, due to the structure of the tree, the conditional probability of a "down-jump" is

$$1 - q(t, n) \equiv Q(i_{t+1} = i(t+1, n) \mid i_t = i(t, n)).$$

Having specified a conditional probability for each branch of the tree (more will be said about this specification shortly), the risk-neutral probability measure $Q$ is now immediate. For each state $\omega \in \Omega$, there is a unique path through the tree, and so $Q(\omega)$ should equal the product of the conditional probabilities along this path.

For the information submodel, that is, the partitions $\{\mathcal{P}_t\}$, we assume that the investors know at each point in time precisely the past and present values of the short-rate process, but nothing more. Except for the specification of the real-world probability measure $P$, this finishes the construction of the binomial interest rate model. The price processes for the zero-coupon bonds now follow from (7.4.3), as described in Section 7.4.

Notice that the binomial tree has exactly $1 + 2 + \cdots + T = T(T+1)/2$ nodes, not counting the $T + 1$ nodes for time $T$. Moreover, corresponding to each of these $T(T+1)/2$ nodes are exactly two parameters: $i(t, n)$ and $q(t, n)$. Thus, a general, $T$-period binomial interest rate model is fully described by exactly $T(T+1)$ parameters. This can be quite a lot. How are they chosen?

The usual approach is to choose these parameters so the time-0 prices of all the zero-coupon bonds are consistent with the observed yield curve. This is called "calibrating the model to the yield curve." To be more precise, the model gives rise to $T$ time-0 prices: $P(0, 1), P(0, 2), \ldots, P(0, T)$, each of which is some function of one or more of the model's $T(T+1)$ parameters. Meanwhile, the yield curve observed in the financial marketplace gives rise to $T$ observed prices, say, $\hat{P}(0, 1), \hat{P}(0, 2), \ldots, \hat{P}(0, T)$. Thus, at least in principle, we can set the model's price $P(0, t)$ equal to the observed price $\hat{P}(0, 1)$, giving rise to a system of $T$ equations in the $T(T+1)$ unknown parameters.

This is some help, but with $T$ equations and $T(T+1)$ unknowns, we still have $T^2$ parameters to be determined. This is where Ho and Lee [93] and Black, Derman, and Toy [13] come to the rescue by adding additional structure.

### The Ho-Lee Model

Ho and Lee [93] make the following assumption:

$$[1 + i(t, n+1)] = k[1 + i(t, n)], \qquad q(t, n) = q, \quad \text{for all } n, t. \qquad (7.6.1)$$

Here $k$ and $q$ are two specified constants.

## The Black-Derman-Toy Model

Black, Derman, and Toy [13] make the following assumption:

$$i(t, n+1) = \sigma(t)i(t, n), \qquad q(t, n) = \frac{1}{2}, \quad \text{for all } n, t \qquad (7.6.2)$$

where $\sigma(1), \ldots, \sigma(T - 1)$ are $T - 1$ specified constants.

The constants $k$ and $q$ for (7.6.1) and $\sigma(t)$ for (7.6.2) can be thought of as measures for the volatility of the short-rate, and they are chosen accordingly. In both cases, the assumptions are such that if you know the value of the parameter $i(t, n)$ at one time-$t$ node, then by (7.6.1) or (7.6.2), you also know the value of the parameter $i(t, n)$ at all other time-$t$ nodes as $n$ varies from 0 to $t$. Thus, in both cases the number of unknown parameters has been reduced from $T(T + 1)$ to only $T$, one for each period. These remaining $T$ parameters can be obtained by calibration to the yield curve, as we describe next.

Assume that the parameters $k$ and $\sigma(t)$ are all greater than 1, so that $i(t, 0)$ are the smallest of all the $i(t, n)$'s having the same value of $t$. It suffices to set the $T$ values of $i(t, 0), t = 0, 1, \ldots, T - 1$, by calibration to the yield curve. This will be done one at a time, beginning with $i(0, 0)$, then setting $i(1, 0)$, and so forth.

Setting $i(0, 0)$ is automatic; we simply use $i(0, 0) = \hat{P}(0, 1)^{-1} - 1$. Note that the values of $i(1, 0), i(2, 0), \ldots, i(T - 1, 0)$ do not affect $P(0, 1)$.

In general, suppose that $i(0, 0), i(1, 0), \ldots,$ and $i(t - 1, 0)$ have all been set in such a way that $P(0, u) = \hat{P}(0, u)$ for $u = 1, \ldots, t$. The next step is to choose $i(t, 0)$ so that $P(0, t + 1) = \hat{P}(0, t + 1)$. To do this, we use (7.4.3):

$$P(0, t + 1) = \mathrm{E}^Q[(1 + i_0)^{-1} \cdots (1 + i_{t-1})^{-1}(1 + i_t)^{-1}]. \qquad (7.6.3)$$

Consider the right-hand side of (7.6.3) as a function of the unknown parameter $i(t, 0)$. As this parameter increases, so do the values of $i(t, n)$ for all $n > 0$ (by either (7.6.1) or (7.6.2)). But the probability distribution (that is, the values of the probabilities) of $i_t$ under $Q$ is not affected, so the right-hand side of (7.6.3) is a decreasing function of $i(t, 0)$. Moreover, setting $i(t, 0)$ either small enough or large enough makes the right-hand side of (7.6.3) either larger than or smaller than, respectively, the observation $\hat{P}(0, t + 1)$ (since $0 < \hat{P}(0, t + 1) < \hat{P}(0, t)$). Thus, to find the value of $i(t, 0)$ satisfying $P(0, t + 1) = \hat{P}(0, t + 1)$, we can use a simple numerical procedure such as the secant method or the bisection method to generate a sequence of "guesses" that converge to the desired value.

To compute the right-hand side of (7.6.3) for a particular set of parameters, we can use backward induction. This is a kind of dynamic programming procedure in which you first compute the conditional expectation $(1 + i_t)^{-1}$ given each time-$t$

node, then you compute the conditional expectation of $(1 + i_{t-1})^{-1}(1 + i_t)^{-1}$ given each time-$(t - 1)$ node, and so forth until, finally, you compute the right-hand side of (7.6.3).

**Example 7.6.1.** Consider a two-period (i.e., $T = 2$) Black-Derman-Toy model (see (7.6.2)) with $\sigma(1) = 11/10$, $\hat{P}(0, 1) = 0.95$, and $\hat{P}(0, 2) = 0.90$. The short rate at time 0 is easily computed to be

$$i(0, 0) = \frac{1}{\hat{P}(0, 1)} - 1 = \frac{20}{19} - 1 = \frac{1}{19} = 0.05263.$$

For the time-1 short-rate values, a guess of $i(1, 0) = i$ implies $i(1, 1) = (1.1)i$, so the conditional expectations associated with the time-1 nodes are $(1+i)^{-1}$ and $(1+1.1i)^{-1}$, corresponding to nodes $(1, 0)$ and $(1, 1)$, respectively.

Proceeding with the backward induction algorithm, we compute the conditional expectation associated with the time-0 node:

$$E^Q[(1 + i_0)^{-1}(1 + i_1)^{-1}] = (1 + i_0)^{-1}E^Q[(1 + i_1)^{-1}]$$

$$= \frac{19}{20}[0.5(1 + i)^{-1} + 0.5(1 + 1.1i)^{-1}].$$

This equals the right-hand side of (7.6.3), of course, so we could set this equal to $\hat{P}(0, 2) = 0.90$. This gives rise to a simple quadratic equation, the solution of which is computed to be $i = i(1, 0) = 0.05292$.

However, with a larger number of periods in the model, a simple equation like this would not be available, and so we illustrate the numerical procedure that can be used in the general situation. Start with an initial guess of $i = i(1, 0) = 0.05$. The backward induction procedure (or substitution in the preceding displayed equation) gives $P(0, 2) = 0.9026$. This value is larger than $\hat{P}(0, 2) = 0.90$, so our initial guess was too low.

For our second guess, try $i = 0.06$. This gives $P(0, 2) = 0.8937$, so the correct value of $i$ is between 0.05 and 0.06. Continuing with a logical sequence of guesses, $i = 0.052$ gives $P(0, 2) = 0.9008$, $i = 0.053$ gives $P(0, 2) = 0.8967$, and so forth. ∎

As illustrated by the preceding example, the algorithm for computing $i(t, 0)$ capitalizes on the fact that the right-hand side of (7.6.3) is decreasing with respect to $i(t, 0)$. By using the backward induction procedure, we can compute the right-hand side of (7.6.3) for a particular choice of $i(t, 0)$, and so we can use the secant iteration procedure to generate a sequence of choices that converges to the value of $i(t, 0)$ that satisfies (7.6.3).

However, if for a given choice of $i(t, 0)$, not only the right-hand side of (7.6.3) but also the derivative of the right-hand side of (7.6.3) with respect to $i(t, 0)$ could be computed, then an iterative procedure might be employed, such as the Newton-Raphson method, that would converge more quickly to the value of $i(t, 0)$, satisfying (7.6.3). It turns out that there is indeed a method for obtaining this derivative for a given choice of $i(t, 0)$: the *forward induction technique*.

The forward induction technique is based upon two key ideas, the first of which is the notion of *Arrow-Debreu* prices. Consider the contingent claim $X$ that pays $1 at time $m$ if the binomial term structure process passes through node $(m, j)$, whereas nothing is paid if the process passes through another time-$m$ node. Consider the price of $X$ at an arbitrary node $(n, i)$ with $n < m$, and let $A(n, i, m, j)$ denote this price. By virtue of the special form of the contingent claim $X$, $A$ is called an *Arrow-Debreu price* or a *Green's function* (because of its continuous-time analog). For instance, if $n = m - 1$, then

$$
A(m - 1, i, m, j) = \begin{cases} \dfrac{1 - q(m - 1, j)}{1 + i(m - 1, j)}, & i = j \\[2ex] \dfrac{q(m - 1, j - 1)}{1 + i(m - 1, j - 1)}, & i = j - 1 \\[2ex] 0, & \text{otherwise.} \end{cases} \tag{7.6.4}
$$

The Arrow-Debreu prices for the earlier nodes can be computed using backward induction, that is, in a recursive manner by which you fix the maturity $m$ and work out the time-$n$ prices in terms of time-$(n + 1)$ prices (this technique should be familiar by now). We are interested in these Arrow-Debreu prices because if $P(n, i, m)$ denotes the price at node $(n, i)$ of the zero-coupon bond maturing at time $m > n$, then

$$
P(n, i, m) = \sum_{j=0}^{m} A(n, i, m, j). \tag{7.6.5}
$$

As it stands, nothing much has been gained, because the backward induction technique for computing the Arrow-Debreu prices is essentially the same as the technique used for computing the right-hand side of (7.6.3) for the secant iteration procedure. However, by exploiting a second idea, the *binomial forward equation*, we can do better. The idea is that there is a second recursive relationship that is satisfied by the Arrow-Debreu prices. Instead of fixing the maturity $m$ and considering the prices at adjacent points in time $n$, fix the time $n$ and consider the prices for adjacent maturities $m$. In particular, it turns out the Arrow-Debreu prices satisfy the following binomial forward equation (for simplicity we assume that $q(t, n) = 1/2$ for all $t$ and

$n$, as in the Black-Derman-Toy model, leaving other cases):

$$A(n, i, m+1, j) = \begin{cases} \dfrac{A(n, i, m, j)}{2[1 + i(m, j)]}, & j = 0 \\[3mm] \dfrac{A(n, i, m, j)}{2[1 + i(m, j)]} + \dfrac{A(n, i, m, j-1)}{2[1 + i(m, j-1)]}, & j = 1, \ldots, m \\[3mm] \dfrac{A(n, i, m, j-1)}{2[1 + i(m, j-1)]}, & j = m+1. \end{cases}$$

$$(7.6.6)$$

The forward induction technique is implemented as follows. Just as with secant iteration we perform $T$ big steps where first the observation $\hat{P}(0, 1)$ is used to compute $i(0, 0)$, then $\hat{P}(0, 2)$ is used to compute $i(1, 0), \ldots$, and, for the $T$-th step $\hat{P}(0, T)$ is used to compute $i(T - 1, 0)$. However, in addition, as part of the first big step, we compute $A(0, 0, 1, 0)$ and $A(0, 0, 1, 1)$ (using (7.6.4)); as part of the second big step, compute $A(0, 0, 2, 0)$, $A(0, 0, 2, 1)$, and $A(0, 0, 2, 2)$ (using the binomial forward equation, in a manner that will described shortly); and so forth.

For a better understanding of how an individual big step is carried out, suppose $m - 1$ big steps have been carried out. By (7.6.5) we have

$$P(0, 0, m) = \sum_{j=0}^{m-1} A(0, 0, m, j),$$

so the first task is to use the binomial forward equation to substitute for the $A(0, 0, m, j)$'s in terms of the known $A(0, 0, m-1, j)$ values as well as the unknown values of the short rates $i(m-1, j)$, $j = 0, 1, \ldots, m-1$. The second task is to substitute the appropriate expression for $i(m - 1, j)$, $j > 0$, as a function of $i(m - 1, 0)$ (this comes from either (7.6.1) or (7.6.2), as explained previously). Thus, we now have a precise analytical function for $P(0, 0, m)$ in terms of $i(m - 1, 0)$, so we can use an efficient algorithm such as the Newton-Raphson procedure to solve for the value of $i(m - 1, 0)$ such that $P(0, 0, m) = \hat{P}(0, m)$. Finally, the last task of the $m$-th step is to substitute this value of $i(m-1, 0)$ in the expressions for the $A(0, 0, m, j)$'s, in order to be ready for step $m+1$.

## Section 7.7
# Implementation of the Black-Derman-Toy Model

The general framework for implementing the additive (Ho-Lee) and the multiplicative (Black-Derman-Toy) interest rate models was described in the previous section. The parameters $k$ and $q$ in (7.6.1) and the scalars $\sigma(1), \ldots, \sigma(T-1)$ in (7.6.2) are crucial in implementing these models. In this section, we describe how to obtain $\sigma(1), \ldots,$ $\sigma(T-1)$ by illustrating numerically the implementation of the Black-Derman-Toy model. We also highlight the importance of the forward induction technique in calibrating the model. A similar illustration can be found in Sherris [178].

Equation (7.6.1) assumes that $\sigma(1), \ldots, \sigma(T-1)$ are known constants so that at each time step we have to deal only with one equation with one unknown. In the original Black-Derman-Toy model, these volatilities had to be inferred from other inputs. Consequently, the actual calibration of the BDT model is more complex than that presented in Section 7.6. The main difference has to do with the volatility parameter. In this derivation, the input volatility is the volatility of the long-term yield, which we denote by $\sigma_y(t)$.

The assumptions made in the original BDT model can be summarized as follows:

1.  The short rate is the fundamental variable; the BDT model is implicitly an approximation of a continuous-time world where the short rates are lognormal random variables.
2.  The model requires two input term structures: the yield curve $Y(0, t)$ and the yield volatility curve $\sigma_y(t)$, for $t = 1, 2, \ldots$. The interest rate lattice constructed is consistent with these market data.
3.  The lattice constructed is a recombining binomial tree, with equal risk-neutral probability of moving to the up-state or the down-state; that is, $q(t, n) = 1/2$ for all $t, n$.
4.  Volatility of the short rate is a function of time and independent of state.

In view of assumptions 1 and 3, it is convenient to imagine that the BDT short rate evolves according to the lattice in Figure 7.2. For any initial value of $i(t-1, n)$, there are two equally probable states one period later: $i(t, n+1)$ in the up-state

FIGURE 7.2 | *Evolution of Short Rates*

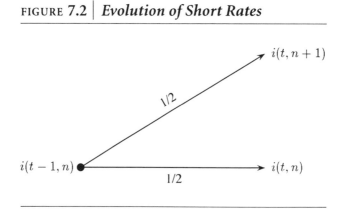

or $i(t, n)$ in the down-state. The volatility of the short rates, $\sigma_r(t)$, can be computed as

$$\sigma_r(t) = \frac{1}{2} \log \frac{i(t, n+1)}{i(t, n)}.$$

Rearranging the above expression, we have

$$i(t, n+1) = i(t, n) \exp\{2\sigma_r(t)\}. \tag{7.7.1}$$

Note that this is related to (7.6.2) by $\sigma(t) = \exp\{2\sigma_r(t)\}$.

Next we define the yield volatility. Recall that $P(n, j, m)$ was introduced in the previous section as the price at node $(n, j)$ of the zero-coupon bond maturing at time $m > n$. Similarly, let $Y(n, j, m)$ denote the corresponding yield rate so that we have the following relationship:

$$P(n, j, m) = [1 + Y(n, j, m)]^{-(m-n)}. \tag{7.7.2}$$

In particular, $Y(1, 1, m)$ and $Y(1, 0, m)$ represent the yield rate at nodes $(1, 1)$ and $(1, 0)$ respectively of the zero-coupon bond maturing at time $m$. Then the current yield volatility for maturity $t$, $\sigma_y(t)$, is defined by

$$\sigma_y(t) = \frac{1}{2} \log \frac{Y(1, 1, t)}{Y(1, 0, t)}$$

or equivalently

$$Y(1, 1, t) = Y(1, 0, t) \exp\{2\sigma_y(t)\} \tag{7.7.3}$$

for $t = 2, 3, \ldots$.

The term structures $Y(0, t)$ and $\sigma_y(t)$ are the two basic set of market data fitted to the BDT model. Based on the forward induction technique described in the previous section, we now illustrate step by step the calibration procedure using the market data in Table 7.1. In a later part of this section, we show that the same calibration process can be used to calibrate other input market data.

**Time-0 Calibration.** At time 0, the one-period zero-coupon bond computed from the lattice must match with the corresponding bond from the market; hence, we have $i(0, 0) = 6\%$ from Table 7.1.[2] Before proceeding with the calibration process, we first

---

[2]Notice that the yield volatility of 20% has no impact on determining this short rate.

TABLE 7.1 | *A Sample of Yield Rates and Volatilities*

| Maturity $t$ | Yield $Y(0, t)$ | Yield Volatility $\sigma_y(t)$ |
|:---:|:---:|:---:|
| 1 | 6% | 20% |
| 2 | 7 | 19 |
| 3 | 8 | 18 |
| 4 | 9 | 17 |
| 5 | 10 | 16 |

initialize the following Green's functions as defined in (7.6.4):

$$A(0, 0, 1, 0) = A(0, 0, 1, 1) = \frac{1}{2[1 + i(0, 0)]} = \frac{1}{2(1.06)} = 0.4717.$$

The usefulness of the Green's functions will become apparent in subsequent calibration.

**Time-1 Calibration.** At time 1, we have $Y(0, 2) = 7\%$ and $\sigma_y(2) = 19\%$. The task is to find $i(1, 0)$ and $i(1, 1)$ such that the interest rate lattice constructed up to this time step is consistent with this market information. To compute the price of a two-period zero-coupon bond from the lattice, (7.6.3) implies

$$P(0, 2) = E^Q[(1 + i_0)^{-1}(1 + i_1)^{-1}]$$

$$= \frac{1}{1 + i_0} \left[ \frac{1}{2} \frac{1}{[1 + i(1, 0)]} + \frac{1}{2} \frac{1}{[1 + i(1, 1)]} \right]$$

$$= \frac{A(0, 0, 1, 0)}{1 + i(1, 0)} + \frac{A(0, 0, 1, 1)}{1 + i(1, 1)}$$

where we have substituted the Green's function obtained in the previous time step. Since the two-period zero-coupon bond price computed from the lattice must match with the current two-period yield rate, we have

$$P(0, 2) = \hat{P}(0, 2) = \frac{1}{(1.07)^2} = \frac{A(0, 0, 1, 0)}{1 + i(1, 0)} + \frac{A(0, 0, 1, 1)}{1 + i(1, 1)}. \tag{7.7.4}$$

The only unknowns in this equation are $i(1, 0)$ and $i(1, 1)$. This equation represents the first calibration equation from matching the yield curve.

To obtain the other calibration equation, we now work with another piece of market information, the yield volatility $\sigma_y(2) = 19\%$. Setting $t = 2$ in (7.7.3), we have

$$Y(1, 1, 2) = Y(1, 0, 2)e^{2\sigma_y(2)} = Y(1, 0, 2)\exp\{2(0.19)\}. \qquad (7.7.5)$$

By construction, $Y(1, 0, 2)$ and $Y(1, 1, 2)$ represent the one-period yield rates at nodes $(1, 0)$ and $(1, 1)$, respectively. In this special case, $Y(1, 0, 2)$ and $Y(1, 1, 2)$ are coincidentally equivalent to the short rates at these nodes. Hence, we have

$$Y(1, 0, 2) = i(1, 0)$$

and

$$Y(1, 1, 2) = i(1, 1).$$

Substituting these two expressions into (7.7.5) gives

$$i(1, 1) = i(1, 0)\exp\{2(0.19)\}. \qquad (7.7.6)$$

This equation again involves the two unknowns $i(1, 0)$ and $i(1, 1)$. It is the second calibration equation that results from matching the yield volatility. Using (7.7.4) and (7.7.6), we jointly solve for $i(1, 0)$ and $i(1, 1)$. These two equations are nonlinear, and to solve them simultaneously, we need to use numerical techniques such as the Newton-Raphson iteration method. Solving gives $i(1, 0) = 6.52\%$ and $i(1, 1) = 9.54\%$.

Once the short rates at time 1 are known, the Green's function $A(0, 0, 2, 0)$, $A(0, 0, 2, 0)$, and $A(0, 0, 2, 2)$ is updated according to (7.6.6) as follows:

$$A(0, 0, 2, 0) = \frac{A(0, 0, 1, 0)}{2[1 + i(1, 0)]},$$

$$A(0, 0, 2, 1) = \frac{A(0, 0, 1, 0)}{2[1 + i(1, 0)]} + \frac{A(0, 0, 1, 1)}{2[1 + i(1, 1)]}, \qquad (7.7.7)$$

$$A(0, 0, 2, 2) = \frac{A(0, 0, 1, 1)}{2[1 + i(1, 1)]}.$$

In addition to these values, we also need the following values in subsequent calibration:

$$A(1, 0, 2, 0) = A(1, 0, 2, 1) = \frac{1}{2[1 + i(1, 0)]},$$

$$A(1, 1, 2, 1) = A(1, 1, 2, 2) = \frac{1}{2[1 + i(1, 1)]},$$

$$A(1, 0, 2, 2) = A(1, 1, 2, 0) = 0.$$

***Time-2 Calibration.*** To extend the lattice to time 2, we are confronted with three unknowns, $i(2, 0)$, $i(2, 1)$, and $i(2, 2)$. However, we have only two pieces of market data, $Y(0, 3)$ and $\sigma_y(3)$. Finding three unknowns from two quantities does not in general give a unique solution. Thus, it seems that we have an infinite number of possible solutions.

To solve this problem, recall that in this model the short rate is assumed to be lognormally distributed with a volatility of the logarithmic short rate depending only on time. Letting $t = 1$ and $n = 0$ and 1 in (7.7.1) and with appropriate substitution, we have

$$i(2, 1) = i(2, 0)\sigma(2), \tag{7.7.8}$$

$$i(2, 2) = i(2, 1)\sigma(2) = i(2, 0)\sigma(2)^2 \tag{7.7.9}$$

where $\sigma(2) = \exp\{2\sigma_r(2)\}$. The above analysis implies that solving three unknowns $i(2, 0)$, $i(2, 1)$, and $i(2, 2)$ boils down to solving only two unknowns $i(2, 0)$ and $\sigma(2)$. Once these two quantities are found, the other two short rates can be computed.

To find the first calibration equation for solving $i(2, 0)$ and $\sigma(2)$, we must compute the three-period zero-coupon bond price, $P(0, 3)$, from the lattice. One technique is to use the usual backward induction method as follows:

$$
P(0, 3) = \frac{1}{1 + i(0, 0)} \left\{ \frac{1}{2[1 + i(1, 0)]} \left( \frac{1}{2[1 + i(2, 0)]} + \frac{1}{2[1 + i(2, 1)]} \right) \right.
$$
$$
\left. + \frac{1}{2[1 + i(1, 1)]} \left( \frac{1}{2[1 + i(2, 1)]} + \frac{1}{2[1 + i(2, 2)]} \right) \right\}
$$

$$
= \left\{ \frac{1}{4[1 + i(0, 0)][1 + i(1, 0)]} \right\} \frac{1}{1 + i(2, 0)}
$$
$$
+ \left\{ \frac{1}{4[1 + i(0,0)][1 + i(1,0)]} + \frac{1}{4[1 + i(0,0)][1 + i(1,1)]} \right\} \frac{1}{1 + i(2, 1)}
$$
$$
+ \left\{ \frac{1}{4[1 + i(0, 0)][1 + i(1, 1)]} \right\} \frac{1}{1 + i(2, 2)}. \tag{7.7.10}
$$

This recursive valuation approach, however, is computationally burdensome. It requires rolling back the lattice from the maturity of the bond to time 0 each time the value of the zero-coupon bond is needed.

A more efficient approach is to make use of Green's functions. Comparing (7.7.10) to the Green's functions defined in (7.7.7), we see that the three-period bond price is more conveniently determined by

$$
P(0, 3) = \frac{A(0, 0, 2, 0)}{1 + i(2, 0)} + \frac{A(0, 0, 2, 1)}{1 + i(2, 1)} + \frac{A(0, 0, 2, 2)}{1 + i(2, 2)}.
$$

Using (7.7.8) and (7.7.9), the three unknowns in the above equation can further be simplified to only two unknowns as

$$P(0, 3) = \frac{A(0, 0, 2, 0)}{1 + i(2, 0)} + \frac{A(0, 0, 2, 1)}{1 + i(2, 0)\sigma(2)} + \frac{A(0, 0, 2, 2)}{1 + i(2, 0)\sigma(2)^2}$$

$$= \sum_{j=0}^{2} \frac{A(0, 0, 2, j)}{1 + i(2, 0)\sigma(2)^j}.$$

The bond price computed from the lattice must match with the current yield rate. Hence, the first calibration equation for solving $i(2, 0)$ and $\sigma(2)$ becomes

$$\hat{P}(0, 3) = \frac{1}{[1 + Y(0, 3)]^3} = \frac{1}{(1.08)^3} = \sum_{j=0}^{2} \frac{A(0, 0, 2, j)}{1 + i(2, 0)\sigma(2)^j}. \qquad (7.7.11)$$

We now describe how to use the volatility information $\sigma_y(3) = 18\%$ to arrive at the other calibration equation. Letting $t = 3$ in (7.7.3) yields

$$Y(1, 1, 3) = Y(1, 0, 3) \exp\{2\sigma_y(3)\} = Y(1, 0, 3) \exp\{2(0.18)\} \qquad (7.7.12)$$

where $Y(1, 0, 3)$ and $Y(1, 1, 3)$ represent the yield rate of a two-period zero-coupon bond at nodes $(1, 0)$ and $(1, 1)$, respectively. It follows from (7.7.2) that

$$P(1, m, 3) = [1 + Y(1, m, 3)]^{-2}$$

or equivalently

$$Y(1, m, 3) = P(1, m, 3)^{-1/2} - 1$$

for $m = 0, 1$. Substituting the above expression into (7.7.12), we have

$$P(1, 1, 3)^{-1/2} - 1 = [P(1, 0, 3)^{-1/2} - 1] \exp\{2(0.18)\}. \qquad (7.7.13)$$

However, $P(1, m, 3)$ denotes the price of a two-period zero-coupon bond at node $(1, m)$. These values can be determined from the lattice as

$$P(1, 0, 3) = \frac{1}{1 + i(1, 0)} \left\{ \frac{1}{2[1 + i(2, 0)]} + \frac{1}{2[1 + i(2, 1)]} \right\}$$

$$= \frac{A(1, 0, 2, 0)}{1 + i(2, 0)} + \frac{A(1, 0, 2, 1)}{1 + i(2, 1)}$$

$$= \sum_{j=0}^{2} \frac{A(1, 0, 2, j)}{1 + i(2, j)} = \sum_{j=0}^{2} \frac{A(1, 0, 2, j)}{1 + i(2, 0)\sigma(2)^j} \qquad (7.7.14)$$

and

$$P(1, 1, 3) = \frac{1}{1 + i(1, 1)} \left\{ \frac{1}{2[1 + i(2, 1)]} + \frac{1}{2[1 + i(2, 2)]} \right\}$$

$$= \frac{A(1, 1, 2, 1)}{1 + i(2, 1)} + \frac{A(1, 1, 2, 2)}{1 + i(2, 2)}$$

$$= \sum_{j=0}^{2} \frac{A(1, 1, 2, j)}{1 + i(2, j)} = \sum_{j=0}^{2} \frac{A(1, 1, 2, j)}{1 + i(2, 0)\sigma(2)^j} \qquad (7.7.15)$$

where the required Green's functions are known quantities at time 2. Substituting (7.7.14) and (7.7.15) into (7.7.13), we obtain

$$\left( \sum_{j=0}^{2} \frac{A(1, 1, 2, j)}{1 + i(2, 0)\sigma(2)^j} \right)^{-\frac{1}{2}} - 1 = \left[ \left( \sum_{j=0}^{2} \frac{A(1, 0, 2, j)}{1 + i(2, 0)\sigma^j(2)} \right)^{-\frac{1}{2}} - 1 \right] e^{0.36}.$$

$$(7.7.16)$$

This equation involves only two unknowns, $i(2, 0)$ and $\sigma(2)$. Together with (7.7.11), these two unknowns can be determined numerically. Exercise 7.13 asks you to verify that the solution to (7.7.11) and (7.7.16) is $i(2, 0) = 6.949\%$ and $\sigma(2) = 1.4119$. Hence, the short rates $i(2, 1)$ and $i(2, 2)$ are computed as

$$i(2, 1) = i(2, 0)\sigma(2) = (6.949)(1.4119) = 9.812\%$$

and

$$i(2, 2) = i(2, 0)\sigma(2)^2 = (6.949)(1.4119)^2 = 13.854\%.$$

Similarly, once these short rates are determined, the values $A(0, 0, 3, j)$, $A(1, 0, 3, j)$, and $A(1, 1, 3, j)$ for $j = 0, \ldots, 3$ are updated accordingly using (7.6.6) before proceeding to the next time step.

***Time-t Calibration.*** The above procedure is now readily generalized to calibrating the time-$t$ short rates. In general, the calibrating procedure involves solving two simultaneous nonlinear equations. One equation is obtained from matching the yield rate, and the other equation is derived from matching the yield volatility. A crucial observation in setting up these equations is to recognize that the volatility structure is only time-dependent, not state-dependent. Thus, we could derive the following implied recursive relation between the short rates (see Exercise 7.14):

$$i(t, n) = i(t, 0)\sigma(t)^n \qquad (7.7.17)$$

for $t = 1, 2, \ldots$ and $n = 1, 2, \ldots, t$. This recursive relationship plays an important role in calibration. At time $t$, although we are confronted with $t + 1$ unknown short rates, the existence of the implied recursive relation reduces the $t + 1$ unknowns to only two unknowns, namely, $i(t, 0)$ and $\sigma(t)$. Once these two unknowns are evaluated, the rest of the short rates are computed using (7.7.17).

The use of the Green's functions further facilitates the calibration process. For instance, the first equation from matching the yield rate is conveniently expressed as

$$P(0, t + 1) = \sum_{j=0}^{t} \frac{A(0, 0, t, j)}{1 + i(t, 0)\sigma(t)^j}. \tag{7.7.18}$$

Similarly, the second equation from matching the yield volatility is given by

$$Y(1, 1, t + 1) = Y(1, 0, t + 1)e^{2\sigma_y(t+1)} \tag{7.7.19}$$

where

$$Y(1, m, t + 1) = \left( \sum_{j=0}^{t} \frac{A(1, m, t, j)}{1 + i(t, 0)\sigma(t)^j} \right)^{-\frac{1}{t}} - 1$$

for $m = 0, 1$. When we conduct the calibration procedure in a forward direction for $t = 0, 1, 2, \ldots$, then at any time-$t$ calibration, the short rates $i(j, n)$, $j = 0, 1, \ldots$, $t - 1, n = 0, 1, \ldots, j$ are already known. Therefore, as long as we keep updating the required Green's functions, the calibration equations are obtained easily and (7.7.18) and (7.7.19) involve only two unknowns, $i(t, 0)$ and $\sigma(t)$. Numerical techniques such as the Newton-Raphson iteration method can be used to solve for these two unknowns.

Figure 7.3 shows the five-period calibrated BDT binomial lattice. If we examine how the short rates evolve over time, we notice that the lowest value of the short rate is increasing over the first four periods. This behavior would often be viewed as unreasonable for an interest rate generator. However, we must emphasize that the BDT lattice has been computed using the $Q$ measure. There is no assurance that this probability distribution corresponds to the physical distribution. Recall once again that a $Q$ measure is used for pricing derivative securities. For real-world projections, the $P$ measure must be used.

The calibration procedure described above involves fitting two market term structures simultaneously. In general, the same algorithm can be used to fit other choices of term structure. For instance, we may be interested in calibrating the short-rate volatilities or the prices of derivative such as interest rate caps as opposed to the yield volatilities. We now discuss how to handle these situations.

FIGURE **7.3** | *The Calibrated BDT Binomial Lattice*

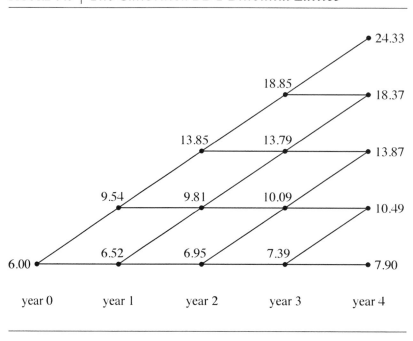

First, consider the formal case of fitting the yield curve and the short-rate volatility curve simultaneously. It turns out that the calibrating these two curves is less laborious. At each time-step calibration, there is only one equation with one unknown to be solved. To see this, first note that the $\sigma(t)$ in (7.7.18) is the short-rate volatility at time $t$. This is precisely the input market short-rate volatility curve. Hence, (7.7.18) contains only one unknown $i(t, 0)$, and the numerical techniques such as the Newton-Raphson method can be used to solve for the unknowns. Once $i(t, 0)$ is determined, the rest of the short rates are derived recursively.

Note that by construction, it is not possible to fit both volatility curves simultaneously to the BDT model. If one of the volatility curves is fitted, the other volatility curve will be left unspecified as discussed in the following example.

***Example 7.7.1.*** In this example, we demonstrate the limitation inherent in the BDT model. This may have important implications in choosing the appropriate interest rate model. For simplicity, we construct a 30-year lattice with a yearly time step based on the following two sets of market term structures:

a.  A flat 8% yield curve and a flat 10% yield volatility curve.

b.  A flat 8% yield curve and a flat 10% short-rate volatility curve.

For each calibrated lattice, we compute the implied volatility curve that is not fitted to the model. The implied volatility curves are depicted in Figure 7.4. For this particular example, it is interesting to note that the future short-rate volatilities must be increasing in order to accommodate a flat current yield volatility curve while the yield volatilities must be decreasing to fit a flat short-rate volatility curve. ∎

FIGURE **7.4** | *Comparisons of the Implied Volatility Curves*

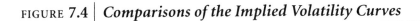

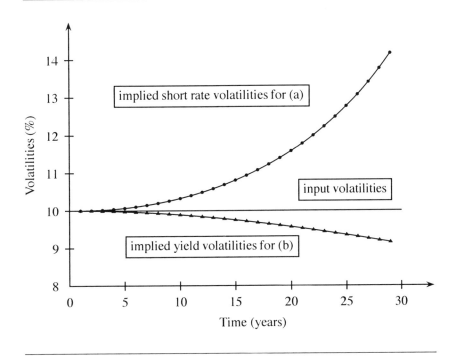

So far we have considered fitting the volatility curve. In practice, it may be important that the interest rate lattice constructed be able to reproduce current market derivative prices such as interest rate caps, floors, or swaptions. For these situations, the calibration procedure described above still applies. For simplicity, assume that the market prices of a series of caplets settled in arrears are available. Now, the calibration objective is to fit both the current yield curve and the cap price curve to the interest rate lattice. The first calibration equation resulting from matching the yield curve still corresponds to (7.7.18) with the unknowns $i(t, 0)$ and $\sigma(t)$. To set up the second equation, we first need to compute the time-0 price of the caplet settled in arrears at time $t + 1$ from the lattice. Let $c_t$ denote the caplet price computed from the lattice while $\hat{c}_t$ denotes the market caplet price. Hence, we have

$$
c_t = \sum_{j=0}^{t} \frac{A(0, 0, t, j)}{1 + i(t, j)} [i(t, j) - \kappa_t]^+
$$

$$
= \sum_{j=0}^{t} \frac{A(0, 0, t, j)}{1 + i(t, 0)\sigma(t)^j} [i(t, 0)\sigma(t)^j - \kappa_t]^+
$$

where $\kappa_t$ is the strike rate for the corresponding caplet. Because the caplet prices, $\hat{c}_t$, computed from the lattice must be equal to the market price of the corresponding caplet, the unknowns $i(t, 0)$ and $\sigma(t)$ must be selected such that

$$\hat{c}_t = c_t = \sum_{j=0}^{t} \frac{A(0, 0, t, j)}{1 + i(t, 0)\sigma(t)^j}[i(t, 0)\sigma(t)^j - \kappa_t]^+. \qquad (7.7.20)$$

This equation represents the second calibration equation resulting from matching the caplet at time $t$. Trial-and-error approaches can be used to solve (7.7.18) and (7.7.20) simultaneously to achieve the fitting criteria.

Similar to the case of fitting the volatility curves, it is generally not possible to fit a whole range of derivative security prices to the BDT lattice at the same time. In this situation, one has to use an optimization algorithm to find the values $i(t, 0)$ and $\sigma(t)$ that best fit the input market data.

# Section 7.8
# Interest Rate Futures

The basic concepts about futures markets were introduced in Section 2.3. In particular, T-bill and T-bond futures contracts were discussed, as was the idea of valuing a T-bill futures contract by using the formula for the price of a comparable forward contract, a formula that was derived with an arbitrage argument. However, this formula is at best an approximation for futures, because in a world with stochastic interest rates the prices of comparable forward and futures contracts will in general not be the same.

What, then, is a better way to value the price of a futures contract? The answer is provided in Chapter 11, where we explain how to construct a securities market model that includes futures prices. The idea is simple. First, build an ordinary, arbitrage-free securities market model, making sure to include the assets or securities that underlie the contemplated futures contract. Second, set the date, say, time $\tau$, when the contemplated futures contract expires. Third, work out the value, which will be denoted $X_\tau$, of the futures contract when it expires. This is straightforward because we know the value of the underlying security at time $\tau$, and $X_\tau$ should be a logical function of this value. For instance, if the underlying value is the price of a stock index, then $X_\tau$ should be set equal to the time-$\tau$ price of this index. Of course, $X_\tau$ will be a random variable because it will be a function of one or more random variables. In fact, $X_\tau \in \mathcal{P}_\tau$, that is, the time-$\tau$ value of the futures contract will be a function of the information available at time $\tau$.

In the case of some interest rate futures, the time-$\tau$ price $X_\tau$ might be a somewhat complicated function of two or more underlying securities. In all cases, however,

$X_\tau$ will be a function of the time-$\tau$ curve of zero-coupon bond prices, a curve that is fully observable at time $\tau$. Thus, in principle it is always possible to specify the expiration price of an interest rate futures contract as a random variable $X_\tau \in \mathcal{P}_\tau$. For instance, as explained in Section 2.3, the expiration price of a T-bond futures contract is based on the price of the T-bond that is the cheapest to deliver among a group of more than one dozen T-bonds. Knowing the time-$\tau$ curve of zero-coupon prices, we can readily compute the time-$\tau$ price of any T-bond; so at time-$\tau$ we can deduce which T-bond is the cheapest to deliver, and thus we can work out exactly what $X_\tau$ must be.

Returning to the development of the futures price model, it remains for us to work out the futures prices at all times preceding the expiration date $\tau$. This is done by exploiting the fact that *in an arbitrage-free securities market the futures prices are martingales under the risk-neutral probability measure(s)*. Note that this statement refers to the ordinary prices of futures contracts, not the discounted prices. As explained in Chapter 11, this principle results from the fact that from the theoretical standpoint an investor can buy and sell futures contracts without putting up any capital. A margin account must be opened with a futures broker, but the collateral used can be interest-bearing securities, or the cash held by the broker can earn interest. Consequently, if a situation ever arises when the futures price is sure to go up (or sure to go down), then an arbitrage opportunity exists. Conversely, if no arbitrage opportunities are present, then at each point in time the possibility of the futures price going up must be balanced by the possibility of the price going down. It follows that the futures price must be a martingale under some probability measure. Moreover, this probability measure must be such that the discounted prices of the ordinary securities in the model are also martingales, so no-arbitrage opportunities can be constructed by trading the futures contract in conjunction with one or more of the ordinary securities. Consequently, the futures prices must be martingales under the risk-neutral probability measure (see Pliska [146] for a rigorous proof of this result).

Putting the pieces together gives the following relationship for the time-$t$ futures price $X_t$:

$$X_t = \mathrm{E}_t^Q[X_\tau], \quad 0 \le t \le \tau. \tag{7.8.1}$$

Because the futures price is a martingale under the risk-neutral probability measure $Q$, it follows by the martingale property that its time-$t$ price equals the expectation of its price at a future time. For this future time, we have selected $\tau$, the expiration date, because we know the futures price is given by $X_\tau$ on this date. Thus, (7.8.1) can be used to specify the stochastic process $X$ giving the futures prices at all times $t < \tau$.

*Example 7.8.1 (T-Bill Futures).* As explained in Section 2.3.2, the futures price at expiration equals the price of a T-bill that matures 3 months later. To illustrate how this might be modeled, we take the three-period term structure model in Example 7.4.2.

However, for simplicity we assume time is measured in years and that at delivery, which is taken to be time $\tau = 2$, the underlying T-bill matures in one period, that is, in 1 year.

A T-bill is a zero-coupon bond, so the price $X_2$ of the futures contract must be at expiration can be determined easily; it is precisely equal to $P(2, 3)$ (ignoring for simplicity the factor of 100), as displayed in the table for Example 7.4.2. We know the risk-neutral probability measure ($Q(\omega_k) = 1/12$ for $k = 1, \ldots, 12$), so using the martingale property, we can quickly compute the futures prices at times 0 and 1. For instance, if the short rate $i_1 = 6\%$, then the time-1 futures price is

$$X_1(\omega_k) = E_1^Q[P(2, 3)] = 0.5(0.9390) + 0.5(0.9479) = 0.9435$$

for $k = 1, \ldots, 4$. Similarly we compute $X_1(\omega_k) = 0.9524$ for $k = 5, \ldots, 8$ and $X_1(\omega_k) = 0.9616$ for $k = 9, \ldots, 12$, and finally the time-0 futures price (which is the same for all $\omega$)

$$X_0 = E^Q[P(2, 3)] = \frac{1}{6}[0.9390 + \cdots + 0.9662] = 0.9525. \qquad \blacksquare$$

# Section 7.9
# Callable Bonds

Once an interest rate lattice is constructed, the resulting lattice can be used to value many interest-rate-dependent securities. These applications include the pricing of bond options, caps, floors, and swaptions. The early exercise of the options can also be captured using the backward induction techniques described in Chapter 6. In this section, we consider the pricing of coupon bonds and callable bonds using the Black-Derman-Toy interest rate lattice constructed in Section 7.7.

**Coupon Bonds**

A coupon bond pays a stream of fixed coupon payments at different times plus a balloon payment equal to the redemption value of the bond at maturity. Therefore, a coupon bond can be decomposed into a portfolio of zero-coupon bonds with different maturities. The price of the coupon bond can be calculated by aggregating the prices of these zero-coupon bonds. To illustrate, consider a 4-year par bond with an annual coupon rate of 10%. This bond pays an annual coupon payment of 10 for the next 4 years. At maturity, which is at the end of the fourth year, an additional amount equal to the redemption value of the bond, which is 100 in this case, is also paid. Thus, this particular bond can be decomposed into three zero-coupon bonds with maturities 1, 2, and 3 years and maturity value 10 and a zero-coupon bond with maturity 4 years and maturity value 110. The price of the bonds can be calculated as (see also (7.2.1))

$$\text{coupon bond price} = \text{sum of the zero-coupon bond prices}$$

$$= \sum_{t=1}^{3} \frac{10}{[1 + Y(0, t)]^t} + \frac{110}{[1 + Y(0, 4)]^4}.$$

Using the term structure from Table 7.1, we compute the price of the coupon bond as 104.03.

A coupon bond can be priced from any interest rate lattice. This method uses the backward recursion technique discussed in Chapter 6. Let $B(t, n)$ and $C(t, n)$ denote the value of the underlying security and the cash flow when $(t, n)$ is realized. Figure 7.5 shows how the values of $B$ and $C$ evolve for any subbranch of the interest rate lattice. At node $(t, n)$ with short rate $i(t, n)$, the underlying security pays the amount $C(t, n)$ and is worth $B(t, n)$. One period later, the short rate will change to $i(t + 1, n)$ with probability $1 - q$ and $i(t + 1, n + 1)$ with probability $q$. If node $(t + 1, n)$ is realized, the underlying security pays $C(t + 1, n)$ and is worth $B(t + 1, n)$, otherwise the security pays $C(t + 1, n + 1)$ and is worth $B(t + 1, n + 1)$ at node $(t + 1, n + 1)$.

FIGURE 7.5 | *Subbranch of the Binomial Lattice*

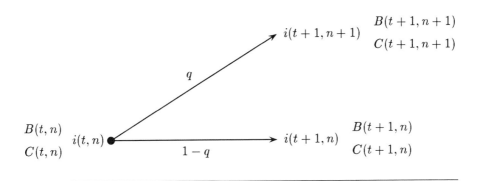

To avoid arbitrage, the value of the security at node $(t, n)$ must be equal to the expected present value of the one-period values. Thus, the following relationship must hold:

$$B(t, n) = \frac{1}{1 + i(t, n)} q[C(t + 1, n + 1) + B(t + 1, n + 1)]$$

$$+ \frac{1}{1 + i(t, n)} (1 - q)[C(t + 1, n) + B(t + 1, n)]. \quad (7.9.1)$$

This expression gives the general algorithm for rolling back the values from time $t + 1$ to time $t$. The backward recursive technique can now be described as follows: Starting at the maturity of the underlying security with $t = T$, determine the value of $B(T, n)$ and $C(T, n)$ for $n = 0, 1, \ldots, T$. Then, use (7.9.1) to compute $B(T - 1, n)$ for $n = 0, 1, \ldots, T - 1$. This procedure is repeated for $t = T - 2, T - 3, \ldots$ until $t = 0$, which yields $B(0, 0)$, the price of the security at time 0. This procedure works as long as the maturity value of the underlying security as well as the cash flow at each node can be determined.

In our coupon-bond example, we have

$$B(4, n) = 100,$$

for $n = 0, \ldots, 4$ and

$$C(t, n) = 10$$

for $t = 1, 2, 3, 4, n = 0, 1, e, \ldots, t$. Using the calibrated interest rate lattice from Figure 7.3, Figure 7.6 shows the intermediate values of $V$ computed from (7.9.1). The bond price value $B(0, 0)$ is the same as that obtained from the first approach. We can also use Green's function to compute the required bond price, as illustrated in Exercise 7.17.

FIGURE 7.6 | *The Bond Price Lattice* $(B(t, n))$

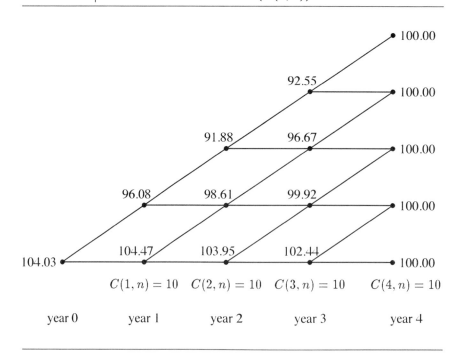

We now discuss the valuation of callable bonds. The key distinction between a noncallable bond and a callable bond lies in the embedded-option component of the callable bond. A callable bond has a call provision that allows the issuer to redeem the bonds before the maturity for a certain specified price known as the call (strike) price. We will use the term structure price in this context since it makes things clearer. Consequently, the cash flow of a callable bond is contingent on variables such as the future short rates. This is in contrast to the cash flow of a coupon bond, which is deterministic.

Essentially, the price of a callable bond can be decomposed into two components: the noncallable bond and the embedded call option on bond; that is, we have

$$\text{callable bond price} = \text{noncallable bond price} - \text{call option price}. \qquad (7.9.2)$$

The option component refers to the right to buy the bond at a specified strike price, and this value is subtracted from the corresponding noncallable bond because the owner of the callable bond has shorted the option. Relationship (7.9.2) implies that the pricing of a callable bond is equivalent to pricing the noncallable bond and the embedded call option. The price of the noncallable is readily computed from the current term structure of interest rates or from the technique described in the previous subsection. We now discuss the pricing of the underlying call options.

The value of the embedded call option is a contingent claim and depends on future interest rates. Unfortunately, traditional analysis of callable bonds tends to ignore the interest rate dependence of these options. Typically, two types of yield rates, the *yield-to-maturity* and the *yield-to-call*, are calculated. The yield-to-maturity is computed by assuming the call option is not exercised, whereas the yield-to-call assumes the bond is called at the earliest possible call date. The lesser of these yields is known as the *yield-to-worst*. The bond price corresponding to the yield-to-worst is the price-to-worst and is assumed to be the price of the callable bond.

With the development of option price theory, a slightly more sophisticated approach is adopted by first pricing the embedded option component and then using relation (7.9.2) to arrive at the callable bond price. The option is priced using the Black-Scholes model, which assumes that the underlying option is European with the first call date as the maturity of the option.

This model is an improvement over the traditional approach. Nevertheless, it suffers from several drawbacks. First, it does not capture the American nature of the underlying option. The callable bond typically has a period of call protection, during which the option cannot be exercised. However, the bond is callable at any time after this protection period. Second, the strike price of a callable bond normally starts at a price above par and declines steadily until it reaches par. The Black-Scholes model uses a single strike price and a single maturity. Also, most embedded options in callable bonds are long-dated, and the constant interest rate and constant volatility assumptions made in the Black-Scholes framework become questionable. A better approach for overcoming these problems is to rely on stochastic interest rate model so that various characteristics of the bond option can be captured.

Before we get into the stochastic details of pricing the embedded call options, it is instructive to present some of the key differences in how callable and noncallable bonds behave in response to interest rate changes. Figure 7.7 plots the prices of two noncallable 10% bonds against different flat yield curves. The curve with the steeper slope has a 30-year maturity, and the other curve has a 5-year maturity. This figure also illustrates that any shift in interest rates has a larger impact on bonds with longer maturities. Also, for a high level of interest rates, the price of the bond with the longer maturity is less than the price of the corresponding bond with the shorter maturity.

FIGURE **7.7** │ *Noncallable Bond Price Versus Short Rate*

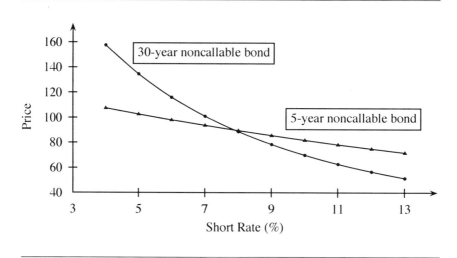

Consider next a 10%, 30-year bond callable at par at any time after 5 years. When the interest rates are high, the likelihood of a call is low, and the callable bond behaves more like a 30-year noncallable bond. When the interest rates are low, the price of the 30-year bond is well above par and increases the chance of being called in the fifth year; thus, we would expect that the price of the callable bond closely resembles the 5-year noncallable bond in this case. For any intermediate level of interest rates, the price of the callable bond is always less than the lesser price of these noncallable bonds. Thus, the lesser value of these two noncallable bonds provides an upper bound for the callable bonds.

We next illustrate the pricing of a callable bond based on the Black-Derman-Toy interest rate lattice. Consider a 4-year 10% coupon bond that is callable at par at any time on or after the second year. The noncallable bond is equivalent to the coupon bond discussed in the previous subsection; therefore, the price of the noncallable bond is 104.03. Because the embedded bond option can be exercised after the second year, the backward induction method described in Chapter 6 can be used to determine the appropriate option value.

At each call period, two components must be computed, the exercise value and the holding value. The exercise value, $E(t, n)$, represents the payoff if the option is exercised at node $(t, n)$, and the holding value, $H(t, n)$, represents the value of the option when the option is not exercised at node $(t, n)$. Therefore, we have

$$E(t, n) = [B(t, n) - K]^+$$

where $K$ is the strike price and $B(t, n)$ is the price of the underlying bond at node $(t, n)$. In our example, these values are displayed in Figure 7.6. We also have

$$H(t, n) = \frac{qV(t+1, n+1) + (1-q)V(t+1, n)}{1 + i(t, n)}$$

where $V(i, j)$ denotes the value of the option at node $(i, j)$. The recursive valuation algorithm involves comparing the exercise value to the holding value. The larger of the two values is the option value for node $(t, n)$; that is,

$$V(t, n) = \max[E(t, n), H(t, n)].$$

Figure 7.8 shows the values of the exercise values, the holding values and the option values at each node of the lattice as a result of pricing the bond call option in our example. For instance, at node $(2, 0)$, $B(2, 0) = 103.95$ from Figure 7.6, thus $E(2, 0) = [103.95 - 100]^+ = 3.95$ because the call price is 100. Also, the holding value $H(2, 0)$ is calculated as

$$H(2, 0) = \frac{1}{1 + i(2, 0)} \left[ \frac{V(3, 0)}{2} + \frac{V(3, 1)}{2} \right]$$

$$= \frac{2.44 + 0}{2(1 + 0.0695)} = 1.14.$$

Therefore, $V(2, 0) = \max[3.95, 1.14] = 3.95$, indicating that it is optimal to exercise the option at this node. Note that in years 1 and 0, early exercise is not permitted, and thus the the option values are simply discounted at the then prevailing short rates. The option value at time 0 is 0.87, and so the corresponding callable bond price is $104.03 - 0.87 = 103.16$.

Next, consider how the price of a callable bond changes as interest rates change. Figure 7.9 is similar to Figure 7.7 except that the price behavior of a 10% 30-year callable bond is also plotted. Consistent with the earlier discussion, when the

FIGURE 7.8 | *The Pricing of Embedded Call Options*

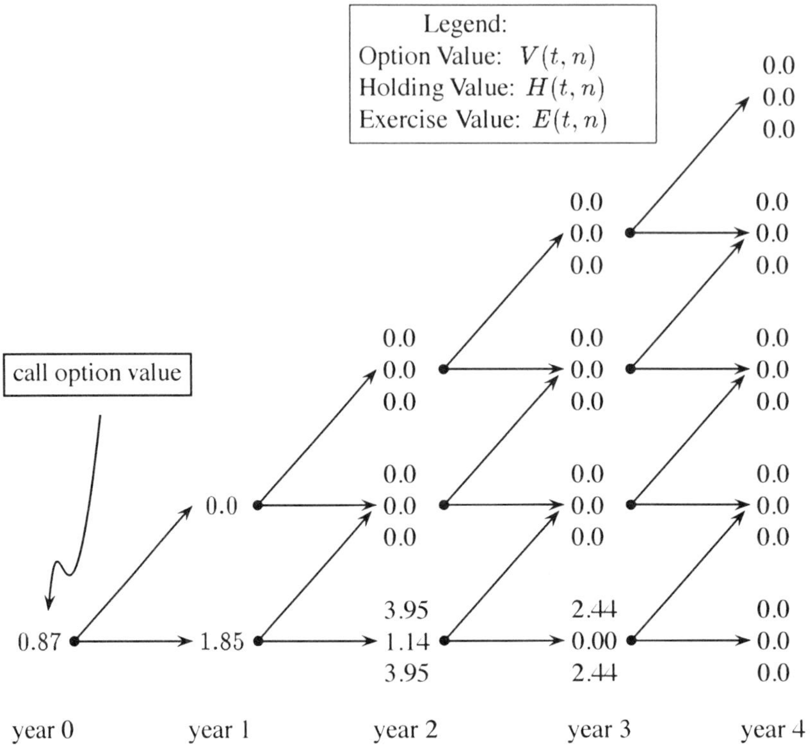

interest rates are high, the callable bond price mimics the 30-year noncallable bond price. When the rates are low, the callable bond is more likely to be called and behaves more like the 5-year noncallable bond. In this situation, the price of the callable bond is substantially less than the corresponding price of a 30-year non-callable bond. This effect is known as *price compression*. The embedded call option reduces the price of the otherwise identical noncallable bond. Figure 7.9 also illustrates that for intermediate levels of interest rates, the upper bound substantially overestimates the price of the callable bonds. The upper bound corresponds to the prices obtained from the traditional yield-to-worst approach and thus gives a good approximation to the callable bond price only when the interest rates are quite high or quite low. Note also that the price curve for the callable bonds is not a straight line. In fact, when the rates are low, the bond's price behavior exhibits negative convexity, and when the rates are high, the bond's price behavior illustrates positive convexity.

This section shows how the price sensitivities of a callable bond can be computed using a stochastic interest rate model. The price sensitivity of callable bonds will be important in the context of asset-liability management. We have seen that the

FIGURE 7.9 | *Price Behavior of Noncallable and Callable Bonds*

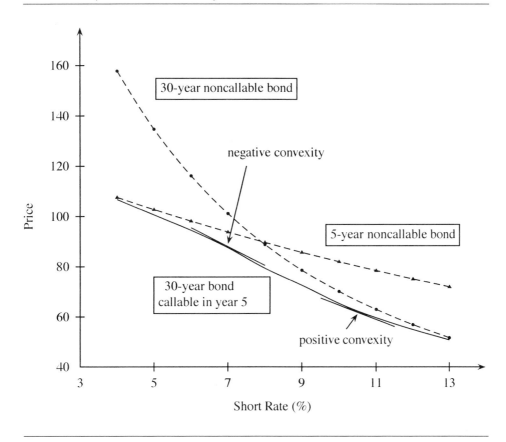

traditional methods do not fully capture the entire picture. A stochastic interest rate model is needed to properly model the price behavior.

# Section 7.10
# Mortgage-Backed Securities

The valuation of mortgage-backed securities (see Section 2.8) basically involves an application of (3.7.4). As background to mortgage-backed securities, we first discuss conventional fixed-rate mortgages.

## SECTION 7.10.1 | FIXED-RATE MORTGAGES

A fixed-rate mortgage contract is a common type of residential mortgage in the United States. The term of the mortgage can be as long as 30 years, and it is repaid by level, periodic installments over its term. The amount of the repayment is based on the mortgage interest rate at the inception of the contract, which we call the *contract rate*. Note that this interest rate is established at inception and is the rate used to compute the outstanding balance should the mortgage be prepaid. We adopt the following notation:

$n =$ term of the mortgage

$B_t =$ outstanding balance on mortgage at time $t$ allowing for principal repaid at time $t$; by construction, $B_0$ is the original amount of the loan

$c_0 =$ mortgage contract interest rate per period

$A =$ level payment on the mortgage at the end of each period

$I_t =$ the interest repaid in the $t$-th payment

$P_t =$ the principal repaid in the $t$-th payment.

The amount of the level payment is found from

$$B_0 = \sum_{t=1}^{n} \frac{A}{(1 + c_0)^t}.$$

(7.10.1)

Since $A$ is a constant independent of $t$ we have

$$A = \frac{B_0}{\sum_{t=1}^{n}(1 + c_0)^{-t}}.$$

(7.10.2)

The interest component of the $t$-th payment is

$$I_t = c_0 B_{t-1}, \quad t = 1, 2, \ldots, n.$$

(7.10.3)

In each payment, the principal plus the interest is constant and equal to $A$:

$$A = I_t + P_t, \quad t = 1, 2, \ldots, n.$$

(7.10.4)

The outstanding principal after the $t$-th payment is

$$B_t = A \sum_{s=1}^{n-t} \frac{1}{(1 + c_0)^s}, \quad t = 1, 2, \ldots, n.$$

(7.10.5)

Note that the outstanding balance is computed with reference to the rate $c_0$, which was established at contract inception. The amount $B_t$ represents the amount the homeowner would pay if he or she refinanced the mortgage at time $t$.[3] If interest rates

---

[3] Assuming there is no penalty to refinance.

have fallen to $c_1 (< c_0)$ since the mortgage was first taken out, this may be an attractive possibility since the new mortgage would involve lower periodic payments. Suppose the new mortgage is amortized over the remaining term $(n - t)$. The revised periodic payment $A_1$ is given by

$$A_1 \sum_{s=1}^{n-t} \frac{1}{(1 + c_1)^s} = A \sum_{s=1}^{n-t} \frac{1}{(1 + c_0)^s} = B_t. \tag{7.10.6}$$

It is clear that $A_1 < A$.

**Example 7.10.1.** Suppose a 30-year fixed-rate mortgage was taken out at a contract rate of 10% per year with annual payments. The initial amount of the loan was 100,000. Find the level yearly payment and compute the current balance outstanding after the tenth payment. If current mortgage rates have dropped to 6% per year (when the tenth payment has just been made), find the revised yearly payment that would amortize the mortgage over the next 20 years.

Using the formulas given above we find the following:
- Level yearly payment is 10,607.92.
- Outstanding balance after 10 years is 90,311.24.
- Revised yearly payment for next 20 years is 7,873.75. ∎

If there are no penalties associated with prepayments, it is rational for the homeowner to repay the mortgage when mortgage interest rates fall. Essentially, the homeowner has an embedded call option.

The incentive to repay as interest rates fall has consequences for the asset-liability management of the financial institution that holds a portfolio of residential mortgages in its asset portfolio. As interest rates fall, mortgages are prepaid, and the duration of these assets shortens. To make matters worse, the repayments have to be reinvested at lower interest rates. As we saw earlier, this prepayment risk can be shifted to other investors by issuing mortgage-backed securities.

## SECTION 7.10.2 | MODELING PREPAYMENTS

There are several factors that influence a homeowner's propensity to prepay. We have already noted that the level of interest rates will affect the incidence of prepayments. A very simple framework for discussing prepayments is a convenient way to begin. First, assume that prepayments are deterministic and only depend on time. There is a useful correspondence between prepayments and the traditional actuarial survival function used to model mortality in life contingencies.

Imagine that there is a large pool of identical mortgage loans. Each mortgage is to be amortized over $n$ periods. Let $l_0$ denote the number of mortgages in the pool. If there are no prepayments, the number of mortgages would remain constant throughout the entire term. We can use the life-table framework to analyze the case when there are prepayments. Prepayments correspond to *deaths*. Let $l_t$ denote the number of mortgage loans outstanding at the end of period $t$ and let $d_t$ denote the number of mortgages repaid during the period $(t, t + 1]$. We have

$$d_t = l_t - l_{t+1}. \tag{7.10.7}$$

This survival table summarizes the mortgage prepayment experience, and although it is written just as a function of time, we are able to include other relevant state variables, such as the prevailing interest rate. We provide a simple example in Table 7.2 in which we start with 100,000 loans and 5% of them are prepaid at the end of each year.

Suppose an investor purchases a pass-through mortgage-backed security in which the prepayment experience corresponds to Table 7.2. The investor's share of the total periodic cash flows from the pool of loans includes not only the scheduled periodic payments but also the principal repayments resulting from prepayments. It is instructive to illustrate the pattern of the cash flows on a pass-through security under this prepayment assumption. The total cash flows on the entire pool at period $t$ are

$$l_{t-1}(I_t + P_t) + d_{t-1}B_t. \tag{7.10.8}$$

The total payment at time $t$ consists of the regular scheduled payments on all loans that were in force at time $t - 1$, together with the repayments for the loans that are repaid at time $t$.

### TABLE 7.2 | *Survival Table Based on 5% Decrement Each Year*

| Year | Number of Mortgages at Start of Year | Number of Mortgages Repaid at End of Year | Number of Mortgages at End of Year |
|------|--------------------------------------|-------------------------------------------|------------------------------------|
| 1 | 100,000 | 5,000 | 95,000 |
| 2 | 95,000 | 4,750 | 90,250 |
| 3 | 90,250 | 4,513 | 85,737 |
| 4 | 85,737 | 4,287 | 81,450 |
| 5 | 81,450 | 4,072 | 77,378 |

Suppose that the original pool consists of identical fixed-rate 30-year term mortgages. Assume the initial mortgage contract rate is 10% per year. We saw in Example 7.10.1 that the level yearly payment in this case is 10,607.92. A pass-through security with initial face value of 1,000 would receive 106.08 every year if there were no prepayments. In Table 7.3, we provide details of the cash flows on a pass-through security both for a 5% and 0% prepayment assumptions.

TABLE **7.3** | *Composition of Cash-Flow Payments on a 1,000 Face Amount Pass-Through MBS with Different Deterministic Prepayment Assumptions: Contract Rate = 10% per Year, Mortgage Term = 30 Years*

| Prepayment Assumption | Year | Scheduled Principal | Interest | Principal from Prepayments | Total |
|---|---|---|---|---|---|
| 5% per year | 1 | 6.08 | 100.00 | 49.70 | 155.78 |
| | 2 | 6.35 | 94.42 | 46.89 | 147.67 |
| | 3 | 6.64 | 89.10 | 44.22 | 139.95 |
| | 4 | 6.94 | 84.01 | 41.66 | 132.61 |
| | 5 | 7.25 | 79.15 | 39.21 | 125.62 |
| 0% per year | 1 | 6.08 | 100.00 | 0 | 106.08 |
| | 2 | 6.69 | 99.39 | 0 | 106.08 |
| | 3 | 7.36 | 98.72 | 0 | 106.08 |
| | 4 | 8.09 | 97.99 | 0 | 106.08 |
| | 5 | 8.90 | 97.18 | 0 | 106.08 |

## SECTION **7.10.3** | INTEREST-SENSITIVE PREPAYMENTS

Prepayments depend on a number of factors. For simplicity, we just assume that they consist of a deterministic component as well as an interest-sensitive component. To model the dependence on interest rates, we make further simplifying assumptions. We assume that the propensity to prepay is proportional to the difference between the current interest rate and some reference rate. The reference rate could well be the original contract rate in the mortgage. This means that the number of surviving mortgages depends on both the time and a state variable that determines the interest rate. If we use a recombining lattice model (such as the Black-Derman-Toy model), the same framework can be used to model the prepayments. In general, the prepayments will depend on the interest rate path.

Suppose that the relevant interest rate evolves according to a more general lattice model. At time 0, the rate is $i(0, 0)$. At time 1, the rate is either $i(1, 0)$ or $i(1, 1)$. We do not necessarily assume that the lattice recombines so that at time 2 there are four possible values of the rate. Suppose we label the numbers of mortgages that survive in a given pool using the same notation. The initial number of mortgages is $l(0, 0)$, and the numbers at time 1 are $l(1, 0)$ and $l(1, 1)$. The structure is given in Figure 7.10.

FIGURE **7.10** | *Structure of the General Interest Rate Lattice*

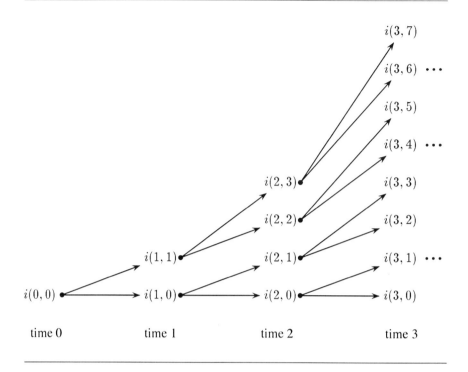

At time $t$, there are $2^t$ states, and we label these states as

$$\{0, 1, 2, \ldots, (2^t - 1)\}. \tag{7.10.9}$$

The node $(t, k)$ has the two following successors at time $t + 1$: $(t + 1, 2k)$ and $(t + 1, 2k + 1)$. We assume that the rate of prepayments at time $t$ in state $k$ has the following form:

$$\frac{d(t, k)}{l(t, k)} = g(i(t, k)), \quad k = 0, 1, \ldots, 2^{t-1}, \tag{7.10.10}$$

that $g$ is a nonincreasing function of the current short-term interest rate $i(t, k)$, and that $0 \leq g \leq 1$. This means that as the current short-term rate falls the rate of prepayments increases. Considerable econometric research has gone into the determinants of prepayment experience. Later we assume a simple prepayment assumption that captures the essence of these types of securities.

The numbers of survivors at time $t+1$ in the two successor states are $l(t+1, 2k)$ and $l(t + 1, 2k + 1)$ where

$$l(t + 1, 2k) = l(t, k) - d(t, k)$$

and

$$l(t + 1, 2k + 1) = l(t, k) - d(t, k).$$

We see that these two values are equal so that the number of survivors after a down-move from state $k$ to state $2k$ is equal to the number of survivors after an up-move from state $k$ to state $2k + 1$.

### SECTION 7.10.4 | NUMERICAL EXAMPLE OF MBS VALUATION

To give a numerical example of the valuation of a pass-through mortgage-backed security, we use a short-term (3-year) mortgage so that we can display most of the steps in the calculations. First, assume the initial loan is 100,000, the amortization rate is 9% per year, and the yearly payment is 39,505.48. We now assume that the lattice of short-term interest rates is given in Figure 7.11. These rates are used for discounting future cash flows and also for determining the interest-sensitive component of prepayments.[4]

### FIGURE 7.11 | *General Interest Rate Lattice Example (Rates in %)*

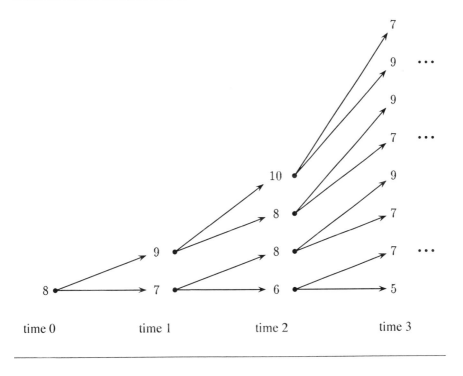

<hr>

[4]In practice mortgage rates are more likely to be based on the long interest rates than the short rates.

Suppose that the prepayment rate based on this interest rate lattice depends on the current short-term interest rate and the reference rate, $i_0$. The prepayment function is a table look-up form as shown in Table 7.4. The rate is structured in such a way that it depends only on the difference between the reference rate and the current short-term rate. For instance, suppose the reference is 8% and the current short-term rate is 7%, then the prepayment rate is 15% according to Table 7.4.

### TABLE 7.4 | *Prepayment Rates*

| $i_0 - i(t, k)$ | Prepayment Rate $d(t, k)$ |
|:---:|:---:|
| $\geq 3\%$ | 0.3 |
| 2 | 0.25 |
| 1 | 0.15 |
| 0 | 0.05 |
| $-1$ | 0.04 |
| $-2$ | 0.03 |
| $\leq -3$ | 0.02 |

We also assume that there are $l(0, 0) = 100{,}000$ identical mortgages at time 0 in the initial pool. We can compute the numbers of survivors along each interest rate path using the prepayment rates in Table 7.4 and the interest rate lattice in Figure 7.11. The results are given in Figure 7.12.

For example, if the short-term interest rates over the first 3 years are 8%, 9%, and 8% corresponding to nodes $(0, 0)$, $(1, 1)$, and $(2, 2)$, and the reference rate is 8%, the number of survivors along this path are 100,000, 95,000, 91,200, and 86,640. The cash flows that arise along this interest rate path can be computed as we saw earlier in Table 7.2; we assume an initial notional amount of 10,000. The schedule of payments for this path is given in Table 7.5. The present value of these cash flows is obtained by discounting them along the interest rate path actually experienced:

$$10{,}118.59 = \frac{4{,}298.02}{1.08} + \frac{3{,}890.75}{(1.08)(1.09)} + \frac{3{,}602.90}{(1.08)(1.09)(1.08)}.$$

Using the same approach, we can obtain the cash flows along each of the eight interest rate paths and the present value of these cash flows by discounting them by the interest rates along the path. The value of the MBS is obtained by weighting the present value along each path by the probability of that path occurring. If we assume that the one-period probabilities of an up-jump in the interest rate lattice are each equal to one-half, then the probability of each path is 1/8. On this basis the current market value of the MBS is 10,173.56. The intervening steps in this calculation are summarized in Table 7.6.

FIGURE **7.12** │ *Survival Numbers under Prepayment Function*

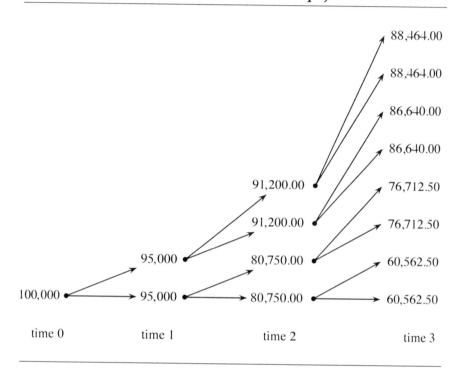

TABLE **7.5** │ *Schedule of Payments under 10,000 MBS for Interest Rate Path {8%, 9%, 8%}: Original Mortgage 3-Year Term, Contract Rate 9%*

| Year | Short Rate | Interest | Scheduled Principal | Principal from Prepayments | Total |
|------|------|----------|-----------|------------|-------|
| 1 | 8% | 900.00 | 3,050.55 | 347.47 | 4,298.02 |
| 2 | 9 | 594.18 | 3,158.84 | 137.73 | 3,890.75 |
| 3 | 8 | 297.49 | 3,305.49 | 0.00 | 3,602.90 |

| Present Value of Payments | | | | | 10,118.59 |

TABLE 7.6 | *Value of Payments under 10,000 MBS for All Eight*
*Interest Rate Paths: Original Mortgage*
*3-Year Term, Contract Rate 9%*

| Path | Short-Term Rate | | | Value of Cash Flows along Path |
| | Year 1 | Year 2 | Year 3 | |
| --- | --- | --- | --- | --- |
| 1 | 8% | 7% | 6% | 10,278.53 |
| 2 | 8 | 7 | 6 | 10,278.53 |
| 3 | 8 | 7 | 8 | 10,230.30 |
| 4 | 8 | 7 | 8 | 10,230.30 |
| 5 | 8 | 9 | 8 | 10,118.59 |
| 6 | 8 | 9 | 8 | 10,118.59 |
| 7 | 8 | 9 | 10 | 10,067.07 |
| 8 | 8 | 9 | 10 | 10,067.07 |

# Section 7.11
# Single-Premium Deferred Annuities

In this section we discuss the valuation of single-premium deferred annuities (SPDAs), which were introduced in Chapter 2. The valuation problem is similar to the valuation of mortgage-backed securities, presented in the previous section. SPDA cash flow is interest sensitive, as we explain below, and therefore its valuation is similar to the valuation of a mortgage-backed security.

There are, of course, fundamental differences between mortgage-backed securities and single-premium deferred annuities. The MBS is a traded security that provides its owner a share of cash flows from a dedicated pool of mortgages. On the other hand, the SPDA usually is not a security for U.S. regulatory purposes. It is classified as an insurance contract, but most SPDA buyers (and companies that sell them) consider the SPDA to be an investment contract just as bank certificate of deposit (CD) buyers (and issuing banks) consider CDs to be investment contracts. Normally, SPDA owners do not consider cash flow from the contract to be derived from a pool of assets, although the issuing company may have a portfolio dedicated to its SPDA liabilities.

We see that the typical SPDA provides the owner with an option to surrender the contract early and that this option is analogous to the option that mortgage borrowers have to prepay their loans. As interest rates rise, SPDA owners tend to surrender and reinvest in higher-yielding alternatives; this is analogous to the mortgage borrowers' propensity to prepay and refinance their loans when interest rates drop.

Experience studies have shown that owners of these options exercise them in different ways, which we cannot hope to model on an individual basis. This leads us to a model based on the probability of surrender (analogous to the prepayment option of mortgage borrowers). A mortagage-backed security investor buys a contract and receives cash flow from the pool, which varies as underlying prepayment options are exercised. A single-premium deferred annuity investor buys a contract and receives no cash flow until it matures, unless the investor exercises the option to take the cash back early (subject to a surrender charge). The MBS owner is short a prepayment option, whereas the SPDA owner is long a prepayment option.

## SECTION 7.11.1 | SPDA CONTRACT TERMS

We use as much of the model from Section 7.10 as possible to take advantage of the analogy between the contracts and the previously developed short-rate paths. First, let us survey briefly typical policy terms of the SPDA.

The typical SPDA sold in the U.S. is intended for individual investors. Many investors consider the SPDA to be an alternative to a CD issued by a bank.[5] SPDA customers make single cash payments to the insurance company. The company credits the customer's deposit with interest it earns, subject to a guaranteed minimum interest rate over the term of the contract, usually 3 to 10 years. At any time, the customer can surrender the contract for the cash value (that is, the principal and interest), subject to a surrender charge that diminishes with time. The customer can hold the policy to maturity at which time the accumulated value can be taken in cash or converted to an annuity. The annuity conversion rate may be guaranteed. Most SPDA contracts allow the customer to convert to an annuity any time without paying a surrender charge.

The SPDA death benefit is usually the account value without application of the surrender charge. Although the death benefit and annuity conversion option provide an element of mortality risk, the major risk the company bears comes from the interest guarantees and the surrender option. Costs of issuing an annuity (mainly commissions to agents or brokers) are paid at the time of issue, but the company earns its profit over the life of the contract. So, if a customer surrenders early, the company may not make a profit, even though it collects the surrender charge. Because the mortality guarantee is a small part of the valuation problem and most readers will have already mastered life insurance mathematics, we omit the death benefit and annuity conversion option from further consideration. Thus, we can consider the

---

[5]In the U.S., the SPDA has a tax advantage relative to a bank-issued CD. The SPDA customer pays no tax on interest until it is received as cash, but the CD customer pays taxes as interest is credited, whether or not it is actually received. This disparity of tax treatment on nearly identical products has lead the U.S. banking industry to lobby Congress for equal treatment, so far without success.

SPDA to be a loan by the customer to the insurance company, which can be called early by the customer, subject to a penalty.

The typical surrender charge is expressed as a percentage of the cash value. For a 10-year contract, typical surrender charges might be 7% during the first year, 6% in the second year, eventually grading down to 1% in the seventh year, and no surrender charge thereafter. For this section, we use $s(t)$ to denote the surrender charge factor to be applied if the customer surrenders at time $t$.

The interest rate that the company credits to the policyholder's account is based on a strategy it develops. Presumably the crediting rate is linked to assets that are earmarked to support the policy. For our discussion, we denote the credited rate applied at time $t$ in state $k$ by $i_c(t, k)$. In practice, the crediting rate is a function of the short rate, but for ease of exposition we assume that it is simply the short rate, subject to a minimum rate guarantee. Of course, the crediting rate could be based on a more complicated formula. For example, a company could offer the current 5-year rate. To model this, we would just have to calculate the price of a 5-year bond at each node in the lattice corresponding to the term of the SPDA. The lattice would run 5 years beyond the expiration of the SPDA, but otherwise there is no problem in doing this. However, for this discussion we assume that $i_c(t, k) = \max(i(t, k), i_1)$, where $i_1$ is the guaranteed rate.

The surrender option, like the MBS prepayment option, may not be exercised optimally. Some customers need their money sooner than planned and are willing to bear the surrender charge to get it. Some customers do not surrender even if competitive alternatives seem better to other customers. We know from a Society of Actuaries study [118] that customers tend to avoid surrendering when $s(t)$ is positive. In addition, they are more likely to surrender when there are better alternative interest rates available, just as borrowers are more likely to repay when borrowing rates drop. The alternative competitive rate is analogous to the reference rate in the MBS model, so we continue to refer to it as the reference rate.

In practice, the reference rate varies with time and the state of the short rate, but for ease of exposition we assume that the reference rate is a constant $i_0$. Usually the probability of surrender is determined by a a function of the surrender charge $s(t)$ and the spread $i_0 - i_c(t, k)$ of the reference rate over the credited rate, and a base surrender probability $q \geq 0$. As in the previous section, $l(t, k)$ denotes the number of contracts surviving to time $t$ in state $k$ and $d(t, k)$ denotes the number of contracts terminating between $t$ and $t + 1$. A reasonable choice for the surrender probability is

$$\frac{d(t, k)}{l(t, k)} = \min\{1, q \exp\{-b_1 s(t) - b_2[i_0 - i_c(t, k)]\}\}.$$

Because there cannot be more surrenders than there are contracts (no contracts are reinstated), we must have $0 \leq d(t, k) \leq l(t, k)$. This is provided by the formula because the exponential function is positive, and we have a maximum of one. The Society of Actuaries study [118] showed that SPDA surrenders increase as the surrender change decreases and surrenders increase as the spread increases, both intuitively reasonable. This means that $b_1$ and $b_2$ are positive. In the next subsection, we show how surrenders and cash flows develop along short-rate paths.

## SECTION 7.11.2 | INTEREST-SENSITIVE SURRENDERS

We focus now on a 4-year SPDA for illustrative purposes. The crediting rate is the short rate subject to a minimum guarantee $i_1$ of 7.5% per year. The surrender charge is $s(1) = 10\%$ in the first year, $s(2) = 6\%$ in the second year, $s(3) = 3\%$ in the third year, and zero in the fourth year. Some reasonable values for the function defining the probability of surrender are $i_0 = 0.08$, $q = 0.03$, $b_1 = 0.5$, and $b_2 = 0.4$. These values are consistent with the Society of Actuaries study but are used here for purposes of illustration only.

We suppose that the company issues a large enough number of annuities so that we can assume that the expected cash flows given by the model are very likely to be close to the actual future values. Consider a unit of $10,000 in the company's SPDA pool, all issued under the stated conditions.

The interest rate structure is the same as the one we used in the MBS example given in Figure 7.11. For each path, apply the minimum rate guarantee to get credited rates. From the credited rates, calculate the accumulated value of 10,000 along each path, conditional on no surrenders. We need this to calculate the annual cash flow to contract owners who surrender and the maturity value for those who do not. This is very much like the calculation of expected cash flows to a portfolio of endowment insurance policyholders. The accumulated cash flows are shown in Table 7.7.

TABLE 7.7 | *Accumulated Cash Values Calculated from the Credited Rates along Each Path That Are Available to Surviving Contract Owners*

| Path | \multicolumn{5}{Cash Values} | | | | |
|------|--------|--------|--------|--------|--------|
|      | 0 | 1 | 2 | 3 | 4 |
| 1 | 10,000 | 10,800 | 11,610 | 12,481 | 13,417 |
| 2 | 10,000 | 10,800 | 11,610 | 12,481 | 13,417 |
| 3 | 10,000 | 10,800 | 11,610 | 12,539 | 13,479 |
| 4 | 10,000 | 10,800 | 11,610 | 12,539 | 13,667 |
| 5 | 10,000 | 10,800 | 11,772 | 12,714 | 13,667 |
| 6 | 10,000 | 10,800 | 11,772 | 12,714 | 13,858 |
| 7 | 10,000 | 10,800 | 11,772 | 12,949 | 14,115 |
| 8 | 10,000 | 10,800 | 11,772 | 12,949 | 14,374 |

Next calculate the survival probabilities along each path, which are shown in Table 7.8. Using the survival probabilities and the cash values conditional on survival to each contract anniversary, we can calculate the expected payments of surrender values at time $t < 4$ and the expected maturity payment at $t = 4$. The expected surrender cash flow at $t = 2$ on path 2 is $(0.9715 - 0.9433) \times 11,610 = 307$. The expected maturity value at $t = 4$ on path 2 is $0.8883 \times 13,417 = 11,918$. Table 7.9 shows the expected cash flows along each path. The last column gives the present value of the cash flows discounted along each path (using the short rates). The value to the insurance company of the liability to make the expected surrender and maturity payments is the average over all eight paths. This amounts to 9,769 per 10,000 of

TABLE 7.8 | *Survival Probabilities along a Path Given the Probability of a Contract Surviving to Time t along the Given Path*

| Path | Survival Probabilities $l(t, k)/l(0, 0)$ | | | | |
|------|--------|--------|--------|--------|--------|
|      | 0      | 1      | 2      | 3      | 4      |
| 1    | 1.0000 | 0.9715 | 0.9433 | 0.9156 | 0.8885 |
| 2    | 1.0000 | 0.9715 | 0.9433 | 0.9156 | 0.8883 |
| 3    | 1.0000 | 0.9715 | 0.9433 | 0.9154 | 0.8881 |
| 4    | 1.0000 | 0.9715 | 0.9433 | 0.9154 | 0.8878 |
| 5    | 1.0000 | 0.9715 | 0.9431 | 0.9152 | 0.8879 |
| 6    | 1.0000 | 0.9715 | 0.9431 | 0.9152 | 0.8876 |
| 7    | 1.0000 | 0.9715 | 0.9431 | 0.9150 | 0.8874 |
| 8    | 1.0000 | 0.9715 | 0.9431 | 0.9150 | 0.8872 |

TABLE 7.9 | *Expected Cash Flows at Time t along Each Path*

| Path | Expected Cash Flows | | | | | Present Value |
|------|---|-----|-----|-----|--------|---------------|
|      | 0 | 1   | 2   | 3   | 4      |               |
| 1    | 0 | 277 | 307 | 335 | 11,921 | 10,065 |
| 2    | 0 | 277 | 307 | 335 | 11,918 | 9,889  |
| 3    | 0 | 277 | 307 | 339 | 11,970 | 9,758  |
| 4    | 0 | 277 | 307 | 339 | 12,134 | 9,714  |
| 5    | 0 | 277 | 314 | 344 | 12,135 | 9,714  |
| 6    | 0 | 277 | 314 | 344 | 12,301 | 9,670  |
| 7    | 0 | 277 | 314 | 353 | 12,526 | 9,670  |
| 8    | 0 | 277 | 314 | 353 | 12,752 | 9,668  |

deposits accepted from SPDA customers at $t = 0$. The difference $10,000 - 9,769 = 231$ is the value of the minimum rate guarantee the company provides (offset by the surrender charges).

## SECTION 7.11.3 | OTHER ISSUES IN SPDA MODELING

The term of an SPDA is typically 3 to 10 years, and the interest model may have nodes at monthly intervals. This would allow modeling cash flow monthly, but the number of paths would be enormous; even for a 3-year contract we would have $2^{3 \times 12 - 1} \geq 34$ billion paths. Usually we would select a sample of the paths, perhaps only 10,000 to 50,000 paths, and calculate the present value of cash flows along each sample path. The average over the sample is an estimate of the average over the entire population of paths. The issue of how many sample paths to take is considered by Robbins et al. [158].

The model we discussed for valuing the company's liability at the time the policy is issued can be adapted to determine the value of the company's liability sometime after the policies are issued. This method would give a value related to the bond market through the term structure model. Note that this may be different from the liability the company may be required to carry in its statutory financial statements.

Some companies offer an additional benefit, called a *bail-out* option. The bail-out option allows the customer to surrender without a surrender charge if the crediting rate drops below a certain level. For example, the bail-out rate might be 6%, and the guarantee minimum rate might be 4%. If the current crediting rate of 8% falls below 6%, some customers will surrender, and they will not pay a surrender change. Others will not, perhaps because competitive rates have dropped too. These customers continue getting the credited rate subject to the 4% minimum.

Interesting variations of the SPDA are being developed all the time. The *CD annuity* is like a bank CD in that it provides no surrender values. Like the usual SPDA, the entire cash value is available as a death benefit, and it can be annuitized without penalty. The CD annuity can pay a higher rate of return because it does not provide a surrender value. This higher rate of return is attractive to investors with low liquidity needs, and in the U.S. it has the advantage of deferral of tax on accumulation of interest. The CD annuity is not really a CD, of course. As an insurance contract it is not transferable. Although CDs cannot be "surrendered," they can be sold in a secondary market, so bank CD owners have greater liquidity than annuity CD owners.

Another recent development is an SPDA with a minimum rate keyed to an equity index. This presents a much more difficult valuation problem because the index introduces another random factor. These SPDAs are called *equity-indexed* annuities, and insurance companies use options to hedge these equity-index guarantees.

# Section 7.12
# Exercises

### Exercise 7.1

Show that if the term structure of zero-coupon bond prices $P(t, t + T)$ is not nonincreasing in $T$, then an arbitrage opportunity exists, and some forward interest rate is negative.

### Exercise 7.2

Show that if the fixed rate in a forward swap is equal to the swap rate, then the prices of the corresponding payer and receiver swaptions are equal to each other.

### Exercise 7.3

Suppose the fixed interest rate in a swap is equal to the swap rate. Show that the price of the corresponding cap (i.e., it has the same payment times, and the cap rate equals the swap rate) equals the price of the corresponding floor.

### Exercise 7.4

Consider Example 7.4.2 with the short rates as given. However, instead of starting with $P(t, 3)$ as indicated and with $Q(\omega) = 1/12$ for all $\omega \in \Omega$, suppose the martingale measure is $Q(\omega_1) = \cdots = Q(\omega_8) = 0.08$ and $Q(\omega_9) = \cdots = Q(\omega_{12}) = 0.09$. Use (7.4.3) to derive the zero-coupon bond prices $P(t, T)$ for all $t < T$; $T = 1, 2, 3$, and all $\omega \in \Omega$.

### Exercise 7.5

Verify that $v_0$ and the three values of $v_1$ are correct for the swap in Example 7.5.1 by showing they equal the expected discounted values of the cash flows. (Reminder: Use the martingale measure.)

### Exercise 7.6

Suppose the current term structure of zero-coupon bond prices is given by $P(0, 1) = 0.9512$, $P(0, 2) = 0.8958$, $P(0, 3) = 0.8378$, $P(0, 4) = 0.7772$, $P(0, 5) = 0.7189$, $P(0, 6) = 0.6650$, $P(0, 7) = 0.6126$, and $P(0, 8) = 0.5667$. What is the swap rate for a payer forward start swap with initial payment at time 3 and final payment at time 8?

## Exercise 7.7

Compute $v_0$ and the three values of $v_1$ for the swap in Example 7.5.1, assuming, however, that the fixed rate is 5.5% instead of 4.5%.

## Exercise 7.8

Compute the time-0 value of the payer swaption that corresponds to the swap in Exercise 7.7 and is exercised at time 1. Compute the time-0 price of the corresponding receiver swaption, using both risk-neutral valuation and the appropriate parity relationship.

## Exercise 7.9

Show that the time-$t$ price of a floorlet that is settled in arrears at time $\tau$ is

$$\pi_t = B_t E_t^Q \left[ \frac{(1 + \kappa) \max\{0, \, P(\tau - 1, \tau) - (1 + \kappa)^{-1}\}}{B_{\tau-1}} \right].$$

Use this to verify that the floor in Example 7.5.3 has initial value approximately equal to $2,912.

## Exercise 7.10

Compute the time-0 value of the floor in Example 7.5.3 by calculating the expectation under the martingale measure of the discounted cash flow.

## Exercise 7.11

Compute the time-0 value of the cap analyzed in Example 7.5.3, assuming, however, that the cap rate is 5.5% instead of 4.5%.

## Exercise 7.12

Verify the binomial forward equation discussed in Section 7.6.

## Exercise 7.13

Show that the solution to (7.7.11) and (7.7.16) is $i(2, 0) = 6.949\%$ and $\sigma(2) = 1.4119$.

## Exercise 7.14

Show that the recursive relation (7.7.17) holds under the Black-Derman-Toy model.

## Exercise 7.15

Consider a European call option on the futures price of Example 7.8.1. The expiration date is time 1, and the exercise price is 0.95. Show that the time-0 price of this call is 0.0044. Compute the time-0 price of the European put having the same exercise price and expiration date.

## Exercise 7.16

Specify the futures price process at times 0 and 1 as in Example 7.8.1, assuming, however, that the risk-neutral probability measure is $Q(\omega_1) = \cdots = Q(\omega_8) = 0.08$ and $Q(\omega_9) = \cdots = Q(\omega_{12}) = 0.09$. Then compute the initial prices of the European put and call options as in Exercise 7.15.

## Exercise 7.17

Verify that the following valuation formula involving Green's function can be used to compute the price of the coupon bond in Section 7.9:

$$\text{Price} = \sum_{t=1}^{3}\sum_{n=0}^{t} A(0, 0, t, n)C(t, n) + \sum_{n=0}^{4} A(0, 0, 4, n)[C(4, n) + V(4, n)].$$

## Exercise 7.18

Construct a 5-year Black-Derman-Toy interest rate lattice with a yearly time step using the following term structures.

| Maturity $t$ | Yield $Y(0, t)$ | Short-Rate Volatility $\sigma_y(t)$ |
|:---:|:---:|:---:|
| 1 | 6% | 20% |
| 2 | 7 | 19 |
| 3 | 8 | 17.24846 |
| 4 | 9 | 15.62123 |
| 5 | 10 | 14.05365 |

Note that the yield curve is similar to Table 7.1. Compare the calibrated lattice to Figure 7.3. What do you conclude?

## Exercise 7.19

Construct an interest rate lattice. Assume that initially all interest rates are 8% per year and that the term structure of the volatilities (in % per year) of the short rate for term $t$ (in years) is

$$\sigma(t) = 25.5 - \frac{t}{2}.$$

Write a program to compute a 30-year Black-Derman-Toy interest rate lattice with yearly time steps.

## Exercise 7.20

Consider three different mortgage pools:

- Pool A consists of fixed-rate mortgages with term equal to 5 years.
- Pool B consists of fixed-rate mortgages with term equal to 10 years.
- Pool C consists of fixed-rate mortgages with term equal to 30 years.

Suppose that the initial contract rate for all mortgages is 8.5% per year and that the prepayment rate is given by

$$\frac{d(t, k)}{l(t, k)} = g(t) \max[1, e^{10(0.08 - i(t, k))}]$$

$$g(t) = \begin{cases} 0.02t, & 0 < t \le 5 \\ 0.12 - 0.004t, & 5 < t \le 30 \end{cases}$$

where $i(t, k)$ is the short rate at time $t$ and state $k$. In the case of each pool, find the value to a purchaser of a pass-through mortgage-backed security with face value of 10,000. Assume that there is an expense charge of 1/2% per year and that this is deducted from the interest component pool cash flow before payments are made to the MBS holders. The MBS holder thus receives interest computed at 8.0% instead of 8.5%. Based on the Black-Derman-Toy lattice from Exercise 7.19, and using simulation, find the values of the MBS

a. For Pool A

b. For Pool B

c. For Pool C

## Exercise 7.21

A company issues an SPDA that matures in 5 years. Determine the company's initial liability per 10,000 of SPDA deposits at the time of deposit, subject to the following information. Surrender charges are 10% in year 1, 8% in year 2, 4% in year 3, 2% in year 4, and zero in year 5. The crediting rate is the short rate plus 0.5% subject to a minimum guarantee of 8%. The interest rate model is the one you developed for Exercise 7.19 with annual effective rates. The reference rate and other surrender probability parameters are as follows:

$$\frac{d(t, k)}{(t, k)} = \min\{1, q \exp(-b_1 s(t) - b_2(i_0 - i(t, k)))\}$$

with $q = 0.03$, $i_0 = 0.08$, $b_1 = 0.5$, and $b_2 = 0.4$.

# CHAPTER 8

## PORTFOLIO SELECTION

## *Section 8.1*
## *Introduction*

In this chapter, we deal with discrete-time portfolio analysis. Typical assets are common stocks, bonds, domestic or foreign cash, and real estate. An investment in an asset over one period of time leads to a rate of return

$$R = \frac{S_1 - S_0 + D(0, 1)}{S_0}$$

where $S_0$ and $S_1$ denote the price of the asset at the beginning and the end of the period and $D(0, 1)$ represents the value (at the end of the period) of the net cash flows during the holding period (dividends, coupon payments, etc.). We assume that there are $N$ assets, and that the rates of return over one period are given by the random variables $R_1, R_2, \ldots, R_N$.

If an investor chooses a portfolio

$$\boldsymbol{x}^T = (x_1, \ldots, x_N), \quad \sum_{i=1}^{N} x_i = 1$$

where $x_i$ denotes the proportion of wealth invested in asset $i$, then the portfolio rate of return is given by the random variable

$$R_{\boldsymbol{x}} = \sum_{i=1}^{N} x_i R_i.$$

The first two moments of $R_x$ are given by

$$\mu_x = E[R_x] = \sum_{i=1}^{N} x_i E[R_i] = \sum_{i=1}^{N} x_i \mu_i \tag{8.1.1}$$

and

$$\begin{aligned}
\sigma_x^2 &= \text{Var}(R_x) \\
&= \sum_{i=1}^{N} \sum_{j=1}^{N} x_i x_j \text{Cov}(R_i, R_j) \\
&= \sum_{i=1}^{N} \sum_{j=1}^{N} x_i \sigma_{ij} x_j
\end{aligned} \tag{8.1.2}$$

where $\Sigma = (\sigma_{ij})$ denotes the covariance matrix.

Typically, asset returns are positively correlated (see Figure 8.1 and Table 8.1). Therefore, the law of large numbers does not apply, and diversification allows us only to reduce, not to eliminate, the risk of portfolio returns.

For the one-period portfolio problem two basic approaches are available, Markowitz's mean variance and utility maximization.

FIGURE **8.1** | *Evolution of the Market*

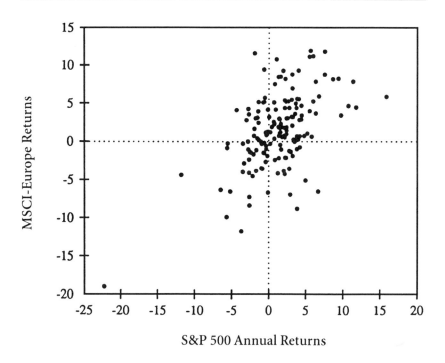

TABLE **8.1** | *Correlation Coefficients and Standard Deviations*

|  | U.S. Cash | U.S. Bond | Japan Bond | Euro Bond | U.S. Equity | Japan Equity | Euro Equity |
|---|---|---|---|---|---|---|---|
| U.S. cash | 1.00 | 0.20 | −0.04 | 0.12 | 0.08 | −0.02 | 0.12 |
| U.S. bond | 0.20 | 1.00 | 0.22 | 0.34 | 0.33 | 0.13 | 0.30 |
| Japan bond | −0.04 | 0.22 | 1.00 | 0.68 | −0.07 | 0.53 | 0.30 |
| Euro bond | 0.12 | 0.34 | 0.68 | 1.00 | −0.04 | 0.38 | 0.51 |
| U.S. equity | 0.08 | 0.33 | −0.07 | −0.04 | 1.00 | 0.21 | 0.61 |
| Japan equity | −0.02 | 0.13 | 0.53 | 0.38 | 0.21 | 1.00 | 0.49 |
| Euro equity | 0.12 | 0.30 | 0.30 | 0.51 | 0.61 | 0.49 | 1.00 |
| Standard deviation | 0.50 | 5.23 | 14.66 | 12.52 | 14.45 | 26.19 | 17.06 |

Based on US$ total return from January 1985 until April 1996.

**Markowitz Mean Variance**

Among practitioners, Markowitz's [128] method is the most popular.[1] Given the constraint on portfolio weights, investors have two objectives:

- Maximization of the expected value $\mu_x$ of the portfolio return
- Minimization of portfolio risk, which is measured by $\sigma_x^2$ or $\sigma_x$.

According to individual preferences, an investor puts weights on these conflicting objectives and maximizes

$$2\tau\mu_x - \sigma_x^2, \quad \text{with } \tau \geq 0.$$

The parameter $\tau$ is called *risk tolerance*.[2] Hence, according to Markowitz, the optimization problem to be solved is[3]

$$
\begin{array}{l}
\max_{x \in \mathfrak{R}^N} \left\{ 2\tau\mu_x - \sigma_x^2 \right\} \\[2mm]
\text{subject to } \sum_{i=1}^{N} x_i = 1
\end{array}
$$

---

[1] A similar approach can be found in the work of de Finetti [46].

[2] Later we discuss the relationship with the Arrow-Pratt risk measures.

[3] Instead of choosing a risk tolerance $\tau \geq 0$ the investor can fix an appropriate lower level $c$ for the expected value of $\mu_x$ of the portfolio return. This leads to the equivalent optimization problem:

$$\min_{x \in \mathfrak{R}^N} \sigma_x^2, \quad \text{subject to} \quad \mu_x \geq c \quad \text{and} \quad \sum_{i=1}^{N} x_i = 1.$$

or more explicitly

$$\max_{x \in \mathfrak{R}^N} \left\{ 2\tau \sum_{i=1}^{N} \mu_i x_i - \sum_{i=1}^{N} \sum_{j=1}^{N} x_i \sigma_{ij} x_j \right\}$$

$$\text{subject to } \sum_{i=1}^{N} x_i = 1$$

(8.1.3)

This approach has several important advantages:

- The preferences of the investor enter in a most simple way. Only the risk tolerance $\tau$ has to be determined.
- Only the first and second moments $\mu_i$ and $\sigma_{ij}$ of the asset returns are needed.[4]
- Even if additional linear equality or inequality constraints on $x^T = (x_1, \ldots, x_N)$ are imposed, the optimization problem remains quadratic convex, and powerful numerical algorithms can be used.[5]
- Without additional constraints the optimality conditions are linear in $x^T = (x_1, \ldots, x_N)$ and in the Lagrange multiplier. From this fact the most popular results in modern portfolio theory were derived, such as structure of the efficient frontier, mutual fund theorems, and the capital-asset-pricing model.

**Utility Maximization**

From the point of view of decision theory, it is most natural to maximize the expected utility of end-of-period wealth. Let $W_0$ denote the initial wealth of an investor. Then a portfolio $x$ leads to the final wealth

$$W_0(1 + R_x) = W_0 \left( 1 + \sum_{i=1}^{N} x_i R_i \right)$$

at the end of one period. The optimization problem of the investor is then given by

$$\max_{x \in \mathfrak{R}^N} E[u(W_0(1 + R_x))]$$

$$\text{subject to } \sum_{i=1}^{N} x_i = 1$$

(8.1.4)

---

[4]A drawback of the Markowitz approach is its inability to cover situations where the distribution of the portfolio rate of return cannot be fully characterized by the first two moments. In particular, this applies to all situations where options are involved.

[5]Of course, the Markowitz method should not be applied on subportfolios. Due to correlations, an isolated treatment of subportfolios leads to inefficiency.

The preferences of the investor are represented by the utility function $u(\cdot)$. For practical purposes this second approach is rarely used. Preferences and the distributions of expected returns enter in a complex way, and the numerical calculation of optimal portfolios is rather difficult. However, in contrast to the Markowitz method, maximization of expected utility has a sound theoretical foundation.

For some distributions of the stochastic returns (e.g., multivariate normal) or if the utility function is quadratic, both methods yield the same result. Hence, for the one-period portfolio problem we can conclude that the Markowitz method is appropriate for practical purposes and is consistent with decision theory under proper assumptions.

For the multiperiod portfolio problem in discrete time, the situation is more difficult. No satisfactory extension of the Markowitz method is available for a $T$-period framework. Let us assume that an investor wants to maximize the expected utility of final wealth. To do this, a portfolio choice

$$\boldsymbol{x}^T(t) = (x_1(t), \ldots, x_N(t)), \quad t = 1, \ldots, T$$

has to be made in each point of time $t - 1$. This leads to a dynamic programming problem, which can be solved by backward induction. Typically, the optimal portfolio choice $\boldsymbol{x}^*(t)$ at a point of time $t-1$ will depend on the realized asset returns in preceding periods.

This chapter concentrates on one-period portfolio optimization. In Section 8.2 the Markowitz model and its main properties are presented, and the capital-asset-pricing model is derived (see Sharpe [174] and Lintner [122]). Section 8.3 deals with additional linear constraints (no short selling of assets, constraints on asset categories, etc.). An interpretation of the corresponding Lagrange multipliers is given, and we show that inequality constraints may lead to kinks in the efficient frontier. In Section 8.4 the Markowitz model is extended to an asset-liability model. We discuss the structure of efficient portfolios and explain the use of liability hedging credits (see Sharpe and Tint [176]).

Section 8.5 deals with shortfall constraints. A shortfall occurs if the rate of return on a portfolio falls below some given level (for example, 0% or $-2\%$). Very often investors put a limit on the probability of a shortfall (for example, 5% or 10%). Under a multivariate normal distribution of asset returns shortfall constraints have a simple analytical form, and the corresponding optimization problem has interesting properties. Factor models are introduced in Section 8.6; in particular, the arbitrage pricing theory (APT) is based on a factor model. In practice, factor models are used for risk control.

In Section 8.7 the relationship between the Markowitz approach and expected utility maximization in a one-period model is analyzed. The multiperiod portfolio problem is formulated in Section 8.8, and dynamic programming is applied to this problem in Section 8.9. Finally, in Section 8.10 we show how a risk-neutral computational approach can be used to solve the multiperiod problem.

# Section 8.2
# The Markowitz Model and Its Properties

### SECTION 8.2.1 │ THE MARKOWITZ MODEL

Markowitz's 1952 pioneering work influenced the further development of portfolio theory in many ways. At that time, it was the major breakthrough in developing a model that fully took into account the covariances between asset returns. Moreover, the mathematical structure of his model allowed for the derivation of the capital-asset-pricing model and for mutual fund theorems.

In the Markowitz model no distinction is made between capital income and the price changes of assets. There are $N$ risky assets (common stocks or stock indices, domestic and foreign bonds or bond indices, foreign cash, real estate, commodities, etc.) with stochastic returns $R_1, \ldots, R_N$.

We assume that the first and second moments of $R_1, \ldots, R_N$ exist. Then the vector of expected values and the covariance matrix are given by

$$\boldsymbol{\mu}^T = (\mu_1, \ldots, \mu_N), \quad \text{with } \mu_i = \mathrm{E}[R_i], \quad i = 1, \ldots, N,$$

and

$$\boldsymbol{\Sigma} = (\sigma_{ij})_{i,j=1,\ldots,N}, \quad \text{with } \sigma_{ij} = \mathrm{Cov}(R_i, R_j), \quad i, j = 1, \ldots, N.$$

As mentioned before, the rate of return on a portfolio

$$\boldsymbol{x}^T = (x_1, \ldots, x_N), \quad \sum_{i=1}^{N} x_i = 1$$

is given by

$$R_x = \sum_{i=1}^{N} x_i R_i.$$

According to (8.1.1) and (8.1.2) we obtain

$$\mu_x = \mathrm{E}[R_x] = \boldsymbol{\mu}^T \boldsymbol{x} \tag{8.2.1}$$

and

$$\sigma_x^2 = \mathrm{Var}(R_x) = \boldsymbol{x}^T \boldsymbol{\Sigma} \boldsymbol{x}. \tag{8.2.2}$$

In mean-variance portfolio analysis efficiency is defined as follows:

**Definition 8.2.1.** *A portfolio $x^*$ is called (mean-variance) efficient if there exists no portfolio $x$ with $\mu_x \geq \mu_{x^*}$ and $\sigma_x^2 < \sigma_{x^*}^2$.*

The Markowitz method deals with the calculation of efficient portfolios. There are several ways to do this; the variant we present is widely used in practice. To get efficient portfolios, practitioners use a very simple type of objective function. They maximize (see Figure 8.2)

$$2\tau\mu_x - \sigma_x^2, \quad \tau \geq 0 \tag{8.2.3}$$

where the parameter $\tau$ is the *risk tolerance* of the investor. In fact, it can be shown that $\tau$ is closely related to the corresponding Pratt-Arrow risk measure.[6] Hence, for an investor with risk tolerance $\tau$ ($\tau \geq 0$) we must solve the optimization problem

$$\boxed{\begin{aligned} &\max_{x \in \mathfrak{R}^N} \left\{2\tau\mu_x - \sigma_x^2\right\} \\ &\text{subject to } \sum_{i=1}^{N} x_i = 1 \end{aligned}}.$$

---

[6]Given initial wealth $W_0$, then under a portfolio choice $x$ end-of-period wealth is given by $W_0(1 + R_x)$. An approximation by a Taylor polynomial of second order leads to

$$u[W_0(1 + R_x)] \approx u(W_0) + W_0 \cdot u'(W_0) \cdot R_x + \frac{1}{2} W_0^2 u''(W_0) \cdot R_x^2.$$

Ignoring third and higher noncentral moments, we can approximate that expected utility by

$$\begin{aligned} E[u[W_0(1 + R_x)]] &\approx u(W_0) + W_0 \cdot u'(W_0) \cdot \mu_x + \frac{1}{2} W_0^2 u''(W_0) \cdot \left[\sigma_x^2 + \mu_x^2\right] \\ &\approx u(W_0) - \frac{W_0^2}{2} u''(W_0) \cdot \left[-\frac{2u'(W_0)}{W_0 u''(W_0)}\mu_x - \left(\sigma_x^2 + \mu_x^2\right)\right]. \end{aligned}$$

Given this approximation, maximizing expected utility is approximately equivalent to the maximization of

$$\frac{2}{R_R}\mu_x - \left(\sigma_x^2 + \mu_x^2\right)$$

where $R_R$ denotes the Arrow-Pratt measure of relative risk aversion. Furthermore, if the term $\mu_x^2$ can be neglected, our objective function becomes

$$\frac{2}{R_R}\mu_x - \sigma_x^2,$$

which is equivalent to (8.2.3). Of course, ignoring $\mu_x^2$ as well as third and higher noncentral moments makes sense only in some cases with an extremely short investment period. See also Grauer [79].

FIGURE **8.2** | *Comparing Portfolios*

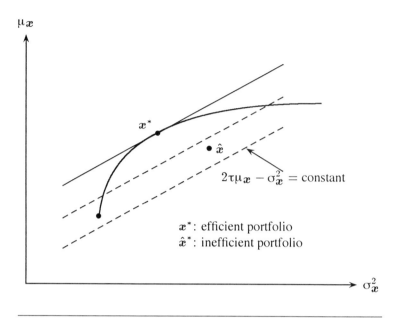

or

$$\max_{x \in \Re^N}\{2\tau\mu^T x - x^T \Sigma x\}$$

$$\text{subject to } e^T x = 1$$

(8.2.4)

with $e^T = (1, 1, \ldots, 1) \in \Re^N$. Without giving a proof, we note that solving (8.2.4) for all $\tau \in [0, +\infty)$ leads to the whole set of efficient portfolios. The set of all points in the $(\mu_x, \sigma_x^2)$-diagram that correspond to efficient portfolios is called the *efficient frontier* (see Figure 8.3). The efficient portfolio corresponding to $\tau = 0$ is called the *minimum variance* portfolio $x^{\text{MIN}}$.

Next we discuss the mathematical properties of the optimization problem (8.2.4). Since any covariance matrix $\Sigma$ is positive semi-definite, the objective function is quadratic concave. Hence, (8.2.4) is a quadratic convex optimization problem. Its Lagrangian function is given by

$$\mathcal{L}(x, \lambda) = 2\tau\mu^T x - x^T \Sigma x + \lambda(e^T x - 1).$$

FIGURE **8.3** | *Set of Efficient Portfolios*

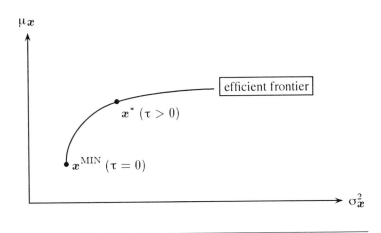

Because of the Kuhn-Tucker theorem,[7] the optimality conditions

$$2\tau\mu - 2\Sigma x + \lambda e = 0, \tag{8.2.5}$$

$$e^T x = 1 \tag{8.2.6}$$

are necessary and sufficient for a global optimum. Moreover, they are linear in the portfolio weights $x^*$ and the Lagrange multiplier $\lambda$.

To calculate the set of efficient portfolios we assume the following:

***Assumption A.1.*** (i) $\Sigma$ is positive definite,[8] and

(ii) $e, \mu$ are linearly independent.

---

[7]The Kuhn-Tucker theorem (see the appendix to this chapter) deals with convex optimization. It assumes a concave objective function, a convex feasible set, and some regularity conditions. According to the Kuhn-Tucker theorem the Lagrange conditions are necessary and sufficient for a global optimum.

[8]Hence the covariance matrix $\Sigma$ has to be nonsingular. A singular covariance matrix $\Sigma$ is equivalent to the condition

$$\text{Var}(a_1 R_1 + \cdots + a_N R_N) = 0, \quad \text{for some } (a_1, \ldots, a_N) \neq (0, \ldots, 0).$$

If the covariance matrix $\Sigma$ is singular, then one of the following situations occurs:

1. There exists a riskless investment strategy.
2. One asset is a combination of other assets (e.g., a stock index and its subindices may be available as investment opportunities).
3. The market allows for arbitrage.

### Set of Efficient Portfolios

Setting $\tau = 0$ in (8.2.5) leads to the minimum variance portfolio

$$x^{\text{MIN}} = \frac{1}{e^T \Sigma^{-1} e} \Sigma^{-1} e.$$

After some calculations, we obtain for fixed $\tau > 0$

$$x^* = \frac{1}{e^T \Sigma^{-1} e} \Sigma^{-1} e + \tau \left( \Sigma^{-1} \mu - \frac{e^T \Sigma^{-1} \mu}{e^T \Sigma^{-1} e} \Sigma^{-1} e \right) \qquad (8.2.7)$$

or[9]

$$x^* = x^{\text{MIN}} + \tau z^*, \quad \text{with } z^* = \Sigma^{-1} \mu - \frac{e^T \Sigma^{-1} \mu}{e^T \Sigma^{-1} e} \Sigma^{-1} e. \qquad (8.2.8)$$

To summarize, all efficient portfolios are of the form

$$x^* = x^{\text{MIN}} + \tau z^*, \quad \tau \geq 0 \qquad (8.2.9)$$

where $x^{\text{MIN}}$ is the minimum variance portfolio, which depends on the covariance matrix $\Sigma$ but not on the vector $\mu$, and $z^*$ depends on $\Sigma$ and $\mu$ and has the property

$$\sum_{i=1}^{N} z_i^* = 0.$$

Hence, $z^*$ is a self-financing portfolio in the sense that long positions are financed by corresponding short positions. Formula (8.2.9) may be interpreted as follows: the portfolio $x^{\text{MIN}}$ leads to a minimum-risk position. This position is corrected by investing in the self-financing return-generating portfolio $z^*$. This is illustrated in Figure 8.4 for $N = 3$.

### Efficient Frontier

Formula (8.2.9) allows an easy calculation of the *efficient frontier*. Using

$$\text{Cov}(R_{x^{\text{MIN}}}, R_{z^*}) = z^{*T} \Sigma x^{\text{MIN}} = 0$$

we obtain

$$\mu_{x^*} = \mu_{x^{\text{MIN}}} + \tau \mu_{z^*}$$

---

[9]In Exercise 8.3, you are asked to verify these formulas.

FIGURE **8.4** | *Efficient Portfolios*

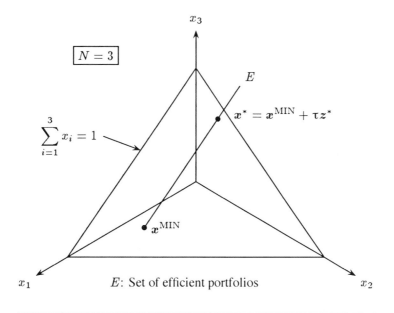

$E$: Set of efficient portfolios

and

$$\sigma_{x^*}^2 = \sigma_{x^{\mathrm{MIN}}}^2 + \tau^2 \sigma_{z^*}^2.$$

Hence, the efficient frontier is parabolic in the $(\mu_x, \sigma_x^2)$-diagram and hyperbolic in the $(\mu_x, \sigma_x)$-diagram (see Figure 8.5).

### SECTION **8.2.2** | THE MARKOWITZ MODEL WITH A RISKLESS ASSET

Very often domestic cash is assumed to be riskless. In this subsection we show that the foregoing results do not change dramatically if a riskless asset is available. We assume that in addition to the risky assets $i = 1, \ldots, N$ with covariance matrix $\Sigma = (\sigma_{ij})_{i, j=1,\ldots,N}$ and expected values $\mu = (\mu_i)_{i=1,\ldots,N}$, a riskless asset ($i = 0$) exists with a deterministic rate of return $R_0 = r$.[10] Then a portfolio

$$\mathbf{x}^T = (x_0, x_1, \ldots, x_N), \quad \sum_{i=0}^{N} x_i = 1$$

---

[10]We use $r$ instead of $i$ as the one-period rate of interest.

FIGURE **8.5** | *Efficient Frontiers*

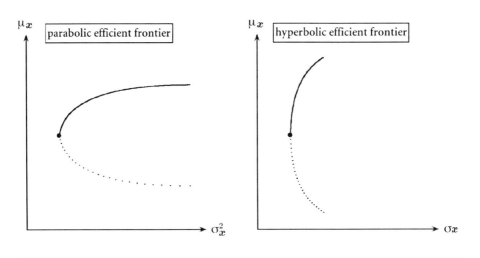

has the total rate of return

$$R_x = \sum_{i=0}^{N} x_i R_i.$$

Assumption A.1 has to be modified as follows:

**Assumption A'.1.**    (i) $\Sigma$ is positive definite, and
(ii) $r \neq \mu_i$ for some $i \in \{1, \ldots, N\}$.

Under A'.1 we can show the following:

1.    Efficient portfolios are of the form[11]

$$x^* = x^{\text{MIN}} + \tau z^*$$

with

$$x^{\text{MIN}} = (1, 0, \ldots, 0)^T \in \Re^{N+1}$$

and

$$\sum_{i=0}^{N} z_i^* = 0.$$

2.    The efficient frontier is parabolic in the $(\mu_x, \sigma_x^2)$-diagram and linear in the $(\mu_x, \sigma_x)$-diagram (see Figure 8.6).

---

[11] To avoid tedious notation, we do not give an explicit formula for $z^*$ in this case.

FIGURE **8.6** | *Efficient Portfolios and Frontiers*

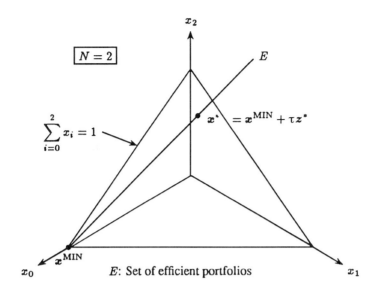

$E$: Set of efficient portfolios

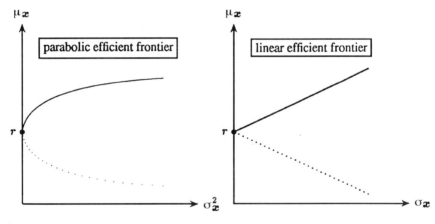

## Practical Issues

If a riskless asset $i = 0$ with a rate of return $R_0 = r$ is available, an efficient portfolio $\boldsymbol{x}^{*T} = (x_0^*, x_1^*, \ldots, x_N^*)$ satisfies the optimality conditions

$$2\tau r + \lambda = 0, \tag{8.2.10}$$

$$2\tau\hat{\mu} - 2\Sigma\hat{x}^* + \lambda\hat{e} = 0, \tag{8.2.11}$$

$$\sum_{i=0}^{N} x_i^* = 1 \tag{8.2.12}$$

where

$$\hat{\mu}^T = (E([R_1]), \ldots, E([R_N])), \qquad \hat{e}^T = (1, 1, \ldots, 1) \in \mathfrak{R}^N,$$

$$\Sigma = (\mathrm{Cov}(R_i, R_j))_{i,j=1,\ldots,N}, \qquad \hat{x}^{*T} = (x_1^*, \ldots, x_N^*).$$

From the optimality conditions several useful relationships for practical portfolio management can be derived.

### Reverse Optimization

The Markowitz approach is used for portfolio problems with hundreds of investment opportunities. However, in some important applications the investment opportunities are asset categories such as domestic cash, domestic stock and bond indices (or subindices), and foreign indices. In such a framework the number of asset categories rarely exceeds 20 ($N \le 20$).

For the practical application of the Markowitz method, estimates for the covariance matrix $\Sigma$ and the vector of expected returns $\hat{\mu}$ are needed. Most practitioners use historical data for the estimation of $\Sigma$ (for details see Grinold and Kahn [80]). Very often the estimate is based on monthly data over a period of 5 years (60 observations). The results are more or less satisfactory. In downside markets, the variances and correlation coefficients are typically larger than in upside markets. Moreover, the correlation coefficients between currencies are not very stable.

A major problem in portfolio management is the estimation of $\hat{\mu}$. Typically, the optimal portfolio $x^*$ is very sensitive with respect to $\hat{\mu}$. Therefore, a precise estimate of $\hat{\mu}$ is crucial. It is tempting to calculate arithmetic or geometric means over the last few years. However, with such a method, long periods of sharp stock price increases (declines) would be naively extrapolated into the future. An indirect method is more promising. From the optimality conditions (8.2.10) and (8.2.11) we obtain

$$2\tau(\hat{\mu} - r\hat{e}) = 2\Sigma\hat{x}^*$$

or

$$\begin{pmatrix} E[R_1] - r \\ \vdots \\ E[R_N] - r \end{pmatrix} = \frac{1}{\tau}\Sigma\hat{x}^*. \tag{8.2.13}$$

Formula (8.2.13) is applied as follows:

- $\Sigma$ is estimated with historical data.
- $r$ is known (for example, return on domestic cash).
- For $x^*$ we use a portfolio that is representative for an average investor.

- An appropriate choice of the risk tolerance $\tau$ guarantees that the risk premia $E[R_i] - r$ correspond to the very long historical level (for example, 5% for equities).

This method is called *reverse optimization*, and the corresponding values for $\hat{\mu}$ are called *neutral returns*. For tactical asset allocation, these neutral returns are corrected according to the forecasts of the investment research department.

### Estimation of the Risk Tolerance

Sometimes we know quite well the type of portfolio that could be appropriate for an investor (such as 40% equities and 60% fixed income). However, for the fine-tuning of strategic asset allocation (for example, investments in foreign bond and equity markets), the risk tolerance $\tau$ would be needed. In fact, given an efficient portfolio $x^*$ the calculation of the implied risk tolerance $\tau$ is straightforward. From (8.2.10) to (8.2.12) we conclude

$$2\tau(r x_0^* + \hat{\mu}^T \hat{x}^*) - 2\hat{x}^{*T}\Sigma\hat{x}^* + \lambda = 0. \tag{8.2.14}$$

Combining this result with (8.2.10) leads to

$$2\tau(E[R_{x^*}] - r) - 2\,\text{Var}(R_{x^*}) = 0$$

or

$$\tau = \frac{\text{Var}(R_{x^*})}{E[R_{x^*}] - r}. \tag{8.2.15}$$

### Marginal Utilities of Portfolio Changes

Typically an investor starts with an inefficient initial portfolio $x$. Very often the solution $x^*$ of

$$\max_{x}\{2\tau(r x_0 + \hat{\mu}^T \hat{x}) - \hat{x}^T\Sigma\hat{x}\}$$
$$\text{subject to } \sum_{i=1}^{N} x_i = 1$$

cannot be implemented for institutional reasons and due to high transaction costs.[12] In such a situation the "marginal utilities" are a very useful tool.

---

[12]Transaction costs can be fully taken into account by a proper modification of the optimization problem. However, the new problem is considerably more complex.

Substituting

$$x_0 = 1 - \sum_{i=1}^{N} x_i$$

into the objective function leads to

$$F(\hat{x}) = 2\tau[r + (\hat{\mu} - r\hat{e})^T \hat{x}] - \hat{x}^T \Sigma \hat{x}.$$

The components $(\partial/\partial x_i) F(\hat{x})$ of the gradient

$$\text{grad } F(\hat{x}) = 2\tau(\hat{\mu} - r\hat{e}) - 2\Sigma \hat{x}$$

$$= (2\tau(\mathrm{E}[R_i] - r) - 2 \operatorname{Cov}(R_x, R_i))_{i=1,\dots,N} \qquad (8.2.16)$$

are called *marginal utilities*. In fact, an increase $dx_i$ in the weight of asset $i$ and a corresponding reduction of the riskless asset leads to a marginal change $(\partial/\partial x_i) F(\hat{x}) dx_i$ of the objective function. By increasing (decreasing) the positions with high (low) marginal utilities, an inefficient portfolio $x$ can be considerably improved.

### SECTION 8.2.3 | AN EXAMPLE: PORTFOLIO CHOICE OF A SWISS INVESTOR

As an example we illustrate the portfolio problem for a Swiss investor. The investor wants to invest in the asset categories ($N = 9$):

- Swiss cash, Swiss bonds, Swiss equities
- Euro bonds, Euro equities
- U.S. bonds, U.S. equities
- Japan bonds, Japan equities.

The reference currency is the Swiss franc; therefore, all returns have to be calculated in Swiss francs. Furthermore, all asset categories including Swiss cash are considered to be risky. The annualized covariance matrix $\Sigma$ was estimated on the basis of quarterly data from 1980 to 1993. A modified reverse optimization method led to an estimation for $\hat{\mu}$ (see Subsection 8.2.2). Using the formulas in Section 8.2.1, we can calculate $x^{\mathrm{MIN}}$ and $z^*$ (Table 8.2). According to (8.2.9), all efficient portfolios $x^*$ are of the form

$$x^* = x^{\mathrm{MIN}} + \tau z^*, \quad \tau \geq 0.$$

For example, the efficient portfolio $x^*$ corresponding to $\tau = 0.194$ has an expected return $\mu_x^* = 6\%$ (Table 8.2).

Obviously, the negative portfolio weight for U.S. bonds is not very convincing. We return to this example in Sections 8.3 and 8.4.

TABLE **8.2** │ *Portfolio Choice of a Swiss Investor*

| Asset Category | $\mu$ | $x^{\text{MIN}}$ | $z^*$ | $x^*$ ($\tau = 0.194$) |
|---|---|---|---|---|
| Swiss cash | 4.0% | 96.2% | −277.0% | 42.5% |
| Swiss bonds | 4.5 | −0.1 | 88.3 | 16.9 |
| Swiss equities | 9.0 | −0.5 | 28.6 | 5.1 |
| Euro bonds | 5.5 | 3.0 | 43.1 | 11.4 |
| Euro equities | 9.5 | 0.9 | 116.6 | 23.5 |
| U.S. bonds | 6.5 | −0.7 | −64.5 | −13.2 |
| U.S. equities | 9.5 | −0.2 | 32.1 | 6.1 |
| Japan bonds | 6.0 | −0.4 | 36.2 | 6.6 |
| Japan equities | 9.5 | 1.8 | −3.4 | 1.1 |

## SECTION **8.2.4** │ THE CAPITAL-ASSET-PRICING MODEL

Sharpe [174] and Lintner [122] developed an equilibrium model for asset prices. Beyond general assumptions such as frictionless markets, their model is structured as follows:

1. There is a riskless asset, ($i = 0$), and $N$ risky assets $i = 1, \ldots, N$.
2. There are $K$ investors, $k = 1, \ldots, K$, with the following characteristics:

  a. Investors $k = 1, \ldots, K$ agree on the first and second moments of returns on assets $i = 1, \ldots, N$; that is,

$$\hat{\mu}^{(k)} = \hat{\mu}, \qquad \Sigma^{(k)} = \Sigma, \quad k = 1, \ldots, K.$$

  b. Assumption A'.1 is satisfied.
  c. All investors have a planning horizon of one period.
  d. Each investor $k$ invests an initial wealth $W_k > 0$.
  e. Each investor $k$ has a risk tolerance $\tau_k > 0$ and chooses the corresponding mean-variance efficient portfolio.

As we know from Section 8.2.2, each investor $k = 1, \ldots, K$ chooses a portfolio

$$x^{(k)} = x^{\text{MIN}} + \tau_k z^*.$$

Total demand results in a portfolio

$$x^{M.d} = \frac{1}{W} \sum_{k=1}^{K} W_k x^{(k)}$$

with

$$W = \sum_{k=1}^{K} W_k,$$

or

$$x^{M.d} = x^{MIN} + \tau_M z^*$$

with

$$\tau_M = \frac{1}{W} \sum_{k=1}^{K} W_k \tau_k.$$

Hence, $x^{M.d}$ is an efficient portfolio and satisfies the optimality conditions (8.2.10)–(8.2.12). In analogy to (8.2.13) and (8.2.15), we obtain

$$\Sigma \hat{x}^{M.d} = \begin{pmatrix} \mathrm{Cov}(R_1, R_{x^{M.d}}) \\ \vdots \\ \mathrm{Cov}(R_N, R_{x^{M.d}}) \end{pmatrix} = \tau_M \begin{pmatrix} \mathrm{E}[R_1] - r \\ \vdots \\ \mathrm{E}[R_N] - r \end{pmatrix} \qquad (8.2.17)$$

and

$$\mathrm{Var}(R_{x^{M.d}}) = \tau_M(\mathrm{E}[R_{x^{M.d}}] - r). \qquad (8.2.18)$$

Dividing (8.2.17) by (8.2.18) leads to

$$\mathrm{E}(R_i) - r = \frac{\mathrm{Cov}(R_i, R_{x^{M.d}})}{\mathrm{Var}(R_{x^{M.d}})}(\mathrm{E}[R_{x^{M.d}}] - r), \quad i = 1, \ldots, N. \qquad (8.2.19)$$

We have used only the efficiency of the total demand portfolio $x^{M.d}$. In equilibrium, total demand has to be equal to total supply. Total supply is given by the market portfolio $x^M$, where all assets are held in proportion to their market values. Due to the equilibrium condition

$$x^{M.d} = x^M,$$

the market portfolio $x^M$ has to satisfy (8.2.19) as well. Using the notation $R^M = R_{x^M}$, we obtain the capital-asset-pricing model relationship

$$\mathrm{E}[R_i] - r = \frac{\mathrm{Cov}(R_i, R^M)}{\mathrm{Var}(R^M)}(\mathrm{E}[R^M] - r)$$

$$= \beta_i(\mathrm{E}[R^M] - r), \quad i = 1, \ldots, N. \qquad (8.2.20)$$

**Comments**

1. In practical applications, the return on a stock index (or on a combination of stock and bond indices) is used as a proxy for $R^M$.

2. The coefficient $\beta_i = \text{Cov}(R_i, R^M)/\text{Var}(R^M)$ is called the *beta coefficient* of asset $i$.

3. The difference $E[R_i] - r$ is the *risk premium* on asset $i$.

4. The difference $E[R^M] - r$ is the *risk premium* on the market portfolio.

5. The CAPM relationship tells us that $\text{Cov}(R_i, R^M)$ and not $\text{Var}(R_i)$ is relevant for the risk premium on asset $i$. This insight led to a dramatic change in economic modeling.[13]

6. Under stationarity and normality assumptions, we can estimate the beta coefficient by applying the ordinary least-square method to

$$R_i - r = \alpha_i + \beta_i(R^M - r) + \varepsilon_i.$$

The term $\beta_i(R^M - r)$ corresponds to the systematic risk, which cannot be diversified. The error term $\varepsilon_i$ satisfies $\text{Cov}(\varepsilon_i, R^M) = 0$ and corresponds to the unsystematic risk. Hence the following decomposition of total risk as measured by the variance is possible:

$$\text{Var}(R_i) = \beta_i^2 \text{Var}(R^M) + \text{Var}(\varepsilon_i).$$

Very often, monthly data over a period of 5 years are used for the estimation of the beta coefficients. However, there is no general agreement about this.

7. Typically, the observed beta coefficients are positive. A negative beta coefficient occurs only in the rare case where $\text{Cov}(R_i, R^M)$ is negative. In other words, the risk premium $E[R_i] - r$ can only be negative if asset $i$ represents a partial insurance against market risk.

8. According to the CAPM relationship, each asset $i$ can be represented by a point $(\beta_i, E[R_i])$ that lies on the theoretical market line

$$E[R_i] = r + (E[R^M] - r)\beta_i.$$

Often the empirical market line, which is based on estimations for $\beta_i$, $E[R_i]$, $E[R^M]$, deviates substantially as portrayed in Figure 8.7 (see, for example, Black, Jensen, and Scholes [14]).

---

[13]In 1990 Markowitz, Miller, and Sharpe were honored with the Nobel Prize for their pathbreaking work in financial economics.

FIGURE **8.7** │ *Market Lines*

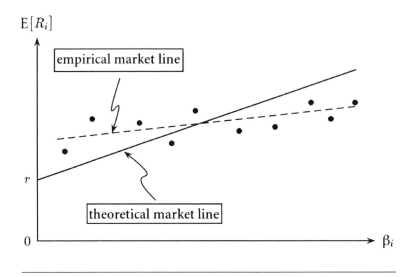

9.   As shown in Black, Jensen, and Scholes [14], Blume and Friend [17], Fama and
     Macbeth [60], Roll [161], and elsewhere, the empirical evidence in favor of the
     CAPM is rather weak. Roll [161] pointed out that the market portfolio should
     contain all types of bonds, real estate, human capital, and so on. Due to the
     fact that such a portfolio cannot be reasonably approximated, Roll questioned
     the empirical testability of the CAPM.

10.  In particular, the following anomalies exist:
     - *Small-Firm Effect.* For firms with a low market value, the CAPM underes-
       timates the risk premium. Lack of liquidity would be a natural explanation
       for the small-firm effect. However, despite the fact that liquid small-firm
       funds were created, the small-firm effect seems to persist.
     - *Value/Growth Effect.* Value (growth) stocks are characterized by a low
       (high) P/E (price to earnings) or P/B (price to book) ratio. After correcting
       for the beta coefficient, it can be shown that in the long run value stocks
       perform better than growth stocks. This phenomenon cannot be fully
       explained by taxes.

11.  Under the assumptions of the CAPM, it is optimal for each investor to combine
     the market portfolio with the riskless investment.[14] Because of this fact, pas-
     sive strategies in which investors simply combine some stock and bond market
     indices became quite popular.

---

[14]More abstractly, a result showing that each investor can attain the optimal asset allocation by
combining some fixed reference portfolios is called a *mutual fund theorem.*

**Extensions of the CAPM**

The CAPM has been extended in many ways. Black [12] developed a CAPM without a riskless asset, and Litzenberger and Ramaswamy [124] analyzed a CAPM with taxes. Furthermore, consumption-based versions of the CAPM exist. Probably the most important extension was the international capital-asset-pricing model (ICAPM). In a world with several currency areas with stochastic exchange rates no asset is riskless for all investors. In the ICAPM developed by Solnik [184], Stultz [188], and others there are several groups of investors. Each group has a different reference currency and considers domestic cash to be riskless. An alternative equilibrium model (arbitrage pricing theory) is presented in Section 8.6.

# Section 8.3
# The Markowitz Model with Additional Linear Constraints

### SECTION 8.3.1 | PRACTICAL EXAMPLES FOR LINEAR CONSTRAINTS

In most practical applications, a portfolio $x$ has to satisfy several types of linear constraints. Very often, the following types occur.

*Nonnegativity Constraints.* For some assets, short selling has to be excluded, that is,

$$x_i \geq 0, \quad i = 1, \ldots, N.$$

A nonnegativity constraint is quite natural for real estate. Moreover, many investors do not allow short selling of equities and bonds.

*Institutional Constraints.* Because of regulations or for other reasons, many investors put an upper limit on the holdings of foreign assets. Sometimes total investment in equities is bounded as well. For some investors, the list of institutional constraints can be quite long. However, if there are too many constraints the set of feasible portfolios becomes small, and the Markowitz approach loses its power.

*Constraints Resulting from Currency Hedging.* The risk of a portfolio can be substantially reduced by international diversification. But there is some controversy over to which extent currency risks are compensated by risk premia. Therefore, many investors want to hold foreign assets without running the corresponding currency risk. In practice, investors hedge currency risk by selling futures or forwards on the foreign currency. These strategies can be decomposed in a short position ($x_{f.\text{cash}} \leq 0$) in foreign cash and a long position ($x_{d.\text{cash}} \geq 0$) in domestic cash. Hence, a full currency hedging of a position in foreign equities ($x_{f.\text{equity}} \geq 0$) and a position ($x_{f.\text{bond}} \geq 0$) in foreign bonds is achieved by the constraint

$$x_{f.\text{equity}} + x_{f.\text{bond}} + x_{f.\text{cash}} = 0.$$

Very often an investor is interested in *partial* currency hedging, and the appropriate constraint is given by

$$x_{f.\text{equity}} + x_{f.\text{bond}} + x_{f.\text{cash}} \geq 0.$$

## SECTION 8.3.2 | THEORETICAL FRAMEWORK

To simplify the analysis we assume that all assets $i = 1, \ldots, N$ are risky. Since each equality constraint can be replaced by two inequality constraints, the Markowitz model with linear constraints is of the form

$$\begin{array}{l} \max\limits_{x \in \Re^N}\{2\tau\mu^T x - x^T \Sigma x\} \\ \text{subject to } Ax \leq b \end{array} \tag{8.3.1}$$

Due to the additional constraints some of the properties of the standard Markowitz model (8.1.3) do not hold any more. But (8.3.1) is still a convex optimization problem with a quadratic objective function and a polyhedral feasible set. If the covariance matrix $\Sigma$ is positive definite, then the solution of (8.3.1) is unique, and very powerful numerical methods are commercially available. A careful and detailed discussion of (8.3.1) can be found in Best and Grauer [7].

*Analysis of the Optimality Conditions.* The Lagrangian function of (8.3.1) is given by

$$\mathcal{L}(x, \lambda) = 2\tau\mu^T x - x^T \Sigma x - \lambda^T (Ax - b).$$

Because of the Kuhn-Tucker theorem, the optimality conditions

$$2\tau\mu - 2\Sigma x - A^T \lambda = 0, \tag{8.3.2}$$

$$Ax \leq b, \tag{8.3.3}$$

$$\lambda^T (Ax - b) = 0, \quad \lambda \geq 0 \tag{8.3.4}$$

are necessary and sufficient for a global optimum of (8.3.1). Equation (8.3.2) and the binding constraints in (8.3.3) form a system of linear equations for the optimal portfolio weights $x^*$ and the corresponding Lagrange multipliers. Best and Grauer [7] discuss the regularity of this system and derived an explicit solution.

The optimality conditions (8.3.2) to (8.3.4) can also be used for a sensitivity analysis. Under regularity and for a fixed set of binding constraints the optimal portfolio weights $x^*$ are linear in the risk tolerance $\tau$. At some critical levels $\tau_1, \tau_2, \ldots$ the set of binding constraints may change. Hence, the optimal portfolio weights are piecewise linear functions $x^*(\tau)$ of the risk tolerance with kinks possible, occurring at $\tau = \tau_1, \tau_2, \ldots$.

**The Efficient Frontier.** Using similar arguments as in Section 8.2.1, we can show that piecewise linear portfolio weights $x^*(\tau)$ lead to a piecewise hyperbolic efficient frontier in the $(\mu_x, \sigma_x)$-diagram as in Figure 8.8.

FIGURE **8.8** │ *Piecewise Hyperbolic Efficient Frontier*

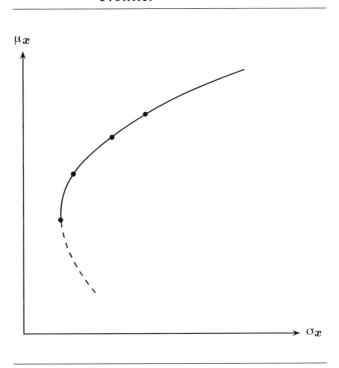

**Interpretation of the Lagrange Multipliers.** What is the influence of additional constraints on the optimal portfolio $x^*$ and the corresponding value of the objective function? Best and Grauer [8] have shown that under regularity conditions the portfolio weights $x^*$ and the Lagrange multipliers $\lambda$ are piecewise linear in $b$. The risk-adjusted return on portfolio $x_b^*$ is given by

$$F(b) = \mathrm{E}[R_{x_b^*}] - \frac{1}{2\tau}\mathrm{Var}(R_{x_b^*})$$

$$= \mu^T x_b^* - \frac{1}{2\tau}x_b^{*T}\Sigma x_b^*.$$

Using the envelope theorem[15] we obtain

$$\frac{\partial}{\partial b_j}F(b) = \frac{1}{2\tau}\lambda_j, \quad j = 1, 2, \ldots. \tag{8.3.5}$$

Formula (8.3.5) tells us how much the risk-adjusted return can be improved if a constraint $j = 1, 2, \ldots$ is relaxed.

## SECTION 8.3.3 | AN EXAMPLE: PORTFOLIO CHOICE OF A SWISS INVESTOR (CONTINUED)

In Section 8.2.3, we calculated an efficient portfolio $x^*$ for a Swiss investor. It turned out that the portfolio weight for U.S. bonds was negative. We continue our example by imposing nonnegativity constraints. This leads to the new optimization problem (see Sections 8.3.1, 8.3.2):

$$\max_{x \in \mathfrak{R}^N}\{2\tau\mu^T x - x^T\Sigma x\}$$

$$\text{subject to } \sum_{i=1}^{N} x_i = 1, \quad x_i \geq 0, i = 1, \ldots, N$$

.

For a risk tolerance $\tau = 0.20$ we obtain the efficient portfolio $x^{**}$ with the expected return $\mu_{x^{**}} = 6\%$.

Compare the portfolios $x^*$ and $x^{**}$ (see Table 8.3). Both portfolios have the same expected return $\mu_{x^*} = \mu_{x^{**}} = 6\%$. Of course, under nonnegativity constraints, a slightly larger risk tolerance is needed to obtain this level of return. The portfolio $x^{**}$ may be more or less appropriate for a private Swiss investor. However, for a pension fund with liabilities reaching into the far-distant future, a portfolio with a cash position of 46.0% would hardly be acceptable.

---

[15]According to the envelope theorem, Lagrange multipliers can be interpreted as "shadow prices" for the corresponding constraints. A precise formulation of the envelope theorem can be found in Takayama [190, p. 132].

TABLE 8.3 | *Portfolio Choice of a Swiss Investor (Continued)*

| Asset Category | $\mu$ | $x^{**}$ Efficient Portfolio with Nonnegativity Constraints $\tau = 0.20$ $\mu_{x^{**}} = 6\%$ | $x^*$ Efficient Portfolio without Nonnegativity Constraints $\tau = 0.194$ $\mu_{x^*} = 6\%$ |
|---|---|---|---|
| Swiss cash | 4.0% | 46.0% | 42.5% |
| Swiss bonds | 4.5 | 10.0 | 16.9 |
| Swiss equities | 9.0 | 5.5 | 5.1 |
| Euro bonds | 5.5 | 7.5 | 11.4 |
| Euro equities | 9.5 | 23.5 | 23.5 |
| U.S. bonds | 6.5 | – | −13.2 |
| U.S. equities | 9.5 | – | 6.1 |
| Japan bonds | 6.0 | 4.5 | 6.6 |
| Japan equities | 9.5 | 3.0 | 1.1 |

# Section 8.4
# The Asset-Liability Model

## SECTION 8.4.1 | THE PENSION PLAN

In this section, we present the asset-liability model as a further extension of the Markowitz approach. For didactical purposes, the asset-liability model is derived in the context of pension finance. Later we see that it can be applied in a much broader framework.

The liabilities of a pension fund result from the difference between future benefits and contributions. These liabilities are not readily marketable; therefore a market value can hardly be determined.[16] Here we assume that some specific accounting rules are used to calculate an initial value $L_0$ of the future net obligations. If the same method is applied one period later, a value $L_1$ results. Hence, from the present point of view, the growth rate of the liabilities is given by the random variable

$$R_L = \frac{L_1 - L_0}{L_0}.$$

---

[16]The work of Wilkie [203] and Wise [209, 210, 211, 212, 213] is directed partly toward finding a suitable present value.

Typically $R_L$ depends on changes of the interest-rate structure, inflation, and real wages. On the other hand, assets are valued according to market prices, and their initial value is denoted by $A_0$. For simplicity we assume that all investment opportunities $i = 1, \ldots, N$ are risky. The investment strategy of the pension fund is given by a portfolio choice $x$. Therefore, the market value of assets after one period is given by

$$A_1 = A_0(1 + R_x).$$

### Surplus Optimization

Depending on its portfolio choice $x$, a pension fund with initial surplus

$$S_0 = A_0 - L_0$$

obtains the surplus after one period

$$S_1 = A_1 - L_1 = A_0(1 + R_x) - L_0(1 + R_L).$$

Our goal is to apply mean-variance analysis to the increase in surplus

$$S_1 - S_0 = A_0 \cdot R_x - L_0 \cdot R_L.$$

Following Sharpe and Tint [176], we use the normalization

$$R_S = \frac{S_1 - S_0}{A_0} = R_x - \frac{1}{f_0} R_L \qquad (8.4.1)$$

where $f_0 = A_0/L_0$ denotes the initial funding ratio.

Markowitz's methodology leads to the optimization problem (see also Shiu [181])[17]

$$\max_{x \in \mathfrak{R}^N} \left\{ 2\tau E\left[ R_x - \frac{1}{f_0} R_L \right] - \text{Var}\left( R_x - \frac{1}{f_0} R_L \right) \right\}$$

$$\text{subject to } \sum_{i=1}^{N} x_i = 1 \qquad (8.4.2)$$

.

---

[17]In the literature, the normalizations $(S_1 - S_0)/L_0$ and $(S_1 - S_0)/S_0$ for $S_0 > 0$ are also used. However, with a proper adjustment of the risk tolerance parameter $\tau$, all types of normalization lead to the same optimal portfolio.

**Applications of the Asset-Liability Model**

- To simplify the problem of a pension fund slightly, it may be appropriate to set

$$R_L = c_0 + c_1 R_{\text{bond}} + c_2 R_{\text{inflation}} + c_3 R_{\text{economic}}$$

where $R_{\text{bond}}$ is the rate of return on a bond index, $R_{\text{inflation}}$ is the rate of inflation, and $R_{\text{economic}}$ is the rate of economic growth. [18]

- Solnik [185] looked at the problem of an investor interested in real returns. His model is obtained by setting $R_L = R_{\text{inflation}}$ and $f_0 = 1$.

- For a portfolio manager optimizing relative to a benchmark portfolio with return $R_{bm}$ we have to set $R_L = R_{bm}$ and $f_0 = 1$ (see Roll [162]).

- As Sharpe and Tint [176] pointed out, the asset-liability model is appropriate not only for very different types of liabilities (foreign currency obligations, debt structure, etc.) but also in the case in which investors have some fixed asset holdings (human capital, ownership of a house, etc.). In this case, the fixed asset holdings represent negative liabilities.

### SECTION 8.4.2 | PROPERTIES OF THE ASSET-LIABILITY MODEL

The mathematical structure of the asset-liability model was first studied by Solnik [185] in his paper on portfolio choice under inflation. Later Sharpe and Tint [176] used the same model in their work on liability hedging credits. Our presentation is based on Keel and Mueller [110].

Obviously (8.4.2) is equivalent to

$$\max_{x \in \Re^N} \left\{ 2\tau E[R_x] - \text{Var}(R_x) + \frac{2}{f_0} \text{Cov}(R_x, R_L) \right\}$$
$$\text{subject to } \sum_{i=1}^{N} x_i = 1$$

or more formally

$$\max_{x \in \Re^N} \{ 2\tau \mu^T x + 2\gamma^T x - x^T \Sigma x \}$$
$$\text{subject to } e^T x = 1 \tag{8.4.3}$$

---

[18]This results from changes due to demography—deaths, disability, and withdrawals not equal to what is expected. Moreover, the factors $R_{\text{bond}}$, $R_{\text{inflation}}$, and $R_{\text{economic}}$ typically have a nonlinear influence on $R_L$. The given formula may be considered as an approximation.

where

$$\Sigma = (\sigma_{ij})_{ij=1.....N}, \qquad \text{with} \quad \sigma_{ij} = \text{Cov}(R_i, R_j),$$

$$\mu^T = (\mu_1, \dots, \mu_N), \qquad \text{with} \quad \mu_i = \text{E}[R_i],$$

$$\gamma^T = (\gamma_1, \dots, \gamma_N), \qquad \text{with} \quad \gamma_i = \frac{1}{f_0} \text{Cov}(R_i, R_L),$$

$$e^T = (1, 1, \dots, 1) \in \Re^N.$$

## Comment

A comparison of (8.4.3) and (8.2.4) shows that the only change consists in the term $2\gamma^T x$. In other words,

$$\mu^T = (\text{E}[R_i])_{i=1.....N}$$

has to be replaced by

$$\mu^T + \frac{1}{\tau}\gamma^T = \left(\text{E}[R_i] + \frac{1}{\tau}\cdot\frac{1}{f_0}\text{Cov}(R_i, R_L)\right)_{i=1.....N}.$$

The correction terms $\text{Cov}(R_i, R_L)/(\tau f_0)$, $i = 1, \dots, N$ are called *liability hedging credits* (see Sharpe and Tint [176]).

## Optimality Conditions

The Lagrangian function of (8.4.3) is given by

$$\mathcal{L}(x, \lambda) = 2\tau\mu^T x + 2\gamma^T x - x^T\Sigma x + \lambda(e^T x - 1).$$

Because of the Kuhn-Tucker theorem, the optimality conditions

$$2\tau\mu + 2\gamma - 2\Sigma x + \lambda e = 0, \tag{8.4.4}$$

$$e^T x = 1 \tag{8.4.5}$$

are necessary and sufficient for a global optimum.

As in Section 8.2 we assume hereafter that A.1 holds.

## The Set of Efficient Portfolios

- Setting $\tau = 0$ in (8.4.4) leads to the minimum variance portfolio under liabilities

$$x^{\text{MIN}} = \Sigma^{-1}\gamma + \frac{\lambda}{2}\Sigma^{-1}e.$$

Taking into account (8.4.5) we obtain

$$x^{\text{MIN}.L} = \frac{1}{e^T \Sigma^{-1} e} \Sigma^{-1} e + \left[ \Sigma^{-1} \gamma - \frac{e^T \Sigma^{-1} \gamma}{e^T \Sigma^{-1} e} \Sigma^{-1} e \right]. \tag{8.4.6}$$

The first term in (8.4.6)

$$x^{\text{MIN}} = \frac{1}{e^T \Sigma^{-1} e} \Sigma^{-1} e \tag{8.4.7}$$

is the minimum variance portfolio from Section 8.2. The second term in (8.4.6)

$$z^L = \left[ \Sigma^{-1} \gamma - \frac{e^T \Sigma^{-1} \gamma}{e^T \Sigma^{-1} e} \Sigma^{-1} e \right], \quad \text{with} \ \sum_{i=1}^{N} z_i^L = 0 \tag{8.4.8}$$

corrects for the liabilities. Hence the minimum variance portfolio under liabilities is given by

$$x^{\text{MIN}.L} = x^{\text{MIN}} + z^L. \tag{8.4.9}$$

• Setting $\tau > 0$ in (8.4.4) leads to the efficient portfolios

$$x^* = x^{\text{MIN}.L} + \tau z^*$$

with

$$z^* = \Sigma^{-1} \mu - \frac{e^T \Sigma^{-1} \mu}{e^T \Sigma^{-1} e} \Sigma^{-1} e, \quad \sum_{i=1}^{N} z_i^* = 0. \tag{8.4.10}$$

From (8.4.9) and (8.4.10) we can conclude that efficient portfolios are of the form

$$x^* = x^{\text{MIN}} + z^L + \tau z^*, \quad \tau \geq 0. \tag{8.4.11}$$

**Comments**

1. As in Section 8.2 the risk tolerance $\tau$ and the vector of expected returns $\mu$ occur only in the last term.

2. Liabilities are fully taken into account by the second term $z^L$. Hence, the occurrence of liabilities leads only to parallel shifts of the set of efficient portfolios (see Figure 8.9).

**Efficient Frontier**

Using a similar argument as in Section 8.2.1 note the following:

1. The efficient frontier is hyperbolic in the $(E[R_x], \sigma[R_x])$-diagram.

FIGURE **8.9** | *Efficient Portfolios*

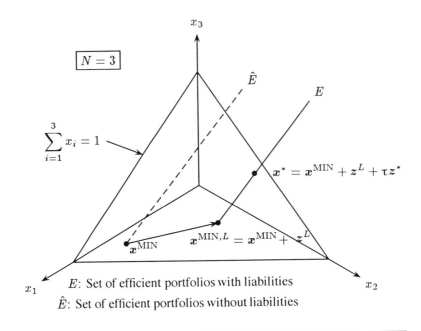

$E$: Set of efficient portfolios with liabilities
$\hat{E}$: Set of efficient portfolios without liabilities

2. The efficient frontier is hyperbolic in the $(E[R_x - (1/f_0)R_L], \sigma[R_x - (1/f_0)R_L])$-diagram provided that the liabilities cannot be fully tracked by a portfolio; that is, $\text{Var}(R_{x^{\text{MIN},L}} - (1/f_0)R_L) > 0$.

## SECTION **8.4.3** | AN EXAMPLE: PORTFOLIO CHOICE OF A SWISS PENSION FUND

Typically, the obligations of a pension fund reach in the far-distant future. More over, we assume that the Swiss pension fund intends a full adjustment of all benefits to the consumer price index. In this situation we apply the asset-liability model with

$$f_0 = 1,$$
$$R_L = c_0 + R_{\text{bond}} - E[R_{\text{bond}}] + R_{\text{inflation}} - E[R_{\text{inflation}}],$$

where $R_{\text{bond}}$ is the rate of return on a bond index and $R_{\text{inflation}}$ is the rate of inflation. Hence, the optimization problem is given by

$$\max_{x \in \mathbb{R}^N}\{2\tau E[R_x] - \text{Var}(R_x) + 2\,\text{Cov}(R_x, R_L)\}$$
$$\text{subject to } \sum_{i=1}^{N} x_i = 1$$

.

According to (8.4.11), the efficient portfolios are given by

$$x^* = x^{\text{MIN}} + z^L + \tau z^*, \quad \tau \geq 0.$$

Table 8.4 contains the numerical values of $x^{\text{MIN}}, z^L, z^*$ for the data of our earlier example. In addition, the efficient portfolio $x^*$ corresponding to a risk tolerance $\tau = 0.163$ ($\text{E}[R_{x^*}] = 6\%$) is calculated.

### TABLE 8.4 | Portfolio Choice of a Swiss Pension Fund

| Asset Category | $x^{\text{MIN}}$ | $z^L$ | $z^*$ | $x^*$ ($\tau = 0.163$) |
|---|---|---|---|---|
| Swiss cash | 96.2% | −91.3% | −277.0% | −40.5% |
| Swiss bonds | −0.1 | 90.0 | 88.3 | 105.3 |
| Swiss equities | −0.5 | −0.3 | 28.6 | 3.9 |
| Euro bonds | 3.0 | 3.8 | 43.1 | 13.9 |
| Euro equities | 0.9 | −4.3 | 116.6 | 15.7 |
| U.S. bonds | −0.7 | 2.0 | −64.5 | −9.3 |
| U.S. equities | −0.2 | 1.7 | 32.1 | 6.8 |
| Japan bonds | −0.4 | −0.9 | 36.2 | 4.7 |
| Japan equities | 1.8 | −1.7 | −3.4 | −0.5 |

At first sight, the portfolio $x^*$ does not look very convincing. However, the weights of Swiss cash (−40.5%) and Swiss bonds (105.3%) have to be interpreted in the sense that 64.8% must be invested in a Swiss bond subportfolio with a properly increased duration. Nevertheless, we can hardly justify the negative weight of U.S. bonds (−9.3%). Again, we should impose nonnegativity constraints on all portfolio weights except Swiss cash.

# Section 8.5
# Shortfall Constraints

## SECTION 8.5.1 | INTRODUCTION

Very often an investor who faces liabilities wants to avoid excessive short-term nominal losses in a portfolio. A shortfall occurs if the rate of return on a portfolio $R_x$ does not attain some given level $c$ (for example, $c = -10\%$ or $c = 0\%$). A shortfall constraint puts an upper limit $\delta$ ($\delta < 1/2$) on the probability of such an event; that is,

$$\Pr\{R_x \leq c\} \leq \delta. \tag{8.5.1}$$

Again we assume that all assets $i = 1, \ldots, N$ are risky. Moreover, we introduce the following assumption:

**Assumption A.2.** The probability distribution of $(R_1, \ldots, R_N)$ is multivariate normal.

Under A.2 the shortfall constraint (8.5.1) becomes

$$E[R_x] - z_\delta \cdot \sigma(R_x) \geq c \tag{8.5.2}$$

with $z_\delta$ representing the $(1 - \delta)$-th quantile of the normal distribution; that is,

$$\frac{1}{\sqrt{2\pi}} \int_{-\infty}^{z_\delta} e^{-x^2/2} \, dx = 1 - \delta.$$

Hence, introducing a shortfall constraint in the asset-liability model leads to the optimization problem

$$\max_{x \in \Re^N} \left\{ 2\tau E\left[ R_x - \frac{1}{f_0} R_L \right] - \text{Var}\left( R_x - \frac{1}{f_0} R_L \right) \right\}$$
$$\text{subject to } E[R_x] - z_\delta \sigma(R_x) \geq c$$
$$\text{and } \sum_{i=1}^{N} x_i = 1 \tag{8.5.3}$$

.

## SECTION 8.5.2 | PROPERTIES OF OPTIMIZATION UNDER SHORTFALL CONSTRAINTS

Using the notation of Section 8.4.2, the optimization problem[19] (8.5.3) is equivalent to

$$\max_{x \in \Re^N}\{2\tau\mu^T x + 2\gamma^T x - x^T\Sigma x\}$$
$$\text{subject to } e^T x = 1,$$
$$\text{and } \mu^T x - z_\delta(x^T\Sigma x)^{1/2} \geq c \tag{8.5.4}$$

.

Since $h(x) = (x^T\Sigma x)^{1/2}$ is a convex function,[20] the feasible set of (8.5.4) is convex. Therefore we are still in the framework of convex optimization; this fact considerably

---

[19]See also Brockett and Xia [30].

[20]We have to show that for any $x_0, w \in \Re^N$,

$$g(s) = [(x_0 + sw)^T\Sigma(x_0 + sw)]^{1/2}$$

is convex in the $s \in \Re$. Since $\Sigma$ is positive semi-definite, we obtain

$$(x_0 + sw)^T\Sigma(x_0 + sw) = x_0^T\Sigma x_0 + 2sx_0^T\Sigma w + s^2 w^T\Sigma w \geq 0.$$

The square root of a quadratic nonnegative function is convex. This proves the convexity of $g(s)$.

simplifies the calculation of numerical solutions. Moreover the Kuhn-Tucker theorem can be applied on (8.5.4).

**Optimality Conditions**

The Lagrangian function of (8.5.4) is given by

$$\mathcal{L}(x, \lambda, v) = 2\tau\mu^T x + 2\gamma^T x - x^T \Sigma x$$
$$+ \lambda[\mu^T x - z_\delta(x^T \Sigma x)^{1/2} - c]$$
$$+ v[e^T x - 1].$$

For $c$ sufficiently small, the Kuhn-Tucker theorem holds,[21] and the necessary and sufficient conditions for a global optimum are given by

$$(2\tau + \lambda)\mu + 2\gamma - \left[2 + \frac{\lambda z_\delta}{(x^T \Sigma x)^{1/2}}\right]\Sigma x + v e = 0, \qquad (8.5.5)$$

$$e^T x = 1, \qquad (8.5.6)$$

$$\mu^T x - z_\delta(x^T \Sigma x)^{1/2} \geq c, \qquad \lambda \geq 0,$$

and

$$\lambda[\mu^T x - z_\delta(x^T \Sigma x)^{1/2} - c] = 0. \qquad (8.5.7)$$

Using the notation of Section 8.4.2, we can show that the optimal portfolio is of the form[22]

$$x^* = x^{\text{MIN}} + \alpha z^L + \beta z^*, \qquad 0 < \alpha \leq 1, \ \beta \geq 0, \qquad (8.5.8)$$

as illustrated in Figure 8.10.

**Comment**

Formula (8.5.8) tells us that a shortfall constraint reduces the effect of liabilities on the optimal asset allocation (see Figure 8.10). This may explain why liabilities are not fully taken into account by many institutional investors (see Sharpe and Tint [176]).

---

[21] Some feasible portfolio $x$ has to satisfy the shortfall constraint with strict inequality.

[22] Bucher [31] proved the same result in a different context.

FIGURE **8.10** | *Optimality with Shortfall Constraints*

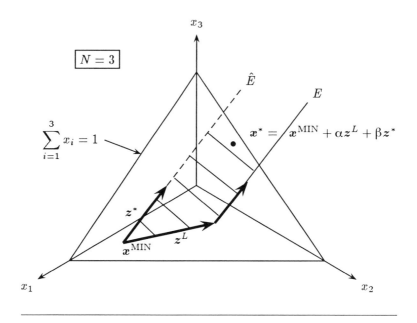

# *Section 8.6*
# *Factor Models*

Typically, asset returns are (positively) correlated. Factor models explain this correlation structure by few common factors. In other words, the asset returns $R_i$, $i = 1, \ldots, N$ are of the form

$$R_i = E[R_i] + c_{i1} F_1 + \cdots + c_{iK} F_K + \varepsilon_i \tag{8.6.1}$$

where $F_k$, $k = 1, \ldots, K$ denotes the stochastic factor return with $E[F_k] = 0$, and $\varepsilon_i$ denotes the residual with $\mathrm{Cov}(\varepsilon_i, \varepsilon_j) = 0$ for $i \neq j$ and $\mathrm{Cov}(\varepsilon_i, F_k) = 0$ for $k = 1, \ldots, K$.

In this section we discuss the two main applications of factor models: arbitrage-pricing theory (APT) and risk control. APT was proposed by Ross [163]. The factors satisfy $\mathrm{Cov}(F_h, F_k) = 0$ for $h \neq k$ and may not have a direct economic interpretation. Under a strengthened assumption about the absence of arbitrage, factor risk premia $\lambda_1, \ldots, \lambda_K$ can be determined. The factor risk premium $\lambda_k$, $k = 1, \ldots, K$, is the risk premium stemming from a unit exposure to factor $F_k$. On average, the expected asset returns $E[R_i]$ can be explained by these factor risk premia. In empirical applications of APT the factors are constructed by principal-component analysis or maximum-likelihood methods. In comparison to CAPM, APT has at least two advantages:

1.  APT is based only on the absence of arbitrage. Therefore, we can also apply it on submarkets (e.g., equity markets of continental Europe).

2.  According to empirical tests conducted by Lehmann and Modest [119], APT is able to explain some anomalies of the CAPM.

Slightly different factor models are used for risk control. Formula (8.6.1) still holds, but instead of statistical factors we use (see, for example, Grinold and Kahn [80])

1.  Economic factors (interest rates, exchange rates, unexpected inflation, economic growth, etc.), or

2.  Characteristics of the assets (dividend yield, firm size, industry group the firm belongs to, etc.).

In risk control, the factor sensitivities of a portfolio are compared with the corresponding sensitivities of the benchmark. The factor model just described is also used for the calculation of the covariance matrix $\Sigma$ (see Grinold and Kahn [80, pp. 45–46]).

## SECTION 8.6.1 | ARBITRAGE PRICING THEORY

As already mentioned, arbitrage pricing theory is based on a factor model of the type

$$R_i = \mathrm{E}[R_i] + \sum_{k=1}^{K} c_{ik} F_k + \varepsilon_i, \quad i = 1, \ldots, N \tag{8.6.2}$$

with

$$\mathrm{E}[F_k] = 0, \quad k = 1, \ldots, K, \quad \mathrm{Cov}(F_k, F_h) = 0, \quad k \neq h,$$
$$\mathrm{E}[\varepsilon_i] = 0, \quad i = 1, \ldots, N, \quad \mathrm{Cov}(\varepsilon_i, \varepsilon_j) = 0, \quad i \neq j, \text{ and}$$
$$(F_k, \varepsilon_i) = 0.$$

Using vector notation we obtain

$$R = \mu + \sum_{k=1}^{K} c_k F_k + \varepsilon \tag{8.6.3}$$

with

$$\mu^T = (\mu_1, \ldots, \mu_N), \quad \mu_i = \mathrm{E}[R_i], \quad i = 1, \ldots, N,$$
$$c_k^T = (c_{1k}, \ldots, c_{Nk}), \quad k = 1, \ldots, K.$$

Before dealing with the general case, we look at a highly simplified model.

### A Simplified Model

For this simplified model, we assume that $R_i$ can be fully explained by the factors $F_1, \ldots, F_K$:

**Assumption B.1.**   $\varepsilon_i \equiv 0$,   $i = 1, \ldots, N$; and

**Assumption B.2.**   There are no arbitrage opportunities.

Under B.1, the return of a portfolio $w \in \Re^N$ is given by

$$R^T w = \mu^T w + \sum_{k=1}^{K} c_k^T w F_k. \tag{8.6.4}$$

A portfolio $w \in \Re^N$ is self-financing if

$$\sum_{i=1}^{N} w_i = 0,$$

or

$$e^T w = 0, \quad \text{with} \quad e^T = (1, \ldots, 1) \in \Re^N.$$

The self-financing portfolios without factor exposure are characterized by

$$e^T w = 0, \tag{8.6.5}$$

$$c_k^T w = 0, \quad k = 1, \ldots, K. \tag{8.6.6}$$

Since the portfolios satisfying (8.6.5) and (8.6.6) are riskless, absence of arbitrage (B.2) implies

$$\mu^T w = 0. \tag{8.6.7}$$

In other words, every solution $w$ of (8.6.5) and (8.6.6) is also a solution of (8.6.7). Hence, according to a theorem in linear algebra, there exist $\lambda_0, \lambda_1, \ldots, \lambda_K$ such that

$$\mu = \lambda_0 e + \sum_{k=1}^{K} \lambda_k c_k \tag{8.6.8}$$

or

$$E[R_i] = \lambda_0 + \sum_{k=1}^{K} \lambda_k c_{ik}, \quad i = 1, \ldots, N. \tag{8.6.9}$$

For the special case, where a riskless investment opportunity with return $R_0 = r$ is available, we conclude that

$$\lambda_0 = r.$$

In this special case, the risk premium on asset $i$

$$E[R_i] - r = \sum_{k=1}^{K} \lambda_k c_{ik} \tag{8.6.10}$$

is obtained by multiplying the factor risk premia $\lambda_1, \ldots, \lambda_K$ with the corresponding factor loadings.

**The General Model**

Now we allow for stochastic residuals. Assumption B.1 is replaced by a new assumption:

**Assumption C.1.** There exists $a > 0$, such that $\mathrm{Var}(\varepsilon_i) < a$, $\quad i = 1, \ldots, N$.

To handle the nonsystematic risk that stems from the residuals, we need an infinity of assets, that is, $N \to \infty$. For this model, we need to introduce the concept of asymptotic arbitrage opportunities.

**Definition 8.6.1.** *Asymptotic arbitrage opportunities are available if there exist*

1.   *A sequence of self-financing portfolios* $w^2, w^3, \ldots, w^N, \ldots$

$$w^N \in \mathfrak{R}^N, \qquad \sum_{i=1}^{N} w_i^N = 0, \qquad and$$

2.   *A number $d > 0$ such that*

$$E\left[ \sum_{i=1}^{N} w_i^N R_i \right] \geq d, \quad N = 2, 3, \ldots,$$

$$\mathrm{Var}\left( \sum_{i=1}^{N} w_i^N R_i \right) \to 0, \quad for \; N \to \infty.$$

The interpretation of this definition is that the returns of a self-financing portfolio $w^N$ have

•     An expected value with a positive lower bound $d$,
•     A variance tending to zero.

As Ingersoll [99, pp. 171–72] points out, a market with asymptotic arbitrage opportunities would allow for infinite wealth with probability one. Assumption B.2 has to be replaced by the following:

*Assumption C.2.* There exist no asymptotic arbitrage opportunities.

Now the following result can be derived (see Ingersoll [99, pp. 172–74]).

**Theorem 8.6.1.** *Under the assumptions C.1 and C.2, there exist $\lambda_0, \lambda_1, \ldots, \lambda_K \in \Re$ such that*

$$E[R_i] = \lambda_0 + \sum_{k=1}^{K} c_{ik}\lambda_k + v_i, \quad i = 1, 2, \ldots$$

*with*

$$\lim_{N \to \infty} \frac{1}{N} \sum_{i=1}^{N} v_i^2 = 0.$$

**Comment**

Some error terms $v_i$ may be quite large. However, in the quadratic mean they tend to zero.

In the empirical tests (see Lehmann and Modest [119]), the factors are determined with a statistical method such as principal-component analysis. Thereafter, $K$ portfolios are constructed that are only exposed to one factor and have minimum unsystematic risk. These $K$ portfolios are used to explain asset returns. In Lehmann and Modest's study, with exception of the small-firm effect, most anomalies of the CAPM could be explained by this procedure.

## SECTION 8.6.2 | RISK CONTROL BY FACTOR MODELS

In Section 8.4.1, it was pointed out that most portfolio managers have to optimize relative to a benchmark portfolio

$$\boldsymbol{b}^T = (b_1, \ldots, b_N), \qquad \sum_{i=1}^{N} b_i = 1.$$

For performance measurement, the managed portfolio $\boldsymbol{x}$ will be compared with the benchmark $\boldsymbol{b}$. In such a situation, the tracking error $\sigma(R_x - R_b)$ plays the most important part in risk control. Nevertheless, a factor model can give additional insight. One can compare $\boldsymbol{x}$ and $\boldsymbol{b}$ with respect to their factor exposures. Using the notation of (8.6.1), the net exposure to factor $k$ is given by

$$\sum_{i=1}^{N} c_{ik}(x_i - b_i), \quad k = 1, \ldots, K.$$

Statistical factors without a direct economic interpretation are rarely used for this purpose. Using macroeconomic factors such as interest rates and exchange rates would allow us to control the corresponding net exposures. However, according to Grinold and Kahn [80] (p. 47) factor models of this type are rather unstable. They favor factor models that are based on asset characteristics such as dividend yield and firm size.

# Section 8.7
# Expected Utility Maximization in a One-Period Model

In the preceding sections portfolio optimization is fully based on the Markowitz approach. On theoretical grounds, expected utility maximization is more desirable. In this section, we look at a one-period investment model without consumption. This model is characterized as follows:

- $W_0$ denotes the initial wealth of the investor.
- There exist $N + 1$ assets $i = 0, 1, \ldots, N$ with rates of return $R_i$. Asset $i = 0$ is riskless; assets $i = 1, \ldots, N$ are risky.
- A portfolio choice

$$x^T = (x_0, x_1, \ldots, x_N), \quad \text{with} \sum_{i=0}^{N} x_i = 1$$

leads to a final wealth

$$W_1 = W_0(1 + R_x), \quad \text{with } R_x = \sum_{i=0}^{N} x_i R_i.$$

- The optimal portfolio choice $x^*$ is the solution of the optimization problem

$$
\max_{x \in \mathfrak{R}^{N+1}} \; E[u[W_0(1 + R_x)]] \\
\text{subject to} \; \sum_{i=0}^{N} x_i = 1
$$
(8.7.1)

where $u(\cdot)$ denotes the von Neumann-Morgenstern utility function of the investor. The constraint in (8.7.1) can be written as

$$x_0 = 1 - \sum_{i=1}^{N} x_i.$$

Therefore, (8.7.1) is equivalent to the unconstrained optimization problem

$$\max_{(x_1,\ldots,x_N)\in\Re^N} E\left[u[W_0(1 + r + \sum_{i=1}^{N} x_i(R_i - r))]\right]. \qquad (8.7.2)$$

## SECTION 8.7.1 | OPTIMALITY CONDITIONS

The following assumptions are useful for the analysis of (8.7.1) or (8.7.2), respectively:

**Assumption D.1.** The utility function $u(\cdot)$ is increasing, strictly concave, and continuously differentiable.

**Assumption D.2.** The random variables are bounded.

Under D.1 and D.2, the portfolio $x^*$ is a solution of (8.7.1) and (8.7.2) if and only if [23]

$$E[u'[W_0(1 + R_{x^*})](R_i - r)] = 0, \quad i = 1, \ldots, N. \qquad (8.7.3)$$

From (8.7.3) we can derive some important results in comparative statics.

## SECTION 8.7.2 | INITIAL WEALTH AND PORTFOLIO CHOICE

The answer to how the composition of an optimal portfolio $x^*$ is related to initial wealth $W_0$ depends on the preferences of the investor. As shown, for example in Merton [134, p. 20]), both the absolute risk-aversion function

$$R_A(w) = -\frac{u''(w)}{u'(w)}$$

and the relative risk-aversion function

$$R_R(w) = -\frac{w\,u''(w)}{u'(w)} = w\,R_A(w)$$

fully characterize the preferences of an investor. For the case of one risky asset ($N = 1$), the following result holds (see, for example, Huang and Litzenberger [96, pp. 21–24]):

**Theorem 8.7.1.** *If a portfolio* $x^{*T}(W_0) = (x_0^*(W_0), x_1^*(W_0))$, *with* $x_1^*(W_0) > 0$ *satisfies the optimality condition* (8.7.3), *then it has the following properties:*

---

[23] Under D.1 and D.2 the objective function (8.7.2) is well defined and concave in $(x_1, \ldots, x_N)$. Due to D.1 and D.2, Lebesgue's convergence theorem [164] allows us to reverse the order of differentiation and integration.

1.   *Provided that the relative risk aversion function $R_R(w)$ is monotone, then*

$$\frac{dx_1^*}{dW_0} \geq 0 \iff R'_R(w) \leq 0$$

*and*

$$\frac{dx_1^*}{dW_0} \leq 0 \iff R'_R(w) \geq 0.$$

2.   *Provided that the absolute risk-aversion function $R_A(w)$ is monotone, then*

$$\frac{d(x_1^* \cdot W_0)}{dW_0} \geq 0 \iff R'_A(w) \leq 0$$

*and*

$$\frac{d(x_1^* \cdot W_0)}{dW_0} \leq 0 \iff R'_A(w) \geq 0.$$

Note that $x_1^*$ denotes the fraction of wealth and $x_1^* \cdot W_0$ the amount of money that is invested in the risky asset.

**Example 8.7.1 (*Power Utility*).** For power utility functions $u(w) = [(w-a)^\alpha - 1]/\alpha$, for $w \geq a$ and $\alpha \in (0, 1)$,

$$R_R(w) = (1 - \alpha)\frac{w}{w - a}.$$

Hence, property 1 implies

$$\frac{dx_1^*}{dW_0} > 0, \quad \text{for } a > 0$$

and

$$\frac{dx_1^*}{dW_0} < 0, \quad \text{for } a < 0. \qquad \blacksquare$$

**Example 8.7.2 (*Exponential Utility*).** For exponential utility functions $u(w) = 1 - e^{-aw}$, $a > 0$, one obtains $R_A = a$. According to property 2, the amount invested in the risky asset does not depend on initial wealth $W_0$. $\qquad \blacksquare$

***Example 8.7.3 (Quadratic Utility).*** For quadratic utility functions

$$u(w) = w - \frac{1}{2b}w^2, \quad b > 0, \quad 0 \le w \le b$$

the absolute risk aversion $R_A(w) = 1/(b - w)$ is increasing. From property 2, an increase in initial wealth leads to a decrease of the amount invested in the risky asset. Due to this unrealistic investment behavior most economists ban quadratic utility functions from portfolio theory. ∎

## SECTION 8.7.3 │ CONSISTENCY OF THE MARKOWITZ APPROACH WITH EXPECTED UTILITY MAXIMIZATION

The Markowitz approach (mean-variance analysis) in its most general version corresponds to the optimization problem

$$
\boxed{
\begin{aligned}
&\max_{x \in \mathfrak{R}^{N+1}} F(\mu_x, \sigma_x) \\
&\text{subject to } \sum_{i=0}^{N} x_i = 1
\end{aligned}
}
\tag{8.7.4}
$$

where $F(\mu_x, \sigma_x)$ is a function of the expected value $\mu$ and the standard deviation with partial derivatives

$$\frac{\partial F}{\partial \mu} > 0, \qquad \frac{\partial F}{\partial \sigma} < 0.$$

We have seen that the Markowitz methodology is very appropriate for practical purposes. To get a sound theoretical foundation, consistency of (8.7.4) with expected utility maximization (8.7.1) is needed. Two cases are known in which this consistency holds:

- Quadratic utility functions
- Multivariate normal distributions of asset returns.

**Quadratic Utility Functions**

Without an assumption on the distribution of asset returns, (8.7.4) and (8.7.1) can be consistent only for linear or quadratic utility functions.[24] Hence for risk-averse investors, one is restricted to quadratic utility functions

$$u(w) = w - \frac{1}{2b}w^2, \quad b > 0.$$

---

[24] For all other utility functions, third and higher moments of the returns enter in (8.7.1).

For $w > b$, these functions are decreasing. Moreover, because of increasing absolute risk aversion $R_A(w) = 1/(w - b)$, they lead to very unrealistic investment behavior (see Subsection 8.7.2). Consequently a satisfactory theoretical basis for the Markowitz methodology can be found only under an appropriate assumption on the distribution of asset returns.

### Multivariate Normal Distributions of Assets Returns

We introduce the following assumption:

**Assumption D.3.**  The returns on the risky assets $R = (R_1, \ldots, R_N)^T$ have a multivariate normal probability distribution with a density

$$f(R) = (2\pi)^{-\frac{N}{2}} (\det \Sigma)^{-\frac{1}{2}} \exp \left\{ -\frac{1}{2} (R - \mu)^T \Sigma^{-1} (R - \mu) \right\}.$$

Now the following result holds (see, for example, Merton [134, pp. 47–48]).

**Theorem 8.7.2.** *Suppose D.1 and D.3 are satisfied. If $x^*$ solves (8.7.1) for some u, then $x^*$ solves (8.7.4) for some F with $\partial F / \partial \mu > 0$ and $\partial F / \partial \sigma < 0$.*

Hence, under multivariate normality, the Markowitz methodology is consistent with expected utility maximization.

As shown by Ingersoll [99, pp. 104–10], the theorem holds for a larger class of probability distributions. This class contains, for example, the multivariate student $T$-distribution.

# Section 8.8
# Multiperiod Expected Utility Maximization: Formulation

The problem of maximizing expected utility of one-period wealth can readily be extended to the problem of maximizing expected utility of wealth after $T$ periods. This multiperiod problem is formulated in this section, and then two solution procedures, dynamic programming and the risk-neutral computational approach are described in the following sections. Note that the ideas here are closely related to the equilibrium-pricing approach for multiperiod models studied in Section 4.7.

Given a probability space $(\Omega, \mathcal{F}, P)$ with time horizon $T < \infty$ and filtration $\boldsymbol{F} = \{\mathcal{F}_t; \ t = 0, \ldots, T\}$, we suppose there are $N$ risky assets having return processes $R_i = \{R_i(t); \ t = 1, \ldots, T\}, i = 1, \ldots, N$. Thus $R_i(t)$ is the one-period return for asset $i$ from time $t - 1$ to time $t$, exactly as described in Section 8.1. We assume that each stochastic process $R_i$ is adapted to the filtration; that is, the information $\mathcal{F}_t$ known to the investors at each time $t$ includes full knowledge of the past and present values of all $N$ return processes.[25] Mathematically we write this as $R_i(t) \in \mathcal{F}_t$ and say that $R_i(t)$ is measurable with respect to the $\sigma$-algebra $\mathcal{F}_t$. Note that for many model formulations, the time-$t$ information $\mathcal{F}_t$ consists of precisely the past and present values (the history) of the return processes, and nothing more.

There is also a riskless asset with constant interest rate $r \geq 0$. Sometimes it is convenient to let $R_0$ denote its return process, so $R_0(t) = r$ for $t = 1, \ldots, T$.

Investors may want to adjust their portfolio positions each period, so it will be necessary to describe an investor's trading strategy by a vector-valued stochastic process $\boldsymbol{X} = (X_0, \ldots, X_N)$, where each component is itself a stochastic process $X_i = \{X_i(t); \ t = 1, \ldots, T\}, i = 0, \ldots, N$. It is convenient to denote $\boldsymbol{X}(t) = \{X_0(t), \ldots, X_N(t)\}$. Of course, these processes must satisfy the constraints

$$\sum_{i=0}^{N} X_i(t) = 1, \quad t = 1, \ldots, T, \tag{8.8.1}$$

because $X_i(t)$ represents the proportion of portfolio wealth that is invested in asset $i$ from time $t-1$ to time $t$. Since we want the investors to be rational but not clairvoyant, we must require the trading strategies to be *predictable* stochastic processes. This means that for each $t$ the trading position $\boldsymbol{X}(t)$ established at time $t - 1$ must be based on the information $\mathcal{F}_{t-1}$ available at time $t - 1$, and nothing more. Mathematically we write this as $\boldsymbol{X}(t) \in \mathcal{F}_{t-1}$ and say that $\boldsymbol{X}(t)$ is measurable with respect to the $\sigma$-algebra $\mathcal{F}_{t-1}$. In summary, a predictable vector-valued stochastic process $\boldsymbol{X}$ satisfying (8.8.1) is called an *admissible trading strategy*.

Let $W_t$ represent the time-$t$ wealth, that is, the time-$t$ value of the portfolio under a particular trading strategy $\boldsymbol{X}$. Then $W_{t-1} X_i(t)$ is the amount of dollars invested in asset $i$ at time $t - 1$, and this becomes $W_{t-1} X_i(t)[1 + R_i(t)]$ at time $t$.

---

[25] See Appendix A for explanations about the filtrations and other probabilistic concepts that are used here.

Hence,

$$W_t = \sum_{i=0}^{N} W_{t-1} X_i(t)[1 + R_i(t)]$$

$$= W_{t-1}\left[1 + \sum_{i=0}^{N} X_i(t) R_i(t)\right]$$

$$= W_{t-1}[1 + R_X(t)]$$

where $R_X$ is the stochastic process $\{R_X(t); \ t = 1, \ldots, T\}$ and $R_X(t) = \sum_{i=0}^{N} X_i(t) R_i(t)$. It follows that

$$W_t = W_0 \prod_{s=1}^{t}[1 + R_X(s)], \quad t = 1, \ldots, T.$$

Note that both $W$ and $R_X$ are adapted stochastic processes.

Suppose there is an investor who starts with initial wealth $W_0 > 0$ and wishes to choose a trading strategy $X$ that will maximize the expected utility of time-$T$ wealth $W_T$. We assume this investor's utility function is a concave, increasing, real-valued function $u$ whose domain includes, at least, $(0, \infty)$ (for example, $u(W) = \log(W)$ or $u(W) = 1 - e^{-aW}$). From the mathematical standpoint, therefore, this investor wishes to solve the following problem:

> Maximize $E[u(W_T)]$
> subject to $X$ is an admissible trading strategy

.

The following two sections describe two approaches for solving this problem, but first here is an example.

***Example 8.8.1.*** Consider an economy in which there are $N = 2$ risky assets as well as a riskless asset with constant interest rate $R_0 = r = 0.10$ per period. During each period the economy will be in one of three states: *boom*, with probability 0.25, *normal*, with probability 0.5, or *recession*; with probability 0.25 independent of the previous states.

The returns on the risky assets are assumed to be independently and identically distributed in each period, as indicated in Table 8.5. Suppose we are interested in a two-period problem, so $T = 2$, and for some utility function $u$ and some initial wealth $W_0$ we seek to maximize $E[u(W_2)]$. We thus build a two-period model with

### TABLE 8.5 | *Probability Distribution of the Risky Assets*

| State of the Economy | $R_1(t)$ | $R_2(t)$ | Probability |
|---|---|---|---|
| Boom | 0.25 | 0.20 | 0.25 |
| Normal | 0.15 | 0.10 | 0.50 |
| Recession | −0.10 | 0.00 | 0.25 |

$\Omega = \{\omega_1, \ldots, \omega_9\}$ and the probability measure $P(\omega)$ and filtration $\mathcal{F}$ as displayed in Figure 8.11. Note by Exercise 8.10 that this model is indeed free of arbitrage opportunities. We come back to this example below. The other quantities appearing in Figure 8.11 are explained in Example 8.10.2. ∎

### FIGURE 8.11 | *The Two-Period Model in Example 8.8.1*

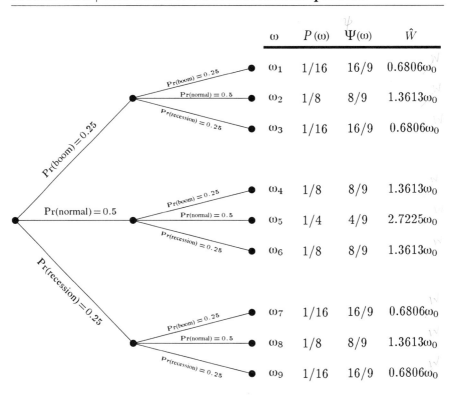

| $\omega$ | $P(\omega)$ | $\Psi(\omega)$ | $\hat{W}$ |
|---|---|---|---|
| $\omega_1$ | 1/16 | 16/9 | $0.6806\omega_0$ |
| $\omega_2$ | 1/8 | 8/9 | $1.3613\omega_0$ |
| $\omega_3$ | 1/16 | 16/9 | $0.6806\omega_0$ |
| $\omega_4$ | 1/8 | 8/9 | $1.3613\omega_0$ |
| $\omega_5$ | 1/4 | 4/9 | $2.7225\omega_0$ |
| $\omega_6$ | 1/8 | 8/9 | $1.3613\omega_0$ |
| $\omega_7$ | 1/16 | 16/9 | $0.6806\omega_0$ |
| $\omega_8$ | 1/8 | 8/9 | $1.3613\omega_0$ |
| $\omega_9$ | 1/16 | 16/9 | $0.6806\omega_0$ |

# Section 8.9
# Multiperiod Expected Utility Maximization: Dynamic Programming

It may not be clear from the problem statement, but many constraints and variables are implicit. Most of the constraints are due to the requirement that the trading strategy be a predictable stochastic process. In other words, the choice of $X(t)$ at time $t - 1$ is restricted so that it cannot depend on the future returns of the assets. At the same time, the choice of $X(t)$ should depend on $W_{t-1}$ as well as, in general, all of the current information $\mathcal{F}_{t-1}$. Keeping in mind that $X(t)$ is a random variable and thus a function of $\omega \in \Omega$ as well as $t$, this means a great number of scalar-valued decision variables must be chosen at time $t - 1$, all chosen subject to the requirement that $X(t) \in \mathcal{F}_{t-1}$.

In general, the portfolio position $X(t)$ selected at time $t - 1$ will need to depend on the history of returns. However, in the special case where the returns in successive periods are independent random variables, the optimal value of $X(t)$ need depend only on $t$ and the current wealth $W_{t-1}$. But even in this case there are many decision variables, usually too many to solve the portfolio problem as a straightforward constrained optimization problem. Other approaches must be taken.

One approach is to use dynamic programming. The idea is to solve a sequence of one-period problems, working backward in time. At each stage the maximum expected utility of time $T$ wealth as a function of the current information (which includes knowledge of the current wealth) is computed. The optimal portfolio position $X(t)$, which also depends on the current information, is tracked. By working backwards in time in a recursive manner, the optimal value of the original problem is eventually obtained, and the optimal trading strategy pieced together.

To be more specific, let the random variable $U_t$ denote the maximum expected utility of time-$T$ wealth $W_T$ conditioned on the time-$t$ information $\mathcal{F}_t$. In other words,

$$U_t(W_t) = \max \mathrm{E}[u(W_T) \mid \mathcal{F}_t]$$

where the maximum is respect to the portfolio positions $X(t + 1) \in \mathcal{F}_t, \ldots, X(T) \in \mathcal{F}_{T-1}$ over all the remaining periods, and we have made explicit the dependence on the time-$t$ wealth $W_t$.

Setting $U_T(W) = u(W)$, we thus have for $t = T - 1$:

$$U_{T-1}(W_{T-1}) = \max_{X(T)} \mathrm{E}[U_T(W_T) \mid \mathcal{F}_{T-1}].$$

Note that $U_{T-1}(W_{T-1})$ is a random variable (although we have not explicitly denoted its dependence on $\omega \in \Omega$) that is a function of the scalar parameter $W_{T-1}$. We can just as well replace $W_{T-1}$ by the scalar $W$, so by an earlier equation we can rewrite this as

$$U_{T-1}(W) = \max_{X(T)} E\left[ U_T\left[ W\left(1 + \sum_{i=0}^{N} X_i(T) R_i(T)\right)\right] \Big| \mathcal{F}_{T-1}\right].$$

Recalling Section 8.7, we see that this is mathematically the same as a one-period maximum expected utility problem. The solution of this problem gives the optimal value of $X(T)$ as a function of the time $(T-1)$ information $\mathcal{F}_{T-1}$ as well as the wealth $W_{T-1} = W$. Note that the maximizing value of $X(T)$ will automatically satisfy the constraint $X(T) \in \mathcal{F}_{T-1}$ since the function being maximized will be $\mathcal{F}_{T-1}$-measurable.

Suppose we have computed the random variables $U_{T-1}(\cdot), \ldots, U_t(\cdot)$ recursively and we are ready to compute $U_{t-1}(\cdot)$. We do this by using the *dynamic programming functional equation*:

$$U_{t-1}(W) = \max_{X(t)} E\left[ U_t\left[ W\left(1 + \sum_{i=0}^{N} X_i(t) R_i(t)\right)\right] \Big| \mathcal{F}_{t-1}\right].$$

As with the computation of $U_{T-1}$, the solution of this one-period problem gives the optimal value of $X(t) \in \mathcal{F}_{t-1}$. Continuing backward in time in a recursive manner, we eventually compute $U_0(\cdot)$, thereby providing the solution to the original problem.

Notice that the dynamic programming method provides a bit more than what was originally asked for: it gives the optimal solution for all possible initial wealths $W$, not just the one $W_0$ in the original specification.

If the returns $R_i(t)$ are independent from one period to the next, then the solution is greatly simplified. The probability distribution for $R(t)$ does not depend on the information $\mathcal{F}_{t-1}$, and so the conditional expectation becomes an ordinary, unconditional expectation. In other words, the dynamic programming functional equation becomes

$$U_{t-1}(W) = \max_{X(t)} E\left[ U_t\left[ W\left(1 + \sum_{i=0}^{N} X_i(t) R_i(t)\right)\right]\right].$$

This means each $U_t(\cdot)$ as well as the corresponding optimal value of the portfolio position $X(t)$ will actually be deterministic functions of time and wealth. Intuitively, if the returns across time are independent, all that matters for the current choice of the one-period portfolio positions are the current wealth, the number of periods to go, and the forecast of the future (with the latter being independent of the past).

*Example 8.9.1.* Consider the two-period problem introduced in Example 8.8.1, and suppose the utility function is logarithmic, that is, $u(W) = \log(W)$ (see Example ?? for another situation involving logarithmic utility). Since the returns for this example are independent across time, we expect the optimal strategy to depend, at most, on the current wealth, the number of periods to go, and the probability distribution for the future returns. In fact (this is a special property of the logarithmic utility function), the optimal strategy will turn out to be also independent of the level of wealth.

To solve this problem with dynamic programming, we begin by setting $U_2(W) = \log(W)$ and addressing the dynamic functional equation

$$U_1(W) = \max_{X(2)} \mathrm{E}\left[\log\left[W\left(1 + \sum_{i=0}^{2} X_i(2)\, R_i(2)\right)\right]\right]$$

(recall the returns are independently distributed across time, so this expectation need not be conditioned on the time-1 information $\mathcal{F}_1$). The trading strategy $X(2)$ must satisfy $X_0(2) + X_1(2) + X_2(2) = 1$, so at this point we can conveniently introduce the notation $X_i(2) = x_i$ and then substitute $x_0 = 1 - x_1 + x_2$, thereby giving

$$U_1(W) = \max \mathrm{E}[\log[W(1 + r + (R_1(2) - r)x_1 + (R_2(2) - r)x_2)]]$$

$$= \log W + \max \mathrm{E}[\log(1 + r + (R_1(2) - r)x_1 + (R_2(2) - r)x_2)]$$

$$= \log W + \max \left\{ \frac{1}{4} \log[1.1 + 0.15x_1 + 0.10x_2] \right.$$

$$\left. + \frac{1}{2} \log[1.1 + 0.05x_1] + \frac{1}{4} \log[1.1 - 0.20x_1 - 0.10x_2] \right\},$$

where the maximum is over all real numbers $x_1$ and $x_2$ (we are assuming, for simplicity, that there are no short-sales restrictions nor any restrictions on the amount of funds that can be borrowed at the fixed interest rate $r = 10\%$). Notice that, as a direct consequence of the log utility function, the maximizing values of $x_1$ and $x_2$, and thus the optimal values of the trading positions established at time 1, will be independent of time-1 wealth $W$.

Next, we find the maximizing values of $x_1$ and $x_2$ by setting the partial derivatives of the argument equal to zero:

$$0 = \frac{1}{4}\frac{0.15}{1.1 + 0.15x_1 + 0.1x_2} + \frac{1}{2}\frac{0.05}{1.1 + 0.05x_1} + \frac{1}{4}\frac{-0.20}{1.1 - 0.2x_1 - 0.1x_2},$$

$$0 = \frac{1}{4}\frac{0.10}{1.1 + 0.15x_1 + 0.1x_2} + \frac{1}{2}\frac{0}{1.1 + 0.05x_1} + \frac{1}{4}\frac{-0.10}{1.1 - 0.2x_1 - 0.1x_2}.$$

Solving these two equations easily yields the unique solution $x_1 = 11$ and $x_2 = -77/4$. Thus for every dollar of time-1 wealth (note that this is independent of whether the first period was a boom, normal, or a recession), it is optimal to sell short 77/4 dollars of the second asset, thereby providing a total of $1 + 77/4 = 81/4$ dollars, which are divided up by putting 11 dollars in the first asset and the balance, $1 - 11 - (-77/4) = 37/4$ dollars, in the bank at 10%.

Substituting these values in the above expression for the optimal objective value yields

$$U_1(W) = \log W + \frac{1}{4} \log\left[1.1 + 0.15(11) + 0.10\left(-\frac{77}{4}\right)\right]$$

$$+ \frac{1}{2} \log[1.1 + 0.05(11)] + \frac{1}{4} \log\left[1.1 - 0.2(11) - 0.10\left(-\frac{77}{4}\right)\right]$$

$$= \log W + 0.1542.$$

This completes the first iteration of the dynamic programming algorithm.

For the second iteration of the dynamic programming algorithm, we compute $(x_1 = X_1(1), \text{etc.})$

$$U_0(W) = \max E[U_1[W(1 + r + (R_1(1) - r)x_1 + (R_2(1) - r)x_2)]]$$

$$= 0.1542 + \max E[\log[W(1 + r + (R_1(1) - r)x_1 + (R_2(1) - r)x_2)]]$$

$$= 0.1542 + \max E[\log[W(1.1 + (R_1(1) - r)x_1 + (R_2(1) - r)x_2)]]$$

$$= 0.1542 + \log W + \max \left\{ \frac{1}{4} \log[1.1 + 0.15x_1 + 0.10x_2] \right.$$

$$\left. + \frac{1}{2} \log[1.1 + 0.05x_1] + \frac{1}{4} \log[1.1 - 0.20x_1 - 0.10x_2] \right\}.$$

But we recognize this last term as the same as before; it equals 0.1542, corresponding to the same maximizing values $x_1 = 11$ and $x_2 = -77/4$. Thus, the optimal objective function for the original problem is

$$U_0(W) = 0.3084 + \log W,$$

and the optimal position established at time-0 is specified by $X_0(1) = 37/4$, $X_1(1) = 11$, and $X_2(1) = -77/4$, independent of the time-0 wealth $W_0$. ∎

## Section 8.10
## Multiperiod Expected Utility Maximization: The Risk-Neutral Computational Approach

As discussed in Chapter 5, if the multiperiod model is a reasonable one, then there cannot be any arbitrage opportunities, and thus a risk-neutral probability (i.e., martingale) measure $Q$ must exist. If the risk-neutral measure $Q$ is unique, that is, if the model is complete, then $Q$ can be used to great advantage in an alternative computational approach.

The basic idea is quite simple. The original optimal portfolio problem can be viewed as finding the admissible trading strategy $X$ that maximizes the function $E[u(W_T)]$, a real-valued function with domain the set of all admissible trading strategies: that is, a certain set of stochastic processes.

However, this function can be decomposed into the composition of two functions. The first function $X \rightarrow W_T$ maps the set of all admissible trading strategies into $W$, which denotes the set of all time-$T$ *wealths* that can be generated by a trading strategy $X$ starting with initial wealth $W_0$. The second function $W_T \rightarrow E[u(W_T)]$ maps $W$ into the real line.

This decomposition allows us to solve the optimal portfolio problem with a three-step process:
- First, characterize the set $W$ of *attainable wealths.*
- Second, solve the optimization problem of maximizing $E[u(W)]$ over all $W \in W$, thereby giving the *optimal attainable wealth*, which we denote by $\hat{W}$.
- Third, find the optimal trading strategy, that is, the strategy $\hat{X}$ that generates $\hat{W}$.

The first step is easy in the case of a complete market; this is shown below. Moreover, the second step is easy, because our assumption that the utility function $u$ is concave means that step 2 is nothing more than a convex optimization problem. With some modest additional assumptions about the utility function, an explicit formula for $\hat{W}$ and the optimal objective value can be readily obtained, as is shown below. Finally, the third step is easy, at least in principle, because it is nothing more than the problem of hedging the contingent claim $\hat{W}$. In other words, step 3 is the same as finding the trading strategy that replicates the European option having time-$T$ payoff $\hat{W}$. This kind of problem was extensively studied in Chapters 5 and 6.

We now take a more detailed look at step 1. Recall from Chapter 5 that under the risk-neutral measure $Q$ and under any trading strategy $X$ the corresponding discounted wealth process, namely $(1 + r)^{-t} W_t$, will be a martingale. This means $E^Q[(1 + r)^{-T} W_T] = W_0$ for all trading strategies $X$. Furthermore, if the market is complete (as we are assuming), then for any random variable $W$ there exists some trading strategy $X$ and some initial wealth $W_o$ such that the corresponding wealth process satisfies $W_T = W$. This means, in particular, that if $W$ satisfies $E^Q[(1 + r)^{-T} W] = W_0$ for the specified number $W_0$, then the trading strategy $X$ that replicates $W$ must be such that the corresponding initial wealth is precisely $W_0$. Putting this all together, we have our characterization of the set $W$:

$$W = \{\text{all random variables } W : E^Q[(1 + r)^{-T} W] = W_0\}.$$

So much for step 1; we now turn to step 2. In view of our characterization of $W$, we can write the step 2 subproblem as follows:

$$\boxed{\begin{array}{l} \max \; E[u(W)] \\ \text{subject to } E^Q[(1 + r)^{-T} W] = W_0 \end{array}}.$$

To solve this constrained convex optimization problem, we introduce a Lagrange multiplier $\lambda$, thereby creating an equivalent unconstrained convex optimization problem:

$$\max \; E[u(W)] - \lambda E^Q[(1 + r)^{-T} W].$$

Next we introduce the state price density $\psi(\omega) \equiv Q(\omega)/P(\omega)$, $\omega \in \Omega$. This random variable is closely related to the state price process introduced in Chapter 5. It allows us to rewrite the unconstrained convex optimization problem as

$$\max \; E[u(W) - \lambda(1 + r)^{-T} \psi \cdot W].$$

Then we consider the necessary condition for the random variable $W$ to maximize this expression. Assuming the utility function $u$ is differentiable, and remembering that the random variables $W$ and $\psi$ are functions of $\omega \in \Omega$, this necessary condition is

$$u'(W(\omega)) = \lambda(1 + r)^{-T} \psi(\omega), \quad \text{all } \omega \in \Omega$$

where it is assumed that $\Omega$ is finite with $P(\omega) > 0$, all $\omega \in \Omega$.

This last equation can be used to solve for the optimal $W$. Let $h(\cdot)$ denote the inverse of the marginal utility function $u'(\cdot)$. Assuming the decreasing function $u'(w)$

ranges from $\infty$ to 0 as the scalar $w$ increases from 0 to $\infty$ (a property satisfied by many important utility functions), this equation can be rewritten as

$$W = h(\lambda(1 + r)^{-T}\psi).$$

(If this property does not hold, then the basic method still goes through, but the results might not be so straightforward.)

All that remains is to determine the correct value of the Lagrange multiplier $\lambda$. This is the scalar such that the original constraint is satisfied when the preceding expression is substituted for $W$. In other words, with $\hat{\lambda}$ denoting the value of $\lambda$ such that

$$E^Q[(1 + r)^{-T}h(\lambda(1 + r)^{-T}\psi)] = W_0,$$

we finally have

$$\hat{W} = h(\hat{\lambda}(1 + r)^{-T}\psi).$$

The optimal objective value is thus given by $E[u(\hat{W})]$. All this is illustrated in the following two examples; additional examples are given in Exercises 8.17 to 8.19.

***Example 8.10.1 (Logarithmic Utility).*** With $u(w) = \log(w)$ one has $u'(w) = 1/w$, in which case $h(i) = 1/i$. The equation for $\hat{\lambda}$, the correct value of the Lagrange multiplier, is

$$W_0 = E^Q\left[\frac{(1 + r)^{-T}}{\hat{\lambda}(1 + r)^{-T}\psi}\right] = \frac{1}{\hat{\lambda}}E^Q\left[\frac{1}{\psi}\right]$$

$$= \frac{1}{\hat{\lambda}}E^Q\left[\frac{P}{Q}\right] = \frac{1}{\hat{\lambda}}E[1] = \frac{1}{\hat{\lambda}}.$$

Hence, $\hat{\lambda} = W_0^{-1}$, in which case the optimal attainable wealth is

$$\hat{W} = \frac{W_0(1 + r)^T}{\psi}$$

and the optimal objective value is

$$E[\log(\hat{W})] = E\left[\log\left(\frac{W_0(1 + r)^T}{\psi}\right)\right] = \log(W_0(1 + r)^T) - E[\log(\psi)]. \quad\blacksquare$$

***Example 8.10.2.*** The plan here is to use the results of Example 8.10.1 to solve the two-period problem introduced in Example 8.9.1. As stated in Exercise 8.11, the risk-neutral probability measure for this model is unique (so the model is complete) and is given by $Q(\omega) = 1/9$, all $\omega \in \Omega$. Hence, the state price density $\psi$ is easily computed; the values for $\psi(\omega)$, all $\omega \in \Omega$, are displayed in Figure 8.11.

Having derived $\psi$, we can easily compute the optimal objective value:

$$E[\log(\hat{W})] = \log W_0 + 2\log(1.1) - E[\log(\psi)]$$
$$= \log W_0 + 0.1906 + 0.1178$$
$$= \log W_0 + 0.3084,$$

which is in precise agreement with the dynamic programming calculation of Example 8.9.1.

The next task is to compute the optimal attainable wealth $\hat{W}$. By Example 8.10.1, this is given by $\hat{W} = (1.1)^2 W_0/\psi$, so the individual values of $\hat{W}(\omega)$ are easily worked out to be as displayed in Figure 8.11.

This completes the second principal step of the risk-neutral computational approach. All that remains is to derive the trading strategy that generates the contingent claim $\hat{W}$. To do this, we can start by computing the optimal position to establish at time 1 if the first period was a boom:

$$W_1[1.25x_1 + 1.20x_2 + (1 - x_1 - x_2)(1.1)] = 0.6806 W_0,$$
$$W_1[1.15x_1 + 1.10x_2 + (1 - x_1 - x_2)(1.1)] = 1.3613 W_0,$$
$$W_1[0.90x_1 + x_2 + (1 - x_1 - x_2)(1.1)] = 0.6806 W_0.$$

The solution is easily found to be $W_1 = 0.825 W_0$, $x_1 = 11$, and $x_2 = -77/4$ (after adjustment due to round-off error). The trading positions to establish in the other time-1 situations as well as at time 0 are computed in a similar manner. The result will be the same trading strategy that was computed in Example 8.9.1 ∎

# Section 8.11
# Appendix: Kuhn-Tucker Theorem

In this chapter, we deal with optimization problems of the type

$$
\begin{array}{ll}
\max_{x \in \Re^N} f(x) & \\
\text{subject to } g_i(x) \geq 0, & i = 1, \ldots, m_1 \\
\text{and } g_i(x) = 0, & i = m_1 + 1, \ldots, m
\end{array}
\tag{8.11.1}
$$

The Lagrangian is given by

$$\mathcal{L}(\boldsymbol{x}, \boldsymbol{\lambda}) = f(\boldsymbol{x}) + \sum_{i=1}^{m} \lambda_i g_i(\boldsymbol{x}).$$

The following version of the Kuhn-Tucker theorem is appropriate for our purposes.

**Theorem 8.11.1.** *Assume*

1.   $f : \Re^N \to \Re$ *is concave.*
2.   $g_i : \Re^N \to \Re, \quad i = 1, \ldots, m_1$ *are concave,*
     $g_i : \Re^N \to \Re, \quad i = m_1 + 1, \ldots, m$ *are linear.*
3.   *There exists $\hat{x} \in \Re^N$ with*
     $g_i(\hat{x}) > 0, \quad i = 1, \ldots, m_1,$
     $g_i(\hat{x}) = 0, \quad i = m_1 + 1, \ldots, m.$

*Then $x^*$ solves (8.11.1) if and only if there exists $\boldsymbol{\lambda} = (\lambda_1, \ldots, \lambda_m)$ with $\lambda_1, \ldots, \lambda_{m_1} \geq 0, \lambda_{m1+1}, \ldots, \lambda_m \in \Re$ such that*

$$\mathcal{L}(\boldsymbol{x}^*, \boldsymbol{\lambda}') \geq \mathcal{L}(\boldsymbol{x}^*, \boldsymbol{\lambda}) \geq \mathcal{L}(\boldsymbol{x}, \boldsymbol{\lambda}),$$

$$\forall \boldsymbol{x} \in \Re^N, \qquad \forall \boldsymbol{\lambda}' \in \Re^m, \quad \text{with } \lambda'_1, \ldots, \lambda'_{m_1} \geq 0.$$

**Corollary 8.11.2.** *Under the assumptions of the theorem and if $f(\boldsymbol{x}), g_1(\boldsymbol{x}), \ldots, g_{m1}(\boldsymbol{x})$ are differentiable in $\boldsymbol{x}^*$ we obtain the following: $\boldsymbol{x}^*$ solves (8.11.1) if and only if there exists $\boldsymbol{\lambda} = (\lambda_1, \ldots, \lambda_m)$ with $\lambda_1, \ldots, \lambda_{m_1} \geq 0, \lambda_{m_1+1}, \ldots, \lambda_m \in \Re$ such that*

1.   $\text{grad } f(\boldsymbol{x}^*) + \sum_{i=1}^{m} \lambda_i \text{ grad } g_i(\boldsymbol{x}^*) = \boldsymbol{0}$
2.   $g_i(\boldsymbol{x}^*) \geq 0, \qquad \lambda_i g_i(\boldsymbol{x}^*) = 0, \quad i = 1, \ldots, m_1$
3.   $g_i(\boldsymbol{x}^*) = 0, \quad i = m_1 + 1, \ldots, m.$

These results are a special case of Arrow, Hurwicz, and Uzawa [1]. For an easy reference see Takayama [189, Theorem 1.D.4.iii, pp. 97–98, and diagram 1.15, p. 100].

# Section 8.12
# Exercises

## Exercise 8.1

The random variables $R_1$, $R_2$ denote the rates of return on two subindices. Furthermore, the rate of return on the index is given by

$$R_3 = 0.7 R_1 + 0.3 R_2.$$

If $\mathrm{Var}(R_1) = 0.04$, $\mathrm{Var}(R_2) = 0.0225$, $\mathrm{Cov}(R_1, R_2) = 0.018$, the covariance matrix $\Sigma = (\mathrm{Cov}(R_i, R_j))_{i,j=1,2,3}$ can be calculated. Show that $\Sigma$ is positive semi-definite but not positive definite.

## Exercise 8.2

Show that

$$\Sigma = \begin{pmatrix} 0.04 & -0.012 & -0.012 \\ -0.012 & 0.01 & -0.004 \\ -0.012 & -0.004 & 0.01 \end{pmatrix}$$

cannot be a covariance matrix. (Hint: Calculate the eigenvalues or use a Cholesky decomposition.)

## Exercise 8.3

Verify (8.2.7) and (8.2.8).

## Exercise 8.4

$N = 3$ risky assets are available, with

$$\Sigma = \begin{pmatrix} 0.0025 & -0.002 & 0.003 \\ -0.002 & 0.01 & 0.01 \\ 0.003 & 0.01 & 0.04 \end{pmatrix}, \qquad \mu = \begin{pmatrix} 0.06 \\ 0.08 \\ 0.11 \end{pmatrix}.$$

a. Calculate $x^{\mathrm{MIN}}$, $z^*$.
b. Calculate the efficient frontiers in the $(\mu_x, \sigma_x^2)$- and in the $(\mu_x, \sigma_x)$-diagrams.

## Exercise 8.5

A riskless asset and two risky assets with rates of return $R_0$, $R_1$, $R_2$ are available:
$R_0 = 0.05$, $\mathrm{E}[R_1] = 0.07$, $\mathrm{E}[R_2] = 0.11$
$\mathrm{Var}(R_1) = 0.01$, $\mathrm{Var}(R_2) = 0.04$, $\mathrm{Cov}(R_1, R_2) = 0.01$.
a. Calculate $\mathrm{E}[R_x]$ and $\sigma(R_x)$ for a portfolio $x^T = (0.3, 0.2, 0.5)$.
b. Calculate the optimal portfolio $x^*$ for an investor with a risk tolerance $\tau = 0.3$.

## Exercise 8.6

Riskless cash, a bond index, and a stock index with rates of return $R_0$, $R_1$, $R_2$ are available as investment opportunities. For an investor with a risk tolerance $\tau = 0.3$ and without any additional constraints, the optimal portfolio choice is

$x^{*T} = (0.2, 0.3, 0.5)$. Furthermore, $R_0 = 0.06$, $\text{Var}(R_1) = 0.01$, $\text{Var}(R_2) = 0.03$, $\text{Cov}(R_1, R_2) = 0.005$ are known. Use reverse optimization to calculate $E[R_1]$, $E[R_2]$.

## Exercise 8.7

Calculate the "marginal utilities" for an investor with a risk tolerance $\tau = 0.4$ in Exercise 8.5.

## Exercise 8.8

In this exercise the CAPM is assumed to hold. The rates of return on the risk-free asset and on the market portfolio are denoted by $R_0$ and $R^M$.

a. Let $\beta_i$ be the beta coefficients of the risky assets $i = 1, \ldots, N$. What is the beta coefficient of a portfolio $x^T = (x_0, x_1, \ldots, x_N)$?

b. Given $R_0 = 0.05$, $E[R^M] = 0.10$, calculate the beta coefficient of an asset $i$ with $E[R_i] = 0.11$.

c. Given $R_0 = 0.06$, $E[R^M] = 0.12$, calculate the beta coefficient of an efficient portfolio $x^*$ with $E[R_{x^*}] = 0.105$. What do you know about $\rho(R_{x^*}, R^M)$?

d. Given $R_0 = 0.04$, $E[R^M] = 0.09$, $\sigma(R^M) = 0.20$, calculate the systematic and unsystematic risk (measured by variance) of an asset $i$ with $E[R_i] = 0.10$, $\sigma(R_i) = 0.30$.

e. A share of a firm is expected to have a value of \$50 1 year from now. No dividends are paid, and the beta coefficient is 0.9. Given the market conditions $R_0 = 0.06$, $E[R^M] = 0.11$, how would you price this share today?

## Exercise 8.9

Use standard software to solve the optimization problem

$$
\begin{array}{|l|}
\hline
\max_{x \in \mathbb{R}^N} \{2\tau\mu^T x - x^T \Sigma x\} \\[2mm]
\text{subject to } \sum_{i=1}^{N} x_i = 1, \quad x \geq 0 \\
\hline
\end{array}
$$

with

$$
\Sigma = \begin{pmatrix} 0.0004 & -0.001 & 0 \\ -0.001 & 0.01 & 0.01 \\ 0 & 0.010 & 0.04 \end{pmatrix}, \qquad \mu = \begin{pmatrix} 0.06 \\ 0.08 \\ 0.12 \end{pmatrix}
$$

for the risk tolerance levels $\tau = 0.2, 0.4, 0.5, 0.6, 0.7$.

## Exercise 8.10

Show that the two-period model in Example 8.8.1 is free of arbitrage opportunities by showing that the risk-neutral probability measure $Q$ is unique and satisfies $Q(\omega) = 1/9$ for all $\omega \in \Omega$.

## Exercise 8.11

Use dynamic programming to solve the two-period problem in Example 8.9.1, adding the stipulation that short sales are prohibited.

## Exercise 8.12

Use dynamic programming to solve the two-period problem in Example 8.9.1, dropping the assumption that the state of the economy is independently distributed from one period to the next. Instead, assume that the economy just finished a normal period, that it evolves like a Markov chain, and that from one period to the next the economy remains in the same state with probability $1/2$, whereas with equal probabilities it changes next period to one of the other two states.

## Exercise 8.13  (Power Utility)

Use dynamic programming to solve the two-period problem in Example 8.9.1, the only change being that the utility function is a power function (see Examples 4.2.4 and 8.7.1).

## Exercise 8.14  (Exponential Utility)

Use dynamic programming to solve the two-period problem in Example 8.9.1, the only change being that the utility function is exponential (see Examples 4.2.3 and 8.7.2).

## Exercise 8.15  (Quadratic Utility)

Use dynamic programming to solve the two-period problem in Example 8.9.1, the only change being that the utility function is quadratic (see Examples 4.2.2 and 8.7.3).

## Exercise 8.16

Verify the last statement of Example 8.10.1 by showing that the optimal trading strategy of Example 8.9.1 generates the optimal attainable wealth $\hat{W}$.

## *Exercise 8.17 (Power Utility)*

With the power utility function show that the optimal attainable wealth is

$$\hat{W} = \frac{W_0 \{\psi(1+r)^{-T}\}^{-1/(1-\alpha)}}{\mathrm{E}\left[\{\psi(1+r)^{-T}\}^{-\alpha/(1-\alpha)}\right]}$$

and that the optimal objective value is

$$\mathrm{E}[u(\hat{W})] = \frac{W_0^\alpha}{\alpha} \left(\mathrm{E}\left[\{\psi(1+r)^{-T}\}^{-\alpha/(1-\alpha)}\right]\right)^{1-\alpha}.$$

Then use the risk-neutral computational approach to solve the two-period problem in Example 8.9.1, the only change being this change of utility function.

## *Exercise 8.18 (Exponential Utility)*

With an exponential utility function show that the optimal attainable wealth is

$$\hat{W} = \frac{W_0 + a^{-1}\mathrm{E}[\psi(1+r)^{-T} \log\{\psi(1+r)^{-T}\}]}{\mathrm{E}[\psi(1+r)^{-T}]} - a^{-1} \log\{\psi(1+r)^{-T}\}$$

and that the optimal objective value is

$$\mathrm{E}[u(\hat{W})] = 1 - \mathrm{E}[\psi(1+r)^{-T}] \exp\left\{\frac{-aW_0 - \mathrm{E}[\psi(1+r)^{-T} \log\{\psi(1+r)^{-T}\}]}{\mathrm{E}[\psi(1+r)^{-T}]}\right\}.$$

Then use the risk-neutral computational approach to solve the two-period problem in Example 8.9.1, the only change being this change of utility function.

## *Exercise 8.19 (Quadratic Utility)*

With a quadratic utility function show that the optimal attainable wealth is

$$\hat{W} = b + \frac{\{(1+r)^T W_0 - b\}\psi}{\mathrm{E}^Q[\psi]}$$

and that the optimal objective value is

$$\mathrm{E}[u(\hat{W})] = \frac{(b/2)\{\mathrm{E}^Q[\psi] - 1\} + (1+r)^T W_0 - (1+r)^{2T} W_0^2/(2b)}{\mathrm{E}^Q[\psi]}.$$

Then use the risk-neutral computational approach to solve the two-period problem in Example 8.9.1, the only change being this change of utility function.

# Chapter 9

## Investment Return Models

---

## Section 9.1
## Introduction

The practical application of financial economic theory includes determining strategic and tactical asset allocations for insurance and pension funds, assessing the solvency requirements for these funds, and pricing and valuation of various assets and liabilities. A very common method used by fund managers and asset consultants to assist in determining a strategic asset allocation is an "optimizer" based on mean-variance analysis and the concept of the efficient set. Mean-variance analysis optimizes an asset allocation by trading off expected return for variance using an investor's risk tolerance. Mean-variance optimization was an early development in financial economics and is the underlying model for the development of the capital asset pricing model (CAPM). This methodology has been adapted to incorporate liabilities by treating these as a negative asset class or by modeling factors, such as rates of inflation, that influence the liabilities.

Factor models of security returns, as used in the development of arbitrage pricing theory (APT), are also used in establishing asset allocation strategies. These models assume a linear relationship between returns and explanatory factors such as GDP growth, inflation, and interest rates. They are used to select portfolios that have desired sensitivities to the selected factors. Chapter 8 covers these topics in some detail.

Option pricing is based on a multiperiod model of asset returns and a dynamic investment strategy that finances the option payoffs. This multiperiod dynamic approach has also found applications to investment strategy in the form of portfolio insurance, which replicates a synthetic put option, and constant proportion portfolio insurance, which is a dynamic asset allocation with an equity component equal to a multiple of the surplus in a fund. Option-pricing strategies can be considered as a form of matching. Pricing an option involves determining an asset allocation strategy that finances the option cash flows exactly. In a similar manner, matching is an investment strategy, using fixed-interest securities or other interest-sensitive securities, that selects assets exactly matching the liability cash flows (see Chapter 3).

The assumptions underlying mean-variance optimization and standard option pricing are idealized; asset returns are usually assumed to follow a multivariate normal (or lognormal) distribution. Changes in asset values are often assumed to be independent and identically distributed. For most models, this means that asset values have no serial correlation, which is consistent with the notion of efficient markets. These models are used as part of the process of determining asset portfolios that meet requirements of return and risk, often without considering the underlying nature of the liabilities that the assets are required to meet.

Empirical studies of equity returns have provided evidence that the independent and identically distributed multivariate normal (or lognormal) model often used to model changes in asset values in financial economic theory is at best a crude approximation to the return-generating process underlying asset returns. Studies have provided evidence that the variance of asset returns is time-varying, and various models have been proposed to capture this time variability. There is also some debate about whether or not there is "long-run" mean reversion in equity values. Evidence of nonlinear dependence in equity values can be found even though the evidence for serial correlation is weak. The independent and identically distributed normal (or lognormal) model is also inadequate for modeling returns on fixed-interest securities, and the interrelationship between economic variables, such as inflation, and asset returns is a matter of debate.

For many applications including setting asset strategies and managing solvency reserves for insurance and pension funds, it is necessary to model the factors that influence the liabilities and the interaction between the assets and the liabilities. This process is referred to as asset-liability modeling; an example is the modeling of interest rates for the immunization of a set of annuity liabilities. In many applications, the underlying factors that are assumed to influence the liability values include economic inflation. This is the case for salary-related pension benefits and for many insurance classes such as those covering bodily injury and property values.

Against this background, models for asset returns and the factors influencing insurance and pension liabilities have been developed based on both theoretical relationships between asset returns and economic variables and empirically estimated relationships. This is an area of active current research, but one critical to the application of financial economic theory to practical actuarial problems.

This chapter begins with an outline of the common models used in finance as investment-return models for asset values and returns: the random-walk model and the autoregressive or mean reverting models. We discuss briefly empirical studies related to these models, the modeling of liabilities, and the link between inflation and asset returns. Multivariate models are introduced, and the technique for generating multivariate normal returns are outlined. We discuss econometric models such as the VAR models along with the concepts of unit roots, cointegration, and GARCH models. Stochastic investment return models, including the Wilkie model, that have been developed for insurance and pension applications are explained, as well as insurance and pension applications where these stochastic investment return models have been applied.

# Section 9.2
# Financial Models

### SECTION 9.2.1 | RANDOM WALK

In financial economics, equity values are usually assumed to follow a random walk. This model represents an equity-indexed value:

$$\log P(t + h) = \log P(t) + \mu h + \sigma \sqrt{h}\, \varepsilon_{t+h} \tag{9.2.1}$$

where $P(t)$ is the level of the equity index at time $t$, $h$ is a time increment, $\mu$ and $\sigma$ are constants, and $\varepsilon_{t+h}$ are independent, identically distributed random variables with zero mean and unit variance. This can also be written as

$$\Delta \log P(t) = \mu h + \sigma \sqrt{h}\, \varepsilon_{t+h}$$

where $\Delta Y(t) = Y(t + h) - Y(t)$. Note that the first differences of $\log P(t) \equiv \Delta \log P(t) = \log P(t + h) - \log P(t)$ equal the continuously compounded growth rates of $P$.

Equation (9.2.1) can be rewritten as

$$\log P(t + h) - \mu \cdot (t + h) = \log P(t) - \mu t + \sigma \sqrt{h}\, \varepsilon_{t+h}$$

or

$$\Delta[\log P(t) - \mu t] = \sigma \sqrt{h}\, \varepsilon_{t+h}. \tag{9.2.2}$$

Note the following key points about (9.2.1) and (9.2.2):

- The first differences of $\log P(t)$ are stationary (that is, do not depend on $t$) with mean and variance proportional to $h$ and have zero serial correlation.

- The variance of $\log\{P(t + \tau h)/P(t)\}$ grows linearly with $\tau$ so that "long-horizon" returns have variances that are linearly proportional to "short-horizon" returns.

- The departure of $\log P(t)$ from the growth trend determined by $\mu t$, $[\log P(t) - \mu t]$, is not stationary, but $\Delta[\log P(t) - \mu t]$ is stationary, so $[\log P(t) - \mu t]$ is "difference stationary."

- $\Delta[\log P(t) - \mu t]$ does not depend on $[\log P(t) - \mu t]$ so that changes in $[\log P(t) - \mu t]$ are stochastic and hence not predictable.

- The serial correlations of $[\log P(t + \tau h)]^2$ and $|\log P(t + \tau h)|$ are zero so that there is no "nonlinear" dependence.

Often $\varepsilon_{t+h}$ is assumed to be normally distributed, in which case $\log P(t)$ is normal (i.e., $P(t)$ is lognormal) with independent and identically distributed increments with mean $\mu h$ and variance $\sigma^2 h$. In this case, the parameter values are estimated by the sample mean and variance of $\Delta \log P(t)$ using historical data. When this model is used to project the future distribution of $P(t)$, parameter uncertainty (that is, sampling error) must be allowed for; otherwise the sample estimates are being treated as the (unknown) population parameters of the index-generating process.

## SECTION 9.2.2 | AUTOCORRELATION

Consider what happens if $\Delta \log P(t)$ depends on $\log P(t)$ in the following manner:

$$\Delta \log P(t) = \gamma[\log P(t) - \mu t] + \mu h + \sigma\sqrt{h}\,\varepsilon_{t+h} \qquad (9.2.3)$$

or

$$\Delta[\log P(t) - \mu t] = \gamma[\log P(t) - \mu t] + \sigma\sqrt{h}\,\varepsilon_{t+h} \qquad (9.2.4)$$

where $\gamma < 0$.

In this case, if $\log P(t)$ departs from the trend $\mu t$, then the expected change in the next time period will pull $\log P(t + h)$ back toward the trend by an amount determined by $\gamma$. Such a process is said to be *autoregressive* or *mean-reverting* with speed of adjustment $\gamma$. In this case, departures from the trend have a stationary distribution. To see this, define $Y(t) = [\log P(t) - \mu t]$ as the departures from the "trend." Using the backshift function $B$, defined such that $BY(t) = Y(t - h)$, (9.2.4) can be written as

$$Y(t) = (1 + \gamma)Y(t - h) + \sigma\sqrt{h}\,\varepsilon_t$$
$$= [(1 + \gamma)B]Y(t) + \sigma\sqrt{h}\,\varepsilon_t.$$

Taking all terms containing $Y(t)$ to the left-hand side and multiplying both sides by $[1 - (1 + \gamma) B]^{-1}$ gives

$$
\begin{aligned}
Y(t) &= [1 - (1 + \gamma) B]^{-1} \sigma \sqrt{h}\, \varepsilon_t \\
&= \sigma \sqrt{h}\, [1 - (1 + \gamma) B]^{-1} \varepsilon_t \\
&= \sigma \sqrt{h}\, [1 + (1 + \gamma) B + (1 + \gamma)^2 B^2 + \cdots] \varepsilon_t \\
&= \sigma \sqrt{h}\, [\varepsilon_t + (1 + \gamma) \varepsilon_{t-h} + (1 + \gamma)^2 \varepsilon_{t-2h} + \cdots].
\end{aligned} \qquad (9.2.5)
$$

The key points to note about (9.2.3), (9.2.4), and (9.2.5) are the following:
- $Y(t)$ is stationary for $|1 + \gamma| < 1$ or $-2 < \gamma < 0$, in which case $\log P(t)$ is "trend stationary" around the trend $\mu t$.
- The case where $\gamma = 0$ reduces to (9.2.1) and (9.2.2) is "difference stationary."
- The variance of $Y(t)$ is

$$
\sigma^2 h [1 + (1 + \gamma)^2 + (1 + \gamma)^4 + \cdots] = \frac{\sigma^2 h}{1 - (1 + \gamma)^2}.
$$

- The autocovariance of the series $Y(t)$ for lag $k$ is

$$
\sigma^2 h \sum_{j=0}^{\infty} (1 + \gamma)^j (1 + \gamma)^{j+k} = \frac{\sigma^2 h (1 + \gamma)^k}{1 - (1 + \gamma)^2}.
$$

In this case, the series is autocorrelated, which implies that information about the history of the series can be used to forecast future values of the series. The process is not Markovian, unlike the random walk assumption for traded asset prices.

## SECTION 9.2.3 | PRICES AND RETURNS

In efficient financial markets, some financial theories suggest that prices should not exhibit any autocorrelation because this could, in theory, be used to earn excess returns. This has led to the use of the random walk assumption for share prices in financial economics. Thus, in portfolio theory and option-pricing theory, it is usually assumed that increments in prices are independent and identically distributed, usually with a normal or lognormal distribution, and so prices are usually assumed to be "difference" stationary. On the other hand, interest rates on bonds are sometimes modeled using a mean-reverting process. Such a process assumes that interest rates are "trend" stationary rather than difference stationary.

## SECTION 9.2.4 | EMPIRICAL ISSUES

Numerous empirical studies of prices and interest rates have tried to determine the nature of the process driving equity prices and interest rates. These studies have identified departures in price and returns data from the commonly used assumptions covered earlier. There has been some debate about the empirical evidence and the statistical veracity of the tests and the economic meaning of the results. However, these issues must be understood if the standard assumptions are used.

Most studies of equity returns and other financial data find them to be lepto-kurtic as compared with the normal distribution. This means that the return distributions are peaked at the mean and fat-tailed compared with the normal distribution. The distribution of price changes becomes more normal as the horizon over which these are measured is increased. Thus, annual returns are closer to normal than monthly returns. This "fat-tailed" feature of returns can be modeled in a number of ways, such as to use a heteroscedastic, or time-varying volatility, model for returns.

A number of studies of equity returns have found that the variance of price changes for longer horizons does not increase linearly as would be expected if equity prices followed a random walk. The variance was found to grow at a slower than linear rate, suggesting that equity values exhibit long-run mean reversion.

Studies of equity returns, interest rates, and foreign exchange rates have also found significant nonlinear dependence with absolute values of returns and squared returns significantly autocorrelated. These studies generally do not find evidence of serial correlation in the prices themselves.

The nonlinear dependence of squared returns suggests that the returns series could be heteroscedastic, and not homoscedastic as the random-walk model assumes. Studies of stock market volatility over long periods of time in a number of markets suggest that financial market volatility varies in certain systematic ways. For example, volatility of equity markets has tended to increase in recessions and financial crises and to be lower in bull markets than in bear markets. This latter phenomenon is usually explained by the effect of leverage where negative shocks result in proportionally higher volatility. Markets also exhibit volatility clustering where large and small "shocks" tend to cluster together. Large changes in returns tend to be followed by large changes and small changes by small changes. This feature of asset returns is indicative of nonlinear dependence in the returns series.

## SECTION 9.2.5 | INSURANCE AND PENSION LIABILITY ISSUES

Modeling insurance or pension liabilities and their interaction with asset cash flows requires a model of economic inflation. The major factor often assumed to impact on both asset values and liability claim payments is economic inflation. Future payments from pension funds are salary-linked, and salary growth is closely linked to rates of inflation in the economy. Claim payments for liability insurance products often provide compensation for lost earnings and are influenced by inflation. In a similar way, automobile and property insurance claims can be influenced by economic inflation, although not to the same extent as for earnings-related benefits.

The values of fixed-interest securities reflect current market yields to maturity, and new and maturing cash flows will often be invested at the market yields to maturity. As market yields to maturity rise and fall, so does the value of fixed interest investments. A term structure model as covered in Chapter 7 based on financial economic theory is needed for the valuation of fixed-interest and interest-sensitive asset and liability cash flows. Future market yields to maturity will be required for asset-liability projections, and these yields are often assumed to be influenced by inflation rates or expected inflation rates. A standard deterministic actuarial approach often assumes that the rate of interest maintains a constant margin over the rate of salary inflation. In a stochastic model, the rate of inflation is often assumed to have an influence on interest rates. Time-series techniques based on transfer functions and cross-correlations, as in Box and Jenkins [20], have been used to estimate the relationship between inflation and interest rates.

A contentious issue is the relationship between equity values, dividend growth rates, and inflation. Most actuaries would assume that equity values and dividends are influenced by inflation. Time-series analysis of equity returns carried out by authors developing models for asset-liability studies (see Carter [34], FitzHerbert [63], Harris [83], Huber [97], and Thomson [191]) suggest that there is little direct correlation between rates of equity growth for share price indices and the rate of inflation. Sharp [172] finds common stock returns are negatively related to inflation using year-to-year data. He also provides a brief review of studies of the relationship between stock returns and inflation found in U.S. data. These studies should be interpreted carefully because more recent developments in time-series and econometric analysis can be used to determine if equity values and inflation indices "move together" even though the rates of growth in these indices exhibit no significant cross-correlations. This is the notion of cointegration of the series originally developed by Engle and Granger [55] and discussed in Holden and Perman [95], Mills [135], and Perman [145]. Equity assets are often used as an inflation "hedge," and so the nature of this relationship is fundamental for asset-liability modeling and strategic asset allocation. This is discussed further in Section 9.3.

## SECTION 9.2.6 | MULTIVARIATE NORMAL RETURNS

Asset-liability studies are often performed using the quadratic optimization approach developed in portfolio theory. An assumption is made that one or more factors influence the liabilities, often an inflation rate such as the Consumer Price Index or a wages index, and the correlation matrix between different asset class returns and the liability factor is estimated and input into a quadratic optimizer to determine the efficient frontier for asset-allocation purposes. As usually implemented in practice the asset-liability model is a single-period model based on a "horizon" date for the liabilities. Asset and liability values are projected to the horizon date. The assumption is then made that these asset and liability returns are multivariate normal or lognormal random variables. This approach treats the asset-allocation problem as a single-period, not a dynamic, problem. For asset-liability studies a small group of asset classes is modeled. Typically this includes domestic equities, domestic fixed interest, domestic real property, domestic cash, international equities, and international fixed interest. Chapter 8 covered this approach in detail.

## SECTION 9.2.7 | GENERATING MULTIVARIATE NORMAL RANDOM VARIABLES

For actuarial modeling, simulation to generate the future distribution of cash flows or asset and liability values is often necessary. The models often involve a number of asset classes and some economic variables and are used to project asset returns and liability values. They are usually based on the normal or lognormal random walk model, and so multivariate normal random variables must be generated.

Assume that a vector of $n$ normal random variables is required with mean vector

$$\mu = \begin{bmatrix} \mu_1 \\ \mu_2 \\ \vdots \\ \mu_n \end{bmatrix}$$

and covariance matrix

$$\Sigma = [\sigma_{i,j}] = \begin{bmatrix} \sigma_1^2 & \rho_{12}\sigma_1\sigma_2 & \cdots & \rho_{1n}\sigma_1\sigma_n \\ \rho_{12}\sigma_1\sigma_2 & \sigma_2^2 & \cdots & \rho_{2n}\sigma_2\sigma_n \\ \vdots & \ddots & \cdots & \vdots \\ \rho_{1n}\sigma_1\sigma_n & \rho_{2n}\sigma_2\sigma_n & \cdots & \sigma_n^2 \end{bmatrix}.$$

Note that $\Sigma$ can be written as $\Sigma = \sigma^T C \sigma$ where

$$\sigma = \begin{bmatrix} \sigma_1 \\ \sigma_2 \\ \vdots \\ \sigma_n \end{bmatrix}$$

is the standard deviation vector and

$$C = \begin{bmatrix} 1 & \rho_{12} & \cdots & \rho_{1n} \\ \rho_{12} & 1 & \cdots & \rho_{2n} \\ \vdots & \ddots & \cdots & \vdots \\ \rho_{1n} & \rho_{2n} & \cdots & 1 \end{bmatrix}$$

is the correlation matrix.

A vector of normal random variables with any mean and covariance matrix can be generated from multivariate standard normal variables. To do this let the vector $Y = \mu + S\varepsilon$ where

$$\varepsilon = \begin{bmatrix} \varepsilon_1 \\ \varepsilon_2 \\ \vdots \\ \varepsilon_n \end{bmatrix}$$

is a vector of $n$ independent standard univariate standard normal variables generated from a standard normal random number generator. The mean vector and variance matrix of $Y$ are

$$E[Y] = \mu,$$
$$\text{Var}(Y) = E[(Y - \mu)(Y - \mu)^T]$$
$$= E[(S\varepsilon)(S\varepsilon)^T]$$
$$= E[S\varepsilon\varepsilon^T S^T]$$
$$= SS^T$$

where $E[\varepsilon\varepsilon^T] = I$, the identity matrix, since these are independent normal variables.

For the random variates in $Y$ to have the required mean and variance, a matrix $S$ must be found such that

$$SS^T = \Sigma.$$

The matrix $S$ can be determined using the modified Cholesky decomposition (square root) of $\Sigma$, a positive definite matrix. This process is covered in practically all numerical analysis textbooks (see, for example, Conte and de Boor [41]), and many programming languages have prewritten subroutines to perform Cholesky decomposition.

The multivariate i.i.d. normal (or lognormal) model suffers from a number of major problems from an asset-liability modeling perspective. First, the model is inherently single-period and does not allow dynamic asset allocation strategies to be analyzed or developed. There is a need for a proper multiperiod model for projections to handle dynamic asset allocation. A second problem, the assumption that none of the return series are autocorrelated, is particularly troublesome with the fixed-interest asset class where it is common to assume mean reversion or some other process with autocorrelation. Finally, the modeling of interest rates as the return on an asset class is problematic when it would be more appropriate to model a term structure of interest rates using one or more factors.

These models also assume that the variance is constant. Empirical evidence indicates that, particularly in the equity markets but also in other financial asset markets, large shocks tend to be followed by large shocks (of either sign) and small shocks tend to be followed by small shocks. This phenomenon is referred to as volatility clustering. The empirical evidence indicates correlation between absolute returns and between squared returns. This is often modeled using a GARCH model, which is described in Section 9.3.4.

# *Section 9.3*
# *Econometric Models*

## SECTION 9.3.1 | VARMA MODELS

Vector autoregressive (VAR) models are commonly used in econometric modeling. A VAR model can be written as

$$x_t = \sum_{j=1}^{m} A_{t-j} x_{t-j} + \varepsilon_t$$

where $x_t = y_t - \mu$ is a mean-adjusted vector of the $p$ series included in the model, $A_{t-j}$ is a matrix of parameters, and $\varepsilon_t$ is a vector of zero mean serially uncorrelated disturbances. Such models have the advantage of allowing feedback between the different asset returns and economic variables in the model; they capture all possible linear relationships between current and past values of the series being modeled. The structure of the model is determined empirically, although we can impose constraints. One of the estimation problems with such models is that there are often too many estimated parameters. For example, if the model includes $m$ lags and $p$ series, then this will involve $mp^2$ coefficients and $p(p+1)/2$ terms in the correlation matrix. The result is that the model appears to have a high statistical fit to the historical data, but it will be unstable for projecting since it is overparameterized. Often the parameters in the model are highly correlated, suggesting the need for a more parsimonious model that incorporates theoretical relationships as far as possible. Deaves [46] fits a VAR model to Canadian inflation and interest-rate data, and Wilkie [205] fits a VAR to U.K. wage and price inflation data.

Vector autoregressive moving average (VARMA) models are more general than VAR models because they allow for moving average terms, and they are often more parsimonious than VAR models because fewer lags in the autoregressive terms are required and because a moving average model is in theory equivalent to an infinite-order autoregressive model. Frees et al. [66] develop a VARMA model with GARCH errors for use with U.S. data for inflation, wages, interest rates, and unemployment rates to employ with Social Security projections; and Sherris, Tedesco, and Zehnwirth [180] fit VARMA models to Australian inflation and investment returns data.

**Example 9.3.1.** Historical data on the Australian share price equity index and the Australian consumer price inflation index from September 1948 to March 1995 was used to fit a VARMA model to these series (Sherris et al. [180]). The resulting VARMA model was

$$\begin{bmatrix} y_{t+1} \\ x_{t+1} \end{bmatrix} = \begin{bmatrix} 0.905 & 0 \\ 0 & 0 \end{bmatrix} \begin{bmatrix} y_t \\ x_t \end{bmatrix} \begin{bmatrix} \varepsilon_{t+1} \\ \eta_{t+1} \end{bmatrix} + \begin{bmatrix} -0.473 & 0 \\ 0 & 0 \end{bmatrix} \begin{bmatrix} \varepsilon_t \\ \eta_t \end{bmatrix}$$

where $y_t$ is the mean adjusted continuously compounded rate of inflation and $x_t$ is the mean adjusted continuously compounded rate of growth in the equity index

$$\begin{bmatrix} y_t \\ x_t \end{bmatrix} = \begin{bmatrix} (y_t - y_{t-1}) - 0.0153 \\ (x_t - x_{t-1}) - 0.0161 \end{bmatrix}$$

where $y_t = \log$ (consumer price index at quarter $t$) and $x_t = \log$ (share price index at quarter $t$).

The covariance matrix for the errors was

$$\Sigma = \text{Var} \begin{bmatrix} \varepsilon_{t+1} \\ \eta_{t+1} \end{bmatrix} = \begin{bmatrix} 8.84 \times 10^{-3} & -7.18 \times 10^{-5} \\ -7.18 \times 10^{-5} & 8.39 \times 10^{-3} \end{bmatrix}$$

so that the standard deviation was 0.094 for the quarterly continuously compounded equity return and 0.0092 for the continuously compounded inflation rate. The correlation between the residuals was $-0.0834$. ∎

State-space models are a more general modeling framework that contain as special cases the transfer function models and VARMA models. Both VAR and VARMA models have equivalent representations in the state-space modeling framework (Harvey [84]). A state-space model can be written in the form of a state equation

$$z_t = Fz_{t-1} + G\varepsilon_t$$

and an observation equation

$$y_t = Hz_t$$

where $z_t$ is the state of the model at time $t$, $F$, $G$, and $H$ are matrices of parameters, and $\varepsilon_t$ is the mean zero vector of serially uncorrelated disturbances. Statistical techniques for fitting such models can be found in many statistical packages such as SAS.

Developing and estimating investment return models requires knowledge and skills in time series and econometrics. In practice, input from an expert who is familiar with modern time series and econometric tools may be obtained to assist in developing a structure for a model and for estimating parameters. Often the hardest issue is deciding on the appropriate structure and testing if this structure is consistent with the historical data. Such model building is a mixture of art and science. There is, however, a large body of literature in finance, economics, and econometrics covering the empirical analysis of financial data and the economic theory underlying such models.

In developing a model, consider first some basic issues about the structure of the model. These concern assumptions about stationarity of the series and long-run relationships between the different series that are being modeled. Econometricians have developed tests for such assumptions. These tests, applications of which to a number of the U.K. data series can be found in Wilkie [206], have been applied to Australian data in Sherris et al. [180]. An examination of these assumptions is useful before developing a model structure.

## SECTION 9.3.2 | UNIT ROOTS

An important issue in modeling investment series is whether or not the series is stationary. For instance, if the level of interest rates is stationary, then an autoregressive model or a model using the levels of interest rates would be appropriate for model structure, parameter estimation using standard statistical techniques, and projection of the series. If the level of a series is found to be nonstationary, then the differences of the series are taken and these are examined for stationarity. If the first differences of the series are stationary, then the series is said to contain a "unit root" or be "difference stationary." In this case, the trend in the level of the series is stochastic, and "shocks" have a permanent effect on the series, whereas if the level of the series is stationary, then the trend in the series is deterministic and "shocks" are transitory. The importance of recognizing if a series has stationary levels or stationary differences has resulted in econometricians developing tests that are referred to as "unit-root" tests (see Mills [135] and Wilkie [206]).

Sherris et al. [180] apply standard unit-root tests to Australian quarterly investment data and find empirical evidence to support the assumption that the following series are stationary: the continuously compounded rate (force) of inflation, the continuously compounded return on the share (stock) price index, the continuously compounded growth rate of share dividends, differences in the dividend yields, and differences in interest rates. In this analysis, the equity price index was found to be best represented as a random walk with drift and long-term interest rates close to a random walk with drift. Such analysis suggests that these stationary variables should be the series included in a stochastic investment model for model fitting, parameter estimation, and projection. Note that structural breaks in a series can result in a stationary series appearing to have a unit root using these tests and that there is evidence of such structural breaks.

## SECTION 9.3.3 | COINTEGRATION AND ERROR-CORRECTION MODELS

The concept of cointegration between different series has been developed in the econometrics literature to model long-run equilibrium relationships. If a number of series are difference stationary and have stochastic trends, then it is possible for these series to "move together" or have common stochastic trends if there is a long-run equilibrium relationship between them. For example, interest rates of different maturities might be expected to maintain long-run equilibrium relationships as might share dividends and share prices. Asset returns and inflation might also be expected to maintain a long-run equilibrium relationship. Tests for such linear equilibrium relationships have been developed in econometrics.

To illustrate the cointegration concept, consider the interest rate at time $t$, denoted by $r_t$, and a measure of inflation at time $t$, denoted by $F_t$. If both these series are difference stationary, then the level of the series is a random walk and both have stochastic trends. If $r_t - \alpha F_t$, where $\alpha$ is the regression coefficient from a regression of $r_t$ on $F_t$, is stationary, then this linear relationship represents a long-run equilibrium between the series. Engle and Granger [55] have shown that where such a cointegrating relationships exists an error-correction model can be developed for the series. The error-correction model for the interest rate, taking into account the long-run equilibrium relationship with $F_t$, is

$$r_{t+1} - r_t = \Delta r_t = a + b(r_t - \alpha F_t) + \varepsilon_t,$$

and a similar model holds for $\Delta F_t$. Thus $r_t$ behaves like a random walk with drift but has a tendency to "revert" toward the long-run equilibrium $\alpha F_t$ through the error-correction term.

The Wilkie model [206] assumes that dividends and share prices are cointegrated and finds empirical support for this assumption especially for monthly U.K. data.

### SECTION 9.3.4 │ GARCH MODELS

Generalized autoregressive conditionally heteroscedastic (GARCH) models allow for the variance of a series to be heteroscedastic by relating the variance to previous values of the variance of the series and to past "shocks" in the series. A GARCH($p$, $q$) process for the variance $h_t$ of a series $y_t$ takes the form

$$h_t = \alpha_0 + \sum_{j=1}^{p} \phi_j h_{t-j} + \sum_{j=1}^{q} \alpha_j \varepsilon_{t-j}^2$$

where $\alpha_j$ ($0 \leq j \leq q$) and $\phi_j$ ($1 \leq j \leq p$) are estimated parameters and $\varepsilon_{t-1} = y_{t-1} - \hat{y}_{t-1}$, which is assumed to be i.i.d. and normally distributed for parameter estimation and model-projection purposes. GARCH(1, 1) models have been found to provide a satisfactory empirical fit for inflation series in the United States, the United Kingdom, and Australia.

**Example 9.3.2.** The following GARCH(1, 1) model for Australian quarterly inflation is series fitted in Sherris et al. [180]:

$$y_t = 0.0104 + \varepsilon_t,$$
$$h_t = 0.00001 + 0.651 h_{t-1} + 0.287 \varepsilon_{t-1}^2.$$ ∎

# Section 9.4
# Actuarial Stochastic Investment Models

### SECTION 9.4.1 │ THE WILKIE MODEL

The earliest actuarial investment-return models were deterministic. An important technique for assessing the financial impact of uncertain future outcomes in these models is the use of scenario analysis. This technique projects cash flows in a deterministic manner for a range of possible outcomes. More recent asset-liability models use stochastic investment-return models. The earliest work in this area in the actuarial profession was by the U.K. actuary David Wilkie [204], who developed work carried out by the Maturity Guarantees Working Party of the Institute of Actuaries.

These models reflect financial economic theory as well as the salient features of historical data for asset returns and economic variables. They also focus on the long-run behavior of asset returns and the long-run relationships between these returns and economic factors. This is in contrast to models that emphasize short-run prediction used in market-timing investment strategies. Thus the modeling of the impact of inflation must incorporate realistic long-run properties and correlations with other asset classes. These models also must capture the risk properties of the different asset-class returns and the economic factors, such as inflation, that are included in the model.

A number of actuarial investment-return models have been proposed for asset-liability modeling purposes. These have been developed for the most part using traditional time-series techniques and historical investment returns and economic inflation data. Transfer function modeling has been used to model the interrelationship between the different series by assuming inflation, or other returns series, influences the asset returns. The earliest studies using this approach were by Wilkie [204] and [206].

Wilkie [204] developed a stochastic investment model for the United Kingdom. The variables used in the model are the

- Retail prices index
- Share dividends index
- Dividend yield on share indexes
- Consols yield (long-term government interest rate).

The model is structured such that variables are ordered and depend only on lagged values of themselves and variables of a lower order. This cascade structure is illustrated in Figure 9.1. The model has been extended to include other interest rates and other asset returns (Wilkie [206]). Carter [34], employing the same methodology used by Wilkie, derived a stochastic investment model for the Australian experience. Both Wilkie and Carter use the standard Box-Jenkins [20] times-series methodology.

FIGURE **9.1** | *Cascade Structure for the Wilkie Model*

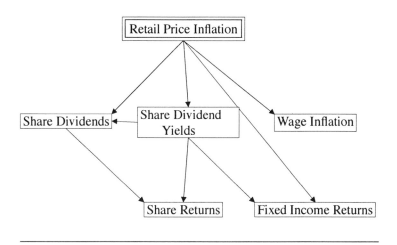

Models such as the Wilkie model and variations of it are used by actuaries. Although we should bear in mind the shortcomings of such models in practical applications, it is also important to recognize the usefulness of a stochastic approach to asset-liability modeling. To illustrate the main features of these models, we outline and discuss the basic structure of the Wilkie model. In practice, the model structure must be appropriate for the problem that is being addressed. Hence, parameter estimates need to take into account the most current information.

The Wilkie model was originally estimated as an annual frequency model. Other frequencies, monthly series in particular, were examined in Wilkie [206], and quarterly series have been examined in Carter [34]. Note that the structure and assumptions of a model with an annual frequency might not be appropriate for higher frequency models. Carter finds that the Wilkie model structure, developed on annual U.K. data, does not fit well to quarterly Australian data.

The Wilkie model uses a "cascade" structure where variables have a hierarchical relationship so that variables further down the hierarchy are influenced by only the variables further up the hierarchy. In the Wilkie model structure, inflation is assumed to influence share yields, and both share yields and inflation are assumed to influence share dividends. Inflation is also assumed to influence interest rates. Such a structure allows for both a simple interpretation of the model dependencies and estimation using transfer function techniques in time series. The structure also allows different components of the model to be used for asset-liability modeling without having to generate all of the series included in the complete model. Parameters of the model are fitted from historical data. The model estimation procedure is not covered here; see the original papers (Wilkie [204], [206]) or standard time-series texts and software (Harvey [84], SAS [168]). It is worth noting that some empirical studies suggest that investment returns can influence inflation and that the link between inflation and investment returns may not be unidirectional (see, for example, Carter [34] for quarterly Australian data). If these interactions are considered important, then a VAR or VARMA model will include them and allow them to be tested for significance.

In the Wilkie model, price inflation is assumed to be a factor influencing the returns on the assets in the model. The model uses a first-order autoregressive AR(1) model for the continuously compounded rate of inflation. Such a model can be written as (see Wilkie [206])

$$I(t) - \mu_Q = \alpha_Q \cdot [I(t-1) - \mu_Q] + \sigma_Q \cdot Z_Q(t)$$

where $I(t) = \log[Q(t)/Q(t-1)]$, $Q(t)$ is the level of the inflation index, $Z_Q(t)$ is an i.i.d. standardized normal variable, and $\mu_Q$, $\alpha_Q$, and $\sigma_Q$ are parameters to be estimated. Data from a range of countries indicate that such a model is a reasonable representation of the historical inflation series but that the normal distribution assumption is not always appropriate. There is evidence of heteroscedasticity in the inflation series so that $\sigma_Q$ cannot be assumed to be a constant. In an annual model, the parameter value for $\alpha_Q$ for a range of countries is typically found to be in the range 0.4 to 0.8 so that when projecting using this model the variability of future inflation is greater than that of a random-walk assumption for the inflation index.

**Example 9.4.1.** Wilkie [206] estimated the parameters for his inflation model from long periods of U.K. annual data. The model based on data from 1919 to 1982 is the AR(1) model

$$I(t) - 0.0364 = 0.6[I(t-1) - 0.0364] + 0.0543\,Z_Q(t).$$

Parameter estimates are also given for differing time periods and for revised data. Table 9.1 gives some of these. Standard errors for the parameters are in brackets.

TABLE **9.1** │ *Some Parameter Values for the Wilkie Inflation Model (Standard Errors Are in Parentheses)*

| Parameter | 1919–82 | 1923–94 |
|-----------|---------|---------|
| $\mu_Q$ | 0.0364 | 0.0473 |
|          | (0.0169) | (0.0120) |
| $\alpha_Q$ | 0.5977 | 0.5773 |
|          | (0.0926) | (0.0798) |
| $\sigma_Q$ | 0.0543 | 0.0427 |
|          | (0.0048) | (0.0036) |

Sharp [173] has fitted an autoregressive model the same as Wilkie's to annual Canadian inflation data from 1924 to 1981 and obtains the model

$$I(t) - 0.0308 = 0.6812[I(t-1) - 0.0308] + 0.0324\,Z_Q(t).$$

Wilkie [206] has fitted his model to inflation data from twenty-three countries for differing time periods. For U.S. data from 1926 to 1989, the model given is

$$I(t) - 0.03 = 0.65[I(t-1) - 0.03] + 0.035\,Z_Q(t). \qquad \blacksquare$$

Wilkie also models wages using a first-order autoregressive model. When constructing models for other variables the assumption is made in the model that the inflation series influences the other variables. Thus wages are assumed to depend on prices. Models with this one-way dependency are fitted using transfer-function models in time series and allow one series to depend on current and lagged values of itself and another series.

Share dividend yields are modeled as

$$\log Y(t) - \log \mu_Y = \alpha_Y I(t) + Y_N(t)$$

where $Y_N(t) = \beta_Y Y_N(t-1) + \sigma_Y Z_Y(t)$, $Y(t)$ is the dividend yield on the share index at time $t$, $Z_Y(t)$ is a standardized i.i.d. normal variable, and $\mu_Y$, $\alpha_Y$, $\beta_Y$, and $\sigma_Y$ are parameters to be estimated. Note that the (logarithm of the) dividend yield is influenced by the rate of inflation and has a first-order autoregressive component. Wilkie finds that the inflation parameter $\alpha_Y$ is significant and positive for U.K. data, implying that high inflation leads to high dividend yields in the model.

Share dividends are modeled using a more complicated structure in which the continuous compounding dividend growth rate is modeled as a function of current and past inflation, the previous year's dividend-yield "shock," and a first-order moving average component. Wilkie [206] gives the model as

$$K(t) = I_D(t) + \mu_D + \phi_D \varepsilon_Y(t-1) + \gamma_D \varepsilon_D(t-1) + \varepsilon_D(t)$$

where $K(t) = \log[D(t)/D(t-1)]$, $D(t)$ is the value of the dividend index for shares,

$$I_D(t) = \alpha_D M_D(t) + \beta_D I(t),$$
$$M_D(t) = \delta_D I(t) + (1-\delta_D) M_D(t-1),$$
$$\varepsilon_Y(t-1) = \sigma_Y Z_Y(t-1),$$
$$\varepsilon_D(t) = \sigma_D Z_D(t),$$

and $\mu_D$, $\alpha_D$, $\beta_D$, $\gamma_D$, $\delta_D$, $\phi_D$, and $\sigma_Y$ are parameters to be estimated. Wilkie [205] provides a justification for this structure of the model and extensive details on parameter estimates for different countries and for different time periods. Refer to the original paper for an excellent coverage of many of the topics discussed in this chapter.

Once the dividend yield and the share dividends are modeled in this fashion, it is then a simple matter to determine the equity (or share) price index $P(t)$ since $P(t) = D(t)/Y(t)$. Note that some models would model the share-price index as a random walk, and the dividend yield as a first-order autoregressive model, rather than model the dividend series and the dividend yield to derive the share price index. The model structure should be representative of the relationships and distribution assumptions that the historical data suggest.

The links between these different modeling approaches have not been fully explored. For instance, there is empirical evidence supporting the random-walk assumption for equity values based on annual data, but the model structure suggested by Wilkie is not consistent with the random-walk assumption for equity values over long investment horizons (this is noted in Wilkie [206]). There are studies, however, that suggest that equity values demonstrate long-run "mean reversion," which is inconsistent with the random-walk assumption.

For long-term nominal interest rates, Wilkie suggests a model that has an inflation component and a real, or inflation-adjusted, yield modeled as a third-order autoregressive component. The inflation component is described as an "exponentially weighted moving average of past inflation." The real yield has a third-order autoregressive component and an effect from the current dividend-yield "shock." The model is relatively complex compared with the models covered earlier in Chapter 7 for term structure modeling.

Wilkie also models the short interest rate by modeling the logarithm of the ratio between the long-term interest rate and the short-term interest rate using a first-order autoregressive model. In essence, the interest rate model developed by Wilkie is similar in concept to a two-factor interest rate model using factors similar to those used in Brennan and Schwartz [26] who develop an equilibrium term structure model that is equivalent to using the long interest rate and the spread between the long and the short rates as factors. Note that the selection of the structure and parameters of the Brennan and Schwartz model requires extreme care to ensure the simulated values from such a model are sensible (see, for example, Hogan [94]).

Wilkie [206] also develops models for property returns, index-linked securities (which are traded in the UK), and exchange rates. Readers are referred to the original paper for more details on these models. He also fits his model structure to historical data from a number of different countries.

## SECTION 9.4.2 | OTHER MODELS

The Wilkie model was the earliest published stochastic investment model that was specifically developed for insurance and pension applications. The paper by Mulvey and Thorlacius [138] describes another model, although not with the same detail that is available for the Wilkie model. It is of interest to outline some of the details of this model as another example of a stochastic investment-return model for use in insurance and pension applications. There is insufficient published detail to set out explicit functional relationships for the model. In particular, there appears to be no published empirical or econometric analysis to demonstrate how well the model represents investment-return series based on historical data.

This model is used to generate representative scenarios for key investment returns and economic variables using simulation. It includes price and wage inflation, interest rates for different maturities (both real and nominal), stock dividend yields and dividend growth rates, and exchange rates. The cascade structure of the model is set out in Figure 9.2. The model consists of submodels for individual countries linked together to form an international investment-return model with the U.S., German, and Japanese economies forming the cornerstones.

FIGURE **9.2** | *Cascade Structure for the Stochastic Investment*
*Model Described in Mulvey and Thorlacius [138]*

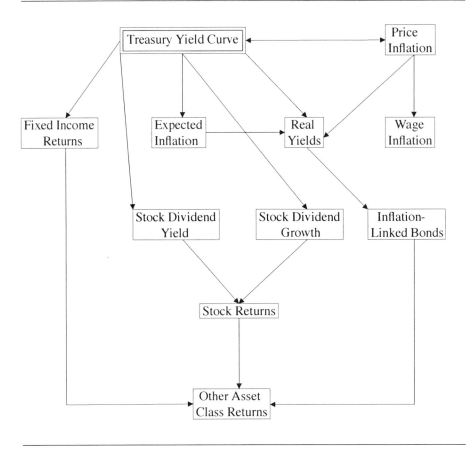

The model for an individual country is based on a cascade structure similar to that of the Wilkie model. Interest rates are generated using a two-factor model similar to that of Brennan and Schwartz [26] using short- and long-term spot rates as the factors. Interest rates are modeled as autoregressive but with changes in interest rates influenced by the level of inflation. Yields for other maturities are interpolated using a double exponential formula.

Price inflation is generated in conjunction with the yield curve with changes in the short-term spot rate directly influencing changes in it. Changes are also influenced by the level of the short- and long-term spot rates and a stochastic factor. Inflation is modeled with stochastic volatility, which is autoregressive. Wage inflation is generated from price inflation with a lag since it can be assumed that wages react slowly to changes in price inflation. Wage inflation is used for modeling pension plan liabilities directly linked to salaries.

Real interest rates are generated from interest rates and inflation. Changes in long-term real interest rates are influenced by changes in long-term spot rates as well as the level of long-term rates and of price inflation and a stochastic factor.

Currencies are determined by modeling the relative strength of each country's currency. Exchange rates are influenced by the average cost of goods in foreign countries relative to domestic cost, short-term spot interest rates, and price inflation along with a stochastic factor. Thus currencies reflect purchasing power parity.

Stock returns are generated by modeling dividend yields and dividend growth rates. Changes in dividend growth rates are influenced by price inflation and a stochastic factor. Changes in dividend yields are assumed to be influenced by changes in short- and long-term spot interest rates, changes in exchange rates as well as the level of interest rates and real yields, and a stochastic factor. Dividend yields are assumed to be autoregressive. The volatility of the dividend yield depends on the dividend growth rate.

Parameters for the model for scenario generation are determined by incorporating risk premiums into the expected return for the different asset classes using both historical returns and normative assumptions. The volatility parameters are calibrated to target values based on historical data and expert judgment. The model is implemented using simulation, and variance reduction procedures, such as antithetic variates, are used where appropriate.

Thomson [192] develops a cascade structure for a stochastic investment model for actuarial applications using annual South African data. The structure of the model, different from that of the Wilkie model, was determined using time-series techniques and transfer-function modeling. The model includes inflation rates, short- and long-term interest rates, dividend growth rates, dividend rates, rental growth rates, and rental yields. Thomson provides extensive details on the models used for these variables. The model is significantly different from those of Wilkie [204] and Mulvey and Thorlacius [138] outlined earlier. In particular, the equity dividend growth rate influences inflation. Dividend yields are not influenced by inflation and follow a first-order autoregressive process.

Sharp [173] uses time-series techniques to model Canadian inflation using annual data from 1924 to 1991. He finds that an autoregressive model similar to that used in the Wilkie model fits the Canadian data well. Sharp [172] examines the relationship between investment returns and inflation using Canadian data. Deaves [46] examines nominal and real interest rates and inflation in Canada; he uses ARIMA and VAR models and examines the predictive performance of these models.

## SECTION 9.4.3 | OTHER ISSUES

Models used for asset-liability management are based on assumptions about the structure of the model and require estimates of model parameters. The model structure and parameters are estimated from historical data and from current market data. In some cases, subjective input also influences the model choice, especially of the parameters for projection purposes. In any asset-liability model, awareness of model risk, which arises from the model being an approximation to a complex economic system, and parameter risk, which arises from treating the estimated parameters as the actual parameter values, is important. Allowing for these sources of risk increases the uncertainty of future outcomes beyond that formally allowed for in a model that does not take them into account.

These models have been designed for projection and dynamic solvency-testing purposes. They represent the real-world distribution for investment returns and are not "arbitrage-free" models by construction. The models can be adapted for use in valuation of asset and liability cash flows by ensuring that they are arbitrage free. To do this, the real-world probabilities must be adjusted to the equivalent martingale probabilities for the $Q$ measure. This requires estimating a market price of risk for the risk factors in the model. Conceptually, the way to do this is to adjust the expected returns on the different traded assets in the model, using the model structure and assumptions, so that the model will reproduce the current market values of traded assets when the model is used to value these assets. Tilley [195] sets out how to do this for an interest-rate model. For a multifactor and multi-asset model the procedure for generating an arbitrage-free model in practice is likely to be more complex and to involve significant numerical computation, especially since asset values usually need to be generated using simulation with a complex model structure.

# Section 9.5
## Insurance and Pension Applications

### SECTION 9.5.1 | INVESTMENT STRATEGY AND PORTFOLIO INSURANCE

Setting a long-run strategic asset-allocation policy for an insurance or pension fund is an important application of an asset-liability model. This asset allocation sets the weighting for the main asset classes as a benchmark asset allocation to see if they are adding value in the investment process. It is essential that this strategic or long-term benchmark reflects the nature of the liabilities and the risk tolerance of the fund. The fund manager will depart from the strategic asset allocation to take advantage of market anomalies, to take views on the relative values of the different asset classes, or to take advantage of superior information or information-processing skills or tools.

Tactical asset allocation strategies are often based on a quantitative investment-return model that is used to set asset allocation strategies that depart from the agreed-on long-run strategic asset allocation. Factor models of asset returns are also used to construct portfolios with factor exposures that are expected to outperform the asset class index that will be used for performance measurement.

Asset-liability models are used to examine the impact of a pension fund's asset allocation strategy on the variability of the contribution required to fund the benefits and on the funding level. They can also be used to examine the benefit of derivative-based strategies, including the use of portfolio insurance strategies designed to place a floor on the return earned on the fund.

If the fund adopts a passive investment management strategy, then it uses a prespecified long-run or strategic asset allocation to set the percentage of the fund to be invested in each asset class. These percentages are kept constant through time by rebalancing the percentage of the fund in each asset class from time to time as the value of each asset class changes. For instance, this could be done at fixed time intervals, such as on a monthly or quarterly basis. Such strategies are known as time-based strategies. Alternatively, the rebalancing could occur only after a specified percentage move in one or more of the asset classes. This is known as a moved-based strategy. The choice of rebalancing method is dependent on transaction costs and how closely the fund wishes to track the optimal asset allocation.

If a passive strategy is adopted then for each asset class, securities are selected to replicate the asset-class index that is used for performance measurement. Rebalancing the portfolio asset-class percentages to maintain a constant strategic asset allocation is known as a constant mix strategy. Such a strategy sells from the asset classes that rise in value and buys assets in asset classes that fall in value in order to maintain the constant mix percentages for each of the asset classes.

Many insurance and pension funds are concerned about downside risk and place constraints on asset allocations to limit the chance of the value of the assets falling below the value of the liabilities. A strategy that can be used to ensure that the value of the assets does not fall below a specified level is option-based portfolio insurance. To use such a strategy, a time horizon must be decided upon, and a desired floor on the assets determined. To see how this works, consider a fund with a 5-year horizon: current liabilities with value $L_0$ that are estimated to grow to $L_5$ in 5 years. The fund is assumed to invest in two asset classes: one is a risky asset class and the other a risk-free asset class. The risk-free asset class is usually a Treasury bond portfolio with a duration equal to the investment horizon, which needs to be rebalanced to keep the duration equal to the planning horizon. The risky asset class is a portfolio of equity assets for which an estimate of the volatility is available. The current value of the assets is $A_0$ with $A_0 > L_0$. The objective of the fund is to invest the assets so that the value of the assets in 5 years is always greater than $L_5$. For this purpose, we assume that the fund invests an amount of the assets equal to the current value of liabilities.

One way of meeting this investment objective is to use some of the surplus of $S_0 = A_0 - L_0$ to purchase a 5-year put option on the risky asset portfolio value, with initial value $L_0$ and a strike value of $L_5$, and invest fully in the risky asset class. Note that at the very most the value of $L_5$ cannot be greater than $L_0(1 + i_f)$ where $i_f$ is the return on the risk-free asset class over the 5-year horizon. Otherwise, the fund is not able to meet its floor objective even if it invested 100% in the risk-free portfolio without using the current surplus.

Thus, the payoff in 5 years from the risky assets plus the put option is

$$L_0(1 + i_e) + \max[L_5 - L_0(1 + i_e), 0] = L_0(1 + i_e), \quad \text{if } L_0(1 + i_e) > L_5,$$

or

$$L_0(1 + i_e) + \max[L_5 - L_0(1 + i_e), 0] = L_0(1 + i_e) + L_5 - L_0(1 + i_e) = L_5,$$
$$\text{if } L_0(1 + i_e) < L_5$$

where $i_e$ is the (uncertain) return on the risky equity portfolio over the 5- year horizon. Note that this strategy requires assets totaling $P + L_0$ where $P$ is the cost of the put option. Thus a surplus equal to the cost of the put option is required to provide the portfolio insurance for the initial value of the liabilities.

For the cost of the put option, the fund has ensured that the value of the invested assets always exceeds a floor equal to the estimated value of the liabilities in 5 years. Note also that the fund could, in theory, have purchased a call option on the risky equity portfolio for a cost of $C$, for the same amount and strike price as for the put option, and invested the present value of $L_5$ at the risk-free rate into the duration-matched Treasury bond portfolio. Assuming that the liability value increases at the risk-free rate then the present value of $L_5$ at the risk-free rate is $L_0$. From put-call parity, ignoring any income and outgo on assets and liabilities, we have $P + L_0 = C + L_5/(1 + i_f)$ so that the total amount of assets (and surplus) required for both strategies is the same.

In practice, the value of the liability at the end of the planning horizon should be treated as a random variable so that the portfolio insurance option is an option to exchange the asset portfolio for an amount equal to the value of the liabilities. If the value of the asset portfolio does not exceed the value of the liabilities then the option is exercised, and the asset portfolio is exchanged for an amount equal to the value of the liabilities. To illustrate the concept of portfolio insurance, we continue to assume that $L_5$ is a fixed and known value. It is also necessary to incorporate asset income and (expected) liability outgo in the calculations. For instance, for an insurance fund an allowance is needed for death claims and surrenders. For a pension fund, an allowance is needed for deaths, withdrawals, and retirements.

Given that the equity portfolio is often a portfolio similar to the equity market index, it is (in theory) possible to purchase these put, or call, options on the equity market index. In practice, it is not viable to buy put options for such long horizons.

The prices quoted by market makers in such options incorporate a large spread, and the market is illiquid. Thus, to implement such a portfolio insurance strategy, it is necessary to "roll your own" options using dynamic hedging.

Portfolio insurance is the term used for dynamic hedging strategies that aim to replicate the payoff on a put option on a portfolio. To see how this works, consider the above case with the amount $L_0$ invested into the equity assets and a put option being replicated. The initial portfolio that is set up will total in value $L_0 + P$. From the Black-Scholes formula, assuming there are no income or outgo cash flows, we have for a 5-year European put

$$P = \frac{L_5}{(1 + i_f)} N(-d_2) - L_0 N(-d_1) \qquad (9.5.1)$$

where

$$d_1 = \frac{\log\left[\dfrac{L_0}{L_5/(1 + i_f)}\right] + \dfrac{\sigma^2 T}{2}}{\sigma\sqrt{T}}$$

and

$$d_2 = d_1 - \sigma\sqrt{T}.$$

The replicating portfolio for the put option initially contains an amount of $-L_0 N(-d_1)$ (a short holding) of the risky portfolio and an amount invested in the risk-free Treasury fund of $L_5/(1 + i_f)N(-d_2)$. Thus instead of investing $L_0$ into the equity portfolio and buying the put option, the dynamic hedging strategy would initially hold $[L_0 - L_0 N(-d_1)] = L_0[1 - N(-d_1)]$ in the risky asset portfolio and $L_5/(1 + i_f)N(-d_2)$ in the duration-matched Treasury fund. As time passes, the replicating portfolio must be rebalanced since the put option is equivalent to a trading strategy that replicates the option payoff. In theory, this is done continuously, but in practice it can be done only at discrete-time points using either a time- or a move-based strategy.

This trading strategy used to replicate the put option will require the sale and purchase of the equity portfolio as the hedge ratio changes through time. This can be expensive because of transaction costs and illiquidity in the market. Program trading is used to buy and sell portfolios of equities and can be used to implement a portfolio insurance program. An alternative to dealing in the physical portfolio of equity securities is to use futures on an equity index to adjust the required exposure to the equity market while leaving the underlying equity portfolio unchanged. The different methods of implementing such an insurance strategy involves consideration of transactions costs and tracking error. Tracking error usually refers to the standard deviation of the difference between the actual return and the target return. One of the risks involved in the implementation of portfolio insurance using dynamic hedging is that of "jump" risk where the market "gaps," and it is not possible to trade at the required price. Examples of this are market "crashes" or "corrections" such as in October 1987.

A drawback with option-based portfolio insurance is that, for long-run investors such as a defined benefit pension fund, a fixed time horizon is unlikely to be appropriate. Also, as the time horizon moves close to the final date, if the value of the assets is close to the target liability value, then the gamma of the put option is high, and the hedge ratio, given by $-N(d_1)$, changes significantly. The result is that there is increased trading activity required to replicate the put-option payoff and increased and often unnecessary transaction costs. For this reason the time horizon for the portfolio insurance is often reset prior to the horizon date. Thus, the option is in effect "rolled over" prior to expiry to a new horizon.

With portfolio insurance, as the value of the equity portfolio rises the proportion of the total fund that is held in equity assets rises and as the value of the equity portfolio falls the proportion of the total fund held in equity assets falls. Thus, portfolio insurance involves buying the risky asset as the asset value rises and selling the risky asset as its value falls. Compare this with the constant-mix strategy, which involves selling the risky asset as its value rises and buying the risky asset as its value falls. Thus constant-mix investors are "sellers" of portfolio insurance.

As mentioned already, a problem with option-based portfolio insurance for long-run investors such as pension funds and for some life insurance fund products is that it has a fixed horizon. A dynamic strategy that has been developed to handle this problem is constant proportion portfolio insurance (CPPI) (see the paper by Black and Jones [?]). The concept underlying CPPI is to determine the proportion of the fund that is invested in the equity assets based on the current surplus in the fund. This is determined using a fixed multiplier, $m$, of the surplus as the amount of equity assets to hold.

The formula for determining the amount invested in the equity (or risky) assets is

$$E = m\,C$$

where $E$ is the equity exposure, $m$ is the multiplier, and $C$ is the "cushion," which equals the difference between the value of the assets and the floor. For a fund with liabilities of $L_0$ and assets with value $A_0$, the cushion would be taken as $S_0 = A_0 - L_0$. The floor need not be a fixed value and can grow at the risk-free rate or be set in some other manner. The multiplier $m$ reflects the risk aversion of the investor.

The equation above can be rewritten as

$$C = \frac{1}{m} E$$

so that $1/m$ is the proportion of the equity value that can be lost before the fund will reach the floor. As an example, an investor with a $100 million fund and a floor of $90 million using a multiple of 4 would invest $4 \times \$10 = \$40$ million in equities and $60 million in the risk-free asset. If the equity fund falls in value by 1/4 then the cushion is completely eliminated. Note that as the value of the equity assets change so does the cushion and hence the proportion of the fund in the equity assets. In fact, as the equity asset values increase, the fund increases its exposure to equity assets and vice versa in a way similar to option-based portfolio insurance.

Insurance companies require an asset allocation strategy that matches the liability cash flows as closely as possible if the fund does not have sufficient capital reserves or margins in its pricing to take investment risks or if the fund is very risk averse. This is the case for fixed-annuity funds in which the pricing is competitive and directly linked to returns on fixed-interest securities. This involves the selection of assets with cash flows that match the timing and interest rate (and perhaps other factor) sensitivity of the liabilities. Variable annuities and equity-linked annuities, with minimum death-benefit guarantees, require more sophisticated matching techniques including the use of "exotic" derivatives or specially designed dynamic hedging strategies.

## SECTION 9.5.2 | VALUATION OF INSURANCE LIABILITIES

Asset-liability models are used both for projection of cash flows for assets and liabilities and for valuation of these cash flows. For the purposes of projecting cash flows, the model parameters should be selected to produce realistic distributions of future cash flows based on historical data and current information. However, for the purposes of valuation, it is important to select parameters that are risk adjusted. The most straightforward method is to determine parameters of the model that will reproduce the market values of the assets when the model is used to value the assets. By doing this, the valuation of the liabilities using the model will be on a basis consistent with that used for the valuation of assets. Once the parameters are consistent with the market values for assets, the model can be used for valuing the liability cash flows. The insurance policy values generated by the model can then be used as input into the pricing process for policy liabilities. Actual insurance prices are influenced by a host of factors such as the competitive nature of the insurance market, the volume of business, and other goals of the company since insurance markets are not as "perfectly competitive" as asset markets. Liability values will also often be influenced by risk factors that are not traded in financial markets. This requires an incomplete market model for the valuation of liabilities.

It is important to understand that when the model is used for pricing or valuation on a basis consistent with the market value of the assets, it is using a "risk-adjusted" distribution for the asset returns. Such a distribution assumption is only appropriate for valuation and not for projection of the cash flows of the fund for solvency purposes. In practice, valuation assumptions used in actuarial liability valuations are changed only slowly and are often based on conservative assumptions. However, if the valuation of the assets is based on market values, then such a conservative approach to the valuation of liabilities will not be consistent with the asset values.

Option-pricing techniques have been adapted to the valuation of interest-rate-sensitive insurance liabilities. They are based on interest-rate "scenario" or "path" generators that are constructed to be "arbitrage free." They also model policyholder behavior such as lapse rates as well as company product features such as interest-crediting strategies. These lapse rates and interest-crediting strategies can depend on the path of interest rates so that the valuation of these liabilities is "path dependent."

Typical examples of such interest-sensitive insurance products are single premium deferred annuities (SPDAs) and universal life (UL) contracts. SPDAs are insurance products that credit an earnings rate linked to fixed interest returns. Crediting rates are usually determined at specified intervals referred to as the reset frequency. Annual resets are common. A minimum crediting rate is sometimes guaranteed. Policyholders are allowed to withdraw a specified percentage, such as 10%, of the accumulated account value without penalty. Otherwise, surrenders are subject to a charge as a percentage of the account value in the early years of the policy, declining to zero over a period of, say, 8 years. Policyholder surrenders are assumed to be related to the difference between the crediting rate and current Treasury interest rates. These policies have initial expenses that are recovered over the life of the policy through a margin in the crediting rate or in the surrender charge as well as renewal expenses.

In valuing interest-sensitive cash flows, the standard techniques used in practice are covered in Chapter 7. These techniques apply to default-free securities and do not take into account other market frictions such as market liquidity. For many interest-sensitive securities, the market requires a premium over default-free Treasury yields to cover default, liquidity, and other risks. This is reflected in the yield quoted in the market for these securities.

### Option-Adjusted Spread

Securities can also be "mispriced" relative to Treasury bonds, in which case arbitrage opportunities are possible. Often, especially in actively traded markets, any apparent mispricing is not sufficient to cover the transaction costs required to take advantage of the arbitrage. The term structure models used in practice are often "calibrated" to the current Treasury yield curve. If other interest-sensitive securities are valued with a model calibrated to the current Treasury curve and the market value differs from the term structure model price then this suggests that the security is mispriced. Often in practice such mispricing just reflects factors not taken into account in the term structure model used for valuation, such as transaction costs, market liquidity, and taxes.

A method of quantifying this "mispricing" used in the fixed-interest markets is the option-adjusted spread method. Recall that the value of an interest-sensitive security is often estimated using a sample of interest-rate paths (see Chapter 3). If the market value of an interest-sensitive security differs from this estimate, then a constant addition is made to all the short interest rates along all the paths so that the value obtained from this procedure equals the quoted market value of the security. This constant addition to all the interest rates is referred to as the option-adjusted spread (OAS).

Interest-sensitive insurance liabilities can be valued using similar techniques, but an appropriate option-adjusted spread must be used. There is no generally agreed basis for doing this since insurance liability cash flows are influenced by many factors different to those prevailing in fixed and interest-sensitive asset markets and do not have an actively traded market. This approach to determining an OAS for insurance liability cash flows is similar in concept to determining "risk-adjusted" discount rates for insurance cash flows.

**Fair Value of Liabilities**

Accounting standards increasingly require the valuation of assets at market value. Liabilities should be valued on a basis consistent with that of the assets. A valuation of liabilities on a basis consistent with that of the market value of assets is usually referred to as a "fair" value of the liabilities. Valuation of liabilities in such a manner is a current area of development, and there are many unresolved issues, some of which are closely related to corporate finance and often draw on financial theory, including option pricing.

Actuaries have developed appraisal value and embedded-value techniques for assessing the value of insurance company liabilities. These methods use cash-flow projection techniques for the liabilities using actuarial models for mortality, lapses, and surrenders and relevant accounting and actuarial standards to determine liability reserves on future dates. The net cash flows after establishing the necessary reserves can be valued at an appropriate "risk-adjusted" discount rate to determine the value of the company. Different accounting and actuarial standards produce different patterns of net cash flows from an insurance company so that statutory rules often produce different net cash-flow patterns to generally accepted accounting principles (GAAP).

The issues in the area of valuation of insurance company liabilities not only are complex but also require an understanding of many corporate finance issues not covered in detail in this book. They involve issues about allowing for taxes, determining "risk-adjusted" rates of return for valuing liability cash flows where no active market exists for such liability cash flows, allowing for agency problems between management, policyholders, and shareholders, plus many more challenging research issues. The application of "arbitrage-free" valuation techniques and stochastic investment models to insurance liabilities is only one aspect of this important area.

### SECTION 9.5.3 │ MATURITY GUARANTEES AND MINIMUM DEATH BENEFITS

Insurance companies sell products that provide guarantees related to the investment performance of the assets where the assets are invested in equities as well as fixed-interest assets; these products are found in various countries. For example, in Australia they are referred to as capital guaranteed investment account products. These products are single-premium investment account products, in which the premiums are invested in a mix of equity and other classes of assets, and a guarantee of a return of the premium, sometimes with a low rate of interest, is given to the policyholder. In Canada, segregated fund insurance products are similar in that they also contain a guarantee of a return of premiums, or perhaps of 75% of the premiums. The premiums are invested in stock or bond funds. In the United States, the recent popularity of variable insurance products including variable annuities in which returns are linked to equity returns has increased the emphasis on modeling equity returns as well as an interest rates. The common feature of these products is that the assets backing the liability are invested in securities with volatile returns, and at the same time a return guarantee is given to the policyholder. In some cases, the guarantee can be in a form similar to the exotic options covered in Chapter 6.

Equity-indexed annuities (EIAs) are deferred annuities that provide a minimum guaranteed return on the premium invested. The premium, or 90% of the premium in many cases, is usually guaranteed to be returned with an annual rate of interest of 3% since this is required under the nonforfeiture laws for SPDA contracts. The return on the EIA is linked to the growth of a stock market index such as the S&P 500. This is a price index and not an accumulation index so that it does not include the dividends on the index as part of the return. The EIA is usually credited with a percentage, referred to as the "participation rate," of the gain to the index (ignoring dividends) over a term typically in the range of 1 to 7 years. There are a variety of methods of determining the credited returns, from those that credit a final percentage participation ranging from 60% to 100% of the gain in the index from inception to maturity, to those that credit the highest return during the term of the policy and provide a form of lookback option on the index value. (Chapter 6 discussed this type of exotic option.) Some products lock in returns during the term of the product in a similar manner to ratchet and cliquet options.

Actuaries have used stochastic investment models to analyze the reserving requirements for such investment-guarantee products dating back to the Maturity Guarantees Working Party of the Institute of Actuaries in London. This work was in fact the genesis of the Wilkie stochastic investment model discussed earlier. The approach used by actuaries is to establish a reserve so that under various alternative investment strategies used by the company the guarantee will be met with a high degree of confidence. Thus the stochastic investment model is used to project investment returns and the accumulation of the insurance product premiums to the maturity date of the contract. The financial cost of the guarantee is then determined for each simulation as well as an overall proportion of simulations in which the company cannot meet the guarantee. An amount of capital, or reserve, is then established so that the proportion of simulations in which the company will not meet the guarantee is below a required level such as 1%.

An alternative approach based on option pricing can be used. This approach is covered in Boyle and Schwartz [?] and Bacinello and Ortu [?]. The guarantee is treated as a form of put option. Option-based portfolio insurance can then be used as a dynamic investment strategy to ensure that the company can meet the guarantee. This strategy must take into account transaction costs and incorporate discrete rebalancing. The option-pricing approach not only determines the cost of the guarantee, that is, the initial reserve for the guarantee, but also establishes the dynamic investment strategy that should be used by the company to ensure that it will have sufficient assets to meet the guarantee.

Because the dynamic strategy can only be implemented at discrete intervals in practice, the guarantee cannot be exactly replicated, and there will be hedging or tracking error. There will also be transaction costs to take into account each time the portfolio is rebalanced.

To analyze the cost of these guarantees, it is also necessary to take into account surrenders and deaths. In the case of surrenders, there is often no guarantee, although in some countries certain insurance products allow for minimum surrender values. In the case of deaths, the benefit can involve a guarantee in the form of a return of premiums if this is greater than the fund value. Thus pricing and reserving for these products must allow for these decrements. The simulation approach using a stochastic investment model can incorporate decrements in the projection of future commitments under the guarantee. This approach involves scenario or "pathwise" generation of returns, the calculation of policy payments for decrements and maturities along each scenario or path, the discounting of the payments along each path, and the calculation of an average value of the discounted payments for all paths. A standard error for this expected value can also be calculated to indicate if sufficient paths have been used to obtain an accurate estimate of the expected value.

Note that such an approach requires an "arbitrage-free" model for valuation and that a term structure model should be incorporated to determine values along the paths. This arbitrage-free model will have different parameters from those of the model used in the actuarial stochastic model approach for establishing reserves based on a solvency probability. For projecting the asset and liability flows and examining solvency it is important to use parameters that are representative of future experience. Many of the issues in constructing stochastic investment models for cash-flow projection of insurance and pension liabilities have been mentioned earlier in this chapter.

## SECTION 9.5.4 | SOLVENCY

An important aspect of managing an insurance business is the determination and management of the capital required to support the paying of claims and running of the business. Ensuring that the company is solvent is important in attracting new business. Because policyholders do not typically diversify their exposure to insurance companies when buying automobile, home, or life insurance, the risk of insolvency of an insurance company is an important concern of insurance industry regulators. Solvency can be considered as a financial position where the current market values of the assets of the company exceed the value of the liabilities. More generally, it can be considered as an ability of the company to continue to pay future claims. This latter case is usually referred to as capital adequacy.

An asset-liability model is used to establish the capital adequacy of an insurance company by projecting the asset and liability cash flows into the future. Similarly, a model is required to determine the value of assets and liabilities for solvency purposes. Usually solvency is measured using book values rather than market values of assets and liabilities. Accounting standards are placing more emphasis on the use of market values of assets for accounting purposes and regulators are placing more emphasis on market values. For management purposes, the market values of both assets and liabilities should be determined on a consistent basis.

For pension funds, solvency is often assessed using the ratio of assets to liabilities and usually reflects statutory requirements in the method used to value the assets and liabilities. An asset-liability model can be used to assess both statutory and market-value-based solvency where the market or "fair" values of assets and liabilities are used. The objective of ensuring that the statutory requirements are met is best incorporated into an asset-liability model as a constraint rather than as a basic objective. The primary objective should be strategies that optimize the return on the fund allowing for the liabilities using market or "fair" values. These strategies should also be designed to meet the statutory solvency requirements.

# Section 9.6
## Exercises

### Exercise 9.1

Consider the following data for an index of equity price as at the end of each month during a year.

| Month | Index Value $P(t+h)$ |
|-------|---------------------|
| Dec | 3,042.45 |
| Jan | 3,050.05 |
| Feb | 3,141.50 |
| Mar | 3,220.04 |
| Apr | 3,123.44 |
| May | 3,217.14 |
| Jun | 3,056.28 |
| Jul | 3,089.90 |
| Aug | 3,126.98 |
| Sep | 3,186.40 |
| Oct | 3,361.64 |
| Nov | 3,328.03 |
| Dec | 3,444.51 |

a. Calculate sample estimates for $\mu$ and $\sigma$ using these data assuming that $P(t)$ follows the random-walk model given in (9.2.1).

b. Calculate the monthly rates of return given by $P(t+h)/P(t) - 1$ for each month of this year and the arithmetic average of these rates of return.

c. Explain why your estimate for $\mu$ in (a) and the arithmetic average rate of return in (b) differ.

### Exercise 9.2

Assume that an equity index follows the autoregressive process given in (9.2.3) over a time interval of $h = 1/12$ of a year (1 month) with $\gamma = -0.01$, $\mu = 0.12$, and $\sigma = 0.2$. Determine the form of (9.2.4) that annual observations generated from this process would follow (i.e., give the parameter values to generate annual values of the process).

## Exercise 9.3

Show that for the three-dimensional case in Section 9.2.7,

$$S = LD^{1/2} = \begin{bmatrix} 1 & 0 & 0 \\ \rho_{12}\dfrac{\sigma_2}{\sigma_1} & 1 & 0 \\ \rho_{12}\dfrac{\sigma_2}{\sigma_1} & \dfrac{\sigma_3}{\sigma_2}\dfrac{(\rho_{23}-\rho_{13}\rho_{12})}{(1-\rho_{12}^2)} & 1 \end{bmatrix}$$

$$\times \begin{bmatrix} \sigma_1 & 0 & 0 \\ 0 & \sigma_2\sqrt{1-\rho_{12}^2} & 0 \\ 0 & 0 & \sigma_3\sqrt{\dfrac{(1-\rho_{13}^2)(1-\rho_{12}^2)-(\rho_{23}-\rho_{13}\rho_{12})^2}{1-\rho_{12}^2}} \end{bmatrix}$$

$$= \begin{bmatrix} \sigma_1 & 0 & 0 \\ \rho_{12}\sigma_2 & \sigma_2\sqrt{1-\rho_{12}^2} & 0 \\ \rho_{13}\sigma_3 & \dfrac{\sigma_3(\rho_{23}-\rho_{13}\rho_{12})}{\sqrt{(1-\rho_{12}^2)}} & \sigma_3\sqrt{\dfrac{(1-\rho_{13}^2)(1-\rho_{12}^2)-(\rho_{23}-\rho_{13}\rho_{12})^2}{1-\rho_{12}^2}} \end{bmatrix}.$$

## Exercise 9.4

Assume that the returns for the three asset classes, equities, fixed income, and property (real estate), are multivariate normal random variables with mean vector

$$\mu = \begin{bmatrix} 0.12 \\ 0.06 \\ 0.085 \end{bmatrix} = \begin{bmatrix} \text{equities} \\ \text{fixed income} \\ \text{property} \end{bmatrix}$$

and covariance matrix

$$\begin{bmatrix} 0.04 & 0.003 & 0.014 \\ 0.003 & 0.0025 & -0.0015 \\ 0.014 & -0.0015 & 0.01 \end{bmatrix}.$$

Generate a sample of 1,000 returns for each of these three asset classes using

$$r = \mu + S\varepsilon$$

where $\varepsilon$ is a vector of i.i.d. standard normal variates and $S$ is determined using the result in Exercise 9.3. Calculate simple mean and standard deviations for the returns for each asset class from this sample.

## Exercise 9.5

Consider a 5-year single-premium equity-indexed annuity guaranteeing a return on maturity of 90% of the single premium with 3% annual interest. The EIA credits 90% of the gain in the S&P 500 index over the 5-year term subject to the minimum guarantee.

a. Write the maturity value of the single premium in terms of an option on the S&P 500 index.

b. Use the binomial model results in Chapter 6 to derive an expression for the value of the maturity payoff and evaluate this expression if the S&P 500 index is assumed to have an annual volatility of 20% over the 5-year term and the risk-free rate is assumed to be 4% per year (semiannual compounding).

c. Outline how you would use an actuarial stochastic investment model to assist in assessing the solvency of an insurance company issuing only this type of EIA.

d. Discuss how traded options could be used by the insurance company to manage the risk of these products.

# Chapter 10

## Option Pricing in Continuous Time

### Section 10.1
### Introduction

This chapter presents an accessible approach to continuous-time option pricing. The reader has encountered the principal ideas of option pricing in Chapters 2, 4, 5, and 6, in which time is a discrete variable. The continuous-time model has the advantages that some of the analyses or calculations can be done more elegantly and that in some cases explicit answers are obtained. Furthermore, the continuous-time model appears to be closer to reality in many situations.

There are two classical approaches to the continuous-time model in the finance literature. One approach is to start out with the model, for example, assuming that the stock price follows a geometric Brownian motion. To carry out the analyses rigorously, challenging technical tools such as *stochastic calculus* are needed; these are beyond the scope of this book. The other classical approach is to start with the binomial model, as discussed earlier, and to reach the continuous-time model by taking appropriate limits. In the binomial model both state space and time space are discrete, and in the limit both become continuous. In this sense, the transition to the limit is not a simple, but perhaps an awkward, operation.

Here we present an intermediate approach that is particularly suitable for actuaries. We begin with a continuous-time model that is based on the Poisson process; actuaries are familiar with this from risk theory. The Poisson process has the great advantage that it has simple sample paths. Hence, it is easy to see what is going on in a sample path, for example, when a self-financing portfolio is constructed. This model is richer than the classical geometric Brownian motion model; it has one more parameter, so that it can incorporate the asymmetry of the logarithm of the stock prices. The classical model can be retrieved as a limit, and so results for the classical model can be obtained by taking appropriate limits. This is a transparent operation since time is continuous from the outset.

The model based on the Poisson process is a complete market model. In an infinitesimal time interval, only two things can happen: a fixed-size jump occurs, or no jump occurs. Consequently, any European-type contingent claim can be replicated by a self-financing portfolio. Then, by the principle of no arbitrage, the price of an option must be equal to the value of this portfolio. This is proved in Section 10.5, in which we have a continuous-time version of the *fundamental theorem of asset pricing*: the price of an option is the expected discounted value of the payoff, where the expectation is taken with respect to the risk-neutral probability measure (equivalent martingale measure). In Section 10.6, results for the classical geometric Brownian motion model, the Black-Scholes formula in particular, are obtained as limits. Certain options are based on the prices of two stocks; for example, the European Margrabe option (exchange option) gives the right to exchange a share of a given stock against a share of another stock at a given date. We discuss the pricing of such options in Section 10.7. In Sections 10.10 to 10.12, American options are also considered. To obtain simpler answers, we assume that these options are perpetual, that there is no finite expiry date. Anyone not familiar with Brownian motion will find Section 10.13 useful; it is a heuristic and accessible introduction to Brownian motion (the Wiener process), a more rigorous development of which is presented in Appendix A.

An interesting historical note is that the Poisson process was first studied by the Swedish actuary Filip Lundberg in his 1903 doctoral thesis. The mathematics of Brownian motion was investigated by Louis Bachelier in his 1900 thesis; this work appeared 5 years before Albert Einstein's famous paper on Brownian motion. Bachelier was interested in option pricing, but unfortunately he modeled the stock prices (and not their logarithm) by a Brownian motion.

# Section 10.2
## Contingent Claims

A *contingent claim* is a random payment due at a future time $T$. In most of this chapter we consider claims that are contingent on a single asset, and to help fix ideas we assume that this asset is a non-dividend-paying stock. The no-dividend condition will be relaxed in Section 10.8. Let $S(t)$ denote the price of a share of the stock at time $t$, $t \geq 0$. Some common contingent claims are European call options and put options on the stock. A contingent claim is described by a nonnegative continuous payoff function $\Pi(s)$, $s \geq 0$, and a maturity date (exercise date) $T$, $T > 0$. The holder (or owner) of the contingent claim receives the amount $\Pi(S(T))$ at time $T$, and contingent claims can be traded. The problem is to price the contingent claim at each time $t$, $0 \leq t < T$. To find an answer, we have to formulate a model for the stock-price process.

We also consider American options, in Sections 10.10–10.12. For an American option, the option-exercise date $T$ is not fixed but can be chosen by the holder of the option.

# Section 10.3
# A Model for the Stock Price Process

We assume

$$S(t) = S(0)e^{kN(t)-ct}, \quad t \geq 0 \tag{10.3.1}$$

where $S(0)$ is the initial stock price, $k$ and $c$ are two constants, and $\{N(t)\}$ is a Poisson process, say, with parameter $\lambda$. Sample paths of shifted Poisson processes $\{kN(t)-ct\}$, with $k > 0$ and $c > 0$, are shown in Figure 10.1.

We assume that coexistence with a riskless asset, which earns interest at a continuously compounded rate $r$, is not a priori excluded. This is the condition that $k$ and $c + r$ have the same sign (both positive or negative). If this condition were not satisfied, for example, if $k > 0$ and $c + r \leq 0$, we would have

$$S(t) = S(0)e^{kN(t)-ct} \geq S(0)e^{rt}, \quad t \geq 0 \tag{10.3.2}$$

with strict inequality holding as soon as $N(t) \geq 1$. But then no one would invest in the riskless asset, because the investor could always earn more by investing in the stock.

In a "small" time interval, only two scenarios are possible for the Poisson process $\{N(t)\}$: either there is a jump (of size 1) or else there is no jump. Hence, for the stock price process $\{S(t)\}$ two scenarios have to be examined for each $t$, $t > 0$:

a.    At time $t$, the stock price jumps from $S(t)$ to $S(t)e^k$.

b.    There is no jump in an open interval containing $t$, and so $S(t)$ is differentiable at $t$ with

$$S'(t) = -cS(t). \tag{10.3.3}$$

FIGURE **10.1** │ *Sample Paths of Two Shifted Poisson Processes with μ = 0 and σ² = 1*

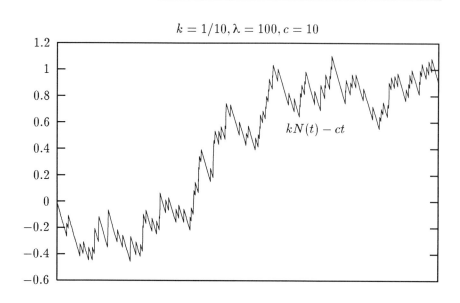

$k = 1/10, \lambda = 100, c = 10$

$kN(t) - ct$

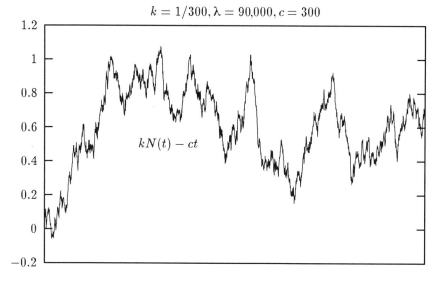

$k = 1/300, \lambda = 90{,}000, c = 300$

$kN(t) - ct$

The three parameters of the stock-price model can be expressed in terms of the first three moments of the exponent in (10.3.1). Let

$$Y(t) = kN(t) - ct. \tag{10.3.4}$$

Since $\{Y(t)\}$ is a process with stationary and independent increments, we can write

$$E[Y(t)] = \mu t, \tag{10.3.5}$$

$$\text{Var}[Y(t)] = \sigma^2 t, \tag{10.3.6}$$

and

$$E[(Y(t) - E[Y(t)])^3] = \gamma t \tag{10.3.7}$$

where $\mu$, $\sigma^2$, and $\gamma$ are the mean, variance, and third central moment per unit time. On the other hand, the moment generating function of $Y(t)$ is

$$
\begin{aligned}
E[e^{zY(t)}] &= E[e^{zkN(t)}]e^{-zct} \\
&= \exp([\lambda(e^{kz} - 1) - cz]t),
\end{aligned}
\tag{10.3.8}
$$

from which (or otherwise) we get

$$E[Y(t)] = (k\lambda - c)t, \tag{10.3.9}$$

$$\text{Var}[Y(t)] = k^2\lambda t, \tag{10.3.10}$$

and

$$E[(Y(t) - E[Y(t)])^3] = k^3\lambda t. \tag{10.3.11}$$

This way we obtain

$$\mu = k\lambda - c, \tag{10.3.12}$$

$$\sigma^2 = k^2\lambda, \tag{10.3.13}$$

and

$$\gamma = k^3\lambda. \tag{10.3.14}$$

The model parameters thus can be expressed in terms of $\mu$, $\sigma^2$, and $\gamma$ as

$$k = \frac{\gamma}{\sigma^2}, \tag{10.3.15}$$

$$\lambda = \frac{\sigma^6}{\gamma^2}, \tag{10.3.16}$$

$$c = \frac{\sigma^4}{\gamma} - \mu. \tag{10.3.17}$$

**Remark.** In Exercise 10.4, you are asked to show that, for given values of $\mu$ and $\sigma^2$, the moment generating function of $Y(t)$, which is given by (10.3.8), converges to

$$\exp\left(\mu tz + \frac{1}{2}\sigma^2 tz^2\right) \tag{10.3.18}$$

as $\gamma \to 0$, with $k$, $\lambda$, and $c$ varying according to (10.3.15), (10.3.16), and (10.3.17), respectively. Thus in the limit, $Y(t)$ has a normal distribution (with mean $\mu t$ and variance $\sigma^2 t$), and $\{Y(t)\}$ is a Brownian motion (Wiener process). Such an $\{S(t)\}$ is called a *geometric Brownian motion*. Some of the fascinating properties of the Brownian motion are explained in Section 10.13 and also in Appendix A. The graph in the lower panel of Figure 10.1 may look like a sample path from a Brownian motion, but, in fact, it is a simulated sample path from a shifted Poisson process. The parameter values underlying the two graphs in Figure 10.1 have been chosen to produce identical values for $\mu$ and $\sigma^2$, but the value of $k$ in the lower panel is 30 times smaller than the one in the upper panel.

# Section 10.4
# *Self-financing Portfolios*

We assume here that the two securities (the stock and the riskless asset) can be traded continuously and that trading is frictionless: that is, that the buying price and selling price are the same, there is no restriction on short sales or borrowing, there are no taxes, the volume of trading does not affect the price, and so on. We are interested in portfolios of the stock and riskless asset that are *self-financing*. The idea of a self-financing portfolio is that at any time a certain percentage of the total value of the portfolio is invested in the stock and the complement in the riskless asset. This percentage may be negative or exceed 100% and may depend on time and on past history. The portfolio is called self-financing if the changes of its value are exclusively due to the investment gains and losses; that is, no external funds are added to or subtracted from the portfolio.

    We look at a particular form of a portfolio, whose value at time $t$ depends only on $t$ and $S(t)$ and is denoted by $W(S(t), t)$. In this portfolio the amount invested in the stock at time $t$, denoted by $\eta(S(t), t)$, depends only on the stock price $S(t)$. Thus, at time $t$, $\eta(S(t), t)$ will be invested in the stock, and the complement, $W(S(t), t) - \eta(S(t), t)$, in the riskless asset. The portfolio is self-financing if, at each point of time and under each scenario, the change of value is equal to the algebraic investment gain (which can be positive or negative). What are the mathematical conditions for the functions $W(s, t)$ and $\eta(s, t)$ under which the portfolio is self-financing? To answer this question, we examine the two scenarios discussed in Section 10.3.

Under scenario (a), where at time $t$ the price of the stock jumps from $S(t)$ to $S(t)e^k$, the value of the portfolio jumps from $W(S(t), t)$ to $W(S(t)e^k, t)$, and the instantaneous investment gain is

$$\eta(S(t), t)e^k - \eta(S(t), t). \tag{10.4.1}$$

Thus, the self-financing condition is that

$$W(S(t)e^k, t) - W(S(t), t) = \eta(S(t), t)(e^k - 1). \tag{10.4.2}$$

Therefore the amount invested in the stock at time $t$ must be

$$\eta(S(t), t) = \frac{W(S(t)e^k, t) - W(S(t), t)}{e^k - 1}. \tag{10.4.3}$$

Under scenario (b), there is no jump in an open interval containing $t$, so $S(t)$ is differentiable, with

$$S'(t) = -cS(t).$$

For notational simplicity, we assume that the function $W(s, t)$ is differentiable with respect to its variables. By the chain rule, the rate of change of the value of the portfolio is

$$\begin{aligned}
\frac{d}{dt} W(S(t), t) &= W_s(S(t), t)S'(t) + W_t(S(t), t) \\
&= -cS(t)W_s(S(t), t) + W_t(S(t), t)
\end{aligned} \tag{10.4.4}$$

where subscripted symbols denote partial derivatives. However, under this scenario, the investment gain is realized continuously, at a rate of

$$-c\eta(S(t), t) + r[W(S(t), t) - \eta(S(t), t)]. \tag{10.4.5}$$

It follows from (10.4.4) and (10.4.5) that the self-financing condition is

$$\begin{aligned}
-cS(t)W_s(S(t), t) + W_t(S(t), t) \\
= -c\eta(S(t), t) + r[W(S(t), t) - \eta(S(t), t)] \\
= rW(S(t), t) - (c + r)\eta(S(t), t).
\end{aligned} \tag{10.4.6}$$

If we replace $\eta$ in (10.4.6) according to (10.4.3), we obtain

$$-cS(t)W_s(S(t), t) + W_t(S(t), t)$$
$$= rW(S(t), t) - \frac{c+r}{e^k - 1}[W(S(t)e^k, t) - W(S(t), t)],$$

or

$$-csW_s(s, t) + W_t(s, t) = rW(s, t) - \frac{c+r}{e^k - 1}[W(se^k, t) - W(s, t)]. \qquad (10.4.7)$$

On one hand, by considering whether the stock jumps or not, we translate the self-financing condition mathematically as (10.4.3) and (10.4.6), which, in turn, imply (10.4.7). On the other hand, if we have a function $W(s, t)$ satisfying (10.4.7), then we can use (10.4.3) to determine $\eta(S(t), t)$, and then (10.4.6) is satisfied. Hence, a portfolio, whose value at time $t$ depends only on $t$ and the stock price at $t$, is self-financing if and only if its value function $W(s, t)$ satisfies (10.4.7). The amount invested in the stock at time $t$ is given by (10.4.3). We call (10.4.7) the *self-financing equation*.

Observe that, in deriving (10.4.7), we did not use the assumption that $\{N(t)\}$ is a homogeneous Poisson process. A weaker assumption is sufficient for obtaining (10.4.7), that, in each infinitesimal time interval, exactly two scenarios are possible: a jump with known magnitude, or no jumps.

# *Section 10.5*
# *The Price of a Contingent Claim*

For a contingent claim given by the payoff function $\Pi(s)$ and maturity date $T$, we construct a self-financing portfolio whose value at time $T$ is $\Pi(S(T))$. Then, by the principle of no arbitrage, the price of the contingent claim at any time before $T$ must be equal to the value of this *replicating portfolio* at that time.

Let the function $V(s, t)$ be defined as a conditional expected value of the discounted payoff:

$$V(s, t) = E^*[e^{-r(T-t)}\Pi(S(T)) \mid S(t) = s]$$
$$= e^{-r(T-t)}E^*[\Pi(S(T)) \mid S(t) = s], \quad 0 \le t < T \qquad (10.5.1)$$

where the asterisk with the expectation operator indicates that the conditional expectation is calculated with respect to a new Poisson parameter $\lambda^*$, which is yet to be determined; in earlier chapters the notation $E^Q$ was used. Note that, if $t$ is close to

$T$, $V(s, t)$ is $\Pi(se^{c(T-t)})$ plus a correction term in the order of $T - t$ that is due to discounting and the possibility of jumps occurring between $t$ and $T$. From this it follows that

$$V(S(t), t) \to \Pi(S(T))\ \ \ \ \ \ \ \ \ \ (10.5.2)$$

for $t \uparrow T$. The question is whether we can choose $\lambda^*$ such that there is a self-financing portfolio whose value at time $t$ is $V(S(t), t)$, $0 \le t < T$.

We now derive an equation for the function $V$ by applying the law of iterated expectations to the right-hand side of (10.5.1). For $0 \le t < T$, let $0 < h < T - t$, and $S(t) = s$. Consider whether or not there is a jump between time $t$ and time $t + h$. The probability that there are no jumps between time $t$ and time $t + h$ is $e^{-\lambda^* h}$, and the probability that the first jump after time $t$ occurs between time $t + \tau$ and time $t + \tau + d\tau$ is $e^{-\lambda^* \tau} \lambda^* d\tau$. By conditioning on the time of the first such jump, we obtain

$$V(s, t) = e^{-(r+\lambda^*)h} V(se^{-ch}, t + h) + \lambda^* \int_0^h e^{-(r+\lambda^*)\tau} V(se^{k-c\tau}, t + \tau)\, d\tau. \ \ \ (10.5.3)$$

Differentiating (10.5.3) with respect to $h$ and setting $h = 0$ yields

$$0 = -(r + \lambda^*)V(s, t) - cs V_s(s, t) + V_t(s, t) + \lambda^* V(se^k, t). \ \ \ \ \ \ (10.5.4)$$

Thus, the function $V(s, t)$ satisfies (10.4.7) provided that we set

$$\lambda^* = \frac{c + r}{e^k - 1}, \ \ \ \ \ \ \ \ \ \ (10.5.5)$$

which is a positive number because $k$ and $c + r$ are assumed to have the same sign (see Section 10.3). As we can have a replicating portfolio whose value at time $t$ is $V(S(t), t)$, the price of the contingent claim at time $t$ must be $V(S(t), t)$, the discounted conditional expectation of the payoff, where the expectation is calculated according to the Poisson parameter $\lambda^*$ given by (10.5.5). Thus, with $S(t) = s$, the price of the contingent claim at time $t$, $0 \le t < T$, is calculated by

$$V(s, t) = e^{-r(T-t)} E^*[\Pi(S(T)) \mid S(t) = s]$$

$$= e^{-r(T-t)} \sum_{n=0}^{\infty} \Pr^*[N(T) - N(t) = n] \Pi(se^{nk - c(T-t)})$$

$$= e^{-(r+\lambda^*)(T-t)} \sum_{n=0}^{\infty} \frac{[\lambda^*(T - t)]^n}{n!} \Pi(se^{nk - c(T-t)}). \ \ \ (10.5.6)$$

Furthermore, in the replicating portfolio, the amount invested in the stock at time $t$ is

$$\eta(S(t), t) = \frac{V(S(t)e^k, t) - V(S(t), t)}{e^k - 1}$$

$$= \frac{\lambda^*}{c + r}[V(S(t)e^k, t) - V(S(t), t)]. \qquad (10.5.7)$$

Formula (10.5.1) means that, under the probability measure according to the Poisson parameter $\lambda^*$, the expected rate of return of a contingent claim is the same as the rate of return of the riskless asset. As a check, consider $\Pi(z) = z$; then, for $t$, $h \geq 0$,

$$E^*[S(t + h) \mid S(t) = s] = sE^*[e^{kN(h) - ch}]$$

$$= s\exp([\lambda^*(e^k - 1) - c]h)$$

$$= se^{rh}.$$

The analysis in this section can be generalized to pricing options on more than one risky asset. (See Gerber and Shiu [75].) Furthermore, the argument can be adapted to path-dependent options, which are options with payoffs depending not only on the terminal value of the stock price.

# *Section 10.6*
# *The Geometric Brownian Motion Case*

The classical continuous-time stock-price model assumes a geometric Brownian motion for the stock-price process. We treat it as a limiting case. The remark in Section 10.3 (and Exercise 10.4) points out that in the limit $\gamma \to 0$ (with the parameters $k$, $\lambda$, and $c$ varying according to (10.3.15), (10.3.16), and (10.3.17), respectively), the process $\{Y(t)\}$ is a Brownian motion with drift $\mu$ and infinitesimal variance $\sigma^2$.

Now, the moment generating function of $Y(t)$ with respect to the new Poisson parameter $\lambda^*$ is

$$E^*[e^{zY(t)}] = \exp[\lambda^* t(e^{kz} - 1) - ctz] \qquad (10.6.1)$$

where the parameters $k$ and $c$ are given by (10.3.15) and (10.3.17), respectively, and $\lambda^*$ is expressed in terms of $k$ and $c$ according to (10.5.5). In Exercise 10.16 you are asked to show that the right-hand side of (10.6.1) converges to

$$\exp\left(\mu^* tz + \frac{1}{2}\sigma^2 tz^2\right), \qquad (10.6.2)$$

as $\gamma \to 0$, with

$$\mu^* = r - \frac{1}{2}\sigma^2. \qquad (10.6.3)$$

Expression (10.6.2), of course, is the moment generating function of a normal random variable with mean $\mu^* t$ and variance $\sigma^2 t$. Hence, in the probability measure defined by the new Poisson parameter $\lambda^*$, $\{Y(t)\}$ becomes in the limit a Brownian motion with the new drift parameter $\mu^*$ and unchanged infinitesimal variance $\sigma^2$ (and $\{S(t)\}$ is a geometric Brownian motion).

Given $S(t) = s$, the price of the contingent claim at time $t$ must be

$$\begin{aligned} V(s, t) &= e^{-r(T-t)} E^*[\Pi(S(T)) \mid S(t) = s] \\ &= e^{-r(T-t)} \int_{-\infty}^{\infty} \Pi(se^x) f(x; \mu^*(T-t), \sigma^2(T-t))\, dx \quad (10.6.4) \end{aligned}$$

where

$$f(x; \mu, \sigma^2) = \frac{1}{\sqrt{2\pi}\,\sigma} \exp\left[-\frac{(x-\mu)^2}{2\sigma^2}\right], \quad -\infty < x < \infty \qquad (10.6.5)$$

is the normal probability density function with parameters $\mu$ and $\sigma^2$. Furthermore, if we take the limit $k \to 0$ in (10.5.7), we see that the amount invested in the stock in the replicating portfolio must be

$$\eta(S(t), t) = S(t) V_s(S(t), t). \qquad (10.6.6)$$

Hence, the number of shares of the stock in the replicating portfolio is

$$\frac{\eta(S(t), t)}{S(t)} = V_s(S(t), t), \qquad (10.6.7)$$

which is usually called *delta* and denoted as $\Delta$ in the literature (see also Section 6.7.1).

**Example 10.6.1.** Calculate the price of a European call option on the stock with exercise price $K$ and exercise date $T$. Here,

$$\Pi(s) = (s - K)^+. \qquad (10.6.8)$$

For simplicity, consider $t = 0$. Let $S(0) = s$ and

$$\kappa = \log\left(\frac{K}{s}\right). \qquad (10.6.9)$$

Applying (10.6.4) yields

$$
\begin{aligned}
V(s,0) &= e^{-rT} \int_{\kappa}^{\infty} (se^x - K) f(x; \mu^* T, \sigma^2 T) \, dx \\
&= e^{-rT} \left[ s \int_{\kappa}^{\infty} e^x f(x; \mu^* T, \sigma^2 T) \, dx - K \int_{\kappa}^{\infty} f(x; \mu^* T, \sigma^2 T) \, dx \right] \\
&= s e^{-rT} \int_{\kappa}^{\infty} e^x f(x; \mu^* T, \sigma^2 T) \, dx - K e^{-rT} [1 - F(\kappa; \mu^* T, \sigma^2 T)]
\end{aligned}
$$

$$(10.6.10)$$

where $F(x; \mu, \sigma^2)$ is the normal distribution function with parameters $\mu$ and $\sigma^2$. Using the identity

$$
e^x f(x; \mu, \sigma^2) = \exp\left( \mu + \frac{1}{2}\sigma^2 \right) f(x; \mu + \sigma^2, \sigma^2)
$$

$$(10.6.11)$$

we obtain

$$
\int_{\kappa}^{\infty} e^x f(x; \mu^* T, \sigma^2 T) \, dx = \exp\left( \mu^* T + \frac{1}{2}\sigma^2 T \right) [1 - F(\kappa; (\mu^* + \sigma^2) T, \sigma^2 T)].
$$

$$(10.6.12)$$

Let $\Phi(\cdot)$ denote the standard normal distribution function. It follows from (10.6.10) and (10.6.12) that

$$
\begin{aligned}
V(s,0) &= s e^{(-r+\mu^*+\frac{1}{2}\sigma^2)T} [1 - F(\kappa; (\mu^* + \sigma^2) T, \sigma^2 T)] \\
&\quad - K e^{-rT} [1 - F(\kappa; \mu^* T, \sigma^2 T)] \\
&= s e^{(-r+\mu^*+\frac{1}{2}\sigma^2)T} \left[ 1 - \Phi\left( \frac{\kappa - (\mu^* + \sigma^2) T}{\sigma\sqrt{T}} \right) \right] \\
&\quad - K e^{-rT} \left[ 1 - \Phi\left( \frac{\kappa - \mu^* T}{\sigma\sqrt{T}} \right) \right] \\
&= s e^{(-r+\mu^*+\frac{1}{2}\sigma^2)T} \Phi\left( \frac{-\kappa + (\mu^* + \sigma^2) T}{\sigma\sqrt{T}} \right) \\
&\quad - K e^{-rT} \Phi\left( \frac{-\kappa + \mu^* T}{\sigma\sqrt{T}} \right).
\end{aligned}
$$

$$(10.6.13)$$

Substituting (10.6.3) into (10.6.13) we obtain the *Black-Scholes formula*,

$$
V(s,0) = s \Phi\left( \frac{-\kappa + rT + \frac{1}{2}\sigma^2 T}{\sigma\sqrt{T}} \right) - K e^{-rT} \Phi\left( \frac{-\kappa + rT - \frac{1}{2}\sigma^2 T}{\sigma\sqrt{T}} \right).
$$

$$(10.6.14)$$

More generally, with $S(t) = s$,

$$V(s, t) = s\, \Phi\left(\frac{\log(s/K) + \left(r + \frac{1}{2}\sigma^2\right)(T - t)}{\sigma\sqrt{T - t}}\right)$$

$$- K e^{-r(T-t)} \Phi\left(\frac{\log(s/K) + \left(r - \frac{1}{2}\sigma^2\right)(T - t)}{\sigma\sqrt{T - t}}\right), \quad (10.6.15)$$

which is the same as (2.11.1).                    ∎

The Black-Scholes formula can be used to price contingent claims with piece-wise linear payoff functions. Every piecewise linear function can be written as a linear combination of a constant, the linear function $s$, and functions of the form $(s - K_j)^+$. Thus, the price of a contingent claim with a piecewise linear payoff function is the corresponding linear combination of the discounted value of the constant, the stock price, and call option prices. For example, in the case of a European put option, we start with

$$(K - s)^+ = K - s + (s - K)^+, \quad (10.6.16)$$

substitute $s$ by $S(T)$, and then take discounted expectations. The resulting formula is called *put-call parity*.

From (10.6.7), we know that the number of shares in the replicating portfolio is given by $V_s(S(t), t)$. In the particular case of a European call option we can calculate this partial derivative. Differentiating (10.6.15) with respect to $s$ and simplifying, we obtain

$$V_s(S(t), t) = \Phi\left(\frac{\log(S(t)/K) + \left(r + \frac{1}{2}\sigma^2\right)(T - t)}{\sigma\sqrt{T - t}}\right). \quad (10.6.17)$$

# Section 10.7
# Options on Two Stocks

Consider two non-dividend-paying stocks with their prices at time $t$ denoted by $S_1(t)$ and $S_2(t)$, respectively, $t \geq 0$. We limit our discussion to the geometric Brownian motion model. Let $Y_i(t)$ be defined by

$$S_i(t) = S_i(0) \exp[Y_i(t)] \quad (10.7.1)$$

and assume that $\{Y_1(t), Y_2(t)\}$ is a bivariate Brownian motion, with drift parameters $\mu_1, \mu_2$, infinitesimal variances $\sigma_1^2, \sigma_2^2$, and correlation coefficient $\rho$. This process can be characterized by the properties (1) that it has independent and stationary increments and (2) that the joint distribution of $Y_1(t)$ and $Y_2(t)$ is bivariate normal, with means $\mu_1 t$, $\mu_2 t$, variances $\sigma_1^2 t$, $\sigma_2^2 t$, and covariance $\rho\sigma_1\sigma_2 t$.

Here a contingent claim is defined by a continuous payoff function $\Pi(s_1, s_2) \geq 0$ and a maturity date $T$, at which time the holder of the contingent claim will receive the amount $\Pi(S_1(T), S_2(T))$. For $S_1(t) = s_1$, $S_2(t) = s_2$, $0 \leq t < T$, we denote the price of the contingent claim at time $t$ as $V(s_1, s_2, t)$. The price can be shown to be again equal to a conditional expectation of the discounted payoff,

$$V(s_1, s_2, t) = E^*[e^{-r(T-t)}\Pi(S_1(T), S_2(T)) \mid S_1(t) = s_1, S_2(t) = s_2]$$
$$= e^{-r(T-t)}E^*[\Pi(S_1(T), S_2(T)) \mid S_1(t) = s_1, S_2(t) = s_2],$$
$$0 \leq t < T. \quad (10.7.2)$$

The asterisk with the expectation operator indicates that the conditional expectation is calculated with respect to a changed probability measure, which is obtained by replacing $\mu_1$ and $\mu_2$ with $\mu_1^*$ and $\mu_2^*$, but leaving the parameters $\sigma_1$, $\sigma_2$, and $\rho$ unchanged. Let

$$f(x_1, x_2; \mu_1, \mu_2, \sigma_1^2, \sigma_2^2, \rho), \quad -\infty < x_1, x_2 < \infty \quad (10.7.3)$$

denote the bivariate normal probability density function with parameters $\mu_1$, $\mu_2$, $\sigma_1$, $\sigma_2$, $\rho$. Then the expectation in (10.7.2) is

$$E^*[\Pi(S_1(T), S_2(T)) \mid S_1(t) = s_1, S_2(t) = s_2] = \int_{-\infty}^{\infty}\int_{-\infty}^{\infty}\Pi(s_1 e^{x_1}, s_2 e^{x_2})$$
$$\times f(x_1, x_2; \mu_1^*(T-t), \mu_2^*(T-t), \sigma_1^2(T-t), \sigma_2^2(T-t), \rho)\, dx_1\, dx_2. \quad (10.7.4)$$

The new drift parameters, $\mu_1^*$ and $\mu_2^*$, are such that (10.7.2) gives the right price for both stocks:

$$e^{-r(T-t)}E^*[S_i(T) \mid S_1(t) = s_1, S_2(t) = s_2] = s_i, \quad i = 1, 2. \quad (10.7.5)$$

Since

$$E^*[S_i(T) \mid S_1(t) = s_1, S_2(t) = s_2] = E^*[s_i \exp[Y_i(T-t)]]$$
$$= s_i \exp\left[\mu_i^*(T-t) + \frac{1}{2}\sigma_i^2(T-t)\right], \quad (10.7.6)$$

(10.7.5) is equivalent to

$$\mu_i^* = r - \frac{1}{2}\sigma_i^2, \quad i = 1, 2. \quad (10.7.7)$$

**Example 10.7.1.** Consider the right (but not the obligation) to exchange stock 1 for stock 2 at time $T$. This is a European option with payoff function

$$\Pi(s_1, s_2) = (s_2 - s_1)^+, \tag{10.7.8}$$

and so the price at time 0 is

$$
\begin{aligned}
V(s_1, s_2, 0) &= e^{-rT} E^*[(S_2(T) - S_1(T))^+ \mid S_1(0) = s_1, S_2(0) = s_2] \\
&= s_2 e^{-rT} \iint_D e^{x_2} f(x_1, x_2; \mu_1^* T, \mu_2^* T, \sigma_1^2 T, \sigma_2^2 T, \rho)\, dx_1\, dx_2 \\
&\quad - s_1 e^{-rT} \iint_D e^{x_1} f(x_1, x_2; \mu_1^* T, \mu_2^* T, \sigma_1^2 T, \sigma_2^2 T, \rho)\, dx_1\, dx_2
\end{aligned}
$$
$$\tag{10.7.9}$$

where the region of integration is

$$
\begin{aligned}
D &= \{(x_1, x_2) \mid s_2 e^{x_2} \geq s_1 e^{x_1}\} \\
&= \left\{ (x_1, x_2) \mid x_2 - x_1 \geq \log\left(\frac{s_1}{s_2}\right) \right\}. \tag{10.7.10}
\end{aligned}
$$

Using the identities

$$
\begin{aligned}
&e^{x_2} f(x_1, x_2; \mu_1, \mu_2, \sigma_1^2, \sigma_2^2, \rho) \\
&\quad = \exp\left(\mu_2 + \frac{1}{2}\sigma_2^2\right) f(x_1, x_2; \mu_1 + \rho\sigma_1\sigma_2, \mu_2 + \sigma_2^2, \sigma_1^2, \sigma_2^2, \rho) \tag{10.7.11}
\end{aligned}
$$

and

$$
\begin{aligned}
&e^{x_1} f(x_1, x_2; \mu_1, \mu_2, \sigma_1^2, \sigma_2^2, \rho) \\
&\quad = \exp\left(\mu_1 + \frac{1}{2}\sigma_1^2\right) f(x_1, x_2; \mu_1 + \sigma_1^2, \mu_2 + \rho\sigma_1\sigma_2, \sigma_1^2, \sigma_2^2, \rho) \tag{10.7.12}
\end{aligned}
$$

we can express the double integrals as probabilities, yielding

$$
\begin{aligned}
V(s_1&, s_2, 0) \\
&= s_2 \exp\left[\left(-r + \mu_2^* + \frac{1}{2}\sigma_2^2\right) T\right] \\
&\quad \times \Pr\left[X_2 - X_1 \geq \log\left(\frac{s_1}{s_2}\right); (\mu_2^* + \rho\sigma_1\sigma_2)\, T, (\mu_2^* + \sigma_2^2)\, T, \sigma_1^2 T, \sigma_2^2 T, \rho\right] \\
&\quad - s_1 \exp\left[\left(-r + \mu_1^* + \frac{1}{2}\sigma_1^2\right) T\right] \\
&\quad \times \Pr\left[X_2 - X_1 \geq \log\left(\frac{s_1}{s_2}\right); (\mu_1^* + \sigma_1^2)\, T, (\mu_2^* + \rho\sigma_1\sigma_2)\, T, \sigma_1^2 T, \sigma_2^2 T, \rho\right].
\end{aligned}
$$

To evaluate these two probabilities, note that the random variable $X_2 - X_1$ has a normal distribution in both cases with variance

$$\left(\sigma_2^2 + \sigma_1^2 - 2\rho\sigma_1\sigma_2\right) T = v^2 T \tag{10.7.13}$$

where

$$v^2 = \sigma_2^2 + \sigma_1^2 - 2\rho\sigma_1\sigma_2.$$

In the first probability term, the mean of $X_2 - X_1$ is

$$\left(\mu_2^* + \sigma_2^2\right) T - \left(\mu_1^* + \rho\sigma_1\sigma_2\right) T = \left(r - \frac{1}{2}\sigma_2^2 + \sigma_2^2\right) T - \left(r - \frac{1}{2}\sigma_1^2 + \rho\sigma_1\sigma_2\right) T$$

$$= \frac{1}{2}\left(\sigma_2^2 + \sigma_1^2 - 2\rho\sigma_1\sigma_2\right) T$$

$$= \frac{1}{2}v^2 T; \tag{10.7.14}$$

in the second probability term, the mean of $X_2 - X_1$ is

$$\left(\mu_2^* + \rho\sigma_1\sigma_2\right) T - \left(\mu_1^* + \sigma_1^2\right) T = \left(r - \frac{1}{2}\sigma_2^2 + \rho\sigma_1\sigma_2\right) T - \left(r - \frac{1}{2}\sigma_1^2 + \sigma_1^2\right) T$$

$$= -\frac{1}{2}\left(\sigma_2^2 + \sigma_1^2 - 2\rho\sigma_1\sigma_2\right) T$$

$$= -\frac{1}{2}v^2 T. \tag{10.7.15}$$

Thus, we have a surprisingly simple formula, known as *Margrabe's formula*, for the price of the exchange option:

$$V(s_1, s_2, 0)$$

$$= s_2 \left[1 - \Phi\left(\frac{\log(s_1/s_2) - \frac{1}{2}v^2 T}{v\sqrt{T}}\right)\right] - s_1 \left[1 - \Phi\left(\frac{\log(s_1/s_2) + \frac{1}{2}v^2 T}{v\sqrt{T}}\right)\right]$$

$$= s_2 \Phi\left(\frac{\log(s_2/s_1) + \frac{1}{2}v^2 T}{v\sqrt{T}}\right) - s_1 \Phi\left(\frac{\log(s_2/s_1) - \frac{1}{2}v^2 T}{v\sqrt{T}}\right). \tag{10.7.16}$$

■

# *Section 10.8*
# *Dividends*

So far we have excluded the payment of dividends, at least in the time interval from 0 to $T$. The easiest way to include dividends in the model is to assume that dividends are paid continuously at a constant proportional rate $\delta \geq 0$; that is, the stockholder will receive between time $t$ and time $t + dt$ a dividend $\delta S(t) \, dt$. (See Subsection 6.3.6 for the discrete-time analogue of this analysis.)

The analysis in the preceding sections can be adapted as follows. Under scenario (b) of Section 10.4, the investment gain is now at a rate of

$$(\delta - c)\eta(S(t), t) + r[W(S(t), t) - \eta(S(t), t)]$$
$$= r W(S(t), t) - (c - \delta + r)\eta(S(t), t). \tag{10.8.1}$$

Equating this with the rate of change of the value of the portfolio yields

$$-c S(t) W_s(S(t), t) + W_t(S(t), t) = r W(S(t), t) - (c - \delta + r)\eta(S(t), t), \tag{10.8.2}$$

which generalizes (10.4.6). Substituting for $\eta$ according to (10.4.3), we obtain

$$-c S(t) W_s(S(t), t) + W_t(S(t), t)$$
$$= r W(S(t), t) - \frac{c - \delta + r}{e^k - 1}[W(S(t)e^k, t) - W(S(t), t)],$$

or

$$-cs W_s(s, t) + W_t(s, t) = r W(s, t) - \frac{c - \delta + r}{e^k - 1}[W(se^k, t) - W(s, t)]. \tag{10.8.3}$$

Thus a portfolio, whose value at time $t$ depends only on $t$ and the (dividend-paying) stock price at $t$, is self-financing if and only if it satisfies the self-financing equation (10.8.3).

Because of (10.5.4), the function $V(s, t)$ defined by (10.5.1) satisfies (10.8.3) if we modify (10.5.5) as

$$\lambda^* = \frac{c - \delta + r}{e^k - 1}. \tag{10.8.4}$$

Hence, the price of the contingent claim is still given by a conditional expectation of the discounted payoff, $V(S(t), t)$, but the conditional expectation is taken with respect to the modified Poisson parameter (10.8.4).

As a check, assume that all dividends are immediately reinvested in the stock. For each share of the stock at time 0, there will be $e^{\delta t}$ shares of the stock at time $t$. Thus, $S(0)$ must be the price of the payoff of the amount of $e^{\delta t} S(t)$ at time $T$; this is the condition that

$$S(0) = e^{-rT} E^*[e^{\delta T} S(T)]$$
$$= e^{-(r-\delta)T} E^*[S(T)]$$
$$= e^{-(r-\delta)T} S(0) E^*[e^{kN(T)-cT}]$$
$$= e^{-(r-\delta)T} S(0) \exp([\lambda^*(e^k - 1) - c]T),$$

or

$$0 = -(r - \delta) + \lambda^*(e^k - 1) - c,$$

which is the same as (10.8.4).

Analogous reasoning can be used as a quick way to obtain the new value of $\mu^*$ in the geometric Brownian motion model. The condition for $\mu^*$ is that

$$S(0) = e^{-(r-\delta)T} E^*[S(T)]$$
$$= e^{-(r-\delta)T} S(0) E^*[e^{Y(T)}]$$
$$= e^{-(r-\delta)T} S(0) \exp\left(\mu^* T + \frac{1}{2}\sigma^2 T\right);$$

hence,

$$\mu^* = r - \delta - \frac{1}{2}\sigma^2. \qquad (10.8.5)$$

Substituting this in (10.6.13) yields the generalized Black-Scholes formula for the price of a European call option on a dividend-paying stock:

$$V(s, 0) = s e^{-\delta T} \Phi\left(\frac{-\kappa + (r - \delta)T + \frac{1}{2}\sigma^2 T}{\sigma\sqrt{T}}\right)$$
$$- K e^{-rT} \Phi\left(\frac{-\kappa + (r - \delta)T - \frac{1}{2}\sigma^2 T}{\sigma\sqrt{T}}\right) \qquad (10.8.6)$$

where $\kappa$ is defined by (10.6.9) (see also Exercise 2.10). Formula (10.8.6) may be used to price currency exchange options, with $S(t)$ denoting the spot exchange rate at time $t$, $r$ the domestic continuously compounded rate of interest, and $\delta$ the foreign continuously compounded rate of interest. In this context (10.8.6) is known as the *Garman-Kohlhagen formula*.

Finally, we return to the two-stock model in Section 10.7 and assume that stock $i$ pays dividends continuously at a constant proportional rate $\delta_i \geq 0$, $i = 1, 2$. Then we must set

$$\mu_i^* = r - \delta_i - \frac{1}{2}\sigma_i^2, \quad i = 1, 2, \qquad (10.8.7)$$

and the basic conclusions can be easily adapted. For example, the price for the right to exchange stock 1 for stock 2 at time $T$ is simply obtained by using the new values of $\mu_1^*$ and $\mu_2^*$, which yield

$$V(s_1, s_2, 0) = e^{-\delta_2 T} s_2 \Phi\left(\frac{\log(s_2/s_1) + (\delta_1 - \delta_2 + \frac{1}{2}v^2)T}{v\sqrt{T}}\right)$$

$$- e^{-\delta_1 T} s_1 \Phi\left(\frac{\log(s_2/s_1) + (\delta_1 - \delta_2 - \frac{1}{2}v^2)T}{v\sqrt{T}}\right); \qquad (10.8.8)$$

this generalizes Margrabe's formula (10.7.16). Again, note that the rate of interest $r$ does not appear in the formula.

# Section 10.9
## Incomplete Market Models

In the models of the earlier sections of this chapter, the payoff of each contingent claim can be obtained as the terminal value of a self-financing portfolio. Hence, the price of the contingent claim at any time before the maturity date must be the value of this replicating portfolio at that time. In general, for richer (and sometimes more realistic) stock price process models, replicating portfolios do not exist for most contingent claims. Thus, there are no unique prices for contingent claims: a priori a multitude of internally consistent price systems can be constructed. We consider one particular construction, which is based on *Esscher transforms*. In 1932 the Swedish actuary F. Esscher [56] suggested that the Edgeworth approximation (a refinement of the normal approximation) yields better results if it is applied to a modification or transformation of the original distribution of aggregate claims. We define this Esscher transform more generally as a change of measure for certain stochastic processes (see Gerber and Shiu [73], [74], [75]).

We suppose that

$$S(t) = S(0)e^{Y(t)}, \quad t \geq 0 \qquad (10.9.1)$$

where $\{Y(t)\}$ is a process with independent and stationary increments, such that

$$E[e^{zY(t)}] = E[e^{zY(1)}]^t. \qquad (10.9.2)$$

(Some authors call such $\{Y(t)\}$ a *Lévy process.*) Define

$$M(z) = E[e^{zY(1)}], \qquad (10.9.3)$$

the moment generating function of $Y(1)$. The idea is to construct a one-parameter family of associated probability measures, called *Esscher measures,* and then to determine the parameter to achieve compatibility with the observed stock price.

The expectation and probability with respect to the Esscher measure of parameter $h$ are denoted as $E[\cdot; h]$ and $\Pr[\cdot; h]$, and the process $\{Y(t)\}$ has independent and stationary increments such that the moment generating function of $Y(t)$ is

$$E[e^{zY(t)}; h] = \frac{E[e^{(z+h)Y(t)}]}{E[e^{hY(t)}]}$$

$$= \left(\frac{M(z+h)}{M(h)}\right)^t, \quad t \geq 0. \tag{10.9.4}$$

Let

$$F(x, t) = \Pr[Y(t) \leq x]$$

and

$$F(x, t; h) = \Pr[Y(t) \leq x; h].$$

An interpretation of the Esscher transform is that the original distribution function $F(x, t)$ of $Y(t)$ is replaced by $F(x, t; h)$ through the formula

$$dF(x, t; h) = \frac{e^{hx} dF(x, t)}{M(h)^t} \tag{10.9.5}$$

where differentiation is with respect to the $x$ variable.

Now the price of a contingent claim with payoff function $\Pi(s)$ and maturity date $T$ is *defined* as the conditional expectation of the discounted payoff:

$$V(s, t) = E[e^{-r(T-t)}\Pi(S(T)) \mid S(t) = s; h^*]$$
$$= e^{-r(T-t)}E[\Pi(S(T)) \mid S(t) = s; h^*], \quad 0 \leq t \leq T. \tag{10.9.6}$$

Here $h^*$ is the parameter value that reproduces the observed stock price; this is the condition that

$$S(0) = e^{-rT}E[S(T); h^*]$$

$$= e^{-rT}S(0)E[e^{Y(T)}; h^*]$$

$$= e^{-rT}S(0)\left(\frac{M(1+h^*)}{M(h^*)}\right)^T. \tag{10.9.7}$$

Hence, $h^*$ is the solution of the equation

$$e^r = \frac{M(1+h^*)}{M(h^*)}. \tag{10.9.8}$$

The existence of $h^*$ is a consequence of some regularity conditions. In Exercise 10.26 you are asked to show that the solution of (10.9.8) is unique.

**Example 10.9.1.** Calculate the price of a European call option with exercise price $K$ and maturity date $T$. The payoff function is

$$\Pi(z) = (z - K)^+, \quad z \geq 0,$$

and, given $S(0) = s$,

$$V(s, 0) = e^{-rT} E[(S(T) - K)^+; h^*]$$

$$= e^{-rT} \left[ s \int_\kappa^\infty e^x \, dF(x, T; h^*) - K \int_\kappa^\infty dF(x, T; h^*) \right]$$

$$= se^{-rT} \int_\kappa^\infty e^x \, dF(x, T; h^*) - Ke^{-rT}[1 - F(\kappa, T; h^*)]. \quad (10.9.9)$$

Because

$$e^x dF(x, t; h) = \frac{e^{(1+h)x} \, dF(x, t)}{M(h)^t}$$

$$= \left( \frac{M(1 + h)}{M(h)} \right)^t \frac{e^{(1+h)x} \, dF(x, t)}{M(1 + h)^t}$$

$$= \left( \frac{M(1 + h)}{M(h)} \right)^t dF(x, t; 1 + h)$$

and (10.9.8) holds, we have

$$\int_\kappa^\infty e^x \, dF(x, T; h^*) = \left( \frac{M(1 + h^*)}{M(h^*)} \right)^T \int_\kappa^\infty dF(x, T; 1 + h^*)$$

$$= \left( \frac{M(1 + h^*)}{M(h^*)} \right)^T [1 - F(\kappa, T; 1 + h^*)]$$

$$= e^{rT}[1 - F(\kappa, T; 1 + h^*)], \quad (10.9.10)$$

and so the price of the call option price on the non-dividend-paying stock is

$$V(s, 0) = s[1 - F(\kappa, T; 1 + h^*)] - e^{-rT} K[1 - F(\kappa, T; h^*)], \quad (10.9.11)$$

which generalizes the Black-Scholes formula (10.6.14). ∎

If the model is a complete market model, the unique prices of the contingent claims are obtained by this method. For example, if the stock-price process is a geometric Brownian motion as in Section 10.6, we get

$$M(z) = E[e^{zY(1)}]$$
$$= \exp\left(\mu z + \frac{1}{2}\sigma^2 z^2\right).$$

Applying this to (10.9.4) and simplifying yields

$$E[e^{zY(t)}; h] = \exp\left(\left[(\mu + h\sigma^2)z + \frac{1}{2}\sigma^2 z^2\right]t\right), \tag{10.9.12}$$

which is the moment generating function of a normal random variable. Hence the transformed stock price process is still a geometric Brownian motion, with $\mu$ replaced by

$$\mu(h) = \mu + h\sigma^2, \tag{10.9.13}$$

and unchanged value of $\sigma^2$. (There is a slight abuse of notation here; we use $\mu$ to denote both a constant and a function.)

Condition (10.9.8) for $h^*$ is now

$$e^r = \exp\left(\mu + \frac{1}{2}\sigma^2 + h^*\sigma^2\right). \tag{10.9.14}$$

It follows from (10.9.13) and (10.9.14) that

$$\mu(h^*) = \mu + h^*\sigma^2$$
$$= r - \frac{1}{2}\sigma^2, \tag{10.9.15}$$

which is the same as (10.6.3). To evaluate the first term in the right-hand side of (10.9.11), we also need the value $\mu(1 + h^*)$, which by (10.9.13) and (10.9.15) is

$$\mu(h^*) + \sigma^2 = r - \frac{1}{2}\sigma^2 + \sigma^2$$
$$= r + \frac{1}{2}\sigma^2.$$

Consider an example of an incomplete market model. Suppose that $\{Y(t)\}$ is a shifted compound Poisson process,

$$Y(t) = Z(t) - ct, \quad t \geq 0 \tag{10.9.16}$$

where $\{Z(t)\}$ is a compound Poisson process with Poisson parameter $\lambda$ and jump sizes that are exponentially distributed with parameter $\beta$. (Because the jump size is random, self-financing portfolios cannot be constructed.) Hence,

$$M(z) = E[e^{zY(1)}]$$

$$= \exp\left[\lambda\left(\frac{\beta}{\beta - z} - 1\right) - cz\right]. \tag{10.9.17}$$

Applying (10.9.17) to (10.9.4) yields

$$E[e^{zY(1)}; h^*] = \exp\left[\lambda\left(\frac{\beta}{\beta - z - h} - \frac{\beta}{\beta - h}\right) - cz\right]$$

$$= \exp\left[\frac{\lambda\beta}{\beta - h}\left(\frac{\beta - h}{\beta - h - z} - 1\right) - cz\right]. \tag{10.9.18}$$

Thus, the transformed process is of the same type, with $\beta$ replaced by

$$\beta(h) = \beta - h, \tag{10.9.19}$$

$\lambda$ replaced by

$$\lambda(h) = \frac{\lambda\beta}{\beta - h}$$

$$= \frac{\lambda\beta}{\beta(h)}, \tag{10.9.20}$$

and unchanged $c$. (Again we are abusing notation in using $\beta$ and $\lambda$ to denote both constants and functions.)

From (10.9.8) we get the condition for $h^*$:

$$e^r = \exp\left[\lambda\left(\frac{\beta}{\beta - 1 - h^*} - \frac{\beta}{\beta - h^*}\right) - c\right], \tag{10.9.21}$$

or

$$c + r = \frac{\lambda\beta}{(\beta - 1 - h^*)(\beta - h^*)}$$

$$= \frac{\lambda\beta}{[\beta(h^*) - 1]\beta(h^*)}, \tag{10.9.22}$$

which is a quadratic equation in $\beta(h^*)$. Since $\beta(h^*)$ is positive,

$$\beta(h^*) = \frac{1}{2} + \sqrt{\frac{1}{4} + (c + r)\lambda\beta}. \tag{10.9.23}$$

It follows from (10.9.20) that

$$\lambda(h^*) = \frac{\lambda\beta}{\beta(h^*)}. \tag{10.9.24}$$

A simple consequence of the method of Esscher transforms is the following factorization formula. Let $g(\cdot)$ be a (measurable) function and $h$, $k$, and $t$ be real numbers, $t \geq 0$; then

$$
\begin{aligned}
\mathrm{E}[S(t)^k g(S(t)); h] &= \frac{\mathrm{E}[S(t)^k g(S(t)) e^{hY(t)}]}{\mathrm{E}[e^{hY(t)}]} \\
&= \frac{\mathrm{E}[S(t)^{h+k} g(S(t))]}{\mathrm{E}[S(t)^h]} \\
&= \frac{\mathrm{E}[S(t)^{h+k}]}{\mathrm{E}[S(t)^h]} \frac{\mathrm{E}[S(t)^{h+k} g(S(t))]}{\mathrm{E}[S(t)^{h+k}]} \\
&= \mathrm{E}[S(t)^k; h]\mathrm{E}[g(S(t)); h+k]. \tag{10.9.25}
\end{aligned}
$$

As an example, apply (10.9.25) with $k = 1$, $h = h^*$, and $g(x) = I(x > K)$, where $I(A) = 1$ if $A$ is true and $I(A) = 0$ if $A$ is false:

$$
\begin{aligned}
\mathrm{E}[S(T)I(S(T) > K); h^*] &= \mathrm{E}[S(T); h^*]\mathrm{E}[I(S(T) > K); h^* + 1] \\
&= \mathrm{E}[S(T); h^*]\Pr[S(T) > K; h^* + 1] \\
&= S(0)e^{rT}\Pr[S(T) > K; h^* + 1]. \tag{10.9.26}
\end{aligned}
$$

The last equality holds because of the first equality in (10.9.7). Thus, we obtain

$$
\begin{aligned}
\mathrm{E}[e^{-rT}(S(T) - K)^+; h^*] &= e^{-rT}\mathrm{E}[(S(T) - K)I(S(T) > K); h^*] \\
&= e^{-rT}\{\mathrm{E}[S(T)I(S(T) > K); h^*] - K\mathrm{E}[I(S(T) > K); h^*]\} \\
&= S(0)\Pr[S(T) > K; h^* + 1] - Ke^{-rT}\Pr[S(T) > K; h^*], \tag{10.9.27}
\end{aligned}
$$

which is the same as (10.9.11).

# Section 10.10
# American Options

An American option has the additional feature that its holder can choose the time at which he or she wants to exercise it. The time of option exercise, $T$, may depend on the observed stock prices and other information and is a random variable. In mathematical terminology, $T$ is called a *stopping time* (see Appendix A).

We assume that we have a complete market model so that, for each fixed future time $t$, the value at time 0 of the random payment, $\Pi(S(t))$, paid at time $t$ is

$$\mathrm{E}^*[e^{-rt}\Pi(S(t))]. \qquad (10.10.1)$$

The function

$$V(s) = \sup_T \mathrm{E}^*[e^{-rT}\Pi(S(T)) \mid S(0) = s] \qquad (10.10.2)$$

is the *price function* of the American option, and an *optimal exercise strategy* is a stopping time $T$ for which the supremum is attained.

Most American options have a finite expiry date $\tau$, $\tau < \infty$; that is, only stopping times $T$ satisfying $T \le \tau$ are admitted. The resulting optimization problem does not have a simple solution in general and is beyond the scope of this book. A notable exception is an American call option, with exercise price $K$ and finite expiry date $\tau$, on a non-dividend-paying stock. The no-dividend condition implies that the price of the stock at a stopping time $T$, $T \le \tau$, is the conditional expectation of the discounted stock price at time $\tau$,

$$S(T) = \mathrm{E}^*[e^{-r(\tau-T)}S(\tau) \mid T, S(T)]. \qquad (10.10.3)$$

Using (10.10.3) and then Jensen's inequality we obtain

$$\begin{aligned}
e^{-rT}(S(T) - K)^+ &= e^{-rT}(\mathrm{E}^*[e^{-r(\tau-T)}S(\tau) \mid T, S(T)] - K)^+ \\
&= e^{-r\tau}(\mathrm{E}^*[S(\tau) \mid T, S(T)] - e^{r(\tau-T)}K)^+ \\
&\le e^{-r\tau}\mathrm{E}^*[(S(\tau) - e^{r(\tau-T)}K)^+ \mid T, S(T)] \\
&\le e^{-r\tau}\mathrm{E}^*[(S(\tau) - K)^+ \mid T, S(T)]. \qquad (10.10.4)
\end{aligned}$$

From this and the law of iterated expectations, it follows that

$$\mathrm{E}^*[e^{-rT}(S(T) - K)^+] \le \mathrm{E}^*[e^{-r\tau}(S(\tau) - K)^+].$$

But this shows that the optimal strategy is to exercise the call option at the expiry date. Hence, the prices of American and European call options are identical, provided that the underlying stock does not pay any dividends.

The optimization problem is also simplified for *perpetual options*, which are American options without a finite expiry date. The reason is that, in this case, the form of the optimal exercise strategy is simpler (and can often be guessed), and the remaining problem is to determine the optimal values of one or two parameters.

In the following we assume, as in Section 10.6, that the stock-price process is a geometric Brownian motion. Hence the sample paths are continuous, which simplifies the analysis. For certain payoff functions $\Pi(\cdot)$, which are typically $U$-shaped, for example,

$$\Pi(z) = |z - K|, \quad z \geq 0,$$

it is sufficient to consider strategies of the following form:

$$T_{u,v} = \min\{t \mid S(t) = u \text{ or } S(t) = v\}, \quad (10.10.5)$$

with $0 < u \leq s = S(0) \leq v$ (see Figure 10.2). Thus, the strategy is to exercise the option as soon as the stock price rises to the level $v$ or falls to the level $u$ for the first time; and the value of this strategy is (see Figure 10.3)

$$V(s; u, v) = E^*[e^{-rT_{u,v}} \Pi(S(T_{u,v})) \mid S(0) = s], \quad u \leq s \leq v. \quad (10.10.6)$$

FIGURE **10.2** | *The Stopping Time $T_{u,v}$*

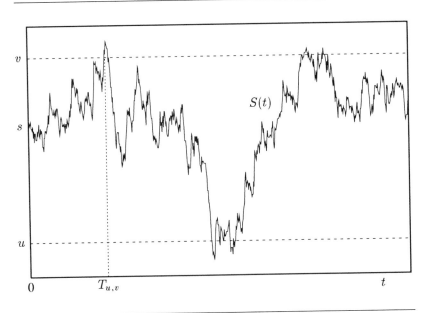

With the definitions

$$A(s; u, v) = E^*[e^{-rT_{u,v}} I(S(T_{u,v}) = u) \mid S(0) = s], \quad u \leq s \leq v \quad (10.10.7)$$

and

$$B(s; u, v) = E^*[e^{-rT_{u,v}} I(S(T_{u,v}) = v) \mid S(0) = s], \quad u \leq s \leq v, \quad (10.10.8)$$

FIGURE **10.3** | *The Value of the Strategy $T_{u,v}$*

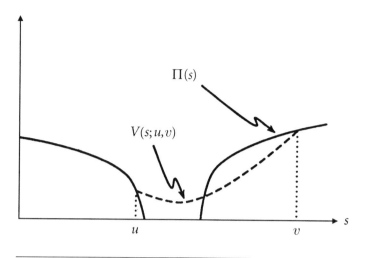

we can rewrite (10.10.6) as

$$V(s; u, v) = \Pi(u) A(s; u, v) + \Pi(v) B(s; u, v), \qquad (10.10.9)$$

which is valid for $0 < u \le s \le v < \infty$. Luckily, explicit expressions are available for the functions $A$ and $B$, and we only have to make the appropriate substitutions $[a = \log(u/s)$ and $b = \log(v/s)]$ in (10.13.14) and (10.13.15). Thus,

$$A(s; u, v) = \frac{v^{\theta_2} s^{\theta_1} - v^{\theta_1} s^{\theta_2}}{v^{\theta_2} u^{\theta_1} - v^{\theta_1} u^{\theta_2}} \qquad (10.10.10)$$

and

$$B(s; u, v) = \frac{s^{\theta_2} u^{\theta_1} - s^{\theta_1} u^{\theta_2}}{v^{\theta_2} u^{\theta_1} - v^{\theta_1} u^{\theta_2}}. \qquad (10.10.11)$$

Here $\theta_1$, $\theta_2$ are the solutions of the quadratic equation

$$\frac{1}{2}\sigma^2\theta^2 + \mu^*\theta - r = 0, \qquad (10.10.12)$$

which is the same as (10.13.18) but with $\mu$ changed to $\mu^* = r - \delta - (1/2)\sigma^2$ according to (10.8.5). We note that $\theta_1 < 0$, and that $\theta_2 > 1$ if $\delta > 0$ and $\theta_2 = 1$ if $\delta = 0$. The remaining problem is to find $\bar{u}$ and $\bar{v}$, the values of $u$ and $v$ maximizing $V(s; u, v)$. They are obtained from the first-order conditions:

$$V_u(s; \bar{u}, \bar{v}) = 0, \qquad (10.10.13)$$
$$V_v(s; \bar{u}, \bar{v}) = 0. \qquad (10.10.14)$$

Exercise 10.27 shows that (10.10.13) and (10.10.14) are equivalent to

$$V_s(\tilde{u}; \tilde{u}, \tilde{v}) = \Pi'(\tilde{u}), \qquad (10.10.15)$$

$$V_s(\tilde{v}; \tilde{u}, \tilde{v}) = \Pi'(\tilde{v}). \qquad (10.10.16)$$

These equations are known as the *smooth pasting condition*; they show that the option price has a continuous first derivative (see Figure 10.4).

FIGURE **10.4** | *The Price of the Perpetual Option*

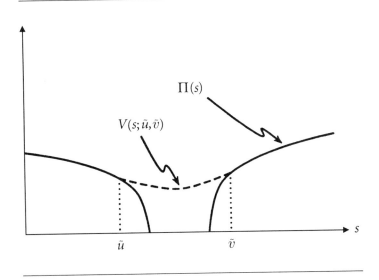

For another kind of payoff function, typically decreasing, it is sufficient to consider strategies such that the perpetual option is exercised as soon as the stock price falls to a certain level $u$. For $0 < u \le s = S(0)$, let

$$T_u = \min\{t \mid S(t) = u\} \qquad (10.10.17)$$

and

$$V(s; u) = E^*[e^{-rT_u}\Pi(S(T_u)) \mid S(0) = s]$$
$$= \Pi(u)E^*[e^{-rT_u} \mid S(0) = s]. \qquad (10.10.18)$$

Because

$$E^*[e^{-rT_u} \mid S(0) = s] = \lim_{v \to \infty} A(s; u, v)$$
$$= \left(\frac{s}{u}\right)^{\theta_1},$$

we obtain

$$V(s; u) = \Pi(u)\left(\frac{s}{u}\right)^{\theta_1},$$

(10.10.19)

valid for $0 < u \le s < \infty$. Hence $\bar{u}$, the optimal option-exercise stock price, is the value of $u$ that maximizes the expression

$$\frac{\Pi(u)}{u^{\theta_1}}.$$

(10.10.20)

**Example 10.10.1.** Consider the perpetual *put* option with exercise price $K$. Then

$$\Pi(z) = (K - z)^+, \quad z \ge 0.$$

It is clear that the optimal option-exercise stock price, $\bar{u}$, is less than $K$. Hence, the problem is to maximize

$$\frac{K - u}{u^{\theta_1}}.$$

(10.10.21)

The solution is

$$\bar{u} = \frac{-\theta_1}{1 - \theta_1} K.$$

(10.10.22)

The price of the perpetual put option at time 0 is $K - s$ for $0 < s = S(0) \le \bar{u}$, and

$$V(s; \bar{u}) = (K - \bar{u})\left(\frac{s}{\bar{u}}\right)^{\theta_1}$$

(10.10.23)

for $s > \bar{u}$. Note that the derivative of (10.10.23) with respect to $s$ tends to

$$(K - \bar{u})\frac{\theta_1}{\bar{u}} = -1$$

as $s \downarrow \bar{u}$. Thus, the option price has a continuous first derivative. ∎

For a third kind of payoff function, typically increasing, it is sufficient to consider strategies where the option is exercised as soon as the stock price rises to a certain level $v$. Let $V(s; v)$ be the value of such a strategy. By letting $u \downarrow 0$ in (10.10.11) we obtain

$$V(s; v) = \Pi(v)B(s; 0, v) = \Pi(v)\left(\frac{s}{v}\right)^{\theta_2},$$

(10.10.24)

valid for $0 < s \leq v < \infty$. Then $\bar{v}$, the optimal option-exercise stock price, is the value of $v$ that maximizes the expression

$$\frac{\Pi(v)}{v^{\theta_2}}. \tag{10.10.25}$$

**Example 10.10.2.** Consider the perpetual *call* option with exercise price $K$:

$$\Pi(z) = (z - K)^+, \quad z \geq 0.$$

It is clear that $\bar{v}$, if it exists, is greater than $K$. First assume that the underlying stock pays dividends at a constant proportional rate $\delta > 0$, which implies that $\theta_2 > 1$. Then the maximal value of

$$\frac{v - K}{v^{\theta_2}} \tag{10.10.26}$$

is attained for

$$\bar{v} = \frac{\theta_2}{\theta_2 - 1} K. \tag{10.10.27}$$

The price of the perpetual call option at time 0 is $s - K$ for $s \geq \bar{v}$, and

$$V(s; \bar{v}) = (\bar{v} - K)\left(\frac{s}{\bar{v}}\right)^{\theta_2} \tag{10.10.28}$$

for $0 < s < \bar{v}$.

In the absence of dividends, we have $\theta_2 = 1$ and

$$V(s; v) = (v - K)\frac{s}{v} = \left(1 - \frac{K}{v}\right)s \tag{10.10.29}$$

for $s < v$. This is an increasing function in $v$, and its supremum is

$$\lim_{v \to \infty} V(s; v) = s. \tag{10.10.30}$$

However, the price of the call option cannot be greater than $s$, the current price of the stock. Thus the only candidate for the option price would be $s$. Unfortunately, no exercise strategy exists with which this price can be attained. This is illustrated by the fact that, as $\theta_2 \downarrow 1$,

$$\bar{v} = \frac{\theta_2}{\theta_2 - 1} K \to \infty. \tag{10.10.31}$$

■

# Section 10.11
# *Russian Options*

For certain options, the payoff is not only a function of the stock price at the time of exercise, but it depends also on the previously observed stock prices in some way. Some authors use the term "exotic options" or "path-dependent options" to describe such securities. As an example, we discuss *Russian options*, a term coined by Shepp and Shiryaev [177] in honor of the famous Russian mathematician Kolmogorov. Again we assume a geometric Brownian motion as the stock-price model and dividends paid at a constant proportional rate $\delta > 0$. Let $s = S(0)$ and $m \geq s$. We define

$$M(t) = \max\Big\{m, \max_{0\leq\tau\leq t} S(\tau)\Big\}, \qquad (10.11.1)$$

which is the maximal observed stock price until time $t$ ($m$ has the role of an initial value or the historical stock-price maximum up to time 0) (see Figure 10.5).

FIGURE **10.5** | *The Stock Price Maximum*

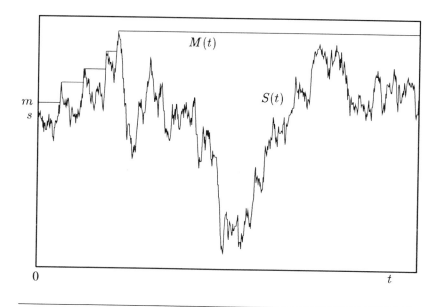

For the owner of a stock, a major concern is missing the right moment to sell the stock. Such an investor might prefer, instead of holding the stock, to own a security, called a Russian option, which pays $M(T)$ if the owner chooses to exercise it at time $T$. For $0 < s \le m < \infty$, the price at time 0 of this perpetual option is

$$V(s, m) = \sup_{T} E^*[e^{-rT} M(T) \mid S(0) = s, M(0) = m]. \qquad (10.11.2)$$

It is sufficient to consider option-exercise strategies of the form

$$T_{\varphi} = \inf\{t \mid S(t) = \varphi M(t)\}, \qquad (10.11.3)$$

where $0 < \varphi < 1$ and $0 < s = S(0) \le m = M(0) < \infty$; the value of such a strategy at time 0 is denoted by $V(s, m; \varphi)$. By distinguishing whether the stock price first rises to the level $m$ or first falls to the level $\varphi m$ (in which case the payoff of $m$ takes place), we obtain, for $0 < s \le m$,

$$V(s, m; \varphi) = V(m, m; \varphi) B(s; \varphi m, m) + m A(s; \varphi m, m)$$

$$= V(m, m; \varphi) \frac{(s/m)^{\theta_2} \varphi^{\theta_1} - (s/m)^{\theta_1} \varphi^{\theta_2}}{\varphi^{\theta_1} - \varphi^{\theta_2}} + m \frac{(s/m)^{\theta_1} - (s/m)^{\theta_2}}{\varphi^{\theta_1} - \varphi^{\theta_2}},$$

$$(10.11.4)$$

because of (10.10.10) and (10.10.11). We note that

$$V(m, m; \varphi) = m V(1, 1; \varphi); \qquad (10.11.5)$$

hence, (10.11.4) becomes

$$V(s, m; \varphi) = m \frac{V(1, 1; \varphi)[(s/m)^{\theta_2} \varphi^{\theta_1} - (s/m)^{\theta_1} \varphi^{\theta_2}] + (s/m)^{\theta_1} - (s/m)^{\theta_2}}{\varphi^{\theta_1} - \varphi^{\theta_2}}.$$

$$(10.11.6)$$

To determine $V(1, 1; \varphi)$, we use the following heuristic reasoning. If $s$ is "close" to $m$, we are practically sure that the stock price will attain (and therefore exceed) the level $m$ before the option is exercised. Thus, with very high probability, the maximum will be increased, which implies that the exact initial value of $m$ is "irrelevant." Mathematically, this means that

$$V_m(m, m; \varphi) = 0. \qquad (10.11.7)$$

Therefore, differentiating (10.11.6) with respect to $m$, and then setting $s = m$, we obtain the condition

$$0 = V(1, 1; \varphi)(\varphi^{\theta_1} - \varphi^{\theta_2}) - V(1, 1; \varphi)(\theta_2 \varphi^{\theta_1} - \theta_1 \varphi^{\theta_2}) - (\theta_1 - \theta_2)$$

$$= V(1, 1; \varphi)[(1 - \theta_2)\varphi^{\theta_1} - (1 - \theta_1)\varphi^{\theta_2}] - (\theta_1 - \theta_2), \qquad (10.11.8)$$

which yields

$$V(1, 1; \varphi) = \frac{\theta_2 - \theta_1}{(\theta_2 - 1)\varphi^{\theta_1} - (\theta_1 - 1)\varphi^{\theta_2}}. \tag{10.11.9}$$

If we substitute (10.11.9) in (10.11.6) and simplify, we obtain the explicit formula

$$V(s, m; \varphi) = m\frac{(\theta_2 - 1)(s/m)^{\theta_1} - (\theta_1 - 1)(s/m)^{\theta_2}}{(\theta_2 - 1)\varphi^{\theta_1} - (\theta_1 - 1)\varphi^{\theta_2}}, \qquad \varphi m \le s \le m. \tag{10.11.10}$$

Thus $\bar{\varphi}$, the optimal value of $\varphi$, is the one that minimizes the denominator, whose derivative is

$$(\theta_2 - 1)\theta_1 \varphi^{\theta_1 - 1} - (\theta_1 - 1)\theta_2 \varphi^{\theta_2 - 1}.$$

Hence,

$$\bar{\varphi} = \left(\frac{-\theta_1(\theta_2 - 1)}{\theta_2(1 - \theta_1)}\right)^{\frac{1}{\theta_2 - \theta_1}}. \tag{10.11.11}$$

Finally, the price of the Russian option is $m$ if $s \le \bar{\varphi} m$ and $V(s, m; \bar{\varphi})$ if $\bar{\varphi} m \le s \le m$. For further discussions on the Russian option, see Gerber, Michaud, and Shiu [72] and Gerber and Shiu [76]

# Section 10.12
## Lookback Options without Expiry Date

Evidently, the price of a Russian option is higher than $m$, which in turn is higher than the current price of the stock, making it an expensive security. If the investor already owns the stock, then a preference might be the cheaper option that provides a payoff of only

$$M(T) - S(T), \tag{10.12.1}$$

instead of $M(T)$. This is the *perpetual lookback put option*. Here we consider a generalization of the Russian option, a security that pays its holder

$$M(T) - \kappa S(T), \tag{10.12.2}$$

if the holder chooses to exercise it at time $T$. Here $\kappa$ is a constant between 0 and 1. If $\kappa = 0$, we have the Russian option; if $\kappa = 1$, we have the perpetual lookback put option. The analysis of this generalization can be carried out in a parallel fashion, step by step.

Again we only have to consider exercise strategies of the form (10.11.3). With a slight abuse of notation, we denote their values by the symbol $V(s, m; \varphi)$, which was used in the last section for the case $\kappa = 0$. Since the payoff is now

$$M(T_\varphi) - \kappa S(T_\varphi) = (1 - \kappa\varphi) M(T_\varphi), \tag{10.12.3}$$

we start with

$$V(s, m; \varphi) = V(m, m; \varphi) B(s; \varphi m, m) + (1 - \kappa\varphi) m A(s; \varphi m, m). \tag{10.12.4}$$

Proceeding step by step as before, we get

$$V(1, 1; \varphi) = (1 - \kappa\varphi) \frac{\theta_2 - \theta_1}{(\theta_2 - 1)\varphi^{\theta_1} - (\theta_1 - 1)\varphi^{\theta_2}} \tag{10.12.5}$$

and

$$V(s, m; \varphi) = m(1 - \kappa\varphi) \frac{(\theta_2 - 1)(s/m)^{\theta_1} - (\theta_1 - 1)(s/m)^{\theta_2}}{(\theta_2 - 1)\varphi^{\theta_1} - (\theta_1 - 1)\varphi^{\theta_2}}. \tag{10.12.6}$$

Hence, the optimal value of $\varphi$ is now chosen to maximize the expression

$$\frac{1 - \kappa\varphi}{(\theta_2 - 1)\varphi^{\theta_1} - (\theta_1 - 1)\varphi^{\theta_2}}. \tag{10.12.7}$$

# Section 10.13
# Appendix: A Layman's Guide to Brownian Motion (Wiener Process)

In Section 10.6 we considered the classical model in which

$$S(t) = S(0)e^{W(t)} \tag{10.13.1}$$

where $\{W(t)\}$ is a Brownian motion (Wiener process) with drift parameters $\mu$ and diffusion coefficient $\sigma$. This is a process with stationary and independent increments, whereby the increment over an interval of length $t$ is normally distributed with mean $\mu t$ and variance $\sigma^2 t$. Brownian motion is surrounded by a certain mystique (which perhaps explains its popularity) that is due to certain properties of its sample paths:

- As a function of $t$, $W(t)$ is continuous but nowhere differentiable.
- The *absolute variation* or *total variation* over any interval $(a, b)$ is infinite,

$$\int_a^b |dW(t)| = \infty. \tag{10.13.2}$$

An explanation of this phenomenon is that the process has heavily oscillating sample paths.

- The *quadratic variation* over an interval $(a, b)$ is nonrandom, and there is an explicit formula:

$$\int_a^b |dW(t)|^2 = \sigma^2(b - a). \tag{10.13.3}$$

A consequence of this formula is that in theory there is no estimation problem for $\sigma^2$. If a sample path is observed for a certain time interval, $\sigma^2$ can be directly computed: calculate the quadratic variation of the sample path and divide it by the length of the interval.

The French often add the abbreviation "p.s." following (10.13.2) and (10.13.3), where p.s. stands for *presque sûrement* (almost surely). We now show that p.s. could also stand for *peu surprenant* (little surprising).

Brownian motion $\{W(t)\}$ with parameters $\mu$ and $\sigma^2$ can be obtained as a limit of shifted Poisson processes $\{Y_k(t)\}$ as $k \to 0$, where

$$Y_k(t) = k N_k(t) - c_k t, \tag{10.13.4}$$

$$c_k = \frac{\sigma^2}{k} - \mu, \tag{10.13.5}$$

and the parameter for the Poisson process $\{N_k(t)\}$ is

$$\lambda_k = \frac{\sigma^2}{k^2} \tag{10.13.6}$$

(see Exercise 10.3). We are now ready to explain the behavior of the sample paths of $\{W(t)\}$:

- The discontinuities of $Y_k(t)$, $t \geq 0$, are of size $k$; hence, they disappear in the limit $k \to 0$. The function $Y_k(t)$ cannot be differentiated at the points where $N_k(t)$ has a jump. In the limit $k \to 0$ ($\lambda_k \to \infty$), the jumps will be dense; this explains why $W(t)$ does not have a derivative.

- The absolute variation of $Y_k(t)$ over $(a, b)$ is

$$\int_a^b |dY_k(t)| = |k|[N_k(b) - N_k(a)] + |c_k|(b - a)$$
$$\geq |c_k|(b - a). \tag{10.13.7}$$

In view of (10.13.5), this lower bound tends to infinity for $k \to 0$, which explains (10.13.2).

- The quadratic variation of $Y_k(t)$ over $(a, b)$ is

$$\int_a^b |dY_k(t)|^2 = k^2[N_k(b) - N_k(a)], \tag{10.13.8}$$

which is a random variable with mean

$$k^2 \lambda_k(b - a) = \sigma^2(b - a), \tag{10.13.9}$$

and variance

$$k^4 \lambda_k(b - a) = k^2 \sigma^2(b - a) \tag{10.13.10}$$

that vanishes in the limit as $k \to 0$. This explains (10.13.3).

For the Brownian motion $\{W(t)\}$, given by the parameters $\mu$ and $\sigma^2$, there is an explicit result about the time of first passage through one of two barriers. Let $a < 0 < b$. We define the stopping time

$$T = \min\{t \mid W(t) = a \text{ or } W(t) = b\}. \tag{10.13.11}$$

For $r > 0$, we introduce functions

$$\mathcal{A}(a, b) = E[e^{-rT} I(W(T) = a)] \tag{10.13.12}$$

and

$$\mathcal{B}(a, b) = E[e^{-rT} I(W(T) = b)]. \tag{10.13.13}$$

A well-known result, easily proven by applying the optional sampling theorem to certain martingales (see Appendix A), is that

$$\mathcal{A}(a, b) = \frac{e^{\theta_2 b} - e^{\theta_1 b}}{e^{\theta_2 b + \theta_1 a} - e^{\theta_1 b + \theta_2 a}}, \tag{10.13.14}$$

$$\mathcal{B}(a, b) = \frac{e^{\theta_1 a} - e^{\theta_2 a}}{e^{\theta_2 b + \theta_1 a} - e^{\theta_1 b + \theta_2 a}}, \tag{10.13.15}$$

where $a \leq 0 \leq b$. Here

$$\theta_1 = \frac{-\mu - \sqrt{\mu^2 + 2r\sigma^2}}{\sigma^2} \tag{10.13.16}$$

and

$$\theta_2 = \frac{-\mu + \sqrt{\mu^2 + 2r\sigma^2}}{\sigma^2} \tag{10.13.17}$$

are the solutions of the quadratic equation

$$\frac{1}{2}\sigma^2\theta^2 + \mu\theta - r = 0. \tag{10.13.18}$$

### Remarks

- With $r > 0$, we have $\theta_1 < 0$ and $\theta_2 > 0$.
- In the limit $r \to 0$, we get $\theta_1 = -2\mu/\sigma^2$ and $\theta_2 = 0$. Then

$$\mathcal{A}(a, b) = \frac{1 - e^{\theta_1 b}}{e^{\theta_1 a} - e^{\theta_1 b}} \tag{10.13.19}$$

  is the probability that the first barrier to be crossed is the lower barrier at $a$, and

$$\mathcal{B}(a, b) = \frac{e^{\theta_1 a} - 1}{e^{\theta_1 a} - e^{\theta_1 b}} \tag{10.13.20}$$

  is the probability that the first barrier to be crossed is the upper barrier at $b$.
- In financial applications, $r$ can be interpreted as an instantaneous rate (force) of interest, and $\mathcal{A}$ and $\mathcal{B}$ are expected discounted values. However, if we consider $r$ as a variable, then $\mathcal{A}$ and $\mathcal{B}$ are Laplace transforms. To illustrate this, suppose that $\mu > 0$ and that there is only an upper barrier at $b$ (thus, we let $a \downarrow -\infty$). Then

$$\mathcal{B}(-\infty, b) = \exp(-\theta_2 b)$$
$$= \exp\left[\frac{\mu b}{\sigma^2}\left(1 - \sqrt{1 + 2\left(\frac{\sigma}{\mu}\right)^2 r}\right)\right] \tag{10.13.21}$$

is the Laplace transform of the first passage time through the barrier at $b$. Identification is possible in this case: the underlying distribution is the *inverse Gaussian* distribution, with shape parameter

$$\alpha = \frac{\mu b}{\sigma^2} \tag{10.13.22}$$

and scale parameter

$$\beta = \left(\frac{\mu}{\sigma}\right)^2. \tag{10.13.23}$$

The probability density function of the stopping time $T$ is

$$f_T(t) = \frac{\alpha}{\sqrt{2\pi\beta}} t^{-3/2} e^{-\frac{(\beta t - \alpha)^2}{2\beta t}}, \quad t > 0. \tag{10.13.24}$$

- To calculate the price of an option we use the risk-neutral probability measure, but to calculate the distribution of the time to exercise an option we use the physical or actual probability measure.

# *Section 10.14*
# *Exercises*

## *Exercise 10.1*
Show that, if $k$ and $c + r$ have opposite signs, then the model contains arbitrage opportunities.

## *Exercise 10.2*
For $c$ and $\lambda$ given by (10.3.12) and (10.3.13), show that

$$\lambda(e^{kz} - 1) - cz = \left(\frac{\sigma}{k}\right)^2 (e^{kz} - 1) - \left(\frac{\sigma^2}{k} - \mu\right) z.$$

## *Exercise 10.3*
Prove that, for given $\mu$ and $\sigma^2$, as $k \to 0$ (with $c$ and $\lambda$ varying according to (10.3.12) and (10.3.13)),

$$\lambda(e^{kz} - 1) - cz \to \mu z + \frac{1}{2}\sigma^2 z^2.$$

## *Exercise 10.4*
Prove that, for given $\mu$ and $\sigma^2$, as $\gamma \to 0$ (with $k$, $\lambda$, and $c$ varying according to (10.3.15), (10.3.16), and (10.3.17), respectively),

$$\lambda(e^{kz} - 1) - cz \to \mu z + \frac{1}{2}\sigma^2 z^2.$$

## Exercise 10.5

Show that

$$V(s, t) = e^{-rh}[(1 - \lambda^* h) V(se^{-ch}, t + h) + \lambda^* h V(se^{k-ch}, t + h)] + o(h) \quad (10.14.1)$$

where the quantity $o(h)$ satisfies

$$\lim_{h \to 0} \frac{o(h)}{h} = 0.$$

Deduce (10.5.4) by rearranging (10.14.1), dividing it by $h$, and letting $h$ tend to 0.

## Exercise 10.6

Show that, for $s > 0$ and $0 \le u < T$,

$$V(s, u) = e^{-(r+\lambda^*)(T-u)} \Pi(se^{-c(T-u)})$$
$$+ \lambda^* \int_u^T e^{-(r+\lambda^*)(t-u)} V(se^{k-c(t-u)}, t) \, dt. \quad (10.14.2)$$

## Exercise 10.7

Let $L$ be the linear operator defined by

$$Lf(s, w) = \lambda^* \int_w^T e^{-(r+\lambda^*)(t-w)} f(se^{k-c(t-w)}, t) \, dt, \quad s > 0, \ 0 \le w < T.$$
$$(10.14.3)$$

Show that (10.14.2) can be written as

$$(I - L)V(s, u) = e^{-(r+\lambda^*)(T-u)} \Pi(se^{-c(T-u)}) \quad (10.14.4)$$

where $I$ denotes the identity operator.

## Exercise 10.8

For $n \ge 1$, define $L^n = L(L^{n-1})$. Show by induction that

$$L^n f(s, u) = \lambda^* \int_u^T e^{-(r+\lambda^*)(t-u)} \frac{[\lambda^*(t - u)]^{n-1}}{(n - 1)!} f(se^{nk-c(t-u)}, t) \, dt. \quad (10.14.5)$$

## Exercise 10.9

Interpret the quantity $\lambda^* e^{-\lambda^*(t-u)} [\lambda^*(t - u)]^{n-1}/(n - 1)! \, dt$ as a probability.

## Exercise 10.10

Show that, with

$$f(s, u) = e^{-(r+\lambda^*)(T-u)} \Pi(se^{-c(T-u)}),$$

(10.14.5) becomes

$$L^n f(s, u) = e^{-(r+\lambda^*)(T-u)} \frac{[\lambda^*(T-u)]^n}{n!} \Pi(se^{nk-c(T-u)}). \qquad (10.14.6)$$

## Exercise 10.11

Assuming the validity of

$$(I - L)^{-1} = I + L + L^2 + L^3 + \cdots,$$

use (10.14.4) and (10.14.6) to give another proof of (10.5.6).

## Exercise 10.12

Rewrite (10.5.6) as

$$V(s_0 e^{-c(t-t_0)}, t) = e^{-(r+\lambda^*)(T-t)} \sum_{n=0}^{\infty} \frac{[\lambda^*(T-t)]^n}{n!} \Pi(s_0 e^{nk-c(T-t_0)}). \qquad (10.14.7)$$

Verify that

$$\frac{d}{dt} V(s_0 e^{-c(t-t_0)}, t) = (r + \lambda^*) V(s_0 e^{-c(t-t_0)}, t) - \lambda^* V(s_0 e^{k-c(t-t_0)}, t).$$

## Exercise 10.13

Show that the price of a contingent claim that provides a payoff $S(T)^\alpha$ at time $T$ is

$$V(s, t) = s^\alpha \exp\{(T-t)[\lambda^*(e^{\alpha k} - e^k) + (1 - \alpha)c]\}.$$

## Exercise 10.14

For given $\mu$ and $\sigma^2$, if

$$c = \frac{\sigma^2}{k} - \mu \qquad (10.14.8)$$

and $\lambda^*$ is defined by (10.5.5), show that

$$\lim_{k \to 0} \lambda^* k - c = r - \frac{1}{2}\sigma^2,$$

which is the right-hand side of (10.6.3). Note that $\mu$ does not appear in the limit.

---

### Exercise 10.15

Prove that, for given $\mu$ and $\sigma^2$, as $k \to 0$ (with $c$ and $\lambda^*$ varying according to (10.14.8), and (10.5.5), respectively),

$$\lambda^*(e^{kz} - 1) - cz \to \mu^* z + \frac{1}{2}\sigma^2 z^2$$

with $\mu^*$ given by (10.6.3).

---

### Exercise 10.16

Prove that, for given $\mu$ and $\sigma^2$, as $\gamma \to 0$ (with $k$, $c$, and $\lambda^*$ varying according to (10.3.15), (10.3.17), and (10.5.5), respectively),

$$\lambda^*(e^{kz} - 1) - cz \to \mu^* z + \frac{1}{2}\sigma^2 z^2$$

with $\mu^*$ given by (10.6.3).

---

### Exercise 10.17

Applying the Taylor expansion or otherwise, show that, for given $\mu$, $\sigma^2$, and twice-differentiable function $g(s)$, as $k \to 0$ (with $c$ and $\lambda^*$ varying according to (10.14.8) and (10.5.5), respectively),

$$\lambda^*[g(se^k) - g(s)] + (-c)sg'(s) \to rsg'(s) + \frac{(\sigma s)^2}{2}g''(s).$$

Note: In an infinitesimal interval of length $ds$, $\lambda^* ds$ is the expected number of jumps (in the modified probability measure), and $-cds$ is the relative amount of change in the stock price if there is no jump.

---

### Exercise 10.18

Prove that, for given $\mu$ and $\sigma^2$, in the limit $k \to 0$ with $c$ varying according to (10.14.8), the self-financing equation (10.4.7) becomes

$$W_t(s, t) = r W(s, t) - rs W_s(s, t) - \frac{(\sigma s)^2}{2} W_{ss}(s, t),$$

which is the same as (6.3.17). In the mathematics literature this partial differential equation is classified as a parabolic differential equation. Its derivation in the finance literature usually involves an application of *Itô's lemma*.

## Exercise 10.19

For $V(s, t)$ given by (10.6.15), verify the following:

$$\frac{\partial}{\partial s} V(s, t) = V_s(s, t) = \Phi\left(\frac{\log(s/K) + \left(r + \frac{1}{2}\sigma^2\right)(T - t)}{\sigma\sqrt{T - t}}\right) > 0,$$

$$\frac{\partial}{\partial K} V(s, t) = -e^{-r(T-t)}\Phi\left(\frac{\log(s/K) + \left(r - \frac{1}{2}\sigma^2\right)(T - t)}{\sigma\sqrt{T - t}}\right) < 0,$$

$$\frac{\partial}{\partial r} V(s, t) = K(T - t)e^{-r(T-t)}\Phi\left(\frac{\log(s/K) + \left(r - \frac{1}{2}\sigma^2\right)(T - t)}{\sigma\sqrt{T - t}}\right) > 0,$$

$$\frac{\partial}{\partial T} V(s, t) = \frac{s\sigma}{2\sqrt{T - t}}\phi\left(\frac{\log(s/K) + \left(r + \frac{1}{2}\sigma^2\right)(T - t)}{\sigma\sqrt{T - t}}\right)$$

$$+ rKe^{-r(T-t)}\Phi\left(\frac{\log(s/K) + \left(r - \frac{1}{2}\sigma^2\right)(T - t)}{\sigma\sqrt{T - t}}\right) > 0,$$

$$\frac{\partial}{\partial t} V(s, t) = V_t(s, t) = -\frac{\partial}{\partial T} V(s, t),$$

$$\frac{\partial}{\partial \sigma} V(s, t) = s\sqrt{T - t}\phi\left(\frac{\log(s/K) + \left(r + \frac{1}{2}\sigma^2\right)(T - t)}{\sigma\sqrt{T - t}}\right) > 0,$$

$$\frac{\partial^2}{\partial s^2} V(s, t) = V_{ss}(s, t) = \frac{1}{s\sigma\sqrt{T - t}}\phi\left(\frac{\log(s/K) + \left(r + \frac{1}{2}\sigma^2\right)(T - t)}{\sigma\sqrt{T - t}}\right) > 0$$

where $\phi = \Phi'$ is the standard normal density function.

## Exercise 10.20

a. Show (10.7.11) and (10.7.12) by verifying the more general identity

$$\exp(x_1 z_1 + x_2 z_2) f\left(x_1, x_2; \mu_1, \mu_2, \sigma_1^2, \sigma_2^2, \rho\right)$$

$$= \exp\left[\mu_1 z_1 + \mu_2 z_2 + \frac{1}{2}\left(\sigma_1^2 z_1^2 + 2\rho\sigma_1\sigma_2 z_1 z_2 + \sigma_2^2 z_2^2\right)\right] f\left(x_1, x_2; \bar{\mu}_1, \bar{\mu}_2, \sigma_1^2, \sigma_2^2, \rho\right),$$

with

$$\bar{\mu}_1 = \mu_1 + z_1\sigma_1^2 + z_2\rho\sigma_1\sigma_2,$$

$$\bar{\mu}_2 = \mu_2 + z_2\sigma_2^2 + z_1\rho\sigma_1\sigma_2.$$

b. Use this identity to calculate the moment generating function of the bivariate normal distribution.

## Exercise 10.21

a. Show that, for an invertible, symmetric, $n \times n$ matrix $V$, and $n$-dimensional column vectors $\mu$, $x$, and $z$,

$$z^T x - \frac{1}{2}(x - \mu)^T V^{-1}(x - \mu) = z^T \mu + \frac{1}{2} z^T V z - \frac{1}{2}(x - \mu - V z)^T V^{-1}(x - \mu - V z).$$

b. Generalize the identity in Exercise 10.20 (a) and derive the moment generating function of the $n$-dimensional normal distribution.

## Exercise 10.22

Derive a formula for the price of the European maximum option; that is, with payoff at time $T$ being $\text{Max}[S_1(T), S_2(T)]$, find $V(s_1, s_2, t), 0 \le t < T$.

## Exercise 10.23

For $V(s_1, s_2, 0)$ given by (10.7.16), show that

$$\frac{\partial}{\partial s_1} V(s_1, s_2, 0) = V_{s_1}(s_1, s_2, 0) = -\Phi \left( \frac{\log(s_2/s_1) - \frac{1}{2}v^2 T}{v\sqrt{T}} \right)$$

and

$$\frac{\partial}{\partial s_2} V(s_1, s_2, 0) = V_{s_2}(s_1, s_2, 0) = \Phi \left( \frac{\log(s_2/s_1) + \frac{1}{2}v^2 T}{v\sqrt{T}} \right).$$

## Exercise 10.24

Verify that (see Section 10.8)

$$S(0) = E^* \left[ \delta \int_0^T e^{-rt} S(t) \, dt + e^{-rT} S(T) \right].$$

Interpret the formula.

## Exercise 10.25

Let $\alpha$ be a real number. Interpret the formula (see Section 10.8)

$$S(0) = E^* \left[ (\delta - \alpha) \int_0^T e^{-rt} e^{\alpha t} S(t) \, dt + e^{-rT} e^{\alpha T} S(T) \right].$$

## Exercise 10.26

(Uniqueness of solution to (10.9.8).)

a. Show that

$$\frac{d}{dh} E[Y(t); h] = \mathrm{Var}[Y(t); h]. \qquad (10.14.9)$$

b. Show that the function

$$f(h) = \log[M(1+h)] - \log[M(h)]$$

is an increasing function.

c. Show that (10.9.8) has at most one solution $h = h^*$.

## Exercise 10.27

a. Use (10.10.9) to show that

$$V_u(u; u, v) = \Pi'(u) + \Pi(u) A_u(u; u, v) + \Pi(v) B_u(u; u, v),$$
$$V_s(u; u, v) = \Pi(u) A_s(u; u, v) + \Pi(v) B_s(u; u, v).$$

b. For $u < x < s < v$, interpret the identities

$$A(s; u, v) = A(s; x, v) A(x; u, v),$$
$$B(s; u, v) = A(s; x, v) B(x; u, v) + B(s; x, v).$$

c. By differentiating the identities in (b) with respect to $x$ and setting $x = s = u$, show that

$$A_u(u; u, v) + A_s(u; u, v) = 0,$$
$$B_u(u; u, v) + B_s(u; u, v) = 0.$$

d. Show that

$$V_u(u; u, v) = \Pi'(u) - V_s(u; u, v).$$

## Exercise 10.28

From (10.10.9) to (10.10.11) it follows that

$$V(s; u, v) = Q_1(u, v)s^{\theta_1} + Q_2(u, v)s^{\theta_2}.$$

Set $s = u$ and $s = v$ to obtain two linear equations for $Q_1(u, v)$ and $Q_2(u, v)$. Then determine $Q_1(u, v)$ and $Q_2(u, v)$.

## Exercise 10.29

In Figure 10.3 the values of $u$ and $v$ are not optimal.

a. If we decrease $v$, does $V(s; u, v)$ increase?

b. If we decrease $u$, does $V(s; u, v)$ increase?

## Exercise 10.30

Show that (see Section 10.11)

$$V_s(\varphi m, m; \varphi) = 0$$

if and only if $\varphi = \tilde{\varphi}$.

## Exercise 10.31

The smooth pasting condition

a. From (10.12.6), calculate $V_s(\varphi m, m; \varphi)$.

b. Show that the derivative of (10.12.7) with respect to $\varphi$ can be written as

$$\frac{-\kappa - V_s(\varphi m, m; \varphi)}{(\theta_2 - 1)\varphi^{\theta_1} - (\theta_1 - 1)\varphi^{\theta_2}}.$$

c. What is the value of $V_s(\tilde{\varphi} m, m; \tilde{\varphi})$?

d. Interpret the answer for (c) with Figure 10.6.

FIGURE **10.6** | *The Price of the Generalized Russian Option*

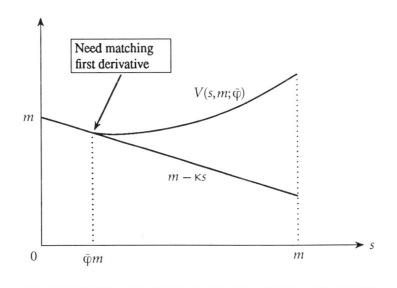

### Exercise 10.32

With payoff given by (10.12.2), let $\bar{\varphi}$ denote the optimal value of $\varphi$. Express $\kappa$ in terms of $\bar{\varphi}$, $\theta_1$, and $\theta_2$.

### Exercise 10.33 (Perpetual Lookback Call Option)

Price the *perpetual lookback call option*, which provides a payoff of

$$S(T) - m(T),$$

if the option is exercised at time $T$. Here $m(T)$ is the historical stock-price minimum up to time $T$.

# CHAPTER 11
## NO-ARBITRAGE PRICING THEORY—ADVANCED

## Section 11.1
## Introduction

In this final chapter we return to no-arbitrage pricing theory, which we have encountered in Chapter 5. This chapter can be read independently of Chapter 5; the treatment presented here is more detailed and rigorous. We use probability concepts such as information structures, filtrations, conditional expectations, martingales, and stopping times. You may find Appendix A, especially Section A.1, helpful in understanding these concepts.

An important application of financial economic theory to insurance is the "fair" valuation or "market" valuation of insurance liabilities. We pointed out in Section 3.3 that Redington had the insight that, because an insurance liability is merely a stream of future cash flows that can be regarded as the negative of asset cash flows, the liability cash-flow stream should be valued by the same method used for valuing asset cash flows. This led us to study the fundamental theorem of asset pricing. This result was proved in Section 5.2 for the single-period model, where it was assumed that there was an asset with strictly positive payoff at time 1.

In Subsection 11.2.4, we use a separating hyperplane theorem to derive the fundamental theorem of asset pricing in the multiperiod case and without the strictly positive asset assumption. Then in Subsection 11.2.10, we present another proof of the fundamental theorem of asset pricing, recently published by Rogers [160]. The remainder of Section 11.2 gives the various equivalent formulas for pricing cash-flow streams that can be spanned or generated by the primitive securities in the model. Section 11.3 discusses no-arbitrage pricing of forward contracts and futures contracts. In particular, it shows that the futures price process is a Doob's martingale under the risk-neutral probability measure. Section 11.4 deals with American options. Mathematically, this is the most difficult section in this book. The results are derived without using advanced probability theory.

Throughout this chapter, we make the following assumptions, which are standard for discrete-time and discrete state-space models of a perfect capital market. The market is frictionless. There are no taxes, transaction costs, or restrictions on short sales. All securities or assets are perfectly divisible. Information is available to all investors simultaneously. Every investor acts rationally. The market clears at discrete points in time, which are separated by regular intervals. For simplicity, each interval is a single unit of time.

# Section 11.2
# *The Multiperiod Model: Revisited*

### SECTION 11.2.1 | NOTATION FOR INFORMATION STRUCTURE

As in Chapter 5, the basic mathematical structure for the multiperiod model consists of a finite collection of sample points $\Omega = \{\omega_1, \omega_2, \ldots, \omega_M\}$, which is sometimes referred to as the *sample space*. The symbol $M$ denotes the generic number of sample points for the model. We sometimes refer to an individual element of this set as a *market outcome* since each $\omega \in \Omega$ is interpreted as corresponding to a particular market history. We can also refer to a particular $\omega$ as a *sample point*, a *sample path*, or a *scenario path*. We assume that each $\omega$ has a positive probability of occurrence.

We further assume that a finite sequence of partitions of $\Omega$ is defined, which we denote as $\{\mathcal{P}_k; k = 0, \ldots, T\}$, satisfying $\mathcal{P}_0 \subseteq \mathcal{P}_1 \subseteq \cdots \subseteq \mathcal{P}_k \subseteq \cdots \subseteq \mathcal{P}_T$. The requirement that the partitions be successive refinements of one another has the interpretation that information is revealed through time in the model. In each of our securities market models we always assume that $\mathcal{P}_0 = \{\{\omega_1, \omega_2, \ldots, \omega_M\}\} \equiv \{\Omega\}$ and $\mathcal{P}_T = \{\{\omega_1\}, \{\omega_2\}, \ldots, \{\omega_M\}\}$. At time 0, the investors know the collection of the $M$ possible market outcomes and the partitions, but they do not know until time $T$ which of the market outcomes will occur. The condition $\mathcal{P}_0 = \{\{\omega_1, \omega_2, \ldots, \omega_M\}\}$ is interpreted as there being no information available at time 0, the start of the trading period, concerning the market outcome. The condition $\mathcal{P}_T = \{\{\omega_1\}, \{\omega_2\}, \ldots, \{\omega_M\}\}$ is interpreted as there being full revelation of information by time $T$, the end of the trading period. The pair $(\Omega, \{\mathcal{P}_k\})$ consisting of the sample space $\Omega$ together with the sequence of partitions $\{\mathcal{P}_k\}$ is referred to as a *filtered space*. The filtered space $(\Omega, \{\mathcal{P}_k\})$ models the revelation of information through time. At time $k$, we are able to distinguish between market outcomes belonging to different elements of $\mathcal{P}_k$ but are unable to distinguish between market outcomes belonging to the same element in $\mathcal{P}_k$.

We require some notation to help us work with the information structures in our securities market models. For a set $\mathcal{A}$, let $\#\mathcal{A}$ denote number of elements or cardinality of $\mathcal{A}$. Suppose that $(\Omega, \{\mathcal{P}_k\})$ is a filtered space. The number of sets of $\omega$'s comprising the partition $\mathcal{P}_k$ is denoted $v_k$ so that $v_k = \#\mathcal{P}_k$ and $\mathcal{P}_k = \{\mathcal{H}_1^{(k)}, \mathcal{H}_2^{(k)}, \ldots, \mathcal{H}_{v_k}^{(k)}\}$. In Chapter 5, we used the term "time-$k$ histories" to describe elements of $\mathcal{P}_k$. Since $\mathcal{P}_0$ consists of the single element $\Omega$, we have $v_0 = 1$ and $\mathcal{P}_0 = \{\mathcal{H}_1^{(0)}\} \equiv \{\Omega\}$. The element of the partition $\mathcal{P}_k$ to which the sample point $\omega$ belongs is denoted $\mathcal{H}^{(k)}(\omega)$. The symbol $v^{(k)}(\omega)$ denotes the number of sample points in the element of $\mathcal{P}_k$ to which $\omega$ belongs, so that $v^{(k)}(\omega) = \#\mathcal{H}^{(k)}(\omega)$. We also make use of representative sets for each partition $\mathcal{P}_k$ in our information structure. The symbol $\Omega^{(k)}$ denotes a set consisting of one representative from each of the sets $\mathcal{H}_1^{(k)}, \mathcal{H}_2^{(k)}, \ldots, \mathcal{H}_{v_k}^{(k)}$ comprising $\mathcal{P}_k$. Hence, $\Omega^{(k)}$ has $v_k$ elements; that is, $\#\Omega^{(k)} = v_k$. Without loss of generality, it may be assumed that $\Omega^{(0)} \subseteq \Omega^{(1)} \subseteq \cdots \subseteq \Omega^{(k)} \subseteq \cdots \subseteq \Omega^{(T)}$.

**Example 11.2.1.** The preceding notation can be illustrated with a simple example, which serves to illustrate our notation. Consider an information structure with the tree representation given in Figure 5.2 in Chapter 5. Then

$$\Omega = \{\omega_1, \omega_2, \ldots, \omega_{22}\}, \quad M = 22;$$

$$\mathcal{P}_1 = \{\mathcal{H}_1^{(1)}, \mathcal{H}_2^{(1)}, \mathcal{H}_3^{(1)}\}, \quad v_1 = 3, \quad \text{with}$$

$$\mathcal{H}_1^{(1)} = \{\omega_1, \omega_2, \ldots, \omega_7\}, \quad v_1^{(1)} = 7,$$

$$\mathcal{H}_2^{(1)} = \{\omega_8, \omega_9, \ldots, \omega_{12}\}, \quad v_2^{(1)} = 5,$$

$$\mathcal{H}_3^{(1)} = \{\omega_{13}, \omega_{14}, \ldots, \omega_{22}\}, \quad v_3^{(1)} = 10;$$

$$\mathcal{P}_2 = \{\mathcal{H}_1^{(2)}, \mathcal{H}_2^{(2)}, \ldots, \mathcal{H}_9^{(2)}\}, \quad v_2 = 9, \quad \text{with}$$

$$\mathcal{H}_1^{(2)} = \{\omega_1, \omega_2, \omega_3\}, \quad v_1^{(2)} = 3,$$

$$\mathcal{H}_2^{(2)} = \{\omega_4, \omega_5\}, \quad v_2^{(2)} = 2,$$

$$\mathcal{H}_3^{(2)} = \{\omega_6, \omega_7\}, \quad v_3^{(2)} = 2,$$

$$\mathcal{H}_4^{(2)} = \{\omega_8, \omega_9, \omega_{10}\}, \quad v_4^{(2)} = 3,$$

$$\mathcal{H}_5^{(2)} = \{\omega_{11}, \omega_{12}\}, \quad v_5^{(2)} = 2,$$

$$\mathcal{H}_6^{(2)} = \{\omega_{13}, \omega_{14}, \omega_{15}\}, \quad v_6^{(2)} = 3,$$

$$\mathcal{H}_7^{(2)} = \{\omega_{16}, \omega_{17}\}, \quad v_7^{(2)} = 2,$$

$$\mathcal{H}_8^{(2)} = \{\omega_{18}, \omega_{19}\}, \quad v_8^{(2)} = 2,$$

$$\mathcal{H}_9^{(2)} = \{\omega_{20}, \omega_{21}, \omega_{22}\}, \quad v_9^{(2)} = 3;$$

$$\mathcal{P}_3 = \{\{\omega_1\}, \{\omega_2\}, \ldots, \{\omega_{22}\}\}, \quad v_3 = 22 = M.$$

Also

$$\mathcal{H}^{(1)}(\omega_6) = \mathcal{H}_1^{(1)} = \{\omega_1, \omega_2, \ldots, \omega_7\}, \quad v^{(1)}(\omega_6) = 7,$$

$$\mathcal{H}^{(1)}(\omega_9) = \mathcal{H}_2^{(1)} = \{\omega_8, \omega_9, \ldots, \omega_{12}\}, \quad v^{(1)}(\omega_9) = 9,$$

$$\mathcal{H}^{(1)}(\omega_{22}) = \mathcal{H}_3^{(1)} = \{\omega_{13}, \omega_{14}, \ldots, \omega_{22}\}, \quad v^{(1)}(\omega_{22}) = 10,$$

and

$$\mathcal{H}^{(2)}(\omega_7) = \mathcal{H}_3^{(2)} = \{\omega_6, \omega_7\}, \quad v^{(2)}(\omega_7) = 2,$$

$$\mathcal{H}^{(2)}(\omega_{18}) = \mathcal{H}_8^{(2)} = \{\omega_{18}, \omega_{19}\}, \quad v^{(2)}(\omega_{18}) = 2,$$

$$\mathcal{H}^{(2)}(\omega_{21}) = \mathcal{H}_9^{(2)} = \{\omega_{20}, \omega_{21}, \omega_{22}\}, \quad v^{(2)}(\omega_{21}) = 3.$$

A particular choice of representative sets $\Omega^{(0)}$, $\Omega^{(1)}$, $\Omega^{(2)}$, $\Omega^{(3)}$, which as we have commented are not unique, is as follows:

$$\Omega^{(0)} = \{\omega_1\},$$

$$\Omega^{(1)} = \{\omega_1, \omega_{11}, \omega_{16}\},$$

$$\Omega^{(2)} = \{\omega_1, \omega_4, \omega_6, \omega_8, \omega_{11}, \omega_{13}, \omega_{16}, \omega_{18}, \omega_{20}\},$$

$$\Omega^{(3)} = \{\omega_1, \omega_2, \ldots, \omega_{22}\} \equiv \Omega.$$

Note that $\#\Omega^{(k)} = v_k$ and that $\Omega^{(0)} \subseteq \Omega^{(1)} \subseteq \Omega^{(2)} \subseteq \Omega^{(3)}$. ∎

Although this notation may at first seem involved, with practice it is natural and easy to remember. To become more comfortable with this notation, it may be helpful to draw some additional information structure trees and identify the various aspects of these trees associated with the preceding notation.

**Definition 11.2.1.** *A **random variable** is a mapping from the sample space $\Omega$ to the real numbers [that is, a mapping $\Omega \to \mathfrak{R}$]. A **stochastic process** or simply a **process** is a mapping $X = X(\cdot, \cdot) : \{0, \ldots, T\} \times \Omega \to \mathfrak{R}$. For $k = 0, \ldots, T$, $X(k) = X(k, \cdot)$ is a random variable. Hence, a process is a sequence of random variables. A process $X$ is commonly written as $\{X(k)\}$ or as $\{X(k); k = 0, \ldots, T\}$. A process $X$ is said to be **adapted** to the information structure $\{\mathcal{P}_k\}$ if for each $k = 0, \ldots, T$, the random variable $X(k)$ is constant on the sample points of each element of $\mathcal{P}_k$. For an adapted process $X$, $k = 1, \ldots, T - 1$, $\mathcal{H} \in \mathcal{P}_k$, we sometimes write $X(k, \mathcal{H})$ for the common value of $X(k, \omega)$, $\omega \in \mathcal{H}$; we can also write $X(0, \omega)$ as $X(0)$. Similarly, by replacing*

$\Re$ with $\Re^n$ and $X$ with $\mathbf{X}$, we define an n-dimensional random variable, n-dimensional stochastic process, and adapted n-dimensional stochastic process.

The notion of a process being adapted corresponds to the idea that, since at time $k$ we can only distinguish between sample points in different elements of $\mathcal{P}_k$, the values of a process must be equal across sample points that we cannot distinguish between. See also the discussion following Definition 5.3.2.

Let $\mathcal{F}_k$ denote the *field* generated by the partition $P_k$; that is, $\mathcal{F}_k$ consists of $\emptyset$, $\Omega$, the elements of $\mathcal{P}_k$ and their unions; see Definition A.1.3 in Appendix A. The sequence of fields, $\mathbf{F} = \{\mathcal{F}_0, \ldots, \mathcal{F}_T\}$, is called a *filtration* (Definition A.1.4). Saying that a process $X$ is adapted to $\{\mathcal{P}_k\}$ is the same as saying that $X$ is adapted to $\mathbf{F}$ (Definition A.1.7). See Table A.1 in Appendix A.

## SECTION 11.2.2 | SECURITIES MARKET MODEL

As in Chapter 5, we assume that there are $N$ primitive assets $S = [S_1, S_2, \ldots, S_N]$ and $M$ states of nature $\Omega = \{\omega_1, \omega_2, \ldots, \omega_M\}$. We also assume that

- Dividends $\mathbf{D} = [D_1, D_2, \ldots, D_N]$ are paid on these securities just before the end of each time interval, and
- Securities are traded at the beginning of each time interval, with the quantities or number of units held denoted by $\theta = [\theta_1, \theta_2, \ldots, \theta_N]^T$.

Time points are denoted $0, \ldots, T$. We use the following notation:

$S_i(k, \omega_j)$: price of security $i$ in state $\omega_j$ at time $k$, just after dividends are paid at time $k$

$D_i(k, \omega_j)$: dividend payment of security $i$ in state $\omega_j$ at time $k$

$\theta_i(k, \omega_j)$: number of shares (or units) held of security $i$ in state $\omega_j$ at time $k$ until just before time $k + 1$

for $i = 1, \ldots, N$; $j = 1, \ldots, M$; $k = 0, \ldots, T$.

The three $N$-dimensional processes $S$, $D$, and $\theta$, defined by

$$S(k, \omega_j) = [S_1(k, \omega_j), S_2(k, \omega_j), \ldots, S_N(k, \omega_j)],$$

$$D(k, \omega_j) = [D_1(k, \omega_j), D_2(k, \omega_j), \ldots, D_N(k, \omega_j)],$$

$$\theta(k, \omega_j) = [\theta_1(k, \omega_j), \theta_2(k, \omega_j), \ldots, \theta_N(k, \omega_j)]^T,$$

are assumed to be adapted. This means that the prices, dividends, and holdings reflect all the information up to the current time. The processes $S$ and $D$ are expressed as row vectors, and $\theta$ as a column vector. The process $\theta$ is known as a *trading strategy* and represents an investor's portfolio holdings over each trading interval.

**Definition 11.2.2.** *The **cash-flow stream financed** or **generated by a trading strategy** $\theta$ is the process $c^\theta$ defined by*[1]

$$c^\theta(k, \omega) = [S(k, \omega) + D(k, \omega)]\theta(k - 1, \omega) - S(k, \omega)\theta(k, \omega),$$

*for $k = 0, \ldots, T$, $\omega \in \Omega$, with $\theta(-1, \omega) = \theta(T, \omega) = 0$.*

The conditions $\theta(-1, \omega) = \theta(T, \omega) = 0$ mean that trading begins at time 0 and that all trading positions are liquidated at time $T$. The process $c^\theta$ is adapted because the processes $S$, $D$, and $\theta$ are adapted. Definition 11.2.2 generalizes (5.3.4) to the dividend-paying case. If $\{c^\theta(k)\}$ is a cash-flow stream financed by the trading strategy $\theta$, then the investor's portfolio dynamics are of the form

$$[S(k, \omega) + D(k, \omega)]\theta(k - 1, \omega) = S(k, \omega)\theta(k, \omega) + c^\theta(k, \omega). \qquad (11.2.1)$$

We use the term *cash-flow stream* to refer to a generic adapted process. The value of the portfolio at time $k$ is $S(k, \omega)\theta(k, \omega)$.

**Example 11.2.2.** We consider a three-period model with the information structure as shown in Figure 11.1 and assume that there are two assets available for trade. The first asset is a zero-coupon bond, and the second asset is a dividend-paying stock. We assume that we have a constant interest rate of 5% per period, so that the bond price is

$$S_1(k, \omega) = (1.05)^{k-3}, \quad k = 0, 1, 2, 3.$$

Ex-dividend stock prices, $S_2(k, \omega)$, and stock dividends, $D_2(k, \omega)$, are shown in Figure 11.2.

Suppose now that an investor adopts a trading strategy consisting of buying and holding one share of stock, which we are associating with asset 2, over the trading period. We thus have

$$\theta(k, \omega) = \begin{bmatrix} 0 \\ 1 \end{bmatrix}, \quad k = 0, 1, 2, \omega \in \Omega.$$

Since the trading interval stops at time 3, by our convention we have $\theta(3, \omega) = 0$, for all $\omega \in \Omega$. The cash-flow stream generated by this trading strategy is

$$c^\theta(0, \omega) = -138.38(1) = -138.38,$$
$$c^\theta(k, \omega) = D(k, \omega)\theta(k - 1, \omega), \quad k = 1, 2,$$
$$c^\theta(3, \omega) = [S(3, \omega) + D(3, \omega)]\theta(2, \omega)$$

---

[1] For aesthetic reasons, the superscript $\theta$ of $c^\theta$ is not typeset in boldface.

FIGURE **11.1** | *Three-Period Information Structure*

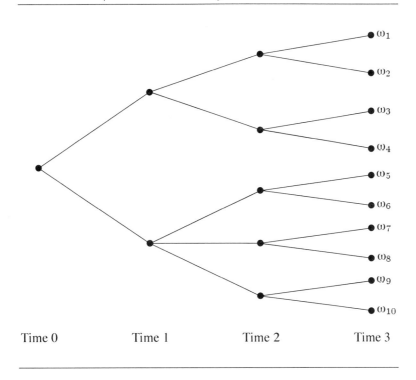

FIGURE **11.2** | *Ex-dividend Stock Prices and Dividends*
*(Dividends Are in Parentheses)*

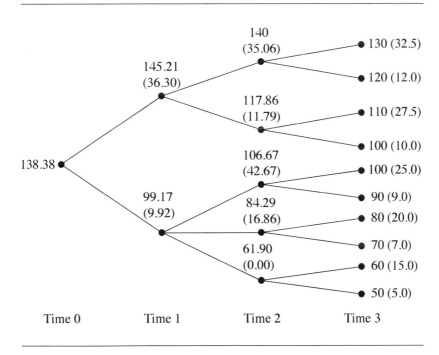

for all $\omega \in \Omega$. Note that $c^\theta(0, \omega)$ does not depend on $\omega$ (because $c^\theta$ is an adapted process and so consists of the single set $\{\Omega\}$).

Now consider a trading strategy $\phi$ as defined in Figure 11.3, where the investor actively changes his or her portfolio holdings. Thus

$$c^\phi(0, \omega) = -100(0.86384) + 2(138.38) = 190.38,$$

$$c^\phi(1, \omega) = \begin{cases} 2(36.30) = 72.60, & \omega \in \{\omega_1, \omega_2, \omega_3, \omega_4\} \\ (-1)99.17 + 2(9.92) = -79.33, & \omega \in \{\omega_5, \dots, \omega_{10}\}. \end{cases}$$

$$c^\phi(2, \omega) = \begin{cases} -100(0.95238) + 2(140.24) + 2(55.06) = 255.36, & \omega \in \{\omega_1, \omega_2\} \\ -1(117.86) + 2(11.79) = -94.28, & \omega \in \{\omega_3, \omega_4\} \\ -100(0.95238) + 106.67 + 3(42.67) = 139.44, & \omega \in \{\omega_5, \omega_6\} \\ -100(0.95238) + 3(16.86) = -44.66, & \omega \in \{\omega_7, \omega_8\} \\ -100(0.95238) - 61.9 = -157.14, & \omega \in \{\omega_9, \omega_{10}\}, \end{cases}$$

$$c^\phi(3, \omega) = \begin{cases} 0, & \omega = \omega_1 \\ 0, & \omega = \omega_2 \\ -100 + 3(110) + 3(27.5) = 312.50, & \omega = \omega_3 \\ -100 + 3(100) + 3(10) = 230, & \omega = \omega_4 \\ 2(100) + 2(25) = 250, & \omega = \omega_5 \\ 2(90) + 2(9) = 198, & \omega = \omega_6 \\ 3(80) + 3(20) = 300, & \omega = \omega_7 \\ 231, & \omega = \omega_8 \\ 300, & \omega = \omega_9 \\ 220, & \omega = \omega_{10}. \end{cases}$$ ∎

**Definition 11.2.3.** *A cash-flow stream $\{c(k); k = 1, \dots, T\}$ is said to be **attainable** if a trading strategy $\theta$ exists such that $c(k, \omega) = c^\theta(k, \omega), \omega \in \Omega, k = 1, \dots, T$.*

According to this definition, a cash-flow stream is attainable if there exists a trading strategy that finances it. Note that, in Definition 11.2.3, the cash-flow stream starts at time 1, not time 0. That is, it is a stream of future cash flows. An important question is how a price for a stream of future cash flows can be determined. If the cash-flow stream is attainable, then an obvious candidate for its price is

$$S(0)\theta(0) = -c^\theta(0).$$

However, there can be more than one trading strategy that finances or generates the cash-flow stream, giving rise to more than one price. Theorem 11.2.9 shows that, if the securities market model is arbitrage free, then an attainable cash-flow stream has a unique price.

FIGURE **11.3** | ***Trading Strategy φ***

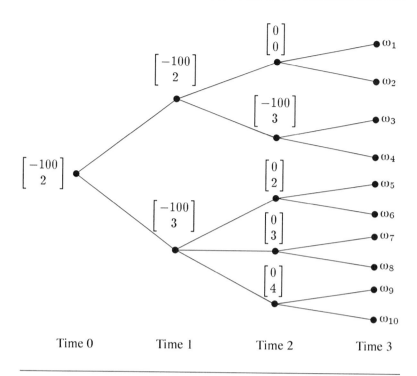

Time 0        Time 1        Time 2        Time 3

***Definition 11.2.4.*** *A trading strategy that finances a single cash flow $c(T)$ payable at time $T$ is said to be **self-financing**. (This means $c(1) = \cdots = c(T-1) = 0$.) The same idea applies to strategies financing single cash flows at other fixed times $k \in \{1, \ldots, T\}$.*

If the primitive assets pay no dividends, then a self-financing strategy for cash flow $c(T)$, payable at time $T$, must satisfy

a.    $S(k, \omega)\theta(k-1, \omega) = S(k, \omega)\theta(k, \omega), \quad$ for $k = 1, \ldots, T-1$,

b.    $S(T, \omega)\theta(T-1, \omega) = c(T, \omega) = c(T)$.

Requirement (a) is the self-financing condition, whereas (b) says that the trading strategy yields the correct terminal cash flow. The concept of self-financing trading strategies was discussed in Section 5.3.2.

## SECTION **11.2.3** | DEFINITION OF ARBITRAGE

The definition of arbitrage for the single-period model in Chapter 5 can be rephrased in terms of our notation for cash flows in the following way:

-    A $\theta$ exists such that $c^\theta(0) \geq 0$ and $c^\theta(1, \omega) > 0$ for at least one $\omega \in \Omega$, or
-    A $\theta$ exists such that $c^\theta(0) > 0$ and $c^\theta(1, \omega) \geq 0$ for all $\omega \in \Omega$.

The definition of arbitrage in the multiperiod model is an extension of these two conditions.

**Definition 11.2.5.** *A one-dimensional process $\{x(k); k = 0, \ldots, T\}$ is said to be **positive** if $x(k, \omega) \geq 0$ for each $\omega$ and each $k$, and at least one pair $(k^*, \omega^*)$ exists such that $x(k^*, \omega^*) > 0$. The process $\{x(k); k = 0, \ldots, T\}$ is said to be **strictly positive** if also $x(k, \omega) > 0$ for each $\omega$ and $k$.*

Note the analogy with the definition of $x > 0$ and $x \gg 0$ for $x \in \mathfrak{R}^n$ in Chapter 5.

**Definition 11.2.6.** *A model admits **arbitrage** if a trading strategy $\{\theta(k); k = 0, \ldots, T\}$ exists such that the generated cash-flow process $\{c^\theta(k); k = 0, \ldots, T\}$ is positive.*

This definition means that a model admits arbitrage if
- The initial cash flow is positive, and all future cash flows are nonnegative, or
- The initial cash flow is nonnegative, and all future cash flows are nonnegative, with at least one of them being positive for some state nature.

In Section 5.3.3, arbitrage was defined in terms self-financing trading strategies only. We can check that Definitions 5.3.1 and 11.2.4 are equivalent in the more restricted model of Chapter 5.

## SECTION 11.2.4 | FUNDAMENTAL THEOREM OF ASSET PRICING

**Definition 11.2.7.** *A **state price process** for the securities market model is a strictly positive adapted process $\{\psi(k); k = 1, \ldots, T\}$ such that, for every financed cash-flow stream $\{c^\theta(k)\}$,*

$$S(0, \omega^*)\theta(0, \omega^*) = \sum_{\omega \in \Omega} \sum_{k=1}^{T} \psi(k, \omega)c^\theta(k, \omega), \quad \omega^* \in \Omega. \qquad (11.2.2)$$

Note that the left-hand side of (11.2.2) is independent of $\omega^*$ (because the processes are adapted) and is sometimes written as $S(0)\theta(0)$. If we define $\psi(0, \omega) = 1/M$ for all $\omega \in \Omega$, then we can rewrite (11.2.2) as

$$0 = \sum_{\omega \in \Omega} \sum_{k=0}^{T} \psi(k, \omega)c^\theta(k, \omega). \qquad (11.2.3)$$

Chapter 5 gave a different, but equivalent, definition for a state price process; see Definition 5.3.5. The equivalence is proved in Theorem 11.2.13, but this definition is presented here because it facilitates the proof of Theorem 11.2.9.

The proof of the fundamental theorem of asset pricing rests on the next result, which is one form of the separating hyperplane theorem. The proof below is more general than the one in Section 5.2.7 because it is for the multiperiod case and it is not assumed that an asset exists with strictly positive payoffs. For more details related to the separating hyperplane theorem, see Gale [68, pp. 44 and 49], Rockafellar [159, Theorem 11.2, p. 96], Karlin [107, Theorem B.3.5, p. 404], or Mangasarian [127, Theorem 6, pp. 50 and 53].

**Theorem 11.2.8 (Separating Hyperplane Theorem).** *Let $\Re^n$ denote the linear space of $n$-dimensional column vectors. Let $V$ be a vector subspace of $\Re^n$ with $V \cap \Re^n_+ = \{0\}$. Then a vector $x \in \Re^n_{++}$ exists such that $x^T v = 0$ for all vectors $v \in V$. This means that a strictly positive vector $x$ exists that is orthogonal to every vector in $V$.*

**Theorem 11.2.9 (Fundamental Theorem of Asset Pricing).** *A securities market model is arbitrage free if and only if there exists a state price process.*

**Proof.** *Suppose a state price process $\psi$ exists for the model. Then (11.2.3) holds for any financed cash-flow stream $\{c^\theta(k)\}$. A cash-flow stream satisfying this condition cannot be positive. Therefore, Definition 11.2.6 cannot be satisfied, and the securities market model is arbitrage free.*

*Conversely, suppose that the securities market model is arbitrage free. We construct a state price process using the separating hyperplane theorem. Let $\theta$ be any trading strategy. We form a vector from all the values $\{c^\theta(k, \omega); k = 0, 1, \ldots, T, \omega \in \Omega\}$. The construction of an adapted state price process is simpler if we do not repeat the values of $c^\theta(k, \omega)$ that are identical. That the cash-flow process $c^\theta$ is adapted means that, for each $k$, the values of the random variable $c(k) = c(k, \cdot)$ are constant on each element of the partition $\mathcal{P}_k$. Recall that $v_k$ denotes the number of elements in $\mathcal{P}_k$. Then*

$$\mathcal{P}_k = \{\mathcal{H}^{(k)}_1, \ldots, \mathcal{H}^{(k)}_{v_k}\}, \quad k = 0, \ldots, T,$$

*where $\mathcal{H}^{(k)}_j$ is the $j$-th elementary set of $\mathcal{P}_k$. We let $c^\theta(k, \mathcal{H}^{(k)}_j)$ denote the common value $c^\theta(k, \omega)$, $\omega \in \mathcal{H}^{(k)}_j$ and form the vector*

$$c^\theta = [c^\theta(0, \mathcal{H}^{(0)}_1), c^\theta(1, \mathcal{H}^{(1)}_1), \ldots, c^\theta(1, \mathcal{H}^{(1)}_{v_1}), \ldots,$$
$$c^\theta(T, \mathcal{H}^{(T)}_1), \ldots, c^\theta(T, \mathcal{H}^{(T)}_M)]^T.$$

*This vector is of dimension $n = v_0 + v_1 + \cdots + v_T$ ($v_0 = 1$ and $v_T = M$). The trading strategy $\theta$ generates an arbitrage if and only if $c^\theta > 0$. Let*

$$V = \{c^\theta; \theta \text{ is a trading strategy}\}$$

be the set of all financed cash-flow streams. Since $c^{a_1\theta^{(1)}+a_2\theta^{(2)}} = a_1 c^{\theta^{(1)}} + a_2 c^{\theta^{(2)}}$ for all scalars $a_1$, $a_2$ and all trading strategies $\theta^{(1)}$, $\theta^{(2)}$, the set $V$ is a vector subspace of $\Re^n$. If $V \cap \Re_+^n$ contains more than the zero vector, then there exists a trading strategy that generates a positive cash-flow stream. Hence, we see that the securities market model is arbitrage free if and only if

$$V \cap \Re_+^n = \{\mathbf{0}\}.$$

By the separating hyperplane theorem, a vector $x \in \Re_{++}^n$, denoted as $x = (x_1, \ldots, x_n)^T$, exists such that

$$x^T c^\theta = 0 \text{ for each trading strategy } \theta,$$

that is,

$$x_1 c^\theta\left(0, \mathcal{H}_1^{(0)}\right) + x_2 c^\theta\left(1, \mathcal{H}_1^{(1)}\right) + \cdots + x_{1+v_1} c^\theta\left(1, \mathcal{H}_{v_1}^{(1)}\right) + \cdots$$
$$+ x_{1+v_1+\cdots+v_{T-1}+1} c^\theta\left(T, \mathcal{H}_1^{(T)}\right) + \cdots + x_n c^\theta\left(T, \mathcal{H}_M^{(T)}\right) = 0.$$

Recall that $\#\mathcal{H}$ denote the number of elements in the set $\mathcal{H}$; that is, $\#\mathcal{H}$ is the number of sample points $\omega$ in $\mathcal{H}$. A state price process for the securities model may be constructed as

$$\psi(0, \omega) = \frac{1}{M}, \qquad \omega \in \mathcal{H}_1^{(0)} = \Omega,$$

$$\psi(1, \omega) = \frac{x_2}{x_1 \# \mathcal{H}_1^{(1)}}, \qquad \omega \in \mathcal{H}_1^{(1)},$$

$$\vdots \qquad\qquad \vdots$$

$$\psi(1, \omega) = \frac{x_{1+v_1}}{x_1 \# \mathcal{H}_{v_1}^{(1)}}, \qquad \omega \in \mathcal{H}_{v_1}^{(1)},$$

$$\vdots \qquad\qquad \vdots$$

$$\psi(k, \omega) = \frac{x_{1+\cdots+v_{k-1}+1}}{x_1 \# \mathcal{H}_1^{(k)}}, \qquad \omega \in \mathcal{H}_1^{(k)},$$

$$\vdots \qquad\qquad \vdots$$

$$\psi(k, \omega) = \frac{x_{1+\cdots+v_{k-1}+v_k}}{x_1 \# \mathcal{H}_{v_k}^{(k)}}, \qquad \omega \in \mathcal{H}_{v_k}^{(k)},$$

$$\vdots \qquad\qquad \vdots$$

$$\psi(T, \omega) = \frac{x_{1+\cdots+v_{T-1}+1}}{x_1}, \qquad \omega \in \mathcal{H}_1^{(T)} = \{\omega_1\},$$

$$\vdots \qquad\qquad \vdots$$

$$\psi(T, \omega) = \frac{x_n}{x_1}, \qquad \omega \in \mathcal{H}_M^{(T)} = \{\omega_M\}. \qquad \blacksquare$$

**Example 11.2.3.** Let $T = 2$, $M = 5$, $\Omega = \{\omega_1, \omega_2, \omega_3, \omega_4, \omega_5\}$, $\mathcal{H}_1^{(1)} = \{\omega_1, \omega_2, \omega_3\}$, $\mathcal{H}_2^{(1)} = \{\omega_4, \omega_5\}$ (see Figure 11.4). Then $n = 1 + 2 + 5 = 8$. The linear subspace $V \subseteq \mathfrak{R}^8$ is spanned by the three $N$-column vectors:

$$[-S_i(0), \; S_i(1, \omega_1) + D_i(1, \omega_1), \; S_i(1, \omega_4) + D_i(1, \omega_4), 0, 0, 0, 0, 0]^T,$$

$$[0, \; -S_i(1, \omega_1), 0, \; S_i(2, \omega_1) + D_i(2, \omega_1), \; S_i(2, \omega_2) + D_i(2, \omega_2),$$
$$S_i(2, \omega_3) + D_i(2, \omega_3), 0, 0]^T,$$

$$[0, 0, \; -S_i(1, \omega_4), 0, 0, 0, \; S_i(2, \omega_4) + D_i(2, \omega_4), \; S_i(2, \omega_5) + D_i(2, \omega_5)]^T,$$

$$i = 1, \ldots, N. \quad \blacksquare$$

FIGURE **11.4** | ***Two-Period Information Structure for Example 11.2.3***

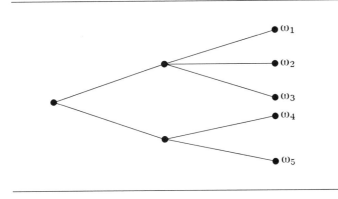

When a securities market model is arbitrage free, (11.2.2) guarantees that each attainable cash-flow stream will have a unique price as given by either side of this equation. The price of an attainable cash-flow stream in an arbitrage-free securities market will be defined as $S(0, \omega^*)\theta(0, \omega^*)$ where $\theta$ is a trading strategy financing the cash-flow stream. If more than one trading strategy finances or generates the cash-flow stream, they give the same price. The price, of course, is independent of $\omega^*$ because the processes are adapted. This result on cash-flow pricing has also been given as Theorem 5.3.11.

In summary, in an arbitrage-free securities market model, we can capture the unique price of an attainable cash-flow stream by using the state-price-weighted sum of future uncertain cash-flow values as given by the right-hand side of (11.2.2).

### SECTION **11.2.5** | COMPLETENESS

In this section we examine whether every future cash-flow stream $c = \{c(k); k = 1, \ldots, T\}$ is attainable. The word *future* emphasizes that there is no cash flow from $c$ at time 0. The next definition is the same as Definition 5.3.13.

***Definition 11.2.10.*** *A securities market model is said to be **complete** if every adapted future cash-flow stream is financed by some trading strategy* $\Theta$.

The notion of completeness is of considerable practical importance as we can price any adapted future cash-flow stream in a complete market. Unfortunately, many insurance products cannot be handled by complete market theory, because their cash-flow streams are not attainable.

***Theorem 11.2.11.*** *An arbitrage-free securities model is complete if and only if there is only one state price process.*

***Proof.*** *Suppose the model is arbitrage free and complete. Then the uniqueness of the state price process* $\psi$ *follows from noting that the (unique) price of a self-financing portfolio yielding a single unit at time k in state* $\mathcal{H}, \mathcal{H} \in \mathcal{P}_k$, *is*

$$\sum_{\omega \in \mathcal{H}} \psi(k, \omega) = \psi(k, \omega^*) \# \mathcal{H}$$

*for each* $\omega^* \in \mathcal{H}$.

*Conversely, suppose the market model is arbitrage free but not complete. We express the processes* $\psi$ *and* $c^\theta$ *in vector form similar to that in the proof of Theorem 11.2.9 but without the first element, that is,*

$$c^\theta = \left[ c^\theta \left(1, \mathcal{H}_1^{(1)}\right), \ldots, c^\theta \left(1, \mathcal{H}_{v_1}^{(1)}\right), \ldots, c^\theta \left(T, \mathcal{H}_1^{(T)}\right), \ldots, c^\theta \left(T, \mathcal{H}_M^{(T)}\right) \right]^T$$

*and*

$$\psi = \left[ \psi \left(1, \mathcal{H}_1^{(1)}\right), \ldots, \psi \left(1, \mathcal{H}_{v_1}^{(1)}\right), \ldots, \psi \left(T, \mathcal{H}_1^{(T)}\right), \ldots, \psi \left(T, \mathcal{H}_M^{(T)}\right) \right].$$

*These two vectors are of dimension*

$$v_1 + v_2 + \cdots + v_T = n - 1.$$

*Let* $G$ *denote the* $(n-1)$ *by* $(n-1)$ *diagonal matrix whose diagonal entries are the cardinalities of the elements of the partitions* $\mathcal{P}_1, \mathcal{P}_2, \ldots, \mathcal{P}_T$,

$$G = \mathrm{diag}\big(\# \mathcal{H}_1^{(1)}, \ldots, \# \mathcal{H}_{v_1}^{(1)}, \ldots, \underbrace{1, \ldots, 1}_{M \text{ times}} \big).$$

*Then the no-arbitrage condition is*

$$\psi G c^\theta = -c^\theta(0)$$

*for each trading strategy* $\Theta$.

We stack the $N$-dimensional column vectors $\theta(k, \mathcal{H})$ vertically one on top of the other, but without the last $M$ ones to form a column vector $\bar{\theta}$ of dimension $N(n - M)$; that is,

$$\bar{\theta} = \left[\theta\left(0, \mathcal{H}_1^{(0)}\right)^T, \theta\left(1, \mathcal{H}_1^{(1)}\right)^T, \ldots, \theta\left(1, \mathcal{H}_{v_1}^{(1)}\right)^T, \ldots,\right.$$

$$\left.\theta\left(T - 1, \mathcal{H}_1^{(T-1)}\right)^T, \ldots, \theta\left(T - 1, \mathcal{H}_{v_{T-1}}^{(T-1)}\right)^T\right]^T.$$

The mapping $\theta \mapsto c^\theta$ is linear. An $(n - 1)$ by $N(n - M)$ matrix $C$ (see the example below) exists such that

$$C\bar{\theta} = c^\theta.$$

If the market is not complete, there is a cash-flow vector $c \in \mathfrak{R}^{n-1}$ with no $\bar{\theta}$ such that $C\bar{\theta} = c$. Hence, rank $C < n - 1$, so a nonzero $(n - 1)$-dimensional row vector $\phi$ exists such that $\phi C = 0$. Then for each real number $\varepsilon$ such that $\psi + \varepsilon \phi G^{-1} \gg 0$,

$$(\psi + \varepsilon \phi G^{-1}) G c^\theta = \psi G c^\theta + \varepsilon \phi G \bar{\theta} = -c^\theta(0).$$

Hence, we find infinitely many state price processes.

**Example 11.2.3 (continued).** Let $N = 3, T = 2, M = 5, \Omega = \{\omega_1, \omega_2, \omega_3, \omega_4, \omega_5\}$, $\mathcal{H}_1^{(1)} = \{\omega_1, \omega_2, \omega_3\}, \mathcal{H}_2^{(1)} = \{\omega_4, \omega_5\}$. Then $n - 1 = 7$. We cannot display $C$, which is a $7 \times 9$ matrix, on one page, so we display the seven rows comprising $C$. Let $S_i^+(k, \omega) = S_i(k, \omega) + D_i(k, \omega)$. Then the rows of $C$ are

$$\left[S_1^+(1, \omega_1), S_2^+(1, \omega_1), S_3^+(1, \omega_1), -S_1(1, \omega_1), -S_2(1, \omega_1), -S_3(1, \omega_1), 0, 0, 0\right],$$

$$\left[S_1^+(1, \omega_4), S_2^+(1, \omega_4), S_3^+(1, \omega_4), 0, 0, 0, -S_1(1, \omega_4), -S_2(1, \omega_4), -S_3(1, \omega_4)\right],$$

$$\left[0, 0, 0, S_1^+(2, \omega_j), S_2^+(2, \omega_j), S_3^+(2, \omega_j), 0, 0, 0\right], \quad j = 1, 2, 3,$$

$$\left[0, 0, 0, 0, 0, 0, S_1^+(2, \omega_j), S_2^+(2, \omega_j), S_3^+(2, \omega_j)\right], \quad j = 4, 5. \qquad \blacksquare$$

## SECTION 11.2.6 | OTHER VALUATION FORMULAS

In Section 11.2.4, we have seen how the absence of arbitrage is equivalent to the existence of a state price process that can be used to price all financed cash-flow streams. Depending on the context in which we are working, it may be convenient to express this fundamental result in one of two equally fundamental forms involving *equivalent martingale measures* or *state price densities*. We discuss these alternative representations of the fundamental theorem of asset pricing and provide some useful implications of the fundamental theorem in terms of each of the state price processes, equivalent martingale measures, and state price densities.

Frequently cash-flow streams must be valued at points in time other than time 0. The following result shows how a state price process can be used for valuation throughout the information structure of a securities market model. Consider the following situation: We are at time $j$ in one of the states in $\mathcal{H}$, $\mathcal{H} \in \mathcal{P}_j$, and we are to receive cash flows $c^\theta(k)$ at times $k = j+1, j+2, \ldots, T$. If the model is arbitrage free, then $S(j, \mathcal{H})\theta(j, \mathcal{H})$ represents the price of these remaining cash flows. Recall the notation that, for an adapted process $X$ and $\mathcal{H} \in \mathcal{P}_j$, the common value of $X(j, \omega)$, $\omega \in \mathcal{H}$, is denoted as $X(j, \mathcal{H})$.

**Theorem 11.2.12 (Price of Remaining Cash Flows).** *A strictly positive adapted process* $\{\psi(k)\}$, *with* $\psi(0, \omega) = 1/M$, *is a state price process if and only if for all* $j = 0, \ldots, T-1$, *and for all trading strategies* $\theta$ *the following relation holds:*

$$\sum_{\omega \in \mathcal{A}} \psi(j, \omega) S(j, \omega) \theta(j, \omega) = \sum_{\omega \in \mathcal{A}} \sum_{k=j+1}^{T} \psi(k, \omega) c^\theta(k, \omega), \quad \mathcal{A} \in \mathcal{P}_j. \quad (11.2.4)$$

*In particular, if* $\psi$ *is a state price process, then for* $\mathcal{H} \in \mathcal{P}_j$,

$$S(j, \mathcal{H})\theta(j, \mathcal{H}) = \frac{1}{\psi(j, \mathcal{H})\#\mathcal{H}} \sum_{\omega \in \mathcal{H}} \sum_{k=j+1}^{T} \psi(k, \omega) c^\theta(k, \omega). \quad (11.2.5)$$

**Proof.** *Suppose* $\{\psi(k)\}$ *is a state price process, and let* $\theta$ *be a trading strategy. Define a new strategy*

$$\theta^*(k, \omega) = \begin{cases} \theta(k, \omega), & \text{if } \omega \in \mathcal{A} \text{ and } k = j, j+1, \ldots, T \\ 0, & \text{otherwise.} \end{cases}$$

*Then* (11.2.4) *follows from the definition of a state price process applied to* $\theta^*$. *The converse assertion follows from the same definition (set* $j = 0$ *and* $\mathcal{A} = \Omega$*). Equation* (11.2.5) *results from noting that* $S(j, \omega)$, $\theta(j, \omega)$, *and* $\psi(j, \omega)$ *are constant for* $\omega \in \mathcal{H}$ *for each* $\mathcal{H} \in \mathcal{P}_j$, *since the processes are adapted.*

The following result provides an equivalent characterization of a state price process. This relation is a useful computational tool in its own right, but it also provides us with an elegant means of linking state price processes and equivalent martingale measures, which we discuss later, and links prices in successive time periods. This is the definition for a state price process in Chapter 5, where the securities are assumed to pay no dividends; see Definition 5.3.5.

**Theorem 11.2.13 (Recursive State Price Property).** *A strictly positive adapted process* $\psi = \{\psi(k)\}$, *with* $\psi(0, \omega) = 1/M$, *is a state price process if and only if*

$$\sum_{\omega \in \mathcal{A}} \psi(k, \omega) S(k, \omega) = \sum_{\omega \in \mathcal{A}} \psi(k+1, \omega)[S(k+1, \omega) + D(k+1, \omega)] \quad (11.2.6)$$

*for all* $\mathcal{A} \in \mathcal{P}_k$, *for all* $k = 0, \ldots, T - 1$.

**Proof.** *If* $\{\psi(k)\}$ *is a state price process, then* (11.2.6) *follows from* (11.2.4) *by employing the trading strategy that buys* 1 *unit of each asset at time* $k$ *if the state of the world is in the set* $\mathcal{A}$ *at that time and by selling all assets at time* $k + 1$.

*Conversely, we must show that if a strictly positive adapted process* $\{\psi(k)\}$, *with* $\psi(0) = 1/M$, *satisfies* (11.2.6), *then this process satisfies Definition 11.2.7. Thus, we need to show that, for each financed cash-flow stream* $\{c^{\theta}(k)\}$, *the condition* (11.2.6) *implies that*

$$S(0, \omega^*)\theta(0, \omega^*) = \sum_{\omega \in \Omega} \sum_{k=1}^{T} \psi(k, \omega) c^{\theta}(k, \omega),$$

*where* $\omega^*$ *is an arbitrary element of* $\Omega$. *The idea of the proof is to use* (11.2.6) *to inductively roll back the time indices to get to the reduced expression* $S(0, \omega^*)\theta(0, \omega^*)$. *Now,*

$$\sum_{\omega \in \Omega} \psi(n, \omega)[S(n, \omega)\theta(n-1, \omega) + D(n, \omega)\theta(n-1, \omega)]$$

$$= \sum_{\mathcal{H} \in \mathcal{P}_{n-1}} \sum_{\omega \in \mathcal{H}} \psi(n, \omega)[S(n, \omega) + D(n, \omega)]\theta(n-1, \omega)$$

$$= \sum_{\mathcal{H} \in \mathcal{P}_{n-1}} \left\{ \sum_{\omega \in \mathcal{H}} \psi(n, \omega)[S(n, \omega) + D(n, \omega)] \right\} \theta(n-1, \mathcal{H})$$

$$= \sum_{\mathcal{H} \in \mathcal{P}_{n-1}} \#\mathcal{H}\psi(n-1, \mathcal{H})S(n-1, \mathcal{H})\theta(n-1, \mathcal{H}) \quad \text{by (11.2.6)}$$

$$= \sum_{\omega \in \Omega} \psi(n-1, \omega)S(n-1, \omega)\theta(n-1, \omega).$$

*Hence, for* $n = 1, \ldots, T$, *we have*

$$\sum_{\omega \in \Omega} \psi(n, \omega)[S(n, \omega)\theta(n-1, \omega) + D(n, \omega)\theta(n-1, \omega)]$$

$$= \sum_{\omega \in \Omega} \psi(n-1, \omega)S(n-1, \omega)\theta(n-1, \omega). \quad (11.2.7)$$

*Since* $\Theta(T, \omega) = 0$, *it follows from our definition of financed cash-flow stream that*

$$c^\theta(T, \omega) = [S(T, \omega) + D(T, \omega)]\Theta(T - 1, \omega).$$

*Substituting the expression above into (11.2.7) results in*

$$\sum_{\omega \in \Omega} \psi(T, \omega)c^\theta(T, \omega) = \sum_{\omega \in \Omega} \psi(T - 1, \omega)S(T - 1, \omega)\Theta(T - 1, \omega).$$

*Hence, we have*

$$\sum_{\omega \in \Omega}\sum_{k=1}^{T} \psi(k, \omega)c^\theta(k, \omega) = \sum_{\omega \in \Omega}\sum_{k=1}^{T-1} \psi(k, \omega)c^\theta(k, \omega)$$
$$+ \sum_{\omega \in \Omega} \psi(T - 1, \omega)S(T - 1, \omega)\Theta(T - 1, \omega).$$

*Because*

$$c^\theta(T-1, \omega)+S(T-1, \omega)\Theta(T-1, \omega) = [S(T-1, \omega)+D(T-1, \omega)]\Theta(T-2, \omega),$$

*we can apply* (11.2.7) *again to obtain*

$$\sum_{\omega \in \Omega}\sum_{k=1}^{T} \psi(k, \omega)c^\theta(k, \omega) = \sum_{\omega \in \Omega}\sum_{k=1}^{T-2} \psi(k, \omega)c^\theta(k, \omega)$$
$$+ \sum_{\omega \in \Omega} \psi(T - 2, \omega)S(T - 2, \omega)\Theta(T - 2, \omega).$$

*We then proceed inductively until we arrive at*

$$\sum_{\omega \in \Omega}\sum_{k=1}^{T} \psi(k, \omega)c^\theta(k, \omega) = \sum_{\omega \in \Omega} \psi(0, \omega)S(0, \omega)\Theta(0, \omega) = S(0, \omega^*)\Theta(0, \omega^*).$$

*Therefore, $\psi$ is a state price process.*

## SECTION 11.2.7 | STATE PRICE DENSITY PROCESS

In this section we discuss state price density processes, for which we need the concept of conditional expectation with respect to a partition, or equivalently, with respect to the field generated by the partition. We have already encountered conditional expectations in Chapter 5; see (5.3.1).

We let the preceding model be unchanged, except that we assign a probability $P(\omega) > 0$ to each $\omega \in \Omega$. (This agrees with our initial assumption that no event in our model is "impossible.") This assignment may be done in any desired fashion. The only point is to bring us into a securities market model making some assignment of positive probabilities to all market outcomes.

Recall that the *indicator function* of a set $A \subseteq \Omega$ is the function $1_A : \Omega \to \{0, 1\}$ that is equal to 1 for all $\omega \in A$ and equal to 0 otherwise. An indicator function is defined for every subset of $\Omega$.

***Definition 11.2.14 (Conditional Expectation of a Random Variable).*** *Let X be a random variable. The **conditional expectation** of X with respect to the information structure at time k, denoted* $E[X \mid \mathcal{P}_k]$*, is defined as*

$$E[X \mid \mathcal{P}_k](\omega) = \sum_{i=1}^{v_k} \frac{E\left[1_{\mathcal{H}_i^{(k)}} X\right]}{P\left(\mathcal{H}_i^{(k)}\right)} 1_{\mathcal{H}_i^{(k)}}(\omega).$$

From this it is clear that $E[X \mid \mathcal{P}_k]$ is a random variable that is constant on each of the elements of $\mathcal{P}_k$.

***Remark:*** Because $\Omega$ is a finite set, there is a one-to-one correspondence between partitions and fields. Let $\mathcal{F}_k = \sigma(\mathcal{P}_k)$, the field generated by the partition $\mathcal{P}_k$. We use the notation $E[X \mid \mathcal{F}_k]$ and $E[X \mid \mathcal{P}_k]$ interchangeably; see also Definition A.1.12 in Appendix A. Some authors prefer to economize on the notation for conditional expectation and write $E_k[X]$ for $E[X \mid \mathcal{P}_k]$. The symbol $E[\cdot \mid \mathcal{P}_k]$ is interpreted as "conditional on all information available up to time $k$." ∎

We now introduce the notion of a state price density process. If we introduce a new process $\zeta$, defined by $\zeta(k, \omega) = \psi(k, \omega)/P(\omega)$, then the characteristic property of state price processes (11.2.3) can be expressed as

$$0 = \sum_{\omega \in \Omega} \sum_{k=0}^{T} \frac{\psi(k, \omega)}{P(\omega)} c^{\theta}(k, \omega) P(\omega)$$

$$= \sum_{k=0}^{T} E[\zeta(k) c^{\theta}(k)]. \tag{11.2.8}$$

The process $\zeta$ is not in general adapted to the filtration $\mathbf{F} = \{\mathcal{F}_0, \ldots, \mathcal{F}_T\}$. We can obtain a formula similar to the last one, but with an adapted process in place of $\zeta$, simply by defining $Z(k) = E[\zeta(k) \mid \mathcal{F}_k]$, $k = 0, \ldots, T$, and noting that

$$E[\zeta(k) c^{\theta}(k)] = E[E[\zeta(k) c^{\theta}(k) \mid \mathcal{F}_k]]$$
$$= E[c^{\theta}(k) E[\zeta(k) \mid \mathcal{F}_k]]$$
$$= E[Z(k) c^{\theta}(k)].$$

(The first and second equalities are consequences of properties (c) and (d) in Theorem A.1.13 in Appendix A.) Hence, (11.2.8) becomes

$$0 = \sum_{k=0}^{T} \mathrm{E}[\, Z(k) c^{\theta}(k)\,].\qquad(11.2.9)$$

**Definition 11.2.15.** *A **state price density process** is any one-dimensional strictly positive adapted process Z, with $Z(0) = 1$, such that (11.2.9) holds for all trading strategies $\theta$. This equation is equivalent to*

$$S(0)\theta(0) = \sum_{k=1}^{T} \mathrm{E}[\, Z(k) c^{\theta}(k)\,].$$

Observe the similarity between the state price density process and the pricing kernel $Z_j$ of Chapter 4. The next theorems are immediate translations of Theorems 11.2.11, 11.2.13, and 11.2.12 in terms of state price density processes.

**Theorem 11.2.16.** *An arbitrage-free market securities model is complete if and only if there is only one state price density process.*

**Theorem 11.2.17 (Recursive State Price Density Property).** *A strictly positive adapted process $\{Z(k)\}$, with $Z(0) = 1$, is a state price density process if and only if*

$$Z(k, \omega) S(k, \omega) = \mathrm{E}[\, Z(k+1)[S(k+1) + D(k+1)]\,|\,\mathcal{F}_k](\omega)$$

*for all $\omega \in \Omega$ and for $k = 0, \ldots, T-1$.*

**Theorem 11.2.18 (Price of Remaining Cash Flows).** *A strictly positive adapted process $\{Z(k)\}$, with $Z(0) = 1$, is a state price density process if and only if for all $j = 0, \ldots, T$, and for all trading strategies $\theta$ the following relation holds:*

$$Z(j, \omega) S(j, \omega) \theta(j, \omega) = \sum_{k=j+1}^{T} \mathrm{E}[\, Z(k) c^{\theta}(k)\,|\,\mathcal{F}_j](\omega).\qquad(11.2.10)$$

We now turn to the notion of equivalent martingale measures.

## SECTION 11.2.8 | RISK-NEUTRAL OR EQUIVALENT MARTINGALE MEASURES

We reinterpret no-arbitrage valuation in terms of the so-called *risk-neutral* or *equivalent martingale* measure. The idea is that when we can "deflate" all prices using some strictly positive security, absence of arbitrage is equivalent to existence of a probability $Q$ under which deflated prices satisfy the martingale property. The next definition is the same as Definition 5.3.3.

**Definition 11.2.19.** *An adapted process* $\{X(k)\}$ *on the filtered probability space* $(\Omega, P, \{\mathcal{P}_k\})$ *is said to be a* **martingale** *if*

$$E[X(k+1) \mid \mathcal{P}_k](\omega) = X(k, \omega), \quad k = 0, \ldots, T-1, \omega \in \Omega.$$

**Definition 11.2.20.** *A non-dividend-paying security that has strictly positive values at all times and in all states of nature with* $B(0, \omega) = 1$ *is called a* **deflator.**

Any strictly positive security, which pays no dividends, can be used as a deflator by normalizing its time-0 value to 1. (The word *numeraire* is often used for deflator.)

We let the market model include a deflator as one of the traded securities, say, $B = S_1$. In Section 5.3, we used the bank account as the deflator. Suppose $\psi$ is a state price process. From Theorem 11.2.12 (with a trading strategy $\theta$ consisting solely of one unit of $B$ at times $k, \ldots, T-1$) we find that for each $\mathcal{A} \in \mathcal{F}_i$,

$$\sum_{\omega \in \mathcal{A}} \psi(k, \omega) B(k, \omega) = \sum_{\omega \in \mathcal{A}} \psi(T, \omega) B(T, \omega). \tag{11.2.11}$$

In particular, for $k = 0$ and $\mathcal{A} = \Omega$ we have

$$B(0) = 1 = \sum_{\omega \in \Omega} \psi(T, \omega) B(T, \omega), \tag{11.2.12}$$

so we can define a probability measure $Q$ on $(\Omega, \mathcal{F})$ by

$$Q(\omega) = \psi(T, \omega) B(T, \omega), \quad \omega \in \Omega. \tag{11.2.13}$$

Next consider any trading strategy $\theta$, and focus initially on the generated cash flow at time $k$. For $\mathcal{H} \in \mathcal{P}_k$, (11.2.11) implies

$$\sum_{\omega \in \mathcal{H}} \psi(k, \omega) c^\theta(k, \omega) = \sum_{\omega \in \mathcal{H}} \psi(k, \omega) B(k, \omega) \frac{c^\theta(k, \omega)}{B(k, \omega)}$$

$$= \sum_{\omega \in \mathcal{H}} \psi(T, \omega) B(T, \omega) \frac{c^\theta(k, \omega)}{B(k, \omega)}$$

$$= \sum_{\omega \in \mathcal{H}} Q(\omega) \frac{c^\theta(k, \omega)}{B(k, \omega)}$$

$$= E^Q \left[ \frac{c^\theta(k)}{B(k)} 1_{\mathcal{H}} \right].$$

(The second equality holds because $c^\theta(k, \omega)$ and $B(k, \omega)$ are constant for $\omega \in \mathcal{H}$.) By summing over each set $\mathcal{H} \in \mathcal{P}_k$ and each $k = 0, \ldots, T$, the characteristic property of state price processes (11.2.3) is seen to be equivalent to

$$0 = \sum_{k=0}^{T} \mathrm{E}^Q \left[ \frac{c^\theta(k)}{B(k)} \right] \tag{11.2.14}$$

or

$$S(0)\theta(0) = \sum_{k=1}^{T} \mathrm{E}^Q \left[ \frac{c^\theta(k)}{B(k)} \right]. \tag{11.2.15}$$

**Definition 11.2.21.** *Consider an arbitrage-free securities market model with deflator B. A probability measure Q on $(\Omega, \mathcal{F})$ is said to be an* **equivalent martingale measure** *for the securities market model if $Q(\omega) > 0$ for each $\omega \in \Omega$ and (11.2.14) holds for each trading strategy $\theta$.*

The next theorems translate Theorems 11.2.11, 11.2.13, and 11.2.12 into the language of equivalent martingale measures. If the securities pay no dividends, then Theorem 11.2.23 is the same as Definition 5.3.4.

**Theorem 11.2.22.** *Consider an arbitrage-free market securities model with deflator B. The model is complete if and only if there is only one martingale measure.*

**Theorem 11.2.23 (Martingale Property).** *Consider an arbitrage-free securities market model with deflator B. A probability measure Q on $(\Omega, \mathcal{F})$, with $Q(\omega) > 0$ for each $\omega \in \Omega$, is an equivalent martingale measure if and only if*

$$S(k, \omega) = \mathrm{E}^Q \left[ \frac{B(k)}{B(k+1)} [S(k+1) + D(k+1)] \, \middle| \, \mathcal{F}_k \right] (\omega) \tag{11.2.16}$$

*for all $\omega \in \Omega$ and for $k = 0, \ldots, T - 1$.*

With the definitions

$$S^B(k) = \frac{S(k)}{B(k)}$$

and

$$D^B(k) = \frac{D(k)}{B(k)},$$

(11.2.16) is equivalent to

$$S^B(k, \omega) = E^Q[S^B(k+1) + D^B(k+1) \mid \mathcal{F}_k](\omega). \qquad (11.2.17)$$

Let $\Delta$ denote the forward difference operator. Then (11.2.17) can be rewritten as

$$E^Q[D^B(k+1) + \Delta S^B(k) \mid \mathcal{F}_k] = 0.$$

Strictly speaking, (11.2.17) says that the deflated price process $S^B$ is a martingale only when there are no dividends (see Definition 11.2.19). It is nevertheless referred to as the martingale property of deflated prices. The procedure of working with the dynamics in terms of $S^B$ and $D^B$ is known as *change of numeraire*.

**Proof.** *Suppose that (11.2.14) holds and consider $\mathcal{H} \in \mathcal{P}_k$. Consider the trading strategy that buys one share of asset i at time k if the state of the market is in $\mathcal{H}$ and liquidates the asset at time $k+1$. Using these cash flows in (11.2.15) yields*

$$0 = E^Q\left[-\frac{S_i(k)}{B(k)}1_{\mathcal{H}}\right] + E^Q\left[\frac{S_i(k+1) + D_i(k+1)}{B(k+1)}1_{\mathcal{H}}\right].$$

*Thus, we have*

$$E^Q\left[\frac{S_i(k)}{B(k)}1_{\mathcal{H}}\right] = E^Q\left[\frac{S_i(k+1) + D_i(k+1)}{B(k+1)}1_{\mathcal{H}}\right]$$

*for each $\mathcal{H} \in \mathcal{P}_k$, or*

$$\frac{S_i(k, \omega)}{B(k, \omega)} = E^Q\left[\frac{S_i(k+1) D_i(k+1)}{B(k+1)}\,\Big|\,\mathcal{F}_k\right](\omega),$$

*which is the i-th component of the vector equation (11.2.16).*

*Conversely, suppose that (11.2.16) holds and let $\theta$ denote a particular trading strategy. Then*

$$E^Q\left[\frac{c^\theta(T)}{B(T)}\,\Big|\,\mathcal{F}_{T-1}\right](\omega) = E^Q\left[\frac{[S(T) + D(T)]\theta(T-1)}{B(T)}\,\Big|\,\mathcal{F}_{T-1}\right](\omega)$$

$$= \frac{S(T-1, \omega)\theta(T-1, \omega)}{B(T-1, \omega)}.$$

*Because of the law of iterated expectations and*

$$c^\theta(T-1, \omega) = [S(T-1, \omega) + D(T-1, \omega)]\,\theta(T-2, \omega) - S(T-1, \omega)\theta(T-1, \omega),$$

*we have*

$$E^Q \left[ \frac{c^\theta(T-1)}{B(T-1)} + \frac{c^\theta(T)}{B(T)} \right] = E^Q \left[ \frac{c^\theta(T-1)}{B(T-1)} + E^Q \left[ \frac{c^\theta(T)}{B(T)} \,\middle|\, \mathcal{F}_{T-1} \right] \right]$$

$$= E^Q \left[ \frac{[S(T-1) + D(T-1)]\,\theta(T-2)}{B(T-1)} \right].$$

*We can continue rolling backwards in time and using conditioning to find*

$$E^Q \left[ \sum_{k=1}^{T} \frac{c^\theta(k)}{B(k)} \right] = E^Q \left[ \frac{[S(1) + D(1)]\,\theta(0)}{B(1)} \right] = S(0)\theta(0).$$

**Theorem 11.2.24 (Price of Remaining Cash Flows).** *Consider an arbitrage-free securities market model with deflator B. A probability measure Q on $(\Omega, \mathcal{F})$, with $Q(\omega) > 0$ for each $\omega \in \Omega$, is an equivalent martingale measure for the securities market model if and only if for all $j = 0, 1, \ldots, T-1$, and for all trading strategies $\theta$ the following relation holds:*

$$S(j, \omega)\theta(j, \omega) = B(j, \omega) \sum_{k=j+1}^{T} E^Q \left[ \frac{c^\theta(k)}{B(k)} \,\middle|\, \mathcal{F}_j \right] (\omega). \qquad (11.2.18)$$

**Proof.** *Formula (11.2.18) immediately implies (11.2.15) when we set $j = 0$. Conversely, suppose that (11.2.15) holds. Fix a time $j \in \{0, 1, \ldots, T-1\}$ and consider a trading strategy $\theta$. For a given set $\mathcal{A} \in \mathcal{F}_j$, we define a new trading strategy*

$$\tilde{\theta}(k, \omega) = \begin{cases} \theta(k, \omega), & \omega \in \mathcal{A}, k = j, j+1, \ldots, T \\ 0, & \text{otherwise;} \end{cases}$$

*that is,*

$$\tilde{\theta}(k, \omega) = 1_{\{j, j+1, \ldots, T\}}(k) 1_{\mathcal{A}}(\omega) \theta(k, \omega).$$

*Applying (11.2.14), we find that*

$$0 = E^Q \left[ \sum_{k=0}^{T} \frac{c^{\tilde{\theta}}(k)}{B(k)} \right]$$

$$= E^Q[0 - 1_{\mathcal{A}} S(j)\theta(j)] + E^Q \left[ 1_{\mathcal{A}} \sum_{k=j+1}^{T} \frac{c^\theta(k)}{B(k)} \right].$$

*Thus,*

$$S(j, \omega)\theta(j, \omega) = E^Q \left[ \sum_{k=j+1}^{T} \frac{c^\theta(k)}{B(k)} \,\middle|\, \mathcal{F}_j \right](\omega).$$

If no arbitrage opportunities exist, then any deflator $B$ can be used to find a martingale measure $Q$; the dependence of the latter on the particular deflator chosen can be indicated by writing it $Q^B$. Formula (11.2.13) shows that the ratio of the probabilities relating to two deflators $B$ and $B'$ is

$$\frac{Q^{B'}(\omega)}{Q^B(\omega)} = \frac{B'(T, \omega)}{B(T, \omega)}. \tag{11.2.19}$$

This ratio of probabilities bears the name of *Radon-Nikodym derivative*. We now single out an important type of deflator.

**Definition 11.2.25.** *A deflator $B$ is called a **locally risk-free asset, bank account,** or **money market fund** if*

$$B(k, \omega) = \begin{cases} 1, & k = 0 \\ \exp[r(0, \omega) + r(1, \omega) + \cdots + r(k-1, \omega)], & k = 1, \ldots, T, \end{cases} \tag{11.2.20}$$

*where $r = \{r(k)\}$ is an adapted process.*

The process $r$ plays the role of a one-period interest rate or short rate, *which is known at the beginning of the period,* that is to say, $r(k, \omega)$ is the continuously compounded rate of interest for period $(k, k+1)$ and is known at time $k$. It is said to be *locally* risk free, because knowledge of the future only extends to the next period.[2] The quantity $e^{r(k)} - 1$ was denoted as $i_k$ and was called the short rate in Section 5.3.1.

The previous pricing formulas take a particularly appealing form when a locally risk-free asset is used as deflator. For instance, (11.2.16) and (11.2.18) become respectively

$$S(k, \omega) = e^{-r(k,\omega)} E^Q[S(k+1) + D(k+1) \,|\, \mathcal{F}_k](\omega), \tag{11.2.21}$$

$$S(j, \omega)\theta(j, \omega) = \sum_{k=j+1}^{T} E^Q\left[e^{-[r(j)+r(j+1)+\cdots+r(k-1)]} c^\theta(k) \,|\, \mathcal{F}_j\right](\omega). \tag{11.2.22}$$

---

[2]Those who are acquainted with probability theory will recognize that a locally risk-free asset is the same as a *predictable* deflator (see Definition A.1.8 in Appendix A).

Observe that in (11.2.21) the discount factor for period $(k, k+1)$,

$$e^{-r(k,\omega)} = \frac{B(k, \omega)}{B(k+1, \omega)},$$

can be taken out of the expectation, as it is known at time $k$ (or, to express it another way, it is $\mathcal{F}_k$-measurable).

Taking a broader view of the problem of pricing cash flows, we see that, although expected discounted cash flows do not give the correct arbitrage-free prices, discounted expectations are appropriate, but with two very significant modifications:

a.     The discounting rates are the risk-free rates, and

b.     The expectation is not with respect to the "physical" probability $P$ (which is estimated from past data), but with respect to the risk-neutral probability $Q$.

A special case of (11.2.21) is that the price of a financed cash-flow stream is given by the discounted expectation

$$\mathrm{E}^Q \left[ \sum_{k=1}^{T} e^{-[r(0)+\cdots+r(k-1)]} c^{\theta}(k) \right]. \tag{11.2.23}$$

Formula (11.2.23) is among the most widely used formulas in financial economics; see (3.7.3) in Chapter 3.

A direct proof of Theorem 11.2.24 can be given in the case when the deflator for the securities market model is a money market account. This provides an opportunity to see how a change of numeraire is used in conjunction with equivalent martingale measures.

Recall that a cash-flow stream $c$ is financed by the adapted process $\theta$ if

$$[S(k, \omega) + D(k, \omega)]\theta(k-1, \omega) = S(k, \omega)\theta(k, \omega) + c(k, \omega) \tag{11.2.24}$$

for $k = 1, \ldots, T-1$, with $\theta(T, \omega) = 0$. Let $c^*(k, \omega) = c(k, \omega)/S_1(k, \omega)$, $S^*(k, \omega) = S(k, \omega)/S_1(k, \omega)$, and $D^*(k, \omega) = D(k, \omega)/S_1(k, \omega)$. Earlier, $S^*$ and $D^*$ were denoted as $S^B$ and $D^B$, respectively. Then (11.2.24) becomes

$$[S^*(k, \omega) + D^*(k, \omega)]\theta(k-1, \omega) = S^*(k, \omega)\theta(k, \omega) + c^*(k, \omega),$$

or

$$c^*(k, \omega) = S^*(k, \omega)\theta(k-1, \omega) - S^*(k, \omega)\theta(k, \omega) + D^*(k, \omega)\theta(k-1, \omega). \tag{11.2.25}$$

Since

$$S^*(k, \omega)\theta(k-1, \omega) - S^*(k, \omega)\theta(k, \omega)$$

$$= [\Delta S^*(k-1, \omega)]\theta(k-1, \omega) - \Delta[S^*(k-1, \omega)\theta(k-1, \omega)],$$

(11.2.25) can be rewritten as

$$c^*(k, \omega) = [\Delta S^*(k-1, \omega)]\theta(k-1, \omega) - \Delta[S^*(k-1, \omega)\theta(k-1, \omega)]$$
$$+ D^*(k, \omega)\theta(k-1, \omega)$$
$$= -\Delta[S^*(k-1, \omega)\theta(k-1, \omega)]$$
$$+ [\Delta S^*(k-1, \omega) + D^*(k, \omega)]\theta(k-1, \omega).$$

Summing the expression above from $k = n+1$ to $k = T$ and recalling that $\theta(T, \omega) = 0$ yields

$$\sum_{k=n+1}^{T} c^*(k, \omega) = S^*(n, \omega)\theta(n, \omega) + \sum_{k=n+1}^{T} [\Delta S^*(k-1, \omega) + D^*(k, \omega)]\theta(k-1, \omega).$$

$$(11.2.26)$$

**Theorem 11.2.26 (Theorem 11.2.24 Revisited).** *Consider an arbitrage-free market securities model with a money market account as the deflator. The price of the remaining cash flows at time $n$, $n = 0, \ldots, T - 1$, for a financed cash-flow stream $c^\theta$ is given by the discounted conditional expectation under $Q$ of the remaining cash flows; that is,*

$$S(n, \omega)\theta(n, \omega) = E^Q\left[\sum_{k=n+1}^{T} e^{-[r(n)+\cdots+r(k-1)]}c^\theta(k)\,\bigg|\,\mathcal{F}_n\right](\omega).$$

***Proof.***

$$E^Q[\{\Delta S^*(k-1) + D^*(k)\}\theta(k-1) \mid \mathcal{F}_{k-1}](\omega)$$
$$= \{E^Q[S^*(k) + D^*(k) \mid \mathcal{F}_{k-1}](\omega) - S^*(k-1, \omega)\}\,\theta(k-1, \omega)$$
$$= \{0\}\theta(k-1, \omega) = 0.$$

*Using this fact and the law of iterated expectations yields*

$$E^Q\left[\sum_{k=n+1}^{T} [\Delta S^*(k-1) + D^*(k)]\theta(k-1)\,\bigg|\,\mathcal{F}_n\right](\omega) = 0.$$

*Therefore by (11.2.26), we have*

$$S^*(n, \omega)\theta(n, \omega) = E^Q\left[\sum_{k=n+1}^{T} c^*(k)\,\bigg|\,\mathcal{F}_n\right](\omega). \qquad (11.2.27)$$

*Because the deflator is assumed to be the money market account,*

$$S^*(n, \omega) = e^{-[r(0.\omega)+\cdots+r(n-1.\omega)]}S(n, \omega)$$

*and, for $k > n$,*

$$c^*(k, \omega) = e^{-[r(0.\omega)+\cdots+r(n-1.\omega)]}e^{-[r(n.\omega)+\cdots+r(k-1.\omega)]}c(k, \omega).$$

*Canceling like terms across (11.2.27) yields*

$$S(n, \omega)\theta(n, \omega) = E^Q\left[\sum_{k=n+1}^{T} e^{-[r(n)+\cdots+r(k-1)]}c(k)\,\Big|\,\mathcal{F}_n\right](\omega).$$

We have discussed state price density processes and equivalent martingale measures and have indicated how a state price density process or an equivalent martingale measure can be arrived at when a state price process is available. In fact, there is a one-to-one correspondence between state price processes and equivalent martingale measures (or state price density processes). It is left as an exercise to work out the correspondence between state price processes and state price density processes. For definiteness we assume that our securities market model includes a money market fund as a primitive asset. The money market fund serves as the deflator for use with the equivalent martingale measure. We discuss next the correspondence between equivalent martingale measures and state price processes.

**Theorem 11.2.27.** *There exists a probability measure Q on $\Omega$ such that $Q(\omega) > 0$ for each $\omega \in \Omega$ and*

$$S(k, \omega) = E^Q[e^{-r(k)}\{S(k + 1) + D(k + 1)\}\,|\,\mathcal{F}_k](\omega) \qquad (11.2.28)$$

*for $k = 0, \ldots, T - 1$, and $\omega \in \Omega$, if and only if a strictly positive adapted process $\psi$, with $\psi(0) = 1/M$ exists such that*

$$S(k, \mathcal{H}) = \frac{1}{\#\mathcal{H}\psi(k, \mathcal{H})} \sum_{\omega \in \mathcal{H}} \psi(k + 1, \omega)[S(k + 1, \omega) + D(k + 1, \omega)] \quad (11.2.29)$$

*for $k = 0, \ldots, T - 1, \mathcal{H} \in \mathcal{P}_k$.*

From (11.2.16) we know that (11.2.28) is equivalent to the existence of an equivalent martingale measure. Similarly, we know from (11.2.4) that (11.2.29) is equivalent to the existence of a state price process. Consequently, Theorem 11.2.27

says that an equivalent martingale measure for the securities market model exists if and only a state price process for the securities market model exists.

**Proof.** *Suppose that Q satisfying (11.2.28) exists. Then for $\omega^* \in \mathcal{H}, \mathcal{H} \in \mathcal{P}_k$,*

$$S(k, \omega^*) = E^Q[e^{-r(k)}\{S(k+1) + D(k+1)\} \mid \mathcal{F}_k](\omega^*)$$

$$= \frac{1}{Q(\mathcal{H})} \sum_{\omega \in \mathcal{H}} e^{-r(k.\omega)} Q(\omega)[S(k+1, \omega) + D(k+1, \omega)]$$

$$= \frac{1}{Q(\mathcal{H})} \sum_{\omega \in \mathcal{H}} e^{-r(k.\omega)} \frac{Q(\mathcal{H} \cap \mathcal{P}_{k+1})}{\#(\mathcal{H} \cap \mathcal{P}_{k+1})}[S(k+1, \omega) + D(k+1, \omega)]$$

$$= \frac{1}{\#\mathcal{H}} \frac{1}{e^{-[r(0.\omega)+\cdots+r(k-1.\omega)]}} \frac{1}{Q(\mathcal{H})/\#\mathcal{H}} \sum_{\omega \in \mathcal{H}} e^{-[r(0.\omega)+\cdots+r(k.\omega)]}$$

$$\times \frac{Q(\mathcal{H}^{(k+1)}(\omega))}{\#\mathcal{H}^{(k+1)}(\omega)}[S(k+1, \omega) + D(k+1, \omega)].$$

*The third step follows because $e^{-r(k.\omega)}[S(k+1, \omega) + D(k+1, \omega)]$ is $\mathcal{F}_{k+1}$-measurable (that is, constant on each set of the partition $\mathcal{P}_{k+1}$). For the fourth step, recall the notation that $\mathcal{H}^{(k+1)}(\omega)$ is the element of the partition $\mathcal{P}_{k+1}$ to which $\omega$ belongs.*
    *Define*

$$\psi(k, \omega) = e^{-[r(0.\omega)+\cdots+r(k-1.\omega)]} \frac{Q(\mathcal{H})}{\#\mathcal{H}},$$

*for $\omega \in \mathcal{H}, \mathcal{H} \in \mathcal{P}_k$. Then $\{\psi(k)\}$ is strictly positive and adapted. Hence, we have shown*

$$S(k, \omega^*) = \frac{1}{\#\mathcal{H}\psi(k, \omega^*)} \sum_{\omega \in \mathcal{H}} \psi(k+1, \omega)[S(k+1, \omega) + D(k+1, \omega)],$$

*for $\omega^* \in \mathcal{H}$ and $\mathcal{H} \in \mathcal{P}_k$.*
    *Conversely, suppose a strictly positive adapted process $\psi$ exists satisfying (11.2.29). Define a strictly positive function Q on $\Omega$ by*

$$Q(\omega) = e^{r(0.\omega)+\cdots+r(T-1.\omega)}\psi(T, \omega).$$

*The function Q is a probability measure because*

$$\sum_{\omega \in \Omega} Q(\omega) = \sum_{\omega \in \Omega} e^{r(0.\omega)+\cdots+r(T-1.\omega)}\psi(T, \omega) = S_1(0, \omega) = 1,$$

*as the money market fund is a primitive asset.*

*For $\mathcal{H} \in \mathcal{P}_k$,*

$$Q(\mathcal{H}) = \sum_{\omega \in \mathcal{H}} Q(\omega)$$

$$= \sum_{\omega \in \mathcal{H}} e^{r(0.\omega)+\cdots+r(T-1.\omega)}\psi(T, \omega)$$

$$= \frac{\#\mathcal{H}\psi(k, \omega^*)}{\#\mathcal{H}\psi(k, \omega^*)} \sum_{\omega \in \mathcal{H}^{(k)}(\omega^*)} S_1(T, \omega)\psi(T, \omega)$$

$$= \#\mathcal{H}\psi(k, \omega^*)S_1(k, \omega^*)$$

$$= \#\mathcal{H}\psi(k, \omega^*)e^{r(0.\omega^*)+\cdots+r(k-1.\omega^*)} \tag{11.2.30}$$

*where $\omega^*$ is any element of $\mathcal{H}$. The penultimate quality follows from (11.2.29). Thus, by (11.2.29), we have for $\omega^* \in \mathcal{H}, \mathcal{H} \in \mathcal{P}_k$,*

$$S(k, \omega^*) = \frac{1}{\#\mathcal{H}\psi(k, \omega^*)} \sum_{\omega \in \mathcal{H}} \psi(k+1, \omega)[S(k+1, \omega) + D(k+1, \omega)]$$

$$= \frac{1}{Q(\mathcal{H})} \sum_{\omega \in \mathcal{H}} e^{-r(k.\omega)} \frac{Q(\mathcal{H} \cap \mathcal{P}_{k+1})}{\#(\mathcal{H} \cap \mathcal{P}_{k+1})}[S(k+1, \omega) + D(k+1, \omega)]$$

*( from (11.2.30))*

$$= \frac{1}{Q(\mathcal{H})} \sum_{\omega \in \mathcal{H}} e^{-r(k.\omega)} Q(\omega)[S(k+1, \omega) + D(k+1, \omega)]$$

$$= E^Q[e^{-r(k)}\{S(k+1) + D(k+1)\} \mid \mathcal{F}_k](\omega^*).$$

*The second to last step follows because $e^{-r(k.\omega)}[S(k+1, \omega) + D(k+1, \omega)]$ is constant on each set $\mathcal{P}_k$. Therefore, we have shown that*

$$S(k, \omega^*) = E^Q[e^{-r(k)}\{S(k+1) + D(k+1)\} \mid \mathcal{F}_k](\omega^*)$$

*as required.*

Theorem 11.2.27 yields the following version of the fundamental theorem of asset pricing for securities market models with a deflator asset.

***Theorem 11.2.28.*** *The securities market model is arbitrage free if and only if an equivalent martingale measure exists.*

As we have noted, there is a one-to-one correspondence between state price processes and state price densities, and thus a similar version of the fundamental theorem of asset pricing can be stated for state price density.

*Example 11.2.4.* This example illustrates the relationship between state price processes and equivalent martingale measures for a single model. We leave it to you to determine a state price density for this model under the assumption that all states have equal probability.

Suppose we have a two-period model with the information structure depicted in Figure 11.5, and two primitive assets with price processes as indicated in Figure 11.6. Neither asset pays dividends. A state price process for this model is given by

$$\psi(1, \omega_1) = \psi(1, \omega_2) = 0.2,$$

$$\psi(1, \omega_3) = \psi(1, \omega_4) = \psi(1, \omega_5) = 0.15,$$

$$\psi(2, \omega_1) = 0.168,$$

$$\psi(2, \omega_2) = 0.172,$$

$$\psi(2, \omega_3) = 0.18,$$

$$\psi(2, \omega_4) = 0.135,$$

$$\psi(2, \omega_5) = 0.09.$$

FIGURE **11.5** | *Two-Period Information Structure for Example 11.2.4*

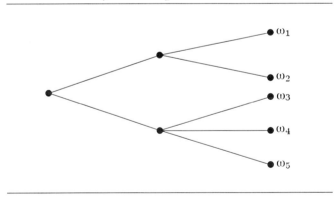

To four digits, an equivalent martingale measure for this model is given by

$$Q(\omega_1) = 0.2325,$$

$$Q(\omega_2) = 0.2381,$$

$$Q(\omega_3) = 0.2353,$$

$$Q(\omega_4) = 0.1764,$$

$$Q(\omega_5) = 0.1177.$$

FIGURE **11.6** │ *Price Processes for Assets 1 and 2*

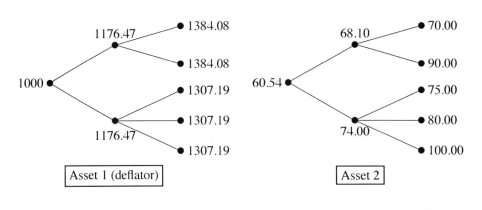

To four digits, one-period interest rates for the deflator asset can be computed as

$$r(0, \omega) = 0.1625,$$

$$r(1, \omega_1) = r(1, \omega_2) = 0.1625,$$

$$r(1, \omega_3) = r(1, \omega_4) = r(1, \omega_5) = 0.1054. \qquad \blacksquare$$

**Example 11.2.5.** Consider a two-period securities market model with the information structure as shown in Figure 11.5. Suppose we have three traded assets whose price processes are given in Figure 11.7. Assume that none of the assets are dividend paying. We show how to compute an equivalent martingale measure for this model assuming that the securities market model is arbitrage free.

Next compute an equivalent martingale measure for this model using asset 1 as numeraire. It is sufficient to compute the conditional probabilities that we have denoted in Figure 11.8. Hence,

$$\frac{139}{93} = \beta \frac{100}{100} + (1 - \beta) \frac{200}{100}$$

from which $\beta = 47/93$. This equation is simply finding $\beta$ such that the martingale condition for asset 2 is valid at the correct node. Similarly,

$$\frac{199}{97} = \gamma_1 \frac{100}{100} + \gamma_2 \frac{200}{100} + (1 - \gamma_1 - \gamma_2) \frac{300}{100}$$
$$= 3 - 2\gamma_1 - \gamma_2,$$

FIGURE **11.7** | *Price Processes of the Three Traded Assets*

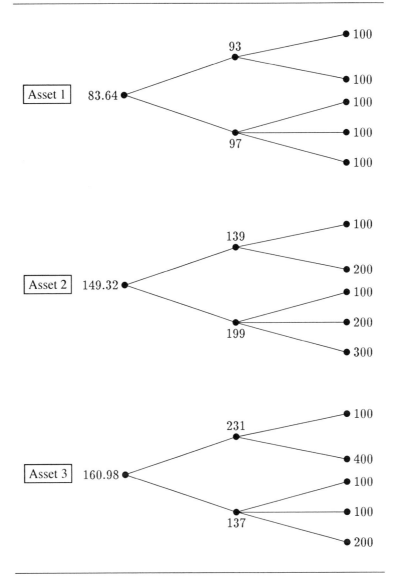

and

$$\frac{137}{97} = \gamma_1 \frac{100}{100} + \gamma_2 \frac{100}{100} + (1 - \gamma_1 - \gamma_2)\frac{200}{100}$$
$$= 2 - \gamma_1 - \gamma_2;$$

that is,

$$2\gamma_1 + \gamma_2 = \frac{92}{97}$$

FIGURE **11.8** | *Risk-Neutral Conditional Probabilities for Example 11.2.5*

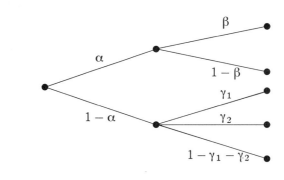

and

$$\gamma_1 + \gamma_2 = \frac{57}{93}.$$

Therefore,

$$\gamma_1 = \frac{35}{97}, \qquad \gamma_2 = \frac{22}{97}.$$

Similarly for the first period:

$$\frac{149.32}{83.64} = \alpha \frac{139}{93} + (1 - \alpha) \frac{199}{97},$$

which yields $\alpha = 0.47812$. Thus, we can fill in the risk-neutral conditional probabilities and generate $Q$ (see Figure 11.9):

$$Q(\omega_1) = 0.47812 \left(\frac{47}{93}\right) = 0.24163,$$

$$Q(\omega_2) = 0.23649,$$

$$Q(\omega_3) = 0.18831,$$

$$Q(\omega_4) = 0.11836,$$

$$Q(\omega_5) = 0.21521.$$

No locally riskless traded asset is found in this model, but since the asset payoffs have full rank at each node of the tree, we can synthetically create an asset that is locally riskless. Therefore, we can speak of the implied interest rates in the model. Consider this for the node at time 1 comprising $\{\omega_1, \omega_2\}$. A portfolio of asset 1 and asset 2,

FIGURE **11.9** | *Risk-Neutral Conditional Probabilities for Example 11.2.5*

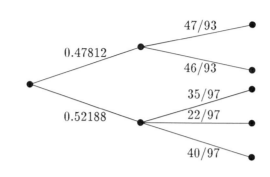

denoted by $\theta_1$ and $\theta_2$ respectively, exists such that

$$\theta_1 S_1(3, \omega) + \theta_2 S_2(3, \omega) = 1, \quad \text{for } \omega \in \{\omega_1, \omega_2\}.$$

Thus,

$$\theta_1 + \theta_2 \frac{S_2(3, \omega)}{S_1(3, \omega)} = \frac{1}{S_1(3, \omega)}, \quad \omega \in \{\omega_1, \omega_2\}.$$

Applying $E^Q[\cdot \mid \mathcal{F}_2]$ to both sides and using the martingale property yields

$$\theta_1 + \theta_2 \frac{S_2(2, \omega_1)}{S_1(2, \omega_1)} = E^Q\left[\frac{1}{S_1(3)} \,\middle|\, \mathcal{F}_2\right](\omega_1).$$

Hence,

$$\theta_1 S_1(2, \omega_1) + \theta_2 S_2(2, \omega_1) = E^Q\left[\frac{S_1(2)}{S_1(3)} \,\middle|\, \mathcal{F}_2\right](\omega_1).$$

Consequently, for $E^Q[S_1(2, \omega)/S_1(3, \omega) \mid \mathcal{F}_2](\omega_1)$ units paid at time 2, the investor receives 1 at time 3 in either of the two possible states. Therefore, the implied interest rate is

$$-\log\left(E^Q\left[\frac{S_1(2)}{S_1(3)} \,\middle|\, \mathcal{F}_2\right](\omega_1)\right).$$

We can compute the implied interest rate at the three relevant nodes as shown in Figure 11.10. ∎

FIGURE **11.10** | *Implied Interest Rate*

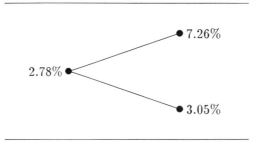

**Example 11.2.6.** The primitive assets in the model are used to compute the risk-neutral probability measure or equivalently the local state prices. We can then use the data to compute the prices of any spanned cash-flow stream that we are interested in. This can be done recursively without the need to compute the trading strategy that finances the cash-flow stream of interest. Of course, if we need the trading strategy to deal with hedging, then we can compute it using linear algebra at each node.

Consider the two-asset, two-period model as given in Figure 11.11. We can compute the risk-neutral conditional probabilities as shown in Figure 11.12. The risk-neutral probability measure is not unique and is indexed by the parameter $s$. This model is not complete because the primitive assets do not span the trinomial node at time 1.

FIGURE **11.11** | *Two-Period Model*

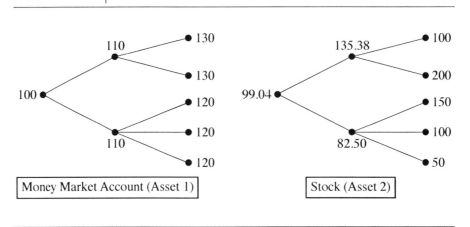

FIGURE **11.12** | *Risk-Neutral Conditional Probabilities for Example 11.2.6*

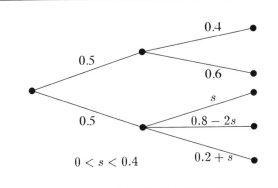

What is the range of prices an investor would be willing to pay for the cash-flow stream depicted in Figure 11.13? Indexing the family of risk-neutral probability measures by $s$ yields the measure (note $0 < s < 0.4$ from Figure 11.12):

$$Q_s = \begin{cases} Q(\omega_1) = (0.5)(0.4) \\ Q(\omega_2) = (0.5)(0.6) \\ Q(\omega_3) = 0.5s \\ Q(\omega_4) = 0.5(0.8 - 2s) \\ Q(\omega_5) = 0.5(0.2 + s). \end{cases}$$

FIGURE **11.13** | *Cash-Flow Stream*

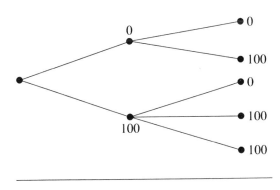

Then the range of prices could be expressed as the interval lying between

$$\inf_{0 < s < 0.4} \ E^{Q_s} \left[ \frac{S_1(0)}{S_1(2)} c(2) + \frac{S_1(0)}{S_1(1)} c(1) \right]$$

and

$$\sup_{0 < s < 0.4} E^{Q_s} \left[ \frac{S_1(0)}{S_1(2)} c(2) + \frac{S_1(0)}{S_1(1)} c(1) \right].$$

Using Figure 11.14, we see that the price range of the cash-flow stream is (48.08, 64.75). ∎

FIGURE **11.14** | *Price of Remaining Cash-Flow Stream*

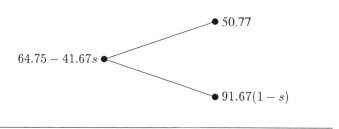

### SECTION **11.2.9** | RECURSIVE RELATION FOR PRICING UNCERTAIN CASH-FLOW STREAMS

As a practical matter, the current price of a cash-flow stream is rarely computed using (11.2.5) or its alternative form (11.2.8). Instead, the cash flows back through the information structure are priced in a recursive fashion. Recall the notation that $v^{(k)}(\omega) = \#\mathcal{H}^{(k)}(\omega)$ and that $\Omega^{(k)}$ denotes a representative set of $\mathcal{P}_k$.

Suppose we are in an arbitrage-free securities market model with state price process $\psi = \{\psi(k)\}$. We further assume that asset 1 is a non-dividend-paying strictly positive asset that can be used as numeraire, $B(k, \omega) = S_1(k, \omega)$ as before, and let $\mathbf{Q}$ denote the risk-neutral probability measure for the numeraire $B$ that is equivalent to the state price process $\psi$. Consider a financed cash-flow stream $\{c^\theta(k)\}$. Define the "value process" as

$$V(k, \omega^*) = \sum_{\omega \in \mathcal{H}^{(k)}(\omega^*)} \sum_{j=k+1}^{T} \frac{\psi(j, \omega)}{v^{(k)}(\omega^*)\psi(k, \omega^*)} c^\theta(j, \omega). \tag{11.2.31}$$

Equivalently,

$$V(k, \omega^*) = E^Q \left[ B(k) \sum_{j=k+1}^{T} \frac{c^\theta(j)}{B(j)} \middle| \mathcal{F}_k \right] (\omega^*). \tag{11.2.32}$$

Thus, $V(k, \omega^*)$ is the price at time $k$ along market outcome $\omega^*$ of the remaining cash flows in our financed cash-flow stream $\{c^\theta(k); \ k = 1, 2, \ldots, T\}$. In other words, $V(k, \omega^*)$ is $S(k, \omega^*)\theta(k, \omega^*)$. We can now derive a recursive relation based on either of the definitions of the value process for $\{c^\theta(k)\}$. When we do not want to indicate explicit dependence of $V$ on $\omega^*$ in (11.2.32), we just write

$$V(k) = E^Q \left[ B(k) \sum_{j=k+1}^{T} \frac{c^\theta(j)}{B(j)} \,\middle|\, \mathcal{F}_k \right].$$

In Chapter 5, $V$ was written as $V^\theta$; see Section 5.3.2. In this chapter, we drop the superscript $\theta$ for notational simplicity. When $\theta$ is a self-financing trading strategy, the next theorem reduces to Proposition 5.3.7.

**Theorem 11.2.29 (Recursive Valuation).**

$$V(k, \omega^*) = E^Q \left[ \frac{B(k)}{B(k+1)} [c^\theta(k+1) + V(k+1)] \,\middle|\, \mathcal{F}_k \right] (\omega^*) \qquad (11.2.33)$$

or equivalently,

$$V(k, \omega^*) = \sum_{\omega \in \mathcal{H}^{(k)}(\omega^*) \cap \Omega^{(k+1)}} \frac{v^{(k+1)}(\omega)\psi(k+1, \omega)}{v^{(k)}(\omega^*)\psi(k, \omega^*)} [c^\theta(k+1, \omega) + V(k+1, \omega)].$$

$$(11.2.34)$$

**Proof.** *It follows from* (11.2.32) *that*

$V(k, \omega^*)$

$$= E^Q \left[ \frac{B(k)}{B(k+1)} c^\theta(k+1) + \frac{B(k)}{B(k+1)} \sum_{j=k+2}^{T} \frac{B(k+1)}{B(j)} c^\theta(j) \,\middle|\, \mathcal{F}_k \right] (\omega^*)$$

$$= E^Q \left[ \frac{B(k)}{B(k+1)} \left\{ c^\theta(k+1) + E^Q \left[ \sum_{j=k+2}^{T} \frac{B(k+1)}{B(j)} c^\theta(j) \,\middle|\, \mathcal{F}_{k+1} \right] \right\} \,\middle|\, \mathcal{F}_k \right] (\omega^*)$$

$$= E^Q \left[ \frac{B(k)}{B(k+1)} [c^\theta(k+1) + V(k+1)] \,\middle|\, \mathcal{F}_k \right] (\omega^*), \qquad (11.2.35)$$

*which is* (11.2.33).

To derive (11.2.34), *recall that* $Q(\omega) = \psi(T, \omega) B(T, \omega)$. *Thus,*

$$Q(\mathcal{H}^{(k)}(\omega^*)) = \sum_{\omega \in \mathcal{H}^{(k)}(\omega^*)} \psi(T, \omega) B(T, \omega)$$

$$= v^{(k)}(\omega^*)\psi(k, \omega^*) \frac{1}{v^{(k)}(\omega^*)\psi(k, \omega^*)} \sum_{\omega \in \mathcal{H}^{(k)}(\omega^*)} \psi(T, \omega) B(T, \omega)$$

$$= v^{(k)}(\omega^*)\psi(k, \omega^*) B(k, \omega^*)$$

*where the last expression follows from* (11.2.5). *In other words, we have*

$$Q(\mathcal{H}^{(k)}(\omega)) = v^{(k)}(\omega)\psi(k, \omega) B(k, \omega).$$

*Thus,*

$$\frac{B(k, \omega)}{B(k + 1, \omega)} \frac{Q(\mathcal{H}^{(k+1)}(\omega))}{Q(\mathcal{H}^{(k)}(\omega))} = \frac{v^{(k)}(\omega)\psi(k + 1, \omega)}{v^{(k)}(\omega)\psi(k, \omega)}. \tag{11.2.36}$$

*By definition of conditional probability, we can check that*

$$Q(\omega \mid \mathcal{F}_k)(\omega^*) = \frac{Q(\omega)}{Q(\mathcal{H}^{(k)}(\omega^*))} 1_{\mathcal{H}^{(k)}(\omega^*)}(\omega).$$

*Thus, the right-hand side of* (11.2.35) *is*

$$\sum_{\omega \in \Omega} \frac{B(k, \omega)}{B(k + 1, \omega)} [c^\theta(k + 1, \omega) + V(k + 1, \omega)] Q(\omega \mid \mathcal{F}_k)(\omega^*)$$

$$= \sum_{\omega \in \mathcal{H}^{(k)}(\omega^*)} \frac{B(k, \omega)}{B(k + 1, \omega)} \frac{Q(\omega)}{Q(\mathcal{H}^{(k)}(\omega^*))} [c^\theta(k + 1, \omega) + V(k + 1, \omega)]$$

$$= \sum_{\omega \in \mathcal{H}^{(k)}(\omega^*) \cap \Omega^{(k+1)}} \frac{B(k, \omega)}{B(k + 1, \omega)} \frac{Q(\mathcal{H}^{(k+1)}(\omega))}{Q(\mathcal{H}^{(k)}(\omega^*))} [c^\theta(k + 1, \omega) + V(k + 1, \omega)]$$

*which yields* (11.2.34) *by applying* (11.2.36).

Define

$$X(k, \omega) = \frac{v^{(k)}(\omega)\psi(k, \omega)}{v^{(k-1)}(\omega)\psi(k - 1, \omega)}.$$

The process $\{X(k)\}$ is referred to as the *local state prices* for the model. Clearly, a knowledge of the local state prices (and the information structure) is equivalent to a knowledge of the state price process as the state price process can be computed by multiplying together the local state prices. Equation (11.2.33) can be interpreted as saying that we can value a cash-flow stream by discounting back one period at a time and using the conditional risk-neutral probabilities. Equation (11.2.34) has the interpretation that we can value a cash-flow stream.

**Example 11.2.7.** Consider the model with information structure and numeraire asset prices as shown in Figure 11.15:

$$Q(\omega_k) = \frac{1}{7}, \qquad k = 1, \dots, 7.$$

FIGURE **11.15** | *Information Structure and Numeraire Asset Prices*

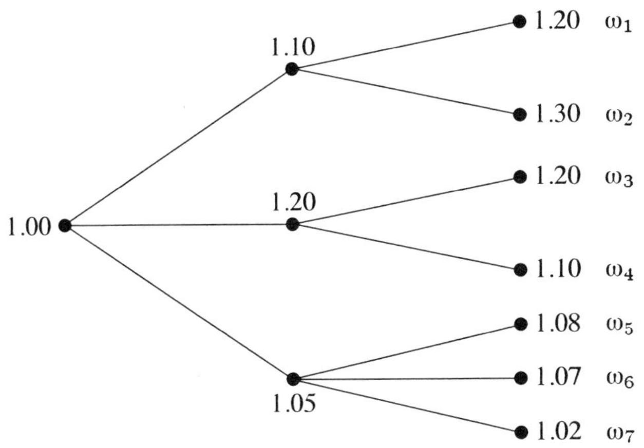

We have determined that the risk-neutral probability measure assigns equal weights to each market outcome:

$$\mathcal{H}^{(1)}(\omega_1) = \{\omega_1, \omega_2\}, \qquad \mathcal{H}^{(1)}(\omega_3) = \{\omega_3, \omega_4\}, \qquad \mathcal{H}^{(1)}(\omega_5) = \{\omega_5, \omega_6, \omega_7\}.$$

We now price the cash-flow stream as shown in Figure 11.16. Working from (11.2.33), proceed as follows:

$$V(1, \omega_1) = \left(\frac{1.1}{1.2}\right) \frac{1}{2}(100) + \left(\frac{1.1}{1.3}\right) \frac{1}{2}(0)$$

$$= 45.83,$$

$$V(1, \omega_3) = \left(\frac{1.2}{1.2}\right) \frac{1}{2}(100) + \left(\frac{1.2}{1.1}\right) \frac{1}{2}(200)$$

$$= 159.09,$$

$$V(1, \omega_5) = \left(\frac{1.05}{1.08}\right) \frac{1}{3}(100) + \left(\frac{1.05}{1.07}\right) \frac{1}{3}(0) + \left(\frac{1.05}{1.02}\right) \frac{1}{3}(100)$$

$$= 66.72,$$

$$V(0, \omega_1) = \left(\frac{1}{1.1}\right) \frac{2}{7}(100 + 45.83) + \left(\frac{1}{1.2}\right) \frac{2}{7}(100 + 159.09) + \frac{1}{1.05} \frac{3}{7}(0 + 66.72)$$

$$= 171.80.$$

FIGURE **11.16** | *Cash-Flow Stream*

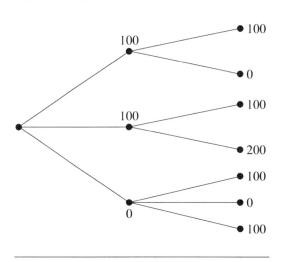

Using (11.2.36), we can compute the local state prices for the model:

$$X(2, \omega_1) = \left(\frac{1.1}{1.2}\right)\frac{1/7}{2/7} = \left(\frac{1.1}{1.2}\right)\frac{1}{2},$$

$$X(2, \omega_2) = \left(\frac{1.1}{1.3}\right)\frac{1/7}{2/7} = \left(\frac{1.1}{1.3}\right)\frac{1}{2},$$

$$X(1, \omega_1) = \left(\frac{1}{1.1}\right)\frac{2/7}{1} = \left(\frac{1}{1.1}\right)\frac{2}{7},$$

$$X(1, \omega_3) = \left(\frac{1}{1.2}\right)\frac{2/7}{1} = \left(\frac{1}{1.2}\right)\frac{2}{7},$$

$$X(1, \omega_5) = \left(\frac{1}{1.05}\right)\frac{3/7}{1} = \left(\frac{1}{1.05}\right)\frac{3}{7}.$$

We can repeat the preceding calculations to obtain

$$159.09 = X(2, \omega_3)100 + X(2, \omega_4)200, \text{ and so on.} \qquad \blacksquare$$

***Example 11.2.8.*** Given the model with numeraire and risk-neutral conditional probabilities as shown in Figure 11.17, we compute the price of a contingent claim payable at time 2 with payments as indicated in Figure 11.17. This can be done as

$$\left(\frac{1.1}{1.3}\right)\frac{1}{4}(100) + \left(\frac{1.1}{1.2}\right)\frac{1}{2}(300) + \left(\frac{1.1}{1.15}\right)\frac{1}{4}(100) = 182.57,$$

$$\left(\frac{1.05}{1.15}\right)\frac{1}{5}(100) + \left(\frac{1.05}{1.1}\right)\frac{4}{5}(200) = 170.99.$$

FIGURE **11.17** | *Numeraire and Risk-Neutral*
*Conditional Probabilities*

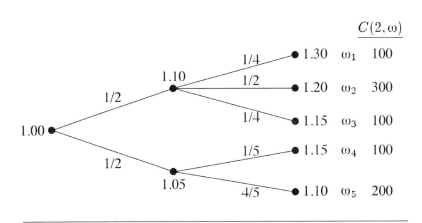

$$C(2, \omega)$$

Hence, the time-0 price of the contingent claim is

$$\left(\frac{1}{1.1}\right)\frac{1}{2}(182.57) + \left(\frac{1}{1.05}\right)\frac{1}{2}(170.99) = 164.41$$

as shown in Figure 11.18.

∎

FIGURE **11.18** | *Price Process of the Contingent Claim*

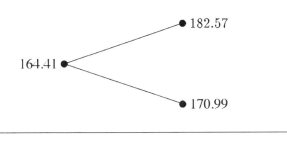

***Example 11.2.9.*** Given a model with local state prices and cash-flow stream as shown in Figure 11.19, we compute the price of the cash-flow stream. The steps are as follows:

$$0.47(100) + 0.22(200) + 0.25(400) = 191,$$
$$0.61(500) + 0.37(0) = 305.$$

FIGURE **11.19** │ *Local State Prices and Cash-Flow Stream*

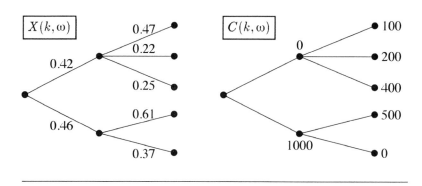

Hence, the price is

$$0.42(0 + 191) + 0.46(1000 + 305) = 680.52.$$  ■

## SECTION 11.2.10 │ A MORE GENERAL FUNDAMENTAL THEOREM OF ASSET PRICING

The version of the fundamental theorem of asset pricing that we prove in this section is from Rogers [160] and has the following features:

- The setting is more general in that the sample space $\Omega$ can be infinite; this allows, in particular, that the security prices be modeled as continuous random variables.

- The proof does not rely on the separating hyperplane theorem.

- An alternative, though equivalent, definition of arbitrage is used.

- A risk-neutral probability measure is explicitly identified, in a form that resembles the Esscher measure of Chapter 10.

We only deal with the one-period case; the same idea works in the multiperiod case, but the mathematics is a little more involved; see the papers by Rogers [160] and by Bühlmann, Delbaen, Embrechts, and Shiryaev [33]. The necessary background on changes of measures can be found in Section A.3 in Appendix A.

Security prices are represented by the row vector of random variables $S = [S_1, \ldots, S_N]$, defined on a probability space $(\Omega, \mathcal{F}, P)$. As before, $S(0)$ is known with certainty. We assume that there is no redundant security, that is to say, there is no nonzero column vector $\theta$ such that $S(1)\theta$ vanishes identically. We further assume the existence of a deflator (numeraire), $S_1$, and that prices have already been deflated; thus, $S_1(0) = S_1(1) = 1$. The following definition of "arbitrage in the ordinary sense" is the same as the one used previously when the sample space was finite, since it was then assumed that $P(\omega) > 0$ for all $\omega$.

**Definition 11.2.30.** *The **gain generated by** $\theta$ is defined as $[S(1) - S(0)]\,\theta$. A (trading) strategy $\theta$ is an **arbitrage in the ordinary sense** if*

$$S(0)\theta \leq 0, \qquad S(1)\theta \geq 0, \quad \text{and} \quad P([S(1) - S(0)]\theta > 0) > 0. \qquad (11.2.37)$$

*A strategy $\theta$ is an **arbitrage in the alternative sense** if*

$$[S(1) - S(0)]\,\theta \geq 0 \quad \text{and} \quad P([S(1) - S(0)]\theta > 0) > 0. \qquad (11.2.38)$$

These two definitions of arbitrage turn out to be the same in our model.

**Theorem 11.2.31.** *There is no arbitrage in the ordinary sense if and only if there is no arbitrage in the alternative sense.*

**Proof.** *Suppose $\theta$ is an arbitrage in the ordinary sense. Then it is clearly an arbitrage in the alternative sense.*

*Suppose $\theta$ is an arbitrage in the alternative sense. Condition (11.2.38) does not guarantee that $S(0)\theta \leq 0$ and $S(1)\theta > 0$. We can circumvent this potential problem because of the existence of a deflator. Define a new trading strategy*

$$\theta' = \theta - [S(0)\theta]\,(1, 0, \ldots, 0)^{T}.$$

*Then $S(0)\theta' = 0$ because $S_1(0) = 1$, and $S(1)\theta' = [S(1) - S(0)]\,\theta$ because $S_1(0) = S_1(1) = 1$. Thus, $\theta'$ is an arbitrage in the ordinary sense.*

**Theorem 11.2.32.** *There is no arbitrage in the alternative sense if and only if there is a risk-neutral probability, that is to say, there is a probability measure $Q$, equivalent to $P$, such that*

$$E^{Q}[S(1)] = S(0).$$

**Proof.** *Suppose a risk-neutral probability measure $Q$ exists. Then for each strategy $\theta$*

$$E^{Q}[S(1) - S(0)]\theta = 0,$$

*so that $\theta$ cannot satisfy (11.2.38).*

*Conversely, suppose there is no arbitrage in the alternative sense. Let $G = S(1) - S(0)$. We assume that the function*

$$\phi(\theta) = E^{P}[\exp(G\theta)]$$

*exists and is finite for all* $\theta \in \Re^N$. *Exercise 11.1 shows that if this is not so, then a preliminary change of measure*

$$\frac{dP'}{dP} = \frac{\exp(-GG^T/2)}{E^P[\exp(-GG^T/2)]} \tag{11.2.39}$$

*implies that* $E^{P'}[\exp(G\theta)]$ *is finite for all* $\theta$.

*The function* $\phi$ *has continuous first derivatives. For the moment, let us assume that* $\phi$ *has a local minimum at some* $\theta^* \in \Re^N$. *Then the first-order derivatives of* $\phi$ *vanish at* $\theta^*$, *meaning that, for* $i = 1, \ldots, N$,

$$0 = \frac{\partial}{\partial \theta_i} \phi(\theta^*) = E^P[(S_i(1) - S_i(0)) \exp(G\theta^*)],$$

*which implies*

$$E^P[S_i(1) \exp(G\theta^*)] = E^P[S_i(0) \exp(G\theta^*)] = S_i(0)E^P[\exp(G\theta^*)].$$

*The probability measure Q defined by*

$$\frac{dQ}{dP} = \frac{\exp(G\theta^*)}{E^P[\exp(G\theta^*)]}$$

*is a risk-neutral measure.*

*The only problem left is proving that* $\phi$ *must have a local minimum. Suppose this is not the case. Then there is an infinite sequence of N-dimensional vectors* $\{\theta_n\}$ *such that (a)* $\|\theta_n\| \to \infty$ *as* $n \to \infty$, *and (b)* $\{\phi(\theta_n)\}$ *is a strictly decreasing sequence. Let*

$$\beta_n = \frac{\theta_n}{\|\theta_n\|}.$$

*The sequence* $\{\beta_n\}$ *is an infinite subset of the closed and bounded set of elements of* $\Re^N$ *with norm equal to 1 and thus has at least one limit point, say,* $\beta^*$. *A subsequence* $\{\beta_{n_k}\}$ *tends to* $\beta^*$, *and so* $\{G\beta_{n_k}\}$ *converges in distribution to* $G\beta^*$.

*Observe that since there is no arbitrage in the alternative sense, and since we have made the assumption that there are no redundant securities, we must have* $P(G\theta < 0) > 0$ *and* $P(G\theta > 0) > 0$ *for all nonzero* $\theta \in \Re^N$. *The vector* $\beta^*$ *is nonzero (it has norm 1), and thus strictly positive numbers* $\delta$ *and* $\varepsilon$ *exist such that*

$$P(G\beta_{n_k} > \delta) > \varepsilon \tag{11.2.40}$$

*for all k. Hence,* $\phi(\theta_{n_k}) \to \infty$ *(see Exercise 11.3), a contradiction.*

*It is relatively easy to see that* $\phi$ *can have only one absolute minimum, since it is strictly convex. This is explored in Exercise 11.4.*

# Section 11.3
# Forward and Futures Prices

In this section we study the prices of forward and futures contracts. Familiarity with the basic aspects and institutional details of forward and futures contracts as described in Chapters 2 and 7 is assumed. To facilitate the analysis of forward and futures contracts, we use an abstract definition of each type of contract that captures the important features of each contract. We employ the securities market model described in the first part of this chapter and assume that we are working in an arbitrage-free securities market model that is also complete. Consequently, a unique equivalent martingale (risk-neutral) measure exists that can be used for valuation. We apply the equivalent martingale measure valuation formulas developed earlier.

We assume that there is a locally riskless asset in the model; see Definition 11.2.25. Although the pricing theory for forward and futures contracts can be developed without the assumption of a locally riskless asset, we find it more convenient to follow the usual development based on the assumption of a locally riskless asset. Last, for $0 \le n < m \le T$, the symbol $P(n, m)$ is defined by the relation

$$P(n, m) = \mathrm{E}^{Q}\left[e^{-[r(n)+r(n+1)+\cdots+r(m-1)]} \,\middle|\, \mathcal{P}_n\right].$$

Since the securities market model is assumed to be complete, we interpret $P(n, m)$ as the price at time $n$ of a zero-coupon bond maturing for unit amount at time $m$.

## SECTION 11.3.1 | FORWARD PRICES

As we know from Chapters 2 and 7, a forward contract on a security is an agreement to exchange the security at a particular time in the future, known as the *delivery date*, at a price that is fixed at the *contract initiation date* and for which the cost to enter the contract is 0. The price that is fixed at the contract initiation date is called the forward price. In our securities market model, an investor can take a long position or a short position in the forward contract. Hence, it follows from the principle of no arbitrage that we determine the forward price from the requirement that the cost to enter the forward contract is 0. For every security in the model and for each choice of times $n$ and $m$ with $0 \le n < m \le T$, there is a forward contract on that security with contract initiation date $n$ and delivery date $m$. If such a forward contract is made on a particular security, we denote the forward price for this contract by $F(n, m)$. For each fixed value of $m$ the adapted process of forward prices, $\{F(0, m), F(1, m), \ldots, F(m-1, m)\}$, can be considered for a forward contract on a particular security with delivery date $m$. This is an adapted process because the forward price $F(n, m)$ is fixed at time $n$. We now give a formal definition of forward contract and characterize the forward prices.

**Definition 11.3.1.** *A **forward contract** on an asset with price process S and with contract initiation date n and delivery date m, $0 \leq n < m \leq T$, is a security with cash-flow stream equal to*

$$c(k) = \begin{cases} S(m) - F(n, m), & k = m \\ 0, & otherwise, \end{cases} \qquad (11.3.1)$$

*where the **forward price** $F(n, m)$ is such that the time-n value of the cash-flow stream is 0.*

Figure 11.20 illustrates the cash flows of the forward contract on a time diagram.

FIGURE **11.20** | *Cash Flow of a Forward Contract*

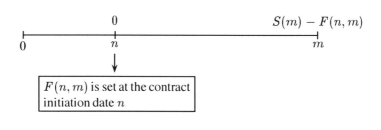

**Theorem 11.3.2.** *For each choice of contract initiation date n and delivery date m, $0 \leq n < m \leq T$, the forward price is*

$$F(n, m) = \frac{S(n)}{P(n, m)},$$

*if the asset does not pay dividends between time n and time m.*

**Proof.** *The cash-flow stream for the forward contract is required to have zero value at the contract initiation date. Consequently,*

$$0 = E^Q \left[ e^{-[r(n)+r(n+1)+\cdots+r(m-1)]} \{ S(m) - F(n, m) \} \,\big|\, \mathcal{P}_n \right]$$
$$= S(n) - F(n, m) P(n, m).$$

*Therefore,*

$$F(n, m) = \frac{S(n)}{P(n, m)}.$$

## SECTION 11.3.2 | FUTURES PRICES

As discussed in Chapter 2, futures contracts differ from forward contracts in several important institutional details. The most significant difference is that futures contracts are marked to market. The pricing of futures contracts will proceed in analogy to that of forward contracts. As was the case for forward contracts, for every security in the model and each choice of times $n$ and $m$ with $0 \le n < m \le T$, a futures contract on that security exists with contract initiation date $n$ and delivery date $m$. If such a futures contract is made on a particular security, we denote the futures price for this contract by $f(n, m)$. For each fixed value of $m$ we can consider the adapted process of futures prices $\{f(0, m), f(1, m), \ldots, f(m-1, m)\}$. These futures prices will be determined so that the value of the remaining cash-flow stream is equal to zero at each point in time. We now give a formal definition of a futures contract and characterize the futures prices.

**Definition 11.3.3.** *A **futures contract** on an asset with price process S and with contract initiation date n and delivery date m, $0 \le n < m \le T$, is a security with cash-flow stream equal to*

$$c(k+1) = \begin{cases} f(k+1, m) - f(k, m), & k = n, n+1, \ldots, m-2 \\ S(m) - f(m-1, m), & k = m-1 \end{cases} \qquad (11.3.2)$$

*where the **futures prices** $f(n, m)$ are such that the value of the remaining cash-flow stream is 0 at each point in time.*

Figure 11.21 illustrates the key points of the futures contract on a time-line diagram.

### FIGURE 11.21 | Cash-Flow Stream of a Futures Contract

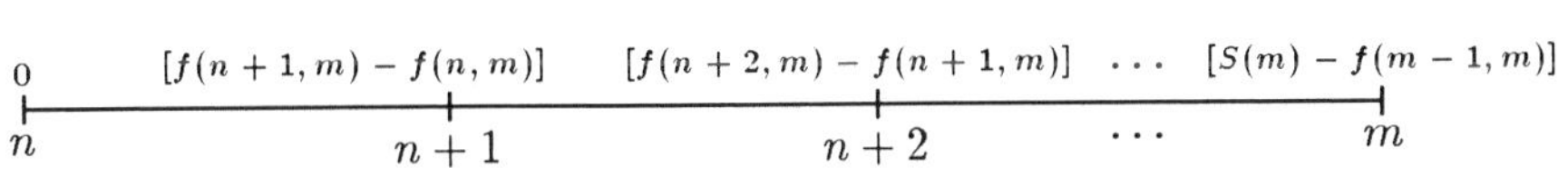

**Theorem 11.3.4.** *For each choice of contract initiation date n and delivery date m, $0 \le n < m \le T$, the futures price satisfies*

$$f(n, m) = E^Q[S(m) \mid \mathcal{P}_n]. \qquad (11.3.3)$$

**Proof.** *Recall that the value process $V = \{V(n)\}$ for a cash-flow stream $\{c(k); k = 1, \ldots, m\}$ is given by*

$$V(n) = \mathrm{E}^Q \left[ \sum_{k=n+1}^{m} e^{-[r(n)+\cdots+r(k-1)]} c(k) \,\middle|\, \mathcal{P}_n \right];$$

*see Theorem 11.2.26 and (11.2.32). For the futures contract, the cash-flow stream is given by (11.3.2).*

*The recursive valuation formula (11.2.33) for the futures contract takes the form*

$$V(n) = \mathrm{E}^Q \left[ e^{-r(n)} [\, f(n+1, m) - f(n, m)] + e^{-r(n)} V(n+1) \,\middle|\, \mathcal{P}_n \right].$$

*Since the value process is always $0$, $V(n) = V(n+1) = 0$, and we have*

$$0 = \mathrm{E}^Q \left[ e^{-r(n)} [\, f(n+1, m) - f(n, m)] \,\middle|\, \mathcal{P}_n \right]. \tag{11.3.4}$$

*Hence, $f(n, m) = \mathrm{E}^Q[\, f(n+1, m) \mid \mathcal{P}_n]$. Since $f(m, m) = S(m)$, the result follows by iterated expectations.*

Equation (11.3.4) can be interpreted as follows. An investor buys or takes a long position in a futures contract at time $n$. The futures price at time $n$ is such that the value of the position is zero, which is the left-hand side of (11.3.4). (At each point of time, an investor can take a long position or a short position in the futures contract; the futures price at that time is such that the value of taking either position is zero.) Marking to market occurs at the time $n + 1$; the investor receives the amount $f(n + 1, m) - f(n, m)$ (or pays, if the amount is negative). The time-$n$ value of this amount is the right-hand side of (11.3.4). After marking to market, the futures contract confers on the investor no other value; hence, we have (11.3.4).

It follows from (11.3.3) that the futures price process $\{ f(n, m); n = 0, \ldots, m\}$ is a martingale under the risk-neutral probability measure $Q$. This fact has been asserted in Section 7.8; (11.3.3) and (7.8.1) are the same. Furthermore, $f(m, m) = S(m)$, the asset price at time $m$. Hence, for a futures contract with delivery date $m$, the futures price process and the asset price process "converge" at time $m$. The futures price process is an example of Doob martingales; see Example A.5.3.

### SECTION 11.3.3 | WHEN INTEREST RATES ARE DETERMINISTIC, FUTURES AND FORWARD PRICES AGREE

**Theorem 11.3.5.** *If interest rates are deterministic, that is, if*

$$r(n, \omega) \equiv r_n, \quad \omega \in \Omega,$$

*for $n = 0, \ldots, T - 1$, then $f(n, m) = F(n, m)$, $n = 0, \ldots, m$.*

**Proof.**

$$f(n, m) = \mathrm{E}^Q[S(m) \mid \mathcal{P}_n]$$

$$= e^{r_n + \cdots + r_{m-1}} \mathrm{E}^Q\left[e^{-(r_n + \cdots + r_{m-1})} S(m) \mid \mathcal{P}_n\right]$$

$$= e^{r_n + \cdots + r_{m-1}} S(n),$$

$$F(n, m) = \frac{S(n)}{P(n, m)}$$

$$= e^{r_n + \cdots + r_{m-1}} S(n).$$

**Example 11.3.1.** Consider a two-period model with risk-neutral conditional probabilities and short rate of interest (compounded continuously) as shown in Figure 11.22. The asset on which a futures or forward contract with delivery date at time 2 is written is assumed to follow the price process shown in Figure 11.23.

FIGURE **11.22** | *Risk-Neutral Conditional Probabilities and Short Rates of Interest*

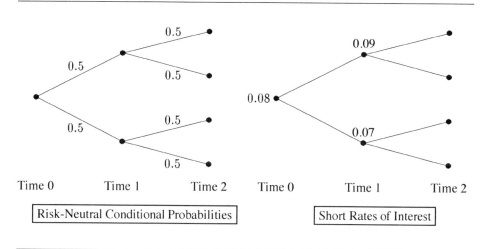

Risk-Neutral Conditional Probabilities

Short Rates of Interest

We can compute the prices of zero-coupon bonds as indicated in Figure 11.24:

$$e^{-0.09} = 0.91393,$$

$$e^{-0.07} = 0.93239,$$

$$P(0, 2) = e^{0.08}(0.5e^{-0.09} + 0.5e^{-0.07}) = 0.85219.$$

FIGURE **11.23** | *Asset Price Process*

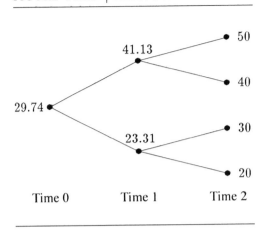

FIGURE **11.24** | *Zero-Coupon Bond Prices*

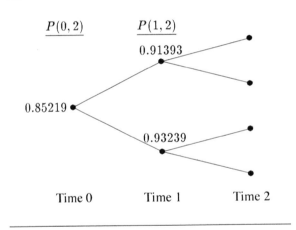

The futures contract prices for the model are shown in Figure 11.25 and are calculated as follows:

$$f(1, 2) = E^Q[S(2) \mid \mathcal{P}_1],$$

$$45 = 0.5(50) + 0.5(40),$$

$$25 = 0.5(30) + 0.5(20),$$

$$f(0, 2) = E^Q[S(2)]$$

$$= 0.25(50) + 0.25(40) + 0.25(30) + 0.25(20)$$

$$= 35.$$

FIGURE **11.25** | *Futures Prices*

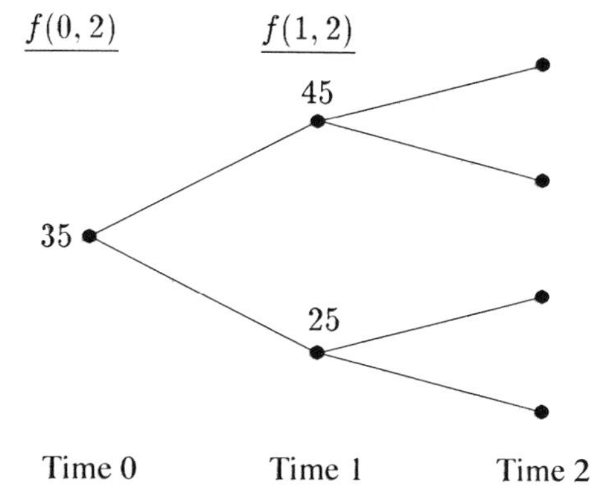

$f(0, 2)$        $f(1, 2)$

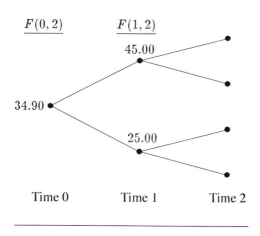

Alternatively, we can calculate $f(0, 2)$ as $E^Q[f(1, 2)]$. Note that in Figure 11.25 we did not label the futures contract prices at time 2 because they are just the asset price at that time. The forward contract prices for this model are shown in Figure 11.26 and are computed as follows:

$$F(1, 2) = \frac{S(1)}{P(1, 2)},$$

$$45.00 = \frac{41.13}{0.91393},$$

$$25.00 = \frac{23.31}{0.93239}.$$

FIGURE **11.26** | *Forward Prices*

$F(0, 2)$        $F(1, 2)$

Note that $F(1, 2) = f(1, 2)$. The forward and futures prices at each node at time 1 agree because, with one period to the delivery date, interest rates are deterministic. Finally,

$$F(0, 2) = \frac{S(0)}{P(0, 2)}$$

$$= \frac{29.74}{0.85219} = 34.90,$$

which is different from $f(0, 2)$. ∎

**Example 11.3.2.** The primitive assets in this and the next examples consist of the locally riskless money market account and the asset on which the futures or forward contract is written. Each model is arbitrage free and complete. Figure 11.27 gives the local state prices and the asset price process for the asset on which the forward or futures contract is written.

FIGURE **11.27** │ *Local State Prices and Asset Price Process for Example 11.3.2*

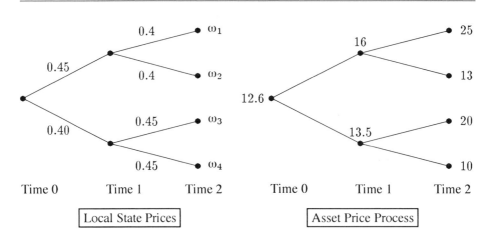

Recall that the implied discount factors are obtained by summing the local state prices of each node of the information structure. For instance,

$$e^{-r(0)} = 0.45 + 0.40 = 0.85.$$

The implied discount factors are

$$e^{-r(0)} = 0.85, \qquad e^{-r(1.\omega_1)} = 0.8, \qquad e^{-r(1.\omega_3)} = 0.9.$$

Therefore, interest rates are fully stochastic and not deterministic. Futures prices for delivery at time 2 are depicted in Figure 11.28. These were computed as follows. We use the symbol $f$ as a dummy variable to denote the futures price we are solving for at each node. For the upper node at time 1,

$$0 = 0.4(25 - f) + 0.4(15 - f);$$

hence, $f = 20$. For the lower node at time 1,

$$0 = 0.45(20 - f) + 0.45(10 - f),$$

yielding $f = 15$. Finally, for the node at time 0,

$$0 = 0.45(20 - f) + 0.4(15 - f),$$

yielding $f = 17.65$.

FIGURE **11.28** | *Futures Prices for Delivery at Time 2 for Example 11.3.2*

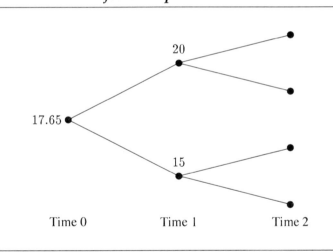

Since there is only one period remaining to delivery at time 1, we know that $F(1, 2) = f(1, 2)$. The price at time 0 of a two-period zero-coupon bond is

$$P(0, 2) = 0.45(0.8) + 0.4(0.9) = 0.36 + 0.36 = 0.72.$$

Therefore, the forward price at time 0 is

$$F(0, 2) = \frac{12.6}{0.72} = 17.5.$$

Notice that $F(0, 2) \neq f(0, 2)$.  ∎

**Example 11.3.3.** Figure 11.29 gives the local state prices and the asset price process for the asset on which the forward or futures contract is written. We can verify that the implied discount factors are

$$e^{-r(0)} = 0.85, \qquad e^{-r(1.\omega_1)} = e^{-r(1.\omega_3)} = 0.9.$$

In particular, interest rates are deterministic.

FIGURE **11.29** | *Local State Prices and Asset Price Process for Example 11.3.3*

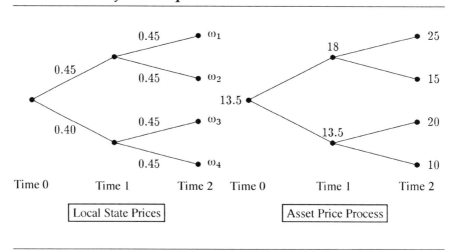

The futures prices for delivery at time 2 are shown in Figure 11.30. Again, we let $f$ denote a dummy variable for the futures price we are computing. The sequence of calculations is as follows:

$$0 = 0.45(25 - f) + 0.45(15 - f)$$

from which $f = 20$;

$$0 = 0.45(20 - f) + 0.45(10 - f)$$

from which $f = 15$; and

$$0 = 0.45(20 - f) + 0.4(15 - f)$$

from which $f = 17.65$.

Since interest rates are deterministic, we know that the futures and forward prices are the same in this model. We can check this by direct calculation of $F(0, 2)$. We compute the price at time 0 of a two-period zero-coupon bond as

$$P(0, 2) = 0.45(0.9) + 0.4(0.9) = 0.765.$$

FIGURE **11.30** | *Futures Prices for Delivery at Time 2 for Example 11.3.3*

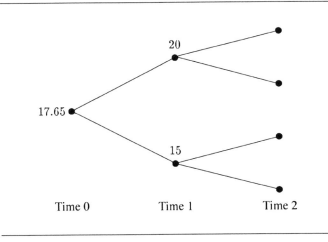

Time 0                Time 1                Time 2

Therefore,

$$F(0, 2) = \frac{13.5}{0.765} = 17.65.$$

Example 11.3.2 shows that when interest rates are stochastic, the futures and forward prices will generally be different. For Examples 11.3.2 and 11.3.3, the implied risk-neutral conditional probabilities are shown in Figure 11.31. Therefore, the

FIGURE **11.31** | *Risk-Neutral Conditional Probabilities for Examples 11.3.2 and 11.3.3*

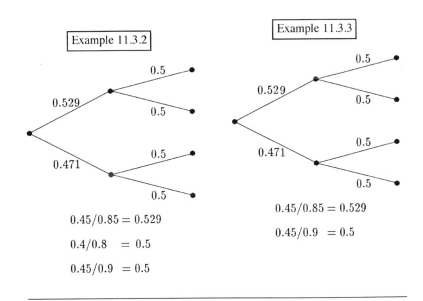

risk-neutral conditional probabilities, and thus the risk-neutral probabilities, are identical for these two examples. Since $f(n, m) = E^Q[S(m) \mid \mathcal{P}_n]$, this explains why the futures prices in both models are the same. Indeed, $Q$ is the same in both models and $S(2)$ are the same in both models, even though $S(1)$ and $S(0)$ differ across the two examples.

# Section 11.4
# Valuation Theory for American Options

The pricing of American options is significantly more complicated than the pricing of adapted cash-flow streams that we have been discussing thus far. Not only are the cash flows associated with an American option stochastic, but since the option holder can exercise the option on a discretionary basis, the cash flows associated with an American option cannot be described as a standard cash-flow stream. Therefore, the valuation of American options requires some additional theory that was not developed as part of our framework for pricing adapted cash-flow streams.

The holder of an American option is able to choose the time to exercise the option subject only to the requirement that the decision to exercise the option at a particular point in time must be made only on the basis of the information available up to that point in time. Mathematically, we are requiring that the time at which the option is exercised be a stopping time; see Subsection A.1.5 of Appendix A for a discussion of stopping times. Aside from the requirement that the decision to exercise the option at a particular point in time be made only on the basis of the information available up to that point in time, option holders are free to exercise the option in any manner they choose. In particular, the writer of the American option does not know which stopping time the option holder will employ. Consequently, the writer of the American option needs to have enough money on hand at each point in time to pay all possible exercise patterns allowable under the option. Our analysis of the pricing of American options will involve this requirement.

Stopping times are used to represent the time at which an action is taken under circumstances in which the decision to act or not at time $k$ depends only on the information available at time $k$, $k \leq T$. It is convenient to think of stopping times in these terms. Recall that, from our interpretation of the information structure, at time $k$ we can tell apart only market outcomes that belong to separate elements of $\mathcal{P}_k$. Thus, if a particular action is decided upon at time $k$ along market outcome $\omega^*$, the same action will be taken at time $k$ for all market outcomes in $\mathcal{H}^{(k)}(\omega^*)$, because $\omega^*$ cannot be distinguished from any of the elements in $\mathcal{H}^{(k)}(\omega^*)$ on the basis of the information available at time $k$. Consequently, the collection of market outcomes for which the decision to act at time $k$ is made will be either empty or a union of a subset of the elements of $\mathcal{P}_k \equiv \{\mathcal{H}_1^{(k)}, \ldots, \mathcal{H}_{v_k}^{(k)}\}$. This leads us to the formal definition of a stopping time.

**Definition 11.4.1.** *A mapping* $\tau : \Omega \rightarrow \{0, 1, \ldots\}$ *is said to be a* **stopping time** *if for each* $k \in \{0, 1, \ldots\}$, *the set* $\{\omega \mid \tau(\omega) = k\}$ *is either empty or equal to a union of a subset of the elements of* $\mathcal{P}_k$.[3]

The symbol $\mathcal{S}^{(0)}$ is used to denote the collection of stopping times, $\tau : \Omega \rightarrow \{1, \ldots, T\}$ on the filtered probability space $(\Omega, P, \{\mathcal{P}_k\})$. Since the probability space is finite and the range of $\tau$ is finite, there are only finitely many stopping times in $\mathcal{S}^{(0)}$. For each $k \in \{1, \ldots, T\}$ and $i \in \{1, \ldots, v_k\}$, the symbol $\mathcal{S}_i^{(k)}$ is used to denote the collection of stopping times, $\tau : \mathcal{H}_i^{(k)} \rightarrow \{0, \ldots, T - k\}$ on the filtered probability space $(\mathcal{H}_i^{(k)}, P(\cdot \mid \mathcal{H}_i^{(k)}), \{\mathcal{H}_i^{(k)} \cap \mathcal{P}_{k+1}, \ldots, \mathcal{H}_i^{(k)} \cap \mathcal{P}_T\})$. The set $\mathcal{S}_i^{(k)}$ is finite. We let $\mathcal{S}^{(k)} = \bigcup_{i=1}^{v_k} \mathcal{S}_i^{(k)}$. We now assume that we are in an arbitrage-free and complete market securities market model. Furthermore, all assets are assumed to be non-dividend paying, although it is possible to remove this restriction.

**Definition 11.4.2.** *An* **American option** *with* **pay off** *or* **payment characteristics** *defined by the nonnegative adapted process* $\{g(k)\}$ *is a security that can deliver any one of the random cash flows* $\{g(\tau) \mid \tau \in \mathcal{S}^{(0)}\}$ *and that will deliver the random cash flow* $\{g(\tau^*)\}$ *for some* $\tau^* \in \mathcal{S}^{(0)}$ *as selected by the option holder. Of course,* $\tau^*$ *is not known to the market ex ante.*

The definition formalizes the idea that an American option can be exercised any time prior to its expiration date.

**Example 11.4.1.** American options include:

- An American put option written on an asset with price process $\{S_2(k)\}$ and strike price $K$ has the payment characteristics $\{g(k)\} = [K - S_2(k)]^+$.
- An American lookback option written on an asset with price process $\{S_2(k)\}$ has the payment characteristics $\{g(k)\} = \max_{j=0,\ldots,k}\{S_2(j)\}$.
- An American Asian call option written on an asset with price process $\{S_2(k)\}$ and strike price $K$ has the payment characteristics $\{g(k)\} = [\sum_{j=1}^{k} S_2(j)/k - K]^+$. ■

---

[3]Because of the correspondence between the partition $\mathcal{P}_k$ and its generated algebra $\mathcal{F}_k = \sigma(\mathcal{P}_k)$, an equivalent definition of stopping time is the following: "A mapping $G : \Omega \rightarrow \{0, 1, \ldots\}$ is said to be a stopping time if $\{\omega \mid \tau(\omega) = k\} \in \mathcal{F}_k$ for each $k \in \{0, 1, \ldots\}$." This is explained in Section A.1.5 of Appendix A.

**Definition 11.4.3.** *Consider an American option with payment characteristics defined by the adapted process $\{g(k)\}$. A trading strategy, $\theta$, is said to* **dominate** *the American option if $\theta$ is such that*

*a.* $\quad S(k, \omega)\theta(k-1, \omega) \geq g(k, \omega), \quad k = 1, \ldots, T, \omega \in \Omega,$ *and*

*b.* $\quad S(k, \omega)\theta(k-1, \omega) - S(k, \omega)\theta(k, \omega) \geq 0, \quad k = 1, \ldots, T, \omega \in \Omega.$

Sometimes it is convenient to omit the dependence on $\omega$. In such a case, condition (a) would be written as $S(k)\theta(k) \geq g(k)$, and it would be understood this holds across all market outcomes. Condition (a) says that the value of the portfolio is always sufficient to pay the amount (or claim) that can be demanded under the American option. Condition (b) says that no new funds need to be injected into the portfolio after the initial investment is made. The inequality in condition (b) leaves open the possibility that funds can be withdrawn under some circumstances. The collection of trading strategies that dominates the American option is denoted by $\Theta$. As we are assuming that we are in an arbitrage-free securities market model that is also complete, thus we have a unique equivalent martingale measure available for valuation. Equivalently, a unique state price process exists for the model. The numeraire asset associated with the equivalent martingale measure is denoted by $B$.

**Definition 11.4.4.** *Consider an American option with payment characteristics $\{g(k)\}$ and associated family of dominating trading strategies $\Theta$. If $\theta^* \in \Theta$ exists such that*

$$S(0, \omega)\theta^*(0, \omega) = \inf\{S(0, \omega)\theta(0, \omega) \mid \theta \in \Theta\}, \qquad (11.4.1)$$

*then the American option is said to be priced and to have the price equal to $S(0, \omega)\,\theta^*(0, \omega)$.*

Intuitively, then, the price of an American option is the cost of the cheapest trading strategy that can meet all future cash-flow obligations from the option. The value $S(0, \omega)\theta^*(0, \omega)$ does not depend on $\omega$.

**Definition 11.4.5.** *We define an adapted process $V$ as follows:*

$$V(0) = \max_{\tau \in \mathcal{S}^{(0)}} E^Q \left[ \frac{1}{B(\tau)} g(\tau) \right]$$

*and*

$$V(k) = \max_{\tau \in \mathcal{S}^{(k)}} E^Q \left[ \frac{B(k)}{B(\tau)} g(k+\tau) \,\middle|\, \mathcal{P}_k \right]$$

*for $k = 1, \ldots, T$.*

The process $V$ will be referred to as the *value process* for the American option. The value process is critical in establishing our characterization of the price of an American option. We now present a series of results leading to our characterization of the price of an American option. The proofs of these results are given in terms of state prices. The corresponding proofs can be given using the risk-neutral probability measure.

The following result is essential in characterizing the price of an American option. It is also the basis for computing the prices of American option.

***Theorem 11.4.6 (Recursive Pricing Relation).*** *The process* $V = \{V(k)\}$ *satisfies the following recursive relationship:*

$$V(k) = \max \left[ g(k),\ \mathrm{E}^Q \left[ \frac{B(k+1)}{B(k)} V(k+1) \,\middle|\, \mathcal{P}_k \right] \right] \qquad (11.4.2)$$

*for $k = 1, \ldots, T$, or equivalently,*

$$V(k, \omega^*) = \max \left[ g(k, \omega^*),\ \sum_{\omega \in \mathcal{H}^{(k)}(\omega^*) \cap \Omega^{(k+1)}} \frac{v^{(k+1)}(\omega)\psi(k+1, \omega)}{v^{(k)}(\omega)\psi(k, \omega)} V(k+1, \omega) \right],$$
$$(11.4.3)$$

*for $k = 1, \ldots, T$, $\omega^* \in \Omega$.*

***Proof.*** *Since $\mathcal{S}^{(0)}$ is a finite set, $\tau^* \in \mathcal{S}^{(0)}$ exists such that*

$$V(0) = \sum_{\omega \in \Omega} \psi(\tau^*(\omega), \omega) g(\tau^*(\omega), \omega). \qquad (11.4.4)$$

*Here $\tau^*(\omega) \geq 1$ for all $\omega \in \Omega$ so that $\tau^* - 1$ restricted to $\mathcal{H}_j^{(1)}$ is a stopping time in $\mathcal{S}_j^{(1)}$:*

$$\sum_{\omega \in \Omega} \psi(\tau^*(\omega), \omega) g(\tau^*(\omega), \omega)$$

$$= \sum_{\omega \in \Omega^{(1)}} \sum_{\omega' \in \mathcal{H}^{(1)}(\omega)} \psi(\tau^*(\omega'), \omega') g(\tau^*(\omega'), \omega')$$

$$= \sum_{\omega \in \Omega^{(1)}} v^{(1)}(\omega)\psi(1, \omega) \frac{1}{v^{(1)}(\omega)\psi(1, \omega)} \sum_{\omega' \in \mathcal{H}^{(1)}(\omega)} \psi(\omega', \tau^*(\omega')) g(\tau^*(\omega'), \omega')$$
$$(11.4.5)$$

$$= \sum_{\omega \in \Omega^{(1)}} v^{(1)}(\omega)\psi(1, \omega) \frac{1}{v^{(1)}(\omega)\psi(1, \omega)}$$

$$\times \sum_{\omega' \in \mathcal{H}^{(1)}(\omega)} \psi(1 + [\tau^*(\omega', \omega') - 1], \omega') g(1 + [\tau^*(\omega') - 1], \omega'). \quad (11.4.6)$$

*We claim that for each $\omega \in \Omega^{(1)}$,*

$$V(1, \omega) = \frac{1}{v^{(1)}(\omega)\psi(1, \omega)} \sum_{\omega' \in \mathcal{H}^{(1)}(\omega)} \psi(1+[\tau^*(\omega')-1], \omega')g(1+[\tau^*(\omega')-1], \omega').$$

(11.4.7)

*Indeed, if this is not true, then for some $\omega \in \Omega^{(1)}$ a stopping time $U \in \mathcal{S}^{(1)}(\omega)$ exists such that*

$$\frac{1}{v^{(1)}(\omega)\psi(1, \omega)} \sum_{\omega' \in \mathcal{H}^{(1)}(\omega)} \psi(1 + [\tau^*(\omega') - 1], \omega')g(1 + [\tau^*(\omega') - 1], \omega')$$

$$< \frac{1}{v^{(1)}(\omega)\psi(1, \omega)} \sum_{\omega' \in \mathcal{H}^{(1)}(\omega)} \psi(1 + U(\omega'), \omega')g(1 + U(\omega'), \omega'). \quad (11.4.8)$$

*We can then construct a new stopping time $\hat{\tau} \in \mathcal{S}^{(0)}$ by*

$$\hat{\tau}(\omega') = \tau^*(\omega')1_{(\mathcal{H}^{(1)}(\omega))^c}(\omega') + [1 + U(\omega')]1_{\mathcal{H}^{(1)}(\omega)}(\omega').$$

*Since relation (11.4.5) holds for any stopping time in $\mathcal{S}^{(0)}$, combining (11.4.5) and (11.4.8) yields*

$$\sum_{\omega \in \Omega} \psi(\hat{\tau}(\omega), \omega)g(\hat{\tau}(\omega), \omega) > \sum_{\omega \in \Omega} \psi(\tau^*(\omega), \omega)g(\tau^*(\omega), \omega) = V(0),$$

*in contradiction to the definition of $V(0)$. Consequently, (11.4.7) must hold. Combining (11.4.7) with (11.4.6) then implies*

$$V(0) = \sum_{\omega \in \Omega^{(1)}} v^{(1)}(\omega)\psi(1, \omega)V(1, \omega).$$

*The proof of the relation for $V(k, \omega^*)$ is nominally more involved because the zero stopping time in $\mathcal{S}^{(k)}(\omega^*)$ is not an element of $\mathcal{S}^{(k+1)}(\omega)$ for any $\omega \in \mathcal{H}^{(k)}(\omega^*) \cap \Omega^{(k+1)}$. However, we next show that a similar argument suffices.*

*The following algebraic relation is valid for any $\tau \in \mathcal{S}^{(k)}(\omega^*)$:*

$$\frac{1}{v^{(k)}(\omega^*)\psi(k, \omega^*)} \sum_{\omega \in \mathcal{H}^{(k)}(\omega^*)} \psi(k + \tau(\omega), \omega)g(k + \tau(\omega), \omega)$$

$$= \frac{1}{v^{(k)}(\omega^*)\psi(k, \omega^*)}$$

$$\times \sum_{\omega \in \mathcal{H}^{(k)}(\omega^*) \cap \Omega^{(k+1)}} \sum_{\omega' \in \mathcal{H}^{(k+1)}(\omega)} \psi(k + \tau(\omega'), \omega')g(k + \tau(\omega'), \omega')$$

$$= \frac{1}{v^{(k)}(\omega^*)\psi(k, \omega^*)} \sum_{\omega \in \mathcal{H}^{(k)}(\omega^*) \cap \Omega^{(k+1)}} v^{(k+1)}(\omega)\psi(k + 1, \omega)$$

$$\times \frac{1}{v^{(k+1)}(\omega)\psi(k + 1, \omega)} \sum_{\omega' \in \mathcal{H}^{(k+1)}(\omega)} \psi(k + \tau(\omega'), \omega')g(k + \tau(\omega'), \omega').$$
(11.4.9)

Let $\tau^* \in \mathcal{S}^{(k)}(\omega^*)$ be such that

$$V(k, \omega^*) = \frac{1}{v^{(k)}(\omega^*)\psi(k, \omega^*)} \sum_{\omega \in \mathcal{H}^{(k)}(\omega^*)} \psi(k + \tau^*(\omega), \omega)g(k + \tau^*(\omega), \omega).$$
(11.4.10)

Such a $\tau^*$ exists by the definition of $V(k, \omega^*)$. There are two cases: either $\tau^*$ is the zero stopping time or $\tau^*$ is not the zero stopping time.

If $\tau^*$ is the zero stopping time (that is, $\tau^*(\omega) = 0$ for all $\omega \in \mathcal{H}^{(k)}(\omega^*)$), then by (11.4.10), we have

$$V(k, \omega^*) = g(k, \omega^*).$$

Therefore, by definition of V, for each $\tau \in \mathcal{S}^{(k)}(\omega^*)$ we would have

$$g(k, \omega^*) = V(k, \omega^*)$$

$$\geq \sum_{\omega \in \mathcal{H}^{(k)}(\omega^*) \cap \Omega^{(k+1)}} \frac{v^{(k+1)}(\omega)\psi(k + 1, \omega)}{v^{(k)}(\omega^*)\psi(k, \omega^*)} \frac{1}{v^{(k+1)}(\omega)\psi(k + 1, \omega)}$$

$$\times \sum_{\omega' \in \mathcal{H}^{(k+1)}(\omega)} \psi(k + \tau(\omega'), \omega')g(k + \tau(\omega'), \omega'). \qquad (11.4.11)$$

For each $\omega \in \mathcal{H}^{(k)}(\omega^*) \cap \Omega^{(k+1)}$, a stopping time $U_\omega \in \mathcal{S}^{(k+1)}(\omega)$ exists such that

$$V(k + 1, \omega) = \frac{1}{v^{(k+1)}(\omega)\psi(k + 1, \omega)}$$

$$\times \sum_{\omega' \in \mathcal{H}^{(k+1)}(\omega)} \psi(k + 1 + U_\omega(\omega'), \omega')g(k + 1 + U_\omega(\omega'), \omega').$$
(11.4.12)

Define the stopping time $\hat{\tau} \in \mathcal{S}^{(k)}(\omega^*)$ by

$$\hat{\tau}(\omega') = \sum_{\omega \in \mathcal{H}^{(k+1)}(\omega^*) \cap \Omega^{(k+1)}} [1 + U_\omega(\omega')]1_{\mathcal{H}^{(k+1)}(\omega)}(\omega').$$

Then

$$\frac{1}{v^{(k+1)}(\omega)\psi(k + 1, \omega)} \sum_{\omega' \in \mathcal{H}^{(k+1)}(\omega)} \psi(k + \hat{\tau}(\omega'), \omega')g(k + \hat{\tau}(\omega'), \omega')$$

$$= \frac{1}{v^{(k+1)}(\omega)\psi(k+1, \omega)}$$

$$\times \sum_{\omega' \in \mathcal{H}^{(k+1)}(\omega)} \psi(k+1+U_\omega(\omega'), \omega')g(k+1+U_\omega(\omega'), \omega') \quad (11.4.13)$$

$$= V(k+1, \omega) \quad (by \ (11.4.12)) \quad (11.4.14)$$

for each $\omega \in \mathcal{H}^{(k)}(\omega^*) \cap \Omega^{(k+1)}$. Since $\hat{\tau} \in \mathcal{S}^{(k)}(\omega^*)$, we therefore obtain

$$g(k, \omega^*) \geq \sum_{\omega \in \mathcal{H}^{(k)}(\omega^*) \cap \Omega^{(k+1)}} \frac{v^{(k+1)}(\omega)\psi(k+1, \omega)}{v^{(k)}(\omega^*)\psi(k, \omega^*)} V(k+1, \omega) \quad (11.4.15)$$

from combining (11.4.13) with (11.4.11).

If $\tau^*$ is not the zero stopping time, then $\tau^*(\omega) \geq 1$, for all $\omega \in \mathcal{H}^{(k)}(\omega^*)$. Hence, for each $\omega \in \mathcal{H}^{(k)}(\omega^*) \cap \Omega^{(k+1)}$ the restriction of $\tau^* - 1$ to $\mathcal{H}^{(k+1)}(\omega)$ is an element of $\mathcal{S}^{(k+1)}(\omega)$. We claim that

$$V(k+1, \omega) = \frac{1}{v^{(k+1)}(\omega)\psi(k+1, \omega)} \sum_{\omega' \in \mathcal{H}^{(k+1)}(\omega)} \psi(k+1+[\tau^*(\omega')-1], \omega')$$

$$\times g(k+1+[\tau^*(\omega')-1], \omega') \quad (11.4.16)$$

for each $\omega \in \mathcal{H}^{(k)}(\omega^*) \cap \Omega^{(k+1)}$. Otherwise, for some $\omega \in \mathcal{H}^{(k)}(\omega^*) \cap \Omega^{(k+1)}$ a stopping time $U_\omega \in \mathcal{S}^{(k+1)}(\omega)$ must exist such that

$$\frac{1}{v^{(k+1)}(\omega)\psi(k+1, \omega)}$$

$$\times \sum_{\omega' \in \mathcal{H}^{(k+1)}(\omega)} \psi(k+1+[\tau^*(\omega')-1], \omega')g(k+1+[\tau^*(\omega')-1], \omega')$$

$$< \frac{1}{v^{(k+1)}(\omega)\psi(k+1, \omega)}$$

$$\times \sum_{\omega' \in \mathcal{H}^{(k+1)}(\omega)} \psi(k+1+U_\omega(\omega'), \omega')g(k+1+U_\omega(\omega'), \omega'). \quad (11.4.17)$$

We can construct a stopping time $\hat{\tau}$ in $\mathcal{S}^{(k)}(\omega^*)$ by

$$\hat{\tau}(\omega') = \tau^*(\omega')1_{(\mathcal{H}^{(k+1)}(\omega))^c}(\omega') + [1+U_\omega(\omega')]1_{\mathcal{H}^{(k+1)}(\omega)}(\omega').$$

(It can be verified that $\hat{\tau} \in \mathcal{S}^{(k)}(\omega^*)$.) It follows from (11.4.17) and (11.4.9) that

$$V(k, \omega^*) = \frac{1}{v^{(k)}(\omega^*)\psi(k, \omega^*)} \sum_{\omega \in \mathcal{H}^{(k)}(\omega^*)} \psi(k+\tau^*(\omega), \omega)g(k+\tau^*(\omega), \omega)$$

$$< \sum_{\omega \in \mathcal{H}^{(k)}(\omega^*) \cap \Omega^{(k+1)}} \frac{v^{(k+1)}(\omega)\psi(k+1, \omega)}{v^{(k)}(\omega^*)\psi(k, \omega^*)}$$

$$\times \frac{1}{v^{(k+1)}(\omega)\psi(k+1, \omega)} \sum_{\omega' \in \mathcal{H}^{(k+1)}(\omega)} \psi(k + \hat{\tau}(\omega'), \omega')g(k + \hat{\tau}(\omega'), \omega').$$

$$(11.4.18)$$

*Since $\hat{\tau} \in \mathcal{S}^{(k)}(\omega^*)$, (11.4.18) cannot be valid, and thus (11.4.16) must hold. Applying (11.4.16) to (11.4.9) yields* [4]

$$V(k, \omega^*) = \sum_{\omega \in \mathcal{H}^{(k)}(\omega^*) \cap \Omega^{(k+1)}} \frac{v^{(k+1)}(\omega)\psi(k+1, \omega)}{v^{(k)}(\omega)\psi(k, \omega)} V(k+1, \omega). \qquad (11.4.19)$$

*Thus, we have shown that when $\tau^*$ is the zero stopping time:*

a.     $V(k, \omega^*) = g(k, \omega^*)$,

b.     $g(k, \omega^*) \geq \displaystyle\sum_{\omega \in \mathcal{H}^{(k)}(\omega^*) \cap \Omega^{(k+1)}} \frac{v^{(k+1)}(\omega)\psi(k+1, \omega)}{v^{(k)}(\omega)\psi(k, \omega)} V(k+1, \omega)$,

*and that when $\tau^*$ is not the zero stopping time,*

c.     $V(k, \omega^*) = \displaystyle\sum_{\omega \in \mathcal{H}^{(k)}(\omega^*) \cap \Omega^{(k+1)}} \frac{v^{(k+1)}(\omega)\psi(k+1, \omega)}{v^{(k)}(\omega)\psi(k, \omega)} V(k+1, \omega)$

d.     $g(k, \omega^*) \leq V(k, \omega^*)$

$$= \sum_{\omega \in \mathcal{H}^{(k)}(\omega^*) \cap \Omega^{(k+1)}} \frac{v^{(k+1)}\psi(k+1, \omega)}{v^{(k)}(\omega)\psi(k, \omega)} V(k+1, \omega).$$

*Therefore, in each of the two possible cases we see that*

$$V(k, \omega^*) = \max \left[ g(k, \omega^*), \sum_{\omega \in \mathcal{H}^{(k)}(\omega^*) \cap \Omega^{(k+1)}} \frac{v^{(k+1)}(\omega)\psi(k+1, \omega)}{v^{(k)}(\omega)\psi(k, \omega)} V(k+1, \omega) \right].$$

The following lemma is a variation of Theorem 11.2.9. In this section, the assets pay no dividends.

**Lemma 11.4.7.** *Suppose that the cash-flow stream $\{c(k)\}$ is financed by the trading strategy $\theta$. Then for $n = 0, \ldots, T - 1$,*

$$S(n, \omega^*)\theta(n, \omega^*) = \sum_{\omega \in \mathcal{H}^{(n)}(\omega^*) \cap \Omega^{(n+1)}} \frac{v^{(n+1)}(\omega)\psi(n+1, \omega)}{v^{(n)}(\omega)\psi(n, \omega)} S(n+1, \omega)\theta(n, \omega),$$

$$\omega \in \Omega. \qquad (11.4.20)$$

---

[4] Since $v^{(k)}(\omega)\psi(k, \omega)$ is constant on each set of $\mathcal{P}_k$, it is irrelevant whether we write $v^{(k)}(\omega)\psi(k, \omega)$ or $v^{(k)}(\omega^*)\psi(k, \omega^*)$.

**Theorem 11.4.8.** *If the securities market model is complete, then a trading strategy* $\theta$ *exists such that*

$$
\begin{array}{lll}
a. & S(k)\theta(k-1) = V(k), & k = 1, \ldots, T, \text{ and} \\
b. & S(k)\theta(k-1) - S(k)\theta(k) \geq 0, & k = 1, \ldots, T.
\end{array} \tag{11.4.21}
$$

**Proof.** *Define the cash-flow stream* $\{c(k); k = 1, \ldots, T\}$ *by*

$$
c(k, \omega^*) = \begin{cases}
V(k, \omega^*) - \displaystyle\sum_{\omega \in \mathcal{H}^{(k)}(\omega^*) \cap \Omega^{(k+1)}} \frac{v^{(k+1)}(\omega)\psi(k+1, \omega)}{v^{(k)}(\omega)\psi(k, \omega)} V(k+1, \omega), \\
\qquad\qquad\qquad\qquad\qquad\qquad\qquad\qquad \text{for } k = 1, \ldots, T-1 \\
V(T, \omega^*), \qquad\qquad\qquad\qquad\qquad\qquad \text{for } k = T.
\end{cases} \tag{11.4.22}
$$

*By the recursive relationship* (11.4.2) *we can write*

$$
V(k, \omega^*) = \sum_{\omega \in \mathcal{H}^{(k)}(\omega^*) \cap \Omega^{(k+1)}} \frac{v^{(k+1)}(\omega)\psi(k+1, \omega)}{v^{(k)}(\omega)\psi(k, \omega)} V(k+1, \omega)
$$

$$
+ \left[ g(k, \omega^*) - \sum_{\omega \in \mathcal{H}^{(k)}(\omega^*) \cap \Omega^{(k+1)}} \frac{v^{(k+1)}(\omega)\psi(k+1, \omega)}{v^{(k)}(\omega)\psi(k, \omega)} V(k+1, \omega) \right]^+ \tag{11.4.23}
$$

*for* $k = 1, \ldots, T-1$. *Thus, we find*

$$
c(k, \omega^*) = \begin{cases}
\left[ g(k, \omega^*) - \displaystyle\sum_{\omega \in \mathcal{H}^{(k)}(\omega^*) \cap \Omega^{(k+1)}} \frac{v^{(k+1)}(\omega)\psi(k+1, \omega)}{v^{(k)}(\omega)\psi(k, \omega)} V(k+1, \omega) \right]^+, \\
\qquad\qquad\qquad\qquad\qquad\qquad\qquad\qquad \text{for } k = 1, \ldots, T-1 \\
g(T, \omega^*), \qquad\qquad\qquad\qquad\qquad\qquad \text{for } k = T.
\end{cases} \tag{11.4.24}
$$

*Therefore,*

$$
c(k, \omega) \geq 0, \quad k = 1, \ldots, T, \omega \in \Omega.
$$

*It is also useful to rewrite* (11.4.23) *as*

$$
V(k, \omega^*) - c(k, \omega^*) = \sum_{\omega \in \mathcal{H}^{(k)}(\omega^*) \cap \Omega^{(k+1)}} \frac{v^{(k+1)}(\omega)\psi(k+1, \omega)}{v^{(k)}(\omega)\psi(k, \omega)} V(k+1, \omega),
$$

$$
\text{for } k = 1, \ldots, T-1. \tag{11.4.25}
$$

*Since the model is complete, a trading strategy* $\theta$ *exists that finances the cash-flow stream* $\{c(k)\}$. *We now show that conditions* (a) *and* (b) *hold for* $\theta$. *Clearly,*

$$S(T, \omega)\theta(T - 1, \omega) = c(T, \omega) = g(T, \omega).$$

*For a generic $\omega^* \in \Omega$,*

$$S(T - 1, \omega^*)\theta(T - 1, \omega^*)$$

$$= \sum_{\omega \in \mathcal{H}^{(T-1)}(\omega^*) \cap \Omega^{(T)}} \frac{v^{(T)}(\omega)\psi(T, \omega)}{v^{(T-1)}(\omega)\psi(T - 1, \omega)} g(T, \omega) \quad (by\ (11.4.20))$$

$$= V(T - 1, \omega^*) - c(T - 1, \omega^*) \quad (by\ (11.4.25)).$$

*Thus,*

$$S(T - 1, \omega^*)\theta(T - 2, \omega^*) = S(T - 1, \omega^*)\theta(T - 1, \omega^*) + c(T - 1, \omega^*)$$

$$= V(T - 1, \omega^*) - c(T - 1, \omega^*) + c(T - 1, \omega^*)$$

$$= V(T - 1, \omega^*).$$

*Hence, by (11.4.20), we have*

$$S(T - 2, \omega^*)\theta(T - 2, \omega^*)$$

$$= \sum_{\omega \in \mathcal{H}^{(T-2)}(\omega^*) \cap \Omega^{(T-1)}} \frac{v^{(T-1)}(\omega)\psi(T - 1, \omega)}{v^{(T-2)}(\omega)\psi(T - 2, \omega)} V(T - 1, \omega)$$

$$= V(T - 2, \omega^*) - c(T - 2, \omega^*) \quad (by\ (11.4.25)),$$

$$S(T - 2, \omega^*)\theta(T - 3, \omega^*)$$

$$= S(T - 2, \omega^*)\theta(T - 2, \omega^*) + c(T - 2, \omega^*)$$

$$= V(T - 2, \omega^*).$$

*Clearly, we can proceed inductively to obtain*

$$S(k, \omega^*)\theta(k - 1, \omega^*) = V(k, \omega^*), \quad k = 1, \ldots, T.$$

*Furthermore,*

$$S(k, \omega)\theta(k - 1, \omega) - S(k, \omega)\theta(k, \omega) = c(k, \omega),$$

*and we already have noted in (11.4) that $c(k, \omega) \geq 0, k = 1, \ldots, T, \omega \in \Omega$. Hence, $\theta$ satisfies (a) and (b).*

**Theorem 11.4.9.** *Consider an American option with payment characteristics defined by $\{g(k)\}$ and associated value process $\{V(k)\}$. If $\theta$ is a trading strategy that dominates the*

*American option, then*

$$S(k)\theta(k-1) \geq V(k), \quad k = 1, \ldots, T. \tag{11.4.26}$$

**Proof.** *Recall that, if the statement of the theorem is written using the definition of a dominating trading strategy, the claim is "If $\theta$ is a trading strategy such that*

a. $\quad S(k, \omega)\theta(k-1, \omega) \geq g(k, \omega), \quad k = 1, \ldots, T, \omega \in \Omega$

b. $\quad S(k, \omega)\theta(k-1, \omega) - S(k, \omega)\theta(k, \omega) \geq 0, \quad k = 1, \ldots, T, \omega \in \Omega,$

   *then*

$$S(k, \omega)\theta(k-1, \omega) \geq V(k, \omega), \quad k = 1, \ldots, T, \omega \in \Omega."$$

*Since $\theta$ is a dominating trading strategy, we have*

$$S(T, \omega)\theta(T-1, \omega) \geq g(T, \omega) \equiv V(T, \omega),$$

*and*

$$S(T-1, \omega^*)\theta(T-2, \omega^*)$$

$$= S(T-1, \omega^*)\theta(T-1, \omega^*) + c(T-1, \omega^*)$$

$$\geq S(T-1, \omega^*)\theta(T-1, \omega^*) \quad (by\ (b))$$

$$= \sum_{\omega \in \mathcal{H}^{(T-1)}(\omega^*) \cap \Omega^{(T)}} \frac{v^{(T)}(\omega)\psi(T, \omega)}{v^{(T-1)}(\omega)\psi(T-1, \omega)} S(T, \omega)\theta(T-1, \omega) \quad (by\ (11.4.20))$$

$$\geq \sum_{\omega \in \mathcal{H}^{(T-1)}(\omega^*) \cap \Omega^{(T)}} \frac{v^{(T)}(\omega)\psi(T, \omega)}{v^{(T-1)}(\omega)\psi(T-1, \omega)} g(T, \omega).$$

*(We are carrying the term $v^{(T)}(\omega)$, but since there is always full revelation of information at time $T$, $v^{(T)}(\omega) = 1$.) By hypothesis, $S(T-1, \omega^*)\theta(T-2, \omega^*) \geq g(T-1, \omega^*)$. Thus, we have shown*

$$S(T-1, \omega^*)\theta(T-2, \omega^*)$$

$$\geq \max\left[ g(T-1, \omega^*), \sum_{\omega \in \mathcal{H}^{(T-1)}(\omega^*) \cap \Omega^{(T)}} \frac{v^{(T)}(\omega)\psi(T, \omega)}{v^{(T-1)}(\omega)\psi(T-1, \omega)} g(T, \omega) \right]$$

$$= V(T-1, \omega^*),$$

*by the recursive relation (11.4.3). In other words,*

$$S(T-1, \omega^*)\theta(T-2, \omega^*) \geq V(T-1, \omega^*).$$

*Similarly,*

$$S(T - 2, \omega^*)\theta(T - 3, \omega^*)$$

$$= S(T - 2, \omega^*)\theta(T - 2, \omega^*) + c(T - 2, \omega^*)$$

$$\geq S(T - 2, \omega^*)\theta(T - 2, \omega^*) \quad (by\ (b);\ that\ is,\ c(T - 2, \omega^*) \geq 0)$$

$$= \sum_{\omega \in \mathcal{H}^{(T-2)}(\omega^*) \cap \Omega^{(T-1)}} \frac{v^{(T-1)}(\omega)\psi(T - 1, \omega)}{v^{(T-2)}(\omega)\psi(T - 2, \omega)} S(T - 1, \omega)\theta(T - 2, \omega)$$

$$(by\ (11.4.20))$$

$$\geq \sum_{\omega \in \mathcal{H}^{(T-2)}(\omega^*) \cap \Omega^{(T-1)}} \frac{v^{(T-1)}(\omega)\psi(T - 1, \omega)}{v^{(T-2)}(\omega)\psi(T - 2, \omega)} V(T - 1, \omega).$$

*By hypothesis,* $S(T - 2, \omega^*)\theta(T - 3, \omega^*) \geq g(T - 2, \omega^*)$. *Thus, we have shown*

$$S(T - 2, \omega^*)\theta(T - 3, \omega^*)$$

$$\geq \max\left[ g(T - 2, \omega^*), \sum_{\omega \in \mathcal{H}^{(T-2)}(\omega^*) \cap \Omega^{(T-1)}} \frac{v^{(T-1)}(\omega)\psi(T - 1, \omega)}{v^{(T-2)}(\omega)\psi(\omega(T - 2))} V(T - 1, \omega) \right]$$

$$= V(T - 2, \omega^*),$$

*by the recursive relation* (11.4.3). *In other words,*

$$S(T - 2, \omega^*)\theta(T - 3, \omega^*) \geq V(T - 2, \omega^*).$$

*Clearly, we can proceed by induction to show that*

$$S(k, \omega^*)\theta(k - 1, \omega^*) \geq V(k, \omega^*), \quad k = 1, \ldots, T, \quad \omega^* \in \Omega.$$

**Corollary 11.4.10.** *Consider an American option with payment characteristics defined by* $\{g(k)\}$ *and associated value process* $\{V(k)\}$. *If* $\theta$ *is a trading strategy that dominates the American option, then*

$$S(0)\theta(0) \geq V(0). \tag{11.4.27}$$

**Proof.**

$$S(0, \omega^*)\theta(0, \omega^*) = \sum_{\omega \in \Omega^{(1)}} v^{(1)}(\omega)\psi(1, \omega)S(1, \omega)\theta(0, \omega) \quad (by\ (11.4.20))$$

$$\geq \sum_{\omega \in \Omega^{(1)}} v^{(1)}(\omega)\psi(1, \omega)V(1, \omega) \quad (by\ (11.4.27))$$

$$= V(0),$$

*by the recursion relation* (11.4.2).

The preceding results imply the following important characterization of the price of an American option.

**Theorem 11.4.11.** *Consider an American option with payment characteristics defined by* $\{g(k)\}$ *and associated value process* $\{V(k)\}$. *If the securities market model is arbitrage free and complete, then the American option is priced and the price of the option is equal to* $V(0)$. *In other words, the price of the American option can be expressed as*

$$V(0) = \max_{\tau \in S^{(0)}} E^Q \left[ \frac{1}{B(\tau)} g(\tau) \right]. \tag{11.4.28}$$

**Proof.** *Denote the trading strategy shown to exist in Theorem 11.4.8 by* $\hat{\theta}$. *Then*

$$S(0, \omega)\hat{\theta}(0, \omega) = \sum_{\omega \in \Omega^{(1)}} v^{(1)}(\omega)\psi(1, \omega)S(1, \omega)\hat{\theta}(0, \omega) \quad (by\ (11.4.20))$$

$$= \sum_{\omega \in \Omega^{(1)}} v^{(1)}(\omega)\psi(\omega, 1)V(\omega, 1) \quad (by\ (b)\ of\ Theorem\ 11.4.8)$$

$$= V(0),$$

*by the recursive relation* (11.4.2).

*As we have noted,* $\hat{\theta}$ *dominates the American option. Thus,*

$$V(0) = S(0, \omega)\hat{\theta}(0, \omega) \geq \inf\{S(0, \omega)\theta(0, \omega) \mid \theta \in \Theta\}.$$

*By Corollary* 11.4.10,

$$S(0, \omega)\theta(0, \omega) \geq V(0), \quad for\ every\ \theta \in \Theta,$$

*so we conclude that*

$$V(0) = \inf\{S(0, \omega)\theta(0, \omega) \mid \theta \in \Theta\}$$

*and that this infimum is achieved for our particular* $\hat{\theta} \in \Theta$. *Therefore,*

$$V(0) = S(0, \omega)\hat{\theta}(0, \omega) = \min\{S(0, \omega)\theta(0, \omega) \mid \theta \in \Theta\}.$$

*Consequently,* $V(0)$ *is the price of the American option according to Definition* 11.4.4, *the financial definition of price.*

To recapitulate briefly how the previous results permit us to establish Theorem 11.4.11: Theorems 11.4.8 and 11.4.9 show that a trading strategy exists that dominates the American option in a minimal fashion. Since the cost of setting up this trading strategy is $V(0)$, this must be the price of the option.

We emphasize that the price of an American option is equal to the least amount of money required so that a portfolio can be established that always has a value as great as the contingent payment that can be demanded under the American option and that requires no further investment of funds after being established at the beginning of the trading interval. We also emphasize that (11.4.28) is a characterization of the price of an American option and is not the definition of the price of an American option.

We close this section with a heuristic argument that the price of the American option should be equal to $V(0)$. Of course, obviously this argument lies outside the rigorous framework of our pricing theory,[5] with the rigorous notion of price for American options defined as in (11.4.1). In an arbitrage-free securities market model the American option sells for an amount greater than or equal to $V(0)$. Indeed, if the American option sold for less than $V(0)$, then $\tau \in \mathcal{S}^{(0)}$ exists such that the price of the random cash flow $g(\tau)$ is greater than the price of the American option. We could then sell this random cash flow, use the proceeds to purchase the American option, and pocket the positive difference between what we received from the sale of the random cash flow $g(\tau)$ and what we paid for the American option. Since the payments we receive from the American option are always sufficient to cover our obligations to the holder of the random cash flow $g(\tau)$, this transaction would generate an arbitrage. Conversely, in an arbitrage-free securities market model the American option sells for an amount less than or equal to $V(0)$. Indeed, if the American option sold for greater than $V(0)$ we can generate an arbitrage as follows.

Let $\hat{\theta}$ denote a trading strategy that satisfies the condition (11.4.21). As we have shown, $S(0)\hat{\theta}(0) = V(0)$. As we know from condition (11.4.26), the trading strategy $\hat{\theta}$ dominates the American option. Therefore, we can sell the American option, use the resulting proceeds to carry out the trading strategy $\hat{\theta}$, and pocket the positive difference between what we received from the sale of the American option and what we need to make our initial investment of $S(0)\hat{\theta}(0)$ for carrying out the trading strategy $\hat{\theta}$. Since the value of our investment portfolio under the trading strategy $\hat{\theta}$ is always as large as the payment the holder of the American option can lay claim to, this transaction generates an arbitrage. Thus, we conclude that in an arbitrage-free securities market model the American option sells for exactly $V(0)$.

---

[5] Among other things, the American option is not assumed to be a traded asset in our rigorous pricing model. Rather, we use the absence of arbitrage and the existing primitive prices to deduce a price for the American option.

The stopping time $\tau^*$ such that

$$V(0) = E^Q \left[ \frac{1}{B(\tau^*)} g(\tau^*) \right]$$

is referred to as the *optimal exercise policy* for the American option. In some ways this terminology is unfortunate in that, as we have seen, the pricing of an American option is about the amount of money required to construct the cheapest dominating portfolio and not directly about any particular random payment $g(\tau^*)$. Nevertheless, the random payment $g(\tau^*)$ is an adapted cash-flow stream, and thus it may be financed by some trading strategy providing the securities market model is complete.

We then ask whether a hedging strategy for the random payment $g(\tau^*)$ is also a hedging strategy for the American option. It can be argued that, because for each $k = 1, \ldots, T - 1$, the random variable $\tau^* - k$ restricted to $\mathcal{H}^{(\tau^*(\omega))}(\omega)$ is a stopping time in $\mathcal{S}^{(k)}(\omega)$, the value of the hedging strategy for the random payment $g(\tau^*)$ is equal to the value of the process $V$ along each market outcome for each point in time. Therefore, we can obtain a hedging strategy for the American option by obtaining a hedging strategy for the random cash flow $g(\tau^*)$ associated with the optimal exercise policy, and, furthermore, along each market outcome for each point in time the price of the American option is always equal to the price of the random cash flow $g(\tau^*)$.

***Example 11.4.2 (American Put Option).*** Suppose that we are in a securities market model following the binomial model of Chapter 5. Assume that $u = 1.2$, $d = 0.91$, the one-period interest rate is 0.07, and the initial stock price is 20. Recall that the local dynamics of the stock price are as in Figure 11.32. Figure 11.33 shows the price of an American put option on the stock that expires in four periods with a strike price of 17 and describes the optimal exercise policy.

FIGURE **11.32** | *The Local Dynamics of the Stock Price*

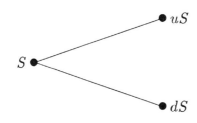

FIGURE **11.33** | ***American Put Option Valuation***
***(Strike = 17)***

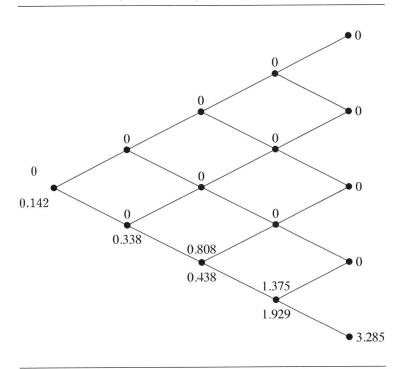

- Price of the American put option: 0.142.
- Price of the corresponding European put option price:

$$\frac{1}{(1.07)^4}(0.448)^4(3.285) = 0.101.$$

- Optimal Exercise Policy: Exercise the put option at time 3 if stock is at \$15.071. In other words, exercise at time 3 if stock has gone down three times.

  We have computed the values at the nodes of the lattice based on the recursive pricing relation (11.4.2):

$$1.375 = \frac{1}{1.07}\left[0.552(0) + 0.448(3.285)\right],$$

$$1.929 = \max[17 - 15.071, 1.375],$$

$$0.808 = \frac{1}{1.07}\left[0.552(0) + 0.448(1.929)\right], \quad \text{and so on.}$$

Effectively, we compute the value of future cash flow at each node when pricing the American put, and then compare with what could be received if the option were exercised. ∎

# Section 11.5
# Exercises

## Exercise 11.1

Prove that, under change of measure (11.2.39), we have $E^{P'}[\exp(G\theta)] < \infty$ for all $\theta \in \mathfrak{R}^N$. (Hint: $(G - \theta^T)(G - \theta^T)^T \geq 0$.)

## Exercise 11.2

a. Prove Holder's inequality: for any variables $X$, $Y$ with $E|X|^p < \infty$, $E|Y|^q < \infty$,

$$E[(|XY|^r)]^{\frac{1}{r}} \leq [E(|X|^p)]^{\frac{1}{p}}[E(|Y|^q)]^{\frac{1}{q}},$$

where $p$, $q$ are real numbers strictly larger than 1, with $1/r = 1/p + 1/q$. The inequality is strict unless either variable vanishes, or there is a constant $c$ such that $P(|X|^p = c|Y|^q) = 1$. (Hint: apply Jensen's inequality to prove that

$$E^Q\left(\frac{|Y|^q}{|X|^p}\right)^{\frac{r}{q}} \leq \left(E^Q\frac{|Y|^q}{|X|^p}\right)^{\frac{r}{q}},$$

and then use the change of measure $dQ/dP = |X|^p/E^P|X|^p$.)

b. Use part (a) to show that the function $\phi$ in the proof of Theorem 11.2.32 is strictly convex and can have at most one minimum.

## Exercise 11.3

Show that (11.2.40) implies $\phi(\theta_{n_k}) \to \infty$ as $k \to \infty$.

## Exercise 11.4

The function $\phi$ (see Section 11.2.10) is said to "tend to infinite radially," since

$$\lim_{t \to \infty} \phi(t\theta) = \infty$$

for all nonzero $\theta$ (under the assumption that no arbitrage exists in the alternative sense and that no securities are redundant). It turns out that $\phi$ has only one minimum, but we can find functions that tend to infinity radially yet fail to have an absolute minimum. Check that this is the case for the following function of two variables:

$$f(x, y) = (x^4 + y^4)(1 - xy)^2 - (x^2 + y^2), \quad x, y \in \mathfrak{R}.$$

Is this function convex?

## Exercise 11.5

In his proof, Rogers [160] uses a strictly increasing, strictly concave utility function $U : \Re \to (-\infty, 0)$ instead of the exponential function (we then maximize $E[U(G\theta)]$, instead of minimizing $E[\exp(G\theta)]$). Retrace the steps of Theorem 11.2.32 to see how the result may be obtained with such a utility function.

Observe that $\theta^*$ depends on the particular function $U$ chosen. How do you reconcile this with the uniqueness of $Q$ when the market is complete?

## Exercise 11.6

Consider a two-period arbitrage-free securities market model. The tree with local state prices is as given.

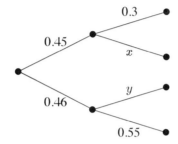

The two cash-flow streams are priced as shown.

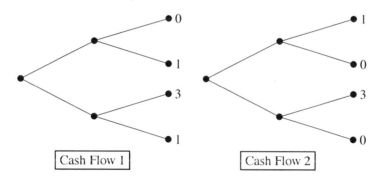

The price of the first cash-flow steam is found to be 1.075, and the price of the second cash-flow stream is 0.687. Determine the numerical values of $x$ and $y$.

## Exercise 11.7

An adapted process $\{X(k)\}$ on the filtered probability space $(\Omega, P, \{\mathcal{P}_k\})$ is said to be a **supermartingale** if

$$E[X(k+1) \mid \mathcal{P}_k](\omega) \le X(k, \omega), \quad k = 0, \dots, T-1, \quad \omega \in \Omega.$$

Consider an American option with payment characteristics defined by the adapted process $\{g(k)\}$. Suppose that asset 1 is a locally riskless asset and that $Q$ is an equivalent martingale measure for the securities market model. Prove that for each trading strategy $\theta$ that dominates the American option, the process $\{S(k)\theta(k)\}$ is a $Q$-supermartingale.

(Hint: Simple algebra allows us to write

$$\Delta[S(k, \omega)\theta(k, \omega)]$$
$$= [\Delta S(k, \omega)]\theta(k, \omega) - [S(k+1, \omega)\theta(k, \omega) - S(k+1, \omega)\theta(k+1, \omega)],$$

$$E^Q[\Delta[S(k)\theta(k)] \mid \mathcal{P}_k]$$
$$= E^Q[[\Delta S(k)]\theta(k) - [S(k+1)\theta(k) - S(k+1)\theta(k+1)] \mid \mathcal{P}_k]$$
$$\leq E^Q[[\Delta S(k)]\theta(k) \mid \mathcal{P}_k]$$
$$= e^{r(k)}E^Q[e^{-r(k)}\Delta S(k) \mid \mathcal{P}_k]\theta(k) = 0.$$

Recall that the condition, $S(k+1, \omega)\theta(k, \omega) - S(k+1, \omega)\theta(k+1, \omega) \geq 0$, is part of the definition of dominating strategy.)

---

## Exercise 11.8

Consider an American option with payment characteristics defined by the adapted process $\{g(k)\}$. Suppose that asset 1 is a locally riskless asset and that $Q$ is an equivalent martingale measure for the securities market model. Let $\hat{\theta}$ be a trading strategy that satisfies condition (11.4.21). Prove, making use of the recursive relation (11.4.2), that the process

$$Z(k, \omega^*) = \sum_{\omega \in \mathcal{H}^{(k)}(\omega^*) \cap \Omega^{(k+1)}} \frac{v^{(k+1)}(\omega)\psi(k+1, \omega)}{v^{(k)}(\omega)\psi(k, \omega)} V(k+1, \omega)$$

is a $Q$-martingale. (The process $\{Z(k)\}$ is recognized as the process $\{S(k)\hat{\theta}(k)\}$ corresponding to a trading strategy $\hat{\theta}$ satisfying the condition (11.4.21). Of course, as we know from the previous exercise, it is the second property of condition (11.4.21) that renders the process $\{S(k)\hat{\theta}(k)\}$ a supermartingale.)

---

## Exercise 11.9

Consider an American option with payment characteristics defined by the adapted process $\{g(k)\}$. Suppose that asset 2 in our securities market model satisfies $S_2(k, \omega) > 0$ for $\omega \in \Omega$, $k = 1, \ldots, T$. Show that a trading strategy that dominates the American option exists, and thus $\Theta$ is not an empty set.

(Hint: Let $m = \min\{S_2(k, \omega) \mid \omega \in \Omega, k = 1, \ldots, T\}$. Fix a number $A$ such that $A > \max\{g(k, \omega) \mid \omega \in \Omega, k = 1, \ldots, T\}$. Let $\theta_*$ denote the strategy that buys and holds and holds $A/m$ shares of asset 2. It is then evident that

$$S(k, \omega)\theta_*(k - 1, \omega) = \frac{A}{m} S_2(k, \omega) \geq A \geq g(k, \omega)$$

and

$$S(k, \omega)\theta_*(k - 1, \omega) = S(k, \omega)\theta_*(k, \omega)$$

for $k = 1, \ldots, T$.)

# APPENDIX A
## PROBABILITY
## BACKGROUND

This appendix provides a background on probability theory: information structures, probability measures, conditional expectations, martingales, stopping times, random walks, and Brownian motion. The first section describes many of the concepts in the simpler case where there is only a finite number of possible outcomes. Section A.1 is sufficient for understanding Chapters 5 and 11. The remaining sections discuss the general case.

## *Section A.1*
## *Finite Sample Spaces*

This section gives an elementary introduction to the probabilistic modeling of securities markets. If you have some familiarity with the subject, you might read only the definitions and theorems. Note: *All the definitions and results specifically concern the case in which the set of possible outcomes Ω is finite; the general theory is described in Section A.2 onwards.*

### SECTION A.1.1 | THE INFORMATION STRUCTURE

Our goal is to build a model for the uncertainty of security prices over time. Each possible evolution is represented by an element of a set Ω ("big omega"), called the *sample space*. The possible outcomes are called "states of nature," or "states of the world," and are often denoted as $\omega$'s ("small omegas"). The time points we consider are $0, \ldots, T$.

***Remark:*** The symbol used to denote a set, such as $\Omega$, can be fixed, but the symbol for an element is a *dummy variable*; as long as no confusion results, we can use any dummy variable $\omega$, $\omega^*$, $\alpha$, and so on, to represent an element of $\Omega$. The same idea applies to functions: the statements "$f(j) = j^3$" and "$f(k) = k^3$" are the same, $j$ and $k$ are dummy variables, and $f$ is the specific function that takes a number as input and outputs that number raised to the power 3. ∎

In order to represent incomplete information (that is, uncertainty), we imagine that an investor only knows that the true state of the world $\omega$ is in some subset of $\Omega$.

***Definition A.1.1.*** *Let $\mathcal{E}$ be a set, and $B_1, \ldots, B_n$ be subsets of $\mathcal{E}$, such that $B_i \cap B_j = \emptyset$ (empty intersection) for all $i \neq j$, and $B_1 \cup \cdots \cup B_n = \mathcal{E}$. The collection $\mathcal{P} = \{B_1, \ldots, B_n\}$ is called a **partition** of $\mathcal{E}$.*

***Example A.1.1.*** Suppose $\Omega = \{\omega_1, \ldots, \omega_{15}\}$. At time 0, investors know nothing, only that the state of the world is some $\omega \in \Omega$. We thus assign the partition $\mathcal{P}_0 = \{\Omega\}$ to time 0. One period later (time 1), events have occurred (stock prices have moved, dividends have been declared, and so on), so investors know a little more; assume, for instance, that they know whether the actual state of the world $\omega$ is in one of the sets

$$A = \{\omega_1, \ldots, \omega_6\}, \qquad B = \{\omega_7, \ldots, \omega_{11}\}, \qquad C = \{\omega_{12}, \ldots, \omega_{15}\}.$$

These sets form a partition $\mathcal{P}_1 = \{A, B, C\}$ of $\Omega$. At time 2, investors have more knowledge; suppose the partition of $\Omega$ at time 2 is

$$\mathcal{P}_2 = \{D, E, F, G, H, I, J\},$$

$$D = \{\omega_1, \omega_2\}, \qquad E = \{\omega_3, \omega_4\}, \qquad F = \{\omega_5, \omega_6\}, \qquad G = \{\omega_7, \omega_8\},$$

$$H = \{\omega_9, \omega_{10}, \omega_{11}\}, \qquad I = \{\omega_{12}, \omega_{13}\}, \qquad J = \{\omega_{14}, \omega_{15}\}.$$

This is illustrated in Figure A.1. For example, investors may find, at time 1, that $\omega \in B$, and, at time 2, that $\omega \in H$. This models the acquiring of more information over time, as $B$ is a smaller set than $\Omega$, and $H$ is a smaller set than $B$. The set $H$ (time 2) is included in $B$ (time 1), and this is consistent with narrowing down the possibilities as time passes. Finally, assume that $\mathcal{P}_3 = \{\{\omega_i\}; i = 1, \ldots, 15\}$ (each set of the partition consists of a single element of $\Omega$). Investors may find at time 3 that the state of nature is $\omega_9$. ∎

FIGURE **A.1** | *Partitions of $\Omega$*

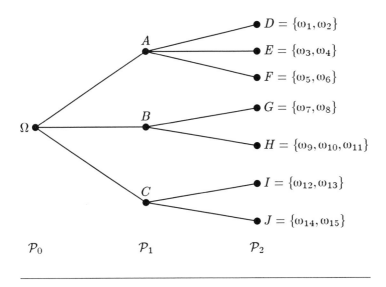

More generally, a $T$-period securities model consists of a sample space $\Omega = \{\omega_1, \ldots, \omega_M\}$ and of successively finer partitions $\mathcal{P}_0, \ldots, \mathcal{P}_T$. Because no information is available at time 0, we let $\mathcal{P}_0 = \{\Omega\}$. At time $T$, complete information can be obtained, so we let $\mathcal{P}_T = \{\{\omega_i\}; i = 1, \ldots, M\}$. ("Successively finer partitions" means that each set $A \in \mathcal{P}_k$ splits into smaller sets $B_1, \ldots, B_n$, which are elements of $\mathcal{P}_{k+1}$. The sets $B_1, \ldots, B_n$ form a partition of $A$.)

**Definition A.1.2.** *Let $\Omega$ be a finite set, and let $\mathcal{G}$ be a set of subsets of $\Omega$. Then $\mathcal{G}$ is a* **field** *(or* **algebra***) if the following conditions are satisfied:*

a.    $\Omega \in \mathcal{G}$,

b.    $B \in \mathcal{G}$ implies $B^c \in \mathcal{G}$ ($B^c$ is the complement of $B$), and

c.    $B_j \in \mathcal{G}; j = 1, \ldots, n$ implies $\bigcup_{j=1}^n B_j \in \mathcal{G}$.

Because $\Omega$ is finite, this definition coincides with that of $\sigma$-*field* (or $\sigma$-*algebra*), which is given in Section A.2. A one-to-one correspondence between partitions and fields over a finite set $\Omega$ is easily established. We can check that the set $\sigma(\mathcal{P})$ defined below is a field; see Section A.2.

**Definition A.1.3.** *The* **field generated by a partition** $\mathcal{P} = \{A_1, \ldots, A_n\}$ *is the following set of subsets of $\Omega$:*

$$\sigma(\mathcal{P}) = \{\emptyset, \Omega, A_1, \ldots, A_n, \text{ and all unions of elements of } \mathcal{P}\}.$$

**Example A.1.2.** In the preceding example, we find

$$\mathcal{F}_0 = \sigma(\mathcal{P}_0) = \{\emptyset, \Omega\},$$

$$\mathcal{F}_1 = \sigma(\mathcal{P}_1) = \{\emptyset, \Omega, A, B, C, A \cup B, A \cup C, B \cup C\},$$

$$\mathcal{F}_2 = \sigma(\mathcal{P}_2) = \{\emptyset, \Omega, D, E, F, G, H, I, J, D \cup E, D \cup F, \ldots\},$$

$$\mathcal{F}_3 = \sigma(\mathcal{P}_3) = \{\text{all subsets of } \Omega\}.$$

Observe that, because the partitions $\mathcal{P}_0, \mathcal{P}_1, \mathcal{P}_2$, and $\mathcal{P}_3$ are successively finer, we have $\mathcal{F}_0 \subset \mathcal{F}_1 \subset \mathcal{F}_2 \subset \mathcal{F}_3$. ∎

In the general securities model we define $\mathcal{F}_k = \sigma(\mathcal{P}_k)$ for each $k = 0, \ldots, T$. The assumption that $\mathcal{P}_{k+1}$ is finer than $\mathcal{P}_k$ implies that $\mathcal{F}_k \subset \mathcal{F}_{k+1}$. *The larger $\mathcal{F}_k$, the more information it contains.*

**Definition A.1.4.** *The family of fields* $\mathbf{F} = \{\mathcal{F}_k; k = 0, \ldots T\}$ *is a filtration if*

$$\mathcal{F}_k \subseteq \mathcal{F}_{k+1}, \quad k = 0, \ldots, T - 1.$$

*In the finite model we always let $\mathcal{F}_0 = \{\emptyset, \Omega\}$ ("uninformative field") and $\mathcal{F} = \mathcal{F}_T = \{all subsets of \Omega\}$ ("field with all the information"); observe that this is not required mathematically.*

Prices of assets corresponding to each $\omega \in \Omega$ are denoted $S(k, \omega)$; dividends are similarly denoted $D(k, \omega)$, for each time point $k = 0, \ldots, T$. Knowledge of the true state of nature $\omega$ means knowledge of $S(k, \omega)$, $D(k, \omega)$ and all the other variables in the model, for all time points $k$. Knowledge of $\omega$ means complete information; an investor possessing this much information at some time $k < T$ could foresee the future.

**Definition A.1.5.** *A random variable (or simply variable) is a mapping that assigns a real number $X(\omega)$ to each $\omega \in \Omega$. A stochastic process (or simply process) is a collection of random variables indexed by $0, \ldots, T$, $X = \{X(k, \omega); k = 0, \ldots, T, \omega \in \Omega\}$. The collection $\{X(k, \omega^*); k = 0, \ldots, T\}$ for a fixed $\omega^* \in \Omega$ is called a path, sample path, or realization of the process $X$.*

The general definition of a random variable is given in Section A.2. In the case of finite probability spaces, it is simpler to use the following equivalent characterization.

**Theorem A.1.6.** *Let $\mathcal{G}$ be the field generated by a partition $\mathcal{P}$, $\mathcal{G} = \sigma(P)$. A random variable $Y$ is **measurable with respect to** $\mathcal{G}$ (or $\mathcal{G}$-**measurable**) if and only if*

$$Y(\omega) \text{ is constant for all } \omega \in A, \quad \text{for each } A \in \mathcal{P}. \tag{A.1.1}$$

*(That is, $Y$ has a constant value on each element of $\mathcal{P}$.) This is equivalent to*

$$\{\omega : Y(\omega) \in K\} \in \mathcal{G}, \quad \text{for each interval } K \subset \mathfrak{R}, \tag{A.1.2}$$

*where $\mathfrak{R}$ denotes the set of real numbers.*

We first observe that no measure is involved in the notion of measurability. Condition (A.1.1) applies only when the field is generated by a finite (or countably infinite) partition of $\Omega$, but it is easier to verify than condition (A.1.2) (which is one form of the general definition).

**Example A.1.3.** Refer to Examples A.1.1 and A.1.2 and let $X$ be the stochastic process

$X(0, \omega) = 12, \quad \omega \in \Omega,$

$X(1, \omega) = 13, \quad \omega \in A, \qquad X(1, \omega) = 11, \quad \omega \in B, \qquad X(1, \omega) = 12, \quad \omega \in C,$

$X(2, \omega) = 14, \quad \omega \in D, \qquad X(2, \omega) = 13, \quad \omega \in E, \qquad X(2, \omega) = 12, \quad \omega \in F,$

$X(2, \omega) = 11, \quad \omega \in G, \qquad X(2, \omega) = 10, \quad \omega \in H, \qquad X(2, \omega) = 19, \quad \omega \in I,$

$X(2, \omega) = 26, \quad \omega \in J, \quad$ and

$X(3, \omega_i) = i + 9, \quad i = 1, \ldots, 15.$

For $k = 0$, 1, 2, or 3, the mapping $\omega \to X(k, \omega)$, $\omega \in \Omega$, is a random variable, denoted $X(k)$ for short. The path of $X$ for $\omega_1$ is (12, 13, 14, 10).

The random variable $X(0)$ is constant on $\Omega$ so $X(0)$ is $\mathcal{F}_0$-measurable. Also, $X(1)$ has a constant value on the sets $A$, $B$, and $C$; thus, $X(1)$ is $\mathcal{F}_1$-measurable. Similarly, $X(2)$ is $\mathcal{F}_2$-measurable, and $X(3)$ is $\mathcal{F}_3$-measurable. In the case of $X(3)$ there was in fact nothing to worry about: $X(3)$ is $\mathcal{F}_3$-measurable whatever its values, because $\mathcal{P}_3$ is made up of sets, each with only one element; another way to arrive at the same conclusion is that requirement (A.1.2) is always satisfied if $\mathcal{G}$ is the set of all subsets of $\Omega$. ∎

We emphasize that partitions of the sample space, or the corresponding fields, are to be interpreted as *information*. The least informative field is $\mathcal{F}_0 = \{\emptyset, \Omega\}$, and the most informative one is $\mathcal{F}_T = \{$all subsets of $\Omega\}$. Any security represented by the process $\{X(k); k = 0, \ldots, T\}$ has to be consistent with the way information increases over time. This leads to the final definition required to specify the *information structure* (see Table A.1).

TABLE **A.1** | *Information Structure for Securities Model Where $\Omega = \{\omega_1, \ldots, \omega_M\}$*

| Time | Partition | Field | Adapted Process |
|------|-----------|-------|-----------------|
| 0 | $\mathcal{P}_0$ | $\mathcal{F}_0 = \{\emptyset, \Omega\}$ | $X(0, \omega)$ (constant) |
| $\vdots$ | $\vdots$ | $\vdots$ | $\vdots$ |
| $k$ | $\mathcal{P}_k$ | $\mathcal{F}_k$ | $X(k, \omega)$ (constant for all $\omega \in A$, for $A \in \mathcal{P}_k$) |
| $k+1$ | $\mathcal{P}_{k+1}$ (finer than $\mathcal{P}_k$) | $\mathcal{F}_{k+1}$ ($\mathcal{F}_k \subset \mathcal{F}_{k+1}$) | $X(k+1, \omega)$ |
| $\vdots$ | $\vdots$ | $\vdots$ | $\vdots$ |
| $T$ | $\mathcal{P}_T = \{\{\omega_i\}; i = 1, \ldots, M\}$ | $\mathcal{F} = \mathcal{F}_T = $ {all subsets of $\Omega$} | $X(T, \omega)$ (always $\mathcal{F}_T$-measurable) |

**Definition A.1.7.** *The process $X = \{X(k); k = 0, \ldots, T\}$ is said to be **adapted** to the filtration $\mathbf{F}$ if $X(k) = X(k, \cdot)$ is $\mathcal{F}_k$-measurable for each $k = 0, \ldots, T$.*

**Example A.1.4.** In the previous example, the process $X$ is adapted to the given filtration. To be adapted is the same as "to be constant over members of the partition at each point in time." If this were not the case, for example, if there were some variations of $X(2, \omega)$ for $\omega \in J = \{\omega_{14}, \omega_{15}\}$, then investors observing stock prices would be able to tell what $\omega$ is the true state of nature, which this model does not allow at time 2. ∎

**Definition A.1.8.** *A process $X = \{X(k); k = 0, \ldots, T\}$ is said to be **predictable** (with respect to the filtration $\mathbf{F} = \{\mathcal{F}_k; k = 0, \ldots T\}$) if*
a.     *$X(0)$ is $\mathcal{F}_0$-measurable, and*
b.     *$X(k)$ is $\mathcal{F}_{k-1}$-measurable for $k = 0, \ldots, T-1$.*

**Example A.1.5.** Some securities, such as T-bills, have the peculiarity that their rates of return over a time period are known at the beginning of the period. Let the information structure be the same as in the previous examples and consider a *money market account* that has a continuously compounded rate of return or force of interest $r(k)$ over the period $(k, k+1)$ $(k = 0, 1, 2)$:

$r(0, \omega) = 0.08, \quad \omega \in \Omega,$

$r(1, \omega) = 0.06, \quad \omega \in A, \quad r(1, \omega) = 0.11, \quad \omega \in B, \quad r(1, \omega) = 0.09, \quad \omega \in C,$

$r(2, \omega) = 0.07, \quad \omega \in D, \quad r(2, \omega) = 0.04, \quad \omega \in E, \quad r(2, \omega) = 0.09, \quad \omega \in F,$

$r(2, \omega) = 0.06, \quad \omega \in G, \quad r(2, \omega) = 0.12, \quad \omega \in H, \quad r(2, \omega) = 0.10, \quad \omega \in I,$

$r(2, \omega) = 0.08, \quad \omega \in J.$

The process $r$ is adapted. Next, define

$$B(k, \omega) = \begin{cases} 1, & \text{if } k = 0 \\ \exp[r(0, \omega) + \cdots + r(k-1, \omega)], & \text{if } k \geq 1. \end{cases}$$

This process represents the accumulated value of 1 unit invested in the money market account at time 0. The word *predictable* is well suited to describe the evolution of $B$, as $B(k)$ is known at time $k - 1$, for $k = 1, 2, 3$. ∎

## SECTION A.1.2 | PROBABILITY, EXPECTATION, CONDITIONAL EXPECTATION

The general definition of a probability measure is given in Section A.3. In the case of finite probability spaces, we use the following result.

***Theorem A.1.9.*** *Let $\Omega = \{\omega_1, \ldots, \omega_M\}$ and $\mathcal{F}$ be the set of all its subsets. A function $P$ that assigns a number $P(\omega)$ to each $\omega \in \Omega$, such that $P(\omega) \geq 0$ for all $\omega \in \Omega$ and $\sum_{i=1}^{M} P(\omega_i) = 1$, is a **probability measure**. Any probability measure $P$ satisfies the following **additivity property**: for each collection $\{A_1, A_2, \ldots, A_n\}$ of disjoint elements of $\mathcal{F}$,*

$$P\left(\bigcup_{i=1}^{n} A_i\right) = \sum_{i=1}^{n} P(A_i).$$

The concept of equivalent probability measure plays an important role in finance (see Chapters 5 and 11). The more technical definition of this concept is given at a later stage (in Section A.3), but the following theorem gives a simple intuitive criterion applicable in the case of finite probability spaces. It says that probability measures are equivalent if they have the same support.

**Theorem A.1.10.** *Two probability measures $P_1$ and $P_2$ defined over all the subsets of a finite set $\Omega$ are equivalent if and only if*

$$P_1(\omega) > 0 \iff P_2(\omega) > 0.$$

It may be said that, as far as financial applications are concerned, the word *equivalent* is ill chosen; for instance, the following probabilities are equivalent, but they are far from being "the same":

$$P_1(\omega_1) = 0.001, \qquad P_1(\omega_2) = 0.999, \qquad P_2(\omega_1) = 0.999, \qquad P_2(\omega_2) = 0.001.$$

We now present definitions of expectation and conditional expectation that are valid when the space is finite; they are particular cases of the general definitions given in Section A.3.

**Definition A.1.11.** *The **expectation** (or **mean**) of a random variable $Y$ defined on the finite probability space $(\Omega, \mathcal{F}, P)$ is*

$$E[Y] = \sum_{i=1}^{M} Y(\omega_i) P(\omega_i).$$

*Suppose $A \in \mathcal{F}$ and $P(A) > 0$. The **conditional expectation of $Y$ given $A$** is*

$$E[Y \mid A] = \frac{1}{P(A)} \sum_{\omega \in A} Y(\omega) P(\omega).$$

**Remark:** When there is more than one probability measure, we indicate the one used to calculate the expectation by a superscript. For example, $E^P[X]$ is the expectation of $X$ with respect to the probability measure $P$.

Conditional expectations given a set of outcomes or an event are common; for example, $E[Y \mid W = \omega]$ or $E[Y \mid W_1 = \omega_1, \ldots, W_1 = \omega_n]$. Finance needs a more general form of conditional expectation, the condition being a field instead of a set. The idea is the following. Consider a partition $\mathcal{P} = \{A_1, \ldots, A_n\}$, with associated field $\mathcal{G} = \sigma(\mathcal{P})$, and suppose all the conditional expectations $E[Y \mid A_i]$, $i = 1, \ldots, n$, have been computed. Imagine then that one set in $\mathcal{P}$ is chosen at random, the probability of choosing $A_i$ being $P(A_i)$. We then obtain a random version of the conditional expectation given a set, call it $Z$, with values

$$Z(\omega) = \begin{cases} E[Y \mid A_1], & \text{if } \omega \in A_1 \\ \vdots & \vdots \\ E[Y \mid A_n], & \text{if } \omega \in A_n. \end{cases}$$

The following definition expresses the previous enumeration in a more concise fashion, with the help of the *indicator variable*[1]

$$I_A(\omega) = \begin{cases} 1, & \text{if } \omega \in A \\ 0, & \text{if } \omega \notin A. \end{cases}$$

The random variable $Y I_A$ equals $Y(\omega)$ if $\omega \in A$; otherwise it equals zero.

**Definition A.1.12.** *Let* $Y$ *be a random variable,* $\mathcal{P} = \{A_1, \ldots, A_n\}$ *be a partition of* $\Omega$*, and* $\mathcal{G} = \sigma(\mathcal{P})$*. The* **conditional expectation of the random variable** $Y$ **given** $\mathcal{G}$ *is the random variable*

$$E[Y \mid \mathcal{G}](\omega) = \sum_{i=1}^{n} \left[ \frac{E(Y I_{A_i})}{P(A_i)} \right] I_{A_i}(\omega).$$

**Remarks:**

1. Observe that the notation for an ordinary expectation is $E[Y]$, not $E[Y(\omega)]$; the dummy variable $\omega$ has been "integrated out" (any other dummy variable might have been used). *But conditional expectations with respect to a field are random variables*, so they have a possibly different value for each $\omega \in \Omega$; we use the notation $E[Y \mid \mathcal{G}](\omega)$ to refer to a specific value of the conditional expectation $E[Y \mid \mathcal{G}]$.

2. The above definition of conditional expectation has to be modified if $P(A_i) = 0$ for some $i$. Because the event $A_i$ is impossible, it does not matter what value we assign to $E[Y \mid A_i]$. This difficulty does not arise in the general definition of conditional expectation (see Section A.3).

3. Because $\Omega$ is finite, there is a one-to-one correspondence between partitions and fields. In Chapter 5, the idea of a field or algebra was not introduced; instead of $E[\cdot \mid \mathcal{G}]$, we used the notation $E[\cdot \mid \mathcal{P}]$, where $\mathcal{P}$ is the partition that generates the field $\mathcal{G}$. In Chapter 11, we used $E[\cdot \mid \mathcal{G}]$ and $E[\cdot \mid \mathcal{P}]$ interchangeably.

**Example A.1.6.** There are eight individuals $\{\omega_1, \ldots, \omega_8\}$ with equal probability of being chosen. Their salaries are the following:

$$Y(\omega_1) = 25{,}000, \quad Y(\omega_2) = 35{,}000, \quad Y(\omega_3) = 50{,}000, \quad Y(\omega_4) = 60{,}000,$$

$$Y(\omega_5) = 70{,}000, \quad Y(\omega_6) = 80{,}000, \quad Y(\omega_7) = 85{,}000, \quad Y(\omega_8) = 95{,}000.$$

---

[1] In Chapters 5 and 11, $1_A$ was also used for $I_A$.

Let $\mathcal{P} = \{A_1, A_2, A_3\}$, where

$$A_1 = \{\omega_1, \omega_2\}, \qquad A_2 = \{\omega_3, \omega_4, \omega_5, \omega_6\}, \qquad A_3 = \{\omega_7, \omega_8\}.$$

The field generated by $\mathcal{P}$ is $\mathcal{F} = \{\emptyset, \Omega, A_1, A_2, A_3, A_1 \cup A_2, A_1 \cup A_3, A_2 \cup A_3\}$. We find

$$E[Y \mid A_1] = 30{,}000, \qquad E[Y \mid A_2] = 65{,}000, \qquad E[Y \mid A_3] = 90{,}000.$$

These are averages over each of the sets (or "salary brackets") $A_1$, $A_2$, $A_3$. But now suppose you pick an individual at random and look for the average salary in that person's salary bracket. The result is the random variable

$$Z(\omega) = E[Y \mid \mathcal{F}](\omega) = \begin{cases} E[Y \mid A_1] = 30{,}000, & \text{if } \omega \in A_1 \\ E[Y \mid A_2] = 65{,}000, & \text{if } \omega \in A_2 \\ E[Y \mid A_3] = 90{,}000, & \text{if } \omega \in A_3. \end{cases}$$

Next, suppose you wish to compute the average salary over the whole population. There are two possibilities: either you add up all the salaries and divide by 8 (this agrees with the definition of expectation), or you weigh the averages over salary brackets (equal to values of the conditional expectation $Z$) with the probabilities of selecting each bracket. From the definition of conditional expectation (with respect to a field), we get

$$\begin{aligned} E[Z] &= P(A_1)E[Y \mid A_1] + P(A_2)E[Y \mid A_2] + P(A_3)E[Y \mid A_3] \\ &= E[Y I_{A_1}] + E[Y I_{A_2}] + E[Y I_{A_3}] \\ &= E[Y(I_{A_1} + I_{A_2} + I_{A_3})] \\ &= E[Y]. \end{aligned}$$

This formula illustrates part (c) in Theorem A.1.13 below. ∎

**Theorem A.1.13 (*Properties of Conditional Expectations*).** *Suppose $Y$ is a random variable defined on $(\Omega, \mathcal{F})$, and that $\mathcal{G}, \mathcal{G}_1 \subset \mathcal{G}_2$ are subfields of $\mathcal{F}$. Then,*

a.    $E[Y \mid \mathcal{G}]$ *is $\mathcal{G}$-measurable.*
b.    $E[Y \mid \mathcal{F}_0] = E[Y]$, *where $\mathcal{F}_0 = \{\emptyset, \Omega\}$.*
c.    $E[E[Y \mid \mathcal{G}]] = E[Y]$.
d.    $E[ZY \mid \mathcal{G}] = ZE[X \mid \mathcal{G}]$, *if $Z$ is $\mathcal{G}$-measurable.*
e.    $E[E[Y \mid \mathcal{G}_1] \mid \mathcal{G}_2] = E[Y \mid \mathcal{G}_1]$.
f.    $E[E[Y \mid \mathcal{G}_2] \mid \mathcal{G}_1] = E[Y \mid \mathcal{G}_1]$.

**Proof.** *Properties (a) and (b) follow from the definition of conditional expectation. Property (c) follows from (b) and (f). Property (d) is immediate when Z is the indicator function $I_A$ of $A \in \mathcal{P}$, if $\mathcal{G} = \sigma(\mathcal{P})$; the more general case follows by linearity. Parts (e) and (f) are left to Exercise A.5.*

## SECTION A.1.3 | INDEPENDENCE

**Definition A.1.14.** *The **field generated by the random variables** $Y_1, \ldots, Y_n$, denoted $\sigma(Y_1, \ldots, Y_n)$, is the smallest field containing the events*

$$\{\omega \mid Y_1(\omega) \in K_1, \ldots, Y_n(\omega) \in K_n\},$$

*for all intervals $K_1, \ldots, K_n$ of $\mathfrak{R}$. It is the smallest field with respect to which the random vector $(Y_1, \ldots, Y_n)$ is measurable. We define the conditional expectation of Z given $Y_1, \ldots, Y_n$ as*

$$E[Z \mid Y_1, \ldots, Y_n] = E[Z \mid \sigma(Y_1, \ldots, Y_n)].$$

**Example A.1.7.** Let $\Omega = \{\omega_1, \omega_2, \omega_3\}$, $\mathcal{F}_0 = \{\emptyset, \Omega\}$, $\mathcal{F} = \mathcal{F}_3 = \{\text{all subsets of } \Omega\}$, and

$$
\begin{aligned}
X_1(\omega_1) &= 0.02, & X_2(\omega_1) &= 0.05, & X_3(\omega_1) &= 0.05, \\
X_1(\omega_2) &= 0.06, & X_2(\omega_2) &= 0.06, & X_3(\omega_2) &= 0.03, \\
X_1(\omega_3) &= 0.06, & X_2(\omega_3) &= 0.05, & X_3(\omega_3) &= 0.04.
\end{aligned}
$$

The process $X = \{X_1, X_2, X_3\}$ might represent the return of an asset over a 3-year period. We can then determine $\sigma(X_t)$, $t = 1, 2, 3$, as well as $\sigma(X_1, X_2)$ and $\sigma(X_1, X_2, X_3)$.

The random variable $X_1$ only takes two values, 0.02 and 0.06. For any interval $K$ of $\mathfrak{R}$ we have only four possibilities: (a) $0.02 \notin K$, $0.06 \notin K$; (b) $0.02 \in K$, $0.06 \notin K$; (c) $0.02 \notin K$, $0.06 \in K$; and (d) $0.02 \in K$, $0.06 \in K$. Thus, $\{\omega \mid X(\omega) \in K\}$ can only be one of four sets: $\emptyset$, $\{\omega_1\}$, $\{\omega_2, \omega_3\}$, or $\Omega$, and

$$\sigma(X_1) = \{\emptyset, \{\omega_1\}, \{\omega_2, \omega_3\}, \Omega\}.$$

In the same way, we find

$$\sigma(X_2) = \{\emptyset, \{\omega_2\}, \{\omega_1, \omega_3\}, \Omega\}, \qquad \sigma(X_3) = \mathcal{F}.$$

Clearly, $\sigma(X_1, X_2)$ includes both $\sigma(X_1)$ and $\sigma(X_2)$, so we must have $\sigma(X_1, X_2) = \mathcal{F}$; therefore, $\sigma(X_1, X_2, X_3) = \mathcal{F}$ also.

Define $\mathcal{F}_1 = \sigma(X_1)$ and $\mathcal{F}_2 = \sigma(X_1, X_2)$; the process $X$ is obviously adapted to the filtration obtained (it is called the *natural filtration* of $X$).

How can we explain these results? If $X_1 = 0.02$, then we know that the state of nature is $\omega_1$, so we have perfect knowledge of $X_2$ and $X_3$ (they are both equal to 0.05). If $X_1 = 0.06$, then the state of nature is either $\omega_2$ or $\omega_3$. The value of $X_2$ is required to determine $\omega$ with certainty. So, in all cases perfect information is obtained by time 2 at most, which is mathematically stated as $\mathcal{F}_2 = \mathcal{F}$. Because this is all the information available, $\mathcal{F}_3$ cannot be any larger. ∎

**Definition A.1.15.** *The fields $\mathcal{G}_1, \ldots, \mathcal{G}_n$ are **independent** if*

$$P(G_1 \cap \cdots \cap G_n) = P(G_1) \cdots P(G_n)$$

*for all sets $G_1 \in \mathcal{G}_1, \ldots, G_n \in \mathcal{G}_n$. The random variables $Y_1, \ldots, Y_n$ are **independent** if the fields $\sigma(Y_1), \ldots, \sigma(Y_n)$ are independent, or, equivalently, if*

$$P(X_1 \in K_1, \ldots, X_n \in K_n) = P(X_1 \in K_1) \cdots P(X_n \in K_n)$$

*for all intervals $K_1, \ldots, K_n$ of $\mathfrak{R}$. If the fields $\sigma(Y)$ and $\mathcal{G}$ are independent, we also say that the random variable $Y$ is independent of $\mathcal{G}$.*

**Example A.1.8 (Binomial Model).** The binomial process can be used to model the stock prices; see Example 5.3.1. Here we consider the sample space as $T$-dimensional row vectors with entries of 0's and 1's; that is, each state of nature $\omega$ is viewed as one such vector. Over the sample space

$$\Omega = \{\omega = (i_1, \ldots, i_T) \mid i_k = 0 \text{ or } 1, k = 1, \ldots, T\} = \{0, 1\}^T$$

define $\mathcal{F}_0 = \{\emptyset, \Omega\}$, as usual, and

$$\mathcal{F}_1 = \sigma(\mathcal{P}_1), \qquad \mathcal{P}_1 = \{\mathcal{H}_1^{(1)}, \mathcal{H}_2^{(1)}\},$$
$$\mathcal{H}_1^{(1)} = \{(i_1, \ldots, i_T) \mid i_1 = 0\}, \qquad \mathcal{H}_2^{(1)} = \{(i_1, \ldots, i_T) \mid i_1 = 1\}.$$

The information at time 1 consists only in knowing what the first component of $\omega$ is, 0 or 1. In the same way, let

$$\mathcal{F}_2 = \sigma(\mathcal{P}_2), \qquad \mathcal{P}_2 = \{\mathcal{H}_1^{(2)}, \mathcal{H}_2^{(2)}, \mathcal{H}_3^{(2)}, \mathcal{H}_4^{(2)}\},$$
$$\mathcal{H}_1^{(2)} = \{(i_1, \ldots, i_T) \mid i_1 = 0, i_2 = 0\}, \qquad \mathcal{H}_2^{(2)} = \{(i_1, \ldots, i_T) \mid i_1 = 0, i_2 = 1\},$$
$$\mathcal{H}_3^{(2)} = \{(i_1, \ldots, i_T) \mid i_1 = 1, i_2 = 0\}, \qquad \mathcal{H}_4^{(2)} = \{(i_1, \ldots, i_T) \mid i_1 = 1, i_2 = 1\}.$$

The information at time 2 consists in knowing what the first and second components of $\omega$ are, and no more. Extend the same idea to times $k = 3, \ldots, T$:

$$\mathcal{F}_k = \sigma(\mathcal{P}_k), \qquad \mathcal{P}_k = \{\mathcal{H}_1^{(k)}, \ldots, \mathcal{H}_{2^k}^{(k)}\},$$

$$\mathcal{H}_1^{(k)} = \{(i_1, \ldots, i_T) \mid i_1 = 0, \ldots, i_k = 0\},$$

$$\vdots \qquad\qquad \vdots \qquad\qquad \vdots$$

$$\mathcal{H}_{2^k}^{(k)} = \{(i_1, \ldots, i_T) \mid i_1 = 1, \ldots, i_k = 1\}.$$

The information at time $k$ consists in knowing the first $k$ components of $\omega$. Then $\mathcal{F}_T$ is the set of all subsets of $\Omega$, representing complete information.

Let $0 < p < 1$ and define

$$P(i_1, \ldots, i_T) = p^{i_1 + \cdots + i_T}(1 - p)^{T - (i_1 + \cdots + i_T)}.$$

By repeating the obvious computation

$$P(i_1, \ldots, i_{T-1}, 0) + P(i_1, \ldots, i_{T-1}, 1) = p^{i_1 + \cdots + i_{T-1}}(1 - p)^{T - (i_1 + \cdots + i_{T-1})} \qquad \text{(A.1.3)}$$

we see that

$$\sum_{\omega \in \Omega} P(\omega) = 1,$$

and $P$ is a probability measure over $\mathcal{F}_T$. (If we think of 0 as "failure" and 1 as "success" in a sequence of $T$ independent trials, the probability of $\omega = (i_1 \ldots, i_T)$ is the probability of observing exactly $k$ successes and $T - k$ failures in precisely the order the 0's and 1's appear in $\omega$.) Define the random variables

$$J_k(i_1, \ldots, i_T) = i_k, \quad k = 1, \ldots, T.$$

Each $J_k$ is clearly $\mathcal{F}_k$-measurable. Moreover, these variables are independent, because

$$P(J_1 = i_1, \ldots, J_T = i_T) = P(i_1, \ldots, i_T) = p^{i_1 + \cdots + i_T}(1 - p)^{T - (i_1 + \cdots + i_T)}$$

and, by reasoning as in (A.1.3),

$$P(J_k = i_k) = \sum_{i_1, \ldots, i_{k-1}, i_{k+1}, \ldots, i_T} p^{i_1 + \cdots + i_T}(1 - p)^{T - (i_1 + \cdots + i_T)}$$

$$= p^{i_k}(1 - p)^{1 - i_k}$$

for all $i_k = 0$ or $1$, $k = 1, \ldots, T$. $\qquad\qquad\blacksquare$

**Theorem A.1.16 (Conditional Expectation and Independence).** *If $Y$ and $G$ are independent, then $E[Y \mid G] = E[Y]$. In particular, if $Y$ and $Z$ are independent, then*

$$E[Y \mid Z] = E[Y].$$

*Moreover, for any two functions $f$ and $g$,*

$$E[f(Y)g(Z)] = E[f(Y)]E[g(Z)].$$

The converse of the first assertion in this theorem is not true. Here is a counter-example. Suppose $X$ and $Z$ are independent random variables with mean 0, and let $Y = XZ$. Then $E[Y \mid Z] = E[Y]$, but $Y$ and $Z$ are not independent. A valid converse to the second assertion exists: if $E[f(Y)g(Z)] = E[f(Y)]E[g(Z)]$ for a sufficiently large class of functions $\{f, g\}$ (for example, all continuous functions), then $Y$ and $Z$ are independent.

## SECTION A.1.4 │ MARTINGALES

**Definition A.1.17.** *Suppose $X = \{X_n; n = 0, 1, \ldots\}$ is adapted to a filtration $\{\mathcal{F}_n; n = 0, 1, \ldots\}$. Then $X$ is a **martingale** if $E[X_{n+1} \mid \mathcal{F}_n] = X_n$, for all $n = 0, 1, \ldots$.*

**Example A.1.9.** In the setting of the previous example, the process

$$X_0 = 1, \qquad X_k = a^k b^{J_1 + \cdots + J_k}, \quad k = 1, \ldots, T$$

is adapted. It is (or should be) intuitively clear that $J_{k+1}$ and $\mathcal{F}_k$ are independent (Exercise A.8). Thus,

$$
\begin{aligned}
E[X_{k+1} \mid \mathcal{F}_k] &= X_k E[ab^{J_{k+1}} \mid \mathcal{F}_k] \\
&= X_k E[ab^{J_{k+1}}] \\
&= X_k a(pb + 1 - p)
\end{aligned}
$$

from the independence of $J_{k+1}$ and $\mathcal{F}_k$. Then $X$ is a martingale if and only if $a(pb + 1 - p) = 1$. ∎

## SECTION A.1.5 │ STOPPING TIMES

In many financial models, the point in time when a particular event occurs is of importance: the time an American option is exercised, the time a down-and-out option becomes worthless, the time of ruin in risk theory. In the real world, we cannot appeal to the future in determining whether an event has occurred or not. For instance, we may very well speak of

$$\tau_1 = \text{first time the price of a stock reaches \$20.}$$

But, if the car you're driving doesn't have a fuel gauge, it is difficult to see how you can determine when

$$\tau_2 = 15 \text{ minutes before running out of gas}$$

occurs, without knowing the future. Mathematicians have much freedom in defining random variables, and both $\tau_1$ and $\tau_2$ are allowed; these variables are known as *random times*. The random times that "do not depend on the future" are called *stopping times*. Both $\tau_1$ and $\tau_2$ above are random times, but only $\tau_1$ qualifies as a stopping time.

A difficulty arises with the definition of stopping times, in that stopping times need not occur at all, depending on chance. For example, the stock price $S$ may (with a certain probability) remain forever under $20, and then $\tau_1$ will not be defined. The convention adopted is to write $\tau_1 = +\infty$ when the event defining the stopping time does not happen. This, of course, does not mean that the event occurs at time $k = +\infty$. The mathematical consequence is that a stopping time $\tau$ takes values in $\{0, \ldots, T\} \cup \{+\infty\}$.

**Definition A.1.18.** *Let $\tau$ be a random variable taking values in $\{0, \ldots, T\} \cup \{+\infty\}$. The variable $\tau$ is a **stopping time** if for all $k = 0, \ldots, T$ the set $\{\omega : \tau(\omega) \leq k\}$ is in $\mathcal{F}_k$. The field $\mathcal{F}_\tau$ is the set of all sets $A$ in $\mathcal{F}$ such that $A \cap \{\omega : \tau(\omega) \leq k\} \in \mathcal{F}_k$ for all $k \geq 0$.*

The requirement for $\tau$ to be a stopping time is thus that at time $k, k = 0, 1, \ldots, T$, enough information be available to determine whether or not $\tau$ has occurred. The field $\mathcal{F}_\tau$ represents the information available at time $\tau$.

**Example A.1.10.** In Example A.1.7, let $\tau$ be the first time the process $X$ goes above 0.05, or, in symbols,

$$\tau = \min\{t : X_t > 0.05\}.$$

On intuitive grounds $\tau$ "does not depend on the future." We first verify this formally and then determine $\mathcal{F}_\tau$.

From the definitions of $X_k$ given previously we obtain

$$\{\omega : \tau(\omega) \leq 1\} = \{\omega_2, \omega_3\} \in \mathcal{F}_1,$$
$$\{\omega : \tau(\omega) \leq 2\} = \{\omega_2, \omega_3\} \in \mathcal{F}_2,$$
$$\{\omega : \tau(\omega) \leq 3\} = \{\omega_2, \omega_3\} \in \mathcal{F}_3,$$

and thus $\tau$ is indeed a stopping time. Next, it is clear that $\emptyset \cap \{\omega : \tau(\omega) \leq k\} = \emptyset \in \mathcal{F}_k$, since each $\mathcal{F}_k$ is a field. Obviously

$$\{\omega_1\} \cap \{\omega : \tau(\omega) \leq k\} = \emptyset \in \mathcal{F}_k, \quad \forall k,$$

but for $i = 2, 3$,

$$\{\omega_i\} \cap \{\omega : \tau(\omega) \leq 1\} = \{\omega_i\} \notin \mathcal{F}_1 = \{\emptyset, \{\omega_1\}, \{\omega_2, \omega_3\}, \Omega\}.$$

Thus, $\mathcal{F}_\tau$ contains only the sets $\emptyset$ and $\{\omega_1\}$, plus their complements, which implies $\mathcal{F}_\tau = \mathcal{F}_1$.

The last result can be interpreted as follows: if we observe the process $X$ up to $\tau$, then we only "see" the event $\{\omega_2, \omega_3\}$, with no possibility of distinguishing between these two states of nature. The complementary event $\{\omega_1\}$ is observed if $\tau$ does not occur. ∎

# Section A.2
# Information Structures, Stochastic Processes in the General Case

We now describe more general concepts from the theory of probability. Comparing the definitions and theorems given in the finite case with the more general ones below will prove beneficial. This section defines some important concepts that do not involve probability.

**Definition A.2.1.** A set is said to be **finite** if the number of its elements is finite. A set is said to be **countable** if it is finite, or if all its elements can be put in a one-to-one correspondence with the natural numbers $1, 2, \ldots$.

It can be shown that the rational numbers are countable, but the real numbers in any interval $(a, b)$ (with $a < b$) are not. (The number of reals in an interval is of a "higher order of infinity.") The set of rational numbers is denoted as $\mathcal{Q}$, and the set of real numbers $\mathfrak{R}$.

**Definition A.2.2.** Let $\Omega$ be a set, and let $\mathcal{F}$ be a set of subsets of $\Omega$. Then $\mathcal{F}$ is a $\sigma$-**field** (or $\sigma$-**algebra**) if the following conditions are satisfied:

a. $\Omega \in \mathcal{F}$,

b. $A \in \mathcal{F}$ implies $A^c \in \mathcal{F}$, and

c. $A_n \in \mathcal{F}, n = 1, 2, \ldots$ implies $\bigcup_{n \geq 1} A_n \in \mathcal{F}$.

*In particular, the σ-field $\mathcal{F}$ generated by the intervals of $\mathfrak{R}$ is called the* **Borel** **σ-field** *and is denoted* $\mathcal{B}(\mathfrak{R})$.

Each σ-field is a field, but a field may not be a σ-field. In the case where $\Omega$ is finite, requirement (c) reduces to finite unions only, and hence each field is a σ-field. In the more general case the possibility of infinite (though countable) unions cannot be avoided. When the sample space $\Omega$ is countable every σ-field is generated by a partition of $\Omega$. In the general case this is no longer true; in particular, $\mathcal{B}(\mathfrak{R})$ is not generated by a partition of $\mathfrak{R}$, and it contains many more sets than just the "countable unions of open intervals and the complements of countable unions of open intervals"; see, for example, Dothan [48, p. 161].

Consider a set $\Omega$ and $\mathcal{F}$ a σ-field of subsets of $\Omega$; this is denoted $(\Omega, \mathcal{F})$.

**Definition A.2.3.** *A mapping $X$ from $(\Omega, \mathcal{F})$ to $(\mathfrak{R}, \mathcal{B}(\mathfrak{R}))$ is a* **random variable** *(abbreviated* **r.v.**) *if*

$$B \in \mathcal{B}(\mathfrak{R}) \text{ implies } \{\omega : X(\omega) \in B\} \in \mathcal{F}. \tag{A.2.1}$$

**Example A.2.1.** Suppose the possible outcomes are $\Omega = \{\omega_1, \omega_2, \omega_3\}$, and $\mathcal{F} = \{\emptyset, \Omega, \{\omega_1\}, \{\omega_2, \omega_3\}\}$. (Equivalently, the σ-field $\mathcal{F}$ is generated by the partition $\mathcal{P} = \{\{\omega_1\}, \{\omega_2, \omega_3\}\}$ of $\Omega$.) Suppose $X$ is the next period's interest rate and is modeled by the mapping

$$\omega_1 \longmapsto 0.05,$$
$$\omega_2 \longmapsto 0.10,$$
$$\omega_3 \longmapsto 0.08.$$

This is the same as writing $X(\omega_1) = 0.05$, $X(\omega_2) = 0.10$, $X(\omega_3) = 0.08$. Is $X$ a random variable (in this particular model)? The answer is no. If we consider the set $B = \{0.08\}$, which is an element of $\mathcal{B}(\mathfrak{R})$ (see Exercise A.13), we see that

$$\{\omega : X(\omega) \in B\} = \{\omega : X(\omega) = 0.08\} = \{\omega_3\} \notin \mathcal{F}.$$

Here $\mathcal{F}$ is "too small," or "contains too little information," to make $X$ a random variable. If we change the σ-field, then $X$ may become a random variable, for instance, when $\mathcal{F}$ is replaced with $\mathcal{G} = \{\text{the set of all subsets of } \Omega\}$. ∎

Stated another way, $X$ is a random variable if "$X$ is $\mathcal{F}/\mathcal{B}(\mathfrak{R})$-measurable." The latter emphasizes that two spaces necessarily exist in the definition of a random variable:

$$(\Omega, \mathcal{F}) \xrightarrow{X} (\Re, \mathcal{B}(\Re)),$$
$$\omega \longmapsto X(\omega).$$

We have more than one way to check the measurability of a mapping; the example above illustrates one possibility. Another way is to verify that

$$\{\omega \mid X(\omega) < a\} \in \mathcal{F}$$

for each real number $a$.

**Definition A.2.4.** A **stochastic process** is a family of random variables $\{X_t; t \in \mathcal{T}\}$ defined on the same space $(\Omega, \mathcal{F})$.

Throughout this book the set of time points $\mathcal{T}$ is either a subset of the natural numbers such as $\{0, \ldots, T\}$ or an interval.

**Definition A.2.5.** The family of $\sigma$-fields $\{\mathcal{F}_t; t \in \mathcal{T}\}$ is a **filtration** if
a. $\mathcal{F}_t \subseteq \mathcal{F}, \quad \forall t \in \mathcal{T}$ (that is, $\mathcal{F}_t$ is a **sub-$\sigma$-field** of $\mathcal{F}$), and
b. $t_1 \leq t_2$ implies $\mathcal{F}_{t_1} \subseteq \mathcal{F}_{t_2}$.
   The process $X = \{X_t; t \in \mathcal{T}\}$ is said to be **adapted** to $\{\mathcal{F}_t; t \in \mathcal{T}\}$ if $X_t$ is $\mathcal{F}_t$-measurable $\forall t \in \mathcal{T}$. For a fixed $\omega \in \Omega$ the set of values $\{X_t(\omega); t \in \mathcal{T}\}$ is called the **realization, trajectory, sample path,** or simply **path** of $X$ for the state of the world $\omega$.

A set $\Omega$ on which are defined a $\sigma$-field $\mathcal{F}$ and a filtration $\mathbf{F} = \{\mathcal{F}_t, t \in \mathcal{T}\}$ will be denoted $(\Omega, \mathcal{F}, \{\mathcal{F}_t, t \in \mathcal{T}\})$, or $(\Omega, \mathcal{F}, \mathbf{F})$.

**Definition A.2.6.** Let $\tau$ be a random variable defined on $(\Omega, \mathcal{F}, \{\mathcal{F}_t; t \in \Re_+\})$ and taking values in $\overline{\Re}_+$. The random variable $\tau$ is a **stopping time** if, for each $t \geq 0$, the set $\{\omega : \tau(\omega) \leq t\}$ is in $\mathcal{F}_t$. The $\sigma$-field $\mathcal{F}_\tau$ is the set of all sets $A$ in $\mathcal{F}$ such that $A \cap \{\omega : \tau(\omega) \leq t\} \in \mathcal{F}_t$ for all $t \geq 0$.

**Remarks:**
1. The measurability requirement has to be suitably modified for random variables, such as stopping times, which may take infinite values.
2. We give here the most basic (and naive) treatment of stopping and hitting times, without due reference to essential technical points such as the right-continuity of the filtration, or properties of the set $B$. For these topics see the more specialized works on stochastic processes, such as Karatzas and Shreve [106]. ∎

An important type of stopping time is when a stochastic process enters a certain region for the first time. Let $X = \{X_t;\ t \in \mathfrak{R}_+\}$ be a stochastic process, $B$ be a subset of $\mathfrak{R}$, and define

$$\tau_B(\omega) = \begin{cases} \inf\{t \in \mathfrak{R}_+;\ X_t(\omega) \in B\} & \text{if this set is not empty,} \\ +\infty & \text{if the set above is empty.} \end{cases}$$

Time $\tau_B$ is called the *hitting time of set* $B$. Very often $B$ is an interval; in Example A.1.10, for instance, $\tau$ is the hitting time of the interval $(0.05, \infty)$.

***Example A.2.2 (Risk Theory).*** Consider two sequences of random variables defined on $(\Omega, \mathcal{F})$: the *individual claims* $\{C_k;\ k \geq 1\}$, and the *arrival times* $\{\tau_k;\ k \geq 1\}$. Claim $C_k$ occurs at time $\tau_k$; we set $\tau_0 = 0$ and assume that for all $\omega$

$$\tau_{k+1}(\omega) > \tau_k(\omega), \quad \forall k \geq 0 \quad \text{and} \quad \lim_{k \to \infty} \tau_k(\omega) = +\infty.$$

We define the number of claims in $[0, t]$ as

$$N_t(\omega) = \max\{k : \tau_k(\omega) \leq t\}, \quad \text{with } N_0(\omega) = 0,$$

and the *aggregate claims process* as

$$S_t(\omega) = \sum_{k=1}^{N_t(\omega)} C_k(\omega).$$

(An empty sum has value 0.) The simplest risk-theoretic model assumes that premiums are paid continuously at a constant rate $c > 0$ and that there is no interest. The insurer's surplus is then

$$U_t(\omega) = u + ct - S_t(\omega), \quad t \geq 0.$$

This is known as the *surplus process*, and $u$ is the *initial surplus* (see Figure A.2).

Ruin is said to occur if some time $t \geq 0$ exists such that $U_t < 0$. We define the *time of ruin*

$$\tau(\omega) = \begin{cases} \inf\{t \in \mathfrak{R}_+ : U_t(\omega) < 0\} & \text{if there is ruin} \\ +\infty & \text{otherwise.} \end{cases}$$

Then $\tau$ is the hitting time of the set $(-\infty, 0)$. It can be shown that $\tau$ is a stopping time. The discrete-time counterpart of this model is considered in Example A.5.2. ∎

Finally, observe that a stochastic process can be seen as a single mapping from one space to another, instead of a whole collection of such mappings (refer to (2.1)).

FIGURE **A.2** | *A Sample Path of the Risk Process*

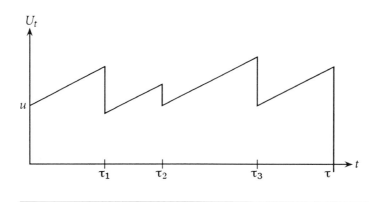

The process $X = \{X_t; t \in \Re_+\}$ can be viewed as a mapping from $\Omega$ to the set of paths

$$(\Omega, \mathcal{F}) \xrightarrow{X} \{\text{function space}\},$$

$$\omega \longmapsto \{X_t(\omega); t \in \Re_+\}.$$

This interpretation agrees with the way stochastic processes are simulated on a computer. For instance, to simulate interest rates $X_1, \ldots, X_n$ we can use, say, $n$ pseudo-random numbers $U_1, \ldots, U_n$. It is then "natural" to think of these as related to a single "state of the world" $\omega$; we then obtain one interest rate path, denoted $X_1(\omega), \ldots, X_n(\omega)$. Each new iteration of $n$ numbers then yields a new interest rate path, which is an element of the set of all possible paths, that is, the set of all vectors $(x_1, \ldots, x_n)$ of real numbers.

# Section A.3
# Probability Measures, Expectations

## SECTION A.3.1 | MEASURES

**Definition A.3.1.** *A real-valued set function $\mu$ on $(\Omega, \mathcal{F})$ is a **measure** if*

a.  $\mu(\emptyset) = 0, \mu(A) \geq 0$ for all $A \in \mathcal{F}$, and

b.  *For any countable collection $\{A_1, A_2, \ldots\}$ of disjoint elements of $\mathcal{F}$,*

$$\mu\left(\bigcup_{i \geq 1} A_i\right) = \sum_{i \geq 1} \mu(A_i).$$

A ***probability measure***, *or simply* ***probability***, *is any measure* $\mu$ *such that* $\mu(\Omega) = 1$.
*If* $\mu$ *is a probability measure, the triple* $(\Omega, \mathcal{F}, \mu)$ *is called a* ***probability space***.

***Example A.3.1 (Lebesgue measure).*** The so-called *Lebesgue measure* $\lambda$ of an interval
is simply its length

$$\lambda([a, b]) = \lambda([a, b)) = \lambda((a, b]) = \lambda((a, b)) = b - a$$

for all $-\infty \leq a < b \leq \infty$. It can be shown that $\lambda(A)$ also makes sense for other
elements of $\mathcal{B}(\mathfrak{R})$. The idea that $\lambda(A)$ is "the length of $A$" becomes less obvious,
however. For instance, the equations above mean that $\lambda(\{x\}) = 0$ for any real number
$x$. Then part (b) of the definition of measure implies that for any countable set $A$ in $\mathfrak{R}$
we have $\lambda(A) = 0$. In particular, the Lebesgue measure of the set of rational numbers,
$Q$, is 0, because the set is countable. But $Q$ is dense in $\mathfrak{R}$; that is, between any two
real numbers there is at least one rational number (and hence an infinity of them).
Thus, $Q$ has no "holes" of positive length and spreads over the whole of $\mathfrak{R}$, whereas
its Lebesgue measure, or "generalized length," is nil.

   If we restrict Lebesgue measure to the interval $(0, 1)$, we then obtain what is
called the *uniform probability measure* on $((0, 1), \mathcal{B}(0, 1))$. ∎

***Example A.3.2.*** Let $\Omega$ be any countable set $\{\omega_1, \omega_2, \ldots\}$, and let $\{a_1, a_2, \ldots\}$ be such
that $a_i \geq 0$ and $\sum_i a_i = 1$. If we set

$$P(\{\omega_i\}) = a_i \quad \text{for all } i,$$

then $P$ is a probability. ∎

***Example A.3.3.*** Let $f$ be any nonnegative function such that

$$\mu([a, b]) = \int_a^b f(x)\, dx$$

exists for all $-\infty \leq a < b \leq \infty$ (it may be infinite). Then, as with Lebesgue measure,
$\mu$ can be shown to extend to a measure on $(\mathfrak{R}, \mathcal{B}(\mathfrak{R}))$. The value of $\mu(A)$ is written

$$\int_A f(x)\, dx$$

even when $A$ is not an interval. (Note: Here the integral has to be interpreted in the
Lebesgue sense; see below.)

This class of measures includes the Lebesgue measure as a special case (set $f(x) \equiv 1$). If $f$ is a nonnegative function such that $\int_{\Re} f(x)\, dx = 1$, then $\mu$ is a probability measure. ∎

## SECTION A.3.2 | DISTRIBUTIONS

Recall that a random variable is a mapping from $(\Omega, \mathcal{F})$ to $(\Re, \mathcal{B}(\Re))$. If a probability measure $P$ exists over $(\Omega, \mathcal{F})$, then $X$ *induces* a probability measure on $(\Re, \mathcal{B}(\Re))$.

**Definition A.3.2.** *The **distribution** of X is the probability measure $P_X$ defined by*

$$P_X(A) = P\{\omega : X(\omega) \in A\}, \quad A \in \mathcal{B}(\Re).$$

*The **distribution function** of X is*

$$F_X(x) = P_X((-\infty, x]) = P\{\omega : X(\omega) \le x\}, \quad x \in \Re.$$

**Example A.3.4 (*The exponential distribution*).** Suppose $\Omega = (0, 1)$, $\mathcal{F} = \mathcal{B}(0, 1)$, $P$ is the uniform probability measure on $(0, 1)$, and

$$X(\omega) = -\log \omega, \quad \omega \in (0, 1).$$

Then for any $x \ge 0$,

$$F_X(x) = P(\omega : -\log \omega \le x) = P(\omega : \omega \ge e^{-x}) = 1 - e^{-x}. \qquad ∎$$

This example describes the usual way to generate the exponential distribution on a computer: generate random numbers with a $U(0, 1)$ distribution, and then apply the transformation $-\log(\cdot)$. The idea we are describing is similar, but more general. The initial space $\Omega$, although not specified, nevertheless represents an urn from which we draw the states of the world $\omega$. The probability measure $P$, plus the particular mapping $X$ (be it one or more random variables), determines the distribution observed in the "real" world $\Re$ (or $\Re^n$).

## SECTION A.3.3 | INTEGRATION, EXPECTATION

**Definition A.3.3.** *A **partition** of $\Omega$ is a countable collection $\{A_1, A_2, \ldots\}$ of disjoint subsets of $\Omega$ with the property that $\bigcup_i A_i = \Omega$. A random variable X is **simple** if there is a finite partition of $\Omega$, $\{A_1, \ldots, A_m\}$, $A_i \in \mathcal{F}$, and real numbers $x_i$, $i = 1, \ldots, m$, such that*

$$X(\omega) = \sum_{i=1}^{m} x_i I_{A_i}(\omega).$$

The **expectation of** $X$, or **integral of** $X$ **with respect to** $P$, is defined as

$$E[X] = \int X \, dP = \sum_{i=1}^{m} x_i P(A_i). \tag{A.3.1}$$

**Example A.3.5.** Let $\Omega = (0, 1)$, $\mathcal{F} = \mathcal{B}(0, 1)$, and $P$ be the uniform probability measure on $(0, 1)$. The sets

$$A_1 = \left(0, \tfrac{1}{8}\right) \cup \left(\tfrac{3}{4}, \tfrac{7}{8}\right), \qquad A_2 = \left[\tfrac{1}{8}, \tfrac{2}{3}\right),$$
$$A_3 = \left(\tfrac{2}{3}, \tfrac{3}{4}\right] \cup \left[\tfrac{7}{8}, 1\right), \qquad A_4 = \left\{\tfrac{2}{3}\right\}$$

form a partition of $\Omega$. Define a simple random variable $X$ as follows:

$$X(\omega) = I_{A_1}(\omega) + 2 I_{A_2}(\omega) + 3 I_{A_3}(\omega) + 500{,}000{,}000 \, I_{A_4}(\omega).$$

Then

$$\int X \, dP = 1 P(A_1) + 2 P(A_2) + 3 P(A_3) + 500{,}000{,}000 \, P(A_4) = \frac{47}{24}.$$

We might have given any value to $X$ on the set $A_4$ without affecting $E[X]$, since $A_4$ has measure 0. ∎

**Definition A.3.4.** An event $A$ occurs **almost surely**, or **with probability one**, if $P(A) = 1$. The random variables $X$ and $Y$ are equal almost surely, or with probability one, if $P(\omega : X(\omega) = Y(\omega)) = 1$. The abbreviations used are **a.s.** and **w.p.1**.

The expectation (if it exists) of an arbitrary random variable is obtained by taking limits of expressions such as (A.3.1). Two variables that are equal a.s. have the same expectation. The following result shows how the expectation of a function of a random variable can be calculated from the distribution of the variable.

**Theorem A.3.5.** Let $X$ be a random variable, and $Y = g(X)$ for some measurable function $g$. Assume $E[Y]$ exists.

a.  Suppose $X$ takes only a countable set of values $\{a_1, a_2, \ldots\} \subset \mathfrak{R}$. Then

$$E[Y] = E[g(X)] = \sum_i g(a_i) P(\omega : X(\omega) = a_i).$$

b.  Suppose $X$ has a density $f_X(\cdot)$; that is, $F_X(x) = \int_{-\infty}^{x} f_X(y) \, dy \; \forall x \in \mathfrak{R}$. Then

$$E[Y] = E[g(X)] = \int_{-\infty}^{\infty} g(x) f_X(x) \, dx.$$

Integration with respect to a measure $\mu$ is defined in the same way as with respect to a probability measure. In the case of Lebesgue measure, the notation used most often is $\int f(x)\,dx$.

## SECTION A.3.4 | ABSOLUTE CONTINUITY, RADON-NIKODYM THEOREM

*Definition A.3.6.* *If $\mu$ and $\nu$ are measures on $(\Omega, \mathcal{F})$, $\mu$ is said to be absolutely continuous with respect to $\nu$ if, for any $A \in \mathcal{F}$, $\nu(A) = 0$ implies $\mu(A) = 0$. This is denoted $\mu \ll \nu$. If $\mu \ll \nu$ and $\nu \ll \mu$, that is, if they are mutually absolutely continuous measures, then $\mu$ and $\nu$ are said to be* **equivalent***.*

*Example A.3.6.* Consider a countable sample space $\Omega = \{\omega_1, \omega_2, \ldots\}$, $\mathcal{F}$ the set of all subsets of $\Omega$, and $P$ a probability measure on $(\Omega, \mathcal{F})$. Define some nonnegative random variable $Z$ on this space. Then the rule

$$Q(A) = \sum_{\omega_i \in A} Z(\omega_i) P(\omega_i) \tag{A.3.2}$$

defines a new measure $Q$ (see the definition of measure at the beginning of this section). It is obvious that $Q \ll P$. The measure $Q$ is a probability measure if and only if $Q(\Omega) = \sum_i Q(\omega_i) = 1$. But by (A.3.2), this is equivalent to $\sum_i Z(\omega_i) P(\omega_i) = 1$. Thus, $Q$ is a probability if and only if $E^P[Z] = 1$. ∎

*Example A.3.7.* Generalize the previous example: consider a nonnegative random variable $Z$ on a space $(\Omega, \mathcal{F}, P)$ and define

$$Q(A) = E^P[ZI_A]. \tag{A.3.3}$$

Then $Q \ll P$; if $P(A) = 0$, then $ZI_A$ is $P$-a.s. equal to the zero random variable, which implies $Q(A) = 0$. Clearly, $Q$ is a probability measure if and only if $E^P[Z] = 1$. ∎

The measure $Q$ defined in (A.3.3) ((A.3.2) being a special case) is denoted as $Z.P$. The last examples show that $Z.P$ is a new measure, which is automatically absolutely continuous with respect to $P$. The next theorem says the converse: any measure $Q$ that is absolutely continuous with respect to $P$ has to be of the form $Z.P$.

*Theorem A.3.7.* [*Radon-Nikodym*] *Let a measure $\mu$ and a probability measure $P$ be defined on $(\Omega, \mathcal{F})$, and assume $\mu \ll P$. Then there exists a nonnegative random variable $Z$ on the same space such that*

$$\mu(A) = \int_A Z\,dP = E^P[ZI_A], \quad \forall A \in \mathcal{F},$$

*that is to say,* $\mu = Z.P$. *The latter is a probability measure if and only if* $E^P[Z] = 1$.

**Definition A.3.8.** *If* $\mu = Z.P$, *then* $Z$ *is called the Radon-Nikodym derivative of* $\mu$ *with respect to* $P$. *Each of the following has exactly the same meaning:*

$$\mu = Z.P, \qquad \frac{d\mu}{dP} = Z, \qquad d\mu = Z dP, \qquad \mu(d\omega) = Z(\omega) P(d\omega).$$

Now consider a probability space $(\Omega, \mathcal{F}, P)$ and a random variable $Z \geq 0$ with $E^P[Z] = 1$. Then $Q = Z.P$ is a probability measure, and the rule $E^Q[I_A] = E^P[Z I_A]$ extends by linearity to simple random variables $X = \sum_{i=1}^m x_i I_{A_i}$. By taking limits, we get the following result:

$$E^Q[X] = E^P[ZX] \tag{A.3.4}$$

whenever one of these expectations exists.

## SECTION **A.3.5** | CONDITIONAL EXPECTATION

The definition of conditional expectation given in Section A.1.2 applies only to the case of finite (or countable) $\Omega$. In the general case, $\sigma$-fields are rarely generated by partitions of $\Omega$, and Definition A.1.12 breaks down. We introduce the concept of conditional expectation ("c.e.") in yet another way, leading to the general definition, based on the Radon-Nikodym theorem. (Another possible line of attack is to first define c.e.'s as orthogonal projections of square-integrable variables on $L^2(\mathcal{G})$, and then to extend them by approximation to simple integrable variables. We do not pursue this idea here; see Exercise A.31.

Suppose $I$ and $Y$ are independent, and that $I$ takes value 0 with probability $p$, and value 1 with probability $q$ $(= 1 - p)$. Let $X = IY$. If $E[Y] = m$, then

$$E[XI = 0] = 0, \qquad E[X \mid I = 1] = m. \tag{A.3.5}$$

We can restate (A.3.5) as follows: the c.e. of $X$ given $I$ is a function of $I$, taking value 0 if $I = 0$ (probability $p$), and value $m$ if $I = 1$ (probability $q$). The c.e. is therefore a random variable, in effect a transformation of $I$:

$$g(i) = E[X \mid I = i],$$

$$(\Omega, \mathcal{F}) \xrightarrow{I} (\Re, \mathcal{B}(\Re)) \xrightarrow{g(\cdot)} (\Re, \mathcal{B}(\Re)),$$

$$E[X \mid I] = g(I) \quad \text{(a random variable)}.$$

Similarly, we may view the c.e. $E[U \mid V]$ as a random variable whose values are $E[U \mid V = v]$. This extends to $E[U \mid V_1, \ldots, V_n]$. However, this is not enough, since in continuous-time models there are often an infinity of variables we condition on, and it becomes very messy (if at all possible) to define a c.e. in the fashion above. The way out is to condition with respect to the $\sigma$-field generated by the random variables.

Returning to (A.3.5), consider the $\sigma$-field

$$\mathcal{G} = \sigma(I) = \{\emptyset, G_0, G_1, \Omega\}$$

where $G_0 = \{\omega \mid I(\omega) = 0\}$ and $G_1 = \{\omega \mid I(\omega) = 1\}$. Define a random variable $Z$ on $(\Omega, \mathcal{G}, P)$ as $Z(\omega) = 0$ on $G_0$ and $Z(\omega) = m$ on $G_1$. Then $Z$ has the same distribution as $E[X \mid I]$. Furthermore,

$$E[ZI_{G_0}] = 0 = E[XI_{G_0}]$$

and

$$E[ZI_{G_1}] = qm = E[XI_{G_1}].$$

Finally, by its very definition, $Z$ is measurable with respect to $\mathcal{G}$, the "information provided by $I$." Hereafter we write indifferently

$$E[X \mid I] \quad \text{or} \quad E[X \mid \mathcal{G}].$$

We now give the general definition of c.e.

**Definition A.3.9.** *Let $X$ be a random variable defined on $(\Omega, \mathcal{F}, P)$ such that $E[|X|] < \infty$, and let $\mathcal{G}$ be a sub-$\sigma$-field of $\mathcal{F}$. A random variable $Z$ satisfying*
*a.     $Z$ is $\mathcal{G}$-measurable, and*
*b.     $E[ZI_G] = E[XI_G]$, for all $G \in \mathcal{G}$,*
*is called the **conditional expectation** of $X$ with respect to $\mathcal{G}$ and is denoted $E[X \mid \mathcal{G}]$. If $\mathcal{G} = \sigma(Y_1, \ldots, Y_n)$ for some random vector $(Y_1, \ldots, Y_n)$, then $Z$ is also denoted $E[X \mid Y_1, \ldots, Y_n]$.*

C.e.'s are not necessarily *unique.* If two or more random variables satisfy the above conditions, then they are a.s. equal. The *existence* of c.e.'s is guaranteed by the Radon-Nikodym theorem. To see this, let $X \geq 0, E[X] < \infty$ be defined on $(\Omega, \mathcal{F}, P)$, and let

$$\mu(G) = E[XI_G], \quad G \in \mathcal{G}.$$

Obviously $\mu$ is a measure on $\mathcal{G}$, and clearly $P(G) = 0$ implies $\mu(G) = 0$, that is, $\mu \ll P$. Thus, a random variable $Z$ exists such that

$$E[XI_G] = \mu(G) = E[ZI_G], \quad G \in \mathcal{G}.$$

($Z$ is necessarily $\mathcal{G}$-measurable, which is what distinguishes it from $X$ in the above equation.) For a random variable $X$ with positive and negative values we proceed separately for $X^+$ and $X^-$, and then combine the resulting c.e.'s.

**Remark:** The relationship between the random variable $E[Y \mid X_1, \ldots, X_n]$ just defined and the *number* $E[Y \mid X_1 = x_1, \ldots, X_n = x_n]$ often encountered in applications is as follows. Define

$$g(x_1, \ldots, x_n) = E[Y \mid X_1 = x_1, \ldots, X_n = x_n].$$

It can be shown that, with probability one,

$$E[Y \mid X_1, \ldots, X_n] = g(X_1, \ldots, X_n).$$

## SECTION A.3.6 | PROPERTIES OF CONDITIONAL EXPECTATION

a. If $X$ is $\mathcal{G}$-measurable, then $E[X \mid \mathcal{G}] = X$ a.s. (If $\mathcal{G}$ contains sufficient information concerning $X$, then conditioning on $\mathcal{G}$ simply returns $X$ itself.)

b. Consider $\sigma$-fields $\mathcal{G}_1 \subset \mathcal{G}_2 \subset \mathcal{F}$. Then

$$E[E[X \mid \mathcal{G}_2] \mid \mathcal{G}_1] = E[X \mid \mathcal{G}_1]$$

and

$$E[E[X \mid \mathcal{G}_1] \mid \mathcal{G}_2] = E[X \mid \mathcal{G}_1].$$

(This is the *law of iterated expectations.* When conditioning successively with respect to different sub-$\sigma$-fields, the end result is always the c.e. with respect to the smallest one.)

c. $E[X \mid \{\emptyset, \Omega\}] = E[X]$. (Conditioning on no information at all returns the least informative c.e.)

d. $E[E[X \mid \mathcal{G}]] = E[X]$. (This is a special case of (b).)

e. If $g$ is a convex function, and if $E[|g(X)|] < \infty$, then $g[E[X \mid \mathcal{G}]] \leq E[g(X) \mid \mathcal{G}]$. (This is *Jensen's inequality.*)

f. If $Y$ is $\mathcal{G}$-measurable, and both $E[X]$ and $E[YX]$ exist, then $E[YX \mid \mathcal{G}] = YE[X \mid \mathcal{G}]$. (This is called *taking out what is known.*)

g. If $X$ and $Y$ are independent, then

$$E[g(X) \mid Y] = E[g(X)].$$

h.  (Dominated convergence theorem) If $X_n \xrightarrow{\text{a.s.}} X$, $|X_n| \leq Y$ for all $n$, and $E[Y] < \infty$, then $E[X_n \mid \mathcal{G}] \xrightarrow{\text{a.s.}} E[X \mid \mathcal{G}]$.

**Remark:** Properties (e) and (h) are often applied to ordinary (unconditional) expectations. These particular cases may be obtained by setting $\mathcal{G} = \{\emptyset, \Omega\}$.

# Section A.4
# Brownian Motion

We list some of the properties of Brownian motion, also called the Wiener process. This process is of great importance in continuous-time finance, which is introduced in Chapter 10. Two intuitive derivations of Brownian motion are given at the end of this section, one as a limit of shifted Poisson processes, and the other as a limit of random walks.

**Definition A.4.1.** *A stochastic process* $\{X_t; t \geq 0\}$ *is said to have* **independent increments** *if all collections of random variables of the form*

$$X_{t_2} - X_{t_1}, \ldots, X_{t_n} - X_{t_{n-1}}$$

*are independent, for any set of points* $0 \leq t_1 < \cdots < t_n$. *The process has* **stationary increments** *if the distribution of* $X_{t'} - X_t$ *only depends on the time difference* $t' - t$, *for any* $t, t', t < t'$.

**Definition A.4.2.** *A process* $B = \{B_t; t \geq 0\}$ *is a* **standard Brownian motion** (*or* **Wiener process**) *if*

a.  $B_0 = 0$ *a.s.*,
b.  $B_t - B_s \sim N(0, t - s)$, *for all* $0 \leq s < t$,
c.  $B$ *has independent increments, and*
d.  *the paths of* $B$ *are a.s. continuous.*
*Any transformation of standard Brownian motion of the form*

$$W_t = \mu t + \sigma B_t, \quad t \geq 0, \ \mu, \sigma \ \text{constants, with } \sigma > 0, \qquad (\text{A.4.1})$$

*is simply called* **Brownian motion**, *with* **drift** $\mu$ *and* **diffusion coefficient** $\sigma$.

The notation $N(0, t - s)$ in $(b)$ means that the random variable $B_t - B_s$ has the normal distribution with mean 0 and variance $t - s$. It is a simple exercise

(Exercise A.33) to verify that, if $B$ is standard Brownian motion, then

$$\text{Cov}(B_s, B_t) = \min(s, t). \tag{A.4.2}$$

We now turn to the behavior of the paths of Brownian motion, which is very different from that of the ordinary functions of calculus.

**Definition A.4.3.** *Let $f$ be a real-valued function defined on $[a, b]$, and consider all the partitions $\pi$ of $[a, b]$. Here a partition means a finite set of points $t_0, t_1, \ldots, t_m$, with $a = t_0 < t_1 < \cdots < t_m = b$. The **total variation** (or **simple variation**) of $f$ over $[a, b]$ is*

$$V_{[a,b]}^f = \sup_{\pi} \sum_{k=0}^{m-1} |f(t_{k+1}) - f(t_k)| \tag{A.4.3}$$

*where the supremum is taken over all the partitions $\pi$ of $[a, b]$.*

Intuitively, the total variation of a function $f$ over an interval is the total distance covered by $f(t)$ in absolute terms. If a function is monotone, then its total variation over $[a, b]$ is simply

$$V_{[a,b]}^f = |f(b) - f(a)|. \tag{A.4.4}$$

It is easy to see that (A.4.4) is correct: if $f$ is increasing, then any sum such as the one in (A.4.3) is composed of terms that all cancel out, except for the first and last ones. If $f$ is a "smooth" function (say, with a continuous derivative), then we may approximate $f$ by a succession of linear segments with slopes agreeing over each subinterval $[t_k, t_{k+1}]$, so

$$|\Delta f(t_k)| \approx |f'(t_k)| \, \Delta t_k$$

where $\Delta t_k = t_{k+1} - t_k$. As the partition gets finer and finer, the sum in (A.4.2) has the obvious limit

$$V_{[a,b]}^f = \int_a^b |df(t)| = \int_a^b |f'(t)| \, dt \tag{A.4.5}$$

(the integral of the absolute value of the speed). The functions we ordinarily see in calculus are smooth enough for this result to hold.

In order to discuss the total variation of Brownian motion, we now introduce the related concept of quadratic variation.

**Theorem A.4.4.** *Suppose B is standard Brownian motion. Then for any sequence of partitions $0 = t_0 < t_1 < \cdots < t_m = T$ such that $\max(\Delta t_k) \to 0$, we have*

$$\lim(P) \sum_{k=0}^{m-1} \left( B_{t_{k+1}} - B_{t_k} \right)^2 = T$$

*where the limit is in the sense of convergence in probability.*

The limit above is called the *quadratic variation of standard Brownian motion*, and the result is sometimes expressed as

$$\int_0^T (d B_t)^2 = T.$$

(This is a relation between random variables, with $T$ being a constant random variable.) For an ordinary Brownian motion $W$ given by (A.4.1), we then have

$$\int_a^b (d W_t)^2 = \sigma^2 (b - a). \tag{A.4.6}$$

An empirical estimation of $\sigma^2$ is then

$$\hat{\sigma}^2 = \frac{1}{b - a} \sum_k \left( \Delta W_{t_k}(\omega) \right)^2,$$

where $\Delta W_{t_k}(\omega) = W_{t_{k+1}}(\omega) - W_{t_k}(\omega)$. By contrast, the drift $\mu$ cannot be recovered from a single Brownian path $\omega$ over a finite interval.

The previous result concerns the quadratic variation of Brownian motion has surprising consequences. Because $|y| > y^2$ for small $y$, we would expect that a finite quadratic variation implies a larger total variation. This, in turn, has implications regarding the differentiability of the trajectories or sample paths. The following theorem makes those ideas more precise. Its proof can be found in the standard texts, for example, Revuz and Yor [156].

**Theorem A.4.5.** *a. Brownian motion has a.s. paths of unbounded variation; that is, for all $\omega$,*

$$\int_a^b |d B_t(\omega)| = +\infty. \tag{A.4.7}$$

*b. Brownian motion has a.s. paths that are nowhere differentiable.*

## SECTION A.4.1 | HITTING TIMES OF BROWNIAN MOTION

For a Brownian motion given by (A.4.1), there is an explicit result concerning the time of first passage through one of two barriers. Let $a < 0 < b$. We define the stopping time

$$\tau = \min\{t \mid W_t = a \text{ or } W_t = b\}.$$

For $r > 0$, we let

$$\mathcal{A}(a, b) = \mathrm{E}\big[e^{-r\tau} I_{\{W_\tau = a\}}\big]$$

and

$$\mathcal{B}(a, b) = \mathrm{E}\big[e^{-r\tau} I_{\{W_\tau = b\}}\big]$$

(where $I_{\{W_\tau = a\}}$ and $I_{\{W_\tau = b\}}$ are the indicator functions of the events "$W$ reaches $a$ first" and "$W$ reaches $b$ first," respectively). We now show that

$$\mathcal{A}(a, b) = \frac{e^{\theta_2 b} - e^{\theta_1 b}}{e^{\theta_2 b + \theta_1 a} - e^{\theta_1 b + \theta_2 a}}, \qquad \mathcal{B}(a, b) = \frac{e^{\theta_1 a} - e^{\theta_2 a}}{e^{\theta_2 b + \theta_1 a} - e^{\theta_1 b + \theta_2 a}}, \qquad (A.4.8)$$

where

$$\theta_1 = \frac{-\mu - \sqrt{\mu^2 + 2r\sigma^2}}{\sigma^2}, \qquad \theta_2 = \frac{-\mu + \sqrt{\mu^2 + 2r\sigma^2}}{\sigma^2}$$

are the solutions of the quadratic equation

$$\frac{1}{2}\sigma^2\theta^2 + \mu\theta - r = 0. \qquad (A.4.9)$$

A stochastic process of the form $\{\exp(-rt + \theta W_t); t \geq 0\}$, where $\theta$ is a number, is a martingale if and only if

$$\mathrm{E}[e^{-rt + \theta W_t}] = e^0 = 1,$$

which gives rise to condition (A.4.9). For $j = 1, 2$, we apply the so-called *optional sampling theorem* to the martingale $\{\exp(-rt + \theta_j W_t); t \geq 0\}$ and the stopping time $\tau$ to obtain

$$1 = \mathrm{E}[e^{-r\tau + \theta_j W_\tau}]$$

$$= \mathcal{A}(a, b)e^{\theta_j a} + \mathcal{B}(a, b)e^{\theta_j b}.$$

These are two linear equations for $\mathcal{A}(a, b)$ and $\mathcal{B}(a, b)$. The solution is given by (A.4.8).

## SECTION A.4.2 │ BROWNIAN MOTION
### IN SEVERAL DIMENSIONS

Often many different time series must be modeled simultaneously, which points to the need for Brownian motions in higher dimensions.

**Definition A.4.6.** *A process* $\boldsymbol{B} = (B^{(1)}, \ldots, B^{(d)})$ *is a* $d$-**dimensional standard Brownian motion** *if*

a.      *Each component* $B^{(k)}$ *is a standard Brownian motion, and*

b.      *All the components are independent.*

**Example A.4.1.** Write two-dimensional standard Brownian motion $\boldsymbol{B}$ as a column vector, and consider a new process $\boldsymbol{W}$ obtained by multiplying $\boldsymbol{B}$ by a constant $2 \times 2$ matrix $\boldsymbol{U} = (u_{i,j})$:

$$\boldsymbol{W}_t = \boldsymbol{U}\boldsymbol{B}_t, \quad t \geq 0.$$

Then $\boldsymbol{W}$ has mean $\boldsymbol{0}$ and covariance matrix

$$\begin{pmatrix} \mathrm{E}\left[(W_t^{(1)})^2\right] & \mathrm{E}\left[W_t^{(1)}W(2)_t\right] \\ \mathrm{E}\left[W_t^{(1)}W_t^{(2)}\right] & \mathrm{E}\left[(W_t^{(2)})^2\right] \end{pmatrix} = \begin{pmatrix} (u_{1.1}^2 + u_{1.2}^2)t & (u_{1.1}u_{2.1} + u_{1.2}u_{2.2})t \\ (u_{1.1}u_{2.1} + u_{1.2}u_{2.2})t & (u_{2.1}^2 + u_{2.2}^2)t \end{pmatrix}.$$

If $u_{1.1}u_{2.1} + u_{1.2}u_{2.2} \neq 0$, then $W^{(1)}$ and $W^{(2)}$ are *correlated*. ∎

## SECTION A.4.3 │ BROWNIAN MOTION AS A LIMIT
### OF POISSON PROCESSES

**Definition A.4.7.** *A process* $N = \{N(t); t \geq 0\}$ *is a* **Poisson process with parameter** $\lambda$ $(\lambda > 0)$ *if*

a.      $N(0) = 0$   *a.s.*

b.      $N(t) - N(s)$ *is a Poisson random variable with mean* $\lambda(t - s)$, *for all* $0 \leq s < t$.

c.      $N$ *has independent increments.*

d.      *The paths of* $N$ *are a.s. continuous from the right.*

A Poisson processes with parameter $\lambda$ can be obtained by letting the waiting times $\{\tau_k - \tau_{k-1}; k = 1, 2, \ldots\}$ be independent exponentially distributed variables (with mean $1/\lambda$) in Example A.2.2.

Poisson processes have stationary and independent increments, just like Brownian motion. By increasing the frequency of the jumps of the Poisson process, while decreasing their size in an appropriate manner, we obtain one-dimensional Brownian motion in the limit. More precisely, a Brownian motion $W$ with parameters $\mu$ and $\sigma^2$ (see (A.4.1)) is the limit of shifted Poisson processes $Y_k = \{Y_k(t)\}$ as $k \to 0$, where

$$Y_k(t) = k N_k(t) - c_k t, \qquad c_k = \frac{\sigma^2}{k} - \mu,$$

and the parameter for the Poisson process $\{N_k(t)\}$ is

$$\lambda_k = \frac{\sigma^2}{k^2}.$$

In Exercise 10.3 the problem is to show the convergence of the moment generating function (and thus of the distribution) of $Y_k(t)$ to that of $W_t$. A more refined analysis shows that the distribution of the whole processes $Y_k$ converges to the distribution of the whole process $W$.

## SECTION A.4.4 | BROWNIAN MOTION AS A LIMIT OF RANDOM WALKS

We first define random walks and then suggest how they can approximate Brownian motion.

**Definition A.4.8.** *A process* $X = \{X_n; n \geq 0\}$ *is a **random walk** if it has the representation*

$$X_n = \varepsilon_1 + \cdots + \varepsilon_n, \quad n \geq 1, \quad X_0 = 0,$$

*where* $\{\varepsilon_k\}$ *are i.i.d. random variables.*

To introduce Brownian motion, consider the particular case where

$$P(\varepsilon_k = 1) = P(\varepsilon_k = -1) = \frac{1}{2},$$

which implies $E[X_n] = 0$ and $\mathrm{Var}(X_n) = n$. The central limit theorem says that

$$\frac{X_n}{\sqrt{n}} \xrightarrow{\text{dist.}} \mathbf{N}(0, 1).$$

A meaningful limit is also obtained if the whole random walk is suitably rescaled. First, transform $X$ into a continuous-time process by setting

$$X_t^{(1)} = X_{\lfloor t \rfloor}, \quad t \in \Re_+, \tag{A.4.10}$$

where $[t]$ is the largest integer smaller than or equal to $t$. Thus, $X^{(1)} = \{X_t^{(1)}\}$ is constant on all intervals $[n, n+1)$, $n$ an integer. Then define

$$X_t^{(n)} = \frac{1}{\sqrt{n}} X_{[nt]}.$$

This includes and extends (A.4.10) (set $n = 1$). The jumps of the "continuous-time" random walk $X^{(n)} = \{X_t^{(n)}\}$ are $\pm 1/\sqrt{n}$, but there are $n$ such jumps in each interval of 1 time unit. As $n \longrightarrow \infty$, the paths of $X^{(n)}$ become continuous. The central limit theorem implies that

$$X_t^{(n)} - X_s^{(n)} \overset{\text{dist.}}{\longrightarrow} N(0, t - s). \tag{A.4.11}$$

Each $X^{(n)}$ has stationary and independent increments, which easily yields

$$\text{Cov}\left(X_s^{(n)}, X_t^{(n)}\right) = \min(s, t) + \mathcal{O}\left(\frac{1}{n}\right) \tag{A.4.12}$$

where $\mathcal{O}(1/n)$ tends to 0 as $n$ goes to $\infty$.

Once again, it can be rigorously shown that $X^{(n)}$ converges to Brownian motion.

**Remark:** There are many other sequences of processes that converge to Brownian motion and that have paths very different from the Poisson process or the random walk shown above.

## Section A.5
## Martingales

Let

$$X_n = \varepsilon_1 + \cdots + \varepsilon_n, \quad X_0 = 0 \tag{A.5.1}$$

be the random walk of the last section, and define $\mathcal{F}_0 = \{\emptyset, \Omega\}$, $\mathcal{F}_n = \sigma(X_1, \ldots, X_n)$. Then, for any $0 \leq m < n$,

$$E[X_n \mid \mathcal{F}_m] = E[X_m + \varepsilon_{m+1} + \cdots + \varepsilon_n \mid \mathcal{F}_m]$$

$$= X_m + E[\varepsilon_{m+1} + \cdots + \varepsilon_n \mid \mathcal{F}_m] \quad (\text{since } X_m \text{ is } \mathcal{F}_m\text{-measurable})$$

$$= X_m \quad (\text{since } \varepsilon_{m+k} \text{ is independent of } \mathcal{F}_m, \text{ and } E[\varepsilon_{m+k}] = 0).$$

Processes having the property "remaining constant in c.e." (such as $X = \{X_n\}$ above) are called martingales and have become very important in probability and finance theory. Discrete- and continuous-time martingales will be described separately, even though the main ideas are the same.

## SECTION A.5.1 | DISCRETE-TIME MARTINGALES

***Definition A.5.1.*** *Suppose* $X = \{X_n; n = 0, 1, \ldots\}$ *is adapted to a filtration* $\{\mathcal{F}_n; n = 0, 1, \ldots\}$ *and that* $E[|X_n|] < \infty$ *for all n. Then X is a*

- ***Martingale*** *if* $E[X_n | \mathcal{F}_m] = X_m,$ *for all* $0 \leq m < n$
- ***Submartingale*** *if* $E[X_n | \mathcal{F}_m] \geq X_m,$ *for all* $0 \leq m < n$
- ***Supermartingale*** *if* $E[X_n | \mathcal{F}_m] \leq X_m,$ *for all* $0 \leq m < n.$

Martingales remain constant in c.e., submartingales increase in c.e., and supermartingales decrease in c.e.

***Example A.5.1.*** Suppose $\{Y_n\}$ is a sequence of i.i.d. random variables, $E[|Y_n|] < \infty$ and $E[|Y_n|] = 1$, and let $X_n = Y_1 \cdots Y_n$, $\mathcal{F}_n = \sigma(Y_1, \ldots, Y_n)$. Then

$$E[X_n | \mathcal{F}_m] = X_m E[Y_{m+1} \cdots Y_n | \mathcal{F}_m] = X_m$$

for any $m < n$, and $X$ is a martingale.

A martingale of this type is obtained in the Cox, Ross, and Rubinstein ("binomial") model (see Section 6.3 and Example A.1.9). ∎

***Example A.5.2 (Risk Theory).*** Consider a discrete-time counterpart to the model in Example A.1.4. The surplus process is

$$U_n = u + \sum_{k=1}^{n} \varepsilon_k, \quad u > 0,$$

where $\varepsilon_k$ is the net result of the company's operation for the $k$-th year (premiums received minus claims paid). It is assumed that the $\{\varepsilon_k\}$ are i.i.d., and that $E[\varepsilon_k] > 0$. Suppose $R > 0$ exists such that $E[e^{-R\varepsilon_k}] = 1$. We let $\mathcal{F}_n$ be the σ-field generated by $\varepsilon_1, \ldots, \varepsilon_n$, which implies that $\{e^{-RU_n}\}$ is a martingale, and that

$$\tau = \min\{n : U_n < 0\} \text{ or } +\infty$$

is a stopping time relative to $\{\mathcal{F}_n\}$. ∎

***Lemma A.5.2.*** *If* $\{X_n\}$ *is a martingale, and* $\tau$ *a stopping time, then for each* $n \geq 0$

$$E[X_n I_{\{\tau \leq n\}}] = E[X_\tau I_{\{\tau \leq n\}}].$$

From the lemma with $X_n = e^{-RU_n}$, for all $n$, we have

$$e^{-Ru} = E[e^{-RU_n}]$$

$$= E\left[e^{-RU_\tau} I_{\{\tau \leq n\}}\right] + E\left[e^{-RU_n} I_{\{\tau > n\}}\right].$$

We see that $U_n$ converges a.s. to $\infty$ (see Exercise A.44) and that $e^{-RU_n} I_{\{\tau > n\}} \leq 1$ for all $n$; the dominated convergence theorem (property (h) of c.e.'s, see Section A.3.6) then implies that the second term on the right-hand side converges to 0 as $n \to \infty$. At the same time, when $n$ increases the indicator variables $I_{\{\tau \leq n\}}$ increase to $I_{\{\tau < \infty\}}$. Consequently,

$$e^{-Ru} = E\left[e^{-RU_\tau} I_{\{\tau < \infty\}}\right]$$

$$= E[e^{-RU_\tau} \mid \tau < \infty] P(\tau < \infty).$$

This yields a fundamental formula for the probability of ruin:

$$P(\tau < \infty) = \frac{e^{-Ru}}{E[e^{-RU_\tau} \mid \tau < \infty]}.$$

An immediate consequence is $P(\tau < \infty) < e^{-Ru}$. The parameter $R$ is called the *adjustment coefficient*.

**Example A.5.3 (Doob martingale).** Suppose $Y$ is integrable, and let $\{\mathcal{F}_n; n \geq 0\}$ be any filtration. Then the random variables

$$X_n = E[Y \mid \mathcal{F}_n], \quad n = 0, 1, \ldots$$

form a martingale, since, for $m < n$

$$E[X_n \mid \mathcal{F}_m] = E[E[Y \mid \mathcal{F}_n] \mid \mathcal{F}_m] = E[Y \mid \mathcal{F}_m] = X_m$$

by property (b) of c.e.'s (Section A.3.6) or by statement ($f$) of Theorem A.1.13.

The intuitive idea is of accumulating information about the variable $Y$. The no-arbitrage pricing of non-dividend-paying contingent claims leads to a martingale of this type (see Chapter 5). ∎

Doob martingales have proved very important in the theory of probability and its applications. First, the martingale $\{E[Y \mid \mathcal{F}_n]\}$ always converges as $n$ tends to infinity. Second, any uniformly integrable martingale $\{X_n\}$ can be put in the form $X_n = E[Y \mid \mathcal{F}_n]$, where $Y$ is the a.s. limit of $X_n$.

*Example A.5.4 (Pure Endowment Insurance).* An insurer will pay 1 unit to an insured at time $N$ (a positive integer) if the insured is still alive. A single premium $\pi$ is paid at time 0. Let $\tau$ be the future lifetime of the insured (completed years), let $\mathcal{F}_n$, $n \geq 1$ be the $\sigma$-field generated by the events $\{\tau \leq 1\}, \ldots, \{\tau \leq n\}$, and let $\mathcal{F}_0 = \{\emptyset, \Omega\}$. Classical insurance mathematics assumes that present values are computed at a fixed interest rate $i$. The loss on this contract is defined as

$$L = v^N I_{\{\tau > N\}} - \pi$$

where $v = 1/(1 + i)$. The reserve at time $0 < n < N$ is defined as

$$V_n = v^{N-n} \mathrm{E}[\, I_{\{\tau > N\}} \mid \mathcal{F}_n\,] = \begin{cases} v^{N-n} P(\tau > N \mid \tau > n), & \text{if } \tau > n \\ 0, & \text{if } \tau \leq n. \end{cases}$$

From the preceding example, the random variables $X_n = \mathrm{E}[L \mid \mathcal{F}_n]$, $n = 0, \ldots, N$ form a martingale $X$. Then, for $n = 1, \ldots, N$,

$$X_n = v^n V_n I_{\{\tau > n\}} - \pi. \tag{A.5.2}$$

For $n = 1, \ldots, N$, let

$$W_n = X_n - X_{n-1}$$

be the increments of $X$. It follows from Exercise A.41 that $W_1, W_2, \ldots$ are uncorrelated. Hence,

$$\mathrm{Var}(L) = \sum_{n=1}^{N} \mathrm{Var}(W_n).$$

This is a particular case of *Hattendorff's theorem*, which says that the same result holds for any life insurance or annuity contract. See Gerber [46, Chapter 3] and Bowers et al. [19, Section 7.10] for more details. ∎

## SECTION A.5.2 | CONTINUOUS-TIME MARTINGALES

*Definition A.5.3.* Suppose $X = \{X_t; t \in \Re_+\}$ is adapted to a filtration $\{\mathcal{F}_t; t \in \Re_+\}$ and that $\mathrm{E}|X_t| < \infty$ for all $t$. Then $X$ is a

- *Martingale if* $\mathrm{E}[X_t \mid \mathcal{F}_s] = X_s$, *for all* $0 \leq s < t$
- *Submartingale if* $\mathrm{E}[X_t \mid \mathcal{F}_s] \geq X_s$, *for all* $0 \leq s < t$
- *Supermartingale if* $\mathrm{E}[X_t \mid \mathcal{F}_s] \leq X_s$, *for all* $0 \leq s < t$.

For technical reasons, we make the following restriction: all continuous-time (sub-, super-)martingales are supposed right-continuous with left-hand limits ("cadlag"). Various regularization theorems say that most (if not all) (sub-, super-) martingales in finance have cadlag modifications.

**Example A.5.5.** Consider a standard Brownian motion $B$ with its filtration $\{\mathcal{F}_t = \sigma(B_s; s \leq t), t \geq 0\}$. Then $B$ is a martingale, because for $0 \leq s < t$

$$E[B_t \mid \mathcal{F}_s] = B_s + E[B_t - B_s \mid \mathcal{F}_s] = B_s,$$

and because the increments of $B$ are independent. This is not surprising: Brownian motion can be constructed as the limit of a sequence of random walks, each of which is a martingale.

The following two processes are also martingales ($t \geq 0$, $\alpha$ a constant):

$$Y_t = B_t^2 - t, \qquad Z_t = \exp\left(\alpha B_t - \frac{\alpha^2 t}{2}\right). \qquad \blacksquare$$

**Example A.5.6.** *Let $N$ be a Poisson process with parameter $\lambda$. The* compound Poisson *process $S$ is defined by introducing another sequence of i.i.d. random variables $\{C_k; k = 1, \ldots\}$, independent of the arrival times $\{\tau_k; k = 1, \ldots\}$ of the Poisson process, and letting*

$$S_0(\omega) = 0, \qquad S_t(\omega) = \sum_{k=1}^{N_t(\omega)} C_k(\omega), \qquad t > 0.$$

*The process $S$ also has stationary and independent increments.* $\blacksquare$

It can be verified that the following two transformations of $S$ are martingales, provided they have finite expectations:

$$Y_t = S_t - \lambda t E[C_1], \qquad Z_t = \exp\{u S_t - \lambda t (E[e^{u C_1}] - 1)\}, \qquad t \geq 0, u \text{ a constant}.$$

For more details on probability theory, see the texts by Billingsley [11], Loève [125], Neveu [139], Revuz and Yor [156], and Williams [207].

# Section A.6
# Exercises

## Exercise A.1

Let $\Omega = \{1, 2, 3, 4\}$. Determine which of the following sets of subsets of $\Omega$ are fields:
a. $\mathcal{F}_1 = \{\emptyset, \Omega\}$
b. $\mathcal{F}_2 = \{\emptyset, \Omega, \{1, 2\}\}$

c. $\mathcal{F}_3 = \{\emptyset, \Omega, \{1, 2\}, \{3, 4\}\}$

d. $\mathcal{F}_4 = \{\text{all possible subsets of } \Omega, \text{including } \emptyset\}$.

## Exercise A.2

Show that $\sigma(\mathcal{P})$, as defined in Definition A.1.3, is a field.

## Exercise A.3

Suppose $\Omega$ is a finite set, and let $\mathcal{P}$, $\mathcal{P}'$ be partitions of $\Omega$. We say that $\mathcal{P}'$ is finer than $\mathcal{P}$ if each set in $\mathcal{P}$ is the union of sets in $\mathcal{P}'$. Show that $\mathcal{P}'$ finer than $\mathcal{P}$ implies $\sigma(\mathcal{P}) \subset \sigma(\mathcal{P})$. Conversely, if $\mathcal{G}$ and $\mathcal{G}'$ are $\sigma$-fields on $\Omega$ with $\mathcal{G} \subset \mathcal{G}'$, then $\mathcal{G} = \sigma(\mathcal{P})$ and $\mathcal{G}' = \sigma(\mathcal{P}')$, where $\mathcal{P}$, $\mathcal{P}'$ are partitions of $\Omega$, and $\mathcal{P}'$ is finer than $\mathcal{P}$.

## Exercise A.4

Show that if a process is predictable, then it is adapted. Interpret this in words.

## Exercise A.5

Provide the missing details in the proof of Theorem A.1.13.

## Exercise A.6

Prove that the definition of c.e. given in Section A.1 is a particular case of the more general one given in Section A.3.

## Exercise A.7

Prove Theorem A.1.16.

## Exercise A.8

In Example A.1.8, prove that $J_{k+1}$ and $\mathcal{F}_k$ are independent.

## Exercise A.9

Prove that, in the setting of Example A.1.8, the following process is a martingale:

$$Y_0 = 0, \qquad Y_k = J_1 + \cdots + J_k - kp, \quad k = 1, \ldots, T.$$

## Exercise A.10

In Example A.1.10, suppose a random time $\tau$ is defined as follows:

$$\tau(\omega_1) = 2, \qquad \tau(\omega_2) = 1, \qquad \tau(\omega_3) = 2.$$

Show that $\tau$ is not a stopping time relative to the "natural" filtration defined in that example.

## Exercise A.11

In Example A.1.10, let

$$\theta(\omega) = \begin{cases} \min\{n : X_n(\omega) < 0.04\}, & \text{if this set is not empty} \\ +\infty, & \text{if the above set is empty.} \end{cases}$$

a. Check that $\theta$ is a stopping time.
b. Verify that $\theta$ does not always occur.
c. Show that $\mathcal{F}_\theta = \mathcal{F}$.

## Exercise A.12

Suppose $\mathcal{F}$ is a $\sigma$-field. Let $A_n \in \mathcal{F}$, $n = 1, 2, \ldots$. Why does it follow that $\bigcap_{n \geq 1} A_n \in \mathcal{F}$?

## Exercise A.13

$\mathcal{B}(\mathfrak{R})$ includes all intervals of the form $[a, b]$, $(a, b]$, $[a, b)$ and $(a, b)$. Check that the following sets are also in $\mathcal{B}(\mathfrak{R})$:

a. $\{x\}$ (the set containing the single element $x$)
b. $\{1, \frac{1}{2}, \frac{1}{3}, \ldots\}$
c. $\mathfrak{R} - \mathcal{Z}$, where $\mathcal{Z}$ is the set of natural numbers
d. $\mathcal{Q}$.

## Exercise A.14

Justify the following claim: "If a $\mathcal{F}$ is the set of all subsets of $\Omega$, then any mapping from $\Omega$ to $\mathfrak{R}$ is a random variable." (This justifies the definition of a random variable given in Section A.1, where the $\sigma$-field $\mathcal{F}$ is always supposed to be the set of all subsets of the sample space.)

## Exercise A.15

Suppose $\Omega = \{1, \ldots, 6\}$ and

$$\mathcal{F} = \{\emptyset, \{1, 2\}, \{3, 4\}, \{5, 6\}, \{1, 2, 3, 4\}, \{1, 2, 5, 6\}, \{3, 4, 5, 6\}, \Omega\}.$$

Determine which of the following mappings are $\mathcal{F}/\mathcal{B}(\Re)$-measurable:

a. $X(\omega) = \omega^2$

b. $X(\omega) = \frac{1}{\omega}$

c. $X(\omega) = [(\omega + 1)/2]$ where $[x]$ is the largest integer smaller than or equal to $x$.

## Exercise A.16

Show that a random variable that is measurable with respect to the uninformative $\sigma$-field $\mathcal{G} = \{\emptyset, \Omega\}$ has to be a constant. More generally, show that if $\mathcal{G}$ is generated by the partition $A_1, \ldots, A_n$ of $\Omega$, then any $\mathcal{G}/\mathcal{B}(\Re)$-measurable mapping is constant on each of the $\{A_k\}$.

## Exercise A.17

Show that "the $\sigma$-field generated by a random variable $Y$ is precisely equal to the family of pre-images of Borel sets," in symbols:

$$\sigma(Y) = \{Y^{-1}(B) \mid B \in \mathcal{B}(\Re)\},$$

with

$$Y^{-1}(B) = \{\omega \mid Y(\omega) \in B\}.$$

## Exercise A.18

Suppose $\tau$ is a stopping time. Show that $\mathcal{F}_\tau$ is a $\sigma$-field.

## Exercise A.19

Suppose $\theta$ and $\tau$ are stopping times. Show that

$$\theta \vee \tau = \max\{\theta, \tau\} \quad \text{and} \quad \theta \wedge \tau = \min\{\theta, \tau\}$$

are also stopping times. Interpret this in words.

## Exercise A.20

Suppose the filtration is indexed by the natural numbers: $\{\mathcal{F}_t; t = 0, 1, \ldots\}$. Show that the following conditions are equivalent:

a. $\{\omega : \tau(\omega) \leq t\} \in \mathcal{F}_t$, for all $t \geq 0$

b. $\{\omega : \tau(\omega) = t\} \in \mathcal{F}_t$, for all $t \geq 0$.

## Exercise A.21

Suppose $\Omega = \{\omega_i; 1 \le i \le 4\}$ and $\mathcal{F}$ is the set of all subsets of $\Omega$. The price of a stock is given in the table below. Let

$$\tau_1(\omega) = \begin{cases} \min\{t : S_t(\omega) = 11\}, & \text{if this set is not empty} \\ +\infty, & \text{if the above set is empty} \end{cases}$$

$$\tau_2(\omega) = \begin{cases} \min\{t : S_t(\omega) = 15\}, & \text{if this set is not empty} \\ +\infty, & \text{if the above set is empty.} \end{cases}$$

| | $S_t(\omega)$ | | |
|---|---|---|---|
| $\omega$ | $t = 1$ | $t = 2$ | $t = 3$ |
| $\omega_1$ | 10 | 12 | 11 |
| $\omega_2$ | 9 | 10 | 8 |
| $\omega_3$ | 10 | 13 | 11 |
| $\omega_4$ | 10 | 13 | 6 |

a. Show that $\tau_1$ and $\tau_2$ are stopping times.

b. Find $\mathcal{F}_{\tau_1}$ and $\mathcal{F}_{\tau_2}$, and give an interpretation in words.

## Exercise A.22

Let $\{\Omega, \mathcal{F}\} = \{(0, 1), \mathcal{B}(0, 1)\}$ and

$$X_t(\omega) = \omega^t, \quad \omega \in (0, 1), t \in \Re_+.$$

a. Is the process $X$ continuous?

b. Show that $\mathcal{F}_0 = \{\emptyset, \Omega\}$ and $\mathcal{F}_t = \mathcal{F}$, for all $t > 0$.

(Observe that the filtration above is not right-continuous, that is to say, $\cap_{t>0}\mathcal{F}_t \neq \mathcal{F}_0$.)

## Exercise A.23 (Risk Theory)

Let $U_t = 10 + t - S_t$, as in Example A.2.2. Suppose that for a certain $\omega$ the following values are known, plus that $U_t \ge U_{21}$ for all $t \ge 21$. What is $\tau(\omega)$? What would the answer be if $c$ were set equal to 2 instead of 1?

| $k$ | 1 | 2 | 3 | 4 | 5 | 6 | 7 |
|---|---|---|---|---|---|---|---|
| $\tau_k(\omega)$ | 3 | 4 | 9 | 15 | 18 | 19 | 21 |
| $C_k(\omega)$ | 4 | 3 | 11 | 9 | 2 | 7 | 1 |

## Exercise A.24

Let $\Omega = (0, 1)$, $\mathcal{F} = \mathcal{B}(0, 1)$, and $P$ be the uniform probability measure on $(0, 1)$, that is,

$$P(a, b) = b - a, \quad \forall\, 0 \le a < b \le 1.$$

Find the distribution of

a. $X_1(\omega) = \omega$
b. $X_2(\omega) = 2 - \omega$
c. $X_3(\omega) = 3 - 2\omega$
d. $X_4(\omega) = \omega^k$, $k$ a constant.

## Exercise A.25

In Example A.3.4, an exponentially distributed random variable with mean 1 is constructed. On the same probability space, construct two other ones with the following distributions:

a. Exponential: $f_Y(y) = \lambda e^{-\lambda y} I_{(0,\infty)}(y)$, $\lambda > 0$
b. Pareto: $f_Y(y) = (c/y^\alpha) I_{(d,\infty)}(y)$, $c, d > 0$, $\alpha > 1$.

## Exercise A.26

Two $\sigma$-fields $\mathcal{G}_i \subset \mathcal{F}$, $i = 1, 2$, are *independent* if

$$P(G_1 \cap G_2) = P(G_1)P(G_2), \quad \forall G_i \in \mathcal{G}_i, i = 1, 2.$$

Two random variables $U$ and $V$ are said to be independent if $\sigma(U)$ and $\sigma(V)$ are independent.

Show that this requirement is equivalent to

$$P(U \in A, V \in B) = P(U \in A)P(V \in B), \quad \forall A, B \in \mathcal{B}(\mathfrak{R}).$$

The above generalizes to any finite number of $\sigma$-fields (or random variables).

## Exercise A.27

Suppose $U$ and $V$ have joint p.d.f. $f_{U,V}$. Show that if $U$ and $V$ are independent (according to the definition in the previous exercise), then we must have

$$f_{U,V}(u, v) = f_U(u) f_V(v), \quad \forall u, v \in \Re,$$

where $f_U$ and $f_V$ are the marginal p.d.f.'s. (This condition is also sufficient for independence.)

## Exercise A.28

In the setting of Example A.3.6, give an example where $Q \ll P$ but $P \not\ll Q$.

## Exercise A.29

Define $\mathrm{Var}(X \mid \mathcal{F}) = \mathrm{E}[(X - \mathrm{E}[X \mid \mathcal{F})^2 \mid \mathcal{F}]$. Show that
a. $\mathrm{Var}(X \mid \mathcal{F}) = \mathrm{E}[X^2 \mid \mathcal{F}] - \{\mathrm{E}[X \mid \mathcal{F}]\}^2$
b. $\mathrm{Var}(X) = \mathrm{E}[\mathrm{Var}(X \mid \mathcal{F})] + \mathrm{Var}(\mathrm{E}[X \mid \mathcal{F}])$.

## Exercise A.30

Show that, if two or more random variables satisfy the conditions of the definition of c.e. (in the general case), then these random variables are a.s. equal.

## Exercise A.31

Suppose $X$ has a finite second moment. Show that $\mathrm{E}[X \mid \mathcal{G}]$ is, among all the variables $Z$ that are $\mathcal{G}$-measurable and have finite second moments, the one that minimizes $\mathrm{E}[(X - Z)^2]$.

## Exercise A.32

Using the properties of conditional expectations, show that if $X$ and $Y$ are independent, then

$$\mathrm{E}[f(X)g(Y)] = \mathrm{E}[f(X)]\mathrm{E}[g(Y)]$$

for any measurable functions $f$ and $g$ such that the two expectations on the right are finite.

## Exercise A.33

Verify (A.4.2).

## Exercise A.34

In the definition of total variation, prove that if $\pi$, $\pi'$ are two partitions of $[a, b]$ such that $\pi' \subset \pi$, then

$$\sum_{\pi'} |f(t_{k+1}) - f(t_k)| \leq \sum_{\pi} |f(t_{k+1}) - f(t_k)|.$$

## Exercise A.35

Suppose $f$ has a continuous derivative over $[a, b]$. Modify the heuristic justification of expression (A.4.5) to show that the length of the curve $\{(t, f(t)); a \leq t \leq b\}$ is

$$\int_a^b \sqrt{1 + f'(t)^2}\, dt.$$

## Exercise A.36

Suppose $B$ is a $d$-dimensional standard Brownian motion, and suppose $U$ is a $d \times d$ orthogonal matrix ($U^T = U^{-1}$). Show that $W = UB$ is also a $d$-dimensional standard Brownian motion.

## Exercise A.37

Verify (A.4.11) and (A.4.12).

## Exercise A.38

Suppose the $\{\varepsilon_k\}$ are i.i.d. but with some arbitrary distribution such that $E[\varepsilon_1] = 0$, $\text{Var}(\varepsilon_1) = 1$.

a. Check that (A.4.11) and (A.4.12) still hold.
b. Find an expression for the total variation of $X^{(n)}$ over interval $[0, T]$, and show that it has an expected value that tends to $+\infty$ as $n \to \infty$.
c. Find an expression for the quadratic variation of $X^{(n)}$ over interval $[0, T]$, and show that its expected value that tends to $T$ as $n \to \infty$.

## Exercise A.39

Show that a partition for the $\sigma$-field $\mathcal{F}_n$ in Example A.5.4 is

$$\{\{\tau \leq 1\}, \{1 < \tau \leq 2\}, \ldots, \{n - 1 < \tau \leq n\}, \{n < \tau\}\}.$$

Use this fact to derive (A.5.2).

## Exercise A.40

A martingale $X = \{X_n\}$ such that $E[X_n^2] < \infty$ for all $n$ is said to be *square-integrable*. Show that the increments of such a martingale are uncorrelated.

## Exercise A.41

Use (A.5.2) to show that, for $n = 2, 3, \ldots, N,$

$$W_n = v^n \big\{ [V_n - (1+i)V_{n-1}] I_{\{\tau > n\}} - (1+i)V_{n-1} I_{\{\tau \in (n-1, n]\}} \big\}.$$

Show that $\{W_n\}$ have mean zero and are uncorrelated.

## Exercise A.42

Show that for $\{X_n\}$ to satisfy the martingale condition $X_m = E[X_n \mid \mathcal{F}_m]$ for all $0 \le m < n$ ($m, n = 0, 1, \ldots$), it is sufficient that $X_n = E[X_{n+1} \mid \mathcal{F}_n]$ for all $n \ge 0$.

## Exercise A.43

Prove Lemma A.5.2.

## Exercise A.44

Suppose the variables $X_n = \varepsilon_1 + \cdots + \varepsilon_n$, $n = 1, 2, \ldots$, form a random walk, with $E[\varepsilon_k] = \mu > 0$. Show that $X_n$ converges a.s. to $+\infty$.

## Exercise A.45

Suppose $0 < \alpha < 1, 0 < \beta < 1$, and $\alpha + \beta = 1$. Let

$$X_{n+1} = \begin{cases} \alpha + \beta X_n, & \text{with probability } X_n \\ \beta X_n, & \text{with probability } 1 - X_n \end{cases}$$

for $n = 0, 1, \ldots$, with $X_0 = x_0 \in (0, 1)$. Show that $X_n \in (0, 1)$ for all $n$ and that $X = \{X_n\}$ is a martingale. Also find the limit distribution of $X_n$. (Hint: Consider $E[X_{n+1}(1 - X_{n+1}) \mid X_n]$.)

## Exercise A.46

Let $\{X_n\}$ be a martingale and $g$ a convex function. Use Jensen's inequality to show that, if $E[|g(X_n)|] < \infty$ for each $n$, then $\{g(X_n)\}$ is a submartingale.

## Exercise A.47

Let $X = \{X_n\}$ be a random walk and let $Y_n = Y_{n-1} + X_n$. Is $Y$ a martingale? Extend this to the continuous-time case by letting $B$ be standard Brownian motion; is $\int_0^t B_s \, ds$ a martingale?

## Exercise A.48

Show that a martingale $M$ has constant expectation: $E[M_t] = E[M_0]$ for all $t$.

# APPENDIX B
## ANSWERS TO SELECTED EXERCISES

## Chapter 1

1.1   a. (i) 5.42%

      (ii) 5.55%

1.3   $7,302,360

1.4   $0.055, 0.058, \ldots, 0.064$

1.6   a. 75.2% per year

    b. $-61.1\%$ per year

1.7   $15.38

1.8   10.22%

1.9   $ab + (1 - a)r_k, \sigma^2$

## Chapter 2

2.5   $0.0161, -0.0154$

2.7   a. 908.71

    b. 19

    c. $\sigma = 0.271$

    d. 40.46

2.8   27.49%

2.10   a. $c = 17.28, p = 4.85$

2.11   a. zero

     b. $1.64 billion

     c. to $20 billion

## Chapter 3

3.2    b.

| $i^{(2)}$ | $n=5$ | $n=10$ | $n=15$ | $n=20$ |
|---|---|---|---|---|
| 4% | 4,581.12 | 8,339.23 | 11,422.19 | 13,951.29 |
| 6 | 4,393.05 | 7,661.90 | 10,094.23 | 11,904.11 |
| 8 | 4,217.67 | 7,066.97 | 8,991.86 | 10,292.24 |
| 10 | 4,053.91 | 6,542.66 | 8,070.54 | 9,008.52 |
| 12 | 3,900.85 | 6,079.06 | 7,295.36 | 7,974.54 |

3.3    b.

| $i^{(12)}$ | $n=10$ | $n=20$ | $n=30$ |
|---|---|---|---|
| 5% | 4,627.61 | 8,405.46 | 11,432.18 |
| 7 | 4,464.74 | 7,787.37 | 10,153.49 |
| 9 | 4,304.34 | 7,201.75 | 9,009.54 |
| 11 | 4,146.97 | 6,653.77 | 8,007.29 |

## Chapter 4

4.13    0.5618

## Chapter 5

5.1    5.33

5.2    no, yes, $(0, 7/3)$

5.4    $(10.385, 14.768)$

5.5    a. 0.6 up, 0.4 down

       b. 0.6 up, 0.4 down

       c. 0%

       d. 11

5.6    yes, yes, $(1/6, 1/6, 1/6, s)^T$ with $s > 0$

5.7    0.54

5.8    $(1, 10/3)$

5.9    $(0.5, 0.2)^T$

5.10   a. no

       b. yes, $(1/12, 1/3, 1/12, 1/2)^T$

5.11   a. 2, 1, 3

       b. 233%, −100%, 67%

       c. 150%, 0%, 150%

5.12   0.101

## Chapter 6

6.5  3 time intervals:

Value: $409.30

Self-financing portfolio: $813.12 in the asset and borrowing of $403.82.

Delta: 40.66

20 time intervals:

Value: $409.35

Self-financing portfolio: $817.87 in the asset and borrowing of $408.52.

Delta: 40.89

6.7  3 time intervals: $0.295

6.8  Value: $0.402

Delta: 0.22

Gamma: 0.08

Theta: $-2.41$

6.9  European: $0.637

American: $0.672

6.10  Answers will depend on random number generator. Authors' results are:

100 simulations: $0.639, standard error 0.098

1000 simulations: $0.633, standard error 0.031

6.11  $1,436

## Chapter 7

7.4  $P(1, 3)$ and $P(2, 3)$ are as in table.

$P(0, 3) = 0.8646$.

$$P(1, 2) = \begin{cases} 0.9434, & i_1 = 6\% \\ 0.9524, & i_1 = 5\% \\ 0.9615, & i_1 = 4\% \end{cases}$$

$P(0, 2) = 0.9075$

$P(0, 1) = 0.9524$

7.6  7.88%

7.7  $v_0 = -\$9,020$

$$v_1 = \begin{cases} \$9,150, & i_1 = 6\% \\ -\$9,285, & i_1 = 5\% \\ -\$28,353, & i_1 = 4\% \end{cases}$$

7.8  Payer: $2,905; Receiver: $11,925

7.11  $1,438 + $1,350 = $2,788

7.15  0.0021

7.16  Time-1 futures price and put and call prices are as before; but time-0 futures price is 0.9530.

## Chapter 8

8.4    a. $(0.766, 0.362, -0.128)$, $(-1.60, 0.33, 1.27)$

8.5    a. $0.084, 0.111$

     b. $(0.4, 0.2, 0.4)$

8.6    $0.78, 0.115$

8.7    $(0.002, 0.004)$

8.8    b. $1.2$

     c. $0.75$, $\rho = 1$

     d. $0.0576, 0.0324$

     e. $\$45.25$

8.9    $(0.5445, 0.2070, 0.2485)$, $(0.1995, 0.2738, 0.5267)$, $(0.0269, 0.3073, 0.6658)$, $(0, 0.2, 0.8)$, $(0.0667, 0.9333)$

## Chapter 10

10.9   This is the probability that a Poisson process with parameter $\lambda^*$ has $n-1$ jumps between times $u$ and $t$ and that the $n$-th jump occurs at time $t$.

10.28  $Q_1(u, v) = \dfrac{\prod(u)v^{\theta_2} - u^{\theta_2}\prod(v)}{u^{\theta_1}v^{\theta_2} - u^{\theta_2}v^{\theta_1}},$

       $Q_2(u, v) = \dfrac{u^{\theta_1}\prod(v) - \prod(u)v^{\theta_1}}{u^{\theta_1}v^{\theta_2} - u^{\theta_2}v^{\theta_1}}.$

10.29  a. yes

      b. yes

      (by reasoning; no calculations necessary)

10.31  $-\kappa$

10.32  $\kappa = \dfrac{(\theta_2 - 1)\theta_1\bar{\varphi}^{\theta_1-1} - (\theta_1 - 1)\theta_2\bar{\varphi}^{\theta_2-1}}{(\theta_2 - 1)(\theta_1 - 1)(\bar{\varphi}^{\theta_1} - \bar{\varphi}^{\theta_2})}$

## Chapter 11

11.6   $0.6, 0.4$

# REFERENCES

1. K. J. Arrow, L. Hurwicz, and H. Uzawa. Constraint qualification in maximization problems. *Naval Research Logistics Quarterly*, 8:175–91, 1961.

2. D. F. Babbel and C. B. Merrill. Valuation of interest-sensitive financial instruments, *SOA Monograph M-FI96-1*. New Hope, Penn.: Frank J. Fabozzi Associates, 1996.

3. S. Babbs. Binomial valuation of lookback options. Working paper. London: Midland Global Markets, 1992.

4. A. Bacinello and F. Ortu. Single and periodic premiums for guaranteed equity-linked insurance under interest-rate risk: The "lognormal + Vasicek" case. In L. Peccati and M. Viren, editors, *Financial Modelling*, pages 1–24. Berlin: Physica-Verlag, 1993.

5. J. Barraquand and D. Martineau. Numerical valuation of high dimensional multivariate American securities. *Journal of Financial and Quantitative Analysis*, 30:383–405, 1995.

6. L. Besant, editor. *Commodity Trading Manual*, Chicago: Chicago Board of Trade, 1985.

7. M. J. Best and R. R. Grauer. The efficient set mathematics when mean-variance problems are subject to general linear constraints. *Journal of Economics and Business*, 42:105–20, 1990.

8. M. J. Best and R. R. Grauer. Sensitivity analysis for mean-variance portfolio problems. *Management Science*, 37:980–89, 1991.

9. G. O. Bierwag. *Duration Analysis: Managing Interest Rate Risk*. Cambridge, Mass.: Ballinger, 1987.

10. G. O. Bierwag, G. G. Kaufman, and A. L. Toevs. Single-factor duration models in a discrete general equilibrium framework. *Journal of Finance*, 37:325–38, 1982.

11. P. Billingsley. *Probability and Measure*, 2nd edition. New York: John Wiley and Sons, 1987.

12. F. Black. Capital market equilibrium with restricted borrowing. *Journal of Business*, 45:444–54, 1972.

13. F. Black, E. Derman, and W. Toy. A one-factor model of interest rates and its applications to Treasury bond options. *Financial Analysts Journal*, 46, no. 1 (Jan.–Feb.):33–39, 1990.

14. F. Black, M. C. Jensen, and M. Scholes. The capital asset pricing model: Some empirical tests. In M. C. Jensen, editor, *Studies in the Theory of Capital Market*, pages 79–124. New York: Praeger, 1972.

15. F. Black and R. Jones. Simplifying portfolio insurance. *Journal of Portfolio Management*, 14(1):48–51, 1987.

16. F. Black and M. Scholes. The pricing of options and corporate liabilities. *Journal of Political Economy*, 81:637–54, 1973.

17. M. Blume and I. Friend. A new look at the capital asset pricing model. *Journal of Finance*, 28:19–34, 1973.

18. Z. Bodie, A. Kane, and A. J. Marcus. *Investments*, 3rd edition. Chicago: Richard D. Irwin, 1996.

19. N. Bowers Jr., H. Gerber, J. Hickman, D. Jones, and C. Nesbitt. *Actuarial Mathematics*, 2nd edition. Schaumburg, Ill.: Society of Actuaries, 1997.

20. G. E. P. Box and G. M. Jenkins. *Time Series Analysis, Forecasting and Control*. San Francisco: Holden-Day, 1976.

21. P. P. Boyle. A lattice framework for option pricing with two state variables. *Journal of Financial and Quantitative Analysis*, 23:1–12, 1988.

22. P. P. Boyle. *Options and the Management of Financial Risk*. Schaumburg, Ill.: Society of Actuaries, 1992.

23. P. P. Boyle and S. H. Lau. Bumping up against the barrier with the binomial method. *Journal of Derivatives*, 1(4):6–14, 1994.

24. P. P. Boyle and X. Lin. Optimal portfolio selection with transaction costs. *North American Actuarial Journal*, 1(2):27–39, 1997.

25. P. P. Boyle and E. S. Schwartz. The pricing of equity-linked life insurance contracts. *Journal of Risk and Insurance*, 44:195–213, 1977.

26. M. J. Brennan and E. S. Schwartz. An equilibrium model of bond pricing and a test of market efficiency. *Journal of Financial and Quantitative Analysis*, 17:301–29, 1982.

27. M. Broadie and J. Detemple. American option valuation: New bounds, approximations, and a comparison of existing methods. *Review of Financial Studies*, 9:1211–50, 1996.

28. M. Broadie and P. Glasserman. Estimating security price derivatives by simulation. *Management Science*, 42:269–85, 1993.

29. M. P. Broadie and P. Glasserman. Pricing American-style securities using simulation. *Journal of Economic Dynamics and Control*, 21:1323–52, 1997.

30. P. L. Brockett and X. Xia. Operations research in insurance: A review. *Transactions of the Society of Actuaries*, 47:1–88, 1995.

31. T. Bucher. Asset/liability: Ansätze in der Portfoliotheorie. Mimeo. Zurich: ETH Zurich, 1994.

32. H. Bühlmann. *Mathematical Methods in Risk Theory*. Berlin: Springer-Verlag, 1970.

33. H. Bühlmann. F. Delbaen, P. Embrechts, and A. N. Shiryaev. On Esscher transforms in discrete finance models. *ASTIN Bulletin*, 1998, in press.

34. J. Carter. The derivation and application of an Australian stochastic investment model. *Transactions of the Institute of Actuaries of Australia*, 1:315–428, 1991.

35. D. R. Chambers, W. T. Carleton, and R. W. McEnally. Immunizing default-free bond portfolios with a duration vector. *Journal of Financial and Quantitative Analysis*, 23:89–104, 1988.

36. Chicago Board of Trade. *PCS Catastrophe Insurance Options*. Chicago: CBT, 1996.

37. H. Y. Cho and K. W. Lee. An extension of the three-jump process model for contingent claim valuation. *Journal of Derivatives*, 3(1):102–8, 1995.

38. N. A. Chriss. *Black-Scholes and Beyond: Option Pricing Models*. Chicago: Richard D. Irwin, 1997.

39. J. Connolly. Viaticals attract institutional money. *National Underwriter*, November 21, 1994, page 3. Life & Health/Financial Services Edition.

40. G. Constantinides. Habit formation: A resolution of the equity premium puzzle. *Journal of Political Economy*, 98:519–43, 1990.

41. S. D. Conte and C. de Boor. *Elementary Numerical Analysis: An Algorithmic Approach*, 3rd edition. New York: McGraw-Hill, 1981.

42. J. C. Cox and C. Huang. Optimum consumption and portfolio policies when asset prices follow a diffusion process. *Journal of Economic Theory*, 49:33–83, 1989.

43. J. C. Cox, J. Ingersoll, and S. A. Ross. An intertemporal general equilibrium model of asset prices. *Econometrica*, 36:363–84, 1985.

44. J. C. Cox, S. A. Ross, and M. Rubinstein. Option pricing: A simplified approach. *Journal of Financial Economics*, 7:229–63, 1979.

45. J. C. Cox and M. Rubinstein. *Options Markets*. Englewood Cliffs, N.J.: Prentice Hall, 1985.

46. R. Deaves. Modelling and predicting Canadian inflation and interest rate. *Proceedings of the Canadian Institute of Actuaries*, 24:600–711, 1994.

47. B. de Finetti. Il problema dei pieni. *Giornale dell'Instituto Italiano degli Attuari*, 3(1):1–88, 1940.

48. M. Dothan. *Prices in Financial Markets*. New York: Oxford University Press, 1990.

49. D. Duffie. *Security Markets: Stochastic Models*. London: Academic Press, 1988.

50. D. Duffie. *Dynamic Asset Pricing Theory*, 2nd edition. Princeton: Princeton University Press, 1996.

51. D. Duffie and J. Pan. An overview of value at risk. *Journal of Derivatives*, 4(3):7–49, 1997.

52. B. Dumas and B. Alliaz. *Financial Securities*. London: Chapman & Hall, 1995.

53. P. H. Dybvig and S. A. Ross. Arbitrage. In J. Eatwell, M. Milgate, and P. Newman, editors, *The New Palgrave: A Dictionary of Economics*, volume 1, pages 100–106. London: Macmillan, 1987. Reprinted in J. Eatwell, M. Milgate, and P. Newman, editors, *The New Palgrave: Finance*, pages 57–71. New York: W. W. Norton, 1989.

54. E. J. Elton and M. J. Gruber. *Modern Portfolio Theory and Investment Analysis*, 5th edition. New York: John Wiley & Sons, 1995.

55. R. F. Engle and C. W. Granger. Co-integration and error correction: Representation, estimation and testing. *Econometrica*, 55:251–76, 1987.

56. F. Esscher. On the probability function in the collective theory of risk. *Skandinavisk Aktuarietidskrift*, 15:175–95, 1932.

57. F. J. Fabozzi and T. D. Fabozzi, editors. *The Handbook of Fixed Income Securities*, 4th edition. Homewood, Ill.: Richard D. Irwin, 1995.

58. E. Falkenstein and J. Hanweck Jr. Minimizing basis risk from non-parallel shifts in the yield curve. *Journal of Fixed Income*, 6(1):60–68, 1996.

59. E. Falkenstein and J. Hanweck Jr. Minimizing basis risk from non-parallel shifts in the yield curve. Part II: Principal components. *Journal of Fixed Income*, 7(1):85–90, 1997.

60. E. F. Fama and J. Macbeth. Risk, return and equilibrium: Empirical test. *Journal of Political Economy*, 81:607–35, 1973.

61. L. Fisher. Evolution of the immunization concept. In Leibowitz [120], pages 21–26.

62. L. Fisher and R. L. Weil. Coping with the risk of interest-rate fluctuations: Returns to bondholders from naive and optimal strategies. *Journal of Business*, 44:408–31, 1971.

63. R. FitzHerbert. Stochastic investment models. *Transactions of the Institute of Actuaries of Australia*, 197–255, 1992.

64. H. G. Fong and O. Vasicek. Return maximization for immunized portfolio. In Kaufmann, Bierwag, and Toevs [109], pages 227–38.

65. H. G. Fong and O. Vasicek. A risk minimizing strategy for portfolio immunization. *Journal of Finance*, 39:1541–46, 1984.

66. E. W. Frees, Y. Kung, M. A. Rosenberg, V. R. Young, and S. Lai. Forecasting social security actuarial assumptions. *North American Actuarial Journal*, 1(4):49–82, 1997.

67. K. A. Froot, B. S. Murphy, A. B. Stern, and S. E. Usher. The emerging asset class: Insurance risk. In Securitization of Insurance Risk: The 1995 Bowles Symposium, *SOA Monograph M-FI97-1*. Schaumburg, Ill.: Society of Actuaries, 1997, pages 37–43.

68. D. Gale. *The Theory of Linear Economic Models*. New York: McGraw-Hill, 1960.

69. G. Gennotte and A. Jung. Investment strategies under transaction costs: The finite horizon case. *Management Science*, 40:385–404, 1994.

70. H. U. Gerber. *An Introduction to Mathematical Risk Theory*. S. S. Huebner Foundation Monograph Series No. 8. Homewood, Ill.: Richard D. Irwin, 1979.

71. H. U. Gerber. *Life Insurance Mathematics*, 3rd edtion. Berlin: Springer-Verlag, 1997.

72. H. U. Gerber, F. Michaud, and E. S. W. Shiu. Pricing Russian options with the compound Poisson process. *Transactions of the 25th International Congress of Actuaries*, (3):243–64, 1995.

73. H. U. Gerber and E. S. W. Shiu. Martingale approach to pricing perpetual American options. *ASTIN Bulletin*, 24:195–220, 1994.

74. H. U. Gerber and E. S. W. Shiu. Option pricing by Esscher transforms. *Transactions of the Society of Actuaries*, 46:99–140, 1994.

75. H. U. Gerber and E. S. W. Shiu. Actuarial bridges to dynamic hedging and option pricing. *Insurance: Mathematics and Economics*, 18:183–218, 1996.

76. H. U. Gerber and E. S. W. Shiu. Martingale approach to pricing perpetual American options on two stocks. *Mathematical Finance*, 6:303–22, 1996.

77. R. C. Goshay and R. L. Sandor. An inquiry into the feasibility of a reinsurance futures market. *Journal of Business Finance*, 5(2):56–66, 1973.

78. M. R. Granito. *Bond Portfolio Immunization.* Lexington, Mass.: Lexington Books, 1984.

79. R. R. Grauer. Normality, solvency and portfolio choice. *Journal of Financial and Quantitative Analysis*, 21:265–78, 1986.

80. R. C. Grinold and R. N. Kahn. *Active Portfolio Management.* Chicago: Probus, 1995.

81. N. H. Hakansson. Capital growth and the mean-variance approach to portfolio selection. *Journal of Financial and Quantitative Analysis*, 6:517–57, 1971.

82. G. H. Hardy, J. E. Littlewood, and G. Pólya. Some simple inequalities satisfied by convex function. *Messenger of Mathematics*, 58:145–48, 1929.

83. G. Harris. Statistical data analysis and stochastic asset model validation. *Transactions of the 25th International Congress of Actuaries*, 3:311–31, 1995.

84. A. C. Harvey. *Forecasting Structural Time-Series Models, and the Kalman Filter.* Cambridge: Cambridge University Press, 1989.

85. G. A. Hawawini, editor. *Bond Duration and Immunization: Early Developments and Recent Contributions.* New York: Garland, 1982.

86. A. T. Haynes and R. J. Kirton. The financial structure of a life office. *Transactions of the Faculty of Actuaries*, 21:141–97, 1952.

87. D. R. Heath, R. Jarrow, and A. Morton. Bond pricing and the term structure of the interest rates: A new methodology. *Econometrica*, 60(1):77–105, 1992.

88. J. C. Hickman. Investments implications of the actuarial design of life insurance products. *Journal of Risk and Insurance*, 38:571–83, 1971.

89. J. R. Hicks. *Value and Capital.* Oxford: Clarendon Press, 1939.

90. R. S. Hiller and C. Schaack. A classification of structured bond portfolio modeling techniques. *Journal of Portfolio Management*, 17, no. 1 (fall):37–48, 1990.

91. T. S. Y. Ho. Key rate durations: Measures of interest rate risks. *Journal of Fixed Income*, 2(2):29–44, 1992.

92. T. S. Y. Ho. Managing illiquid bonds and the linear path space. *Journal of Fixed Income*, 2(1):80–94, 1992. Comment by L. Pohlman and A. Wolf, 3(3):80–88, 1993.

93. T. S. Y. Ho and S. Lee. Term structure movements and pricing interest rate contingent claims. *Journal of Finance*, 41:1011–29, 1986.

94. M. Hogan. Problems in certain two-factor term structure models. *Annals of Applied Probability*, 3:576–81, 1993.

95. D. Holden and R. Perman. Unit roots and cointegration for the economist. In B. B. Rao, editor, *Cointegration for the Applied Economist*, chapter 3. London: Macmillan, 1994.

96. C. Huang and R. H. Litzenberger. *Foundations for Financial Economics*. Englewood Cliffs, N.J.: Prentice Hall, 1988.

97. P. Huber. A review of Wilkie's stochastic investment model. *Transactions of the 25th International Congress of Actuaries*, 3:335–64, 1995.

98. J. C. Hull. *Options, Futures, and Other Derivative Securities*, 3rd edition. Englewood Cliffs, N.J.: Prentice Hall, 1997.

99. J. E. Ingersoll. *Theory of Financial Decision Making*. Totowa, N.J.: Rowman and Littlefield, 1987.

100. R. Jarrow and S. Turnbull. *Derivative Securities*. Cincinnati: South-Western College Publishing, 1996.

101. F. J. Jones and F. J. Fabozzi. *The International Government Bond Markets*. Chicago: Probus, 1992.

102. C. W. Jordan Jr. *Life Contingencies*, 2nd edition. Chicago: Society of Actuaries, 1967.

103. C. Joy, P. P. Boyle, and K. S. Tan. Quasi-Monte Carlo methods in numerical finance. *Management Science*, 42:926–38, 1996.

104. B. Kamrad and P. Ritchken. Multinomial approximating models for options with $k$ state variables. *Management Science*, 37:1640–53, 1991.

105. J. Karamata. Sur un inégalité relative aux fonctions convexes. *Publications Mathématiques de l'Université de Belgrade*, 1:145–48, 1932.

106. I. Karatzas and S. Shreve. *Brownian Motion and Stochastic Calculus*. New York: Springer-Verlag, 1988.

107. S. Karlin. *Mathematical Methods and Theory in Games, Programming, and Economics*. Reading, Mass.: Addison-Wesley, 1959.

108. H. Kat and L. Verdonk. Tree surgery. *RISK*, 8(2):53–57, 1995.

109. G. G. Kaufmann, G. O. Bierwag, and A. Toevs, editors. *Innovations in Bond Portfolio Management: Duration Analysis and Immunization*. Greenwich, Conn.: JAI Press, 1983.

110. A. Keel and H. H. Mueller. Efficient portfolios in the asset liability context. *ASTIN Bulletin*, 25:33–48, 1995.

111. S. G. Kellison. *Theory of Interest*, 2nd edition. Homewood, Ill.: Richard D. Irwin, 1991.

112. S. A. Klugman, H. H. Panjer, and G. E. Willmot. *Loss Models: From Data to Decision*. New York: John Wiley & Sons, 1998.

113. R. Kocherlakota, E. S. Rosenbloom, and E. S. W. Shiu. Algorithms for cash-flow matching. *Transactions of the Society of Actuaries*, 40:477–84, 1988.

114. R. Kocherlakota, E. S. Rosenbloom, and E. S. W. Shiu. Cash-flow matching and linear programming duality. *Transactions of the Society of Actuaries*, 42:281–93, 1990.

115. R. W. Kolb and B. S. Wilson. *Real Data and Exercises for Finance and Economics*. Miami: Kolb, 1993.

116. K. C. Koopmans. *The Risk of Interest Fluctuations in Life Insurance Companies*. Philadelphia: Penn Mutual Life Insurance Company, 1942.

117. M. Lane. The perfume of the premium . . . or pricing insurance derivatives. In *Securitization of Insurance Risk*. Schaumburg, Ill.: Society of Actuaries Monograph Series, 1997. Bowles Symposium, Georgia State University, May 25–26, 1995.

118. P. D. Laporte, S. H. Cox, S. R. Linney, and L. Lombardi. Single premium deferred annuity persistency study. *Transactions of the Society of Actuaries Reports*, 1(1):281–332, 1992.

119. B. N. Lehmann and D. M. Modest. The empirical foundations of arbitrage pricing theory. *Journal of Financial Economics*, 21:213–54, 1988.

120. M. L. Leibowitz, editor. *Pros & Cons of Immunization: Proceedings of a Seminar on the Roles and Limits of Bond Immunization*. New York: Salomon Brothers, 1980.

121. G. J. Lidstone. On the approximate calculation of the values of increasing annuities and assurances. *Journal of the Institute of Actuaries*, 31:68–72, 1893.

122. J. Lintner. The valuation of risky assets and the selection of risky investments in stock portfolios and capital budgets. *Review of Economics and Statistics*, 47:13–37, 1965.

123. R. Litterman and J. Scheinkman. Common factors affecting bond returns. *Journal of Fixed Income*, 1(1):54–61, 1991.

124. R. Litzenberger and K. Ramaswamy. The effect of personal taxes and dividends on capital asset prices: Theory and empirical evidence. *Journal of Financial Economics*, 7:163–96, 1979.

125. M. Loève. *Probability Theory II*, 4th edition. New York: Springer-Verlag, 1978.

126. F. R. Macaulay. *Some Theoretical Problems Suggested by the Movements of Interest Rates, Bond Yields and Stock Prices in the United States since 1856*. New York: Bureau of Economic Research, 1938. Partially reprinted in Leibowitz [120] and Hawawini [85].

127. O. L. Mangasarian. *Nonlinear Programming*. New York: McGraw-Hill, 1969.

128. H. Markowitz. Portfolio selection. *Journal of Finance*, 7:77–91, 1952.

129. H. Markowitz. *Portfolio Selection: Efficient Diversification of Investments*. New York: John Wiley & Sons, 1959.

130. J. F. Marshall. *Futures and Options Contracting Theory and Practice*. Cincinnati: South-Western College Publishing, 1989.

131. J. F. Marshall and V. K. Bansal. *Financial Engineering: A Complete Guide to Financial Innovation*. New York: Allyn & Bacon, 1992.

132. R. C. Merton. Lifetime portfolio selection under uncertainty: The continuous time case. *Review of Economics and Statistics*, 51:247–57, 1969.

133. R. C. Merton. Theory of rational option pricing. *Bell Journal of Economics and Management Science*, 4:141–83, 1973.

134. R. C. Merton. *Continuous Time Finance*. Cambridge, Mass.: Blackwell, 1990.

135. T. C. Mills. *The Econometric Modelling of Financial Time Series*. Cambridge: Cambridge University Press, 1993.

136. R. B. Mitchell. *From Actuarius to Actuary*. Chicago: Society of Actuaries, 1974.

137. D. P. Moll. On the effect of a rise, or fall, in market values of securities, on the financial position and reserves of a life officer: A letter to the editor. *Journal of the Institute of Actuaries*, 43:105–7, 1909. Reprinted in S. Haberman and T. A.

Sibbett, editors, *History of Actuarial Science*, volume 7. London: Pickering & Chatto, 1995.

138. J. M. Mulvey and A. E. Thorlacius. The Towers Perrin global capital market scenario generation system. In W. T. Ziemba and J. M. Mulvey, editors, *World Wide Asset and Liability Modeling*. Cambridge: Cambridge University Press, 1997.

139. J. Neveu. *Bases mathématiques du calcul des probabilités*. Masson, 1970.

140. H. H. Panjer and G. E. Willmot. *Insurance Risk Models*. Schaumburg, Ill.: Society of Actuaries, 1992.

141. S. H. Paskov and J. F. Traub. Faster valuation of financial derivatives. *Journal of Portfolio Management*, 22(1):113–20, 1995.

142. G. Patrik. Reinsurance. In *Foundations of Casualty Actuarial Science*, pages 277–374. New York: Casualty Actuarial Society, 1990.

143. H. W. Pedersen, E. S. W. Shiu, and A. E. Thorlacius. Arbitrage-free pricing of interest-rate contingent claims. *Transactions of the Society of Actuaries*, 41:231–79, 1989.

144. A. Pelsser and T. Vorst. The binomial model and the Greeks. *Journal of Derivatives*, 1(3):45–49, 1994.

145. R. Perman. Cointegration: An introduction to the literature. *Journal of Economic Studies*, 18(3):3–30, 1991.

146. S. R. Pliska. *Introduction to Mathematical Finance: Discrete Time Models*. Oxford: Blackwell, 1997.

147. A. Post, editor. *Anatomy of a Merger*. Englewood Cliffs, N.J.: Prentice Hall, 1994.

148. E. Z. Prizman and Y. Tian. Duration measures, immunization, and utility maximization. *Journal of Banking and Finance*, 17:689–707, 1993.

149. F. M. Redington. Review of the principles of life-office valuations. *Journal of the Institute of Actuaries*, 78:286–315, 1952. Discussion, 316–40.

150. F. M. Redington. The phase of transition: An historical essay. *Journal of the Institute of Actuaries*, 109:83–96, 1982. Reprinted in Redington [151], 492–506.

151. F. M. Redington. *A Ramble through the Actuarial Countryside: The Collected Papers, Essays and Speeches of Frank Mitchell Redington, MA*. Staple Inn, London: Institute of Actuaries Students' Society, 1986.

152. R. R. Reitano. Multivariate duration analysis. *Transactions of the Society of Actuaries*, 43:335–76, 1991.

153. R. R. Reitano. Multivariate immunization theory. *Transactions of the Society of Actuaries*, 43:393–428, 1991.

154. R. R. Reitano. Nonparallel yield curve shifts and convexity. *Transactions of the Society of Actuaries*, 44:479–99, 1992.

155. R. R. Reitano. Multivariate stochastic immunization theory. *Transactions of the Society of Actuaries*, 45:425–61, 1993.

156. D. Revuz and M. Yor. *Continuous Martingales and Brownian Motion*. Berlin: Springer-Verlag, 1991.

157. P. Ritchken. *Derivative Markets: Theory, Strategy and Applications*. New York: HarperCollins, 1996.

158. E. L. Robbins, S. H. Cox, and R. D. Phillips. Application of risk theory to interpretation of stochastic cash-flow-testing results. *North American Actuarial Journal*, 1(2):85–98, 1997.

159. R. T. Rockafellar. *Convex Analysis*. Princeton: Princeton University Press, 1970.

160. L. C. G. Rogers. Equivalent martingale measures and no-arbitrage. *Stochastics and Stochastics Reports*, 51:41–49, 1994.

161. R. Roll. A critique of the asset pricing theory's tests. *Journal of Financial Economics*, 4:129–76, 1977.

162. R. Roll. A mean/variance analysis of tracking error. *Journal of Portfolio Management*, 19:13–22, 1992.

163. S. A. Ross. The arbitrage theory of capital asset pricing. *Journal of Economic Theory*, 13:341–60, 1976.

164. H. L. Royden. *Real Analysis*. New York: Macmillan, 1968.

165. M. Rubinstein. The valuation of uncertain income streams and the pricing of options. *Bell Journal of Economics*, 7:407–25, 1976.

166. P. A. Samuelson. The effects of interest rate increases on the banking system. *American Economic Review*, 35:16–27, 1945.

167. P. A. Samuelson. The fallacy of maximizing the geometric mean in long sequences of investment or gambling. *Proceedings of the National Academy of Sciences*, 68:2493–96, 1971.

168. SAS Institute. *SAS/ETS Software Applications Guide 1*. Version 6. Cary, N.C.: SAS, 1991.

169. U. Schaede. The development of organized futures trading: The Osaka Rice Bill Market of 1730. In W. T. Ziemba, W. Bailey, and Y. Hamao, editors, *Japanese*

*Financial Market Research, Contributions to Economic Analysis*, pages 339–66. Amsterdam: North-Holland, 1991.

170. J. Shanken. Multivariate proxies and asset pricing relations: Living with the Roll critique. *Journal of Financial Economics*, 18:91–110, 1987.

171. V. M. Shante, P. D. Franzetta, J. E. Hohmann, and J. A. Tilley. Securitization of policy loans. *Record of the Society of Actuaries*, 14(3):1395–1423, 1988.

172. K. P. Sharp. Inflation and investment returns: An overview. *Proceedings of the Canadian Institute of Actuaries*, 24:588–99, 1994.

173. K. P. Sharp. Modelling Canadian price and wage inflation. *Proceedings of the Canadian Institute of Actuaries*, 24:565–87, 1994.

174. W. F. Sharpe. Capital asset prices: A theory of market equilibrium under conditions of risk. *Journal of Finance*, 19:425–42, 1963.

175. W. F. Sharpe. A simplified model for portfolio analysis. *Management Science*, 9(2):277–93, 1963.

176. W. F. Sharpe and L. G. Tint. Liabilities: A new approach. *Journal of Portfolio Management*, 17:5–10, 1990.

177. L. Shepp and A. N. Shiryaev. The Russian option: Reduced regret. *Annals of Applied Probability*, 3:631–40, 1993.

178. M. Sherris. A one-factor interest rate model and the valuation of loans with prepayment provisions. *Transactions of the Society of Actuaries*, 46:251–301, 1994.

179. M. Sherris. The valuation of option features in retirement benefits. *Journal of Risk and Insurance*, 62:509–35, 1995.

180. M. Sherris, L. Tedesco, and B. Zehnwirth. Stochastic investment models: Unit roots, cointegration, state space and GARCH models for Australian data. Working Paper No. 33. University of Melbourne: Centre for Actuarial Studies, 1996.

181. E. S. W. Shiu. Immunization of multiple liabilities. *Insurance: Mathematics and Economics*, 7:219–24, 1988.

182. E. S. W. Shiu. On Redington's theory of immunization. *Insurance: Mathematics and Economics*, 9:171–76, 1990.

183. D. R. Siegal and D. F. Siegal. *Futures Markets*. Fort Worth: Dryden Press, 1990.

184. B. H. Solnik. An equilibrium model of the international capital market. *Journal of Economic Theory*, 8:500–525, 1974.

185. B. H. Solnik. Inflation and optimal portfolio choices. *Journal of Financial and Quantitative Analysis*, 13:903–25, 1978.

186. H. R. Stoll and R. E. Whaley. *Futures and Options*. Cincinnati: South-Western College Publishing, 1993.

187. E. Straub. *Non-Life Insurance Mathematics*. Berlin: Springer-Verlag, 1988.

188. R. Stulz. A model of international asset pricing. *Journal of Financial Economics*, 9:382–406, 1981.

189. A. Takayama. *Mathematical Economics*. Cambridge: Cambridge University Press, 1985.

190. A. Takayama. *Analytical Methods in Economics*. New York: Harvester Wheatsheaf, 1994.

191. R. J. Thomson. A stochastic investment model for actuarial use in South Africa. Paper presented to the Actuarial Society of South Africa convention, 1994.

192. R. J. Thomson. Stochastic investment modelling: The case of South Africa. *British Actuarial Journal*, 2:765–802, 1996.

193. J. E. Tiller Jr. and D. Fagerberg. *Life, Health & Annuity Reinsurance*. Winsted, Conn.: ACTEX, 1990.

194. J. A. Tilley. The application of modern techniques to the investment of insurance and pension funds. *Transactions of the 23rd International Congress of Actuaries*, R:301–26, 1988.

195. J. A. Tilley. An actuarial layman's guide to building stochastic interest rate generators. *Transactions of the Society of Actuaries*, 44:509–64, 1992.

196. J. A. Tilley. Valuing American options in a path simulation model. *Transactions of the Society of Actuaries*, 45:499–521, 1994.

197. J. A. Tilley. The latest in financial engineering: Structuring catastrophe reinsurance as a high-yield bond. Technical report. New York: Morgan Stanley, October 1995.

198. S. M. Turnbull and F. Milne. A simple approach to interest rate option pricing. *Review of Financial Studies*, 4:87–120, 1991.

199. I. T. Vanderhoof. The interest rate assumption and the maturity structure of the assets of a life insurance company. *Transactions of the Society of Actuaries*, 24:157–92, 1972. Discussion, 193–205.

200. O. Vasicek. An equilibrium characterization of the term structure. *Journal of Financial Economics*, 5:177–88, 1977.

201. K. L. Walker. *Guaranteed Investment Contracts: Risk Analysis and Portfolio Strategies*, 2nd edition. Homewood, Ill.: Richard D. Irwin, 1992.

202. R. L. Weil. Maucaulay's duration: An appreciation. *Journal of Business*, 46:589–92, 1973.

203. A. D. Wilkie. Portfolio selection in the presence of fixed liabilities: A comment on "The matching of assets to liabilities." *Journal of the Institute of Actuaries*, 112:229–77, 1985.

204. A. D. Wilkie. A stochastic investment model for actuarial use. *Transactions of the Faculty of Actuaries*, 39:341–403, 1986.

205. A. D. Wilkie. Stochastic investment model for 21st century actuaries. *Transactions of the 24th International Congress of Actuaries*, 5:119–37, 1992.

206. A. D. Wilkie. More on a stochastic asset model for actuarial use. *British Actuarial Journal*, 1:777–945, 1995.

207. D. Williams. *Probability with Martingales*. Cambridge: Cambridge University Press, 1991.

208. R. Willner. A new tool for portfolio managers: Level, slope and curvature durations. *Journal of Fixed Income*, 6(1):48–59, 1996.

209. A. J. Wise. The matching of assets to liabilities. *Journal of the Institute of Actuaries*, 111:445–501, 1984.

210. A. J. Wise. A theoretical analysis of the matching of assets to liabilities. *Journal of the Institute of Actuaries*, 111:375–402, 1984.

211. A. J. Wise. Matching and portfolio selection: Part 1. *Journal of the Institute of Actuaries*, 111:113–33, 1987.

212. A. J. Wise. Matching and portfolio selection: Part 2. *Journal of the Institute of Actuaries*, 111:551–68, 1987.

213. A. J. Wise. Matching. *Journal of the Institute of Actuaries*, 116:529–35, 1989.

214. R. Zvan, P. A. Forsyth, and K. R. Vetzal. PDE methods for pricing barrier options. *Journal of Economic and Dynamic Control*, 1998, in press.

# INDEX

# D

# E

## F

## G

# H

# I

# J

# K

FINANCIAL ECONOMICS: WITH APPLICATIONS
TO INVESTMENTS, INSURANCE AND PENSIONS

*Dustjacket, cover, and interior designed by Arc Group, Ltd., Chicago, Illinois*
*Composed by TechBooks, Fairfax, Virginia, in Minion, on the LaTex System*
*Printed and bound by Edwards Brothers, Inc., Ann Arbor, Michigan*
*Dustjacket printed on 100 lb. enamel and interior printed on 60 lb Finch opaque*
*Bound with Rainbow End Sheets in Kivar 7 Book Cloth*